COMPLETE BOOK OF
L A W
SCHOOLS

COMPLETE BOOK OF

L A W
SCHOOLS

2001 EDITION

ERIC OWENS

Random House, Inc.
New York
www.randomhouse.com/princetonreview

Princeton Review Publishing, L.L.C.
2315 Broadway
New York, NY 10024
E-mail: comments@review.com

ISBN: 0-375-76155-1

Production Editor: Julieanna Lambert
Production Coordinator: Scott Harris
Account Manager: Kevin McDonough

Manufactured in the United States of America on partially recycled paper.

9 8 7 6 5 4 3 2 1

2001 Edition

ACKNOWLEDGMENTS

Eric Owens would like to say, "Thank you, John Katzman, for pretty much everything."

He would also really like to thank Wentworth Miller for graciously offering his invaluable advice on how to succeed in law school.

Thanks also to Bob Spruill for his LSAT expertise.

In addition, much thanks should go to Kevin McDonough for his focus, accountability, and inherent ability to stay in character to meet the fickle tastes of our office. High-fives to Amy Kinney and Jennifer Fallon for all of their help. Thanks also to Yojaira Cordero, Chris Blazier, Charlie Looker, Alex Simon, Ian Garrick-Bethell, Melissa Fernandez, Alberto Morales, Douglas Greenfield, Missy Kay, Michael Palumbo, and Jessica Allen for their dedication to proper data collection and input.

As usual, to Chris Wujciak, what would we do without you? Thanks to Chris for his ever-present guidance and patience throughout the book pouring process. To our newest member, Gillian Pancotti, thank you for your eager attitude in learning our process. A big thanks goes to our omnipresent Guidebook Editor, Julie Mandelbaum; she remains a benevolent and attentive force behind the content of this publication.

A special thanks must go to our entire production team, Jason Kantor, Scott Harris, Vanessa Wanderlingh, and Julieanna Lambert. Your commitment, flexibility, and attention to detail are always appreciated in both perfect and crunch times.

Also, a very special thanks to Evan Schnittman and Kristin Campbell for their foresight and direction throughout the production of this book. Thank you to Amy Rotheim for her sales leadership in this new venture, and a big thanks to Tim Serpico, Kyle Jackson, and Ron Foley for their salesmanship.

CONTENTS

Preface   ix

All About Law School   1

    Chapter 1 So You Want to Go to Law School . . .   3

    Chapter 2 Applying to Law School   13

    Chapter 3 The LSAT   21

    Chapter 4 Writing a Great Personal Statement   33

    Chapter 5 Recommendations   41

    Chapter 6 Real Life Work Experience and Community Service   47

    Chapter 7 Interviews   51

    Chapter 8 Choosing a Law School   53

    Chapter 9 Money Matters   59

    Chapter 10 Career Matters   67

    Chapter 11 Law School 101   71

    Chapter 12 How to Get Really Good Grades at *Any* Law School   79

    Chapter 13 How to Use This Book   89

School Profiles   99

Indexes   327

    Alphabetical List of Schools   329

    Law Program Name   331

    Location   333

    Cost   337

    Enrollment of Law School   339

    Average LSAT   341

    Average Undergrad GPA   343

    Environment   345

    Pass Rate for First-Time Bar   347

    Average Starting Salary   349

About the Author   351

PREFACE

Welcome to the *Complete Book of Law Schools*, The Princeton Review's truly indispensable guide for anyone thinking about entering the law school fray. While our newly redesigned book is unique in many ways, it is primarily different in that it is not simply a reprint of the garden-variety fluff from each law school's admissions booklet. What we have attempted to do is provide a significant amount of essential information from a vast array of sources to give you a complete, accurate, and easily digestible snapshot of each and every law school in the country. Here you'll find a wealth of practical advice on admissions, taking and acing the Law School Admissions Test (LSAT), choosing the right school, and doing well once you're there. You'll also find all the information you need on schools' bar exam pass rates, ethnic and gender percentages, tuition, average starting salaries of graduates, and much more. Indeed, with this handy reference, you should be able to narrow your choices from the few hundred law schools in North America to a handful in no time at all.

Never trust any single source too much, though—not even us. Take advantage of all the resources available to you, including friends, family members, the Internet, and your local library. Obviously, the more you explore all the options available to you, the better decision you'll make. We hope you are happy wherever you end up, and that we were helpful in your search for the best law school for you.

Best of luck!

ALL ABOUT LAW SCHOOL

CHAPTER 1
So You Want to Go to Law School . . .

Congrats! Law school is a tremendous intellectual challenge and an amazing experience. It can be confusing and occasionally traumatic—especially during the crucial first year—but the cryptic ritual of legal education really will make you a significantly better thinker, a consummate reader, and a far more mature person over the course of three years.

The application process is rigorous, but it's not brutal. Here's our advice.

Fascinating Acronyms
LSAC: Law School Admission Council, headquartered in beautiful Newtown, Pennsylvania
LSAT: Law School Admissions Test
LSDAS: Law School Data Assembly Service
ABA: American Bar Association

WHAT MAKES A COMPETITIVE APPLICANT?

It depends. One of the great things about law schools in the United States is that there are a lot of them and standards for admission absolutely run the gamut from appallingly difficult to not very hard at all.

Let's just say, for example, you have your heart set on Yale Law School, arguably the finest law school in all the land. Let's also say you have stellar academic credentials: a 3.45 GPA and an LSAT score in the 99th percentile of everyone who takes it. With these heady numbers, you've got a whopping 2 percent chance of getting into Yale, at best. On the other hand, with this same 3.45 GPA and LSAT score in the 99th percentile, you are pretty much a lock at legal powerhouses like Duke University School of Law and Boston College Law School. With significantly lower numbers—say, a 3.02 GPA and an LSAT score in the 81st percentile, you stand a mediocre chance of getting into top-flight law schools like Case Western or Indiana. With a tremendous amount of luck, these numbers could even land you at George Washington or UCLA.

This is good news. The even better news is that there are several totally respectable law schools out there that will let you in with a 2.5 GPA and an LSAT of 148 (which is about the 36th percentile). If you end up in the top 10 percent of your class at one of these schools and have even a shred of interviewing skills, you'll get a job that is just as prestigious and pays just as much money as the jobs garnered by Yale grads. Honest to Christmas. Notice the important catch here, though: You *must* graduate in the top 10 percent of your class at so-called "lesser" schools. Almost every Yale Law grad who wants a high-paying job can land one.

Ultimately, there's a law school out there, somewhere, for you. If you want to get into a "top-flight" or "pretty good" school, though, you're in for some pretty stiff competition. Unfortunately, it doesn't help that the law school admissions process is somewhat formulaic; your LSAT score and your GPA are vastly more important to the process than anything else about you. But if your application ends up in the "maybe" pile, your recommendations, your major, the reputation of your college alma mater, a well-written and nongeneric essay, and various other factors will play a larger role in determining your fate.

THE ADMISSIONS INDEX

The first thing most law schools will look at when evaluating your application is your "index." It's a number (which varies from school to school) that is made up of a weighted combination of your undergraduate GPA and LSAT score. In virtually every case, the LSAT is weighted more heavily than the GPA.

While the process differs from school to school, it is generally the case that your index will put you into what amounts to one of three piles:

(Probably) Accepted. A select few applicants with high LSAT scores and stellar GPAs are admitted pretty much automatically. If your index is very, very strong compared to the school's median or target number, you're as good as in, unless you are a convicted felon or you wrote your personal statement in crayon.

(Probably) Rejected. If your index is very weak compared to the school's median or target number, you are probably going to be rejected without much ado. When admissions officers read weaker applications (yes, at almost every school every application is read) they will be looking for something so outstanding or unique that it makes them willing to take a chance. Factors that can help here include ethnic background, where you are from, or very impressive work or life experience. That said, don't hold your breath, because not many people in this category are going to make the cut.

Admission Decision Criteria
According to the Law School Admission Council, there are no less than 20 factors that law schools might consider in deciding to admit or reject applicants. They are:
- *LSAT score*
- *Undergraduate grade point average (UGPA)*
- *Undergraduate course of study*
- *College attended*
- *Graduate work*
- *Improvement in grades and grade distribution*
- *Extracurricular activities in college*
- *Ethnic background*
- *Character and personality*
- *Letters of recommendation*
- *Writing skills*
- *Personal statement/essay*
- *Work experience and other relevant experience*
- *Community activities*
- *Motivation and reasons for studying law*
- *State of residency*
- *Difficulties overcome*
- *Pre-college preparation*
- *Past accomplishments and leadership*
- *That old catchall: anything else about you*

Well . . . Maybe. The majority of applicants fall in the middle; their index number is right around the median or target index number. Folks in this category have decent enough LSAT scores and GPAs for the school, just not high enough for automatic admission. Why do most people fall into this category? Because for the most part, people apply to schools they think they have at least a shot of getting into based on their grades and LSAT scores; Yale doesn't see very many applicants who got a 140 on the LSAT. What will determine the fate of those whose applications hang in the balance? One thing law schools often look at is the competitiveness of your undergraduate program. Someone with a 3.3 GPA in an easy major from a school where everybody graduates with a 3.3 or higher will face an uphill battle. On the other hand, someone with the same GPA in a difficult major from a school that has a reputation for being stingy with A's is in better shape. Admissions officers will also pore over the rest of your application—personal statement, letters of recommendation, resume, etc.—for reasons to admit you, reject you, or put you on their waiting list.

ARE YOU MORE THAN YOUR LSAT SCORE?

Aside from LSAT scores and GPAs, what do law schools consider when deciding who's in and who's out? It's the eternal question. On the one hand, we should disabuse you hidebound cynics of the notion that they care about nothing else. On the other hand, if you harbor fantasies that a stunning application can overcome truly substandard scores and grades, you should realize that such hopes are unrealistic.

Nonquantitative factors are particularly important at law schools that receive applications from thousands of numerically qualified applicants. A "Top Ten" law school that receives ten or fifteen applications for every spot in its first-year class has no choice but to "look beyond the numbers," as admissions folks are fond of saying. Such a school will almost surely have to turn away hundreds of applicants with near-perfect LSAT scores and college grades, and those applicants who get past the initial cut will be subjected to real scrutiny.

Waiting Lists

If a law school puts you on its waiting list, it means you may be admitted depending on how many of the applicants they've already admitted decide to go to another school. Most schools rank students on their waiting list; they'll probably tell you where you stand if you give them a call. Also, note that schools routinely admit students from their waiting lists in late August. If you are on a school's waiting list and you really, really want to go there, keep your options at least partially open. You just might be admitted in the middle of first-year orientation.

Less competitive schools are just as concerned, in their own way, with "human criteria" as are the Harvards and Stanfords of the world. They are on the lookout for capable people who have relatively unimpressive GPAs and LSAT scores. The importance of the application is greatly magnified for these students, who must demonstrate their probable success in law school in other ways.

CAN PHYSICS MAJORS GO TO LAW SCHOOL?

"What about my major?" is one of the more popular questions we hear when it comes to law school admissions. The conventional answer to this question goes something like "There is no prescribed pre-law curriculum, but you should seek a broad and challenging liberal arts education, and yadda, yadda, yadda."

Here's the truth: It really doesn't matter what you major in. Obviously, a major in aviation or hotel and restaurant management is not exactly ideal, but please—we beg you!—don't feel restricted to a few majors simply because you want to attend law school. This is especially true if those particular majors do not interest you. Comparative literature? Fine. American studies? Go to town. Physics? No problem whatsoever. You get the idea.

Think about it. Because most would-be law students end up majoring in the *same* few fields (e.g., political science and philosophy), their applications all look the *same* to the folks in law school admissions offices. You want to stand out, which is why it is a good idea to major in something *different*. Ultimately, you should major in whatever appeals to you. By the way, of course, if you want to major in political science or philosophy (or you already have), well, that's fine too.

DOES GRAD SCHOOL COUNT?

Your grades in graduate school will not be included in the calculation of your GPA (only the UGPA, the undergraduate grade point average, is reported to the schools) but will be taken into account separately by an admissions committee if you make them available. Reporting grad school grades would be to your advantage, particularly if they are better than your college grades. Admissions committees are likely to take this as a sign of improvement with maturation.

Engineering and Math Majors Make Great Law Students

A disproportionate number of law students with backgrounds in the so-called "hard sciences" (math, physics, engineering, etc.) make very high grades in law school, probably because they are trained to think methodically and efficiently about isolated problems (which is what law students are supposed to do on exams).

Pre-Law Advisors Are Your Pals

It really pays to cozy up to them. Love them. Shower them with gifts. They are an invaluable source of insight and information before, during, and even after the law school admission process. If you are thinking about law school, do yourself a favor and introduce yourself to a pre-law advisor at your undergraduate institution just as soon as possible.

Already graduated? Don't be bashful about calling a pre-law advisor at the old alma mater. The odds are, they'll still be more than happy to help you out.

ADVICE FOR THE "NONTRADITIONAL" APPLICANT

The term "nontraditional" is, of course, used to describe applicants who are a few years or many years older than run-of-the-mill law school applicants.

In a nutshell, there's no time like the present to start law school. It's true that most law students are in their early to mid-twenties, but if you aren't, don't think for a minute that your age will keep you from getting in and having a great experience. It won't. Applicants for full-time and part-time slots at all manner of law schools all over the fruited plain range in age from twenty-one to seventy-one and include every age in between. Some of these older applicants always intended to go to law school and simply postponed it to work, travel, or start a family. Other older applicants never seriously considered law school until after they were immersed in another occupation.

Part-time attendance is especially worth checking into if you've been out of college for a few years. Also, dozens of law schools offer evening programs—particularly in urban centers.

MINORITY LAW SCHOOL APPLICANTS

Things are definitely looking up. Back in 1978, according to figures published by the American Bar Association's Committee on Legal Education, over 90 percent of the law students in the ABA's 163 schools were white. In recent decades, though, the number of nonwhites enrolled in law school has nearly doubled, from about 10 percent to approximately 19 percent. Taking an even longer view, figures have tripled since 1972, when minority enrollment was only 5.9 percent. These days, the American Bar Association and the legal profession in general seem pretty committed to seeking and admitting applicants who are members of historically under-represented minority groups.

MINORITY REPRESENTATION

Here is a sampling of law schools around the United States that boast notably high minority representation among students.

School Name	% Minority
City University of New York, School of Law at Queens College	45
Columbia University, School of Law	35
George Washington University, Law School	30
Glendale University, College of Law	35
Howard University, School of Law	94
Loyola Marymount University, Loyola Law School	39
New College of California, School of Law	43
North Carolina Central University, School of Law	37
Northwestern University, School of Law	30
Rutgers University — Newark, Rutgers School of Law at Newark	31
San Francisco Law School, College of Law	36
Santa Clara University, School of Law	30
Southern University, Law Center	66
Southwestern University School of Law	33
St. Mary's University, School of Law	46
St. Thomas University, School of Law	47
Stanford University, School of Law	32
Texas Southern University, Thurgood Marshall School of Law	77
UCLA School of Law	31
University of California, Hastings College of Law	30
University of Hawaii — Manoa, William S. Richardson School of Law	69
University of Illinois, College of Law	30
University of Miami, School of Law	31
University of New Mexico, School of Law	38
University of Southern California, The Law School	40
University of the District of Columbia, David A. Clarke School of Law	74
University of West Los Angeles, School of Law	53
Western State University, College of Law	35
Whittier College, Whittier Law School	39
Yale University, Yale Law School	33

Making Law Review

Every law school has something called a law review, which is an academic periodical produced and edited by law students. It contains articles about various aspects of law—mostly written by professors. While some schools sponsor more than one law review, there is generally one that is more prestigious than all the others. In order to "make" law review, you will have to finish the all-important first year at (or very, very near) the top of your class or write an article that will be judged by the existing members of the law review. You might have to do both. Making law review is probably the easiest way to guarantee yourself a job at a blue-chip firm, working for a judge, or in academia. In all honesty, it is a credential you will proudly carry for the rest of your life.

WOMEN IN LAW SCHOOL

During the past decade, the number of women lawyers has escalated rapidly, and women undeniably have become more visible in the uppermost echelons of the field. Two women sit on the United States Supreme Court, just for instance, and two women lead the ABA. Also, according to the ABA-compiled statistics, about 12 percent of all law firm partners are women and women have comprised about 30 percent of all federal judicial appointments over the last eight years.

More and more women are going to law school as well. At a solid majority of the ABA-approved law schools in the United States, the percentage of women in the student population is 45 percent or higher, and women make up well over half of the students at a handful of schools.

Unfortunately, gender discrimination certainly lingers in some places. You might want to check certain statistics on the law schools you are interested in, such as the percentage of women on law review and the percentage of female professors who are tenured or on track to be tenured. Also, go to each law school and talk with female students and female professors about how women are treated at that particular law school. Finally, see if the school has published any gender studies about itself. If it has, you obviously ought to check them out, too.

PROPORTION OF FEMALE STUDENTS

Here is a sampling of law schools around the United States that boast notably high percentages of female students.

School Name	% Female
Albany Law School of Union University	52
American University, Washington College of Law	63
California Western School of Law	54
Catholic University of America, Columbus School of Law	52
City University of New York, School of Law at Queens College	63
DePaul University, College of Law	53
Emory University, School of Law	52
Golden Gate University, School of Law	61
Howard University, School of Law	60
Loyola Marymount University, Loyola Law School	52
Loyola University Chicago, School of Law	58
New College of California, School of Law	55
New England School of Law	52
Northeastern University, School of Law	66
Queen's University, Faculty of Law	57
Seattle University, School of Law	57
Stetson University, College of Law	57
University of Baltimore, School of Law	52
University of Calgary, Faculty of Law	54
University of California—Berkeley, Boalt Hall School of Law	55
University of California—Davis, School of Law	52
University of Cincinnati, College of Law	52
University of Denver, College of Law	52
University of Hawaii—Manoa, William S. Richardson School of Law	52
University of Maryland, School of Law	55
University of New Mexico, School of Law	58
University of the District of Columbia, David A. Clarke School of Law	53
University of Windsor	57
Whittier College, Whittier Law School	52
York University, Osgoode Hall Law School	52

Required Reading
These two law review articles discuss the difficulties women face in law school. Check them out.

Lani Guinier, "Becoming Gentlemen: Women's Experiences at One Ivy League Law School," University of Pennsylvania Law Review, *November 1994.*

Catherine Weiss and Louise Melling, "The Legal Education of Twenty Women," Stanford Law Review, *May 1988.*

CHAPTER 2
APPLYING TO LAW SCHOOL

Our advice: Start early. The LSAT alone can easily consume 80 or more hours of prep time, and a single application form might take as much as 30 hours if you take great care with the essay questions. Don't sabotage your efforts through last-minute sloppiness or let this already-annoying process become a gigantic burden.

WHEN TO APPLY

Yale Law School's absolute final due date is February 15, but Loyola University Chicago's School of Law will consider your application up to April 1. There is no pattern. However, the longer you wait to apply to a school, regardless of its deadline, the worse your chances of getting into that school may be. No efficient admissions staff is going to wait for all the applications before starting to make their selections.

If you're reading this in December and hope to get into a law school for the fall but haven't done anything about it, you're in big trouble. If you've got an LSAT score you are happy with, you're in less trouble. However, your applications will get to the law schools after the optimum time and, let's face it, they may appear a bit rushed. The best way to think about applying is to start early in the year, methodically take care of one thing at a time, and *finish by December*.

Early Admissions Options. A few schools have "early admissions" options, so you may know by December if you've been accepted (for instance, New York University's early admission deadline is on or about October 15). Early admission is a good idea for a few reasons. It can give you an indication of what your chances are at other schools. It can relieve the stress of waiting until April to see where you'll be spending the next three years of your life. Also, it's better to get waitlisted in December than April (or whenever you would be notified for regular admission); if there is a "tie" among applicants on the waiting list, they'll probably admit whoever applied first. Of course, not every school's early admission option is the same (and many schools don't even have one).

Rolling Admissions. Many law schools evaluate applications and notify applicants of admission decisions continuously over the course of several months (ordinarily from late fall to midsummer). Obviously, if you apply to one of these schools, it is vital that you apply as early as possible because there will be more places available at the beginning of the process.

Applying on Computer. Almost all law schools want their applications typed. While typing is not exactly rocket science, it is a pain in the neck. A few services can make the process easier. The Princeton Review's very own review.com will allow you to fill out law school applications electronically for free on its site. The LSACD, a CD-ROM/online service (215-968-1001 or www.lsac.org; $50), has a searchable database and applications to ABA-approved schools.

Looking for a Typewriter?
Most libraries will have one you can use for free. Almost all law libraries have typewriters available if you ask nicely.

LAW SCHOOL ADMISSIONS COUNCIL: THE LAW SCHOOL APPLICATION MAFIA

In addition to single-handedly creating and administering the LSAT, an organization called the Law School Admissions Council (LSAC) maintains a stranglehold on communication between you and virtually every law school in the United States. It runs the Law School Data Assembly Service (LSDAS), which provides information (in a standard format) on applicants to the law schools. They—not you—send your grades, your LSAT score, and plenty of other information about you to the schools. You'll send only your actual applications directly to the law schools themselves. Oh, by the way, the fee for this service is almost $100 of your hard-earned money plus $9 (or more) every time you want LSDAS to send a report about you to an additional law school.

THE BIG HURDLES IN THE APPLICATION PROCESS: A BRIEF OVERVIEW

Take the LSAT. The Law School Admission Test is a roughly three-and-a-half-hour multiple-choice test used by law schools to help them select candidates. The LSAT is given in February, June, October (or, occasionally, late September), and December of each year. It's divided into five multiple-choice sections and one (completely useless) writing sample. All ABA-approved and most non-ABA-approved law schools in the United States and Canada require an LSAT score from each and every applicant.

Register for LSDAS. You can register for the Law School Data Assembly Service at the same time you register to take the LSAT; all necessary forms are contained in the *LSAT and LSDAS Registration Information Book* (hence the name).

Get applications from six or seven schools. Why so many? Better safe than sorry. Fairly early—like in July—select a couple "reach" schools, a couple schools to which you've got a good shot at being accepted, and a couple "safety" schools where you are virtually assured of acceptance. Your safety school—if you were being realistic—will probably accept you pretty quickly. It may take a while to get a final decision from the other schools, but you won't be totally panicked because you'll know your safety school is there for you. If, for whatever reason, your grades or LSAT score are extremely low, you should apply to several safety schools.

Write your personal statement. With any luck, you'll only have to write one personal statement. Many, many schools will simply ask you the same question: basically, "Why do you want to obtain a law degree?" However, you may need to write several personal statements and essays—which is one more reason you need to select your schools fairly early.

Obtain two or three recommendations. Some schools will ask for two recommendations, both of which must be academic. Others want more than two recommendations and want at least one to be from someone who knows you outside traditional academic circles. As part of your LSDAS file, the LSAC will accept up to three letters of recommendation on your behalf, and they will send them to all the schools to which you apply. This is one of the few redeeming qualities of the LSAC. The last thing the writers of your recommendations are going to want to do is sign, package, and send copies of their letters all over the continent.

LSDAS Fees

LSDAS Subscription Fee: $95 (This buys you an LSDAS "subscription" for 12 months and a single, solitary report to one law school.)

LSDAS Law School Reports: $9 (when you initially subscribe)

Additional LSDAS Law School Reports: $11 (after you subscribe)

LSDAS Subscription Renewal: $56 (if, for some strange reason, you want to deal with these people for more than one year)

A Legal Education: Priceless

Update/create your resume. Most law school applicants ask that you submit a resume. Make sure yours is up-to-date and suitable for submission to an academic institution. Put your academic credentials and experience first—no matter what they are. This is just a supplement to the rest of the material; it's probably the simplest part of the application process.

Get your academic transcripts sent to LSDAS. When you subscribe to LSDAS, you must request that the registrar at every undergraduate, graduate, and professional school you ever attended send an official transcript to Law Services. Don't even think about sending your own transcripts anywhere; these people don't trust you any farther than they can throw you. *Make these requests in August*. If you're applying for early decision, start sending for transcripts as early as May. Law schools require complete files before making their decisions, and LSDAS won't send your information to the law schools without your transcripts. Undergraduate institutions can and will screw up and delay the transcript process—even when you go there personally and pay them to provide your records. Give yourself some time to fix problems should they arise.

Write any necessary addenda. An addendum is a brief explanatory letter written to explain or support a "deficient" portion of your application. If your personal and academic life has been fairly smooth, you won't need to include any addenda with your application. If, however, you were ever on academic probation, arrested, or if you have a low GPA, you may need to write one. Other legitimate addenda topics are a low/discrepant LSAT score, DUI/DWI suspensions, or any "time gap" in your academic or professional career.

An addendum is absolutely not the place to go off on polemics about the fundamental unfairness of the LSAT or how that evil campus security officer was only out to get you when you got arrested. If, for example, you have taken the LSAT two or three times and simply did not do very well, even after spending time and money preparing with a test prep company or a private tutor, merely tell the admissions committee that you worked diligently to achieve a high score. Say you explored all possibilities to help you achieve that goal. Whatever the case, lay out the facts, but

Fee Waivers

Taking the LSAT, subscribing to LSDAS, and applying to law schools at $50 a pop will cost you an arm and a leg (though these costs are but a drop in the bucket compared to the amount of money you are about to spend on your law school education). The LSAC and most law schools offer fee waiver programs. If you are financially strapped and are accepted into the LSAC program, you get to take the LSAT and subscribe to LSDAS for free. You also get three LSDAS law school reports and a complimentary book of three previously administered LSATs.

You can request a fee waiver packet from Law Services at 215-968-1001, or write to them at:
Law Services
Attn: Fee Waiver Packet
Box 2000
661 Penn Street
Newtown, PA 18940-0998

let them draw their own conclusions. Be brief and balanced. Be fair. Do not go into detailed descriptions of things. Explain the problem and state what you did about it. This is no time to whine.

Send in your seat deposit. Once you are accepted at a particular school, that school will ask you to put at least some of your money where your mouth is. A typical fee runs $200 or more. This amount will be credited to your first-term tuition once you actually register for classes.

Do any other stuff. You may find that there are other steps you must take during the law school application process. You may request a fee waiver, for example. Make extra-special sure to get a copy of the LSAC's *Official LSAT Registration Booklet*, which is unquestionably the most useful tool in applying to law school. It has the forms you'll need, a sample LSAT, admissions information, the current Law Forum schedule, and sample application schedules.

LAW SCHOOL APPLICATION CHECKLIST

(suitable for framing)

The Princeton Review

January	• **Take a practice LSAT.** Do it at a library or some place where you won't be interrupted. Also, take it all at once.
February	• **Investigate LSAT prep courses.** If you don't take one with The Princeton Review, do *something*. Just as with any test, you'll get a higher score on this one if you prepare for it first.
March	• **Obtain an *Official LSAT Registration Booklet*.** The booklets are generally published in March of each year. You can get one at any law school, by calling the LSAC at 215-968-1001, or by stopping by The Princeton Review office nearest you.
April	• **Register for the June LSAT.** • **Begin an LSAT prep course.** At the very, very least, use some books or software.
May	• **Continue your LSAT prep.**
June	• **Take the LSAT.** If you take the test twice, most law schools will consider just your highest LSAT score. Some, however, will average them. Your best bet is to take it once, do exceedingly well, and get it out of your hair forever.
July	• **Register for LSDAS.** • **Research law schools.**
August	• **Obtain law school applications.** You can call or write, but the easiest and cheapest way to get applications sent to you is via the Internet. • **Get your undergraduate transcripts sent to LSDAS.** Make sure to contact the registrar at each undergraduate institution you attended.
September	• **Write your personal statements.** Proofread them. Edit them. Edit them again. Have someone else look them over for all the mistakes you missed. • **Update your resume.** Or create a resume if you don't have one. • **Get your recommendations in order.** You want your recommenders to submit recommendations exactly when you send your applications (in October and November).
October	• **Complete and send early decision applications.**
November	• **Complete and send all regular applications.**
December	• **Chill.** • **Buy holiday gifts.** • **Make plans for New Years.**

CHAPTER 3
The LSAT

As you may know, we at The Princeton Review are pretty much disgusted with most of the standardized tests out there. They make us a lot of money, of course, and we like that, but they are hideously poor indicators of anything besides how well you do on that particular standardized test. They are certainly not intelligence tests. The LSAT is no exception. It is designed to keep you out of law school, not facilitate your entrance into it. For no good reason we can think of, this silly 101-question test is *the single most important factor in all of law school admissions*, and, at least for the foreseeable future, we're all stuck with it.

Unfortunately, with the possible exception of the MCAT (for medical school), the LSAT is the toughest of all the standardized tests. Only 24 of the 101 questions have a "correct" answer (Logic Games), as opposed to Arguments and Reading Comprehension, where you must choose the elusive "best" answer. As ridiculous as they are, the GMAT, GRE, SAT, MCAT, and ACT at least have large chunks of math or science on them. There are verifiably correct answers on these tests, and occasionally you even have to know something to get to them. *Only the LSAT tests require almost no specific knowledge of anything whatsoever, which is precisely what makes it so difficult*. The only infallible way to study for the LSAT is to study the LSAT itself. The good news is that *anybody* can get significantly better at the LSAT by working diligently at it. In fact, your score will increase exponentially in relation to the amount of time and work you put into preparing for it.

HOW IMPORTANT IS THE LSAT?

The LSAT figures very prominently in your law school application, especially if you've been out of school for a few years. Some law schools won't even look at your application unless you achieve a certain score on your LSAT. By the way, each score you receive is valid for five years after you take the test.

LSAT STRUCTURE

Section Type	Sections	Questions	Time
Logical Reasoning (Arguments)	2	24-26	35 minutes
Analytical Reasoning (Games)	1	24	35 minutes
Reading Comprehension	1	26-28	35 minutes
Experimental	1	????	35 minutes
Writing Sample	1	1	30 minutes

Each test has 101 questions. Neither the experimental section nor the writing sample counts toward your score. The multiple-choice sections may be given in any order, but the writing sample is always administered last. The experimental section can be any of the three types of multiple-choice sections and is used by the test writers to test out new questions on your time and at your expense.

Not only is the writing sample not scored, but it is also unlikely that anyone other than you will ever read it. However, the law schools to which you apply will receive a copy of your writing sample, so you should definitely do it. A blank page would stand out like a sore thumb, and you wouldn't want the folks in the admissions office to think you were some kind of revolutionary.

WHAT'S ON THE LSAT, EXACTLY?

We asked the experts in the LSAT Course Division of The Princeton Review for the lowdown on the various sections of the LSAT. Here's what they had to say:

Analytical Reasoning: If you've ever worked logic problems in puzzle books, then you're already somewhat familiar with the Analytical Reasoning section of the LSAT. The situations behind these problems—often called "games" or "logic games"—are common ones: deciding in what order to interview candidates, or assigning employees to teams, or arranging dinner guests around a table. The arrangement of "players" in these games is governed by a set of rules you must follow in answering the questions. Each Analytical Reasoning section is made up of four games, with five to seven questions each. Questions may ask you to find out what must be true under the rules or what could be true under the rules, they may add a new condition that applies to just that question, they may ask you to count the number of possible arrangements under the stated conditions. These questions are difficult mostly because of the time constraints under which they must be worked; very few test-takers find themselves able to complete the twenty-three or twenty-four questions on this section in the time allotted.

Logical Reasoning: Because there are two scored sections of them, Logical Reasoning questions on the LSAT are the most important to your score. Each Logical Reasoning—sometimes called "arguments"—question is made up of a short paragraph, often written to make a persuasive point. These small arguments are usually written to contain a flaw—some error of reasoning or unwarranted assumption that you must identify in order to answer the question successfully. Questions may ask you to draw conclusions from the stated information, to weaken or strengthen the argument, to identify its underlying assumptions, or to identify its logical structure or method. There are most often a total of fifty or fifty-one argument questions between the two sections—roughly half of the scored questions on the LSAT.

Registering for the LSAT
You can register for the LSAT by mail, over the phone, or on the Internet. To register by mail, you will need a copy of the Registration and Information Bulletin, which you may either request from Law Services or pick up from your pre-law advisor. The LSAT fee is currently a whopping $90; if you're late, it's an extra $54. To avoid late fees, mail your registration form at least six weeks—six weeks—before the test. Also, by registering early, you are more likely to be assigned your first choice of test center. You can reach the Law School Admissions Council at:
Phone: 215-968-1001
www.lsac.org
lsacinfo@lsac.org

Reading Comprehension: Reading Comprehension is familiar to anyone who's taken the SAT or virtually any other standardized test. The Reading Comprehension section is made up of four passages, each roughly 500 words in length, with six to eight associated questions. The material of these reading passages is often obscure or esoteric, but answering the questions correctly doesn't depend on any specialized knowledge. Questions may ask you to identify the passage's main idea, to identify descriptions of its structure or purpose, to evaluate the purpose of specific examples or contentions, or to understand its argumentation. Although the form of this section is familiar, the language and length of passages, questions, and answer choices make it challenging; like the Analytical Reasoning section, the Reading Comprehension section is for many test-takers simply too long to finish in the time allotted.

You really ought to prep for this test. You certainly don't have to take The Princeton Review's course (or buy our book, *Cracking the LSAT,* or sign up for our awesome distance learning courses), as much as we'd obviously like it. There are plenty of other books, software products, courses, and tutors. The evil minions who make the LSAT will gleefully sell you plenty of practice tests as well. Whatever your course of action, though, make sure you remain committed to it so you can be as prepared as possible when you take the actual test.

WHEN SHOULD YOU TAKE THE LSAT?

Here is a quick summary of test dates along with some factors to consider for each.

JUNE

The June administration is the only time the test is given on a Monday afternoon. If you have trouble functioning at the ordinary 8 A.M. start-time, June may be a good option. Furthermore, taking the LSAT in June frees up your summer and fall to research schools and complete applications. On the other hand, if you are still in college, you'll have to balance LSAT preparation with academic course work and, in some cases, final exams. Check your exam schedules before deciding on a June LSAT test date.

OCTOBER/SEPTEMBER

The October test date (which is sometimes in late September) will allow you to prepare for the LSAT during the summer. This is an attractive option if you are a college student with some free time on your hands. Once you've taken the LSAT, you can spend the remainder of your fall completing applications.

DECEMBER

December is the last LSAT administration that most competitive law schools will accept. If disaster strikes and you get a flat tire on test day, you may end up waiting another year to begin law school. December testers also must balance their time between preparing for the LSAT and completing law school applications. Doing so can make for a hectic fall, especially if you're still in college. You should also remember that, while a law school may accept December LSAT scores, taking the test in December could affect your chances of admission. Many law schools use a rolling admissions system, which means that they begin making admissions decisions as early as mid-October and continue to do so until the application deadline. Applying late in this cycle could mean that fewer spots are available. Check with your potential law schools to find out their specific policies.

FEBRUARY

If you want to begin law school in the following fall, the February LSAT will be too late for most law schools. However, if you don't plan to begin law school until the *next* academic year, you can give yourself a head start on the entire admissions process by taking the LSAT in February, then spending your summer researching schools and your fall completing applications.

UPCOMING LSAT TEST DATES			
TEST DATE	Registration Deadline	Late Registration Periods by Mail	Registration by Phone/Online
December 2, 2000	November 3	November 4–10	November 4–15
February 10, 2001	January 12	January 13–19	January 13–24

HOW IS THE LSAT SCORED?

LSAT scores currently range from 120 to 180. Why that range? We have no idea. The following table indicates the percentile rating of the corresponding LSAT score. This varies slightly from test to test.

LSAT Score	Percent Below	LSAT Score	Percent Below
180	99.9	160	81.8
179	99.9	159	78.3
178	99.9	158	74.5
177	99.8	157	70.9
176	99.7	156	67.9
175	99.6	155	64.2
174	99.5	154	59.5
173	99.2	153	55.6
172	98.9	152	51.9
171	98.6	151	47.0
170	97.9	150	44.1
169	97.3	149	39.4
168	96.6	148	36.0
167	95.5	147	32.2
166	94.3	146	29.0
165	92.4	145	25.7
164	91.4	144	22.8
163	89.0	143	20.1
162	86.7	142	17.5
161	83.6	141	15.4

A GOOD LSAT SCORE

A good score on the LSAT is the score that gets you into the law school you want to attend. Remember that a large part of the admissions game is the formula of your UGPA (undergraduate grade point average) multiplied by your LSAT score. Chances are, you are at a point in life where your UGPA is pretty much fixed (if you're reading this early in your college career, start getting very good grades pronto), so the only piece of the formula you can have an impact on is your LSAT score.

A LITTLE IMPROVEMENT GOES A LONG WAY

A student who scores a 154 is in the 63rd percentile of all LSAT-takers. If that student's score were 161, however, that same student would jump to the 86th percentile. Depending upon your score, a 7-point improvement can increase your ranking by over 30 percentile points.

Most law schools will consider just your highest LSAT score, rather than average them, which is what they used to do.

COMPETITIVE LSAT SCORES AROUND THE UNITED STATES

The range of LSAT scores from the 25th to 75th percentile of incoming full-time students at U.S. law schools is pretty broad. Here is a sampling.

Law School	Score
Widener University, School of Law	143–151
The John Marshall Law School	145–152
Gonzaga University, School of Law	146–152
University of North Dakota, School of Law	147–154
University of Pittsburgh, School of Law	151–157
Temple University, James E. Beasley School of Law	152–159
Northeastern University, School of Law	153–160
Rutgers University—Newark, Rutgers School of Law at Newark	153–159
University of Florida, Levin College of Law	152–161
University of Missouri–Columbia, School of Law	152–158
University of Tennessee, College of Law	152–160
Case Western Reserve University, School of Law	153–160
University of Alabama, School of Law	155–161
Southern Methodist University, School of Law	154–160
Loyola University Chicago, School of Law	155–161
Brigham Young University, J. Reuben Clark Law School	157–164
Boston University, School of Law	160–163
Emory University, School of Law	158–162
University of Southern California, The Law School	159–166
George Washington University, Law School	160–163
Duke University, School of Law	162–168
University of Michigan, Law School	163–168
Stanford University, School of Law	165–170
New York University, School of Law	167–171
University of Chicago, Law School	165–172
Yale University, Yale Law School	168–175

PREPARING FOR THE LSAT

No matter who you are—whether you graduated *magna cum laude* from Cornell University or you're on academic probation at Cornell College—the first thing you need to do is order a recent LSAT. One comes free with every *Official LSAT Registration Booklet*. Once you get the test, take it, but not casually over the course of two weeks. Bribe someone to be your proctor. Have them administer the test to you under strict time conditions. Follow the test booklet instructions exactly and do it right. Your goal is to simulate an actual testing experience as much as possible. When you finish, score the test honestly. Don't give yourself a few extra points because "you'll do better on test day." The score on this practice test will provide a baseline for mapping your test preparation strategy.

If your practice LSAT score is already at a point where you've got a very high-percentage shot of getting accepted to the law school of your choice, chances are you don't need much preparation. Order a half dozen or so of the most recent LSATs from LSAC and work through them over the course of a few months, making sure you understand why you are making specific mistakes. If your college or university offers a free or very cheap prep course, take it to get more tips on the test. Many of these courses are taught by pre-law advisors who will speak very intelligently about the test and are committed to helping you get the best score you can.

If, after you take a practice LSAT, your score is not what you want or need it to be, you are definitely not alone. Many academically strong candidates go into the LSAT cold because they assume that the LSAT is no more difficult and about the same as their college courses, and frankly, many students are surprised at how poorly they do the first time they take a dry run. Think about it this way: It's better to be surprised sitting at home with a practice test than while taking the test for real.

If you've taken a practice LSAT under exam conditions and it's, say, 10 or 15 points below where you want it to be, you should probably consult an expert. Test preparation companies spend quite a lot of money and time poring over the tests and measuring the improvements of their students. We sure do. Ask around. Assess your financial situation.

Talk to other people who have improved their LSAT scores and duplicate their strategies.

Whatever you decide to do, make sure you are practicing on real LSAT questions—again and again and again.

SOME ESSENTIAL, DOWN-AND-DIRTY LSAT TIPS

Slow down. Way down. The slower you go, the better you'll do. It's that simple. Any function you perform, from basic motor skills to complex intellectual problems, will be affected by the rate at which you perform that function. This goes for everything from cleaning fish to taking the LSAT. You can get twenty-five questions wrong and still get a scaled score of 160, which is a very good score (it's in the 84th percentile). You can get at least six questions wrong per section or, even better, you can ignore the two or three most convoluted questions per section, *still* get a few *more* questions wrong, and you'll get an excellent overall score. Your best strategy is to find the particular working speed at which you will get the most questions correct.

There is no guessing penalty. If you don't have time to finish the exam, it's imperative that you leave yourself at least 30 seconds at the end of each section in which to grab free points by bubbling in some answer to every question before time is called. Pick a letter of the day—like B—don't bubble in randomly. If you guess totally randomly, you might get every single guess right. Of course, you may also get struck by lightning in the middle of the test. The odds are about the same. *You are far more likely to miss every question if you guess without a plan.* On the other hand, if you stick with the same letter each time you guess, you will definitely be right once in a while. It's a conservative approach, but it is also your best bet for guaranteed points, which is what you want. By guessing the same letter pretty much every time as time runs out, you can pick up anywhere from two to four raw points per section. Be careful about waiting until the very last second to start filling in randomly, though, because proctors occasionally cheat students out of the last few seconds of a section.

Use process of elimination all the time. This is absolutely huge. On 75 percent of the LSAT (all the Logical Reasoning and the Reading Comprehension questions), you are *not*

100% Free Stuff at The Princeton Review's Website
There is a substantial amount of good information at our website, www.review.com. One very cool thing you can do online at our site is take a full, timed LSAT to see just how you'd do.

looking for the *right* answer, only the *best* answer. It says so right there in the instructions. Eliminating even one answer choice increases your chances of getting the question right by 20 to 25 percent. If you can cross off two or three answer choices, you are really in business. Also, very rarely will you find an answer choice that is flawless on the LSAT. Instead, you'll find four answer choices that are definitely wrong and one that is the least of five evils. You should constantly look for reasons to get rid of answer choices so you can eliminate them. This strategy will increase your odds of getting the question right, and you'll be a happier and more successful standardized test-taker. We swear.

Attack! Attack! Attack! Read the test with an antagonistic, critical eye. Read it like it's a contract you are about to sign with the devil; look for holes and gaps in the reasoning of arguments and in the answer choices. Many LSAT questions revolve around what is wrong with a particular line of reasoning. The more you can identify what is wrong with a problem before going to the answer choices, the more successful you'll be.

Write all over your test booklet. Actively engage the exam and put your thoughts on paper. Circle words. *Physically cross out wrong answer choices you have eliminated.* Draw complete and exact diagrams for the logic games. Use the diagrams you draw.

Do the questions in whatever order you wish. Just because a logic game question is first doesn't mean you should do it first. There is *no order of difficulty* on the LSAT—unlike some other standardized tests—so you should hunt down and destroy those questions at which you are personally best. If you are doing a Reading Comprehension question, for example, or tackling an argument, and you don't know what the hell is going on, then cross off whatever you can, guess, and move on. If you have no idea what is going on in a particular logic game, don't focus your energy there. Find a game you can do and milk it for points. Your mission is to gain points wherever you can. By the way, if a particular section is really throwing you, it's probably because it is the dastardly experimental section (which is often kind of sloppy and, thankfully, does not count toward your score).

CHAPTER 4
WRITING A GREAT PERSONAL STATEMENT

There is no way to avoid writing the dreaded personal statement. You'll probably need to write only one personal statement, and it will probably address the most commonly asked question: "Why do you want to obtain a law degree?" This question, in one form or another, appears on virtually every law school application form and often represents your only opportunity to string more than two sentences together. Besides your grades and your LSAT score, it is the most important part of your law-school application. Your answer should be about two pages long, and it should amount to something significantly more profound than "A six-figure salary really appeals to me," or "Because I watch *Law and Order* every night."

Unlike your application to undergraduate programs, the personal statement on a law application is not the time to discuss what your trip to Europe meant to you, describe your wacky chemistry teacher, or try your hand at verse. It's a fine line. While you want to stand out, you definitely don't want to be *overly* creative here. You want to be unique, but you don't want to come across as a weirdo or a loose cannon. You want to present yourself as intelligent, professional, mature, persuasive, and concise because these are the qualities law schools seek in applicants.

THE BASICS

Here are the essentials of writing essays and personal statements.

Find your own unique angle. The admissions people read tons of really boring essays about "how great I am" and how "I think there should be justice for everyone." If you must explain why you want to obtain a law degree, strive to find an angle that is interesting and unique to you. If what you write *isn't* interesting to you, we promise that it won't be remotely interesting to an admissions officer. Also, in addition to being more effective, a unique and interesting essay will be far more enjoyable to write.

In general, avoid generalities. Again, admissions officers have to read an unbelievable number of boring essays. You will find it harder to be boring if you write about particulars. It's the details that stick in a reader's mind.

Good writing is writing that is easily understood. You want to get your point across, not bury it in words. Don't talk in circles. Your prose should be clear and direct. If an admissions officer has to struggle to figure out what you are trying to say, you'll be in trouble. Also, legal writing courses make up a significant part of most law school curriculums; if you can show that you have good writing skills, you have a serious edge.

Buy and read *The Elements of Style*, **by William Strunk, Jr. and E. B. White.** We can't recommend it highly enough. In fact, we're surprised you don't have it already. This little book is a required investment for any writer (and, believe us, you'll be doing plenty of writing as a law student and a practicing attorney). You will refer to it forever, and if you do what it says, your writing will definitely improve.

Have three or four people read your personal statement and critique it. If your personal statement contains misspellings and grammatical errors, admissions officers will conclude not only that you don't know how to write but also that you aren't shrewd enough to get help. What's worse, the more time you spend with a piece of your own writing, the less likely you are to spot any errors. You get tunnel vision. Ask friends, boyfriends, girlfriends, professors, brothers, sisters—somebody—to read your essay and comment on it. Use a computer with a spellchecker. *Be especially careful about punctuation!* Another tip: Read your personal statement aloud to yourself or someone else. You will catch mistakes and awkward phrases that would have gotten past you otherwise because it sounded fine in your head.

Don't repeat information from other parts of your application. It's a waste of time and space.

Stick to the length that is requested. It's only common courtesy.

Maintain the proper tone. Your essay should be memorable without being outrageous and easy to read without being too formal or sloppy. When in doubt, err on the formal side.

Being funny is a lot harder than you think. An applicant who can make an admissions officer laugh never gets lost in the shuffle. The clever part of the personal statement is passed around and read aloud. Everyone smiles and the admissions staff can't bear to toss your app into the "reject" pile. But beware! Most people think they're funny, but only a few are able to pull it off in this context. Obviously, stay away from one liners, limericks, and anything remotely off-color.

WHY DO YOU WANT TO GO TO LAW SCHOOL?
Writing about yourself often proves to be surprisingly difficult. It's certainly no cakewalk explaining who you are and why you want to go to law school, and presenting your lifetime of experiences in a mere two pages is nearly impossible. On the bright side, though, the personal statement is the only element of your application over which you have total control. It's a tremendous opportunity to introduce yourself if you'll avoid the urge to communicate your entire genetic blueprint. Your goal should be much more modest.

DON'T GET CARRIED AWAY
Although some law schools set no limit on the length of the personal statement, you shouldn't take their bait. You can be certain that your statement will be at least glanced at in its entirety, but admissions officers are human, and their massive workload at admissions time has an understandable impact on their attention spans. You should limit yourself to two or three typed, double-spaced pages. Does this make your job any easier? Not at all. In fact, practical constraints on the length of your essay demand a higher degree of efficiency and precision. Your essay needs to convey what kind of thinking, feeling human being you are, and a two-page limit allows for absolutely no fat.

MAKE YOURSELF STAND OUT
We know you know this, but you will be competing against thousands of well-qualified applicants for admission to just about any law school. Consequently, your primary task in writing your application is to separate yourself from the crowd. Particularly if you are applying directly from college or if you have been out of school for a very

short time, you must do your best to see that the admissions committee cannot categorize you too broadly. Admissions committees will see innumerable applications from bright twenty-two-year-olds with good grades. Your essay presents an opportunity to put those grades in context, to define and differentiate yourself.

WHAT MAKES A GOOD PERSONAL STATEMENT?

Like any good writing, your law school application should tend towards clarity, conciseness, and candor. The first two of these qualities, clarity and conciseness, are usually the products of a lot of reading, rereading, and rewriting. Without question, repeated critical revision by yourself and others is the surest way to trim and tune your prose. The third quality, candor, is the product of proper motivation. Honesty cannot be superimposed after the fact; your writing must be candid from the outset.

In writing your personal statement for law school applications, pay particularly close attention to the way it is structured and the fundamental message it communicates. Admissions committees will read your essay two ways: as a product of your handiwork and as a product of your mind. Don't underestimate the importance of either perspective. A well-crafted essay will impress any admissions officer, but if it does not illuminate, you will not be remembered. You will not stand out. This is bad. Conversely, a thoughtful essay that offers true insight will stand out unmistakably, but if it is not readable, it will not receive serious consideration.

WHAT, PARTICULARLY, TO WRITE ABOUT

Given the most popular topic—"Why do you want to obtain a law degree?"—this one is pretty obvious. If you are having serious writer's block, try to express in a compelling manner some moment in your life, some experience you've had, or some intellectual slant of personal interest that is directing you to law school.

THINGS TO AVOID IN YOUR PERSONAL STATEMENT

"MY LSAT SCORE ISN'T GREAT, BUT I'M JUST NOT A GOOD TEST TAKER."

If you have a low LSAT score, avoid directly discussing it in your personal statement like the plague. Law school is a test-rich environment. In fact, grades in most law-school courses are determined by a single exam at the semester's end, and as a law student, you'll spend your Novembers and Aprils in a study carrel, completely removed from society. Saying that you are not good at tests will do little to convince an admissions committee that you've got the ability to succeed in law school once accepted.

Consider also that a low LSAT score speaks for itself—all too eloquently. It doesn't need you to speak for it, too. The LSAT may be an awful test but don't go arguing the merits of the test to admissions officers because ordinarily it is the primary factor they use to make admissions decisions. We feel for you, but you'd be barking up the wrong tree here. The attitude of most law school admissions departments is that while the LSAT may be imperfect, it is equally imperfect for all applicants. Apart from extraordinary claims of serious illness on test day, few explanations for poor performance on the LSAT will mean much to the people who read your application.

About the only situation in which a discussion of your LSAT score is necessary is if you have two (or more) LSAT scores and one is significantly better than another. If you did much better in your second sitting than in your first, or vice versa, a brief explanation couldn't hurt. However, your explanation may mean little to the committee, which may have its own hard-and-fast rules for interpreting multiple LSAT scores. Even in this scenario, however, you should avoid bringing up the LSAT in the personal statement. *Save it for an addendum.*

The obvious and preferable alternative to an explicit discussion of a weak LSAT score would be to focus on what you *are* good at. If you really are bad at standardized tests, you must be better at something else, or you wouldn't have gotten as far as you have. If you think you are a marvelous researcher, say so. If you are a wonderful writer, show it.

Let your essay implicitly draw attention away from your weak points by focusing on your strengths. There is no way to convince an admissions committee that they should overlook your LSAT score. You may, however, present compelling reasons for them to look beyond it.

"MY COLLEGE GRADES WEREN'T THAT HIGH, BUT . . ."

This issue is a bit more complicated than the low LSAT score. Law school admissions committees will be more willing to listen to your interpretation of your college performance, but only within limits. Keep in mind that law schools require official transcripts for a reason. Members of the admissions committee will be aware of your academic credentials before ever getting to your essay. Just like with low LSAT scores, your safest course of action is to *save low grades for an addendum.*

Make no mistake: if your grades are unimpressive, you should offer the admissions committee something else by which to judge your abilities. Again, the best argument for looking past your college grades is evidence of achievement in another area, whether in your LSAT score, your extracurricular activities, your economic hardship as an undergraduate, or your career accomplishments.

"I'VE ALWAYS WANTED TO BE A LAWYER."

Sure you have. Many applicants seem to feel the need to point out that they really, really want to become attorneys. You will do yourself a great service by avoiding such throwaway lines. They'll do nothing for your essay but water it down. Do not convince yourself in a moment of desperation that claiming to have known that the law was your calling since age six (when—let's be honest—you really wanted to be a firefighter) will somehow move your application to the top of the pile. The admissions committee is not interested in how much you want to practice law. They want to know *why.*

"I WANT TO BECOME A LAWYER TO FIGHT INJUSTICE."

No matter how deeply you feel about battling social inequity, between us, writing it down makes you sound like a superhero on a soapbox. Moreover, though some people really do want to fight injustice, way down in the cockles

Law School Trivia
Supreme Court justices William Rehnquist and Sandra O'Connor were classmates at Stanford Law School.

of their hearts, most applicants are motivated to attend law school by less altruistic desires. Among the nearly one million practicing lawyers in the United States, there are relatively few who actually earn a living defending the indigent or protecting civil rights. Tremendously dedicated attorneys who work for peanuts and take charity cases are few and far between. We're not saying you don't want to be one of them; we're merely saying that folks in law school admissions won't *believe* you want to be one of them. They'll take your professed altruistic ambitions (and those of the hundreds of other personal statements identical to yours) with a chunk of salt.

If you can in good conscience say that you are committed to a career in the public interest, show the committee something tangible on your application and in your essay that will allow them to see your statements as more than mere assertions. However, if you cannot show that you are already a veteran in the Good Fight, don't claim to be. Law school admissions committees certainly do not regard the legal profession as a Saints vs. Sinners proposition, and neither should you. Do not be afraid of appearing morally moderate. If the truth is that you want the guarantee of a relatively good job a law degree ensures, be forthright. Nothing is as impressive to the reader of a personal statement as the ring of truth. And what's wrong with a good job, anyhow?

CHAPTER 5
RECOMMENDATIONS

The law schools to which you apply will require two or three letters of recommendation in support of your application. Some schools will allow you to submit as many letters as you like. Others make it clear that any more than the minimum number of letters of recommendation is unwelcome. If you've ever applied to a private school (or perhaps a small public school) then you know the drill.

Unlike the evaluation forms for some colleges and graduate programs, however, law school recommendation forms tend toward absolute minimalism. All but a few recommendation forms for law school applications ask a single, open-ended question. It usually goes something like, "What information about this applicant is relevant that is not to be found in other sources?" The generic quality of the forms from various law schools may be both a blessing and a curse. On the one hand, it makes it possible for those writing your recommendations to write a single letter that will suffice for all the applications you submit. This convenience will make everybody a lot happier. On the other hand, if a free-form recommendation is to make a positive impression on an admissions committee, it must convey real knowledge about you.

WHOM TO ASK

Your letters of recommendation should come from people who know you well enough to offer a truly informed assessment of your abilities. Think carefully before choosing whom to ask to do this favor for you, but, as a general rule, pick respectable people you've known for a long time. The better the writers of your recommendations know you and understand the broader experience that has brought you to your decision to attend law school, the more likely they will be able to write a letter that is specific enough to do you some good. You also want people who can and are willing to contribute to an integrated, cohesive application.

The application materials from most law schools suggest that your letters should come, whenever possible, from people in an academic setting. Some schools want at least two recommendations, both of which must be academic. Others explicitly request that the letters come from someone who has known you in a professional setting, especially if you've been out of school for a while.

HELP YOUR RECOMMENDATION WRITERS HELP YOU

Here, in essence, is the simple secret to great recommendations: Make sure the writers of your recommendations know you, your goals, and the overall message you are trying to convey in your application. The best recommendations will fit neatly with the picture you present of yourself in your own essay, even when they make no specific reference to the issues your essay addresses. An effective law school application will present to the admissions committee a cohesive picture, not a pastiche. A great way to point your recommendation writers in the right direction and maximize their ability to contribute to your overall cause is to provide them with copies of your personal statement. Don't be bashful about amiably communicating a few "talking points" that don't appear in your personal statement, as well.

ACADEMIC REFERENCES

Most applicants will (and should) seek recommendations from current or former professors. The academic environment in law school is extremely rigorous. Admissions committees will be looking for assurance that you will be able not just to survive, but to excel. A strong recommendation from a college professor is a valuable corroboration of your ability to succeed in law school.

You want nothing less than stellar academic recommendations. While a perfunctory, lukewarm recommendation is unlikely to damage your overall application, it will obviously do nothing to bolster it. Your best bet is to choose at least one professor from your major field. An enthusiastic endorsement from such a professor will be taken as a sign that you are an excellent student. Second—and we hope that this goes without saying—you should choose professors who do not immediately associate your name with the letter C.

Specifics are of particular interest to admissions officers when they evaluate your recommendations. If a professor can make *specific* reference to a particular project you completed, or at least make substantive reference to your work in a particular course, the recommendation will be strengthened considerably. Make it your responsibility to

Helpful Websites
www.findlaw.com
Findlaw has the mother lode of free information about law, law schools, and legal careers.
www.ilrg.com
Mother lode honorable mention.
www.hg.org/students.html
Another honorable mention.
www.canadalawschools.org
Pretty much everything you ever wanted to know about Canadian law schools, eh.
www.jurist.law.pitt.edu
The University of Pittsburgh School of Law's splendid "Legal Education Network" offers a wealth of useful information.

enable your professors to provide specifics. Drop hints, or just lay it out for them. You might, for example, make available a paper you wrote for them of which you are particularly proud. Or you might just chat with the professor for a while to jog those dormant memories. You might feel uncomfortable tooting your own horn, but it's for the best. Unless your professors are well acquainted with you to be able to offer a very personal assessment of your potential, they will greatly appreciate a tangible reminder of your abilities on which to base their recommendation.

ESCAPING THE WOODWORK

If you managed to get through college without any professors noticing you, it's not the end of the world. Professors are quite talented at writing recommendations for students they barely know. Most consider it part of their job. Even seemingly unapproachable academic titans will usually be happy to dash off a quick letter for a mere student. However, these same obliging professors are masters of a sort of opaque prose style that screams to an admissions officer, "I really have no idea what to say about this kid who is, in fact, a near-total stranger to me!" Although an admissions committee will not dismiss out of hand such a recommendation, it's really not going to help you much.

REELING IN THE YEARS

Obviously, the longer it has been since you graduated, the tougher it is to obtain academic recommendations. However, if you've held on to your old papers, you may still be able to rekindle an old professor's memory of your genius by sending a decent paper or two along with your request for a recommendation (and, of course, a copy of your personal statement). You want to provide specifics any way you can.

NONACADEMIC REFERENCES

Getting the mayor, a senator, or the CEO of your company to write a recommendation helps only if you have a personal and professional connection with that person. Remember, you want the writers of your recommendations to provide specifics about your actual accomplishments. If you're having trouble finding academic recommendations,

Even More Celebrity Lawyers
Henry James, writer
Howard Cosell, sportscaster
David Stern, NBA commissioner
Abraham Lincoln, U.S. president
Tim and Nina Zagat, the people who bring you Zagat's restaurant and hotel guides

choose people from your workplace, from the community, or from any other area of your life that is important to you. If at all possible, talk to your boss or a supervisor from a previous job who knows you well (and, of course, likes you).

SEND A THANK-YOU NOTE

Always a good idea. It should be short and handwritten. Use a blue pen so the recipient knows for sure that your note is no cheap copy. As with any good thank-you note (and any good recommendation), mention a specific. (Send a thank-you note if you have an interview at a law school, too.)

CHAPTER 6
REAL LIFE WORK EXPERIENCE
AND COMMUNITY SERVICE

WORK EXPERIENCE IN COLLEGE

Most law school applications will ask you to list any part-time jobs you held while you were in college and how many hours per week you worked. If you had to (or chose to) work your way through your undergraduate years, this should come as good news. A great number of law schools make it clear that they take your work commitments as a college student into consideration when evaluating your undergraduate GPA.

WORK EXPERIENCE IN REAL LIFE

All law school applications will ask you about your work experience beyond college. They will give you three or four lines on which to list such experience. Some schools will invite you to submit a resume. If you have a very good one, you should really milk this opportunity for all it's worth. Even if you don't have a marvelous resume, these few lines on the application and your resume are the only opportunities you'll have to discuss your post-college experience meaningfully—unless you choose to discuss professional experience in your personal statement as well.

The kind of job you've had is not as important as you might think. What interests the admissions committee is what you've made of that job and what it's made of you. Whatever your job was or is, you want to offer credible evidence of your competence. For example, mention in your personal statement your job advancement or any increase in your responsibility. Most importantly, though, remember your overriding goal of cohesive presentation: you want to show off your professional experience within the context of your decision to attend law school. This does not mean that you need to offer a geometric proof of how your experience in the workplace has led you inexorably to a career in the law. You need only explain truthfully how this experience influenced you and how it fits nicely into your thinking about law school.

COMMUNITY SERVICE

An overwhelming majority of law schools single out community involvement as one of several influential factors in their admissions decisions. Law schools would like to admit applicants who show a long-standing commitment to something other than their own advancement.

It is certainly understandable that law schools would wish to determine the level of such commitment before admitting an applicant, particularly since so few law students go on to practice public interest law. Be forewarned, however, that nothing—*nothing*—is so obviously bogus as an insincere statement of a commitment to public interest issues. It just reeks. Admissions committees are well aware that very few people take the time out of their lives to become involved significantly in their communities. If you aren't one of them, trying to fake it can only hurt you.

CHAPTER 7
INTERVIEWS

The odds are very good that you won't ever encounter an interview in the law school admissions process. Admissions staffs just aren't very keen on them. They do happen occasionally, though, and if you are faced with one, here are a few tips.

Be prepared. Interviews do make impressions. Some students are admitted simply because they had great interviews; less often, students are rejected because they bombed. Being prepared is the smartest thing you can do.

Don't ask questions that are answered in the brochures you got in the mail. This means you have to read those brochures. At breakfast before the interview is an ideal time.

If there is a popular conception of the school (e.g., Harvard is overly competitive), don't ask about it. Your interviewer will have been through the same song and dance too many times. You don't want to seem off the wall by asking bizarre questions; but even more, you don't want to sound exactly like every other boring applicant before you.

Looking good, feeling good. Wear nice clothes. If you aren't sure what to wear, *ask the admissions staff*. Say these words: "What should I wear?" Get a respectable haircut. Don't chew gum. Clean your fingernails. Brush your teeth. Wash behind your ears. You can go back to being a slob just as soon as they let you in.

Don't worry about time. Students sometimes are told that the sign of a good interview is that it lasts longer than the time allowed for it. Forget about this. Don't worry if your interview lasts exactly as long as the secretary said it would. And don't try to stretch out the end of your interview by suddenly becoming long-winded or asking a lot of questions you don't care about.

CHAPTER 8
CHOOSING A LAW SCHOOL

There are some key things you should consider before randomly selecting schools from around the country or just submitting your application to somebody else's list of the Top 10 law schools.

GEOGRAPHY

It's a big deal. If you were born and raised in the state of New Mexico, care deeply about the "Land of Enchantment," wish to practice law there, and want to be the governor someday, then your best bet is to go to the University of New Mexico. A school's reputation is usually greater on its home turf than anywhere else (except for some of the larger-than-life schools, like Harvard and Yale). Also, most law schools tend to teach law that is specific to the states in which they are located. Knowledge of the eccentricities of state law will help you immensely three years down the road when it comes time to pass the bar exam. Even further, the career services office at your school will be strongly connected to the local legal industry. And, as a purely practical matter, it will be much easier to find a job and get to interviews in Boston, for example, if you live there. Still another reason to consider geography is the simple fact that you'll put down professional and social roots and get to know a lot of really great people throughout your law school career. Leaving them won't be any fun. Finally, starting with geographic limitations is the easiest way to dramatically reduce your number of potential schools.

SPECIALIZATION

Word has it that specialization is the trend of the future. General practitioners in law are becoming less common, so it makes sense to let future lawyers begin to specialize in school. At certain schools, you may receive your JD with an official emphasis in, say, taxation. Specialization is a particularly big deal at smaller or newer schools whose graduates cannot simply get by on their school's established reputation of excellence. Just between us, though, it's kind of hard to specialize in anything in most law schools because every graduate has to take this huge exam—the bar—that tests about a dozen topics. Most of your course selections will (and should) be geared toward passing the bar, which leaves precious few hours for specialization.

You'll almost certainly specialize, but it's not something to worry about until you actually look for a job. All of that said, if you already know what kind of law you want to specialize in, you're in good shape. Many schools offer certain specialties because of their location. If you are very interested in environmental law, you'd be better off going to Vermont Law School or Lewis and Clark's Northwestern School of Law than to New York University. Similarly, if you want to work with children as an attorney, check out Loyola University Chicago's Child Law Center. So look at what you want to do in addition to where you want to do it.

JOINT DEGREE PROGRAMS

In addition to offering specialized areas of study, many law schools have instituted formal dual-degree programs. These schools, nearly all of which are directly affiliated with a parent institution, offer students the opportunity to pursue a JD while also working toward some other degree. Although the JD/MBA combination is the most popular joint degree sought, many universities offer a JD program combined with degrees in everything from public policy to public administration to social work. Amidst a perpetually competitive legal market, dual degrees may make some students more marketable for certain positions come job time. However, don't sign up for a dual-degree program on a whim—they require a serious amount of work. (See page 96 for a list of joint degree programs available at some of the schools in this book.)

YOUR CHANCE OF ACCEPTANCE

Who knows how law schools end up with their reputations, but everything else being equal, you really do want to go a to a well-respected school. It will enhance your employment opportunities tremendously. Remember, whoever you are and whatever your background, your best bet is to select a couple "reach" schools, a couple schools at which you've got a good shot at being accepted, and a couple "safety" schools where you are virtually assured of acceptance. Remember also that being realistic about your chances will save you from unnecessary emotional letdowns. Getting in mostly boils down to numbers. Look at the acceptance rates and the average LSATs and GPAs of incoming classes at various schools to assess how you stack up.

Dean's List
According to a letter signed by just about every dean of every ABA-approved law school in the country, here are the factors you should consider when choosing a law school:

- *Breadth and support of alumni network*
- *Breadth of curriculum*
- *Clinical programs*
- *Collaborative research opportunities with faculty*
- *Commitment to innovative technology*
- *Cost*
- *Externship options*
- *Faculty accessibility*
- *Intensity of writing instruction*
- *Interdisciplinary programs*
- *International programming*
- *Law library strengths and services*
- *Loan repayment assistance for low-income lawyers*
- *Location*
- *Part-time enrollment options*
- *Public interest programs*
- *Quality of teaching*
- *Racial and gender diversity within the faculty and student body*
- *Religious affiliation*
- *Size of first-year classes*
- *Skills instruction*
- *Specialized areas of faculty expertise*

PERSONAL APPEAL

A student at a prominent law school in the Pacific Northwest once described his law school to us as "a combination wood-grain bomb shelter and Ewok village." Another student at a northeastern law school told us her law school was fine except for its "ski-slope classrooms" and "East German Functionalist" architecture. While the curriculums at law schools are pretty much the same, the weather, the surrounding neighborhoods, the nightlife, and the character of the student populations are startlingly different. An important part of any graduate program is enjoying those moments in life when you're not studying. If you aren't comfortable in the environment you choose, it's likely to be reflected in the quality of work you do and your attitude. Before you make a $10,000 to $80,000 investment in any law school, you really ought to check it out in person. While you are there, talk to students and faculty. Walk around. Kick the tires. *Then* make a decision.

EMPLOYMENT PROSPECTS

Where do alumni work? How much money do they make? What percentage of graduates is employed within six months of graduation? What is the law school's bar exam passage rate? How many major law firms interview on campus? These are massively important questions, and you owe it to yourself to look into the answers before choosing a school.

YOUR VALUES

It is important that you define honestly the criteria for judging law schools. What do you want out of a law school? Clout? A high salary? A hopping social life? To live in a certain city? To avoid being in debt up to your eyeballs? A noncompetitive atmosphere? Think about it.

MAKE A LIST

Using these criteria (and others you find relevant), develop a list of prospective schools. Ideally, you'll find this book useful in creating the list. Assign a level to each new school you add (something like "reach," "good shot," and "safety").

The Dreaded Bar Exam

Once you graduate, most states require you to take a bar exam before you can practice law. Some state bar exams are really, really hard. New York and California are examples. If you don't want to take a bar exam, consider a law school in beautiful Wisconsin. Anyone who graduates from a state-certified Wisconsin law school does not need to take the state bar exam to practice law in the Badger State.

At your "reach" schools, the average LSAT scores and GPAs of incoming students should be higher than yours are. These are law schools that will probably not accept you based on your numbers alone. In order to get in, you'll need to wow them with everything else (personal statement, stellar recommendations, work experience, etc.).

Your "good shot" schools should be the schools you like that accept students with about the same LSAT scores and GPA as yours. Combined with a strong and *cohesive* application, you've got a decent shot at getting into these schools.

At your "safety" schools, the average LSAT scores and GPAs of their current students should be below yours. These schools should accept you pretty painlessly if there are no major blemishes on your application (e.g., a serious run-in with the law) and you don't just phone in the application. They hate that.

Did You Know?
According to the evil minions who make the LSAT, the average applicant applies to 4.3 law schools.

CHAPTER 9
MONEY MATTERS

Law school is a cash cow for colleges and universities everywhere and, especially at a private school, you are going to be gouged for a pretty obscene wad of cash over the next three years. Take New York University School of Law, where tuition is just over $27,000. If you are planning to eat, live somewhere, buy books, and (maybe) maintain health insurance, you are looking at about $44,000 per year. Multiply that by three years of law school. You should get $132,000. Now faint. Correct for inflation (NYU certainly will), add things like computers and other miscellany, and you can easily spend $140,000 to earn a degree. Assume that you have to borrow every penny of that $140,000. Multiply it by 8 percent over 10 years (a common assumption of law school applicants is that they will be able to pay all their debt back in 10 years or less). Your monthly payments will be around $1,520.

On the bright side, while law school is certainly an expensive proposition, the financial rewards of practicing can be immensely lucrative. You won't be forced into bankruptcy if you finance it properly. There are tried-and-true ways to reduce your initial costs, finance the costs on the horizon, and manage the debt you'll leave school with—all without ever asking "Have you been in a serious accident recently?" in a television commercial.

LAW SCHOOL ON THE CHEAP

Private schools aren't the only law schools and you don't have to come out of law school saddled with tens of thousands of dollars of debt. Many state schools have reputations that equal or surpass some of the top privates. It might be worth your while to spend a year establishing residency in a state with one or more good public law schools. Here's an idea: Pack up your belongings and move to a cool place like Minneapolis or Seattle or Berkeley or Austin or Boulder. Spend a year living there. Wait tables, hang out, listen to music, walk the earth, write the Great American Novel, and *then* study law.

Tuition at ABA-accredited schools has increased 127 percent in the last decade or so. Over the past 20 years the increase has been a whopping 570 percent.

COMPARISON SHOPPING

Here are the full-time tuition costs at law schools around the country. They are randomly paired schools in the same region (one public and one private) and are provided to help you get a feel of what law school costs are going to run you. Those schools that have the same tuition in both columns are private law schools.

Law School	In State	Out of State
Florida State University, College of Law	$4,890	$16,140
University of Miami, School of Law	$23,760	$23,760
Indiana University—Bloomington, School of Law	$6,850	$17,568
Notre Dame Law School	$23,780	$23,780
University of Tennessee, College of Law	$4,626	$12,932
Vanderbilt University, Law School	$24,350	$24,350
University of Iowa, College of Law	$6,822	$17,384
Drake University, Law School	$18,230	$18,230
Loisiana State University, Law Center	$3,586	$9,427
Tulane University, School of Law	$23,500	$23,500
University of California, Hastings College of Law	$11,200	$20,344
Golden Gate University, School of Law	$20,880	$20,880
University of Texas, School of Law	$6,000	$15,060
Baylor University, School of Law	$14,719	$14,719
University of Illinois, College of Law	$8,024	$18,884
Northwestern University, School of Law	$26,850	$26,850
University of Pittsburgh, School of Law	$12,388	$19,362
University of Pennsylvania, Law School	$26,650	$26,650
University of Oregon, School of Law	$10,238	$13,986
Lewis and Clark College, Northwestern School of Law	$21,290	$21,290

LOAN REPAYMENT ASSISTANCE PROGRAMS

If you are burdened with loans, we've got more bad news. The National Association of Law Placement (NALP) shows that less than 20 percent of law-school grads receive starting salaries of $70,000 or above. There are, however, a growing number of law schools and other sources willing to pay your loans for you (it's called loan forgiveness—as if you've sinned by taking out loans) in return for your commitment to employment in public interest law.

While doing a tour of duty in public service law will put off dreams of working in a big firm or becoming the next Johnnie Cochran, the benefits of these programs are undeniable. Here's how just about all of them work. You commit to working for a qualified public service or public interest job. As long as your gross income does not exceed the prevailing public service salary, the programs will pay off a good percentage of your debt. Eligible loans are typically any educational debt financed through your law school, which really excludes only loan sharks and credit-card debts.

MAXIMIZE YOUR AID

A simple but oft-forgotten piece of wisdom: if you don't ask, you usually don't get. Be firm when trying to get merit money from your school. Some schools have reserves of cash that go unused. Try simply asking for more financial aid. The better your grades, of course, the more likely they are to crack open their safe of financial goodies for you Unfortunately, grants aren't as prevalent for law students as for undergrads. Scholarships are not nearly as widely available, either. To get a general idea of availability of aid at a law school, contact the financial aid office.

PARENTAL CONTRIBUTION?!

If you are operating under the assumption that, as a taxpaying grownup who has been out of school for a number of years, you will be recognized as the self-supporting adult you are, well, you could be in for a surprise. Veterans of financial aid battles will not be surprised to hear that even law school financial aid offices have a difficult time recognizing when apron strings have legitimately been cut. Schools may try to take into account your parents'

The Skinny on Loan Repayment Assistance Programs
For a comprehensive listing of assistance programs and for other loan-forgiveness information, call the National Association for Public Interest Law at 202-466-3686, or look them up on the Web at www.napil.org.

income in determining your eligibility for financial aid, regardless of your age or tax status. Policies vary widely. Be sure to ask the schools you are considering exactly what their policy is regarding financial independence for the purposes of financial aid.

BORROWING MONEY

It's an amusingly simple process and several companies are in the business of lending large chunks of cash specifically to law students. Your law school financial aid office can tell you how to reach them. You should explore more than one option and shop around for the lowest fees and rates.

WHO'S ELIGIBLE?

Anyone with reasonably good credit, regardless of financial need, can borrow enough money to finance law school. If you have financial need, you will probably be eligible for some types of financial aid if you meet the following basic qualifications:

- You are a United States citizen or a permanent U.S. resident.

- You are registered for Selective Service if you are a male, or you have the documentation to prove that you are exempt.

- You are not in default on student loans already.

- You don't have a horrendous credit history.

WHAT TYPES OF LOANS ARE AVAILABLE?

There are four basic types of loans: federal, state, private, and institutional.

Federal

The federal government funds federal loan programs. Federal loans, particularly the Stafford Loan, are usually the "first resort" for borrowers. Most federal loans are need-based, but some higher-interest loans are available regardless of financial circumstances.

Let the Law School Pick Up the Tab for Phone Calls Whenever Possible
A lot of schools have free telephone numbers that they don't like to publish in books like this one. If the number we have listed for a particular law school is not an 800-number, it doesn't necessarily mean that you have to pay every time you call the school. Check out the school's Internet site, or ask for the 800-number when you call the first time.

TABLE OF LOANS			
NAME OF LOAN	**SOURCE**	**ELIGIBILITY**	**MAXIMUM ALLOCATION**
Federal Stafford Student Loan (SSL, formerly GSL)	Federal, administered by participating lender	Demonstrated financial need; selective service registration; not in default on any previous student loan	$8,500/year with maximum aggregate of $65,500; aggregate includes undergraduate loans made under the same program and undergraduate and graduate loans made under the Unsubsidized Stafford Student Loan program
Unsubsidized Stafford Student Loan	Federal, administered by participating lender	Not need based; selective service registration; not in default on any previous student loan.	$8,500/year with maximum aggregate of $65,500; aggregate includes undergraduate loans made under the same program and undergraduate and graduate loans made under the Unsubsidized Stafford Student Loan program
Federal Supplemental Loan for Students (SLS)	Federal, administered by participating lender	Not need based, but must first apply for Federal Stafford Student Loan.	$10,000/year, with aggregate of $73,000; aggregate includes undergraduate loans
Perkins Loan (formerly NDSL)	Federal, administered by school	Demonstrated financial need; selective service registration; not in default on student loans.	Aggregate of $18,000; aggregate amount includes undergraduate loans
Law Access Loan (LAL)	Access Group	Not need based	$120,000 for most schools

Private

Private loans are funded by banks, foundations, corporations, and other associations. A number of private loans are targeted to aid particular segments of the population. You may have to do some investigating to identify private loans for which you might qualify. Like always, contact your law school's financial aid office to learn more.

Institutional

The amount of loan money available and the method by which it is disbursed vary greatly from one school to another. Private schools, especially those that are older and more established, tend to have larger endowments and, therefore, can offer more assistance. To find out about the resources available at a particular school, refer to its catalogue or contact—you guessed it—the financial aid office.

TABLE OF LOANS			
REPAYMENT AND DEFERRAL OPTIONS	INTEREST RATE	PROS	CONS
10 years to repay; begin repayment 6 months after graduation; forbearance possible.	Variable, based on 91-day T-Bill plus 3.1%; current cap is *9%	Most common law school loan; interest is subsidized by the feds during school; once you get a loan, any subsequent loans are made at the same rate	None
10 years to repay; principal is deferred while in school, but interest accrues immediately; begin repayment six months after graduation; forbearance possible	Variable, based on 91-day T-Bill plus 3.1%; current cap is *9%	Not need based; same interest rates as Federal Stafford; once you get a loan, any subsequent loans are made at the same rate	Interest accrues immediately and is capitalized if deferred.
10 years to repay; interest accrues immediately	Variable, 52-week T-Bill plus 3.1%; capped at *11%	High aggregate amount	High interest rate; interest accrues while in school and capitalizes if deferred
10 years to repay; begin repayment 9 months after graduation	Fixed, 5%	Low interest rate	Low maximum allocation; primarily restricted to first- and second-year students
20 years to repay; principal repayment begins nine months after graduation.	Varies quarterly; 91-day T-bill rate plus 3.25% with no cap; average rate has recently hovered around *11%	High maximum allocation, not need based	High interest rate

CHAPTER 10
CAREER MATTERS

Okay, it's a long time away, but you really ought to be thinking about your professional career beyond law school from Day One, especially if your goal is to practice with a major law firm. What stands between you and a job as an "associate," the entry-level position at one of these firms, is a three-stage evaluation: first, a review of your resume, including your grades and work experience; second, an on-campus interview; and last, one or more "call-back" interviews at the firm's offices. It's a fairly intimidating ordeal, but there are a few ways to reduce the anxiety and enhance your chances of landing a great job.

YOUR RESUME

The first thing recruiters tend to notice after your name is the name of the law school you attend. Tacky, but true. Perhaps the greatest misconception among law students, however, is that hiring decisions turn largely upon your school's prestige. All those rankings perpetuate this myth. To be sure, there are a handful of schools with reputations above all others, and students who excel at these schools are in great demand. But you are equally well, if not better, situated applying from the top of your class at a strong, less prestigious law school class than from the bottom half of a "Top 10" law school class.

FIRST-YEAR GRADES ARE THE WHOLE ENCHILADA

Fair or not, the first year of law school will unduly influence your legal future. It's vital that you hit the ground running because law school grades are *the* critical factor in recruitment. An even harsher reality is that *first-year grades are by far the most critical in the hiring process*. Decisions about who gets which fat summer jobs are generally handed down before students take a single second-year exam. Consequently, you're left with exactly no time to adjust to law-school life and little chance to improve your transcript if you don't come out on top as a first-year student.

WORK EXPERIENCE

If you're applying to law school right out of college, chances are your most significant work experience has been a summer job. Recruiters don't expect you to have spent these months writing Supreme Court decisions. They are generally satisfied if you have shown evidence that you worked diligently and seriously at each opportunity. Students who took a year or more off after college obviously have more opportunities to impress, but also more of a burden to demonstrate diligence and seriousness.

Work experience in the legal industry—clerkships and paralegal jobs, just for instance—can be excellent sources of professional development. They are fairly common positions among job applicants, though, so don't feel you have to pursue one of these routes just to show your commitment to the law. You'll make a better impression, really, by working in an industry in which you'd like to specialize (e.g., a prospective securities lawyer summering with an investment bank).

THE INTERVIEWS

There are as many "right approaches" to an interview as there are interviewers. That observation provides little comfort, of course, especially if you're counting on a good interview to make up for whatever deficiencies there are on your resume. Think about the purpose of the initial 30-minute interview you are likely to have: it provides a rough sketch not only of your future office personality but also your demeanor under stress. The characteristics you demonstrate and the *impression* you give are more important than anything you say. Composure, confidence, maturity, articulation, an ability to develop rapport—these are characteristics recruiters are looking for. Give them what they want.

CHAPTER 11
LAW SCHOOL 101

IS IT REALLY THAT BAD?

The first semester of law school has the well-deserved reputation of being among the greatest challenges to the intellect and stamina that you'll ever face. It is tons and tons of work and, in many ways, it's an exercise in intellectual survival. Just as the gung-ho army recruit must survive boot camp, so too must the bright-eyed law student endure the homogenizing effects of that first year.

Though complex and difficult, the subject matter in first-year law-school courses is probably no more inherently difficult than what is taught in other graduate or professional schools. The particular, private terror that is shared by roughly 40,000 1Ls every year stems more from law school's peculiar *style*. The method of instruction here unapologetically punishes students who would prefer to learn passively.

THE FIRST-YEAR CURRICULUM

The first-year curriculum in the law school you attend will almost certainly be composed of a combination of the following courses:

TORTS

The word comes from the Middle French for "injury." The Latin root of the word means "twisted." Torts are wrongful acts, excluding breaches of contract, over which you can sue people. They include battery, assault, false imprisonment, and intentional infliction of emotional distress. Torts can range from the predictable to the bizarre, from "Dog Bites Man" to "Man Bites Dog" and everything in between. The study of torts mostly involves reading cases in order to discern the legal rationale behind decisions pertaining to the extent of, and limits on, the civil liability of one party for harm done to another.

CONTRACTS

They may seem fairly self-explanatory but contractual relationships are varied and complicated, as two semesters of contracts will teach you. Again, through the study of past court cases, you will follow the largely unwritten

---

An Old Law School Adage
First year they scare you to death.
Second year they work you to death.
Third year they bore you to death.

law governing the system of conditions and obligations a contract represents, as well as the legal remedies available when contracts are breached.

CIVIL PROCEDURE

Civil procedure is the study of how you get things done in civil (as opposed to criminal) court. "Civ Pro" is the study of the often dizzyingly complex rules that govern not only who can sue whom, but also how, when, and where they can do it. This is not merely a study of legal protocol, for issues of process have a significant indirect effect on the substance of the law. Rules of civil procedure govern the conduct of both the courtroom trial and the steps that might precede it: obtaining information (discovery), making your case (pleading), pretrial motions, etc.

PROPERTY

You may never own a piece of land, but your life will inevitably and constantly be affected by property laws. Anyone interested in achieving an understanding of broader policy issues will appreciate the significance of this material. Many property courses will emphasize the transfer of property and, to varying degrees, economic analysis of property law.

CRIMINAL LAW

Even if you become a criminal prosecutor or defender, you will probably never run into most of the crimes you will be exposed to in this course. Can someone who shoots the dead body of a person he believes to be alive be charged with attempted murder? What if they were both on drugs or had really rough childhoods? Also, you'll love the convoluted exam questions, in which someone will invariably go on a nutty crime spree.

CONSTITUTIONAL LAW

"Con Law" is the closest thing to a normal class you will take in your first year. It emphasizes issues of government structure (e.g., federal power versus state power) and individual rights (e.g., personal liberties, freedom of expression, property protection). You'll spend a great deal of time studying the limits on the lawmaking power of Congress as well.

Good Law School Joke

In contracts class, the professor asked a student, "If you were to give someone an orange, how would you go about it?"

The student replied, "Here's an orange."

The professor was outraged. "No! No!" she exclaimed. "Think like a lawyer!"

The student then replied, "Okay. I'd say, 'I hereby give and convey to you all and singular, my estate and interests, rights, claim, title, and claim of and in, said orange, together with all its rind, juices, pulp, and seeds, and all rights and advantages contained therein, with full power to bite, cut, freeze, and otherwise eat, or give, bequeath, or devise with and without aforementioned rind, juices, pulp, and seeds. Anything herein before or hereinafter or in any deed, or deeds, instruments of whatever nature or kind whatsoever to the contrary in anywise notwithstanding . . . '"

Tips for Classroom Success

Be alert. Review material immediately before class so that it is fresh in your memory. Then review your notes from class later the same day and the week's worth of notes at the end of each week.

Remember that there are few correct answers. The goal of a law school class is generally to analyze, understand, and attempt to resolve issues or problems.

Learn to state and explain legal rules and principles with accuracy.

You don't want to focus on minutiae from cases or class discussions; always be trying to figure out what the law is.

Accept the ambiguity in legal analysis and class discussion; classes are intended to be thought-provoking, perplexing, and difficult.

No one class session will make or break you. Keep in mind how each class fits within the course overall.

Don't write down what other students say. Write down the law. Concentrate your notes on the professor's hypotheticals and emphasis in class.

A simple but effective way of keeping yourself in touch with where the class is at any given time is to review the table of contents in the casebook.

If you don't use a laptop, don't sit next to someone who does. The constant tapping on the keys will drive you crazy, and you may get a sense that they are writing down more than you (which is probably not true).

If you attend class, you don't need to tape record it. There are better uses of your time than to spend hours listening to the comments of students who were just as confused as you were when you first dealt with the material in class.

LEGAL METHODS

One of the few 20th-century improvements on the traditional first-year curriculum that has taken hold nearly everywhere, this course travels under various aliases, such as Legal Research and Writing, or Elements of the Law. In recent years, increased recognition of the importance of legal writing skills has led over half of the U.S. law schools to require or offer a writing course after the first year. This class will be your smallest, and possibly your only, refuge from the Socratic Method. Methods courses are often taught by junior faculty and attorneys in need of extra cash, and are designed to help you acquire fundamental skills in legal research, analysis, and writing. The Methods course may be the least frightening you face, but it can easily consume an enormous amount of time. This is a common lament, particularly at schools where very few credits are awarded for it.

In addition to these course requirements, many law schools require 1Ls to participate in a moot-court exercise. As part of this exercise, students—sometimes working in pairs or even small groups—must prepare briefs and oral arguments for a mock trial (usually appellate). This requirement is often tied in with the methods course so that those briefs and oral arguments will be well researched—and graded.

THE CASE METHOD

In the majority of your law school courses, and probably in all of your first-year courses, your only texts will be things called casebooks. The case method eschews explanation and encourages exploration. In a course that relies entirely on the casebook, you will never come across a printed list of "laws." Instead, you will learn that in many areas of law there is no such thing as a static set of rules, but only a constantly evolving system of principles. You are expected to understand the principles of law—in all of its layers and ambiguity—through a critical examination of a series of cases that were decided according to such principles. You will often feel utterly lost, groping for answers to unarticulated questions. This is not merely normal; it is intended.

In practical terms, the case method works like this: For every class meeting, you will be assigned a number of cases to read from your casebook, which is a collection of (extremely edited) written judicial decisions in actual court cases. The names won't even have been changed to protect the innocent. The cases are the written judicial opinions rendered in court cases that were decided at the appeals or Supreme Court level. (Written opinions are not generally rendered in lower courts.)

Your casebook will contain no instructions and little to no explanation. Your assignments simply will be to read the cases and be in a position to answer questions based on them. There will be no written homework assignments, just cases, cases, and more cases.

You will write, for your own benefit, summaries—or briefs—of these cases. Briefs are your attempts to summarize the issues and laws around which a particular case revolves *By briefing, you figure out what the law is*. The idea is that, over the course of a semester, you will try to integrate the content of your case briefs and your notes from in-class lectures, discussions, or dialogues into some kind of cohesive whole.

THE SOCRATIC METHOD

As unfamiliar as the case method will be to most 1Ls, the real source of anxiety is the way the professor presents it. Socratic instruction entails directed questioning and limited lecturing. Generally, the Socratic professor invites a student to attempt a cogent summary of a case assigned for that day's class. Hopefully, it won't be you (but someday it will be). Regardless of the accuracy and thoroughness of your initial response, the professor then grills you on details overlooked or issues unresolved. Then, the professor will change the facts of the actual case at hand into a hypothetical case that may or may not have demanded a different decision by the court.

The overall goal of the Socratic Method is to forcibly improve your critical reasoning skills. If you are reasonably well prepared, thinking about all these questions will force you beyond the immediately apparent issues in a given case to consider its broader implications. The dialogue between the effective Socratic instructor and the victim-of-the-moment will also force nonparticipating students to question their underlying assumptions of the case under discussion.

WHAT IS CLINICAL LEGAL EDUCATION?

The latest so-called innovation in legal education is ironic in that it's a return to the old emphasis on practical experience. Hands-on training in the practical skills of lawyering now travels under the name "Clinical Legal Education."

HOW IT WORKS

Generally, a clinical course focuses on developing practical lawyering skills. "Clinic" means exactly what you would expect: a working law office where second- and third-year law students counsel clients and serve human beings. (A very limited number of law schools allow first-year students to participate in legal clinics.)

In states that grant upper-level law students a limited right to represent clients in court, students in a law school's clinic might actually follow cases through to their resolution. Some schools have a single on-site clinic that operates something like a general law practice, dealing with cases ranging from petty crime to landlord-tenant disputes. At schools that have dedicated the most resources to their clinical programs, numerous specialized clinics deal with narrowly defined areas of law, such as employment discrimination. The opportunities to participate in such live-action programs, however, are limited.

OTHER OPTIONS

Clinical legal education is a lot more expensive than traditional instruction, which means that few law schools can accommodate more than a small percentage of their students in clinical programs. If that's the case, check out external clinical placements and simulated clinical courses. In a clinical externship, you might work with a real firm or public agency several hours a week and meet with a faculty advisor only occasionally. Though students who participate in these programs are unpaid, they will ordinarily receive academic credit. Also, placements are chosen quite carefully to ensure that you don't become a gopher.

There are also simulated clinical courses. In one of these, you'll perform all of the duties that a student in a live-action clinic would, but your clients are imaginary.

CHAPTER 12
HOW TO GET REALLY GOOD GRADES
AT *ANY* LAW SCHOOL

You are going to get plenty of advice about how to do well in law school—much of it unsolicited. You certainly don't need any from us. We strongly advise, however, that you pay extra-special attention to Wentworth Miller.

WHO THE HECK IS WENTWORTH MILLER?

There are lots of commercial programs and aids designed to assist law students in studying for and writing exams but—trust us—Wentworth Miller's Legal Essay Exam Writing System, "LEEWS" for short, is the best of the bunch. It's something like The Princeton Review for law school exams. It may be the most fruitful eight hours (and $100 or so) you'll spend in law school. If you can, try to check out the one-day LEEWS seminar when it rolls through your town during first semester. And if your first semester grades aren't what you hoped, make absolutely sure to swallow your pride and sign up for LEEWS when it comes through your area again second semester, even if it means traveling a few hours to a metropolitan area.

We know. You're skeptical. Miller's got credentials, though. He is a 1977 Yale Law graduate, a Rhodes scholar, a member of the New York Bar, and a one-time assistant U.S. attorney. He's been prepping students for the bar exam and law school exams for about 20 years, and he puts his money where his mouth is: a B-average minimum or your money back. He also claims nearly 100,000 graduates from over 170 law schools.

We posed a few questions to Miller about the LEEWS program that we thought incoming law students might ask. Here's what he had to say.

Q: **What are the five biggest mistakes first-year law students make?**

A: An opportunity like this pushes my buttons. This entire topic fires me up. An underlying aim of mine—we Yale Law grads always need some higher, overarching purpose—has always been nothing less than to slowly but surely bring about needed instructional change in law schools. Across the board, I think law schools and law professors do a poor job conveying fundamentals of lawyer-like purpose, function, and thinking. I believe they

Contact LEEWS
LEEWS
501 Broad Street, Suite 201
Sewickley, PA 15143
Phone: 800-765-8246
www.leews.com

seek to be something other than the *trade schools* they are, and they end up failing students while milking them for a needless third year of fees. The process also does little to help future clients.

Anyway, **the biggest mistake** first-year law students make is assuming that the study techniques that brought success in college or graduate school will bring similar success in law school. Almost everyone admitted to Harvard, Duke, NYU, or any number of top law schools scored high on the LSAT and had a nearly perfect GPA as an undergrad. Yet fewer than 10 percent of students at those schools consistently get A's. Over half the class doesn't got a single A in a substantive course. Ever. This is true at all law schools. Despite their best efforts, many students receive the first C's, D's, and even F's of their lives in law school. Clearly, something different is going on; new insights, skills, and techniques are needed.

A **second big mistake** is buying into the mythology prevalent in all law schools that some few students—the 5 to 7 percent who get A's consistently—have an innate, mysterious, lawyering aptitude: the "right stuff." It typically happens when a classmate responds impressively during the intimidating "Socratic Q and A" between professor and student. It certainly occurs when the first set of grades come out and someone you feel is no more intelligent than you, and whom you know to be no more—possibly even less—diligent, gets higher grades, even those rare law school A's.

The notion that "you have it or you don't" is fostered by law professors (who typically got A's in law school, and therefore "had it"), top students (who enjoy the aura of "specialness" accorded to them), and most of all by *other* students who work hard but don't do well. Suddenly they have an excuse for mediocre performance. They can got the same B's and C's with a lot less work, so they give up the quest for A's. Years later, after they've been practicing attorneys for a while, those same students will say, "If only I had known in law school what I know now, I would have studied differently. I would have done much better." Well, they're right. Getting A's is not a matter of genes. Some indeed have a knack. But most can learn how to perform like a competent lawyer on exams, which is all any law

All B+'s puts you in the top quarter at most schools, the top fifth at many.

professor wants to see. The trick is to learn the skills and insights of *actual lawyering* before getting out in practice.

A **third important mistake** is not to focus immediately on the only thing that counts in law school, where grades are concerned: the final exam. Responding "not prepared" three times in class *may* result in your grade being lowered by a half (e.g., B to C+), but this threat is primarily a scare tactic. Generally, and this is so hard for new 1Ls to accept, given their extensive class preparation and fear of being "called on," class participation has no bearing on grades. Nor is it indicative of who is likely to do well. There are almost never graded homework or pop quizzes in law school. If there is a midterm at mid-semester, it's merely a practice exam for your benefit. Professors may say, "The midterm can count up to 25 percent," but that's only if it will help your grade. Midterms almost never count against you. *The only thing that counts is the typically three- or four-hour final exam.* Properly understood, it is the end-all and be-all of the law student's existence. Knowing exactly what is needed for the final exam is critical to briefing more efficiently and getting the most out of class discussion. Yet new law students never even look at old exams (typically on file in the library) until late in the term. They don't know what they are like, what is expected, how to pull them apart analytically. They blithely preoccupy themselves with the daily grind of briefing cases when they should be pointing toward the final exam from Day One.

A **fourth major mistake**, which almost can't be avoided given the faith and confidence 1Ls naturally accord someone so awesome and seemingly all-knowing as a law professor, is to assume that the professor will eventually sort out the confusion and uncertainty typically felt from the very first day of class. The primary reason for this confusion and uncertainty is the ignorance concerning exams and how to handle them. You're not sure what you are supposed to be taking away from cases, and where everything is going. If you approach professors about this, they'll smile sympathetically and say, "Don't worry. Brief your cases. Learn the law. It will eventually click . . . fall into place . . . happen, etc. Besides," they'll tell you, "I'll talk about exams, give you what you need to know at the appropriate time." You'll feel better after this conversation, but you'll be no better off.

What the professors really means is, "You either have it, or you don't," and "If you've got the right stuff, it will click for you." And, frankly, the professor will be thinking, "You must not have it," as evidenced by the fact that you came to express confusion. Indeed, precisely because law professors don't believe that doing well on their exams can be reduced to something approaching science, they happily buy into the standard exam-writing wisdom that has been around for decades and that has never helped more than the few with a knack to attain A's.

A **fifth important mistake** is not to know the "black letter law" that applies to the assigned cases *before* coming to class. You must know black letter law *cold*. Most 1Ls wait all semester for the professor to lay out the law for them. It won't happen. They don't see that as their job. Rarely, if ever, will you hear a professor say, "The rule is . . . ." Instead, they'll start talking about an implication of the rule as it relates to a fact scenario. *It is taken for granted that you can learn the law on your on, and that you have.*

Q: **In a nutshell, what's wrong with the typical advice given to law students?**

A: Well, the most obvious problem with the exam-writing and study advice offered up by professors and law student organizations is that it's "too" nutshell in nature. For example, you'll be told to be "lawyer-like" and to spot "issues" lurking in fact patterns. But what does "lawyer-like" mean? What's an "issue" exactly? These foreign concepts are never adequately explained to the neophyte law student. And no one seems to dare ask, perhaps for fear of being seen not to have the "right stuff."

Without exception, the accumulated exam-writing wisdom featured in virtually all law schools and exam-writing programs centers around the Standard Advice of "IRAC." Professors will say, "Follow IRAC. IRAC the exam. Don't bother with that commercial course. IRAC is the only system. It's all you need." The problem, obviously, is that knowing IRAC has never helped the great majority of law students get anything but B's and C's. The problem, really, is how to *implement* IRAC.

IRAC, by the way, is an acronym standing for Issue (as in "state the legal issue"), Rule ("state the relevant legal

A Few More Good Books

A Few More Good Books

Clarence Darrow, The Story of My Life
The original get-down trial lawyer offers his life and times in his own words.

Gerald Gunther, Learned Hand: The Man and the Judge
A contemporary legal giant (Gunther) considers a legal immortal for the ages (Judge Hand). By the way, is "Learned Hand" the absolute perfect name for a famous American judge or what?

Lani Guinier, The Tyranny of the Majority: Fundamental Fairness in Representative Democracy
This tome is a great introduction to the wonderful world of voting theory (with immensely detailed footnotes to boot) by a cutting-edge "democratic idealist."

Geoffrey R. Stone (Editor), The Bill of Rights in the Modern State
This collection of essays by Constitutional heavyweight champions represents the full—and we mean full—range of contemporary interpretations of the first 10 amendments to the Constitution of 1787.

precept"), Application or Analysis ("apply the rule to the facts, and analyze the issue"), Conclusion ("state a conclusion"). As a start in coming to grips with law exams, IRAC is quite useful. It describes what professors want in the treatment of each issue identified for discussion and gives students a handle on exams. It also supports the notion that professors all want the same thing, although some professors cross students up by instructing, "I don't want to see just IRAC." That means they want more policy discussion introduced. New law students feel much better when they learn what IRAC means. Add to IRAC such standard and rather obvious advice as "Read facts carefully, circling 'issue-generating words,'" "Paragraph frequently," "Argue both sides of the issues," "Support conclusions," "Pay attention to time limits," etc., and you have the gist of standard exam-writing instruction. It's a vague strategy, but it sounds wonderful because law school exams are no longer so mysterious. All that remains, it would seem, is to learn the law.

The problem is that such general and rather obvious advice doesn't go nearly far enough. IRAC and the standard advice fall far short in terms of how, systematically, to identify issues, how to perform the analysis that impresses and earns A's, how to present analysis concisely, and therefore how best to study, learn the law, and get the most out of class discussion. For all but the few students with a knack for methodically sorting out issues and concisely presenting "lawyer-like analysis" in the IRAC formula, confidence will be short-lived. When the exam rolls around, the typical law student will be disoriented by professors' often cryptic instructions (e.g., "Imagine you are a law clerk drafting a memo" or, simply, "What result?"), confused by the helter skelter of dense facts, and stressed by the severe time pressure. Moreover, most 1Ls haven't yet learned how to do "lawyer-like analysis," so they are unable to learn the law as well as they should have.

Q: How is the LEEWS method any different?

A: Well, we go way beyond IRAC, and our instruction on how to analyze as a lawyer is simply better than anyone else's. We show how all law exams and all legal problem solving can be understood in exactly the same way and, therefore, approached in the same way. This makes taking exams, writing papers, and even reading cases a predictable exercise, which engenders great confidence.

Our approach to revealing relevant issues, for example, is unique and highly structured. In the LEEWS approach, students don't randomly attempt to "spot issues." It's too haphazard an exercise. Rather, fact patterns are broken down in a series of steps into manageable units that then reveal the relevant issues—sometimes more of them than the professor realizes are present, which tends to impress. We have an equally innovative approach to presenting analysis—we call it "ugly, but effective, or UBE"—that takes "good writer" out of the equation. Presentation in roughly one concise paragraph per issue, satisfying the dictates of IRAC, becomes almost mathematical and as predictable as identifying issues. We also show students how to cut out the busywork and wasted motion of briefing and course outlining. Our students typically brief cases in two to five lines; take a page, and often less, of class notes per class hour; and end the term with course outlines of 10 to 25 pages. Our results have gotten better and better over the years because I'm always tinkering and trying to convey the techniques better, enabling students to see how to apply the system in every conceivable legal situation.

Q: **Any additional tips for first-year law students?**

A: **Lawyering is a game.** Think of being a law student (and being a lawyer) as a game, because that's essentially what it is. The "lawyering game," properly understood and played, is one of the most intellectually competitive, challenging, and stimulating activities out there. What do you think keeps many lawyers eager to go to the office well into their seventies? The game-like quality of lawyering explains why some students seem to be enjoying what most find unbearable. The ones who enjoy it—who have the "right stuff"—have simply figured out the game. If you find yourself not enjoying reading cases, attending classes, and being at law school in general, it's probably because you haven't caught on to the game reflected in every case and every legal transaction. Unfortunately, most law students never do, which is why most report finding practice to be so much more enjoyable than law school. Inevitably, practicing law teaches you the game of lawyering. *But anybody can learn it*. The trick for success in law school is to learn the game the first year.

Use commercial outlines from Day One. Since rules and principles are rarely stated clearly and completely in the abridged cases reproduced in casebooks, students should pick up commercial outlines for each class at the beginning of the term and refer to the outlines for clear statements of the blurry rules and principles found in cases. It doesn't really matter which commercial outlines you obtain. Emanuel's, Gilbert's, Casenotes, Roadmaps, and others set forth the law clearly and completely. Looking for used copies is a money-saving idea.

Don't waste money on new textbooks. Professors typically advise against the use of commercial outlines because they're afraid students won't read the casebooks. (Of course, many 2Ls and 3Ls don't purchase casebooks or even go to class unless it is mandatory.) I am not advising against purchasing and reading casebooks. I would try to find used copies, though, as they are much cheaper. You may also be able to check out a (free) copy from the law library. The crucial thing to remember is that you need much more than casebooks and lecture notes to get the complete law.

Briefing cases is a waste of time. Briefing cases conventionally (using "IRAC" on each case you read) is a waste of time. No one briefs after first semester. The thing to do is to extract relevant law, know how to apply it (the hard part); and incorporate it weekly in a course outline. It is a terrible mistake to concentrate on briefing and class preparation while ignoring the all-important final exam. Don't wait to look at old exams (on file in the library) until days before finals. Then it's too late.

Class participation is for the birds. It is normally unrelated to exam performance or grades. Those people who sound like such geniuses in class? Few of them get A's. So don't worry about being called on. Prepare (from Day One) for what really counts: the final exam.

Law school and law exams are ultimately about conflict resolution. Think about it: *The raison d'etre of a system of law is conflict resolution.* Nothing more. Statutes, legal precedents, lawsuits, and every other law-related thing are first and foremost concerned with the resolution of present or (anticipated) future conflict. All government and legislative bodies concern themselves with responding to conflicts or potential conflicts (e.g., air pollution and those who favor and oppose certain emission restrictions; abortion; highway safety measures; proposed treaties; etc.). When you are thinking about a case or an exam question, approach the problem as a conflict and try to help both sides resolve it in their favor.

CHAPTER 13
HOW TO USE THIS BOOK

It's pretty simple.

The first part of this book provides a wealth of indispensable information covering everything you need to know about selecting and getting into the law school of your choice. There is also a great deal here about what to expect from law school and how to do well. You name it—taking the LSAT, choosing the best school for you, writing a great personal statement, interviewing, paying for it—it's all here.

The second part is the real meat and potatoes of the *Complete Book of Law Schools*. It comprises portraits of more than 200 schools across the United States and Canada. Each school has a directory entry that contains the same basic information and follows the same basic format. Unless noted in the descriptions below, The Princeton Review collected all of the data presented in these directory entries. As is customary with college guides, all data reflects the figures for the academic year prior to publication, unless otherwise indicated. Since law school offerings and demographics vary significantly from one institution to another and some schools report data more thoroughly than others, some entries will not include all the individual data described below.

Some schools have also opted to include a "School Says..." profile, giving extended descriptions of their admissions process, curriculum, internship opportunities, and much more. This is your chance to get in-depth information on programs that interest you. These schools have paid us a small fee for the chance to tell you more about themselves, and the editorial responsibility is solely that of the law school. We think you'll find these profiles add lots to your picture of a school.

WHAT'S IN THE PROFILES

The Heading: The first thing you will see for each profile is (obviously) the school's name. Just below the name, you'll find the school's snail mail address, telephone number, fax number, e-mail address, and Internet site. You can find the name of the admissions office contact person in the heading, too.

INSTITUTIONAL INFORMATION

Public/Private: Indicates whether a school is state-supported or funded by private means.

Affiliation: If the school is affiliated with a particular religion, you'll find that information here.

Environment: Urban, suburban, or rural. Pretty self-explanatory.

Academic Calendar: The schedule of academic terms. Semester—two long terms. Trimester—three terms. Quarter—three terms plus an optional summer term.

Schedule: Whether only full-time or both full- and part-time programs are available.

Student/Faculty Ratio: The ratio of law students to full-time faculty.

Total Faculty: The number of faculty members at the law school.

% Part Time: The percentage of faculty who are part time.

% Female: The percentage of faculty who are women.

% Minority: You guessed it! The percentage of people who teach at the law school who are also members of minority groups.

PROGRAMS

Academic Specialties: Different areas of law and academic programs in which the school prides itself.

Advanced Degrees Offered: Degrees available through the law school, and the length of the program.

Combined Degrees Offered: Programs at this school involving the law school and some other college or degree program within the larger university, and how long it will take you to complete the joint program.

Clinical Program Required? Indicates whether clinical programs are required to complete the core curriculum.

Clinical Programs: Programs designed to give students hands-on training and experience in the practice of some area of law.

Even More Good Books
Law Services, Thinking About Law School: A Minority Guide
This free publication, which offers pointers on finding and getting into the right school for minority applicants, is worth checking out.

Karl N. Llewellyn, The Bramble Bush: On Our Law and Its Study
Law school deans and professors all across the fruited plain will tell you that The Bramble Bush is the consummate introduction to the study of law. If you don't find this book interesting, don't go to law school. Seriously.

Scott Turow, One L: The Turbulent True Story of a First Year at Harvard Law School
This law school primer is equal parts illuminating and harrowing.

Grading System: Scoring system used by the law school.

Legal Writing/Methods Course Requirements: The components of the curriculum included to develop the research, analysis, and writing skills vital to the practice of law.

STUDENT INFORMATION

Enrollment of Law School: The total number of students enrolled in the law school.

% Male/Female: The percentage of students with an X and a Y chromosome and the percentage of students with two X chromosomes, respectively.

% Full Time: The percentage of students who attend the school on a full-time basis.

% Full Time That Are International: The percentage of students that hails from foreign soil.

% Minority: The percentage of students who represent minority groups.

Average Age of Entering Class: On the whole, how old the 1Ls are.

RESEARCH FACILITIES

Computers/Workstations Available: The number of computers on campus.

Computer Labs: The number of rooms full of computers that you can use for free.

Campuswide Network? Indicates whether the campus is wired.

School-Supported Research Centers: Indicates whether the school has on-campus, internally supported research centers.

EXPENSES/FINANCIAL AID:

Annual Tuition (Residents/Nonresidents): What it costs to go to school there for an academic year. For state schools, both in-state and out-of-state tuition is listed.

Room and Board (On/Off campus): This is the school's estimate of what it costs to buy meals and to pay for decent

---

Law School Trivia
The least litigated of the 10 amendments in the Bill of Rights is the Third Amendment, which prohibits the quartering of soldiers in private homes without consent of the owner.

living quarters for the academic year. Where available, on- and off-campus rates are listed.

Books and Supplies: Indicates how much students can expect to shell out for textbooks and other assorted supplies during the academic year.

Financial Aid Application Deadline: The last day on which students can turn in their applications for monetary assistance.

Average Grant: Average amount awarded to students that does not have to be paid back. This figure can include scholarships as well.

Average Loan: Average amount of loan dollars accrued by students for the year.

% of Aid That Is Merit-Based: The percentage of aid not based on financial need

% Receiving Some Sort of Aid: The percentage of the students here presently accumulating a staggering debt.

Average Total Aid Package: How much aid each student here receives on average for the year.

Average Debt: The amount of debt—or, in legal lingo, arrears—you'll likely be saddled with by the time you graduate.

Tuition Per Credit (Residents/Nonresidents): Dollar amount charged per credit hour. For state schools, both in-state and out-of-state amounts are listed when they differ.

Fees Per Credit (Residents/Nonresidents): That mysterious extra money you are required to pay the law school in addition to tuition and everything else, on a per-credit basis. If in-state and out-of-state students are charged differently, both amounts are listed.

ADMISSIONS INFORMATION
Application Fee: The fee is how much it costs to apply to the school.

Regular Application Deadline and "Rolling" Decision: Many law schools evaluate applications and notify applicants of admission decisions on a continuous, "rolling" basis over the course of several months (ordinarily from late fall to midsummer). Obviously, if you apply to one of these schools, you want to apply early because there will be more places available at the beginning of the process.

Regular Notification: The official date on which a law school will release a decision for an applicant who applied using the "regular admission" route.

LSDAS Accepted? A "Yes" here indicates that the school utilizes the Law School Data Assembly Service.

Average GPA/Range of GPA: It's usually on a 4.0 scale.

Average LSAT/Range of LSAT: Indicates the average LSAT score of incoming 1Ls, as reported by the school.

Transfer Students Accepted? Whether transfer students from other schools are considered for admission.

Other Schools to Which Students Applied: The law schools to which applicants to this school also apply. It's important. It's a reliable indicator of the overall academic quality of the applicant pool.

Other Admissions Factors Considered: Additional criteria the law schools considers when admitting applicants.

Number of Applications Received: The number of people who applied to the law school.

Number of Applicants Accepted: The number of people who were admitted to the school's class.

Number of Applicants Enrolled: The number of those admitted who chose to attend that particular institution.

INTERNATIONAL STUDENTS

TOEFL Required of International Students? Indicates whether or not international students must take the TOEFL, or Test of English as a Foreign Language, in order to be admitted to the school.

Minimum TOEFL: Minimum score an international student must earn on the TOEFL in order to be admitted.

EMPLOYMENT INFORMATION

The **bar graph** will let you know in which fields a law school's grads are working. The fields are as follows:

Public Interest: The percentage of (mostly) altruistic graduates who got jobs providing legal assistance to folks who couldn't afford it otherwise and fighting the power in general.

Private Practice: The percentage of graduates who got jobs in traditional law firms of various sizes, or "put out a shingle" for themselves as sole practitioners.

Military: The percentage of lawyers who work to represent the Armed Forces in all kinds of legal matters. Like Tom Cruise in *A Few Good Men*. We knew you could handle the truth.

Judicial Clerkships: The number of graduates who got jobs doing research for judges.

Government: Uncle Sam needs lawyers like you wouldn't even believe.

Business/Industry: The number of graduates who got jobs working in business, in corporations, in consulting, etc. These jobs are sometimes law-related and sometimes not.

Academic: The number of graduates who got jobs at law schools, universities, and think tanks.

Rate of Placement: Placement rate into the job market upon completion of the Juris Doctor.

Average Starting Salary: The amount of money the average graduate of this law school makes the first year out of school.

Employers Who Frequently Hire Grads: Firms where past grads have had success finding jobs.

Prominent Alumni: Those who made it.

State for Bar Exam: The state for which most students from the school will take the bar exam.

Number Taking Bar Exam: Number of students taking the bar.

Pass Rate for First-Time Bar: After three years, the percentage of students who passed the bar exam the first time they took it. It's a crucial statistic. You *don't* want to fail your state's bar.

Law School Trivia
The guarantee that each state must have an equal number of votes in the United States Senate is the only provision in the Constitution of 1787 that cannot be amended.

DECODING DEGREES

Many law schools offer joint or combined degree programs with other departments (or sometimes even with other schools) that you can earn along with your Juris Doctor. You'll find the abbreviations for these degrees in the individual school profiles, but we thought we'd give you a little help in figuring out exactly what they are.

AMBA	Accounting Master of Business
BCL	Bachelor of Civil Law
DJUR	Doctor of Jurisprudence
DL	Doctor of Law
DLaw	Doctor of Law
EdD	Doctor of Education
HRIR	Human Resources and Industrial Relations
IMBA	International Master of Business Administration
JD	Juris Doctor
JSD	Doctor of Juridical Science
JSM	Master of the Science of Law
LLB	Bachelor of Law
LLCM	Master of Comparative Law (for international students)
LLM	Master of Law
MA	Master of Arts
MAcc	Master of Accounting
MALD	Masters of Arts in Law and Diplomacy
MAM	Master of Arts Management
MAM	Master of Management
MANM	Master of Nonprofit Management
MAPA	Master of Public Administration
MAUA	Masters of Arts in Urban Affairs
MBA	Master of Business Administration
MCJ	Master of Criminal Justice
MCL	Master of Comparative Law
MCP	Master of Community Planning
MCRP	Master of City and Regional Planning

MDiv	Master of Divinity		MSIA	Master of Industrial Administration
ME	Master of Engineering OR Master of Education		MSIE	Master of Science in International Economics
MEd	Master of Education		MSJ	Master of Science in Journalism
MED	Master of Environmental Design		MSPH	Master of Science in Public Health
MEM	Master of Environmental Management		MSW	Master of Social Welfare
MFA	Master of Fine Arts		MT	Master of Taxation
MHA	Master of Health Administration		MTS	Master of Theological Studies
MHSA	Master of Health Services Administration		MUP	Master of Urban Planning
MIA	Master of International Affairs		MUPD	Master of Urban Planning and Development
MIB	Master of International Business		MURP	Master of Urban and Regional Planning
MIP	Master of Intellectual Property		PharmD	Doctor of Pharmacy
MIR	Masters in Industrial Relations		PhD	Doctor of Philosophy
MIRL	Masters Industrial and Labor Relations		REES	Russian and Eastern European Studies Certificate
MJ	Master of Jurisprudence		SJD	Doctor of Juridcial Science
MJS	Master of Juridical Study (not a JD)		DVM	Doctor of Veterinary Medicine
MLIR	Master of Labor and Industrial Relations		MALIR	Master of Arts in Labor and Industrial Relations
MLIS	Master of Library and Information Sciences			
MLS	Master of Library Science			
MMA	Masters Marine Affairs			
MOB	Master of Organizational Behavior			
MPA	Master of Public Administration			
MPAFF	Master of Public Affairs			
MPH	Master of Public Health			
MPP	Master of Public Planning OR Master of Public Policy			
MPPA	Master of Public Policy			
MPPS	Master of Public Policy Sciences			
MPS	Master of Professional Studies in Law			
MRP	Master of Regional Planning			
MS	Master of Science			
MSEL	Master of Studies in Environmental Law			
MSES	Master of Science in Environmental Science			
MSF	Master of Science in Finance			
MSFS	Master of Science in Foreign Service			
MSI	Master of Science in Information			

SCHOOL PROFILES

ALBANY LAW SCHOOL
of Union University

Admissions Contact: Assistant Dean of Admissions and Financial Aid, Dawn M. Chamberlaine
80 New Scotland Avenue, Albany, NY 12208
Admissions Phone: 518-445-2326 • Admissions Fax: 518-445-2369
Admissions E-mail: admissions@mail.als.edu • Web Address: www.als.edu

INSTITUTIONAL INFORMATION

Public/Private: Private
Environment: Urban
Academic Calendar: Semester
Schedule: Full time or part time
Student/Faculty Ratio: 17:1
Total Faculty: 41
% Part Time: 50
% Female: 39
% Minority: 17

PROGRAMS

Academic Specialties: Health Law, Intellectual Property Law, Criminal Law, major research on International Human Rights
Advanced Degrees Offered: JD (3 years), JD/MBA (3.5 years), JD/MPA (3.5–4 years)
Combined Degrees Offered: Same as above
Clinical Program Required? No
Clinical Programs: AIDS Law, Disabilities Law, Domestic Violence, Civil Litigation, various placements and externships, semester in government
Grading System: A+ (4.3), A (4.0), A– (3.7), B+ (3.3)

STUDENT INFORMATION

Enrollment of Law School: 688
% Male/Female: 48/52
% Full Time: 94
% Full Time That Are International: 1
% Minority: 19
Average Age of Entering Class: 27

RESEARCH FACILITIES

Computers/Workstations Available: 100

EXPENSES/FINANCIAL AID

Annual Tuition: $21,495
Room and Board (On/Off Campus): $5,930
Books and Supplies: $595
Average Grant: $5,818
Average Loan: $19,500
% of Aid That Is Merit-Based: 2
% Receiving Some Sort of Aid: 93
Average Total Aid Package: $22,700
Average Debt: $65,000
Fees Per Credit: $650

ADMISSIONS INFORMATION

Application Fee: $50
Regular Application Deadline: 3/15
Regular Notification: Rolling
LSDAS Accepted? Yes
Average GPA: 3.1
Range of GPA: 2.8–3.4
Average LSAT: 150
Range of LSAT: 146–153
Transfer Students Accepted? Yes
Other Schools to Which Students Applied: Syracuse University, State University of New York, Western New England College, Cornell University, Boston College, Boston University, Brooklyn Law School, Pace University
Other Admissions Factors Considered: Academic strength of institution, rigor of undergraduate program, uniqueness of life experience and background, and employment experience
Number of Applications Received: 1,455
Number of Applicants Accepted: 851
Number of Applicants Enrolled: 254

EMPLOYMENT INFORMATION

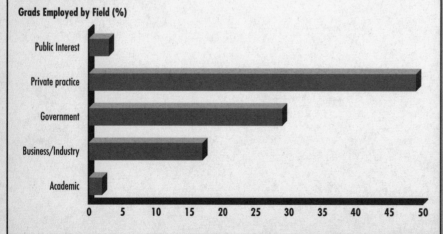

Rate of Placement: 95%
Average Starting Salary: $45,000
Employers Who Frequently Hire Grads: Private law firms, business and industry, and government agencies
Prominent Alumni: Andrew M. Cuomo '82, Secretary of Housing and Urban Development; Richard D. Parsons '71, President, Time Warner; Thomas Vilsack '75, Governor of Idaho

AMERICAN UNIVERSITY
Washington College of Law

Admissions Contact: Director of Admissions, Sandra Oakman
4801 Massachusetts Avenue NW, Washington, DC 20016
Admissions Phone: 202-274-4101 • Admissions Fax: 202-274-4107
Admissions E-mail: admissions@wcl.american.edu • Web Address: www.wcl.american.edu

INSTITUTIONAL INFORMATION

Public/Private: Private
Environment: Urban
Academic Calendar: Semester
Schedule: Full time or part time
Student/Faculty Ratio: 18:1
Total Faculty: 193
% Part Time: 68
% Female: 34
% Minority: 16

PROGRAMS

Academic Specialties: International Law (Human Rights, International Business, International Organizations, Gender), Clinical Education, externships and experiential learning in General Law and Government, Legal Theory (especially History, Jurisprudence)
Advanced Degrees Offered: LLM International Legal Studies (12–18 months), LLM Law and Government (12 months), SJD program newly approved during 1999–2000 academic year (no estimate of program length available)
Combined Degrees Offered: JD/MBA, JD/MBA Health Care Management, JD/MA International Relations, JD/MS Mass Communication, JD/MA Preservation Studies, JD/MPH Public Health, JD/MA Philosophy, JD/LLM Taxation (all 3.5–4 years)
Clinical Program Required? No
Clinical Programs: Criminal Justice, D.C. Civil Litigation, Civil Clinic, Domestic Violence, International Human Rights, Tax, Women and the Law, Community and Economic Development

Grading System: A, A–, B+, B–, C+, C, D, F, with no mandatory curve
Legal Writing/Methods Course Requirements: 26 small sections; 1-year program on legal research, writing, skills

STUDENT INFORMATION

Enrollment of Law School: 1,321
% Male/Female: 37/63
% Full Time: 66
% Full Time That Are International: 4
% Minority: 21
Average Age of Entering Class: 24

RESEARCH FACILITIES

Computers/Workstations Available: 100
School-Supported Research Centers: Assistance for students with laptop configuration for access to the network; high-capacity printer access in the library and labs; every student with a laptop can access the WCL network and internet in each and every classroom; 32 Pentium class and 8 PowerPC class computers, which run Microsoft Windows 95 and Mac OS 8.1 respectively; Lexis-Nexis and Westlaw research software; for students in the Clinic Program, WCL offers a lab of 16 workstations including 10 on which Amicus case management software is installed and a dedicated and secure Novell file server; several online databases support an Externship program, a Clinic program, a Clerkship program and jobs and mentoring opportunities for current students and alumni

EXPENSES/FINANCIAL AID

Annual Tuition: $23,696
Room and Board: $9,126

Books and Supplies: $830
Financial Aid Application Deadline: 3/1
Average Grant: $8,063
Average Loan: $16,926
% of Aid That Is Merit-Based: 2
% Receiving Some Sort of Aid: 80
Average Total Aid Package: $25,042
Average Debt: $53,310
Tuition Per Credit: $382
Fees Per Credit: $837

ADMISSIONS INFORMATION

Application Fee: $55
Regular Application Deadline: 3/1
Regular Notification: Rolling
LSDAS Accepted? Yes
Average GPA: 3.3
Range of GPA: 3.0–3.5
Average LSAT: 156
Range of LSAT: 153–159
Transfer Students Accepted? Yes
Other Schools to Which Students Applied: George Washington University, Georgetown University, Catholic University of America, Boston College, Boston University, University of Maryland, George Mason University, College of William and Mary
Other Admissions Factors Considered: All of the above criteria may be important.
Number of Applications Received: 5,021
Number of Applicants Accepted: 2,117
Number of Applicants Enrolled: 524

INTERNATIONAL STUDENTS

TOEFL Required of International Students? Yes
Minimum TOEFL: 600

EMPLOYMENT INFORMATION

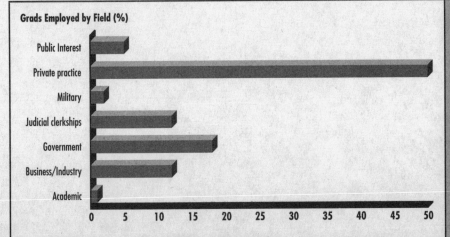

Grads Employed by Field (%)

Rate of Placement: 96%
Average Starting Salary: $49,340
Employers Who Frequently Hire Grads: Akin, Gump, Strauss, Hauer and Feld, LLP; Jones, Day, Reavis and Pogue; Manhattan District Attorney; Department of Justice; Shearman and Sterling; Dickstein, Shapiro and Morin, LLP
Prominent Alumni: Robert Byrd, U.S. senator (D-WV); Enrico Lazio, congressman (R-NY); Carol Crawford, comissioner, International Trade Comission; Joseph Hartaler, chief prosecutor, Oklahoma City bombing case—Timothy McVeigh, Department of Justice
State for Bar Exam: MD
Number Taking Bar Exam: 89
Pass Rate for First-Time Bar: 68%

AMERICAN UNIVERSITY

WCL AT A GLANCE

American University's Washington College of Law (WCL) is a school that places a premium on academic excellence, diversity, and social responsibility. Located in Washington, D.C., the center of the nation's legal institutions, WCL is committed to inculcating in students the intellectual abilities and practical skills required to prepare lawyers to practice in an increasingly complex, transnational world. Founded in 1896 as the first law school in the United States created by and for women (and with women comprising over 60 percent of the entering class and minorities over 26 percent), WCL has both embraced its unique history and adapted its curriculum and activities to today's legal challenges.

PROGRAMS AND CURRICULUM

WCL is well-known for many things. It has a top-flight program in both **public and private international law** (including an LLM degree in **International Legal Studies**), and has a faculty second to none in its background in and commitment to international human rights issues. WCL places an extraordinary focus on **experiential learning**, which comprises both our long-heralded clinical programs and our more recently developed supervised externship program (linking governmental and public interest placements with academic seminars).

Our **Women and the Law Program** (and its offshoot, the **Women in International Law Program**) assess the role of gender in the law school curriculum and in national and international society at large.

As befits our Washington, D.C., location, WCL has a well-developed **Law and Government Program** (including an LLM degree in Law and Government) that emphasizes analysis and understanding of the legal issues that face the mature administrative state. Our **Law and Business Program** examines the relationship between law and legal regulation on the one hand and business on the other. **Intellectual property** and **environmental law** are two of our developing specialties. One of our newest programs, the **Program on Counseling Electronic Commerce Entrepreneurs** connects traditional business planning with cutting-edge issues in cyberspace. These courses and programs are only the tip of the proverbial iceberg: without doubt, WCL has one of the richest, broadest curricula in the country.

FACULTY AND TEACHING

The WCL faculty is noted for its excellence both inside and outside the classroom. Faculty scholarship is broad and impressive, attesting to the existence of a rich, creative intellectual community in which exploration of ideas is valued. But the faculty is not simply interested in scholarship and outside professional activities. The law school faculty care deeply about teaching—and while many law schools "talk the talk" on teaching, at WCL we "walk the walk," constantly searching out ways to improve upon the students' pedagogical experience.

FOCUS ON STUDENTS

WCL offers a **student-centered environment** that is reflected in numerous ways. In our clinical programs, students not only can choose from a startlingly varied array of subject matter—civil practice, community and economic development, criminal justice, domestic violence, international human rights (human rights and asylum), landlord/tenant, tax, women and the law (abuse and neglect, child support and domestic violence)—but also are given primary lawyering responsibility in their cases and legal matters, under the expert supervision and guidance of our clinical faculty.

WCL's student focus is also shown in our revamped **legal writing and research program** (called Legal Method), which is now under the direction of a tenure-track faculty member assisted by three full-time legal writing instructors and experienced adjunct faculty. Sections of Legal Method are kept deliberately small to permit students to receive individualized instruction in legal writing and research. In addition, all first-year students have at least one substantive law class with no more than 45 students (other classes are limited to approximately 95 students per section). Moreover, for the past two years, we have offered a team-taught section of our first-year substantive courses that introduces gender, international law, intellectual property, lawyering skills, law and economics, and legal theory and history while at the same time breaking down some of the artificial barriers between traditional first-year subjects.

Washington College of Law

BEYOND THE CLASSROOM

Outside of the clinic, faculty members regularly include students in their professional activities. For example, in the coming year, Dean Claudio Grossman will argue an international human rights case before the **Inter-American Court of Human Rights in San Jose, Costa Rica**. Five to six students will work with the dean and accompany him to the oral argument in Costa Rica.

Another faculty member's scholarship in the area of the constitutional rights of high school students led eventually to the creation of the **Marshall-Brennan Fellowship Program**, which provides fellowships for law students to teach constitutional law to high school students from the District of Columbia. As one second-year student noted, "My participation in the program, though challenging at times, allowed me to sharpen my legal skills as a counselor, negotiator, and advocate. This was an unforgettable experience."

As our dean has noted, "Without question, our greatest asset is our energetic and heterogeneous student body." Students participate in numerous organizations, committees, and activities, ranging from those concerned with law school issues (such as the faculty appointments committee) to those with national and international foci (such as national and international moot court competitions or international relief efforts). Students, individually and through student organizations, engage in a substantial amount of *pro bono publico* activities, as does the faculty, reflecting the importance of developing a life-long commitment to providing services to underserved populations.

FACILITIES

No law school program takes place in a vacuum, and since 1996 WCL students have taken classes and studied in a **state-of-the-art law building** that has ample space for, among other things, small, medium and large classrooms; three moot court rooms; our numerous student organizations (including four law journals); a new legal writing suite; and the clinical program's law offices. The comprehensive, spacious law library has numerous individual carrels and areas for group and individual study. Most impressively, the law school is "fully wired" with state-of-the-art computer and video technology; the law building has more than a thousand data and telecommunication ports, allowing students to gain access to database and research services from many stations in the library and from virtually any desk or table throughout the building.

Students at WCL are exposed to a learning environment that is rigorous academically while also valuing formal and informal dialogue and other forms of social and professional interaction. Don't just take our word for it; ask any of our students, faculty, staff, or alumni.

Admissions Contact: Director of Admissions, Sandra Oakman
4801 Massachusetts Avenue NW, Washington, DC 20016
Admissions Phone: 202-274-4101 • Admissions Fax: 202-274-4107
Admissions E-mail: admissions@wcl.american.edu • Web Address: www.wcl.american.edu

ARIZONA STATE UNIVERSITY
College of Law

Admissions Contact: Assistant Dean for Student Affairs, Brenda Brock
McAllister and Orange Street, Box 877906, Tempe, AZ 85287-7906
Admissions Phone: 480-965-7896 • Admissions Fax: 480-965-5550
Admissions E-mail: wanda.decrow@asu.edu • Web Address: www.law.asu.edu

INSTITUTIONAL INFORMATION

Public/Private: Public
Environment: Urban
Academic Calendar: Semester
Schedule: Full time only
Student/Faculty Ratio: 14:1
Total Faculty: 35
% Female: 17
% Minority: 11

PROGRAMS

Academic Specialties: Clinical Program; Center for the Study of Law, Science, and Technology; Indian Legal Program; Constitutional Law; Banking; Intellectual Property
Advanced Degrees Offered: JD (3 years)
Combined Degrees Offered: JD/MHSA (4 years), JD/MBA (4 years), JD/PhD Justice Studies (varies)
Clinical Program Required? No
Clinical Programs: The Clinical Program is among the most comprehensive in the country. Over half the law students at ASU participate in 1 of 4 "hands-on" clinics supplemented by innovative simulation courses in trial advocacy, pre-trial discovery practice, negotiation and mediation, and alternative dispute resolution. Students enrolled in the Prosecutor Clinic or Public Defender Clinic represent either the State of Arizona or individual clients in misdemeanor cases. Most students have the opportunity to participate in several trials or hearings and to present at least one case to a jury. Students in the Civil Practice Clinic handle civil cases in local courts and represent clients in contested administrative hearings. In the Mediation Clinic, students explore the problem-solving dimension of lawyering as they work with faculty and professional mediators on nonlitigation solutions to a broad range of disputes.
Grading System: Courses are graded under the following numerical scale: 90–99 Distinguished, 85–89 Excellent, 80–84 Very Good, 75–79 Good, 70–74 Satisfactory, 60–69 Deficient, 59 Failing. A grade of 60 or above is required to receive credit for any course.
Legal Writing/Methods Course Requirements: First-year course, 2 semesters on analysis, research, and writing

STUDENT INFORMATION

Enrollment of Law School: 481
% Male/Female: 53/47
% Full Time: 100
% Full Time That Are International: 2
% Minority: 26
Average Age of Entering Class: 27

RESEARCH FACILITIES

Computers/Workstations Available: 49
School-Supported Research Centers: Clinics, Externships

EXPENSES/FINANCIAL AID

Annual Tuition (Residents/Nonresidents):
$4,938/$12,090
Room and Board (On/Off Campus):
$8,110/$10,150

Books and Supplies: $1,000
Financial Aid Application Deadline: 3/1
Average Grant: $5,026
Average Loan: $13,314
% Receiving Some Sort of Aid: 81
Average Total Aid Package: $14,447
Average Debt: $38,200

ADMISSIONS INFORMATION

Application Fee: $45
Regular Application Deadline: 3/1
Regular Notification: 6/1
LSDAS Accepted? Yes
Average GPA: 3.4
Range of GPA: 3.0–3.7
Average LSAT: 156
Range of LSAT: 153–160
Transfer Students Accepted? Yes
Other Schools to Which Students Applied: University of Arizona, University of Colorado, UCLA School of Law, University of San Diego, Santa Clara University, University of Denver, Brigham Young University, University of New Mexico
Number of Applications Received: 1,862
Number of Applicants Accepted: 441
Number of Applicants Enrolled: 163

INTERNATIONAL STUDENTS

TOEFL Required of International Students? Yes

EMPLOYMENT INFORMATION

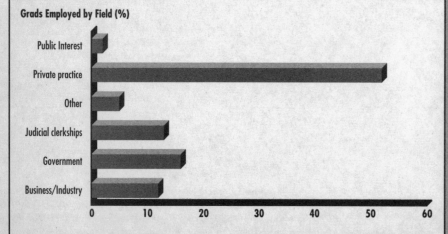

Grads Employed by Field (%)

Average Starting Salary: $43,000
Employers Who Frequently Hire Grads: Snell and Wilmer; Brown and Bain; O'Connor Cavanagh; Lewis and Roca; Streich Lang; Fennemore Craig; and many others throughout Phoenix area. Meyer Hendricks; Osborn Maledon; Bryan Cave; Steptoe Johnson; Squires, Sanders and Dempsey
Prominent Alumni: Judge Michael Hawkins, 9th Circuit, U.S. Court of Appeals; Judge Barry Silverman, 9th Circuit, U.S. Court of Appeals; Judge Roslyn O. Silver, U.S. District Court of Arizona
State for Bar Exam: AZ
Number Taking Bar Exam: 65
Pass Rate for First-Time Bar: 85%

BAYLOR UNIVERSITY
School of Law

Admissions Contact: Admission Director, Becky L. Beck
PO Box 97288, Waco, TX 76798-7288
Admissions Phone: 254-710-1911 • Admissions Fax: 254-710-2316
Admissions E-mail: becky_beck@baylor.edu • Web Address: law.baylor.edu

INSTITUTIONAL INFORMATION

Public/Private: Private
Affiliation: Southern Baptist
Environment: Urban
Academic Calendar: Semester
Schedule: Full time only
Student/Faculty Ratio: 20:1
Total Faculty: 56
% Part Time: 61
% Female: 20
% Minority: 4

PROGRAMS

Academic Specialties: General Civil Litigation, Business Litigation, Estate Planning, Criminal Practice, Business Transaction, Administrative Practice
Combined Degrees Offered: JD/MBA, JD/MT, JD/MPPA (all 3.5–4 years)
Clinical Program Required? Yes
Clinical Programs: Practice courts, internships, District Attorney, Federal Prosecutor, Appellate Courts, Legal Services, Child Support Division, Federal District Court Corp., Business Planning, Estate Planning, and Administration of Estate Capstones
Grading System: Letter and numerical system, 4.0 scale: A (4.0), A– (3.5), B (3.0), B– (2.5), C (2.0), D (1.0), F (0.0)
Legal Writing/Methods Course Requirements: Legal Research—4 quarter hours taught over 3 quaters

STUDENT INFORMATION

Enrollment of Law School: 396
% Male/Female: 60/40
% Full Time: 100
% Full Time That Are International: 1
% Minority: 8
Average Age of Entering Class: 24

RESEARCH FACILITIES

Computers/Workstations Available: 34
School-Supported Research Centers: Through Bearcat, an automated online library system, students have access to a number of database resources from off campus.

EXPENSES/FINANCIAL AID

Annual Tuition: $14,719
Room and Board (On/Off Campus): $8,748/$12,942
Books and Supplies: $600
Financial Aid Application Deadline: 5/1
Average Grant: $4,500
Average Loan: $15,803
% of Aid That Is Merit-Based: 37
% Receiving Some Sort of Aid: 98
Average Total Aid Package: $17,164
Average Debt: $48,554

ADMISSIONS INFORMATION

Application Fee: $40
Regular Application Deadline: 3/1
Regular Notification: Rolling
LSDAS Accepted? Yes
Average GPA: 3.4
Range of GPA: 3.2–3.8
Average LSAT: 160
Range of LSAT: 158–161
Transfer Students Accepted? Yes
Other Schools to Which Students Applied: University of Texas, University of Houston, Texas Tech University, Southern Methodist University, St. Mary's University, Texas A&M University, Vanderbilt University, University of Virginia
Other Admissions Factors Considered: Achievements, evidence of maturity, and strong work ethic
Number of Applications Received: 919
Number of Applicants Accepted: 321
Number of Applicants Enrolled: 65

EMPLOYMENT INFORMATION

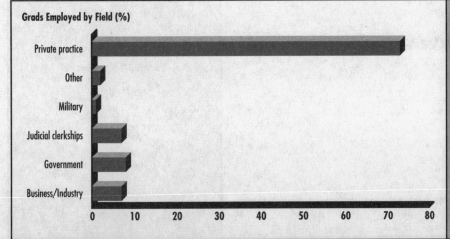

Rate of Placement: 96%
Average Starting Salary: $53,635
Employers Who Frequently Hire Grads: Akin Gump, Jenkins & Gilcrest, Thompson & Knight, Strasburger & Price, Baker & Botts, Haynes & Boone, Bracewell & Patterson, Jackson Walker, Fulbright & Jaworski, Andrews & Kurth, Winstead Sechrest, Liddell Sapp
Prominent Alumni: Leon Jaworski, special prosecutor for Watergate; Fred McClure, congressional legislative liaison for President George Bush; William Sessions, former FBI director
State for Bar Exam: TX
Number Taking Bar Exam: 149
Pass Rate for First-Time Bar: 93%

BOSTON COLLEGE
Law School

Admissions Contact: Director of Admissions, Elizabeth Rosselot
885 Centre Street, Newton, MA 02159
Admissions Phone: 617-552-4350 • Admissions Fax: 617-552-2917
Admissions E-mail: bclawadmis@bc.edu • Web Address: www.bc.edu/lawschool

INSTITUTIONAL INFORMATION

Public/Private: Private
Affiliation: Jesuit
Environment: Urban
Academic Calendar: Semester
Schedule: Full time only
Student/Faculty Ratio: 17:1
Total Faculty: 78
% Part Time: 35
% Female: 27
% Minority: 11

PROGRAMS

Advanced Degrees Offered: JD (3 years)
Combined Degrees Offered: JD/MBA (4 years), JD/MSW (4 years), JD/MEd (4 years)
Clinical Program Required? No
Clinical Programs: Legal Assistance Bureau, Criminal Process, Attorney General Clinical Program, Judicial Process, Urban Legal Laboratory, Juvenile Rights Advocacy, and Immigration Law Clinic
Grading System: Standard A, B, C, D system on a 4.0 scale
Legal Writing/Methods Course Requirements: 5 credits, 2 semesters

STUDENT INFORMATION

Enrollment of Law School: 823
% Male/Female: 49/51
% Full Time: 100
% Full Time That Are International: 1
% Minority: 19
Average Age of Entering Class: 25

EXPENSES/FINANCIAL AID

Annual Tuition: $24,480
Books and Supplies: $840
Average Grant: $8,631
Average Loan: $23,503
% Receiving Some Sort of Aid: 75
Average Debt: $63,500

ADMISSIONS INFORMATION

Application Fee: $65
Regular Application Deadline: 3/1
Regular Notification: Rolling
LSDAS Accepted? Yes
Average GPA: 3.5
Range of GPA: 3.3–3.7
Average LSAT: 161
Range of LSAT: 158–164
Transfer Students Accepted? Yes
Other Schools to Which Students Applied: Boston University, Harvard University, Georgetown University, George Washington University, Suffolk University, Northeastern University, Yale University, Fordham University

INTERNATIONAL STUDENTS

TOEFL Required of International Students? Yes

EMPLOYMENT INFORMATION

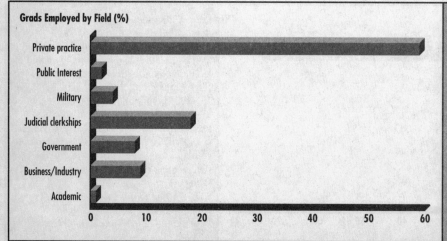

Grads Employed by Field (%)

Rate of Placement: 96%
Average Starting Salary: $83,000
State for Bar Exam: MA
Number Taking Bar Exam: 196
Pass Rate for First-Time Bar: 92%

BOSTON UNIVERSITY
School of Law

Admissions Contact: Director of Admissions and Financial Aid, Barbara J. Selmo
765 Commonwealth Avenue, Boston, MA 02215
Admissions Phone: 617-353-3100 • Admissions Fax: 617-353-0578
Admissions E-mail: bulawadm@bu.edu • Web Address: www.bu.edu/law

INSTITUTIONAL INFORMATION

Public/Private: Private
Environment: Urban
Academic Calendar: Semester
Schedule: Full time only
Student/Faculty Ratio: 14:1
Total Faculty: 133
% Part Time: 53
% Female: 32
% Minority: 10

PROGRAMS

Academic Specialties: Academic specialties of faculty are very broad ranging; special strengths of curriculum include those programs listed below and Civil and Criminal Clinical Programs.
Advanced Degrees Offered: LLM Taxation (1 year full time, up to 6 years part time), LLM Banking (1 year full time, up to 5 years part time), LLM American Law (1 year full time)
Combined Degrees Offered: JD/MBA, JD/MBA Health Care Management, JD/MA International Relations, JD/MS Mass Communication, JD/MA Preservation Studies, JD/MPH (public health), JD/MA Philosophy, JD/LLM Taxation (all 3.5–4 years)
Clinical Program Required? Yes
Clinical Programs: Legislative Services, Criminal Trial Advocacy, Judicial Internship, Legal Externship, Civil Litigation
Grading System: Letter and numerical system on a 4.3 scale
Legal Writing/Methods Course Requirements: Full-year, small-group program for 1Ls

STUDENT INFORMATION

Enrollment of Law School: 892
% Male/Female: 51/49
% Full Time: 100
% Full Time That Are International: 1
% Minority: 24
Average Age of Entering Class: 23

RESEARCH FACILITIES

Computers/Workstations Available: 100
Computer Labs: 4
Campuswide Network? Yes
School-Supported Research Centers: Foreign exchange program with Oxford University; Universite Jean Moulin, Lyon III; Leiden University; Tel Aviv University; Universite Pantheon-Assas, Paris III; Greater Boston Legal Services.

EXPENSES/FINANCIAL AID

Annual Tuition: $24,700
Room and Board: $9,575
Books and Supplies: $1,024
Financial Aid Application Deadline: 3/1
Average Grant: $13,000
Average Loan: $25,042
% of Aid That Is Merit-Based: 2
% Receiving Some Sort of Aid: 82
Average Total Aid Package: $23,865
Average Debt: $64,166

ADMISSIONS INFORMATION

Application Fee: $60
Regular Application Deadline: 3/1
Regular Notification: Rolling
LSDAS Accepted? Yes
Average GPA: 3.4
Range of GPA: 3.2–3.6
Average LSAT: 161
Range of LSAT: 160–163
Transfer Students Accepted? Yes
Other Schools to Which Students Applied: Boston College, University of California—Hastings, George Washington University, New York University, Georgetown University, Fordham University, University of Minnesota, Emory University
Other Admissions Factors Considered: Grade trends, quality and difficulty of courses taken, leadership ability, motivation for study of law, economic or social obstacles overcome by an applicant, and outstanding nonacademic achievements
Number of Applications Received: 4,642
Number of Applicants Accepted: 1,618
Number of Applicants Enrolled: 302

INTERNATIONAL STUDENTS

TOEFL Required of International Students? Yes
Minimum TOEFL: 600

EMPLOYMENT INFORMATION

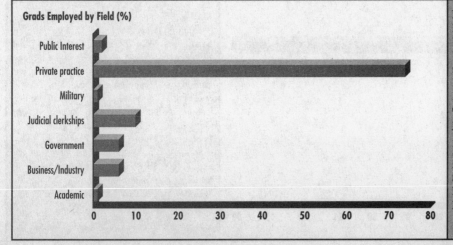

Grads Employed by Field (%)

Rate of Placement: 97%
Prominent Alumni: Hon. William S. Cohen, U.S. secretary of defense; Hon. Judd A. Gregg, U.S. senator; Hon. Barbara C. Jordan, former U.S. representative; Lincoln Almond, governor, Rhode Island; Gary F. Locke, governor, Washington; Hon. Juan R. Torruella, chief judge, U.S. First Circuit Court of Appeals; Hon. Sandra Lynch, judge, U.S. First Circuit Court of Appeals; David E. Kelley, Hollywood movie/TV producer; Rikki J. Klieman, anchor, Court TV; F. Lee Bailey, defense attorney
State for Bar Exam: MA
Number Taking Bar Exam: 204
Pass Rate for First-Time Bar: 89%

BRIGHAM YOUNG UNIVERSITY

J. Reuben Clark Law School

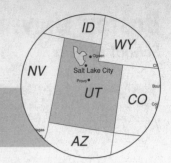

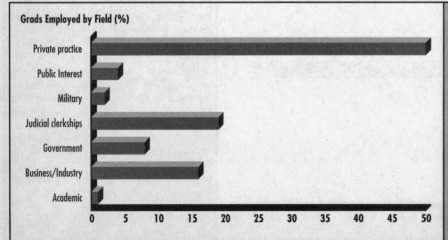

Admissions Contact: Director of Admissions, Lola Wilcock
340 JRCB, Provo, UT 84602
Admissions Phone: 801-378-4277 • Admissions Fax: 801-378-5897
Admissions E-mail: wilcockl@lawgate.byu.edu • Web Address: www.law.byu.edu

INSTITUTIONAL INFORMATION

Public/Private: Private
Affiliation: Latter-day Saints (LDS)
Environment: Urban
Academic Calendar: Semester
Schedule: Full time only
Student/Faculty Ratio: 14:1
Total Faculty: 65
% Part Time: 57
% Female: 25
% Minority: 5

PROGRAMS

Academic Specialties: Each faculty member develops his/her specialty. A variety of specialty classes are offered in International Law, Patent Law, Environmental Law.
Advanced Degrees Offered: Comparative Law (1 school year)
Combined Degrees Offered: JD/MBA, JD/MPA, JD/MAcc, JD/MOB, JD/MEd (all are 4 years), JD/EdD (5 years)
Clinical Program Required? No
Clinical Programs: Law Help is a project designed to provide people with the opportunity to meet with a legal professional who will listen to their legal problem, assess the nature of the problem, and make a recommendation or refer it to an attorney.
Grading System: Students are graded on a 4.0 scale with a set median of 3.2 and no credit for grades under 2.2.

Legal Writing/Methods Course Requirements: Initiated in 1997, Lawyering Skills is a year-long course that combines legal writing, legal research, and an introduction to legal process in a workshop format.

STUDENT INFORMATION

Enrollment of Law School: 450
% Male/Female: 66/34
% Full Time: 100
% Full Time That Are International: 4
% Minority: 14
Average Age of Entering Class: 26

RESEARCH FACILITIES

Computers/Workstations Available: 55
Campuswide Network? Yes

EXPENSES/FINANCIAL AID

Annual Tuition: $5,540
Room and Board (On/Off Campus): $6,100/$7,090
Books and Supplies: $1,230
Average Grant: $2,000
Average Loan: $12,000
% of Aid That Is Merit-Based: 33
% Receiving Some Sort of Aid: 89
Average Total Aid Package: $10,000
Average Debt: $24,000
Fees Per Credit: $308

ADMISSIONS INFORMATION

Application Fee: $30
Regular Application Deadline: 2/1
Regular Notification: Rolling
LSDAS Accepted? Yes
Average GPA: 3.6
Range of GPA: 3.4–3.8
Average LSAT: 160
Range of LSAT: 157–163
Transfer Students Accepted? Yes
Other Schools to Which Students Applied: University of Utah, UCLA School of Law, University of Arizona, Harvard University, University of Idaho, Arizona State University, George Washington University, University of Washington
Other Admissions Factors Considered: Personal statements, three letters of recommendation
Number of Applications Received: 623
Number of Applicants Accepted: 233
Number of Applicants Enrolled: 152

INTERNATIONAL STUDENTS

TOEFL Required of International Students? Yes
Minimum TOEFL: 590

EMPLOYMENT INFORMATION

Grads Employed by Field (%)

- Private practice
- Public Interest
- Military
- Judicial clerkships
- Government
- Business/Industry
- Academic

0 5 10 15 20 25 30 35 40 45 50

Rate of Placement: 99%
Average Starting Salary: $46,500
Employers Who Frequently Hire Grads: Kirkland and Ellis (Los Angeles and Chicago); Army; Utah Fourth District; Novell; Baker and McKenzie; Latham and Watkins; Stoel Reves; Snell and Wilmer; Ray, Quinney and Nebeker; Parsons, Behle and Latimer; LeBoef, Lamb, Greene and MacRae; Vinson and Elkins
Prominent Alumni: Steve Young, San Francisco 49ers; Chris Cannon, Utah congressman; Hon. Dee V. Benson, U.S. District Court, Utah
State for Bar Exam: UT
Number Taking Bar Exam: 92
Pass Rate for First-Time Bar: 97%

BROOKLYN LAW SCHOOL

Admissions Contact: Dean of Admissions and Financial Aid, Henry W. Haverstick III
250 Joralemon Street, Brooklyn, NY 11201
Admissions Phone: 718-780-7906 • Admissions Fax: 718-780-0395
Admissions E-mail: admitg.brooklaw@pcm.brooklaw.edu • Web Address: www.brooklaw.edu

INSTITUTIONAL INFORMATION

Public/Private: Private
Environment: Urban
Schedule: Full time or part time
Student/Faculty Ratio: 20:1
Total Faculty: 148
% Female: 39
% Minority: 6

PROGRAMS

Academic Specialties: Criminal Law (2), Advocacy (1), International Business Law (4), International Human Rights (5), Liability (6), Intellectual Property (3), Public Interest (7)
Combined Degrees Offered: JD/MA Political Science, JD/MS Planning, JD/MBA, JD/MS Library/Information Science, JD/MUP, JD/MPA
Clinical Program Required? No
Clinical Programs: Capital Defender Clinic, Bankruptcy Clinic, Corporate and Real Estate Clinic, Criminal Appeals Clinic, Manhattan District Attorney's Office, Elder Law Clinic, Federal Litigation Clinic, Immigration and Asylum (Safe Harbor Project), Legislation and Law Reform Clinic, Mediation Clinic, Prosecutor's Clinic, Civil Practice Internship, Criminal Practice Internship, Judicial Clerkship Internship. Simulation Courses: Alternative Dispute Resolution, Appellate Advocacy, Civil Practice. Workshops in Class and Derivative Action, Discovery, Evidence, Family Law, Negotiation Seminar, Trial Advocacy.

Grading System: Letter system
Legal Writing/Methods Course Requirements: Legal Writing, 1 year plus 1 upper-division writing elective; Legal Process, one semester in first year

STUDENT INFORMATION

Enrollment of Law School: 1,430
% Male/Female: 52/48
% Full Time: 66
% Full Time That Are International: 1
% Minority: 19
Average Age of Entering Class: 24

EXPENSES/FINANCIAL AID

Annual Tuition: $22,000
Room and Board (On/Off Campus): $10,220
Books and Supplies: $1,200
Average Grant: $4,679
Average Loan: $17,915
% of Aid That Is Merit-Based: 48
% Receiving Some Sort of Aid: 46
Average Total Aid Package: $21,237
Average Debt: $52,633

ADMISSIONS INFORMATION

Application Fee: $60
Regular Application Deadline: Rolling
Regular Notification: Rolling
LSDAS Accepted? Yes
Average GPA: 3.3
Range of GPA: 3.0–3.5
Average LSAT: 157
Range of LSAT: 153–159
Transfer Students Accepted? Yes
Other Schools to Which Students Applied: Fordham University, New York Law School, New York University, St. John's University, Hofstra University, Columbia University, Yeshiva University, Pace University
Other Admissions Factors Considered: Quality of undergraduate institution; major; GPA trends; grade inflation; advanced degree; maturity; moral character; geographic diversity; economic, racial/ethnic, cultural backgrounds; alumni/ae relationship
Number of Applications Received: 2,174

EMPLOYMENT INFORMATION

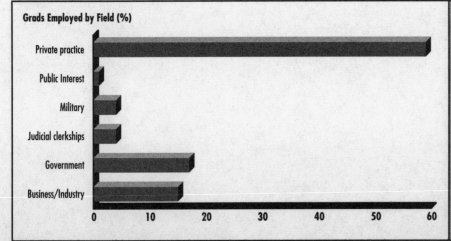

Grads Employed by Field (%)

- Private practice
- Public Interest
- Military
- Judicial clerkships
- Government
- Business/Industry

Rate of Placement: 94%
Average Starting Salary: $74,500
Employers Who Frequently Hire Grads: Fried, Frank, Harris, Shriver and Jacobson; Winthrop, Stimson, Putnam and Roberts; Proskauer Rose; Kings County District Attorney's Office; New York City Law Department; Skadden, Arps, Slate, Meagher and Flom; Stroock and Stroock and Lavan
Prominent Alumni: Herman Badillo, former U.S. congressman and first Puerto Rican to hold that office; David Dinkins, former mayor of New York City; Stuart Subotnick, vice president of Metromedia
State for Bar Exam: NY
Number Taking Bar Exam: 382
Pass Rate for First-Time Bar: 84%

CAL NORTHERN SCHOOL OF LAW

Admissions Contact: Administrative Assistant, Celia Weltner
1395 Ridgewood Drive, Suite 100, Chico, CA 95973
Admissions Phone: 530-891-6900 • Admissions Fax: 530-891-3429
Admissions E-mail: info@calnorthern.edu • Web Address: www.calnorthern.edu

INSTITUTIONAL INFORMATION

Public/Private: Private
Student/Faculty Ratio: 7:1
Total Faculty: 17
% Part Time: 100
% Female: 24
% Minority: 12

PROGRAMS

Academic Specialties: All faculty are practicing attorneys or sitting judges.
Advanced Degrees Offered: JD (4 years)
Clinical Program Required? No

STUDENT INFORMATION

Enrollment of Law School: 75
% Full Time: 0
Average Age of Entering Class: 28

RESEARCH FACILITIES

Computers/Workstations Available: 4

EXPENSES/FINANCIAL AID

Annual Tuition: $5,600
Books and Supplies: $300
Average Grant: $250
Tuition Per Credit: $230

ADMISSIONS INFORMATION

Application Fee: $50
Regular Application Deadline: 5/1
Regular Notification: 7/1
LSDAS Accepted? No
Average GPA: 3.0
Average LSAT: 145
Transfer Students Accepted? Yes
Other Schools to Which Students Applied: University of Idaho, University of Montana, Lincoln Law School of San Jose
Number of Applications Received: 37
Number of Applicants Accepted: 28
Number of Applicants Enrolled: 28

CALIFORNIA PACIFIC SCHOOL OF LAW

Admissions Contact: Dean, Gary Lane
1600 Truxtun Avenue #100, Bakersfield, CA 93301
Admissions Phone: 661-322-5297 • Admissions Fax: 661-322-3409
Admissions E-mail: inquiry@calpaclaw.edu • Web Address: www.calpaclaw.edu

INSTITUTIONAL INFORMATION

Public/Private: Private
Total Faculty: 40
% Part Time: 100
% Female: 25
% Minority: 5

PROGRAMS

Academic Specialties: All faculty are local practitioners—judges, DAs, members of small and large law firms, county counsel—with a keen eye on current practice.
Clinical Program Required? No
Grading System: 4.0 to 0.0, with 2.0 required to graduate
Legal Writing/Methods Course Requirements: 2 quarters, research and writing

STUDENT INFORMATION

Enrollment of Law School: 32
% Male/Female: 100/0
% Full Time: 0
Average Age of Entering Class: 31

RESEARCH FACILITIES

School-Supported Research Centers: Kern County Law Library is one block away.

EXPENSES/FINANCIAL AID

Annual Tuition: $8,580
Books and Supplies: $400
% of Aid That Is Merit-Based: 0
% Receiving Some Sort of Aid: 20
Tuition Per Credit: $8,580
Fees Per Credit: $260

ADMISSIONS INFORMATION

Application Fee: $75
Regular Application Deadline: 6/1
Regular Notification: Rolling
LSDAS Accepted? No
Average GPA: 2.8
Average LSAT: 140
Range of LSAT: 134–150
Transfer Students Accepted? Yes
Other Admissions Factors Considered: Dedication to the study of law

INTERNATIONAL STUDENTS

TOEFL Required of International Students? Yes

EMPLOYMENT INFORMATION

Rate of Placement: 100%
Average Starting Salary: $40,000
Employers Who Frequently Hire Grads: Borton, Petrini and Conron; solo practice; Klein, DeNatale, Goldner
Prominent Alumni: Bob Georgi, attorney with Bakersfield's largest law firm, Borton, Petrini and Conron; Rae Richardson, law offices of Michael Mears, taxation; Steve Lewis, PetroChem

CALIFORNIA WESTERN SCHOOL OF LAW

OVERVIEW

The mission of California Western School of Law is to educate lawyers who will be problem solvers—lawyers who will contribute to improving the lives of their clients and the quality of justice in our society. That is why most students attend law school and why many are anxious to be part of California Western—an institution that has dedicated itself to the law as a problem-solving, helping profession.

Creative problem solving in law has several components, from dealing with community, social, and international problems to the issues presented by clients. The law school is steadfast in its responsibility to influence the profession by training ethical, competent, and compassionate lawyers. The ability of lawyers to help people avoid legal problems, to maintain relationships that work productively, and to creatively resolve disputes is an integral component to the spirit California Western instills in its students.

An energetic faculty with highly diverse interests engages in research and community service as well as teaching. Faculty members constantly strive to engage the students' imaginations and energies in the classroom and in moot court, *Law Review*, and special-interest extracurricular settings. California Western's student/faculty ratio is a low 16:1, which contributes to the quality of education students receive at California Western. Because many faculty members are well-known experts in their fields, students are offered many opportunities to take elective courses taught by experts who may have further developed that area of law.

Since the early 1900s, California Western School of Law has educated ethical and compassionate lawyers to become productive members of the legal profession. California Western's beginnings date back to its charter of 1924. The law school received accreditation by the American Bar Association in 1962 and by the Association of American Law Schools in 1967, distinguished credentials that the school has maintained.

For centuries, the legal profession has improved people's lives. Attorneys have worked with business organizations, neighborhoods, and societies to make them more efficient and just. It is to this noble goal of the legal profession that California Western is dedicated.

LOCATION

California Western is a nonprofit, independent law school in downtown San Diego. A major advantage of attending California Western School of Law is San Diego itself. It is no surprise that San Diego has been ranked fourth on *Money* magazine's list of "Best Places to Live in the West." As Dean Moody, class of 2000 and graduate of Washington State put it, "San Diego is the optimal city for relieving law school stress. Living here is like being on vacation every day with the great weather, beaches, museums, and sports teams. After a hard day of studying, it is nice to go for a relaxing walk on the beach or attend a play or a sporting event. The city really has a lot to offer and I could never imagine living anywhere else."

It would be difficult to think of a better place to endure the rigors of law study. The annual rainfall is nine inches and the average daily temperature ranges from 65 degrees in January to 77 degrees in August. And with 267 days of sunshine a year, students will have plenty of opportunities to explore the 70 miles of accessible beaches that stretch from San Clemente to the Mexican border. Nearby mountains provide hiking trails in summer and challenging ski slopes from late fall to early spring. For desert buffs, a 90-minute drive will put you in the middle of the Anza-Borrego Desert, noted for spectacular spring wildflowers, enormous dunes, and the Salton Sea, a landlocked body of salt water.

Spectacular as they are, these natural advantages are only a small part of what San Diego has to offer. As America's seventh largest city, San Diego offers many cultural and recreational opportunities. There are nearly 200 city parks and recreational facilities, including the 1,017-acre Balboa Park just five minutes from California Western. One of America's largest and loveliest public parks, it is the site of numerous museums, the unique Reuben H. Fleet Space Theatre, the world-famous San Diego Zoo, and the Tony Award–winning Old Globe Theatre.

Local theater thrives in this city. In addition to the Old Globe, there are many other theaters including the San Diego Repertory, the Lamb's Players, and La Jolla Playhouse. The Civic Theater, home of the San Diego Opera, also presents performances by world-class dance companies, and the San Diego Symphony performs at Symphony Hall. The Gaslamp Quarter, called the "historic heart of San Diego"; Seaport Village; Horton Plaza; and Old Town, a small village that is reminiscent of the city's history, offer a splendid variety of restaurants, shops, sights, and entertainment.

Two major universities, the University of California San Diego and San Diego State University, are located within the city. In addition, the Scripps Institute of Oceanography and the Salk Institute, both world-renowned research facilities, are located here.

Should you need even more cultural stimulation, Los Angeles is less than three hours away by car, and the culture of a foreign country is just 20 minutes south, in Mexico's Baja Peninsula. Tijuana, the world's busiest international border crossing, is a great place to go for dinner, duty-free bargains on imported goods, a night of jai alai, or a day at the races. It also boasts an ultra-modern cultural center, which houses a museum and a concert hall. Sixty miles further south is Ensenada, the Mexican fishing capital, where you'll find beach resorts, shopping, and great seafood restaurants.

Sports fans can revel in professional baseball, football, ice hockey, and indoor soccer. San Diego has hosted the Super Bowl two times, and the city will be the site of Super Bowl XXXVII in 2003. San Diego has seen Major League Baseball's World Series championship come to the city twice, most recently in 1998 when the hometown Padres of the National League took on the New York Yankees of the American League. Those who enjoy personal athletic pursuits will find more than 50 public golf courses, miles of jogging and biking paths, tennis, sailing, and surfing, and almost everywhere you look a volleyball game in progress.

As one of the larger cities on the Pacific Rim, San Diego is not just a hub of sporting, cultural, and recreational activities, but it is also home to growing business and industry. Manufacturing, the military, tourism, and agriculture are the major industries of San Diego's diverse economy. With this emerging industry, which includes both research facilities and proprietary companies, comes the need for legal expertise. The wide variety of law firms provides attorneys with a multitude of practice opportunities. San Diego offers everything from small specialty firms to large general practice firms with more than 100 attorneys. Satellite offices also offer students and graduates the opportunity to work for large firms in a smaller setting.

Gina Giannone, a third-year law student who did her undergraduate work at St. Mary's College of California, sums it up this way: "I moved to San Diego to attend California Western and fell in love with it right away. When you need to take a break from studying and to rejuvenate, this is the perfect place to be. The weather is incredible, so you can hike in the nearby mountains, take a run along the beach, or just relax and watch the sunset. I can't think of another place I would rather be."

DEGREES OFFERED

Law students can choose from the following degrees:

- Juris Doctor
- Juris Doctor/Master of Social Work (with San Diego State University)
- Juris Doctor/PhD (Political Science or History, with the University of California San Diego)
- MCL/LLM (for non-U.S. lawyers to study U.S. law)

California Western also offers Areas of Concentration in International Law; Labor and Employment Law; Child, Family, and Elder Law; and Criminal Justice, Criminal Prosecution, and Defense Practice.

SPECIAL PROGRAMS

California Western School of Law offers the following special programs to enhance students' legal studies:

- Two-Year Option
- William J. McGill Center for Creative Problem Solving
- Louis M. Brown Program in Preventive Law
- California Innocence Project
- Institute for Criminal Defense Advocacy
- Study Abroad (New Zealand, London, Malta)
- Center for Telecommunications Law
- Interdisciplinary Training Program in Child Abuse
- Clinical Internship
- Pro Bono Program
- Part-Time Day Program

FINANCIAL AID

California Western administers several financial aid programs that provide financial assistance to more than 85 percent of the student body. Scholarship programs are offered for both entering and continuing students in both the full-time and part-time divisions. Other sources of aid include scholarships and grants offered by organizations not affiliated with the law school, and specific federal and state aid offered to eligible participants. Detailed information about expenses and financial aid is available online at www.cwsl.edu.

ADMISSIONS

Early application is encouraged so that the applicant, if admitted, may take full advantage of financial aid opportunities. Also, because California Western has rolling admissions, acceptance may be more competitive for applicants whose files are received closer to the application deadline.

In order to be considered for admission, an applicant must have, or be scheduled to receive prior to matriculation at California Western, a baccalaureate degree or its equivalent from an accredited college or university of approved standing. Acceptance to California Western is conditioned upon the applicant receiving a bachelor's degree prior to matriculation here. An applicant who has been dismissed from another law school will not be considered for admission to California Western.

Our educational policies, admissions requirements, scholarship programs, loans, and other programs are administered fairly to all. California Western does not discriminate on the basis of race, color, creed, religion, gender, national origin, age, disability, or sexual orientation. Detailed information about admissions policies and procedures are available online at www.cwsl.edu.

Admissions Contact: Ann Kowel, Admissions Director
225 Cedar Street, San Diego, CA 92101
Admissions Phone: 619-525-1401 • Admissions Fax: 619-685-2916
Admissions E-mail: admissions@cwsl.edu • Web Address: www.cwsl.edu

CALIFORNIA WESTERN SCHOOL OF LAW

Admissions Contact: Ann Kowel, Admissions Director
225 Cedar Street, San Diego, CA 92101
Admissions Phone: 619-525-1401 • Admissions Fax: 619-685-2916
Admissions E-mail: admissions@cwsl.edu • Web Address: www.cwsl.edu

INSTITUTIONAL INFORMATION

Public/Private: Private
Environment: Urban
Academic Calendar: Trimester
Schedule: Full time only
Student/Faculty Ratio: 17:1
Total Faculty: 69
% Part Time: 46
% Female: 39
% Minority: 13

PROGRAMS

Advanced Degrees Offered: MCL/LLM (9 months)
Combined Degrees Offered: JD/MSW (4 years)
Clinical Program Required? No
Clinical Programs: Externship Program, Mediation Clinic, Scholastic Internship (1–11 units)
Grading System: 95–50 numerical scale with mandatory curve
Legal Writing/Methods Course Requirements: 3-course series required first, second, third or fourth trimester

STUDENT INFORMATION

Enrollment of Law School: 699
% Male/Female: 46/54
% Full Time: 95
% Full Time That Are International: 2
% Minority: 28
Average Age of Entering Class: 27

RESEARCH FACILITIES

School-Supported Research Centers: San Diego County Law Library, other law school libraries through interlibrary loan

EXPENSES/FINANCIAL AID

Annual Tuition: $21,320
Room and Board (On/Off Campus): $7,816
Books and Supplies: $650
Average Grant: $10,000
Average Loan: $30,000
% of Aid That Is Merit-Based: 10
% Receiving Some Sort of Aid: 85
Average Total Aid Package: $30,000
Average Debt: $78,000
Fees Per Credit: $750

ADMISSIONS INFORMATION

Application Fee: $45
Regular Application Deadline: 4/1
Regular Notification: Rolling
LSDAS Accepted? Yes
Average GPA: 3.1
Range of GPA: 2.8–3.4
Average LSAT: 151
Range of LSAT: 146–152
Transfer Students Accepted? Yes
Other Schools to Which Students Applied: University of San Diego, Southwestern University, Pepperdine University, UCLA School of Law, Whittier College, Golden Gate University, Loyola Marymount University, Santa Clara University
Other Admissions Factors Considered: Work experience, volunteer and extracurricular activities, diversity (ethnic, cultural, age)

INTERNATIONAL STUDENTS

TOEFL Required of International Students? Yes
Minimum TOEFL: 600

EMPLOYMENT INFORMATION

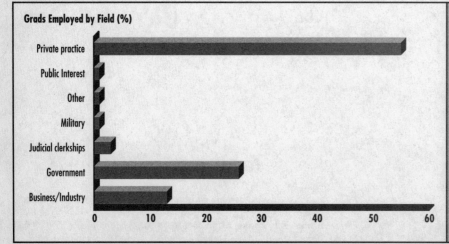

Rate of Placement: 84%
Average Starting Salary: $44,849
Prominent Alumni: Daniel Butler, Civil Rights Division Public Integrity Section U.S. Department of Justice; William C. Johnston, manager, Contracts, Lockheed Missiles and Space Co.; Hon. Thomas Nasslf, former U.S. ambassador to Morocco, chairman of the board/CEO Gulf International Consulting, Inc.; Cynthia Hoover Rosenthal, principal legal advisor, Federal Bureau of Investigation; Edward B. Scott, vice president Chevron Oversea Petroleum; Hon. Garland Burrell, U.S. District Court judge
State for Bar Exam: CA
Number Taking Bar Exam: 91
Pass Rate for First-Time Bar: 75%

CAMPBELL UNIVERSITY
Norman Adrian Wiggins School of Law

Admissions Contact: Associate Dean for Admissions, Alan D. Woodlief, Jr.
PO Box 158, Buies Creek, NC 27506
Admissions Phone: 910-893-1754 • Admissions Fax: 910-893-1780
Admissions E-mail: culaw@webster.campbell.edu • Web Address: http://webster.campbell.edu/culawsch.htm

INSTITUTIONAL INFORMATION

Public/Private: Private
Affiliation: Baptist
Environment: Rural
Academic Calendar: Semester
Schedule: Full time only
Student/Faculty Ratio: 23:1
Total Faculty: 37
% Part Time: 48
% Female: 16
% Minority: 0

PROGRAMS

Academic Specialties: The Trial and Appellate Advocacy Program is a special strength of the curriculum.
Advanced Degrees Offered: JD (3 years, 90 semester hours)
Combined Degrees Offered: JD/MBA
Clinical Program Required? No
Clinical Programs: Legal Externship Program with public service legal office
Grading System: 90–99 Superior, 80–89 Above average, 70–79 Good level, 60–69 Unsatisfactory, 50–59 Failing. Elective courses: H (Honors), S (Satisfactory), UP (Unsatisfactory Pass), UF (Unsatisfactory Fail).
Legal Writing/Methods Course Requirements: 2 semesters

STUDENT INFORMATION

Enrollment of Law School: 297
% Male/Female: 50/50
% Full Time: 100
% Full Time That Are International: 0
% Minority: 6

RESEARCH FACILITIES

School-Supported Research Centers: University library

EXPENSES/FINANCIAL AID

Annual Tuition: $18,500
Books and Supplies: $750
Average Grant: $2,000
Fees Per Credit: $750

ADMISSIONS INFORMATION

Application Fee: $40
Regular Application Deadline: Rolling
Regular Notification: Rolling
Average GPA: 3.2
Range of GPA: 2.9–3.4
Average LSAT: 154
Range of LSAT: 151–156
Transfer Students Accepted? Yes
Other Schools to Which Students Applied: University of North Carolina, Wake Forest University, University of Richmond, North Carolina Central University, University of South Carolina, University of Georgia, Mercer University, Washington and Lee University
Number of Applications Received: 634
Number of Applicants Accepted: 209
Number of Applicants Enrolled: 112

EMPLOYMENT INFORMATION

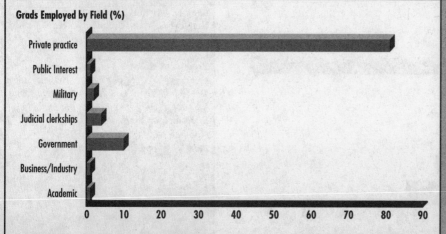

State for Bar Exam: NC
Number Taking Bar Exam: 93
Pass Rate for First-Time Bar: 95%

CAPITAL UNIVERSITY
Law School

Admissions Contact: Assistant Dean of Admissions and Financial Aid, Linda Mihely
665 South High Street, Columbus, OH 43215
Admissions Phone: 614-445-8836 • Admissions Fax: 614-445-7125
Admissions E-mail: law-admissions@capital.edu • Web Address: www.law.capital.edu

INSTITUTIONAL INFORMATION

Public/Private: Private
Affiliation: Lutheran
Environment: Urban
Academic Calendar: Semester
Schedule: Full time or part time
Student/Faculty Ratio: 23:1
Total Faculty: 73
% Part Time: 20
% Female: 30
% Minority: 15

PROGRAMS

Academic Specialties: Dispute Resolution, Business and Tax Law, and Government Law are among the faculty's specialties. Strengths include commitment to teaching, innovative centers and institutes, positive relationships with students, and open access for students.
Advanced Degrees Offered: LLM Taxation (1–6 years), LLM Business and Taxation (1–6 years), MT (1–6 years)
Combined Degrees Offered: JD/MBA (3.5 years full time, 5 years part time), JD/MSN (3.5 years full time, 5 years part time), JD/MSA (3.5 years full time)
Clinical Program Required? No
Clinical Programs: General Civil Litigation Clinic, Mediation Clinic, General Criminal Clinic, externships
Grading System: 4.0 scale A to E
Legal Writing/Methods Course Requirements: 2 semesters of first-year legal writing

STUDENT INFORMATION

Enrollment of Law School: 793
% Male/Female: 54/46
% Full Time: 55
% Full Time That Are International: 23
% Minority: 12
Average Age of Entering Class: 27

RESEARCH FACILITIES

School-Supported Research Centers: Supreme Court Law Library, Columbus Law Library Association, university computer lab, university clinic, and exercise room

EXPENSES/FINANCIAL AID

Annual Tuition: $15,370
Room and Board (Off Campus): $9,748
Books and Supplies: $887
Average Grant: $3,787
Average Loan: $18,400
% of Aid That Is Merit-Based: 38
% Receiving Some Sort of Aid: 93
Average Total Aid Package: $25,400
Average Debt: $44,887
Fees Per Credit: $530

ADMISSIONS INFORMATION

Application Fee: $35
Regular Application Deadline: Rolling
Regular Notification: Rolling
LSDAS Accepted? Yes
Average GPA: 3.0
Range of GPA: 2.7–3.3
Average LSAT: 150
Range of LSAT: 148–157
Transfer Students Accepted? Yes
Other Schools to Which Students Applied: Ohio State University, University of Dayton, University of Akron, University of Cincinnati, University of Toledo, Ohio Northern University, Cleveland State University, Case Western Reserve University
Other Admissions Factors Considered: Socioeconomic status, overcoming hardship, diversity, leadership ability, commitment to justice
Number of Applications Received: 880

EMPLOYMENT INFORMATION

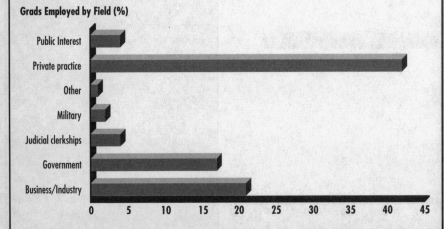

Grads Employed by Field (%)

Average Starting Salary: $46,485
Employers Who Frequently Hire Grads: Law firms, government agencies, business and corporate employers
Prominent Alumni: Robert H. Schottenstein, president, MI Schottenstein Homes, Inc.; Deborah P. Pryce, U.S. representative; Thomas Banasars, president, Ohio State Bar Association
State for Bar Exam: OH
Number Taking Bar Exam: 155
Pass Rate for First-Time Bar: 76%

CASE WESTERN RESERVE UNIVERSITY
School of Law

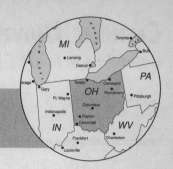

Admissions Contact: Assistant Dean, Barbara Andelman
11075 East Boulevard, Cleveland, OH 44106
Admissions Phone: 800-756-0036 • Admissions Fax: 216-368-1042
Admissions E-mail: lawadmissions@po.cwru.edu • Web Address: www.law.cwru.edu

INSTITUTIONAL INFORMATION

Public/Private: Private
Environment: Urban
Academic Calendar: Semester
Schedule: Full time or part time
Student/Faculty Ratio: 16:1
Total Faculty: 83
% Female: 19
% Minority: 7

PROGRAMS

Academic Specialties: The curriculum is distinguished both for its breadth and depth. Students will find a wide offering of courses in virtually every area of the law. The Health Law, International Law, Constitutional Law, Corporate and Business Law, and Litigation Law offerings are especially strong. Yahoo! Rated CWRU the most "wired" campus in 1999.
Advanced Degrees Offered: LLM Taxation (1 year), LLM U.S. Legal Studies (1 year)
Combined Degrees Offered: JD/MBA (4 years), JD/MNO (nonprofit management) (4 years), JD/MSSA (social work) (4 years), JD/MA Legal History (4 years), JD/MA Bioethics (4 years), JD/MD (medicine) (7 years)
Clinical Program Required? No
Clinical Programs: Civil Law, Health Law, Criminal Law, Family Law
Grading System: A, A–, B+, B, B–, C+, C, C–, D+, D, D–, P, F, WF, W, N; no A+
Legal Writing/Methods Course Requirements: First-year students are required to take "RAW" (Research, Analysis, and Writing), a 2-semester course

taught solely by full-time instructors, each of whom is an experienced attorney. Each RAW section meets in a small group of 20–25 students. During the course of the year, students will undertake a rigorous program of research and legal writing ranging from legal memoranda to contracts to trial briefs to appellate briefs.

STUDENT INFORMATION

Enrollment of Law School: 632
% Male/Female: 55/45
% Full Time: 98
% Full Time That Are International: 1
% Minority: 14
Average Age of Entering Class: 25

RESEARCH FACILITIES

Computers/Workstations Available: 76
School-Supported Research Centers: The Cleveland Public Library is the second largest public library system in the country.

EXPENSES/FINANCIAL AID

Annual Tuition: $21,300
Room and Board: $9,000
Books and Supplies: $800
Financial Aid Application Deadline: 5/1
Average Grant: $14,500
Average Loan: $18,300
% of Aid That Is Merit-Based: 100
% Receiving Some Sort of Aid: 75
Average Total Aid Package: $24,600
Average Debt: $52,000
Tuition Per Credit: $888
Fees Per Credit: $40

ADMISSIONS INFORMATION

Application Fee: $40
Regular Application Deadline: 4/1
Regular Notification: Rolling
LSDAS Accepted? Yes
Average GPA: 3.2
Range of GPA: 2.9–3.5
Average LSAT: 156
Range of LSAT: 153–160
Transfer Students Accepted? Yes
Other Schools to Which Students Applied: Ohio State University, Cleveland State University, University of Michigan, University of Cincinnati, University of Pittsburgh, American University, Boston University, Georgetown University
Other Admissions Factors Considered: Looking at each applicant's file in its entirety, we assess whether we believe the applicant has the intellectual ability to succeed in our program.
Number of Applications Received: 1,411
Number of Applicants Accepted: 883
Number of Applicants Enrolled: 208

EMPLOYMENT INFORMATION

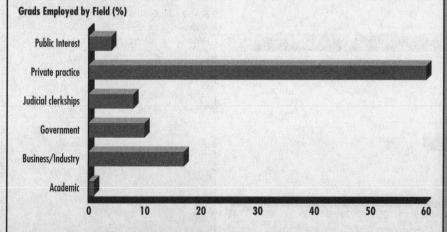

Grads Employed by Field (%)

- Public Interest
- Private practice
- Judicial clerkships
- Government
- Business/Industry
- Academic

Rate of Placement: 97%
Average Starting Salary: $54,098
Prominent Alumni: Barry M. Meyers, executive vice president of Warner Brothers, Inc.; Kathleen McDonald O'Malley, judge, U.S. 6th Circuit Court of Appeals; Richard North Patterson, author; Gary L. Bryenton, managing partner, Baker and Hostetler
State for Bar Exam: OH
Number Taking Bar Exam: 125
Pass Rate for First-Time Bar: 79%

CATHOLIC UNIVERSITY OF AMERICA
Columbus School of Law

Admissions Contact: Director of Admissions, George Braxton
Office of Admissions, Washington, DC 20064
Admissions Phone: 202-319-5151 • Admissions Fax: 202-319-6285
Admissions E-mail: braxton@law.edu • Web Address: www.law.edu

INSTITUTIONAL INFORMATION

Public/Private: Private
Affiliation: Roman Catholic
Environment: Urban
Academic Calendar: Semester
Schedule: Full time or part time
Student/Faculty Ratio: 21:1
Total Faculty: 93
% Part Time: 53
% Female: 34
% Minority: 13

PROGRAMS

Academic Specialties: 3 Institutes/Certificate Programs, Institute for Communications Law Studies, Comparative and International Law Institute, Law and Public Policy
Advanced Degrees Offered: JD (3 years full time, 4 years part time)
Combined Degrees Offered: JD/MA programs in Accounting, Canon Law, History, Philosophy, Psychology, Politics, Library Science, Economics, and Social Work (all 3–4 years)
Clinical Program Required? No
Clinical Programs: General Clinic, Families and the Law Clinic, Advocacy for the Elderly, Advocacy for Victims of Gun Violence, Criminal Prosecution Clinic, D.C. Law Students in Court, legal externships, SEC Training Program
Grading System: Numerical system on 50–100 scale. A letter-based system will be instituted with the entering class of 1999

STUDENT INFORMATION

Enrollment of Law School: 925
% Male/Female: 48/52
% Full Time: 71
% Full Time That Are International: 1
% Minority: 25
Average Age of Entering Class: 24

RESEARCH FACILITIES

Computers/Workstations Available: 300

EXPENSES/FINANCIAL AID

Annual Tuition: $25,360
Room and Board (On/Off Campus): $6,772/$6,620
Books and Supplies: $780
Financial Aid Application Deadline: 3/15
Average Grant: $7,000
Average Loan: $27,000
% of Aid That Is Merit-Based: 25
% Receiving Some Sort of Aid: 84
Average Total Aid Package: $34,500
Average Debt: $68,000
Fees Per Credit: $880

ADMISSIONS INFORMATION

Application Fee: $55
Regular Application Deadline: 3/1
Regular Notification: Rolling
Average GPA: 3.2
Range of GPA: 3.1–3.3
Average LSAT: 156
Range of LSAT: 153–158
Transfer Students Accepted? Yes
Other Schools to Which Students Applied: George Washington University, American University, Georgetown University, University of Maryland, Boston College, University of Baltimore, George Mason University, Syracuse University
Number of Applications Received: 2,110
Number of Applicants Accepted: 840
Number of Applicants Enrolled: 300

INTERNATIONAL STUDENTS

TOEFL Required of International Students? Yes
Minimum TOEFL: 600

EMPLOYMENT INFORMATION

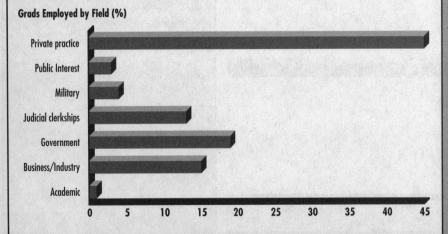

Grads Employed by Field (%)

Rate of Placement: 98%
Average Starting Salary: $50,521
Prominent Alumni: Charlene Barshefsky, JD, U.S. trade representative; Thomas Harkin, JD, U.S. senator; Karen Hastie Williams, JD, senior partner, Crowell and Moring
State for Bar Exam: MD
Number Taking Bar Exam: 104
Pass Rate for First-Time Bar: 70%

CITY UNIVERSITY OF NEW YORK
School of Law at Queens College

Admissions Contact: Director of Admissions, William D. Perez
65-21 Main Street, Flushing, NY 11367
Admissions Phone: 718-340-4210 • Admissions Fax: 718-340-4372
Admissions E-mail: admissions@mail.law.cuny.edu • Web Address: www.law.cuny.edu

INSTITUTIONAL INFORMATION

Public/Private: Public
Environment: Urban
Academic Calendar: Semester
Schedule: Full time only
Student/Faculty Ratio: 11:1
Total Faculty: 50
% Part Time: 26
% Female: 64
% Minority: 36

PROGRAMS

Academic Specialties: CUNY is a public interest/public service law school, and the curriculum is designed to build on the traditional doctrinal core to include policy and lawyering perspectives most relevant to public interest/public service lawyers. All students are required to enroll in a 12–16 credit concentration (externship) or clinical program in their third year that builds on a foundation of 12 credits of lawyering seminars spread over the first 2 years. The academic specialties of the faculty, all of which derive from a mix of scholarly work and lawyering experience, include International Human Rights, Civil Rights, Women's Rights, Health Law, Labor and Workers Law, Environmental Law, and Community Lawyering.
Combined Degrees Offered: None
Clinical Program Required? Yes

Clinical Programs: Battered Women's Clinic, Immigrants and Refugees Rights Clinic, Criminal Defender Clinic, Elder Law Clinic, International Women's Human Rights Clinic, Mediation Clinic
Grading System: A, A–, B+, B, B–, C+, C, C–, D, F; some courses have pass/fail option
Legal Writing/Methods Course Requirements: Primary component of an 8-credit, 2-semester, first-year required Lawyering Seminar course that includes other lawyering skills (interviewing, negotiation, oral advocacy), usually taught through simulation

STUDENT INFORMATION

Enrollment of Law School: 372
% Male/Female: 37/63
% Full Time: 98
% Full Time That Are International: 2
% Minority: 45
Average Age of Entering Class: 28

EXPENSES/FINANCIAL AID

Annual Tuition (Residents/Nonresidents): $5,700/$8,930
Financial Aid Application Deadline: 5/15
Average Grant: $2,652
Average Loan: $9,250
% of Aid That Is Merit-Based: 0
% Receiving Some Sort of Aid: 83
Average Total Aid Package: $18,416
Average Debt: $40,630

ADMISSIONS INFORMATION

Regular Application Deadline: 3/15
LSDAS Accepted? Yes
Average GPA: 3.1
Range of GPA: 2.7–3.3
Average LSAT: 148
Range of LSAT: 142–152
Transfer Students Accepted? Yes
Other Schools to Which Students Applied: New York Law School, St. John's University, Brooklyn Law School, Fordham University, Pace University, Touro College, Yeshiva University
Other Admissions Factors Considered: Experience in public interest or public service

EMPLOYMENT INFORMATION

Rate of Placement: 83%
Employers Who Frequently Hire Grads: Legal Aid Society, NY City; Legal Services Offices, NY City; District Attorneys Offices, NY City
Prominent Alumni: Ruth Lowenkron, director, Disability Law Center, NY Lawyers for the Public Interest; Victoria Ortiz, dean of students, University of California School of Law at Berkeley, Boalthall; Tonya Gonnella Frichner, founder and president, American Indian Law Alliance; Mary Hughes, deputy district attorney, Kings County, NY
States for Bar Exam: CT/NY
Number Taking Bar Exam: 17/111
Pass Rate for First-Time Bar: 59%/63%

CLEVELAND STATE UNIVERSITY
Cleveland-Marshall School of Law

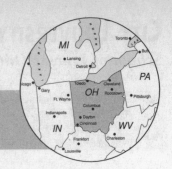

Admissions Contact: Assistant Dean for Admissions, Margaret McNally
1801 Euclid Avenue, Cleveland, OH 44115
Admissions Phone: 216-687-2304 • Admissions Fax: 216-687-6881
Admissions E-mail: admissions@law.csuohio.edu • Web Address: www.law.csuohio.edu

INSTITUTIONAL INFORMATION
Public/Private: Public
Student/Faculty Ratio: 16:1
Total Faculty: 74
% Part Time: 32
% Female: 36
% Minority: 8

PROGRAMS
Academic Specialties: A variety of clinical experiences including in-house clinics and externships with judges and public interest/public service/governmental placements; Criminal Law; Advocacy; Health Law; strong business and tax course offerings
Advanced Degrees Offered: LLM (20–24 credits, may be completed in 1–4 years)
Combined Degrees Offered: JD/MPA, JD/MUPD, and JD/MBA (each may be completed in 4 years full-time)
Clinical Program Required? No
Grading System: A, B+, B, C+, C, D+, D, F on a 4.0 scale
Legal Writing/Methods Course Requirements: First-year, legal writing, full year, 5 credits, includes research, writing, and advocacy; a third semester of legal writing required in second year; upper-level writing required for graduation

STUDENT INFORMATION
Enrollment of Law School: 786
% Male/Female: 53/47
% Full Time: 39
% Full Time That Are International: 1
% Minority: 15
Average Age of Entering Class: 27

RESEARCH FACILITIES
Computers/Workstations Available: 73
School-Supported Research Centers: Access through Ohiolink to research collections in Ohio colleges and universities and online databases

EXPENSES/FINANCIAL AID
Annual Tuition (Residents/Nonresidents): $7,696/$15,392
Room and Board: $7,950
Books and Supplies: $700
Financial Aid Application Deadline: 4/1
Average Grant: $2,155
Average Loan: $14,534
% of Aid That Is Merit-Based: 90
% Receiving Some Sort of Aid: 85
Average Total Aid Package: $16,250
Average Debt: $41,500

ADMISSIONS INFORMATION
Application Fee: $35
Regular Application Deadline: 4/1
Regular Notification: 5/1
LSDAS Accepted? Yes
Average GPA: 3.1
Range of GPA: 2.9–3.5
Average LSAT: 150
Range of LSAT: 147–154
Transfer Students Accepted? Yes
Other Schools to Which Students Applied: Case Western Reserve University, University of Akron, Ohio State University, Ohio Northern University, University of Toledo, University of Cincinnati
Other Admissions Factors Considered: Work experience, other personal experience and information
Number of Applications Received: 1,220
Number of Applicants Accepted: 617
Number of Applicants Enrolled: 254

EMPLOYMENT INFORMATION

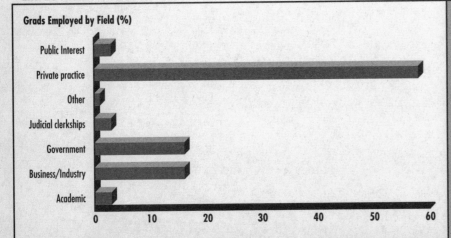

Grads Employed by Field (%)

Rate of Placement: 87%
Average Starting Salary: $48,000
Employers Who Frequently Hire Grads: Jones, Day, Reavis and Pogue; Squire, Sanders and Dempsey; Calfee, Halter and Griswold; Arter and Hadden; Ernst and Young; and McCarthy, Lebit, Crystal and Harman are among the many employers who hire our students. A broad range of employers representing small, medium, and large firms as well as business and government agencies employ our graduates.
State for Bar Exam: OH
Number Taking Bar Exam: 200
Pass Rate for First-Time Bar: 71%

COLLEGE OF WILLIAM & MARY

William & Mary School of Law

Admissions Contact: Associate Dean, Faye F. Shealy
PO Box 8795, Williamsburg, VA 23187-8795
Admissions Phone: 804-221-3785 • Admissions Fax: 804-221-3261
Admissions E-mail: lawadmn@wm.edu • Web Address: www.wm.edu/law/

INSTITUTIONAL INFORMATION

Public/Private: Public
Environment: Suburban
Academic Calendar: Semester
Schedule: Full time only
Student/Faculty Ratio: 18:1
Total Faculty: 74
% Part Time: 61
% Female: 27
% Minority: 7

PROGRAMS

Academic Specialties: With the Institute of Bill of Rights Law in a Center for Constitutional Law, Bill of Rights Study and Public Programs are particular strengths. The Legal Skills Program is a required 2-year program of professional skills and ethics development.
Advanced Degrees Offered: LLM American Legal System (1 year)
Combined Degrees Offered: JD/MPP (4 years), JD/MBA (4 years), JD/MA American Studies (4 years)
Clinical Program Required? No
Clinical Programs: Attorney General, Legal Aid, International Law, Court of Appeals, Environmental Law, Employee Relations
Grading System: A, B+, B, B–, C+, C, C–, D, F on a 4.0 scale
Legal Writing/Methods Course Requirements: The teaching of Legal Writing or Legal Methods is incorporated in our Legal Skills Program, a mandatory two-year program.

STUDENT INFORMATION

Enrollment of Law School: 538
% Male/Female: 57/43
% Full Time: 100
% Full Time That Are International: 3
% Minority: 17
Average Age of Entering Class: 25

RESEARCH FACILITIES

Computers/Workstations Available: 46
School-Supported Research Centers: National Center for State Courts, William and Mary Environmental Science and Policy Cluster, Virginia Institute for Marine Science

EXPENSES/FINANCIAL AID

Annual Tuition (Residents/Nonresidents): $9,074/$18,200
Room and Board: $11,830
Books and Supplies: $1,000
Financial Aid Application Deadline: 2/15
Average Grant: $2,903
Average Loan: $18,060
% of Aid That Is Merit-Based: 35
% Receiving Some Sort of Aid: 89
Average Total Aid Package: $18,778
Average Debt: $52,772

ADMISSIONS INFORMATION

Application Fee: $40
Regular Application Deadline: 3/1
Regular Notification: 4/1
LSDAS Accepted? Yes
Average GPA: 3.3
Range of GPA: 3.1–3.6
Average LSAT: 162
Range of LSAT: 160–165
Transfer Students Accepted? Yes
Other Schools to Which Students Applied: University of Virginia, Washington and Lee University, George Washington University, University of Richmond, Georgetown University, George Mason University, Boston College, American University
Other Admissions Factors Considered: Quality of school(s) attended, difficulty of the major or department in which the degree was earned, hours spent on outside employment or other time-consuming extracurricular activities
Number of Applications Received: 2,267
Number of Applicants Accepted: 718
Number of Applicants Enrolled: 201

INTERNATIONAL STUDENTS

TOEFL Required of International Students? Yes
Minimum TOEFL: 600

EMPLOYMENT INFORMATION

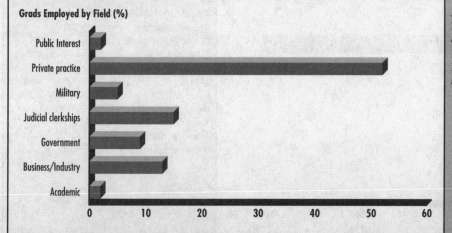

Average Starting Salary: $51,222
Prominent Alumni: John Marshall, chief justice of the United States Supreme Court; Rebecca Beach Smith, U.S. district judge for the Eastern District of Virginia; James McGlothlin, president and CEO, United Co.

COLUMBIA UNIVERSITY
School of Law

Admissions Contact: Dean of Admissions, James Milligan
435 West 116th Street, New York, NY 10027
Admissions Phone: 212-854-2670 • Admissions Fax: 212-854-1109
Admissions E-mail: admissions@law.columbia.edu • Web Address: www.law.columbia.edu

INSTITUTIONAL INFORMATION

Public/Private: Private
Environment: Urban
Academic Calendar: Semester
Schedule: Full time only
Student/Faculty Ratio: 16:1
Total Faculty: 150
% Part Time: 50
% Female: 27
% Minority: 12

PROGRAMS

Academic Specialties: Clinical Education, Corporate Law, Criminal Law, Human Rights, Intellectual Property, International and Comparative Law, mandatory Pro Bono Program, Profession of Law (professional responsibility), Constitutional Law, Critical Race Theory, Feminist Jurisprudence
Advanced Degrees Offered: LLM (1 year), JSD (2 semesters in residence and a dissertation)
Combined Degrees Offered: JD/PhD History, Philosophy, Anthropology, Economics, Political Science, Psychology, Sociology (7 years); JD/MBA (3 or 4 years); JD/MFA Arts Administration (4 years); JD/MS Social Work and Urban Planning (4 years); JD/MS Journalism (3.5 years); JD/MIA (4 years); JD/MPA Public Administration with Columbia (4 years); JD/MPA Public Affairs with Woodrow Wilson School at Princeton (4 years)
Clinical Program Required? No

Clinical Programs: Prisoners and Families, Fair Housing, Law and the Arts, Nonprofit Organizations Mediation
Grading System: A+, A, A−, B+, B, B−, C, F. Some courses and clinicals offer a grade of CR as an option, while others grade CR or F.
Legal Writing/Methods Course Requirements: Legal Writing: Intensive training in the analysis of legal problems and the use of legal materials through seminar discussion, written assignments, and personal conferences—3-week intensive course meets 2 times per week, thereafter, it meets once per week for approximately 8 weeks. Legal Methods: An introduction to legal institutions and processes, and the skills necessary in the professional use of case law and legislation—3-week intensive course that meets 3 hours per day, 5 days per week.

STUDENT INFORMATION

Enrollment of Law School: 1,105
% Male/Female: 55/45
% Full Time: 100
% Full Time That Are International: 5
% Minority: 35
Average Age of Entering Class: 24

RESEARCH FACILITIES

Computers/Workstations Available: 46

EXPENSES/FINANCIAL AID

Annual Tuition: $27,940
Room and Board: $13,830
Books and Supplies: $755
Financial Aid Application Deadline: 3/1
Average Grant: $11,817
Average Loan: $29,112
% of Aid That Is Merit-Based: 0
% Receiving Some Sort of Aid: 76
Average Total Aid Package: $33,000
Average Debt: $78,493

ADMISSIONS INFORMATION

Application Fee: $65
Regular Application Deadline: 2/15
Regular Notification: Rolling
LSDAS Accepted? Yes
Average GPA: 3.6
Average LSAT: 169
Transfer Students Accepted? Yes
Other Schools to Which Students Applied: Harvard University, New York University, Yale University, Georgetown University, Stanford University, University of Pennsylvania, University of Chicago, University of Michigan
Other Admissions Factors Considered: In addition to evaluating a candidate's overall academic history and performance on the LSAT, the committee examines the applicant's personal statement and letters of recommendation. Also considered are course selection, extracuricular involvement, community service.

EMPLOYMENT INFORMATION

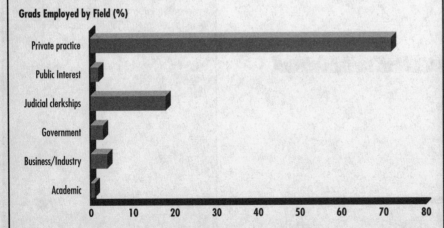

Grads Employed by Field (%)

Private practice
Public Interest
Judicial clerkships
Government
Business/Industry
Academic

Rate of Placement: 100%
Average Starting Salary: $75,535
Prominent Alumni: Ruth Bader Ginsburg, U.S. Supreme Court; Franklin D. Roosevelt, governor of New York and U.S. President; Franklin Thomas, former president of Ford Foundation; George Pataki, New York governor; David Stern, NBA commissioner; Ellen Futter, president, American Museum of Natural History
State for Bar Exam: NY
Number Taking Bar Exam: 272

CORNELL UNIVERSITY
Law School

Admissions Contact: Dean of Admissions, R. Geiger
Myron Taylor Hall, Ithaca, NY 14853
Admissions Phone: 607-255-5141 • Admissions Fax: 607-255-7193
Admissions E-mail: lawadmit@law.mail.cornell.edu • Web Address: www.lawschool.cornell.edu

INSTITUTIONAL INFORMATION

Public/Private: Private
Environment: Suburban
Academic Calendar: Semester
Schedule: Full time only
Student/Faculty Ratio: 12:1
Total Faculty: 43
% Female: 26
% Minority: 10

PROGRAMS

Advanced Degrees Offered: JD (3 years), LLM (1 year), JD/LLM International and Comparative Law (3 years), JD/Maitrise en Driot French Law degree (4 years), JSD (2 years), JD/MLL Prax. Master of German and European Law and Legal Practice (4 years)
Combined Degrees Offered: JD/MBA, JD/MPA, JD/MA, JD/PhD, JD/MIRL, JD/MRP
Clinical Program Required? No
Clinical Programs: Legal Aid, Capital Punishment, Appellate Advocacy, Civil Liberties, Estate Planning, Government Benefits, Women and the Law, Judicial Externship, Legislative Externship, Neighborhood Legal Services Externship, Public International Law Clinic, Law Guardian
Grading System: Letter system

STUDENT INFORMATION

Enrollment of Law School: 546
% Male/Female: 53/47
% Full Time: 100
% Full Time That Are International: 4
% Minority: 25
Average Age of Entering Class: 24

RESEARCH FACILITIES

Computers/Workstations Available: 50

EXPENSES/FINANCIAL AID

Annual Tuition: $25,500
Room and Board: $7,620
Books and Supplies: $760
Financial Aid Application Deadline: 3/15
Average Grant: $7,000

ADMISSIONS INFORMATION

Application Fee: $65
Regular Application Deadline: 2/1
Regular Notification: Rolling
LSDAS Accepted? Yes
Average GPA: 3.6
Range of GPA: 3.3–3.7
Average LSAT: 165
Range of LSAT: 163–166
Transfer Students Accepted? Yes
Other Schools to Which Students Applied: Harvard University, Georgetown University, New York University, Columbia University, Yale University, Duke University, University of Pennsylvania
Other Admissions Factors Considered: Undergraduate and graduate course work, work experience, extracurricular activities, community involvement, and leadership

EMPLOYMENT INFORMATION

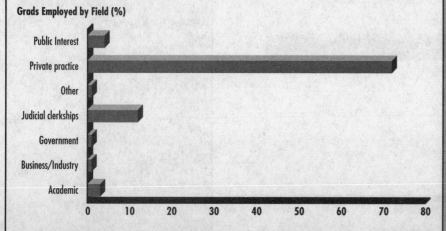

Grads Employed by Field (%)

Rate of Placement: 99%
Average Starting Salary: $79,000
States for Bar Exam: MA/NY
Number Taking Bar Exam: 22/92
Pass Rate for First-Time Bar: 100%/92%

CREIGHTON UNIVERSITY
School of Law

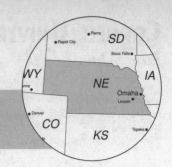

Admissions Contact: Assistant Dean, Andrea D. Bashara
2500 California Plaza, Omaha, NE 68178
Admissions Phone: 402-280-2872 • Admissions Fax: 402-280-3161
Admissions E-mail: admit@culaw.creighton.edu • Web Address: www.creighton.edu/CULAW

INSTITUTIONAL INFORMATION

Public/Private: Private
Affiliation: Catholic
Environment: Urban
Academic Calendar: Semester
Schedule: Full time or part time
Student/Faculty Ratio: 19:1
Total Faculty: 63
% Part Time: 65
% Female: 33
% Minority: 1

PROGRAMS

Academic Specialties: Ethics, Corporate/Commercial/Tax, Constitutional Law, Evidence/Litigation and Alternate Dispute Resolution, Civil Procedure/Federal Courts/Conflict of Laws, Legal Research. Strengths: small classes in first year, heavy faculty/student interaction.
Combined Degrees Offered: JD/MBA (3 years), JD/MS Electronic Commerce (3 years)
Clinical Program Required? No
Clinical Programs: Although no clinics are required, the following clinical programs are offered: Milton R. Abrahams Legal Clinic, clinical and judicial internships with government and legal aid offices
Grading System: 50–100 scale
Legal Writing/Methods Course Requirements: 3-semester legal research and writing program

STUDENT INFORMATION

Enrollment of Law School: 427
% Male/Female: 57/43
% Full Time: 96
% Full Time That Are International: 1
Number of Countries Represented: 2
% Minority: 9
Average Age of Entering Class: 26

RESEARCH FACILITIES

Computers/Workstations Available: 46

EXPENSES/FINANCIAL AID

Annual Tuition: $17,458
Room and Board: $9,900
Books and Supplies: $1,050
Financial Aid Application Deadline: 3/1
Average Grant: $7,500
Average Loan: $18,500
% of Aid That Is Merit-Based: 33
% Receiving Some Sort of Aid: 92
Average Total Aid Package: $20,000
Average Debt: $60,251
Fees Per Credit: $525

ADMISSIONS INFORMATION

Application Fee: $40
Regular Application Deadline: 5/1
Regular Notification: Rolling
LSDAS Accepted? Yes
Average GPA: 3.1
Range of GPA: 2.7–3.4
Average LSAT: 151
Range of LSAT: 148–155
Transfer Students Accepted? Yes
Other Schools to Which Students Applied: University of Nebraska, Drake University
Other Admissions Factors Considered: Life experiences
Number of Applications Received: 700
Number of Applicants Accepted: 469
Number of Applicants Enrolled: 152

EMPLOYMENT INFORMATION

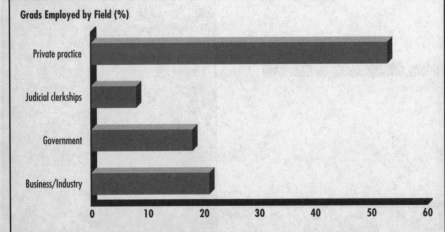

Rate of Placement: 96%
Average Starting Salary: $40,329
Employers Who Frequently Hire Grads: McGrath North, Kutak Rock, Fraser Stryker, Baird Holm, Koley Jessen, Blackwell Sanders, Stinson Mag
Prominent Alumni: Roman L. Hruska, former U.S. senator; Phillip M. Klutznik, former secretary of commerce and real estate developer; John McKay, president, Legal Services Corp., Washington, D.C.
State for Bar Exam: NE
Number Taking Bar Exam: 51
Pass Rate for First-Time Bar: 88%

DALHOUSIE UNIVERSITY
Dalhousie Law School

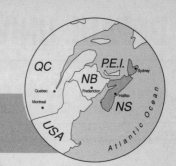

Admissions Contact: Director of Admissions and Placement, Rose Godfrey
Dalhousie Law School, Halifax, NS B3P 1P8 Canada
Admissions Phone: 902-494-1018 • Admissions Fax: 902-494-1316
Admissions E-mail: rose.godfrey@dal.ca • Web Address: www.dal.ca/law/admission.html

INSTITUTIONAL INFORMATION
Public/Private: Public
Student/Faculty Ratio: 13:1
Total Faculty: 35
% Female: 45
% Minority: 6

PROGRAMS
Academic Specialties: Environmental Law, International Law, Marine Law, Maritime Law
Advanced Degrees Offered: LLM, JSD
Combined Degrees Offered: LLB/MBA, LLB/MLIS, LLB/MPA, LLB/MHSA (4 years)
Clinical Program Required? No
Clinical Programs: Legal Aid Clinic, Criminal Clinic
Grading System: Pass/Fail
Legal Writing/Methods Course Requirements: Full year

STUDENT INFORMATION
Enrollment of Law School: 458
% Male/Female: 50/50
% Part Time: 4
% Full Time: 96
% Minority: 12
Average Age of Entering Class: 25

RESEARCH FACILITIES
Computers/Workstations Available: 60

EXPENSES/FINANCIAL AID
Annual Tuition: $5,900
Room and Board (On Campus): $3,500
Books and Supplies: $1,200
Average Grant: $4,212
% of Aid That Is Merit-Based: 43
% Receiving Some Sort of Aid: 57%
Average Total Aid Package: $1,257

ADMISSIONS INFORMATION
Application Fee: $65
Regular Application Deadline: 2/8
Regular Notification: 4/1
Average GPA: 3.7
Average LSAT: 158
Transfer Students Accepted? Yes
Other Schools to Which Students Applied: University of British Columbia, University of New Brunswick, Western University, McGill University, University of Toronto, Queens University, Winsor University, Osgoode University
Number of Applications Received: 1,077
Number of Applicants Accepted: 317
Number of Applicants Enrolled: 161

INTERNATIONAL STUDENTS
TOEFL Required of International Students? Yes
Minimum TOEFL: 600

EMPLOYMENT INFORMATION

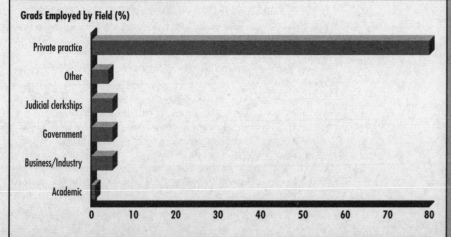

Grads Employed by Field (%)

Rate of Placement: 90%
Employers Who Frequently Hire Grads: Law firms, government, courts
Prominent Alumni: Sir Graham Day, chancellor, Dalhousie University; Purdy A. Crawford, chairman, Imasco Limited; The Honourable Anne MacLellan, justice minister, Canada

DEPAUL UNIVERSITY

OVERVIEW

Your development as a lawyer is shaped by lessons from the real world. What better place to begin that development than in the legal and financial heart of one of the world's greatest cities? Located in Chicago, DePaul College of Law has been educating students for over 100 years, preparing them for a lifetime of career challenges and goals. As part of this dynamic legal community, you will join students from more than 150 colleges and universities, 30 states, and a number of countries as you learn the fundamentals of law and justice.

A CURRICULUM DESIGNED FOR A LIFETIME OF ACHIEVEMENT

DePaul's innovative and rigorous curriculum allows you to tailor your education to your career objectives. The basic core of traditional subjects prepares you for the practice of law, while our three joint degree programs, four certificate programs, two graduate law programs, and extensive collection of advanced-level courses further enrich your options.

Areas of curricular strength include:

- Corporate & Commercial Business Transactions
- Criminal Law & Procedure
- Family/Estate Law
- Health Law
- Intellectual Property Law
- International & Comparative Law
- Litigation & Drafting Skills
- Public Service Management
- Taxation

Joint degree, certificate, and graduate programs include:

- JD/MBA
- JD/MA in International Studies
- JD/MS in Public Service Management
- Certificate in Health Law
- Certificate in Intellectual Property: General
- Certificate in Intellectual Property: Patents
- Certificate in Taxation
- LLM in Health Law
- LLM in Taxation

Six legal clinics provide practical training in the following areas:

- Asylum/Immigration
- Community Development
- Criminal Appeals
- Death Penalty
- Disability Rights
- Technology/Intellectual Property

Five research centers and institutes allow you to contribute directly to the legal community:

Center for Justice in Capital Cases: In conjunction with the Office of the State Appellate Defender, the Center for Justice in Capital Cases trains attorneys appointed to defend individuals charged with a capital crime. Accompanying this center is a Death Penalty Clinic, which provides students an opportunity to acquire outstanding real-world experience by researching cases, locating and interviewing witnesses, writing motions, and participating in a range of other pursuits.

Center for Church/State Studies: The Center for Church/State Studies seeks ways to educate the public and enhance the level of scholarly debate over the liberties and protections of the First Amendment. Through national conferences and local programs, as well as through scholarly lectures and publications, the nondenominational Center explores the role of religion in modern American society. DePaul students work as research assistants on major projects such as the Interfaith Mediation Project and the Centerpiece Project, a study of how law and public policy affect the manner in which religious organizations operate.

Center for Intellectual Property Law: The Center for Intellectual Property Law was established for students, scholars, and professionals to advance and promote the study and practice of this highly progressive field. In addition to training students in the area's technical intricacies through a rigorous curriculum, directed extracurricular activities, and challenging externships, the Center sponsors a range of training workshops, seminars, conferences, and lectures that explore different issues within this ever-evolving area of law.

Center for Law and Science: The Center for Law and Science is devoted to gathering and distributing information in the form of case summaries, bibliographies of legal and scientific articles, website listings, and other materials concerned with how modern science interacts with state and federal courts, as well as with the international legal community. Primary attention is given to identifying, collecting, and analyzing important scientific literature; important trials; and the ongoing appellate reviews of criminal and tort cases that have science issues as important components.

International Human Rights Law Institute: This Institute is dedicated to enhancing awareness and understanding of international human rights law. Hailed by the United Nations, the Institute has initiated and contributed to a wide variety of international projects, including collecting information on humanitarian law violations in order to help the United Nations prosecute war crimes; assisting human rights groups and providing training for human rights lawyers in El Salvador and Guatemala; providing legal assistance to Haitian refugees seeking asylum in the United States; and consulting with the African National Congress' constitutional negotiators in South Africa.

DEVOTED FACULTY PREPARE YOU FOR A LIFETIME OF LEARNING

Under the supervision of a nationally respected faculty, you will learn to consider legal questions from every angle, from every ambiguity, from the most theoretical to the most specific and practical. DePaul students benefit immeasurably from studying with a faculty that is always questioning, exploring, and looking ahead.

You will encounter teachers who will challenge you in the classroom. You will learn not just what the law was yesterday or today, but what it may be tomorrow, and more importantly, why it will be so. DePaul's 50 full-time faculty members—21 of whom are women—are all respected and established scholars, teachers, and practitioners. They bring a variety of professional backgrounds and interests as diverse as the curriculum. Many hold advanced degrees in such fields as biology, business, psychology, political science, archaeology, theatre, public health, and philosophy.

STUDENT ACTIVITIES ENHANCE LEGAL ACUMEN

Recent student achievements include:

- Best Oralist, Frederick Douglass Moot Court Regional Competition, 2000
- Best Brief, Frederick Douglass Moot Court Regional Competition, 2000
- First Place Team, Jessup International Moot Court Regional Competition, 2000
- Best Oralist, Jessup International Moot Court Regional Competition, 2000
- Best Brief, Jessup International Moot Court Regional Competition, 2000
- National Finalists, Lefkowitz Moot Court Competition, 1999

DePaul students also edit and manage four law journals and four digests:

- *DePaul Law Review*
- *DePaul Journal of Health Care Law*
- *DePaul-LCA Journal of Art & Entertainment Law*
- *DePaul Business Law Journal*
- *Environmental Law Digest*
- *International Law Digest*
- *Intellectual Property Law Digest*
- *Women's Law Digest*

PREPARATION FOR A SUCCESSFUL CAREER

DePaul has a consistently strong placement record. In recent years, 93 percent of DePaul graduates have achieved employment within six months of graduation, an excellent record in a competitive legal market. In the most recent survey of current graduates, 93.8 percent reported their employment status:

- 52 percent joined law firms
- 17 percent entered business
- 15 percent entered government
- 1 percent secured judicial clerkships
- 6 percent serve in public interest
- 19 percent serve in other positions

In 1999, average salaries in private practice reached $61,129, and in business, $56,968. The range of yearly starting salaries for all positions was $20,000 to $110,000.

Current students and alumni alike enjoy extensive career opportunities. Recent graduates have been hired by a number of well-known national and international corporations, law firms, government, and public interest organizations.

CHICAGO—A CITY TO EXPLORE

Chicago offers superb education and employment opportunities and is also a wonderful place to live. Three million people in 77 lively neighborhoods enjoy 30 miles of beautiful shoreline, 15 miles of beaches, more than 6,000 restaurants, 40 museums, 6 major sports teams, and countless other possibilities for recreation.

Chicago is famous for the things it does best: jazz and blues music, deep-dish pizza, unrivaled architecture, relentless sports fanaticism, and creative politics. It offers all of the vibrant cultural advantages you would expect of a world-class city, such as an acclaimed symphony and opera, award-winning theater, endless restaurant options, vast parks, and significant historical landmarks.

In some ways, however, Chicago is known better for being a livable city, a city of neighborhoods, a city populated with genuine people. Its diverse, friendly neighborhoods celebrate community. Whether you prefer the classic sophistication of Lincoln Park, the artistic appeal of Bucktown, the authentic Mexican barrio of Pilsen, the eclectic character of Ukrainian Village, or the athletic hub of Wrigleyville, Chicago has a neighborhood for you.

With all that Chicago has to offer, it is not surprising that nearly 8,000 of DePaul's 12,000 law alumni chose to live and work throughout Chicago and its suburbs.

Professionally, culturally, and socially, Chicago offers a lifetime of opportunity.

ACCREDITATION

DePaul College of Law is a member of the Order of the Coif and the Association of American Law Schools and is accredited by the American Bar Association.

Director of Admission, Dennis Shea
25 East Jackon Boulevard, Chicago, IL 60604
Phone: 312-362-6831 or 800-428-7452 • Fax: 312-362-5280
E-mail: lawinfo@wppost.depaul.edu • Web Address: www.law.depaul.edu

DePaul University
DePaul College of Law

Admissions Contact: Director of Admission, Dennis Shea
25 East Jackon Boulevard, Chicago, IL 60604
Admissions Phone: 312-362-6831 • Admissions Fax: 312-362-5280
Admissions E-mail: lawinfo@wppost.depaul.edu • Web Address: www.law.depaul.edu

INSTITUTIONAL INFORMATION

Public/Private: Private
Affiliation: Roman Catholic
Environment: Urban
Academic Calendar: Semester
Schedule: Full time or part time
Student/Faculty Ratio: 21:1
Total Faculty: 110
% Part Time: 55
% Female: 37
% Minority: 7

PROGRAMS

Academic Specialties: Intellectual Property, Health Law, Tax Law, Human Rights Law, Litigation Skills, special IP/Legal Writing integrated program during first year
Advanced Degrees Offered: LLM Health Law (2 years), LLM Tax Law (2 years),
Combined Degrees Offered: JD/MBA (3–4 years)
Clinical Program Required? No
Clinical Programs: Asylum Law, Criminal Appellate, Mediation, Community Development, Family Law, externships
Grading System: A, B+, B, C+, C, D, F with a curve in all years
Legal Writing/Methods Course Requirements: 1 year required (2 courses); multiple electives

STUDENT INFORMATION

Enrollment of Law School: 1,108
% Male/Female: 47/53
% Full Time: 70
% Full Time That Are International: 1
% Minority: 20
Average Age of Entering Class: 25

RESEARCH FACILITIES

Computers/Workstations Available: 250
School-Supported Research Centers: Numerous state, local, and federal libraries as well as Chicago and Illinois Bar Associations and Libraries

EXPENSES/FINANCIAL AID

Annual Tuition: $20,700
Room and Board (Off Campus): $12,500
Books and Supplies: $750
Average Grant: $1,776
Average Loan: $18,500
% of Aid That Is Merit-Based: 20
% Receiving Some Sort of Aid: 80
Average Total Aid Package: $21,000
Average Debt: $60,000
Tuition Per Credit: $725
Fees Per Credit: $725

ADMISSIONS INFORMATION

Application Fee: $40
Regular Application Deadline: 4/1
Regular Notification: 3/1
LSDAS Accepted? Yes
Average GPA: 3.2
Range of GPA: 2.9–3.4
Average LSAT: 153
Range of LSAT: 150–155
Transfer Students Accepted? Yes
Other Schools to Which Students Applied: Loyola University Chicago, Illinois Institute of Technology, John Marshall Law School, Northwestern University, University of Illinois, University of Chicago, University of Notre Dame, Wayne State University
Number of Applications Received: 2,033
Number of Applicants Accepted: 1,274
Number of Applicants Enrolled: 363

INTERNATIONAL STUDENTS

TOEFL Required of International Students? Yes
Minimum TOEFL: 550

EMPLOYMENT INFORMATION

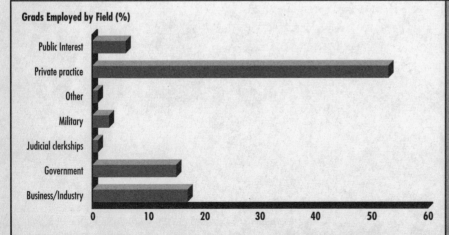

Grads Employed by Field (%)

Rate of Placement: 91%
Average Starting Salary: $50,900
Employers Who Frequently Hire Grads: Cook County State's Attorney's Office; Seyfarth Shaw; City of Chicago, Department of Law; Katten, Muchin & Zavis; Mayer, Brown & Platt; Cook County Public Guardian; DeLoitte and Touche; Arthur Andersen; Ernst and Young; Lake County State's Attorney's Office
Prominent Alumni: Richard M. Daley, mayor, City of Chicago; Jack M. Greenburg, CEO, McDonald's Corporation; Benjamin Hooks, former executive director, NAACP
State for Bar Exam: IL
Number Taking Bar Exam: 238
Pass Rate for First-Time Bar: 89%

DRAKE UNIVERSITY
Law School

Admissions Contact: Director of Admissions and Financial Aid, Kara Blanchard
2507 University Avenue, Des Moines, IA 50311
Admissions Phone: 515-271-2782 • Admissions Fax: 515-271-1990
Admissions E-mail: lawadmit@drake.edu • Web Address: www.law.drake.edu

INSTITUTIONAL INFORMATION

Public/Private: Private
Environment: Urban
Academic Calendar: Semester
Schedule: Full time or part time
Student/Faculty Ratio: 13:1
Total Faculty: 54
% Part Time: 44
% Female: 30
% Minority: 3

PROGRAMS

Academic Specialties: Constitutional Law Resource Center, Agricultural Law Center, clinics and internships, Legislative Center, very strong in Corporate/Commercial offerings and Trial Practice/Litigation offerings
Advanced Degrees Offered: JD (3 years)
Combined Degrees Offered: JD/MBA (6 semesters and 2 summers), JD/MPA (6 semesters and 2 summers), JD/MA (6 semesters and 1 summer), JD/PharmD, JD/MA Political Science (6 semesters and 1 summer), JD/MS Agricultural Economics (6 semesters and 1 summer)
Clinical Program Required? No
Clinical Programs: Administrative Law Clinics, General Clinic, Advanced Criminal Defense/Elder Law Clinic, Environmental Law Internship, Insurance Law Internship, Clerkship Program, Prosecutor Internship
Grading System: 4.0 (A), CR (Credit), I (Incomplete), IP (In Progress)

STUDENT INFORMATION

Enrollment of Law School: 356
% Male/Female: 53/47
% Full Time: 95
% Full Time That Are International: 1
% Minority: 13
Average Age of Entering Class: 25

RESEARCH FACILITIES

Computers/Workstations Available: 104
School-Supported Research Centers: State law library

EXPENSES/FINANCIAL AID

Annual Tuition: $18,230
Room and Board: $7,100
Books and Supplies: $1,100
Financial Aid Application Deadline: 3/1
Average Grant: $9,060
Average Loan: $20,152
% of Aid That Is Merit-Based: 13
% Receiving Some Sort of Aid: 92
Average Total Aid Package: $26,775
Average Debt: $59,000
Tuition Per Credit: $565

ADMISSIONS INFORMATION

Application Fee: $40
Regular Application Deadline: Rolling
Regular Notification: Rolling
Average GPA: 3.2
Range of GPA: 2.9–3.5
Average LSAT: 151
Range of LSAT: 148–156
Transfer Students Accepted? Yes
Other Schools to Which Students Applied: University of Iowa, Creighton University, John Marshall, William Mitchell, Hamline University, Marquette University, DePaul University, Loyola University Chicago
Other Admissions Factors Considered: The full admission committee, consisting of the director and four faculty members, thoroughly reviews each file in detail. All materials and information contained in the application for admission are considered in the decision-making process.
Number of Applications Received: 639
Number of Applicants Accepted: 440
Number of Applicants Enrolled: 116

INTERNATIONAL STUDENTS

TOEFL Required of International Students? Yes
Minimum TOEFL: 560

EMPLOYMENT INFORMATION

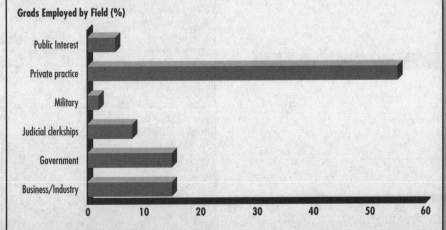

Grads Employed by Field (%)

Rate of Placement: 91%
Average Starting Salary: $41,234
Employers Who Frequently Hire Grads: Davis Brown, Des Moines; Nyemaster Goode, Des Moines; Department of Justice; JAG Corps; Blackwell Sanders, Kansas City; Shughart Thompson, Kansas City; Bryan Cave, Kansas City
Prominent Alumni: Dwight D. Opperman, chairman, Key Investments, Inc.; Terry Branstad, former governor of Iowa; Robert Ray, former governor of Iowa and president of Drake University
State for Bar Exam: IA
Number Taking Bar Exam: 61
Pass Rate for First-Time Bar: 90%

DUKE UNIVERSITY
School of Law

Admissions Contact: Assistant Dean for Admissions and Financial Aid, Dennis J. Shields
Box 90393, Durham, NC 27708-0393
Admissions Phone: 919-613-7020 • Admissions Fax: 919-613-7257
Admissions E-mail: admissions@law.duke.edu • Web Address: http://admissions.law.duke.edu

INSTITUTIONAL INFORMATION

Public/Private: Private
Environment: Urban
Academic Calendar: Semester
Schedule: Full time only
Student/Faculty Ratio: 16:1
Total Faculty: 78
% Part Time: 53
% Female: 27
% Minority: 7

PROGRAMS

Academic Specialties: International and Comparative Law, Corporate Law, Environmental Law, Constitutional Law and Civil Rights, Alternative Dispute Resolution
Advanced Degrees Offered: JD (3 years), LLM (1 year), SJD (1 year—for international students only)
Combined Degrees Offered: JD/MA in 11 fields: English, History, Humanities, Philosophy, Romance Studies, Cultural Anthropology, Economics, Political Science, Psychology, Forestry and Environmental Studies, Public Policy Studies; JD/MS Mechanical Engineering; JD/MBA; JD/MPP; JD/MEM; JD/MTS (4 years); JD/MD (6 years); JD/PhD (7 years); JD/LLM International and Comparative Law (3 years)

Clinical Program Required? No
Clinical Programs: Aids Law Clinic, Death Penalty Clinic, International Development Clinic, Civil/Criminal Trial Practice
Grading System: 4.0 scale
Legal Writing/Methods Course Requirements: 2 semesters first year

STUDENT INFORMATION

Enrollment of Law School: 608
% Male/Female: 54/46
% Full Time: 100
% Full Time That Are International: 3
% Minority: 26
Average Age of Entering Class: 24

RESEARCH FACILITIES

School-Supported Research Centers: All Duke University resources

EXPENSES/FINANCIAL AID

Annual Tuition: $25,500
Room and Board (Off Campus): $7,600
Books and Supplies: $1,200
Financial Aid Application Deadline: 3/15
Average Grant: $8,000
Average Loan: $22,649
% of Aid That Is Merit-Based: 10
% Receiving Some Sort of Aid: 75
Average Total Aid Package: $39,201
Average Debt: $61,000

ADMISSIONS INFORMATION

Application Fee: $65
Regular Application Deadline: 2/1
Regular Notification: Rolling
LSDAS Accepted? Yes
Average GPA: 3.5
Range of GPA: 3.3–3.8
Average LSAT: 165
Range of LSAT: 162–168
Transfer Students Accepted? Yes
Other Schools to Which Students Applied: Harvard University, Georgetown University, Yale University, University of Virginia, Stanford University, Columbia University, University of Michigan, Cornell University
Other Admissions Factors Considered: Demonstrated leadership, dedication to community service, excellence in a field, graduate study in another discipline, work experience, other information indicating academic or professional potential
Number of Applications Received: 3,390
Number of Applicants Accepted: 947
Number of Applicants Enrolled: 238

INTERNATIONAL STUDENTS

TOEFL Required of International Students? Yes
Minimum TOEFL: 600

EMPLOYMENT INFORMATION

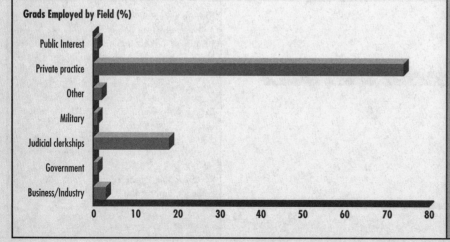

Grads Employed by Field (%)

Rate of Placement: 99%
Average Starting Salary: $77,000
Employers Who Frequently Hire Grads: Over 200 law firms regularly offer positions to Duke Law students.
Prominent Alumni: Pamela Gann, dean, Duke University School of Law; William Campbell, mayor, Atlanta, Georgia; Charlie Rose, talk show host, Bloomberg News.
State for Bar Exam: NC
Number Taking Bar Exam: 51
Pass Rate for First-Time Bar: 100%

DUQUESNE UNIVERSITY
School of Law

Admissions Contact: Dean of Admissions, Joseph Campion
900 Locust Street, Pittsburgh, PA 15282
Admissions Phone: 412-396-6296 • Admissions Fax: 412-396-6283
Admissions E-mail: campion@eduq.edu • Web Address: www.duq.edu

INSTITUTIONAL INFORMATION

Public/Private: Private
Affiliation: Roman Catholic
Environment: Urban
Academic Calendar: Semester
Schedule: Full time or part time
Student/Faculty Ratio: 23:1
Total Faculty: 24
% Female: 21
% Minority: 20

PROGRAMS

Academic Specialties: Strong teaching faculty
Combined Degrees Offered: JD/MBA (4 years), JD/MDiv (4 years), JD/Master of Environmental Science and Management (4 years)
Clinical Program Required? No
Clinical Programs: Development Law Clinic, Criminal Justice Clinic, Family and Poverty Law Clinic
Grading System: Numerical system on 4.0 scale; minimum 3.0 cumulative GPA required to graduate

STUDENT INFORMATION

Enrollment of Law School: 691
% Male/Female: 55/45
% Full Time: 55
% Full Time That Are International: 0
% Minority: 6
Average Age of Entering Class: 23

EXPENSES/FINANCIAL AID

Annual Tuition: $14,942
Room and Board (On/Off Campus): $6,984/$8,000
Average Grant: $4,500
Average Loan: $12,000
% of Aid That Is Merit-Based: 50
% Receiving Some Sort of Aid: 35
Average Total Aid Package: $11,000
Average Debt: $35,000

ADMISSIONS INFORMATION

Application Fee: $50
Regular Application Deadline: 4/1
Regular Notification: Rolling
Average GPA: 3.3
Average LSAT: 154
Transfer Students Accepted? Yes
Other Schools to Which Students Applied: University of Pittsburgh, Pennsylvania State University, Temple University, University of Dayton, University of Akron, Villanova University, University of Baltimore, Case Western Reserve University

INTERNATIONAL STUDENTS

TOEFL Required of International Students? Yes

EMPLOYMENT INFORMATION

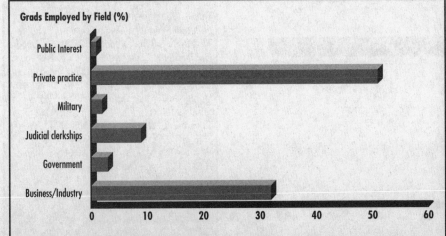

Grads Employed by Field (%)

Rate of Placement: 92%
Average Starting Salary: $46,100
Employers Who Frequently Hire Grads: Reed, Smith, Shaw & McClay, Kirkpatrick & Lockhart, Buchanon Ingersoll
Prominent Alumni: Alan Braverman, general counsel, ABC; William Kostopolous, criminal trial attorney; Carol Los Mansmann, judge, 3rd Circuit Court of Appeals
Number Taking Bar Exam: 147
Pass Rate for First-Time Bar: 73%

EMORY UNIVERSITY
School of Law

Admissions Contact: Assistant Dean for Admissions, Lynell Cadray
Gambrell Hall, 1301 Clifton Road, Atlanta, GA 30322-2770
Admissions Phone: 404-727-6802 • Admissions Fax: 404-727-2477
Admissions E-mail: lawinfo@emory.edu • Web Address: www.law.emory.edu

INSTITUTIONAL INFORMATION

Public/Private: Private
Affiliation: Methodist
Environment: Urban
Academic Calendar: Semester
Schedule: Full time only
Student/Faculty Ratio: 13:1
Total Faculty: 48
% Part Time: 4
% Female: 23
% Minority: 6

PROGRAMS

Academic Specialties: Criminal Law, Constitutional Law, Law and Religion, Commercial Law, Human Rights, International Law, Taxation
Advanced Degrees Offered: LLM (1 year)
Combined Degrees Offered: JD/MBA (4 years), JD/MTS (4 years), JD/MDiv (5 years), JD/MPH (4 years), LLM, JD/REES, JD/PhD, JD/MA (4 years)
Clinical Program Required? No
Grading System: A+ to F; a grade of F is failing. A cumulative average of 2.25 is required for good standing and for graduation. Students with a semester average of 3.45 or higher make the D.

STUDENT INFORMATION

Enrollment of Law School: 615
% Male/Female: 48/52
% Full Time: 100
% Full Time That Are International: 1
% Minority: 20
Average Age of Entering Class: 24

RESEARCH FACILITIES

Computers/Workstations Available: 45
School-Supported Research Centers: The Carter Center, Centers for Disease Control and Prevention

EXPENSES/FINANCIAL AID

Annual Tuition: $25,064
Room and Board: $10,980
Books and Supplies: $1,100
Average Grant: $16,345
Average Loan: $25,264
% of Aid That Is Merit-Based: 2
% Receiving Some Sort of Aid: 80
Average Total Aid Package: $28,000
Average Debt: $49,193
Fees Per Credit: $995

ADMISSIONS INFORMATION

Application Fee: $50
Regular Application Deadline: 3/1
Regular Notification: Rolling
Average GPA: 3.4
Range of GPA: 3.2–3.7
Average LSAT: 160
Range of LSAT: 158–162
Transfer Students Accepted? Yes
Other Schools to Which Students Applied: Boston University, George Washington University, Duke University, Vanderbilt University, Georgetown University, Tulane University, University of Georgia, University of Virginia
Other Admissions Factors Considered: Letters of recommendation, significant obstacles overcome, personal essays, community service, leadership ability, quality and dificulty of undergraduate work, work experience
Number of Applications Received: 2,773
Number of Applicants Accepted: 985
Number of Applicants Enrolled: 184

INTERNATIONAL STUDENTS

TOEFL Required of International Students? Yes
Minimum TOEFL: 600

EMPLOYMENT INFORMATION

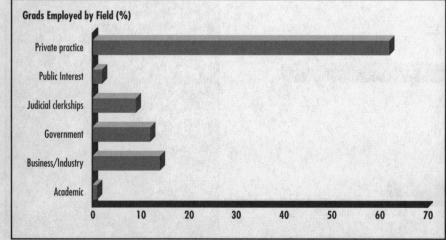

Grads Employed by Field (%)

Rate of Placement: 92%
Average Starting Salary: $58,993
Employers Who Frequently Hire Grads: Cadwalader, Wickersham and Taft; Dewey Ballantine; Milbank, Tweed, Hadley and McCloy; Skadden, Arps, Slate, Meaghert and Flom; Akin Gump; Arent Fox; Alston and Bird; King and Spalding; McDermott, Will and Emery
Prominent Alumni: Hon. Tillie Kidd Fowler '67L, U.S. Congress; Hon. W. Wyche Fowler '69L, ambassador to Saudi Arabia; Robert S. Harkey '65L, general counsel, Delta Air Lines, Inc.
State for Bar Exam: GA
Number Taking Bar Exam: 130
Pass Rate for First-Time Bar: 95%

EMPIRE COLLEGE
School of Law

Admissions Contact: Assistant to Dean, Pat Alley
3035 Cleveland Avenue, Santa Rosa, CA 95403
Admissions Phone: 707-546-4000 • Admissions Fax: 707-546-4058
Admissions E-mail: palley@empirecollege.com • Web Address: www.empcol.com

INSTITUTIONAL INFORMATION

Public/Private: Private
Academic Calendar: Semester
Schedule: Full time only
Student/Faculty Ratio: 40:1
Total Faculty: 47
% Part Time: 100
% Female: 21

PROGRAMS

Academic Specialties: All faculty are practicing attorneys or judges. Small classes. Wide variety of elective courses offered.
Clinical Program Required? No
Clinical Programs: Law Office Clerking, Public Defender, DA's Office
Grading System: 100–65

STUDENT INFORMATION

Enrollment of Law School: 141
% Male/Female: 100/0
% Full Time: 0
% Full Time That Are International: 0
% Minority: 2
Average Age of Entering Class: 38

EXPENSES/FINANCIAL AID

Annual Tuition: $4,580
Books and Supplies: $600
Fees Per Credit: $229

ADMISSIONS INFORMATION

Application Fee: $95
Regular Application Deadline: Rolling
Regular Notification: Rolling
LSDAS Accepted? No
Average GPA: 3.2
Range of GPA: 2.3–4.0
Transfer Students Accepted? Yes
Other Schools to Which Students Applied: University of California—Hastings, University of San Francisco, Golden Gate University, University of California—Berkeley, University of California—Davis, Loyola Marymount University, University of San Diego, Thomas Jefferson School of Law

EMPLOYMENT INFORMATION

Employers Who Frequently Hire Grads: District Attorney's Office, Public Defenders Office, private, business
Prominent Alumni: Jeanne Buckley, Sonoma County Juvenile Court commissioner; Raima Ballinger, Sonoma County Municipal Court judge; Francisca P. Tisher, Napa County Municipal Court judge; Ron Brown, Mendocino County Superior Court judge

FLORIDA COASTAL SCHOOL OF LAW

Admissions Contact: Director of Admissions, Steve Jones
7555 Beach Boulevard, Jacksonville, FL 32216
Admissions Phone: 904-680-7710 • Admissions Fax: 904-680-7776
Admissions E-mail: admissions@fcsl.edu • Web Address: www.fcsl.edu

INSTITUTIONAL INFORMATION

Public/Private: Private
Student/Faculty Ratio: 19:1
Total Faculty: 48
% Part Time: 66
% Female: 44
% Minority: 25

PROGRAMS

Advanced Degrees Offered: JD (3 years full time, 4 years part time)

STUDENT INFORMATION

Enrollment of Law School: 500
% Male/Female: 55/45
% Full Time: 70
% Full Time That Are International: 3
% Minority: 27
Average Age of Entering Class: 27

RESEARCH FACILITIES

Computers/Workstations Available: 50

EXPENSES/FINANCIAL AID

Annual Tuition: $18,420
Room and Board (Off Campus): $11,772
Books and Supplies: $800
Average Grant: $8,500
Average Debt: $12,133

ADMISSIONS INFORMATION

Application Fee: $50
Regular Application Deadline: Rolling
Regular Notification: Rolling
Average GPA: 3.0
Range of GPA: 2.8–3.3
Average LSAT: 151
Range of LSAT: 148–153
Transfer Students Accepted? Yes
Number of Applications Received: 1,500
Number of Applicants Accepted: 400
Number of Applicants Enrolled: 150

INTERNATIONAL STUDENTS

TOEFL Required of International Students? Yes

FLORIDA STATE UNIVERSITY
College of Law

Admissions Contact: Director of Admissions and Records, Sharon J. Booker
425 West Jefferson Street, Tallahassee, FL 32306-1034
Admissions Phone: 850-644-3787 • Admissions Fax: 850-644-7284
Admissions E-mail: admissions@law.fsu.edu • Web Address: www.law.fsu.edu

INSTITUTIONAL INFORMATION
Public/Private: Public
Environment: Urban
Academic Calendar: Semester
Schedule: Full time only
Student/Faculty Ratio: 19:1
Total Faculty: 49
% Part Time: 0
% Female: 33
% Minority: 38

PROGRAMS
Academic Specialties: International, Environmental, Administrative, Cyber, Intellectual Property
Advanced Degrees Offered: JD (minimum 88 credit hours to graduate)
Combined Degrees Offered: JD/MBA, JD/URP, JD/IA, JD/Economics, JD/MPA, JD/SW (most programs take 4 years to complete)
Clinical Program Required? No
Clinical Programs: Students can earn academic credit while learning to assume the role of attorney or judicial clerk at 1 of more than 60 placement sites. The program provides the opportunity for students to be trained in legal practice in numerous agencies and judicial settings in Tallahassee and throughout Florida.
Grading System: 60–100 numerical range with corresponding letter grades ranging from A+ to F
Legal Writing/Methods Course Requirements: 1 year of Legal Writing and Research required

STUDENT INFORMATION
Enrollment of Law School: 683
% Male/Female: 54/46
% Full Time: 100
% Full Time That Are International: 0
% Minority: 21
Average Age of Entering Class: 25

RESEARCH FACILITIES
School-Supported Research Centers: Law students also have access to the main University Library of Florida State University and its branches, as well as to all the libraries of the State University System of Florida.

EXPENSES/FINANCIAL AID
Annual Tuition (Residents/Nonresidents): $4,890/$16,140
Room and Board: $9,000
Books and Supplies: $1,000
Average Grant: $1,500
Average Loan: $18,500
% of Aid That Is Merit-Based: 10
% Receiving Some Sort of Aid: 98
Average Total Aid Package: $18,500
Average Debt: $60,000
Fees Per Credit (Residents/Nonresidents): $155/$513

ADMISSIONS INFORMATION
Application Fee: $20
Regular Application Deadline: 2/15
Regular Notification: Rolling
Average GPA: 3.3
Average LSAT: 155
Range of LSAT: 152–158
Transfer Students Accepted? Yes
Other Schools to Which Students Applied: University of Florida, University of Miami, Emory University, University of Georgia
Other Admissions Factors Considered: Exceptional personal talents, interesting or demanding work experience, service experience, leadership potential, academic rigor, graduate study, maturity
Number of Applications Received: 1,876
Number of Applicants Accepted: 725
Number of Applicants Enrolled: 233

INTERNATIONAL STUDENTS
TOEFL Required of International Students? Yes

EMPLOYMENT INFORMATION

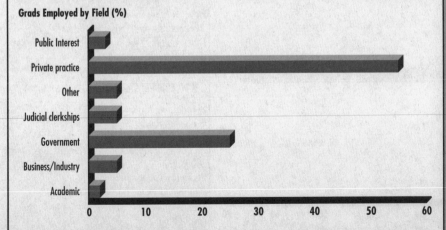

Grads Employed by Field (%)

Rate of Placement: 92%
Average Starting Salary: $40,462
Employers Who Frequently Hire Grads: Law firms, state agencies
Prominent Alumni: John Frost, president, the Florida Bar; Tony La Russa, Jr., St. Louis Cardinals professional baseball team; Mark Ellis, executive director, Central and East European Law Initiative
State for Bar Exam: FL
Number Taking Bar Exam: 156
Pass Rate for First-Time Bar: 82%

FORDHAM UNIVERSITY
School of Law

Admissions Contact: Associate Director of Admissions, John Chalmers
Admissions Office, 140 West 62nd Street, New York, NY 10023
Admissions Phone: 212-636-6810
Admissions E-mail: lawadmissions@mail.lawnet.fordham.edu • Web Address: www.fordham.edu/law

INSTITUTIONAL INFORMATION

Public/Private: Private
Affiliation: Roman Catholic
Environment: Urban
Academic Calendar: Semester
Schedule: Full time or part time
Student/Faculty Ratio: 17:1
Total Faculty: 214
% Part Time: 71
% Female: 28
% Minority: 8

PROGRAMS

Academic Specialties: Constitutional Law, Professional Responsibility and Ethics, Business and Financial Law, Evidence
Advanced Degrees Offered: JD (3 years full time, 4 years part time), LLM (1 year full time)
Combined Degrees Offered: JD/MBA with Fordham Graduate School of Business (4 years full time), JD/MSW with Fordham Graduate School of Social Work (4 years full time)
Clinical Program Required? No
Clinical Programs: Separate clinics for Employment Discrimination, Welfare Rights, Criminal Defense, Battered Women's Rights, Mediation, Civil Rights, etc.
Grading System: Letter grades; mandatory grading curve for first-year courses, grading guidelines for other courses
Legal Writing/Methods Course Requirements: Writing and Research (first year)

STUDENT INFORMATION

Enrollment of Law School: 1,437
% Male/Female: 56/44
% Full Time: 75
% Full Time That Are International: 2
% Minority: 24
Average Age of Entering Class: 24

RESEARCH FACILITIES

Computers/Workstations Available: 200
School-Supported Research Centers: The libraries at Fordham, Columbia, NYU, Penn, and Yale are affiliated so that the students may use any of the 5 libraries.

EXPENSES/FINANCIAL AID

Annual Tuition: $25,035
Room and Board: $17,350
Books and Supplies: $725
Average Grant: $4,865
Average Loan: $3,467
% of Aid That Is Merit-Based: 10
% Receiving Some Sort of Aid: 44
Average Total Aid Package: $7,691
Average Debt: $72,674

ADMISSIONS INFORMATION

Application Fee: $60
Regular Application Deadline: 3/1
Regular Notification: Rolling
LSDAS Accepted? Yes
Average GPA: 3.4
Range of GPA: 3.1–3.6
Average LSAT: 164
Range of LSAT: 161–165
Transfer Students Accepted? Yes
Other Schools to Which Students Applied: New York University, Columbia University, Brooklyn Law School, Boston University, Georgetown University, George Washington University, Yeshiva University, New York Law School
Other Admissions Factors Considered: Prior employment, student activities, service to the community, leadership ability, propensity for public service, communication skills, grade trend, course selection, grades in the major, choice of major, undergraduate institution
Number of Applications Received: 5,030
Number of Applicants Accepted: 1,384
Number of Applicants Enrolled: 454

INTERNATIONAL STUDENTS

TOEFL Required of International Students? Yes
Minimum TOEFL: 600

EMPLOYMENT INFORMATION

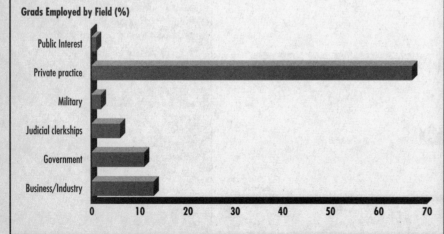

Grads Employed by Field (%)

Rate of Placement: 97%
Average Starting Salary: $79,429
Employers Who Frequently Hire Grads: Cahill, Gordon & Reindel; Department of Justice; Simpson, Thatcher & Bartlett; NY Legal Aid; Skadden, Arps, Slate, Meagher & Flom; AT&T; Merrill Lynch; U.S. Courts
Prominent Alumni: Geraldine Ferraro, former democratic vice presidential candidate; Jack Ford, anchor, NBC *Weekend Today* Show; Joseph M. McGlauglin, judge, U.S. Court of Appeals for the 2nd Circuit
State for Bar Exam: NY
Number Taking Bar Exam: 482
Pass Rate for First-Time Bar: 86%

FRANKLIN PIERCE LAW CENTER

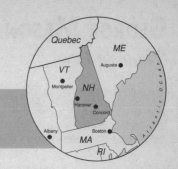

Admissions Contact: Acting Director of Admissions, Lory Attalla
2 White Street, Concord, NH 03301
Admissions Phone: 603-228-9217 • Admissions Fax: 603-228-1074
Admissions E-mail: admissions@fplc.edu • Web Address: www.fplc.edu

INSTITUTIONAL INFORMATION

Public/Private: Private
Environment: Suburban
Academic Calendar: Semester
Schedule: Full time only
Student/Faculty Ratio: 20:1
Total Faculty: 81
% Part Time: 58
% Female: 24
% Minority: 1

PROGRAMS

Academic Specialties: Intellectual Property, Patents, Trademarks, Licensing, Management, Information Law, Entertainment Law, Public Interest and Community Lawyering, Children's Law, Education Law, Health Law, Criminal Law, Nonprofit Organization Law
Advanced Degrees Offered: LLM (1 year), MIP (1 year), Master of Education Law (MEL) pending ABA acquiescence, Certificate of Advanced Graduate Study in Education Law (CAGS in Law) pending ABA acquiescence
Combined Degrees Offered: JD/MIP (3 years)
Clinical Program Required? No
Clinical Programs: Children's Advocacy Clinic, Civil Practice Clinic, Administrative Law and Advocacy, Advanced Civil Practice Clinic, Appellate Defender Clinic, Criminal Practice Clinic, Dispute Resolution in Action, Innovation Clinic, Juvenile

Corrections, Small Claims Mediation Program, Nonprofit Organizations Clinic
Grading System: Anonymous grading using A+ to F. Students may take electives pass/fail. In all classes with more than 15 students, the mean grade in the class will be no higher than B. Waivers of this policy may be sought through the Teaching Effectiveness Committee.

STUDENT INFORMATION

Enrollment of Law School: 384
% Male/Female: 62/38
% Full Time: 100
% Full Time That Are International: 4
% Minority: 14
Average Age of Entering Class: 29

RESEARCH FACILITIES

Computers/Workstations Available: 62

EXPENSES/FINANCIAL AID

Annual Tuition: $18,500
Books and Supplies: $600
Average Grant: $1,800
Average Loan: $21,000
% of Aid That Is Merit-Based: 57
% Receiving Some Sort of Aid: 85
Average Total Aid Package: $24,300
Average Debt: $72,300
Tuition Per Credit: $570

ADMISSIONS INFORMATION

Application Fee: $45
Regular Application Deadline: 5/1
Regular Notification: Rolling
LSDAS Accepted? Yes
Average GPA: 3.0
Range of GPA: 2.0–3.9
Average LSAT: 150
Range of LSAT: 135–166
Transfer Students Accepted? Yes
Other Schools to Which Students Applied: Suffolk University, New England School of Law, Northeastern University, Boston University
Number of Applications Received: 790
Number of Applicants Enrolled: 128

INTERNATIONAL STUDENTS

TOEFL Required of International Students? Yes
Minimum TOEFL: 600

EMPLOYMENT INFORMATION

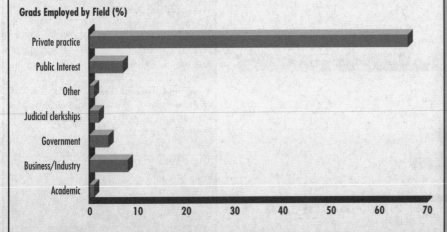

Rate of Placement: 87%
Average Starting Salary: $46,457
Prominent Alumni: Judge Ann Conboy (New Hampshire); Judge Tina Nadeau (New Hampshire); Judge Arthur Brennan (New Hampshire); Doug Wood of Hall, Dickler, Kent, Friedman and Wood (New York)
State for Bar Exam: NH
Number Taking Bar Exam: 126
Pass Rate for First-Time Bar: 87%

GEORGE MASON UNIVERSITY
School of Law

Admissions Contact: Director of Admissions, Anne M. Richard
3401 North Fairfax Drive, Arlington, VA 22201-4498
Admissions Phone: 703-993-8010 • Admissions Fax: 703-993-8260
Admissions E-mail: arichar5@gmu.edu • Web Address: www.law.gmu.edu

INSTITUTIONAL INFORMATION

Public/Private: Public
Environment: Urban
Academic Calendar: Semester
Schedule: Full time or part time
Student/Faculty Ratio: 16:1
Total Faculty: 160
% Part Time: 73
% Female: 14
% Minority: 6

PROGRAMS

Academic Specialties: Law and Economics is a focus of many faculty members. Students are required to take a 1-semester Legal and Economic Methods course. An Intellectual Property Law Program is offered, and a Center for Technology and the Law is being established.
Combined Degrees Offered: None
Advanced Degrees Offered: Juris Master—a master's degree concentrating in policy analysis (2 years, part-time evening program)
Clinical Program Required? No
Clinical Programs: Supervised externships, clinical program
Grading System: Numerical system on a 4.0 scale
Legal Writing/Methods Course Requirements: 2-year, 4-semester, 7-credit writing and research program

STUDENT INFORMATION

Enrollment of Law School: 736
% Male/Female: 52/48
% Full Time: 50
% Full Time That Are International: 0
% Minority: 9
Average Age of Entering Class: 27

RESEARCH FACILITIES

Computers/Workstations Available: 75
School-Supported Research Centers: Prince William Campus Library integrates print, video, and electronic resources to meet the research needs of its patrons. It houses 4 study rooms, 2 media viewing rooms, a focused media and periodicals collection, reference and circulating books, library instruction space, and 20 Pentium processor PCs with access to the Library Catalog, the Library's networked CD-ROMS, and the Internet. At the Fairfax campus, there are 5 reservable labs with 175 Pentium PCs. There is also one Maclab with 20 Macintosh Power PCs. In addition, there are 84 nonreservable PCs located at various labs on the campus.

EXPENSES/FINANCIAL AID

Annual Tuition (Residents/Nonresidents):
$7,784/$18,228
Room and Board (Off Campus): $14,965
Books and Supplies: $750
Average Grant: $7,893
Average Loan: $15,000
% of Aid That Is Merit-Based: 6
Average Debt: $39,914

ADMISSIONS INFORMATION

Application Fee: $35
Regular Application Deadline: 3/1
Regular Notification: 4/15
LSDAS Accepted? Yes
Average GPA: 3.2
Range of GPA: 2.8–3.5
Average LSAT: 157
Range of LSAT: 154–160
Transfer Students Accepted? Yes
Other Schools to Which Students Applied: University of Virginia, George Washington University, American University, College of William and Mary, Catholic University of America, Georgetown University, University of Richmond, Washington and Lee University
Other Admissions Factors Considered: Writing ability as illustrated in LSAT writing sample and personal statement, difficulty of undergraduate curriculum, quality of undergraduate institution, graduate degrees earned, demonstrated commitment to public and community service
Number of Applications Received: 2,004

EMPLOYMENT INFORMATION

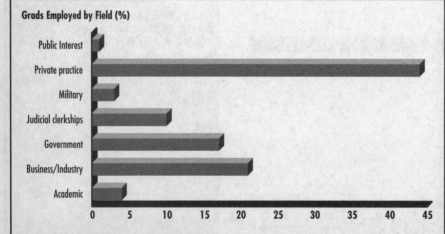

Grads Employed by Field (%)

Field	
Public Interest	
Private practice	
Military	
Judicial clerkships	
Government	
Business/Industry	
Academic	

Rate of Placement: 87%
Average Starting Salary: $60,729
Employers Who Frequently Hire Grads: Hunton and Williams; McGuire, Woods, Battle and Boothe; Finnegan, Henderson, Farabow, Garret and Dunner, LLP
Prominent Alumni: Richard Young, U.S. District Court judge; Leslie Alden, Fairfax County Circuit Court judge
State for Bar Exam: VA
Number Taking Bar Exam: 113
Pass Rate for First-Time Bar: 76%

GEORGE WASHINGTON UNIVERSITY
Law School

Admissions Contact: Assistant Dean for Admissions and Financial Aid, Robert V. Stanek
1819 H Street NW, Washington, DC 20052
Admissions Phone: 202-739-0648 • Admissions Fax: 202-739-0624
Admissions E-mail: jd@admit.nlc.gwu.edu • Web Address: www.law.gwu.edu

INSTITUTIONAL INFORMATION

Public/Private: Private
Environment: Urban
Academic Calendar: Semester
Schedule: Full time or part time
Student/Faculty Ratio: 18:1
Total Faculty: 243
% Part Time: 73
% Female: 27
% Minority: 9

PROGRAMS

Academic Specialties: The JD curriculum is very diverse with over 200 elective courses. Specialized areas of the curriculum include Intellectual Property Law, Environmental Law, International and Comparative Law, and Government Procurement Law.
Advanced Degrees Offered: JD (3 years full time, 4 years part time), LLM (1–2 years), SJD (3 years)
Combined Degrees Offered: JD/MBA, JD/MPA, JD/MA International Affairs, JD/MA History, JD/MA Women's Studies, JD/MPH (each can be completed in 4 years with full-time and summer attendance)
Clinical Program Required? No
Grading System: A+ to F (4.33–0)
Legal Writing/Methods Course Requirements: In the first year, students take Legal Research and Writing in the fall and Introduction to Advocacy in the spring. Both courses are taught in small sections.

STUDENT INFORMATION

Enrollment of Law School: 1,454
% Male/Female: 54/46
% Full Time: 83
% Full Time That Are International: 1
% Minority: 30
Average Age of Entering Class: 24

RESEARCH FACILITIES

Computers/Workstations Available: 90
Campuswide Network? Yes
School-Supported Research Centers: In Washington, D.C., research resources include the collections of the Library of Congress in the various departments of the federal government, and in the libraries of the headquarters of national and international organizations.

EXPENSES/FINANCIAL AID

Annual Tuition: $26,860
Room and Board (Off Campus): $7,700
Books and Supplies: $740
Average Grant: $10,000
Average Loan: $23,000
% of Aid That Is Merit-Based: 5
% Receiving Some Sort of Aid: 72
Average Total Aid Package: $30,000
Average Debt: $65,000
Fees Per Credit: $946

ADMISSIONS INFORMATION

Application Fee: $65
Regular Application Deadline: 3/1
Regular Notification: Rolling
LSDAS Accepted? Yes
Average GPA: 3.4
Range of GPA: 3.3–3.6
Average LSAT: 162
Range of LSAT: 160–163
Transfer Students Accepted? Yes
Other Schools to Which Students Applied: Georgetown University, American University, Boston University, Boston College, New York University, Columbia University, University of Pennsylvania, Fordham University
Number of Applications Received: 7,341
Number of Applicants Accepted: 1,756
Number of Applicants Enrolled: 469

EMPLOYMENT INFORMATION

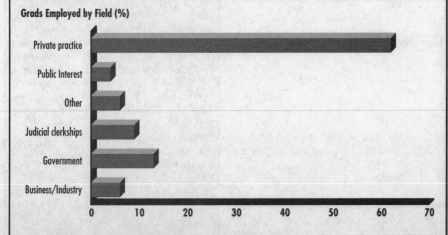

Average Starting Salary: $75,327
Employers Who Frequently Hire Grads: Department of Justice; Howrey and Simon; Finnegan, Henderson et. al.; Akin, Gump, et. al.; Scherman and Sterling; Arnold and Porter; Wiley, Rein and Fielding; various government agencies
Prominent Alumni: Daniel K. Inouye, U.S. senator from Hawaii; William P. Barr, former U.S. attorney general; Judge Joyce Hens Green, U.S. District Court for the District of Columbia
State for Bar Exam: NY
Number Taking Bar Exam: 123
Pass Rate for First-Time Bar: 90%

GEORGETOWN UNIVERSITY
Law Center

Admissions Contact: Assistant Dean for Admissions, Andy Cornblatt
600 New Jersey Avenue NW, Washington, DC 20001
Admissions Phone: 202-662-9010 • Admissions Fax: 202-662-9439
Admissions E-mail: admis@law.georgetown.edu • Web Address: www.law.georgetown.edu/

INSTITUTIONAL INFORMATION

Public/Private: Private
Affiliation: Jesuit
Environment: Urban
Academic Calendar: Semester
Schedule: Full time or part time
Student/Faculty Ratio: 16:1
Total Faculty: 189
% Female: 36
% Minority: 12

PROGRAMS

Academic Specialties: The faculty is particularly strong in the following areas: Administrative Law, Constitutional Law, Corporate and Securities Law, Criminal Law, Environmental Law, Health Law and Policy, International and Comparative Law, Legal Ethics, Legal History, Legal Philosophy, Taxation.
Advanced Degrees Offered: JD (3 years full time, 4 years part time); SJD (3 years); LLM Taxation, LLM Securities Regulation, LLM International and Comparative Law, LLM Individualized (all up to 3 years); LLM Common Law Students (1 year); Certificate in Employee Benefits (10 credits)
Combined Degrees Offered: JD/MBA (4 years), JD/MPH (4 years), JD/MSFS (4 years), JD/Master's in Government (4+ years), JD/Master's in Philosophy (4+ years)
Clinical Program Required? No
Clinical Programs: Appellate Litigation Clinic (1 year), Center for Applied Legal Studies (6 semester hours), Criminal Justice Clinic (12 semester hours),
Domestic Violence Clinic (6 semester hours), Family Opportunities Clinic (6 semester hours), Federal Legislation Clinic
Grading System: 4.0 system: A, A–, B+, B, B–, C+, C, C–, D, F
Legal Writing/Methods Course Requirements: Legal Research and Writing—year-long program introduces students to legal discourse through problem analysis, legal research, writing, oral skills, and legal citation.

STUDENT INFORMATION

Enrollment of Law School: 2,030
% Male/Female: 46/54
% Full Time: 76
% Full Time That Are International: 2
% Minority: 31
Average Age of Entering Class: 24

RESEARCH FACILITIES

School-Supported Research Centers: Library of Congress, National Library of Medicine

EXPENSES/FINANCIAL AID

Annual Tuition: $26,860
Room and Board: $14,466
Average Grant: $8,600
% of Aid That Is Merit-Based: 0
% Receiving Some Sort of Aid: 85
Average Debt: $79,000

ADMISSIONS INFORMATION

Application Fee: $65
Regular Application Deadline: 2/1
Regular Notification: Rolling
LSDAS Accepted? No
Average GPA: 3.5
Range of GPA: 3.3–3.8
Average LSAT: 166
Range of LSAT: 163–168
Transfer Students Accepted? Yes
Other Schools to Which Students Applied: Harvard University, George Washington University, Columbia University, University of Virginia, New York University, Yale University, University of Pennsylvania, Duke University
Number of Applications Received: 7,875
Number of Applicants Enrolled: 587

EMPLOYMENT INFORMATION

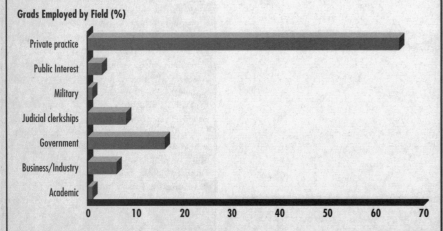

Grads Employed by Field (%)

Rate of Placement: 96%
Average Starting Salary: $73,567
Prominent Alumni: Bob Bennett of Skadden, Arps, Slate, Meagher & Flom, defense attorney for William Jefferson Clinton; Joan Claybrook, president of Public Citizen; George Mitchell of Verner, Liipfert, Berhard, McPherson & Hand, chairman, Peace Commission, former majority leader
State for Bar Exam: MD/NY
Number Taking Bar Exam: 129/158
Pass Rate for First-Time Bar: 82%/91%

GEORGIA STATE UNIVERSITY
College of Law

Admissions Contact: Director of Admissions, Cheryl Jackson
PO Box 4049, Atlanta, GA 30302-4049
Admissions Phone: 404-651-2048 • Admissions Fax: 404-651-1244
Admissions E-mail: lawhld@gsusgi2.gsu.edu • Web Address: http://law.gsu.edu

INSTITUTIONAL INFORMATION
Public/Private: Public
Environment: Urban
Academic Calendar: Semester
Schedule: Full time or part time
Student/Faculty Ratio: 16:1
Total Faculty: 61
% Part Time: 34
% Female: 39
% Minority: 15

PROGRAMS
Academic Specialties: Tax, Commercial Law, Constitutional Law, Alternative Dispute Resolution, Law and Technolog; joint degree programs in Law and Business, Law and Policy, and Law and Philosophy
Combined Degrees Offered: JD/MBA (4 years), JD/MPA (4 years), JD/MA in Philosophy (4 years)
Clinical Program Required? Yes
Clinical Programs: Tax Clinic, Externship Program
Grading System: A (90–100), B (80–89), C (70–79), D (60–69), F (55–59)

STUDENT INFORMATION
Enrollment of Law School: 628
% Male/Female: 68/32
% Full Time: 63
% Full Time That Are International: 2
% Minority: 15
Average Age of Entering Class: 28

EXPENSES/FINANCIAL AID
Annual Tuition (Residents/Nonresidents): $3,132/$12,528
Room and Board: $8,190
Books and Supplies: $590
Financial Aid Application Deadline: 4/1
Average Grant: $3,963
Average Loan: $13,405
% of Aid That Is Merit-Based: 7
% Receiving Some Sort of Aid: 54
Average Total Aid Package: $12,983
Average Debt: $32,082

ADMISSIONS INFORMATION
Application Fee: $30
Regular Application Deadline: 3/5
Regular Notification: Rolling
LSDAS Accepted? No
Average GPA: 3.2
Range of GPA: 2.3–4.0
Average LSAT: 156
Range of LSAT: 146–173
Transfer Students Accepted? Yes
Other Schools to Which Students Applied: University of Georgia, Emory University, Mercer University, University of South Carolina, Florida State University, University of Florida, University of North Carolina
Other Admissions Factors Considered: LSDAS report, letters of recommendation, personal statement, school and community activities, employment experience, advanced study or degrees
Number of Applications Received: 1,710
Number of Applicants Accepted: 481
Number of Applicants Enrolled: 202

INTERNATIONAL STUDENTS
Minimum TOEFL: 680

EMPLOYMENT INFORMATION

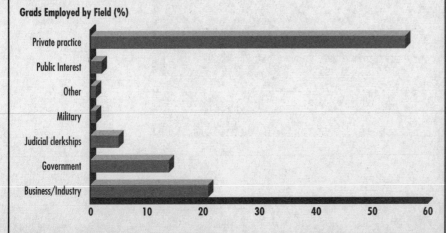

Grads Employed by Field (%)

Rate of Placement: 94%
Average Starting Salary: $49,835
Employers Who Frequently Hire Grads: Alston & Bird; Arnall, Golden & Gregory; Drew Eckl; Kilpatrick & Spalding; Long, Aldridge & Norman; Powell, Goldstein, Frazer & Murphy; Troutman & Sanders; Fisher and Phillips; Long Weinberg; Wilson, Strickland & Benson
Prominent Alumni: Patrica Tate, partner, Long, Aldridge and Norman; Peggy Walker, judge, Douglas County Juvenile Court; Scott Petty, partner, Jones and Askew
State for Bar Exam: GA
Number Taking Bar Exam: 130
Pass Rate for First-Time Bar: 94%

GOLDEN GATE UNIVERSITY

GGU AT A GLANCE

Founded in 1901, Golden Gate University School of Law is an urban law school that draws on the dynamic environment of the legal/business district of San Francisco. Situated in the middle of the legal and financial district, as well as the bustling "Multimedia Gulch," the law school is also a short walk from restaurants, shopping, and downtown plazas.

Students can attend a full-time day program or a part-time evening program. Full-time students may begin their studies in August or January. The low student/faculty ratio of 17:1 strengthens the bond of communication between students and teachers. The School of Law's 700 students include working professionals and recent college graduates from more than 100 undergraduate and graduate institutions. They come from across the United States and from a number of other nations, and represent a wide spectrum of ethnic, economic, and cultural backgrounds.

Golden Gate University School of Law is accredited by the American Bar Association (ABA) and the Committee of Bar Examiners of the State of California and is a member of the Association of American Law Schools (AALS). Graduates qualify to take the bar exam in all 50 states and in the District of Columbia.

A PRACTICAL LEGAL EDUCATION

Golden Gate University School of Law has developed a reputation for providing a strong balance of theory and practical education. The School of Law has one of the most extensive clinical programs in the country, offering students excellent opportunities to experience hands-on, practical legal training. Students can participate in three on-site clinics: the Women's Employment Rights Clinic, the Environmental Law and Justice Clinic, and the Constitutional Law Clinic.

Seven field-placement clinics give students experience in a variety of legal areas, including Criminal Law, Family Law, Landlord-Tenant Issues, Public Interest Law, and Real Estate Law.

The law school also has a comprehensive litigation program, with small classes that allow all students full participation in litigation skills training. Courses such as Trial Advocacy, Mock Trial, and Criminal Litigation give students practical, hands-on experience in preparing for all aspects of trials.

SPECIAL HONORS PROGRAM

In addition to the standard JD program, Golden Gate University offers the unique Integrated Professional Apprenticeship Curriculum (IPAC). This innovative honors program allows students to get the most out of their classroom legal education by combining it with substantive practical experience.

After a first year of foundational courses, IPAC students follow a different schedule in their second and third years. During their second and third summers, they study in intensive simulated law firm settings. In the fall semesters of their second and third year, they participate in two full-time, semester-long professional apprenticeships in law offices and other legal settings. These apprenticeships link work in the legal community with the theory, skills, and values learned in the classroom.

CERTIFICATE AND COMBINED PROGRAMS

JD students can earn specialization certificates in Business Law, Criminal Law, Environmental Law, Intellectual Property, International Law, Labor and Employment Law, Litigation, Public Interest Law, or Real Estate Law. Students may also earn a combined JD/MBA with a focus in a variety of business areas. Other combined degrees include a JD/MA in International Relations and a JD/PhD in Clinical Psychology.

School of Law

GRADUATE PROGRAMS

In recent years, the law school has become a center for graduate legal studies, offering four Master of Laws (LLM) degree programs: International Legal Studies, Environmental Law, Taxation, and United States Legal Studies. In addition, students with an LLM can earn a Doctor of Laws (SJD) in International Legal Studies.

SCHOLARSHIPS AND LOANS

To attract a highly qualified student body, the School of Law awards entering students a number of full-tuition and partial-tuition scholarships based solely on academic merit. In addition, scholarships in the amount of $5,000 are awarded to entering members of minority groups who have demonstrated a commitment to their community. All eligible first-year students are considered for several endowed scholarships. Entering students who are accepted to the Public Interest Scholars Program may be eligible for scholarship assistance. The law school also has a variety of scholarships for continuing students.

CAREER SERVICES, AND PLACEMENT

The Golden Gate University Law Career Services Office provides comprehensive services and support from the time students enter law school through graduation and beyond. All first-year students receive a one-on-one orientation session, a special résumé and cover letter workshop, and a Job Search Guide. Continuing students have access to print and online job listings, career counseling, job search skills workshops, résumé and cover letter review, special programs and job fairs, mock interviews with alumni, recruitment programs, and many other services. Programs and services for graduates are also available. Recent graduates were employed as shown below.

Legal Field	Percentage of Graduates	Average Salary
Academic	1.8%	$63,750
Business	26.3%	$66,667
Government	11.4%	$42,119
Judicial Clerkship	6.1%	$46,285
Private Practice	49.1%	$58,657
Public Interest	5.3%	$32,100

SPECIAL QUALITIES OF GOLDEN GATE UNIVERSITY SCHOOL OF LAW

- Multiple programs, allowing students to attend day or evening classes and start law school in January or August
- Special honors program, the Integrated Professional Apprenticeship Curriculum (IPAC), in which students work in two full-time, semester-long apprenticeships
- Extensive clinical program offering students excellent opportunities to receive hands-on, practical legal training
- Specialization certificates available in nine areas
- Comprehensive litigation program with small classes
- Combined degree programs, including JD/MBA, JD/MA in International Relations, and JD/PhD in Clinical Psychology
- Graduate programs in Taxation, International Legal Studies, Environmental Law, and U.S. Legal Studies
- An excellent downtown location in San Francisco near law firms, government agencies, and courts

Admissions Contact: Cheryl Barnes, Assistant Dean for Admissions and Financial Aid
Address: 536 Mission Street, San Francisco CA 94105-2968
Admissions Phone: 415-442-6630 or 800-GGU-4YOU (press 1, then 2) • Admissions Fax: 415-442-6631
Admissions E-mail: lawadmit@ggu.edu
Web Address: www.ggu.edu/law

GOLDEN GATE UNIVERSITY
School of Law

Admissions Contact: Assistant Dean, Cheryl Barnes
536 Mission Street, San Francisco, CA 94105
Admissions Phone: 415-442-6630 • Admissions Fax: 415-442-6631
Admissions E-mail: lawadmit@ggu.edu • Web Address: www.ggu.edu/law/

INSTITUTIONAL INFORMATION

Public/Private: Private
Environment: Urban
Academic Calendar: Trimester
Schedule: Full time or part time
Student/Faculty Ratio: 18:1
Total Faculty: 150
% Part Time: 78
% Female: 37
% Minority: 10

PROGRAMS

Academic Specialties: Real Estate Law, Environmental Law, Litigation, International Law, Immigration Law, Civil Rights Law (Affirmative Action; Homeless Rights; and Minority, Women, and Gay and Lesbian Issues)
Advanced Degrees Offered: JD (3 years full time, 4 years part time), LLM (1 year)
Combined Degrees Offered: JD/MBA, JD/MPA, JD/MA (4 years), JD/PhD (7 years)
Clinical Program Required? No
Clinical Programs: Students are encouraged to participate. Over half of the students at Golden Gate participate in either the in-house clinics or field placement clinics.
Grading System: Letter and numerical system on a 4.0 scale
Legal Writing/Methods Course Requirements: 2 semesters of Writing and Research in first year; App. Ad. Req. in second year

STUDENT INFORMATION

Enrollment of Law School: 561
% Male/Female: 39/61
% Full Time: 76
% Full Time That Are International: 37
% Minority: 26
Average Age of Entering Class: 28

RESEARCH FACILITIES

Computers/Workstations Available: 75

EXPENSES/FINANCIAL AID

Annual Tuition: $20,880
Room and Board (Off Campus): $11,315
Books and Supplies: $870
Financial Aid Application Deadline: 3/1
Average Grant: $6,000
Average Loan: $21,600
% of Aid That Is Merit-Based: 24
% Receiving Some Sort of Aid: 82
Average Total Aid Package: $30,000
Average Debt: $60,000
Fees Per Credit: $720

ADMISSIONS INFORMATION

Application Fee: $40
Regular Application Deadline: 4/15
Regular Notification: Rolling
LSDAS Accepted? Yes
Average GPA: 3.1
Range of GPA: 2.7–3.4
Average LSAT: 151
Range of LSAT: 145–155
Transfer Students Accepted? Yes
Other Schools to Which Students Applied: University of San Francisco, Santa Clara University, University of California, University of California—Berkeley, University of the Pacific, University of California—Davis, California Western, UCLA School of Law, University of California—Hastings
Other Admissions Factors Considered: Strength of undergraduate program, term-time employment, work experience that engages/develops writing and research skills
Number of Applications Received: 1,585
Number of Applicants Accepted: 923
Number of Applicants Enrolled: 179

INTERNATIONAL STUDENTS

TOEFL Required of International Students? Yes
Minimum TOEFL: 575

EMPLOYMENT INFORMATION

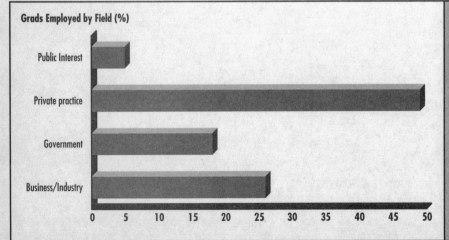

Grads Employed by Field (%)

Rate of Placement: 78%
Average Starting Salary: $50,938
Employers Who Frequently Hire Grads: Small, medium, and large firms; government agencies; public interest organizations; and businesses and corporations
Prominent Alumni: Richard M. Rosenberg, retired chairman and CEO of Bank of America; Philip M. Pro, United States district judge; Marjorie Randolph, VP, Human Resources, Walt Disney Feature Animation
State for Bar Exam: CA
Number Taking Bar Exam: 180
Pass Rate for First-Time Bar: 69%

GONZAGA UNIVERSITY
School of Law

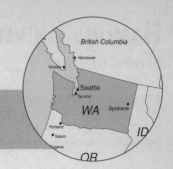

Admissions Contact: Assistant Dean for Admissions, Tamara Martinez
PO Box 3528, Spokane, WA 99220
Admissions Phone: 509-323-5532 • Admissions Fax: 509-323-5710
Admissions E-mail: admissions@lawschool.gonzaga.edu • Web Address: law.gonzaga.edu

INSTITUTIONAL INFORMATION

Public/Private: Private
Affiliation: Jesuit
Environment: Urban
Academic Calendar: Semester
Schedule: Full time only
Student/Faculty Ratio: 16:1
Total Faculty: 45
% Part Time: 38
% Female: 31
% Minority: 2

PROGRAMS

Academic Specialties: Integrated curriculum—skills training and professional ethics and values emphasized throughout the curriculum
Advanced Degrees Offered: JD
Combined Degrees Offered: JD/MBA, JD/MAcc (both 3.5–4 years)
Clinical Program Required? No
Clinical Programs: Award-winning clinic has 3 options: university legal assistance (15 credits over 2 semesters), mini-clinics (3–5 credits), and externship placements
Grading System: Letter and numerical system on a 4.0 scale; students must maintain a cumulative 2.20 GPA
Legal Writing/Methods Course Requirements: 2 credits per semester first year, 1 credit per semester second year

STUDENT INFORMATION

Enrollment of Law School: 458
% Male/Female: 53/47
% Full Time: 96
% Full Time That Are International: 1
% Minority: 16
Average Age of Entering Class: 26

RESEARCH FACILITIES

Computers/Workstations Available: 70

EXPENSES/FINANCIAL AID

Annual Tuition: $19,740
Room and Board (Off Campus): $7,000
Books and Supplies: $900
Financial Aid Application Deadline: 2/1
Average Grant: $7,000
Average Loan: $25,000
% of Aid That Is Merit-Based: 5
Average Total Aid Package: $32,550
Average Debt: $69,000
Tuition Per Credit: $658
Fees Per Credit: $654

ADMISSIONS INFORMATION

Application Fee: $40
Regular Application Deadline: Rolling
Regular Notification: Rolling
LSDAS Accepted? No
Average GPA: 3.1
Range of GPA: 2.9–3.4
Average LSAT: 149
Range of LSAT: 146–152
Transfer Students Accepted? Yes
Other Admissions Factors Considered: Personal statements, work experience, letters of recommendation, comunity service experience
Number of Applications Received: 826
Number of Applicants Accepted: 576
Number of Applicants Enrolled: 152

INTERNATIONAL STUDENTS

TOEFL Required of International Students? Yes

EMPLOYMENT INFORMATION

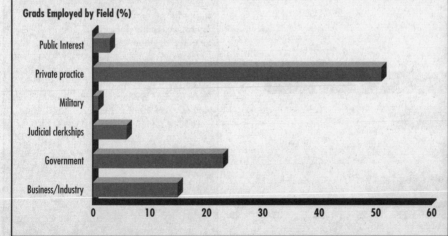

Grads Employed by Field (%)

Rate of Placement: 85%
Average Starting Salary: $38,293
Employers Who Frequently Hire Grads: Various law firms in Spokane and throughout Washington; various local and state government entities
Prominent Alumni: George Nethercutt, US House of Representatives; Christine Gregoire, Washington state attorney general; Washington State Supreme Court Justice Richard Guy
State for Bar Exam: MT/WA
Number Taking Bar Exam: 90/90
Pass Rate for First-Time Bar: 89%/83%

HAMLINE UNIVERSITY
School of Law

Admissions Contact: Office Manager, Diane Ostman
1536 Hewitt Avenue, St. Paul, MN 55104
Admissions Phone: 651-523-2461 • Admissions Fax: 651-523-2435
Admissions E-mail: lawadm@gw.hamline.edu • Web Address: www.hamline.edu/law

INSTITUTIONAL INFORMATION

Public/Private: Private
Affiliation: Methodist
Environment: Metropolis
Academic Calendar: 4-1-4
Schedule: Full time or part time day
Student/Faculty Ratio: 18:1
% Female: 35
% Minority: 8

PROGRAMS

Academic Specialties: Law, Religion, and Ethics; Commercial Law; Children and the Law; Corporate Law; Government and Regulatory Affairs; Labor and Employment Law; Criminal Law; Law and Slavery; Alternative Dispute Resolution
Advanced Degrees Offered: JD (3 years)
Combined Degrees Offered: JD/MAPA (4 years), JD/MBA (4 years), JD/AMBA (4 years), JD/MANM, JD/MAM
Clinical Program Required? No
Clinical Programs: General Practice Clinic, Family Law Mediation, Child Advocacy and Legal Assistance to Minnesota Prisoners (LAMP), Alternative Dispute Resolution Clinic, Education Law Clinic
Grading System: The School of Law uses a 4.0 grading system. All grades are issued on a letter basis: A, B+, B, C+, C, D+, D, F. A few courses are offered on a pass/no pass basis.
Legal Writing/Methods Course Requirements: 1 year, 4 credits

STUDENT INFORMATION

Enrollment of Law School: 488
% Male/Female: 50/50
% Full Time: 95
% Full Time That Are International: 1
% Minority: 11
Average Age of Entering Class: 26

EXPENSES/FINANCIAL AID

Annual Tuition: $17,448
Room and Board (On/Off Campus): $6,000/$9,000
Books and Supplies: $400
Average Grant: $5,500
Average Loan: $22,000
% of Aid That Is Merit-Based: 8
% Receiving Some Sort of Aid: 90
Average Total Aid Package: $26,000
Average Debt: $65,000
Tuition Per Credit: $35
Fees Per Credit: $785

ADMISSIONS INFORMATION

Application Fee: $50
Regular Application Deadline: Rolling
Regular Notification: Rolling
Average GPA: 3.2
Range of GPA: 2.8–3.4
Average LSAT: 153
Range of LSAT: 146–156
Transfer Students Accepted? Yes
Other Schools to Which Students Applied: William Mitchell College of Law, University of Minnesota, University of Wisconsin, Marquette University, Drake University, University of Iowa, University of North Dakota, University of Denver
Other Admissions Factors Considered: Motivation, personal experiences, employment history, graduate education, maturity, letters of recommendation, the ability to articulate one's interest in and suitability for the study of law

INTERNATIONAL STUDENTS

TOEFL Required of International Students? Yes
Minimum TOEFL: 600

EMPLOYMENT INFORMATION

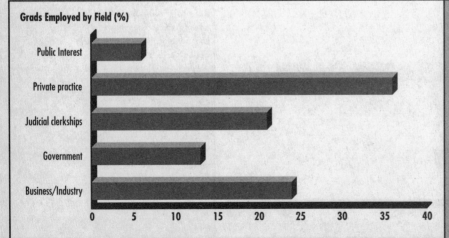

Grads Employed by Field (%)

Rate of Placement: 96%
Average Starting Salary: $36,741
Prominent Alumni: Robert Weisel, judge, U.S. Department of Justice and Immigration; John Peace, General Counsel, Shenadoah Life Ins.; Joanne Smith, judge, 2nd Judicial District
State for Bar Exam: MN/WI
Number Taking Bar Exam: 127/7
Pass Rate for First-Time Bar: 83%/100%

HARVARD UNIVERSITY
Law School

Admissions Contact: Assistant Dean for Admissions and Financial Aid, Joyce Curll
1563 Massachusetts Avenue, Cambridge, MA 02138
Admissions Phone: 617-495-3109 • Admissions Fax: 617-496-7290
Admissions E-mail: jdadmiss@law.harvard.edu • Web Address: www.law.harvard.edu

INSTITUTIONAL INFORMATION

Public/Private: Private
Environment: Urban
Academic Calendar: Semester
Schedule: Full time only
Student/Faculty Ratio: 19:1
Total Faculty: 142
% Part Time: 44
% Female: 20
% Minority: 11

PROGRAMS

Academic Specialties: 251 courses offered; International Law, Taxation, Human Rights, Constitutional Law, Negotiation/Alternative Dispute Resolution, Comparative Law, Family Law
Advanced Degrees Offered: LLM (18/20 credit hours with optional paper), SJD (8 hours of course work, exam, and dissertation)
Combined Degrees Offered: JD/MBA (4 years), JD/MPP-concurrent, JD/MALD-concurrent
Clinical Program Required? No
Clinical Programs: One of the largest clinical programs in U.S., 3 clinics, 5 student practice organizations
Grading System: A+ to F
Legal Writing/Methods Course Requirements: Fall semester course

STUDENT INFORMATION

Enrollment of Law School: 1,658
% Male/Female: 57/43
% Full Time: 100
% Full Time That Are International: 3
% Minority: 27
Average Age of Entering Class: 24

RESEARCH FACILITIES

Computers/Workstations Available: 167

EXPENSES/FINANCIAL AID

Annual Tuition: $25,000
Room and Board: $12,618
Books and Supplies: $900
Average Grant: $12,000
Average Loan: $24,300
% of Aid That Is Merit-Based: 0
% Receiving Some Sort of Aid: 80
Average Total Aid Package: $28,000
Average Debt: $70,000

ADMISSIONS INFORMATION

Application Fee: $70
Regular Application Deadline: 2/1
Regular Notification: Rolling
LSDAS Accepted? Yes
Average GPA: 3.8
Range of GPA: 3.7–3.9
Average LSAT: 170
Range of LSAT: 167–173
Transfer Students Accepted? Yes
Other Schools to Which Students Applied: Yale University, Stanford University
Other Admissions Factors Considered: Letter of reccomendation, extracurricular activities, work experience, leadership, commitment to helping others, personal statement, ability to overcome obstacles. We try to evaluate each applicant in the context of their achievements
Number of Applications Received: 5,818
Number of Applicants Accepted: 845
Number of Applicants Enrolled: 556

EMPLOYMENT INFORMATION

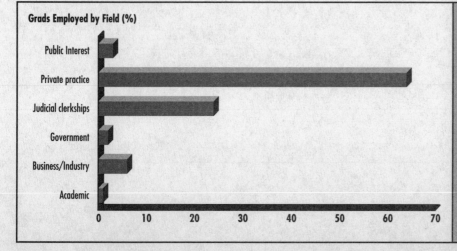

Grads Employed by Field (%)

Rate of Placement: 97%
Average Starting Salary: $81,000
Employers Who Frequently Hire Grads: Major national law firms, federal and state government, investment banks, consulting firms, law schools
Prominent Alumni: Supreme Court Justices Breyer, Ginsburg, Souter, Scalia, Kennedy; Attorney General Janet Reno; Mary Robinson, former president of The Republic of Ireland
State for Bar Exam: MA/NY
Number Taking Bar Exam: 68/199
Pass Rate for First-Time Bar: 100%/92%

HOFSTRA UNIVERSITY

INTRODUCTION

The Hofstra University School of Law is accredited by the ABA and is a member of the AAIS. As a national law school, Hofstra provides a legal education designed to give students fundamental professional training and to prepare them for practice in any jurisdiction. Hofstra promotes considerable faculty/student contact and a strong sense of community.

ENROLLMENT/STUDENT BODY

- 1,867 applicants
- 429 applicants admitted
- 270 applicants enrolled
- 16 percent minority
- 40 percent women

FACULTY

- 75 total
- 54 percent full time
- 46 percent part time or adjunct
- 25 percent women
- 6 percent minority

One of Hofstra's greatest strengths is its faculty. The faculty are persons of academic distinction, and many of them are recognized as national authorities in their fields. They make it a point to be accessible to students outside of the traditional classroom setting. There are frequent lectures and scholarly activities emanating from the 17 endowed chairs and distinguished professorships.

LIBRARY AND PHYSICAL FACILITIES

- 444,000 volumes and equivalents
- Library hours: Monday–Thursday, 8:00 A.M.–Midnight; Friday, 8:00 A.M.– 9:00 P.M.; Saturday, 9:00 A.M.–6:00 P.M.; Sunday, Noon–Midnight
- Lexis-Nexis
- Westlaw
- DIALOG
- 8 full-time librarians
- Library seats 696

CURRICULUM

- Academic Support Program
- 87 credits required to graduate
- Degrees and combined degrees available: JD, JD/MBA
- Range of first year class size: 28–30 (small section); 117–120 (large section)

SPECIAL PROGRAMS

Each entering student at Hofstra is placed in one small section of fewer than 30 students in a substantive course during the first semester of their first year. This small section experience enables a closer relationship between students and faculty in a seminar-like environment.

During the spring semester of their first year, students receive intensive instruction in legal research and writing. During the fall semester of their second year, students participate in the Appellate Advocacy Program, in which they receive instruction in persuasive writing and oral advocacy.

Each January, Hofstra students are able to select a three-credit course on trial techniques, which is patterned on the program of the National Institute for Trial Advocacy. A carefully orchestrated sequence of exercises, covering every aspect of a trial from jury selection to closing arguments, builds the students' abilities so they are able to conduct a full jury trial at the end of the course.

A courthouse of the United States District Court for the Eastern District of New York is located on the Hofstra campus. The court cooperates with the law school in various academic programs and offers the students additional educational and practical experiences.

Civil Externship Program: The Civil Externship Program provides students with opportunities to learn lawyering skills through placements in a variety of nonprofit organizations or government agencies.

Criminal Externship Program: The Criminal Externship Program provides an opportunity for students to learn about all phases of criminal law practice through placements in such agencies as the Nassau, Queens, and Kings County District Attorneys' Offices and New York City, Nassau County, and Suffolk Legal Aid offices. Students work approximately 15 hours per week.

Alternative Dispute Resolution Clinic: The goals of the Alternative Dispute Resolution Clinic are to teach mediation skills, provide clinically supervised mediation experience, and provide direction in the advanced study of theoretical, legal, ethical, and practical issues posed by the use of mediation as an alternative to litigation. The students, under direct faculty supervision, mediate disputes at the Queens Mediation Center concerning claims of property damage and personal injury, consumer and landlord-tenant disagreements, and noise and "life-style" disputes.

Criminal Justice Clinic: This program is a one-semester clinic in which students represent defendants in criminal cases in Nassau County District Court and in Hempstead and Mineola Village courts. Students represent clients in pretrial conferences, witness interviewing, motion and brief writing, case investigations, and trials from jury selection through verdict.

Judicial Externship Program: The Judicial Externship Program provides an opportunity for students to serve as apprentices to state and federal judges for a semester. As judicial externs, for approximately 15 hours per week, students do research, write memoranda, observe court proceedings, and discuss cases with their judge.

Disabilities Law Clinic: The Disabilities Law Clinic is a new clinic that began handling cases in the fall of 1992. It focuses principally on cases involving the Americans with Disabilities Act of 1990, transportation cases, public access cases, and employment discrimination cases.

School of Law

Environmental Law Clinic: This program provides an opportunity to work on current environmental issues with public interest law firms, state or local environmental agencies, and private practitioners engaged in pro bono work in the field.

Housing Rights Clinic: Students handle a wide variety of housing cases for low-income clients, including defenses of eviction cases; actions by tenants against landlords challenging substandard conditions in their apartments; fair housing and exclusionary zoning cases; public utility shut-off cases; and work on behalf of community groups for housing rehabilitation. The course develops lawyering skills with special emphasis on litigation strategy, pre-trial and trial preparation, and trial advocacy.

Pro Bono Student Lawyers Project: The Pro Bono Student Lawyers Project places students with a variety of existing agencies, service organizations, law firms, and private practitioners. Students in the program volunteer their time without compensation or credit to work on pro bono cases.

Unemployment Action Center: The Unemployment Action Center (UAC) is a nonprofit, student-run corporation that offers free advice and representation to persons denied unemployment benefits. The Unemployment Action Center received the New York State Bar Association Law Student Pro Bono Award for 1992.

ADMISSION

- Bachelor's degree required for admission
- Application deadline: April 15
- Modified rolling admission
- LSAT, LSDAS required
- 25th/75th percentile GPA—3.0/3.5
- 25th/75th percentile LSAT—151/158
- Application fee $60

STUDENT ACTIVITIES

Hofstra students publish three journals. The *Hofstra Law Review* enjoys national renown and an international circulation. The *Labor Law Journal* publishes scholarly articles on various aspects of labor and employment law. The *Law and Policy Symposium* focuses on an analysis of a single issue from various perspectives. The inaugural issue will cover state constitutions. Other student organizations include Asian Pacific American Law Students Association (APALSA); Black Law Students Association (BLSA); Coming Out For Civil Rights; *Conscience* (the law school's student newspaper); *Environmental Law Digest;* Environmental Law Society; Federalist Society; Gaelic Law Students Society; Hofstra Law Women; Italian Law Students Association (ILSA); International Law Society; Jewish Law Students Association (JLSA); Lambda Alpha International; Latino-Latina American Law Students Association (LALSA); Phi Alpha Delta (PAD); *Pocket Part* (the law school yearbook); Public Justice Foundation; Republican Law Students Association; Student Bar Association; Trial Advocacy Club; and Unemployment Action Center.

CAREER SERVICES

The Office of Career Services provides a wide range of services to facilitate job placement. The senior assistant dean for career services and the director organize recruitment programs, conduct job development campaigns, teach résumé writing and interviewing techniques, provide career counseling to students and alumni, and maintain employee statistics.

Admissions Contact: Dean for Admissions, Peter Sylver
121 Hofstra University, Hempstead, NY 11550
Admissions Phone: 516-463-5916 • Admissions Fax: 516-463-6264
Admissions E-mail: lawadmissions@hofstra.edu • Web Address: www.hofstra.edu/law

HOFSTRA UNIVERSITY
School of Law

Admissions Contact: Dean for Admissions, Peter Sylver
121 Hofstra University, Hempstead, NY 11550
Admissions Phone: 516-463-5916 • Admissions Fax: 516-463-6264
Admissions E-mail: lawadmissions@hofstra.edu • Web Address: www.hofstra.edu/law

INSTITUTIONAL INFORMATION

Public/Private: Private
Environment: Suburban
Academic Calendar: Semester
Schedule: Full time only
Student/Faculty Ratio: 16:1
Total Faculty: 75
% Part Time: 46
% Female: 25
% Minority: 6

PROGRAMS

Academic Specialties: A rich variety of Family Law courses is offered, including a seminar on Reproductive Technology and workshops in Children's Advocacy and Child Abuse, taught in conjunction with a major hospital. In Trial Advocacy and Alternative Dispute Resolution a variety of simulated and clinical courses is offered, including an Intensive Trial Techniques course culminating in a mock jury trial. Other strengths include International Law and Constitutional Law.
Advanced Degrees Offered: JD (3 years), LLM (1 year)
Combined Degrees Offered: JD/MBA (4 years)
Clinical Program Required? No
Clinical Programs: Criminal Justice Clinic, Housing Rights Clinic, Environmental Law Clinic, Alternative Dispute Resolution Clinic

Grading System: Students are marked on the following scale: A (4.00), A– (3.67), B+ (3.33) through D (1.00) and F (0.00)
Legal Writing/Methods Course Requirements: Legal Writing (2 credits) is taken in second semester of first year; Appel. Adv. (2 credits) is taken in first semester of second year.

STUDENT INFORMATION

Enrollment of Law School: 798
% Male/Female: 60/40
% Full Time: 100
% Minority: 16
Average Age of Entering Class: 24

EXPENSES/FINANCIAL AID

Annual Tuition: $21,800
Room and Board (On/Off Campus): $8,350/ $11,100
Books and Supplies: $900
Financial Aid Application Deadline: 6/1
Average Grant: $4,615
Average Loan: $2,337
% of Aid That Is Merit-Based: 53
% Receiving Some Sort of Aid: 80
Average Total Aid Package: $5,149

ADMISSIONS INFORMATION

Application Fee: $60
Regular Application Deadline: Rolling
Regular Notification: Rolling
Average GPA: 3.3
Range of GPA: 3.0–3.5
Average LSAT: 156
Range of LSAT: 151–158
Transfer Students Accepted? Yes
Other Schools to Which Students Applied: Brooklyn Law School, St. John's University, Fordham University, New York Law School, New York University, Albany Law School, Yeshiva University
Other Admissions Factors Considered: LSAT, GPA, undergraduate school curriculum, work experience, extracurricular activities, recommendations
Number of Applications Received: 1,867
Number of Applicants Accepted: 429
Number of Applicants Enrolled: 270

INTERNATIONAL STUDENTS

TOEFL Required of International Students? Yes
Minimum TOEFL: 570

EMPLOYMENT INFORMATION

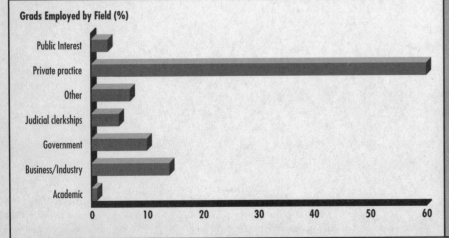

Grads Employed by Field (%)

Rate of Placement: 98%
Average Starting Salary: $51,868
Employers Who Frequently Hire Grads: The most prestigous law firms in New York City and Long Island, government agencies, and public interest orginizations
Prominent Alumni: Hon. Mary Anne Trump Barry, judge, U.S. District Court for the district of New Jersey; Randy L. Levine, deputy mayor for economic development, New York City; Robert Muller, president, Vietnam Veterans of America Foundation, founder of International Campaign to Ban Land Mines, which was awarded the 1997 Nobel Peace Prize
State for Bar Exam: NY
Number Taking Bar Exam: 244
Pass Rate for First-Time Bar: 67%

HOWARD UNIVERSITY
School of Law

Admissions Contact: Assistant Dean, Ruby J. Sherrod
2900 Van Ness Street NW, Washington, DC 20008
Admissions Phone: 202-806-8008 • Admissions Fax: 202-806-8162
Admissions E-mail: admissions@law.howard.edu • Web Address: www.law.howard.edu

INSTITUTIONAL INFORMATION

Public/Private: Private
Environment: Urban
Academic Calendar: Semester
Schedule: Full time only
Student/Faculty Ratio: 16:1
Total Faculty: 56
% Part Time: 14
% Female: 35
% Minority: 60

PROGRAMS

Academic Specialties: Strong faculty with a wide range of interests including Antitrust Law and Religion, Evidence, Critical Race Scholarship, Feminist Scholarship
Advanced Degrees Offered: LLM (foreign lawyers only) (1–2 years)
Combined Degrees Offered: JD/MBA (4 years)
Clinical Program Required? No
Clinical Programs: Criminal Law, Elder Law, Civil Law, Immigration Law, Small Business Law
Grading System: Numerical system; grading is subject to a normalization system
Legal Writing/Methods Course Requirements: Integrated program across 3 years

STUDENT INFORMATION

Enrollment of Law School: 415
% Male/Female: 40/60
% Full Time: 100
% Minority: 94
Average Age of Entering Class: 25

RESEARCH FACILITIES

Computers/Workstations Available: 100
School-Supported Research Centers: Law students have access to numerous research libraries in Washington, D.C., and the surrounding area, including the Library of Congress and numerous other public research centers.

EXPENSES/FINANCIAL AID

Annual Tuition: $12,650
Room and Board: $9,051
Books and Supplies: $1,050
Financial Aid Application Deadline: 2/1
Average Grant: $12,000
Average Loan: $15,000
% of Aid That Is Merit-Based: 28
% Receiving Some Sort of Aid: 95
Average Total Aid Package: $23,000
Average Debt: $55,500
Tuition Per Credit: $505
Fees Per Credit: $703

ADMISSIONS INFORMATION

Application Fee: $60
Regular Application Deadline: 3/31
Regular Notification: Rolling
Average GPA: 3.0
Range of GPA: 2.7–3.2
Average LSAT: 152
Range of LSAT: 148–154
Transfer Students Accepted? Yes
Other Schools to Which Students Applied: Georgetown University, University of Maryland, George Washington University, American University, New York University, Temple University, University of Baltimore, Harvard University
Number of Applications Received: 1,225
Number of Applicants Accepted: 372
Number of Applicants Enrolled: 140

INTERNATIONAL STUDENTS

TOEFL Required of International Students? Yes
Minimum TOEFL: 550

EMPLOYMENT INFORMATION

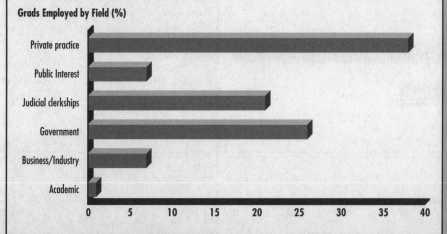

Grads Employed by Field (%)

Average Starting Salary: $85,200
State for Bar Exam: MD/NY
Number Taking Bar Exam: 41/17
Pass Rate for First-Time Bar: 29%/82%

HUMPHREYS COLLEGE
School of Law

Admissions Contact: Admission Officer, Santa Lopez
6650 Inglewood Avenue, Stockton, CA 95207
Admissions Phone: 209-478-0800 • Admissions Fax: 209-478-8721
Admissions E-mail: admissions@humphreys.edu • Web Address: www.humphreys.edu

INSTITUTIONAL INFORMATION

Public/Private: Private
Academic Calendar: Quarter
Schedule: Part time only
Student/Faculty Ratio: 6:1
Total Faculty: 12
% Part Time: 83
% Female: 17
% Minority: 0

PROGRAMS

Academic Specialties: All faculty are practicing attorneys, including private practitioners and public defenders. Several judges are on the faculty.
Clinical Program Required? No
Grading System: 100–90 Excellent, 89–80 Good, 79–70 Satisfactory, 69–55 Unsatisfactory, below 55 Failure
Legal Writing/Methods Course Requirements: 1 quarter in first and fourth years each

STUDENT INFORMATION

Enrollment of Law School: 60
% Male/Female: 100/0
% Full Time: 0
% Full Time That Are International: 0
% Minority: 0
Average Age of Entering Class: 33

EXPENSES/FINANCIAL AID

Annual Tuition: $7,062
Books and Supplies: $650
Average Loan: $14,658
% Receiving Some Sort of Aid: 66
Average Total Aid Package: $14,658
Average Debt: $48,000
Fees Per Credit: $214

ADMISSIONS INFORMATION

Application Fee: $20
Regular Application Deadline: 6/1
Regular Notification: Rolling
LSDAS Accepted? No
Average GPA: 2.8
Average LSAT: 149
Transfer Students Accepted? Yes
Other Schools to Which Students Applied: California State University—Stanislaus, Delta College, California State University—Sacramento
Number of Applications Received: 52
Number of Applicants Accepted: 32
Number of Applicants Enrolled: 19

INTERNATIONAL STUDENTS

TOEFL Required of International Students? Yes
Minimum TOEFL: 450

EMPLOYMENT INFORMATION

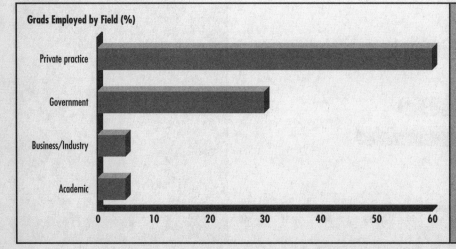

Employers Who Frequently Hire Grads: District Attorney's Offices; police departments
Prominent Alumni: Patti Gharamendi

ILLINOIS INSTITUTE OF TECHNOLOGY
Chicago-Kent College of Law

Admissions Contact: Assistant Dean for Admissions, Michael S. Burns
565 West Adams Street, Chicago, IL 60661
Admissions Phone: 312-906-5020 • Admissions Fax: 312-906-5274
Admissions E-mail: admit@kentlaw.edu • Web Address: www.kentlaw.edu

INSTITUTIONAL INFORMATION

Public/Private: Private
Environment: Urban
Academic Calendar: Semester
Schedule: Full time or part time
Student/Faculty Ratio: 6:1
Total Faculty: 177
% Part Time: 60
% Female: 31
% Minority: 4

PROGRAMS

Academic Specialties: In scholarship, law review articles by the Chicago-Kent faculty are among the most highly cited in court opinions. The members of the faculty are outstanding scholars and instructors. Academic specialties are diverse and include Biotechnology, Information Technology, Environmental Protection, International Business Transactions, New Paradigms in Products Liability, and International Criminal Tribunals.
Advanced Degrees Offered: JD (3 years full time, 4 years part time), LLM (2–8 semesters)
Combined Degrees Offered: JD/MBA (3.5–5 years), JD/LLM (4–5 years), JD/MS Financial Markets (4 to 5 years), JD/MPA (3.5–5 years), JD/MS Environmental Management (3.5 to 5 years)
Clinical Program Required? No
Clinical Programs: Civil, Criminal, Health, Mediation, Tax, Judicial Externship, Advanced Externship

Grading System: Letter and numerical system ranging from A (4.0) to E (0.0); students must maintain a cumulative GPA of 2.1 to remain in good standing and to graduate
Legal Writing/Methods Course Requirements: Chicago-Kent has the most comprehensive legal research and writing program in the country. The 3-year, 5-course curriculum teaches students to analyze a wide range of legal problems and to write about them persuasively. Students in upper-level courses are able to choose special course sections in various areas of specialization.

STUDENT INFORMATION

Enrollment of Law School: 1,143
% Male/Female: 51/49
% Full Time: 70
% Full Time That Are International: 3
% Minority: 16
Average Age of Entering Class: 26

RESEARCH FACILITIES

Computers/Workstations Available: 120

EXPENSES/FINANCIAL AID

Annual Tuition: $22,850
Room and Board (On/Off Campus): $6,632/$13,860
Books and Supplies: $890
Financial Aid Application Deadline: 4/15
Average Grant: $7,330
Average Loan: $24,066
% of Aid That Is Merit-Based: 14

% Receiving Some Sort of Aid: 89
Average Total Aid Package: $24,412
Average Debt: $63,836

ADMISSIONS INFORMATION

Application Fee: $45
Regular Application Deadline: 3/1
Regular Notification: Rolling
LSDAS Accepted? Yes
Average GPA: 3.2
Range of GPA: 2.9–3.4
Average LSAT: 154
Range of LSAT: 150–157
Transfer Students Accepted? Yes
Other Schools to Which Students Applied: Loyola University Chicago, DePaul University, John Marshall Law School, Northwestern University, Northern Illinois University, University of Illinois, American University, George Washington University
Other Admissions Factors Considered: Academic letters of recommendation are highly preferred. The ability to write clearly and effectively is evaluated using the personal statement as a writing sample.
Number of Applications Received: 2,058
Number of Applicants Accepted: 1,299
Number of Applicants Enrolled: 369

INTERNATIONAL STUDENTS

TOEFL Required of International Students? Yes
Minimum TOEFL: 600

EMPLOYMENT INFORMATION

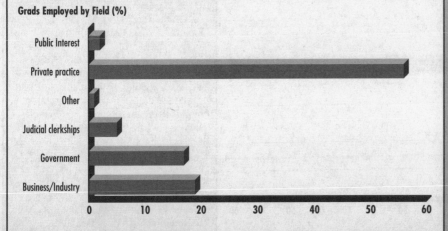

Grads Employed by Field (%)

Rate of Placement: 92%
Average Starting Salary: $49,262
Prominent Alumni: Hon. Abraham Lincoln Marovitz; Hon. Ilana Diamond Rovner; Thomas Demetrio, partner, Corboy and Demetrio
State for Bar Exam: IL
Number Taking Bar Exam: 240
Pass Rate for First-Time Bar: 80%

INDIANA UNIVERSITY — BLOOMINGTON

School of Law

Admissions Contact: Assistant Dean for Admissions, Patricia S. Clark
211 South Indiana Avenue, Bloomington, IN 47405
Admissions Phone: 812-855-4765 • Admissions Fax: 812-855-0555
Admissions E-mail: psclark@indiana.edu • Web Address: www.law.indiana.edu

INSTITUTIONAL INFORMATION

Public/Private: Public
Environment: Urban
Academic Calendar: Semester
Schedule: Full time or part time
Student/Faculty Ratio: 15:1
Total Faculty: 46
% Part Time: 6
% Female: 30
% Minority: 6

PROGRAMS

Academic Specialties: International/Global, Communications, Environmental, Business/Corporations, Interdisciplinary Study of Law (Law and Economics, Law and Psychology, Law and Social Science, etc.)
Advanced Degrees Offered: SJD (1 year in residence, completion of doctoral dissertation), LLM with thesis (completion of 20 credit hours of course work plus completion of thesis), LLM without thesis (completion of 24 credit hours plus a practicum), MCL (completion of 21 credit hours plus a practicum)
Combined Degrees Offered: JD/MBA (4 years), JD/MPA (4 years), JD/MSES (4 years), JD/MLS (4 years), JD/MS Telecommunications (4 years)
Clinical Program Required? No
Clinical Programs: Community Clinic: students represent clients in family law cases. Child Advocacy Program: provides representation for children. Protective Order Project: provides legal assistance to victims of domestic violence. Federal Courts Clinic.
Grading System: 4.0 scale

Legal Writing/Methods Course Requirements: 2-semester 2-credit, pass/fail course in first year

STUDENT INFORMATION

Enrollment of Law School: 612
% Male/Female: 64/36
% Full Time: 99
% Full Time That Are International: 1
% Minority: 14
Average Age of Entering Class: 24

RESEARCH FACILITIES

Computers/Workstations Available: 44
School-Supported Research Centers: The University Library houses one of the largest research collections in the country.

EXPENSES/FINANCIAL AID

Annual Tuition (Residents/Nonresidents): $6,850/$17,568
Room and Board (On/Off Campus): $6,150/$6,325
Books and Supplies: $1,045
Financial Aid Application Deadline: 4/1
Average Grant: $5,479
Average Loan: $16,800
% of Aid That Is Merit-Based: 47
% Receiving Some Sort of Aid: 81
Average Total Aid Package: $18,000
Average Debt: $57,422
Tuition Per Credit (Residents/Nonresidents): $236/$606
Fees Per Credit: $0

ADMISSIONS INFORMATION

Application Fee: $35
Regular Application Deadline: Rolling
Regular Notification: Rolling
LSDAS Accepted? Yes
Average GPA: 3.3
Range of GPA: 3.1–3.7
Average LSAT: 160
Range of LSAT: 153–161
Transfer Students Accepted? Yes
Other Schools to Which Students Applied: Indiana University—Indianapolis, University of Michigan, University of Minnesota, George Washington University, University of Iowa, University of Illinois, Ohio State University, University of Wisconsin
Other Admissions Factors Considered: Faculty evauations, while not required, can be very helpful in the process. Strong writing and analytic skills are highly valued.
Number of Applications Received: 1,493
Number of Applicants Accepted: 692
Number of Applicants Enrolled: 203

INTERNATIONAL STUDENTS

TOEFL Required of International Students? Yes
Minimum TOEFL: 600

EMPLOYMENT INFORMATION

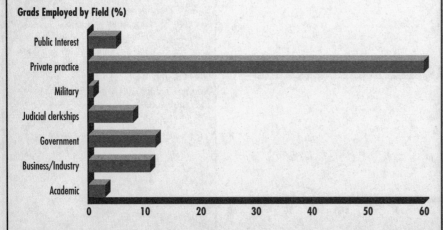

Grads Employed by Field (%)

Rate of Placement: 96%
Average Starting Salary: $52,000
Employers Who Frequently Hire Grads: Barnes & Thornburg; U.S. District Courts; Indiana Court of Appeals; Ice, Miller, Donadio & Ryan; Baker & Daniels; Warner, Norcross & Judd; Lord, Bissell & Brook; Katten, Muckin & Zavis; Kirkland & Ellis; Arnold & Porter
Prominent Alumni: Shirley S. Abrahamson, chief justice, Wisconsin Supreme Court; Lee Hamilton, former U.S. congressman, now head of Woodrow Wilson Center in Washington, D.C.; Birch Bayh, former U.S. senator, now partner in major Washington, D.C. firm
State for Bar Exam: IN
Number Taking Bar Exam: 115
Pass Rate for First-Time Bar: 97%

INDIANA UNIVERSITY — INDIANAPOLIS
School of Law

Admissions Contact: Assistant Dean of Admissions, Angela M. Espada
735 West New York Street, Indianapolis, IN 46202
Admissions Phone: 317-274-2459 • Admissions Fax: 317-274-3955
Admissions E-mail: khmiller@iupui.edu • Web Address: www.iulaw.indy.indiana.edu

INSTITUTIONAL INFORMATION
Public/Private: Public
Environment: Urban
Schedule: Full time or part time
Student/Faculty Ratio: 19:1
Total Faculty: 67
% Part Time: 50
% Female: 19
% Minority: 0

PROGRAMS
Academic Specialties: The faculty includes practitioners as well as scholars, and the curriculum reflects the influence of both.
Combined Degrees Offered: JD/MPA (4 years), JD/MBA (4 years), JD/MHA (4 years)
Clinical Program Required? No
Clinical Programs: Disability, Public Defender, and Civil Law Clinic
Grading System: 4.0 scale with a recommended curve

STUDENT INFORMATION
Enrollment of Law School: 878
% Male/Female: 70/30
% Full Time: 64
% Full Time That Are International: 3
% Minority: 11
Average Age of Entering Class: 27

RESEARCH FACILITIES
Computers/Workstations Available: 40

EXPENSES/FINANCIAL AID
Annual Tuition (Residents/Nonresidents): $7,084/$17,205
Room and Board: $9,900
Books and Supplies: $800
Average Grant: $3,500
Average Loan: $12,500
% of Aid That Is Merit-Based: 20
% Receiving Some Sort of Aid: 60
Average Total Aid Package: $4,500
Average Debt: $39,000
Fees Per Credit (Residents/Nonresidents): $210/$509

ADMISSIONS INFORMATION
Application Fee: $35
Regular Application Deadline: 3/1
Regular Notification: Rolling
LSDAS Accepted? Yes
Average GPA: 3.2
Range of GPA: 3.0–3.5
Average LSAT: 155
Range of LSAT: 151–158
Transfer Students Accepted? Yes
Other Schools to Which Students Applied: Indiana University—Bloomington, University of Notre Dame, Valparaiso University, University of Dayton, University of Louisville, DePaul University, Southern Illinois University, Northern Illinois University
Other Admissions Factors Considered: (For international students) test of written English, a law degree from another institution in their home country
Number of Applications Received: 1,078
Number of Applicants Accepted: 519
Number of Applicants Enrolled: 263

INTERNATIONAL STUDENTS
TOEFL Required of International Students? Yes
Minimum TOEFL: 550

EMPLOYMENT INFORMATION

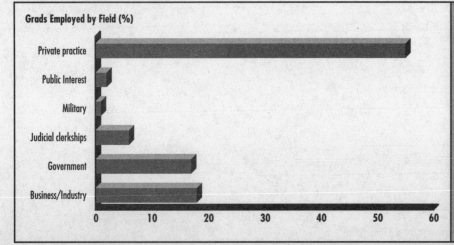

Grads Employed by Field (%)

Rate of Placement: 92%
Average Starting Salary: $47,396
Employers Who Frequently Hire Grads: Private law firms; Baker & Daniels; Barnes & Thornburg; Ice, Miller, Donadio & Ryan
Prominent Alumni: Pamela Carter, first and only African American, female state attorney general; Dan Quayle, former U.S. vice president, and his wife Marilyn Quayle; Greg Garrison, attorney and special prosecutor
State for Bar Exam: IN
Number Taking Bar Exam: 180
Pass Rate for First-Time Bar: 87%

JOHN F. KENNEDY UNIVERSITY
School of Law

547 Ygnacio Valley Road, Walnut Creek, CA 94596
Admissions Phone: 925-295-1800 • Admissions Fax: 925-933-0917
Admissions E-mail: law@jfku.edu • Web Address: www.jfku.edu/law

INSTITUTIONAL INFORMATION

Public/Private: Private
Academic Calendar: Semester
Schedule: Part time only
Student/Faculty Ratio: 30:1

STUDENT INFORMATION

Enrollment of Law School: 249
% Male/Female: 50/50
% Full Time: 0
% Minority: 24
Average Age of Entering Class: 36

EXPENSES/FINANCIAL AID

Annual Tuition: $7,823
Tuition Per Credit: $414

ADMISSIONS INFORMATION

Regular Application Deadline: 5/30
Regular Notification: Rolling
Transfer Students Accepted? No
Other Schools to Which Students Applied:
Golden Gate University, University of California—
Berkeley, University of the Pacific, University of San
Francisco, Stanford University

EMPLOYMENT INFORMATION

Rate of Placement: 89%
Average Starting Salary: $45,076
Employers Who Frequently Hire Grads:
Hinshaw and Culbertson, Cook County State's Attorney, Clausen Miller, City of Chicago Law Department
Prominent Alumni: Hon. William Daley, secretary
of commerce; Hon. Charles Freeman, chief justice
of Illinois; Leo Melamed, chairman emeritus, Chicago Mercantile Exchange; Hon. Joyce E. Tucker,
former comissioner, EEOC; Hon. Blanche Manning, U.S. District Court, Northern District of Illinois
State for Bar Exam: IL
Number Taking Bar Exam: 178
Pass Rate for First-Time Bar: 79%

THE JOHN MARSHALL LAW SCHOOL

Admission Contact: Associate Dean for Admission and Student Affairs, William B. Powers
315 South Plymouth Court, Chicago, IL 60604
Admission Phone: 800-537-4280 • Admission Fax: 312-427-5136
Admission E-mail: admission@jmls.edu • Web Address: www.jmls.edu

INSTITUTIONAL INFORMATION

Public/Private: Private
Environment: Urban
Academic Calendar: Semester
Schedule: Full time or part time
Student/Faculty Ratio: 15:1
Total Faculty: 288
% Part Time: 81
% Female: 17
% Minority: 4

PROGRAMS

Academic Specialties: Excellent programs in Lawyering Skills, Trial Advocacy, and Moot Court are offered in addition to the graduate programs mentioned below.
Advanced Degrees Offered: LLM in Taxation, Intellectual Property, Real Estate, Information Technology, Comparative Legal Studies, International Business and Trade Law, Employee Benefits (1 year full time); MS degree in Information Technology
Combined Degrees Offered: JD/MBA, JD/MPA, JD/MA, JD/LLM
Clinical Program Required? No

Clinical Programs: Trial Advocacy, Fair Housing Clinic, extensive Legal Writing Program, numerous externships and simulation courses available
Grading System: A+ (4.01), A (4.0), A– (3.5), B+ (3.5), B (3.0), B– (2.5), C+ (2.5), C (2.0), C– (1.5), D+ (1.5), D (1.0), F (0)
Legal Writing/Methods Course Requirements: 4 semesters of legal writing are required for a total of 10 semester hours

STUDENT INFORMATION

Enrollment of Law School: 1,152
% Male/Female: 54/46
% Full Time: 62
% Full Time That Are International: 1
% Minority: 19
Average Age of Entering Class: 24

EXPENSES/FINANCIAL AID

Annual Tuition: $21,000
Room and Board (Off Campus): $13,492
Books and Supplies: $700
Average Grant: $8,400
% of Aid That Is Merit-Based: 9
% Receiving Some Sort of Aid: 70
Average Total Aid Package: $18,500
Average Debt: $65,269
Fees Per Credit: $650

ADMISSIONS INFORMATION

Application Fee: $50
Regular Application Deadline: 3/1
Regular Notification: Rolling
LSDAS Accepted? No
Average GPA: 3.0
Range of GPA: 2.7–3.2
Average LSAT: 150
Range of LSAT: 145–152
Transfer Students Accepted? Yes
Other Schools to Which Students Applied: Loyola University Chicago, DePaul University, Illinois Institute of Technology, University of Illinois, Northern Illinois University, University of Dayton, Marquette University, Northwestern University
Number of Applications Received: 1,543
Number of Applicants Accepted: 964
Number of Applicants Enrolled: 287

INTERNATIONAL STUDENTS

TOEFL Required of International Students? Yes
Minimum TOEFL: 600

EMPLOYMENT INFORMATION

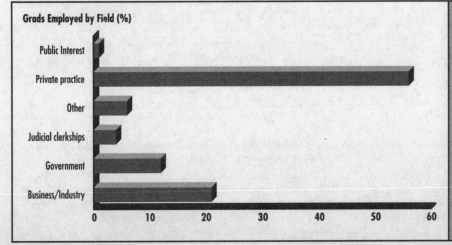

Grads Employed by Field (%)

Rate of Placement: 89%
Average Starting Salary: $45,076
Employers Who Frequently Hire Grads: Hinshaw and Culbertson, Cook County State's Attorney, Clausen Miller, City of Chicago Law Department
Prominent Alumni: Hon. William Daley, secretary of commerce; Hon. Charles Freeman, chief justice of Illinois; Leo Melamed, chairman emeritus, Chicago Mercantile Exchange; Hon. Joyce E. Tucker, former comissioner, EEOC; Hon. Blanche Manning, U.S. District Court, Northern District of Illinois
State for Bar Exam: IL
Number Taking Bar Exam: 178
Pass Rate for First-Time Bar: 79%

THE JOHN MARSHALL LAW SCHOOL

INTRODUCTION

Throughout its history, The John Marshall Law School has upheld a tradition of diversity, innovation, and opportunity that combines an understanding of the theory, the philosophy, and the practice of law. Founded in 1899, The John Marshall Law School today is proud to be recognized as a dynamic independent law school, promoting excellence in all aspects of legal education.

When John Marshall first opened its doors more than 100 years ago, its student body numbered only three. Today, the Law School boasts an enrollment in excess of 1,100 students from more than 30 states and 13 foreign countries.

Cultural and ethnic diversity have been characteristic of The John Marshall Law School student body from the very beginning. John Marshall was founded as a not-for-profit corporation by a small group of distinguished lawyers who believed in the noble principle that admission to the Law School should not be determined by arbitrary and discriminatory factors such as race or religious affiliation.

Over the years, John Marshall's growing success has resulted in a dramatic rise in enrollment and the increasing expansion of the Law School's facilities and academic programs. There are 53 full-time and 235 adjunct faculty members with extensive experience in both legal practice and education. They collaborate in cultivating a personal and practical approach to the teaching of law.

John Marshall's Centers for Excellence offer students the opportunity to engage in penetrating study and practical training in specialized areas of the law, including Advocacy and Dispute Resolution, Fair Housing, Information Technology and Privacy Law, Intellectual Property Law, International Business and Trade Law, Real Estate Law, and Tax Law and Employee Benefits.

FACILITIES

Since 1980, the Law School has expanded its main facility to include a mock courtroom complex with videotape recording and editing facilities and a jury deliberation room; a state-of-the-art computer classroom with 20 workstations; new faculty offices; a 90-seat tiered lecture hall; two 45-seat classrooms; and a full-service conference facility seating more than 150.

In 1990, John Marshall and the Chicago Bar Association entered into a unique partnership. The John Marshall Law School library assumed responsibility for the association's research needs through a totally integrated professional library facility. The seventh floor of the School's library houses the Bar Association collection. The library further boasts a collection of some 360,000 volumes, in addition to a 10,000-volume faculty library to promote scholarly research. John Marshall offers a school-wide computer network, featuring a web of high-speed, digital fiber-optic cabling allowing all students, faculty, and staff access to word processing software, Lexis, WESTLAW, CALI, and the Internet. Furthermore, library study carrels are wired to connect laptop or notebook computers to the School's network.

John Marshall's most recent expansion was the 1996 acquisition of nine floors in the Chicago Bar Association Building at 321 South Plymouth Court. This purchase allows the Law School and the Chicago Bar Association to work even more closely in developing educational programs. The building is adjacent to the law school facilities.

CENTERS FOR EXCELLENCE

John Marshall's seven Centers for Excellence affirm the Law School's mission to teach both the substantive legal knowledge and the professional skills necessary to participate in the profession. They serve as a foundation for our students' academic success.

The Center for Advocacy & Dispute Resolution offers more than 16 courses and seminars on such topics as dispute resolution. Its emphasis on clinical experiences includes fair housing, immigration law, and intellectual property law. The Center also sponsors judicial externships and more than seven interscholastic competitions.

The Center for Information Technology & Privacy Law offers unique LLM and MS degree programs and a curriculum of nearly 30 specialized courses. The Center sponsors an international moot court competition each year and a CLE seminar on new developments in information and comparative law, and publishes *The Journal of Computer and Information Law*.

The Center for Intellectual Property Law runs one of the most successful programs in the country, offering more than 50 IP courses. Its LLM program is regarded among the very best in the nation. Students also benefit from the Center's Master Classes, which are taught by international figures.

The Center for International Business and Trade Law promotes the study of law in an international context. It coordinates agreements with schools in several countries and offers an LLM Program in International Business and Trade Law and an LLM Program in Comparative Legal Studies (for foreign lawyers).

The Center for Real Estate Law offers the most comprehensive program in the country. In addition to its LLM Program in Real Estate Law, the Center's annual Robert Kratovil Seminar in Real Estate Law serves as a forum to bring together the nation's leading scholars and highly regarded practitioners.

The Center for Tax Law & Employee Benefits offers one of the oldest LLM in Tax Law programs in the country, and the nation's only LLM in Employee Benefits. It also offers annual seminars.

The Fair Housing Legal Support Center is one of the nation's leaders in training programs and educational materials dedicated to fair housing law, mortgage discrimination, and disability law. In addition to an online database, the Center works with the Fair Housing Legal Clinic to educate students and assist community members with legal problems.

ACADEMIC PROGRAMS

Since 1899, The John Marshall Law School has sought to maintain diversity in its academic programs. In the early part of this century, that mission included educating women and African-Americans and offering evening courses for working students.

One hundred years later, that mission still includes reaching out to women, minorities, and second-career students. However, much more is demanded of us as we educate 21st-century lawyers. The John Marshall Law School has expanded its curriculum to include such hot areas of law as information technology and international business and trade, as well as such innovative areas as real estate and employee benefits. Of course, we continue to lead the world with our intellectual property program with more than 50 courses available to JD and/or LLM students.

Our curriculum also includes one of the most comprehensive lawyering skills programs in the nation. John Marshall prepares its students for legal practice with four semesters of extensive training in legal research, writing, advocacy, and drafting.

Our commitment to graduate legal education has placed us among the nation's best law schools. With seven LLM programs, The John Marshall Law School is the largest graduate law school in the Midwest and fourth in the nation in number of programs available.

John Marshall offers the Joint Degree Program for JD students who wish to pursue an LLM degree. Available in six areas of law, the joint degree allows students to save both time and money. Other efforts with area schools allow John Marshall students to study at Dominican University for a JD/MBA or at Roosevelt University for a JD/MPA or JD/MA.

Finally, John Marshall prides itself on the strength of its clinical programs. Through these programs, students experience first-hand the challenges and rewards of practicing law. Combined with other academic studies, clinical programs make John Marshall the right choice for students who demand excellence in both legal theory and practical skills education.

ADMINISTRATION AND FACULTY

The John Marshall Law School is proud of its distinguished and comprehensive faculty. Our 53 full-time and 235 adjunct faculty members are knowledgeable in the theory and skilled in the practice of the law. Our professors maintain a balance between the theory of the law and the practice of the law.

Our full-time faculty is well regarded in the legal community. We have some of the top scholars in information technology law, AIDS law, notary law, and contract law. Our adjunct professors are equally accomplished. Among their many areas of expertise, our adjunct faculty members are highly regarded in intellectual property law, real estate law, and fair housing law. More than 10 judges train our students in an extensive array of advocacy skills. Judges also teach John Marshall students in our judicial externship programs.

With all of their scholarly successes, our faculty members remain committed to teaching the law. This emphasis means you will find our professors, both in the classroom and in their offices, always willing to answer questions or discuss current legal issues. Our adjunct professors, most of whom are practicing attorneys or judges, also make themselves available to students.

The Law School also is proud of its administration and staff. Throughout our history, talented professionals have made a commitment to the success of John Marshall that continues to this day.

STUDENT SERVICES

With 1,100 students annually, The John Marshall Law School strives to provide the highest quality of services to one of the largest law school student bodies in the country. This commitment is at the heart of our student-centered mission.

The John Marshall Library is one facet of our students' successes. With more than 360,000 volumes in its collection and more than 50 research and reference computers, the five-floor library is staffed by 24 full-time employees. More than 240 private study carrels, many of which are wired for laptop or notebook computer connections to the Law School's network, are available to our students each semester, as are group study rooms.

A unique partnership with The Chicago Bar Association gives our library the responsibility to service the research needs of the CBA's 22,000 members. Through this partnership, John Marshall can claim a fully professional, totally integrated facility—a true benefit for our students.

Our students also take full advantage of our Career Services Office. The office plans more than 70 programs throughout the academic year to assist students with summer opportunities and the mechanics of job searches, including publishing a series of informative handouts covering these topics. The CSO Resource Center contains up-to-date information on job openings and employer background information, and offers Internet access as well as periodicals and books helpful to both students and alumni.

John Marshall's commitment to students includes a fully staffed Writing Resource Center that helps students develop their writing skills. Three writing advisors, including a full-time director, conduct workshops, visit classes, and assist individual students with the demands of legal writing and the importance of preparation for the legal profession.

John Marshall's commitment to student services does not stop at graduation. The Law School's Office of Alumni Relations organizes events around the country each year and works with alumni chapters in 12 states and the District of Columbia. Alumni also are encouraged to use the Law School's library and Career Services Office throughout their legal careers.

STUDENT LIFE

John Marshall students actively pursue academic and social endeavors to enhance their law school experience. Academically, students engage in two law journals, two national competitions, and moot court activities. Socially, student involvement includes fraternal and legal organizations and social mixers.

The Law School's two journals—*The John Marshall Law Review* and *The John Marshall Journal of Computer and Information Law*—are staffed and edited by more than 100 students. These student-led publications bring both a national and international reputation to the Law School. Students also assist faculty with two nationally regarded competitions, the John Marshall/ABA National Criminal Justice Trial Advocacy Competition and the annual Moot Court Competition in Information Technology and Privacy Law. Through these honors activities, students engage in educational and practical learning that enhances their classroom experiences.

John Marshall is represented by more than 60 students in more than 30 moot court and mock trial competitions annually. Their well-known successes over the last six years—including a World Championship in 1995—highlight the talent of our student body.

Also well known are the visitors and scholars John Marshall welcomes each year. In addition to the typical lectures and/or presentations, these distinguished guests can be found meeting with individual classes or holding round-table discussions with interested students and faculty.

The student Bar Association heads the long list of student organizations. These 30-plus groups engage in social awareness, community service, legal issues discussions, and social activities. They reflect the diversity of our student body and offer a glimpse at the opportunities available to John Marshall students. The highlight of the social year is the annual Barrister's Ball.

CHICAGO LEGAL COMMUNITY

The John Marshall Law School is in the heart of Chicago's legal and financial district. We are located across the street from the Dirksen, Metcalf, and Kluczynski Federal Buildings and within a few blocks of the Circuit Court of Cook County. This proximity enhances our students' efforts to secure employment during law school and after graduation. John Marshall students also have the advantage of being located two blocks from LaSalle Street law firms and directly opposite the department of Immigration and Naturalization Services and the Legal Assistance Foundation.

Admission Contact: Associate Dean for Admission and Student Affairs, William B. Powers
315 South Plymouth Court, Chicago, IL 60604
Admission Phone: 800-537-4280 • Admission Fax: 312-427-5136
Admission E-mail: admission@jmls.edu
Web Address: www.jmls.edu

LEWIS AND CLARK COLLEGE
Northwestern School of Law

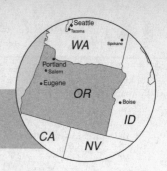

Admissions Contact: Associate Dean, Martha Spence
10015 Southwest Terwilliger Boulevard, Portland, OR 97219-7799
Admissions Phone: 503-768-6616 • Admissions Fax: 503-768-6850
Admissions E-mail: lawadmss@lclark.edu • Web Address: www.lclark.edu/LAW

INSTITUTIONAL INFORMATION

Public/Private: Private
Environment: Urban
Academic Calendar: Semester
Schedule: Full time or part time
Student/Faculty Ratio: 15:1
Total Faculty: 88
% Part Time: 48
% Female: 32
% Minority: 6

PROGRAMS

Academic Specialties: Lewis and Clark has a top-ranked Environmental and Natural Resources Program; certificates in Business Law, Tax Law, and Environmental Law; an emerging specialty in Intellectual Property; and a curriculum that supports specialization in several other subject areas including but not limited to Criminal Law, Tort Litigation, Family Law, Real Estate Transactions, and Employment Law.
Advanced Degrees Offered: LLM Environmental and Natural Resources (12–18 months)
Clinical Program Required? No
Clinical Programs: Students can participate in a live-client clinic in downtown Portland, clinical internship seminars in specific subject areas, summer and full-semester externships, and an environmental practicum. The live clinic offers experience in law, employment, debtor-creditor, small business, landlord-tenant, and domestic violence.
Grading System: A+ to F (4.3 to 0)

Legal Writing/Methods Course Requirements: Year-long course required for first year students includes a number of research and drafting assignments including an appellate brief and a moot court argument

STUDENT INFORMATION

Enrollment of Law School: 672
% Male/Female: 52/48
% Full Time: 73
% Full Time That Are International: 4
% Minority: 10
Average Age of Entering Class: 27

RESEARCH FACILITIES

Computers/Workstations Available: 117

EXPENSES/FINANCIAL AID

Annual Tuition: $21,290
Books and Supplies: $800
Financial Aid Application Deadline: 3/1
Average Grant: $5,475
Average Loan: $24,000
% Receiving Some Sort of Aid: 83
Average Total Aid Package: $29,000
Average Debt: $64,511

ADMISSIONS INFORMATION

Application Fee: $50
Regular Application Deadline: 3/15
Regular Notification: Rolling
LSDAS Accepted? Yes
Average GPA: 3.2
Range of GPA: 2.9–3.5
Average LSAT: 158
Range of LSAT: 154–161
Transfer Students Accepted? Yes
Other Schools to Which Students Applied: University of Oregon, Willamette University, University of Washington, University of Colorado, University of California—Berkeley
Number of Applications Received: 1,384
Number of Applicants Accepted: 839
Number of Applicants Enrolled: 198

INTERNATIONAL STUDENTS

TOEFL Required of International Students? Yes
Minimum TOEFL: 600

EMPLOYMENT INFORMATION

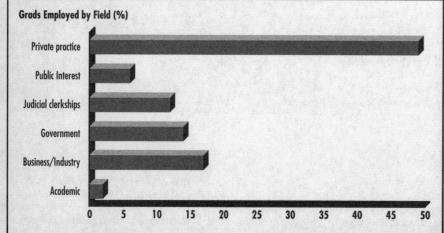

Average Starting Salary: $41,358
Employers Who Frequently Hire Grads: Numerous small and medium-sized firms; state government (Oregon); Multnomah County; United States government; state and federal judiciary; Stoel Rives, LLP
Prominent Alumni: Robert E. Jones, United States district court judge; Philip Pillsbury, Jr., Pillsbury, Levinson and Mills, San Francisco, CA; Earl Blumenauer, U.S. congressman
State for Bar Exam: OR
Number Taking Bar Exam: 140
Pass Rate for First-Time Bar: 82%

LINCOLN LAW SCHOOL OF SACRAMENTO

Admissions Contact: Registrar, Angelia Harlow
3140 J Street, Sacramento, CA 95816
Admissions Phone: 916-446-1275 • Admissions Fax: 916-446-5641
Admissions E-mail: lincolnlaw@lincolnlaw.edu • Web Address: www.lincolnlaw.edu

INSTITUTIONAL INFORMATION

Public/Private: Private
Environment: Urban
Academic Calendar: Semester
Schedule: Part time only
Total Faculty: 24
% Part Time: 100
% Female: 20
% Minority: 10

PROGRAMS

Academic Specialties: All faculty members teach in their fields of expertise.
Advanced Degrees Offered: JD (4 years)
Clinical Program Required? No
Grading System: 4.0 scale
Legal Writing/Methods Course Requirements: Writing Law School Exams, 2 semesters

STUDENT INFORMATION

Enrollment of Law School: 275
% Male/Female: 100/0
% Full Time: 0
Average Age of Entering Class: 35

RESEARCH FACILITIES

Computers Labs: 6
Campuswide Network? No
School-Supported Research Centers: County Law Library; Westlaw software available for home use

EXPENSES/FINANCIAL AID

Annual Tuition: $5,000
Books and Supplies: $500
Financial Aid Application Deadline: 6/1
Average Grant: $500
Average Loan: $10,000
% of Aid That Is Merit-Based: 2
% Receiving Some Sort of Aid: 25
Average Total Aid Package: $5,000
Average Debt: $10,500
Fees Per Credit: $220

ADMISSIONS INFORMATION

Application Fee: $30
Regular Application Deadline: Rolling
Regular Notification: Rolling
LSDAS Accepted? Yes
Average GPA: 2.8
Range of GPA: 2.1–4.0
Average LSAT: 145
Transfer Students Accepted? Yes
Other Schools to Which Students Applied: University of the Pacific, California Western, Golden Gate University, University of California—Davis, University of California—Hastings, Lewis and Clark College, Santa Clara University, UCLA School of Law
Number of Applications Received: 150
Number of Applicants Accepted: 105
Number of Applicants Enrolled: 95

EMPLOYMENT INFORMATION

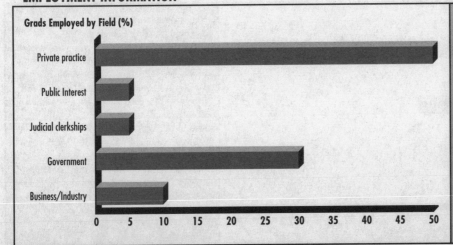

Grads Employed by Field (%)

Average Starting Salary: $40,000
Employers Who Frequently Hire Grads: District Attorney's Office; Attorney Generals Office; Public Defender's Office.
Prominent Alumni: Jan Scully, Sacramento County district attorney; Hon. Ridgely Lazard, Lassen County Municipal Court judge; Hon. Gerald Bakarich, Sacramento Superior Court judge; Steve Cilenti, Amador County district attorney; Bradford Fenocchio, Placet County district attorney; Robert Holzapfel, Glen County district attorney; Hon. Michael Sweet, Yolo County Superior Court judge

LOUISIANA STATE UNIVERSITY
Paul M. Hebert Law Center

Admissions Contact: Director of Admissions/Student Affairs, Michele Forbes
102 Law Center, Baton Rouge, LA 70803
Admissions Phone: 225-388-8646 • Admissions Fax: 225-388-8647
Admissions E-mail: admissions@law.lsu.edu • Web Address: www.law.lsu.edu

INSTITUTIONAL INFORMATION

Public/Private: Public
Environment: Urban
Academic Calendar: Semester
Schedule: Full time only
Student/Faculty Ratio: 20:1
Total Faculty: 60
% Part Time: 47
% Female: 10
% Minority: 5

PROGRAMS

Academic Specialties: The faculty is particularly strong in the areas of Civil Law and International Law. The curriculum is rich in Civil Law offerings.
Advanced Degrees Offered: LLM (1 year), MCL (Master of Civil Law) (1 year)
Combined Degrees Offered: JD/MPA (3 years)
Clinical Program Required? Yes
Clinical Programs: Trial Advocacy, Appellate Advocacy
Grading System: A (82–89), B (76–81), C (65–75), D (55–64), F (54–0)
Legal Writing/Methods Course Requirements: First year fall and spring, 1 hour/week

STUDENT INFORMATION

Enrollment of Law School: 651
% Male/Female: 54/46
% Full Time: 100
% Full Time That Are International: 1
% Minority: 8

EXPENSES/FINANCIAL AID

Annual Tuition (Residents/Nonresidents): $3,586/$9,427
Room and Board (On/Off Campus): $5,200/$9,000
Books and Supplies: $1,500
Average Grant: $4,729
% of Aid That Is Merit-Based: 22
% Receiving Some Sort of Aid: 24

ADMISSIONS INFORMATION

Application Fee: $25
Regular Application Deadline: 2/1
LSDAS Accepted? Yes
Average GPA: 3.3
Range of GPA: 3.1–3.5
Average LSAT: 152
Range of LSAT: 147–156
Transfer Students Accepted? Yes
Other Schools to Which Students Applied: University of Mississippi, Southern University, Loyola University New Orleans, Mississippi College School of Law, University of Texas School of Law, University of Houston, Tulane University, Florida State University
Number of Applications Received: 986
Number of Applicants Accepted: 641
Number of Applicants Enrolled: 314

INTERNATIONAL STUDENTS

TOEFL Required of International Students? Yes
Minimum TOEFL: 600

EMPLOYMENT INFORMATION

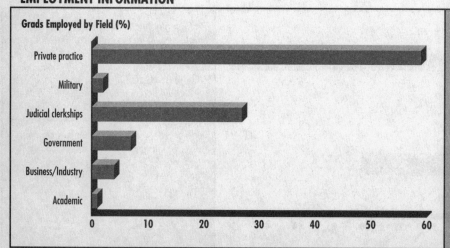

Rate of Placement: 84%
Average Starting Salary: $41,028
Employers Who Frequently Hire Grads: Adams and Reese; Baker and Hostetler; Breazeale, Sachse and Wilson; Phelps Dunbar; McGinchey Stafford Lang; Taylor, Porter, Brooks and Phillips; Stone Pigman; Vinson and Elkins; Chaffe, McCall, Phillips, Toler and Sarpy; Cook, Yancey, King and Galloway; Correro Fishman Haygood Phelps Weiss; Courtenay, Forstall, Hunter and Fontana; Cox and Smith; Crawford and Lewis; Deutsch, Kerrigan and Stiles; Fisher and Phillips; Jackson and Walker; Jenkins and Gilchrist; Jones Walker Waechter Poitevent Carrerre

LOYOLA MARYMOUNT UNIVERSITY
Loyola Law School

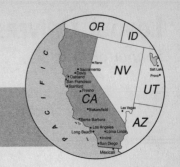

Admissions Contact: Assistant Director of Admissions, Carmen Ramirez
919 S. Albany Street, Los Angeles, CA 90015-1211
Admissions Phone: 213-736-1180 • Admissions Fax: 213-736-6523
Admissions E-mail: admissions@lls.edu • Web Address: www.lls.edu

INSTITUTIONAL INFORMATION

Public/Private: Private
Affiliation: Jesuit
Environment: Urban
Academic Calendar: Semester
Schedule: Full time or part time
Student/Faculty Ratio: 22:1
Total Faculty: 142
% Part Time: 56
% Female: 36
% Minority: 12

PROGRAMS

Academic Specialties: The Law School has extensive offerings in the areas of International and Comparative Law, Law and Social Policy, Legal Skills and Litigation, Jurisprudence, Constitutional Law, and Entertainment/Intellectual Property.
Combined Degrees Offered: JD/MBA (4 years)
Clinical Program Required? No
Clinical Programs: Business and Commercial, Civil Practice/Public Interest, Trial Advocacy, Judicial Administration, State and Local Government
Grading System: 55–100 scale with a normalized grade curve
Legal Writing/Methods Course Requirements: Required Legal Research and Writing course teaches students the basics of legal research and writing. Students are divided into small sections. Research topics covered include: ethical obligations to research, court structure, case reporting and precedent, digests, state and federal statutes and administrative law, periodicals, encyclopedias and treatises, citations form, research strategies, and computer-

ized legal research. Students learn the fundamentals of drafting objective and persuasive legal documents and prepare an office memorandum, a brief or memorandum of points and authorities, and other written work. Professors extensively critique student written work and meet individually with students to review their papers.

STUDENT INFORMATION

Enrollment of Law School: 1,344
% Male/Female: 48/52
% Full Time: 74
% Full Time That Are International: 1
% Minority: 39
Average Age of Entering Class: 23

RESEARCH FACILITIES

Computers/Workstations Available: 121
School-Supported Research Centers: Loyola Marymount Westchster Campus facilities; online library catalogs from USC Law School, Columbia Law School, University of Texas Law School, University of California Libraries, LA Public Library

EXPENSES/FINANCIAL AID

Annual Tuition: $22,530
Room and Board (Off Campus): $8,955
Books and Supplies: $620
Financial Aid Application Deadline: 3/2
Average Grant: $15,800
Average Loan: $23,513
% of Aid That Is Merit-Based: 8
% Receiving Some Sort of Aid: 87
Average Total Aid Package: $25,150
Average Debt: $67,400

ADMISSIONS INFORMATION

Application Fee: $50
Regular Application Deadline: Rolling
Regular Notification: Rolling
LSDAS Accepted? Yes
Average GPA: 3.3
Average LSAT: 158
Range of LSAT: 154–160
Transfer Students Accepted? Yes
Other Schools to Which Students Applied: UCLA School of Law, University of Southern California, Southwestern University, Pepperdine University, University of California—Hastings, University of San Diego, University of California—Davis, University of California—Berkeley
Other Admissions Factors Considered: Undergraduate record, LSAT score, personal statement, letters of recommendation, community/extracurricular involvement, work experience
Number of Applications Received: 2,897
Number of Applicants Accepted: 1,240
Number of Applicants Enrolled: 412

INTERNATIONAL STUDENTS

TOEFL Required of International Students? Yes
Minimum TOEFL: 600

EMPLOYMENT INFORMATION

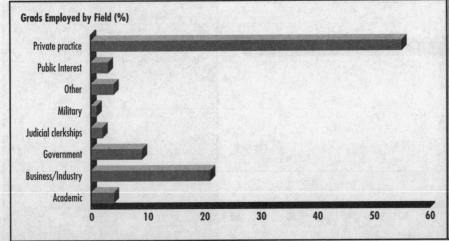

Grads Employed by Field (%)

- Private practice
- Public Interest
- Other
- Military
- Judicial clerkships
- Government
- Business/Industry
- Academic

Rate of Placement: 89%
Average Starting Salary: $67,214
Employers Who Frequently Hire Grads: O'Melveny and Myers; Manatt, Phelps and Phillips; California Attorney General; Los Angeles District Attorney; Dependency Court Legal Services; Skadden, Arps, Slate, Meagher and Flom; Legal Aid Foundation of Los Angeles; Paul Hastings
Prominent Alumni: Benjamin Cayentano, governor of Hawaii; Johnnie Cochran, criminal defense attorney; Helene Hahn, executive vice president of Dreamworks SKG
State for Bar Exam: CA
Number Taking Bar Exam: 359
Pass Rate for First-Time Bar: 84%

LOYOLA UNIVERSITY CHICAGO
School of Law

Admissions Contact: Office of Admission and Financial Aid, Assistant Director
1 East Pearson, Chicago, IL 60611
Admissions Phone: 312-915-7170 • Admissions Fax: 312-915-7906
Admissions E-mail: law-admissions@luc.edu • Web Address: www.luc.edu/schools/law

INSTITUTIONAL INFORMATION

Public/Private: Private
Affiliation: Roman Catholic (Society of Jesus)
Environment: Urban
Academic Calendar: Semester
Schedule: Full time or part time
Student/Faculty Ratio: 18:1
Total Faculty: 132
% Part Time: 77
% Female: 30
% Minority: 10

PROGRAMS

Academic Specialties: Health Law, Corporate Law, Child and Family Law, Litigation, Tax Law, International Law
Advanced Degrees Offered: MJ Health Law, MJ Child Law, MJ Corporate Law (all 22 semester hours); LLM Health Law, LLM Child Law, LLM Corporate Law (all 24 semester hours); SJD Health Law, DLaw in Health Law, (2 years full time)
Combined Degrees Offered: JD/MBA, JD/MSW, JD/HRIR, JD/MA Political Science (4 years)
Clinical Program Required? No
Clinical Programs: Community Law, Tax Law, Child Law, Family Law
Grading System: Letter and numerical system on a 4.0 scale
Legal Writing/Methods Course Requirements: 3 semesters—2 semesters in Illinois, third semester advocacy

STUDENT INFORMATION

Enrollment of Law School: 710
% Male/Female: 42/58
% Full Time: 73
% Full Time That Are International: 4
% Minority: 23
Average Age of Entering Class: 26

RESEARCH FACILITIES

Computers/Workstations Available: 800

EXPENSES/FINANCIAL AID

Annual Tuition: $22,900
Room and Board (Off Campus): $13,240
Books and Supplies: $900
Financial Aid Application Deadline: 3/1
Average Grant: $5,700
Average Loan: $18,500
% of Aid That Is Merit-Based: 54
% Receiving Some Sort of Aid: 90
Average Total Aid Package: $24,200
Average Debt: $61,407
Fees Per Credit: $766

ADMISSIONS INFORMATION

Application Fee: $50
Regular Application Deadline: 4/1
Regular Notification: Rolling
LSDAS Accepted? No
Average GPA: 3.3
Range of GPA: 3.0–3.5
Average LSAT: 158
Range of LSAT: 155–161
Transfer Students Accepted? Yes
Other Schools to Which Students Applied: Northwestern University, Illinois Institute of Technology, University of Illinois, University of Chicago, John Marshall Law School, Boston College, Case Western Reserve University, George Washington University
Other Admissions Factors Considered: Applicant's ability to overcome hardships or disabilities
Number of Applications Received: 2,164
Number of Applicants Accepted: 921
Number of Applicants Enrolled: 230

INTERNATIONAL STUDENTS

TOEFL Required of International Students? Yes
Minimum TOEFL: 600

EMPLOYMENT INFORMATION

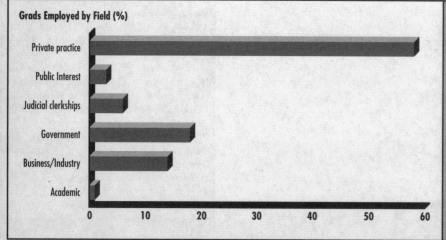

Grads Employed by Field (%)

Rate of Placement: 96%
Average Starting Salary: $57,525
State for Bar Exam: IL
Number Taking Bar Exam: 164
Pass Rate for First-Time Bar: 94%

LOYOLA UNIVERSITY NEW ORLEANS

School of Law

Admissions Contact: Dean of Admissions, Michele Allison-Davis
7214 St. Charles Avenue, New Orleans, LA 70118
Admissions Phone: 504-861-5575 • Admissions Fax: 504-861-5895
Admissions E-mail: ladmit@loyno.edu • Web Address: www.loyno.edu/law

INSTITUTIONAL INFORMATION

Public/Private: Private
Affiliation: Catholic
Environment: Urban
Academic Calendar: Semester
Schedule: Full time or part time
Student/Faculty Ratio: 17:1
Total Faculty: 70
% Part Time: 59
% Female: 34
% Minority: 26

PROGRAMS

Combined Degrees Offered: JD/MBA, JD/Master of Religious Studies, JD/Master of Communications, JD/MPA, JD/MURP. All combined degree programs add an additional year to the JD program.
Clinical Program Required? No
Clinical Programs: Criminal Prosecution and Defenses, Immigration, Civil, Juvenile, Domestic
Grading System: A, B+, B, C+, C, D+, D, F

STUDENT INFORMATION

Enrollment of Law School: 656
% Male/Female: 51/49
% Full Time: 77
% Full Time That Are International: 1
% Minority: 26
Average Age of Entering Class: 26

EXPENSES/FINANCIAL AID

Annual Tuition: $19,685
Room and Board (On/Off Campus): $4,500/$8,600
Books and Supplies: $800
Average Grant: $7,320
Average Debt: $61,587
Fees Per Credit: $766

ADMISSIONS INFORMATION

Application Fee: $20
Regular Application Deadline: Rolling
Regular Notification: Rolling
LSDAS Accepted? Yes
Average GPA: 3.0
Range of GPA: 1.7–4.0
Average LSAT: 152
Range of LSAT: 136–165
Transfer Students Accepted? Yes
Other Schools to Which Students Applied: Tulane University, Southern University, Florida State University, University of Florida, Nova Southeastern University, Stetson University, Georgia State University, St. Mary's University
Other Admissions Factors Considered: Diversity, graduate GPA, date of undergraduate degree
Number of Applications Received: 1,321
Number of Applicants Accepted: 725
Number of Applicants Enrolled: 209

EMPLOYMENT INFORMATION

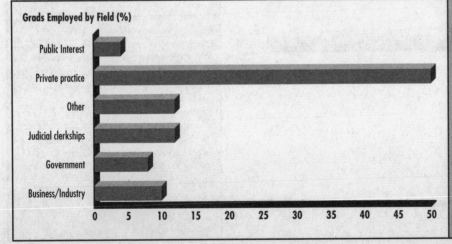

Grads Employed by Field (%)

Public Interest
Private practice
Other
Judicial clerkships
Government
Business/Industry

0 5 10 15 20 25 30 35 40 45 50

State for Bar Exam: LA
Number Taking Bar Exam: 172
Pass Rate for First-Time Bar: 66%

MARQUETTE UNIVERSITY
Law School

Admissions Contact: Assistant Dean for Admissions, Edward A. Kawczynski
1103 West Wisconsin Avenue, PO Box 1881, Milwaukee, WI 53201-1881
Admissions Phone: 414-288-6767 • Admissions Fax: 414-288-0676
Admissions E-mail: law.admissions@marquette.edu • Web Address: www.marquette.edu/law

INSTITUTIONAL INFORMATION

Public/Private: Private
Affiliation: Society of Jesus
Environment: Metropolis
Academic Calendar: Semester
Schedule: Full time only
Student/Faculty Ratio: 15:1
Total Faculty: 32
% Female: 30
% Minority: 3

PROGRAMS

Academic Specialties: Intellectual Property Law, Sports Law, Criminal Law, Civil Litigation, Alternative Dispute Resolution
Combined Degrees Offered: JD/MBA, JD/MA Political Science, JD/MA Political Science International Relations, JD/MA Bioethics (all are 4 years)
Clinical Program Required? No
Grading System: A, B, C, D, F
Legal Writing/Methods Course Requirements:
In addition to stressing commmunication skills in all core classes, Marquette requires you to take specific introductory courses in legal writing, research, and communication. Students all need to meet advanced research and advanced oral communication requuirements with specially designated courses.

STUDENT INFORMATION

Enrollment of Law School: 587
% Male/Female: 55/45
% Full Time: 81
% Full Time That Are International: 0
% Minority: 11
Average Age of Entering Class: 25

RESEARCH FACILITIES

Computers/Workstations Available: 35

EXPENSES/FINANCIAL AID

Annual Tuition: $19,770
Room and Board: $7,560
Books and Supplies: $800
Financial Aid Application Deadline: 3/1
Average Grant: $10,000
Average Loan: $30,000
% Receiving Some Sort of Aid: 90
Average Debt: $62,000
Fees Per Credit: $790

ADMISSIONS INFORMATION

Application Fee: $40
Regular Application Deadline: 4/1
Regular Notification: Rolling
LSDAS Accepted? Yes
Average GPA: 3.1
Range of GPA: 2.9–3.5
Average LSAT: 155
Range of LSAT: 152–157
Transfer Students Accepted? Yes
Other Schools to Which Students Applied: University of Wisconsin, University of Minnesota, DePaul University, Loyola University Chicago, Hamline University, John Marshall Law School, Illinois Institute of Technology, University of Notre Dame
Other Admissions Factors Considered: Diversity of applicant (cultural, educational, experiential) that may enrich the entering class
Number of Applications Received: 840
Number of Applicants Accepted: 748
Number of Applicants Enrolled: 150

INTERNATIONAL STUDENTS

TOEFL Required of International Students? Yes
Minimum TOEFL: 600

EMPLOYMENT INFORMATION

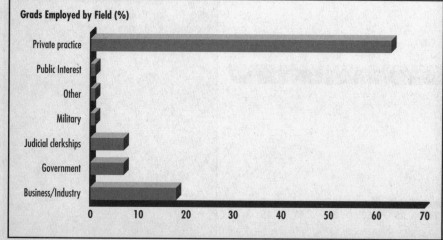

Grads Employed by Field (%)

Private practice
Public Interest
Other
Military
Judicial clerkships
Government
Business/Industry

Rate of Placement: 93%
Average Starting Salary: $50,018
Employers Who Frequently Hire Grads: Michael, Best and Friedrish; Quarles and Brady; Godfrey and Kahn; Von Briesen, Purtell and Roport; Foley and Lardner; Davis and Kualthay; Whyte Hirschboeck Dudek
Prominent Alumni: Justice Janine P. Geske, Wisconsin Supreme Court; Hon. Terence Evans, 7th Circuit Court of Appeals; George G. Lorinczi, Strook, Strook and Lavan; Donald G. Steffes, president and CEO, Washington Casualty

MERCER UNIVERSITY
Walter F. George School of Law

Admissions Contact: Assistant Dean of Admissions and Financial Aid, Marilyn E. Sutton
1021 Georgia Avenue, Macon, GA 31207
Admissions Phone: 912-301-2605 • Admissions Fax: 912-301-2989
Admissions E-mail: deaton_ed@mercer.edu • Web Address: www.law.mercer.edu

INSTITUTIONAL INFORMATION

Public/Private: Private
Affiliation: Baptist
Environment: Urban
Academic Calendar: Semester
Schedule: Full time only
Student/Faculty Ratio: 15:1
Total Faculty: 54
% Part Time: 50
% Female: 19
% Minority: 7

PROGRAMS

Advanced Degrees Offered: JD (3 years)
Clinical Program Required? No
Grading System: A (99–90), B (89–82), C (81–76), D (75–70), F (69–65)

STUDENT INFORMATION

Enrollment of Law School: 415
% Male/Female: 52/48
% Full Time: 100
% Full Time That Are International: 0
% Minority: 12
Average Age of Entering Class: 25

EXPENSES/FINANCIAL AID

Annual Tuition: $19,250
Room and Board (Off Campus): $11,900
Books and Supplies: $600
Financial Aid Application Deadline: 4/1
Average Grant: $13,500
Average Loan: $22,960
% of Aid That Is Merit-Based: 12
% Receiving Some Sort of Aid: 90
Average Total Aid Package: $24,700
Average Debt: $68,855

ADMISSIONS INFORMATION

Application Fee: $45
Regular Application Deadline: 3/15
Regular Notification: Rolling
LSDAS Accepted? Yes
Average GPA: 3.2
Range of GPA: 2.9–3.4
Average LSAT: 153
Range of LSAT: 150–155
Transfer Students Accepted? Yes
Other Schools to Which Students Applied: University of Georgia, Georgia State University, Emory University, Florida State University, Wake Forest University, Stetson University, University of Florida, Samford University
Other Admissions Factors Considered: Letters of recommendation, personal statement, grade point trend, military experience, work experience, community service, evidence of obstacles overcome, writing proficiency
Number of Applications Received: 958
Number of Applicants Accepted: 470
Number of Applicants Enrolled: 154

INTERNATIONAL STUDENTS

Minimum TOEFL: 600

EMPLOYMENT INFORMATION

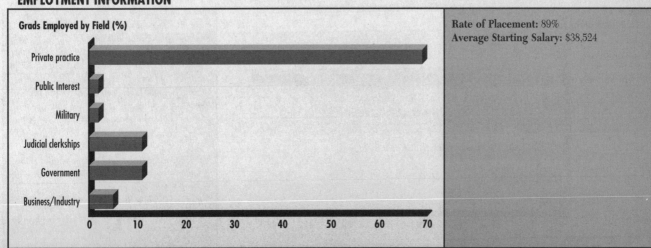

Rate of Placement: 89%
Average Starting Salary: $38,524

MICHIGAN STATE UNIVERSITY
Detroit College of Law

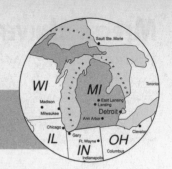

Admissions Contact: Director of Admissions, Andrea Heatley
316 Law Building, East Lansing, MI 48824-1300
Admissions Phone: 517-432-0222 • Admissions Fax: 517-432-0098
Admissions E-mail: law@msu.edu • Web Address: www.dcl.edu

INSTITUTIONAL INFORMATION

Public/Private: Private
Environment: Urban
Schedule: Full time or part time
Student/Faculty Ratio: 23:1
Total Faculty: 30
% Part Time: 40
% Female: 30
% Minority: 2

PROGRAMS

Academic Specialties: 2 concentrations, International Law and Taxation; summer programs in Romania and Ottawa, Canada; joint JD/MBA program
Combined Degrees Offered: JD/MBA (4 years), JD/MPA (4 years), JD/MLIR (4 years), JD/MA (4 years)
Clinical Program Required? No
Clinical Programs: Externships with various courts and government agencies
Grading System: A (4.0) to F (0)

STUDENT INFORMATION

Enrollment of Law School: 715
% Male/Female: 61/39
% Full Time: 78
% Full Time That Are International: 3
% Minority: 19
Average Age of Entering Class: 28

RESEARCH FACILITIES

Computers/Workstations Available: 70
School-Supported Research Centers: The Michigan State University Library System

EXPENSES/FINANCIAL AID

Annual Tuition: $15,584
Room and Board: $6,364
Books and Supplies: $872
Financial Aid Application Deadline: 6/30
Average Grant: $17,000
Average Loan: $16,925
% of Aid That Is Merit-Based: 7
% Receiving Some Sort of Aid: 80
Average Total Aid Package: $18,300
Average Debt: $59,381
Fees Per Credit: $535

ADMISSIONS INFORMATION

Application Fee: $50
Regular Application Deadline: Rolling
Regular Notification: Rolling
Average GPA: 3.2
Range of GPA: 2.9–3.4
Average LSAT: 152
Range of LSAT: 149–156
Transfer Students Accepted? Yes
Other Schools to Which Students Applied: Wayne State University
Number of Applications Received: 1,055
Number of Applicants Accepted: 701
Number of Applicants Enrolled: 210

INTERNATIONAL STUDENTS

TOEFL Required of International Students? Yes
Minimum TOEFL: 600

EMPLOYMENT INFORMATION

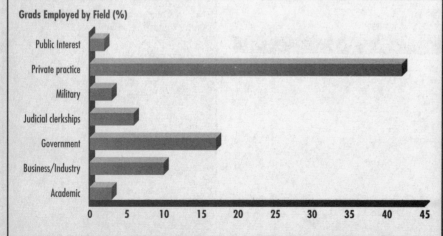

Grads Employed by Field (%)

Rate of Placement: 92%
Average Starting Salary: $43,285
Employers Who Frequently Hire Grads: Clark Hill, PLC; Dykema Gossett, PLLC; Kitch, Drutchas, Wagner and Kenney, PC; Secrest, Wardle, Lynch, Hampton; Truex and Morley
Prominent Alumni: Dennis Archer, mayor of Detroit and former Michigan Supreme Court judge, Hon. Richard Suhrheinrich, judge, U.S. Court of Appeals 6th District Circuit, Michael G. Morris, president and CEO of Consumers Power Company
State for Bar Exam: MI
Number Taking Bar Exam: 194
Pass Rate for First-Time Bar: 76%

MISSISSIPPI COLLEGE
School of Law

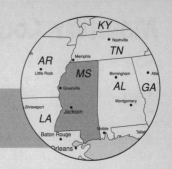

Admissions Contact: Director of Admissions, Patricia H. Evans
151 East Griffith Street, Jackson, MS 39201
Admissions Phone: 601-925-7150 • Admissions Fax: 601-925-7185
Admissions E-mail: pevans@mc.edu • Web Address: www.mc.edu/organizations/acad/law

INSTITUTIONAL INFORMATION

Public/Private: Private
Affiliation: Southern Baptist
Environment: Urban
Academic Calendar: Semester
Schedule: Full time only
Student/Faculty Ratio: 18:1
Total Faculty: 36
% Part Time: 17
% Female: 50
% Minority: 7

PROGRAMS

Academic Specialties: The faculty includes nationally recognized experts in Antitrust, Evidence, and Bankruptcy Law. The curriculum emphasizes both substantive law and skills training.
Advanced Degrees Offered: JD (3 years)
Combined Degrees Offered: JD/MBA: JD (3 years), MBA (1 year)
Clinical Program Required? No
Grading System: A to F
Legal Writing/Methods Course Requirements: 2 semesters first year, upperlevel writing requirement

STUDENT INFORMATION

Enrollment of Law School: 372
% Male/Female: 56/44
% Full Time: 100
% Full Time That Are International: 0
% Minority: 9
Average Age of Entering Class: 27

RESEARCH FACILITIES

Computers/Workstations Available: 27

EXPENSES/FINANCIAL AID

Annual Tuition: $15,469
Room and Board (On/Off Campus): $3,900/ $7,400
Books and Supplies: $900
Financial Aid Application Deadline: 5/1
Average Grant: $9,000
Average Loan: $18,500
% of Aid That Is Merit-Based: 25
% Receiving Some Sort of Aid: 93
Average Total Aid Package: $24,000
Average Debt: $55,000
Tuition Per Credit: $499

ADMISSIONS INFORMATION

Application Fee: $25
Regular Application Deadline: Rolling
Regular Notification: Rolling
LSDAS Accepted? No
Average GPA: 3.1
Range of GPA: 2.8–3.4
Average LSAT: 149
Range of LSAT: 145–152
Transfer Students Accepted? Yes
Other Schools to Which Students Applied: University of Mississippi, Stetson University, Loyola University New Orleans, Louisiana University, Samford University, University of South Carolina
Other Admissions Factors Considered: Extracurricular activities, work experience, letters of recommendation.
Number of Applications Received: 713
Number of Applicants Accepted: 401
Number of Applicants Enrolled: 143

EMPLOYMENT INFORMATION

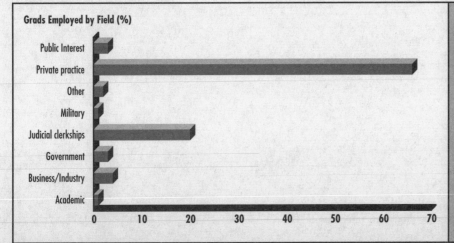

Grads Employed by Field (%)

Rate of Placement: 96%
Average Starting Salary: $40,711
Prominent Alumni: Justice Dan Lee, former chief judge, Mississippi Supreme Court; Eddie Briggs, former lieutenant governor of Mississippi; Dale Danks, former mayor of Jackson

MONTEREY COLLEGE OF LAW

Admissions Contact: Director of Admissions and Student Services, Sandra Riina
404 West Franklin Street, Monterey, CA 93940
Admissions Phone: 831-373-3301 • Admissions Fax: 831-373-0143
Admissions E-mail: admissions@montereylaw.edu • Web Address: www.montereylaw.edu

INSTITUTIONAL INFORMATION

Public/Private: Private
Student/Faculty Ratio: 25:1
Total Faculty: 44
% Part Time: 100
% Female: 23

PROGRAMS

Academic Specialties: Recognizing the special needs of individuals who wish to receive a law degree but cannot attend a full-time program, Monterey provides convenient evening classes taught by practicing attorneys and judges who bring real-world perspective and experiences into the classroom.
Advanced Degrees Offered: JD (4 year evening program)
Clinical Program Required? Yes
Clinical Programs: Under the supervision of a Clinical Studies professor, students give legal advice to clients in a pro bono legal clinic focusing on small claims issues.
Grading System: Numerical grading system (0 to 100) to reflect academic performance
Legal Writing/Methods Course Requirements: Legal Writing classes are required in the first and second years. In the third and fourth years, they are integrated into the curriculum.

STUDENT INFORMATION

Enrollment of Law School: 100
% Full Time: 0
Average Age of Entering Class: 37

RESEARCH FACILITIES

Computers/Workstations Available: 3

EXPENSES/FINANCIAL AID

Annual Tuition: $7,150
Books and Supplies: $600
Average Grant: $750
Average Loan: $5,000
% of Aid That Is Merit-Based: 40
% Receiving Some Sort of Aid: 55
Fees Per Credit: $300

ADMISSIONS INFORMATION

Application Fee: $75
Regular Application Deadline: 6/1
Regular Notification: ASAP
LSDAS Accepted? No
Average GPA: 3.0
Range of GPA: 2.3–4.0
Average LSAT: 150

Transfer Students Accepted? Yes
Other Schools to Which Students Applied: Santa Clara University, Golden Gate University, Lincoln Law School of Sacramento, Lincoln Law School of San Jose
Other Admissions Factors Considered: Selection of students for admission to Monterey College of Law is based on a combination of factors and each application is considered on its own merit. The Admission Committee reviews each applicant's entire file prior to making a decision.

EMPLOYMENT INFORMATION

Employers Who Frequently Hire Grads: Governmental offices, public agencies, private law firms
Prominent Alumni: Hon. Russell Scott, Municipal Court Judge, Monterey County; Hon. Richard Rutledge, Commissioner, Monterey County; Hon. John Salazar, commissioner, Santa Cruz County

NEW COLLEGE OF CALIFORNIA
School of Law

50 Fell Street, San Francisco, CA 94102
Admissions Phone: 415-863-4111 • Admissions Fax: 415-626-5541
Admissions E-mail: lawinfo@infogate.newcollege.edu • Web Address: www.newcollege.edu/pro/law/law.html

INSTITUTIONAL INFORMATION

Public/Private: Private
Academic Calendar: Semester
Schedule: Full time or part time

STUDENT INFORMATION

Enrollment of Law School: 160
% Male/Female: 45/55
% Full Time: 75
% Minority: 43

EXPENSES/FINANCIAL AID

Annual Tuition: $8,515

ADMISSIONS INFORMATION

Application Fee: $45
Regular Application Deadline: 3/1
Regular Notification: Rolling
Transfer Students Accepted? Yes
Number of Applications Received: 200
Number of Applicants Accepted: 70
Number of Applicants Enrolled: 50

NEW ENGLAND SCHOOL OF LAW

Admissions Contact: Director of Admissions, Pamela Jorgensen
154 Stuart Street, Boston, MA 02116
Admissions Phone: 617-422-7210 • Admissions Fax: 617-422-7200
Admissions E-mail: admit@admin.nesl.edu • Web Address: www.nesl.edu

INSTITUTIONAL INFORMATION

Public/Private: Private
Environment: Urban
Academic Calendar: Semester
Schedule: Full time or part time
Student/Faculty Ratio: 20:1
Total Faculty: 93
% Part Time: 60
% Female: 27
% Minority: 8

PROGRAMS

Academic Specialties: International Law, Environmental Law, Business and Tax Law

Clinical Program Required? No

Clinical Programs: The Lawyering Process (Civil Litigation Clinic), The Lawyering Process (Summer Version), The Government Lawyer, Tax Clinic, Administrative Law Clinic, Criminal Procedure II Clinic, Environmental Law Clinic, Family Law Clinic, Health and Hospital Law Clinic

Grading System: Letter and numerical system on a 4.0 scale

Legal Writing/Methods Course Requirements: There are five major objectives of the Legal Methods program: 1) learning to find and analyze the law and to place the law into a variety of legal formats; 2) learning the legal process from initial client interview through final disposition; 3) learning the relationship between courts and other branches of government; 4) learning how legal doctrines develop and change; and 5) learning to recognize and resolve ethical issues that arise in the practice of law.

STUDENT INFORMATION

Enrollment of Law School: 937
% Male/Female: 48/52
% Full Time: 61
% Full Time That Are International: 1
% Minority: 24
Average Age of Entering Class: 27

RESEARCH FACILITIES

Computers/Workstations Available: 79
School-Supported Research Centers: Memberships: New England Law Library Consortium (NELLCO) provides access to 19 major law libraries in the Northeast. Boston Regional Library System (BRLS) provides research and interlibrary loan service amongst its members—from the largest university library, to mid-size public libraries to small corporate libraries. Bilateral agreements exist between New England and Tufts Health Sciences Library and between New England and Wentworth Institute of Technology Library.

EXPENSES/FINANCIAL AID

Annual Tuition: $15,950
Room and Board (Off Campus): $12,600
Books and Supplies: $850
Financial Aid Application Deadline: 4/15
Average Grant: $5,340
Average Loan: $19,125
% of Aid That Is Merit-Based: 65
% Receiving Some Sort of Aid: 78
Average Total Aid Package: $20,950
Average Debt: $62,870
Tuition Per Credit: $610

ADMISSIONS INFORMATION

Application Fee: $50
Regular Application Deadline: 6/1
Regular Notification: Rolling
LSDAS Accepted? Yes
Range of GPA: 2.7–3.3
Average LSAT: 148
Range of LSAT: 143–153
Transfer Students Accepted? Yes
Other Schools to Which Students Applied: Suffolk University, Boston College, Northeastern University, Boston University, Western New England College, New York Law School, Syracuse University, Quinnipac University School of Law
Number of Applications Received: 2,224
Number of Applicants Accepted: 1,524
Number of Applicants Enrolled: 337

INTERNATIONAL STUDENTS

TOEFL Required of International Students? Yes

EMPLOYMENT INFORMATION

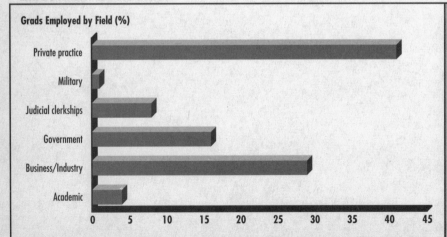

Grads Employed by Field (%)

Rate of Placement: 89%
Average Starting Salary: $46,287
Employers Who Frequently Hire Grads: A partial list of employers who have hired New England School of Law graduates can be found on our website www.nesl.edu/career/employ.htm
Prominent Alumni: Susan Crawford, judge, U.S. Court of Appeals for the Armed Forces; John Simpson, former director of the Secret Service; Gregory Phillips, presiding justice, Roxbury District Court; Joyce London Alexander, chief U.S. magistrate judge, U.S. District Court for District of Massachusetts; Judge Thomas A. Adams, New York Supreme Court; Joseph Mondello, Republican National Comitteeman for New York

NEW YORK LAW SCHOOL

Admissions Contact: Director of Admissions, Pamela McKenna
57 Worth Street, New York, NY 10013
Admissions Phone: 212-431-2888 • Admissions Fax: 212-966-1522
Admissions E-mail: admissions@nyls.edu • Web Address: www.nyls.edu

INSTITUTIONAL INFORMATION

Public/Private: Private
Environment: Urban
Academic Calendar: Semester
Schedule: Full time or part time
Student/Faculty Ratio: 21:1
Total Faculty: 124
% Part Time: 56
% Female: 32
% Minority: 8

PROGRAMS

Academic Specialties: Constitutional Law, Civil and Human Rights, Corporations and Business Transactions, Communications and Media Law, externships and judicial internships
Advanced Degrees Offered: JD (3 years full time, 4 years part time)
Combined Degrees Offered: JD/MBA with Baruch College (4 years of full-time course load)
Clinical Program Required? No
Clinical Programs: Civil and Human Rights Clinic focusing on housing discrimination and political asylum cases
Grading System: A to F, with some courses designated P/F

STUDENT INFORMATION

Enrollment of Law School: 1,405
% Male/Female: 52/48
% Full Time: 66
% Full Time That Are International: 1
% Minority: 23
Average Age of Entering Class: 27

EXPENSES/FINANCIAL AID

Annual Tuition: $22,114
Room and Board (Off Campus): $9,945
Books and Supplies: $800
Average Grant: $7,150
Average Loan: $21,000
% Receiving Some Sort of Aid: 84
Average Total Aid Package: $29,000
Average Debt: $49,000

ADMISSIONS INFORMATION

Application Fee: $50
Regular Application Deadline: Rolling
Regular Notification: Rolling
LSDAS Accepted? Yes
Average GPA: 3.1
Range of GPA: 2.9–3.3
Average LSAT: 154
Range of LSAT: 151–156
Transfer Students Accepted? Yes
Other Schools to Which Students Applied: Brooklyn Law School, Fordham University, St. John's University, Hofstra University, Seton Hall University, New York University, American University, Pace University
Number of Applications Received: 4,240
Number of Applicants Accepted: 2,035
Number of Applicants Enrolled: 509

INTERNATIONAL STUDENTS

TOEFL Required of International Students? Yes
Minimum TOEFL: 600

EMPLOYMENT INFORMATION

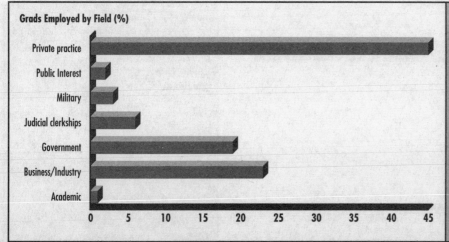

Grads Employed by Field (%)

Rate of Placement: 93%
Average Starting Salary: $60,000
Prominent Alumni: U.S. Supreme Court Justice John Marshall Harlan; Arnold Kopelson, Academy Award–winning producer (*Platoon*)

NEW YORK UNIVERSITY
School of Law

Admissions Contact: Assistant Dean of Admissions, Kenneth J. Kleinrock
110 West Third Street, Second Floor, New York, NY 10012
Admissions Phone: 212-998-6060 • Admissions Fax: 212-995-4527
Admissions E-mail: law.moreinfo@nyu.edu • Web Address: www.law.nyu.edu

INSTITUTIONAL INFORMATION

Public/Private: Private
Environment: Urban
Academic Calendar: Semester
Schedule: Full time only
Student/Faculty Ratio: 13:1
Total Faculty: 185
% Part Time: 38
% Female: 33
% Minority: 10

PROGRAMS

Advanced Degrees Offered: LLM, JSD
Clinical Program Required? No

STUDENT INFORMATION

Enrollment of Law School: 1,328
% Male/Female: 50/50
% Full Time: 100
% Full Time That Are International: 4
% Minority: 23

RESEARCH FACILITIES

Computers/Workstations Available: 200

EXPENSES/FINANCIAL AID

Annual Tuition: $27,540
Room and Board (On Campus): $15,455
Books and Supplies: $650
Financial Aid Application Deadline: 3/15
% Receiving Some Sort of Aid: 78

ADMISSIONS INFORMATION

Application Fee: $65
Regular Application Deadline: 2/1
Regular Notification: 4/15
Average GPA: 3.7
Range of GPA: 3.5–3.8
Average LSAT: 168
Range of LSAT: 167–171
Transfer Students Accepted? Yes
Other Schools to Which Students Applied: Columbia University, Georgetown University, Harvard University, Yale University, University of Pennsylvania, Fordham University, Stanford University, University of Michigan
Number of Applications Received: 6,481
Number of Applicants Enrolled: 415

INTERNATIONAL STUDENTS

TOEFL Required of International Students? Yes

EMPLOYMENT INFORMATION

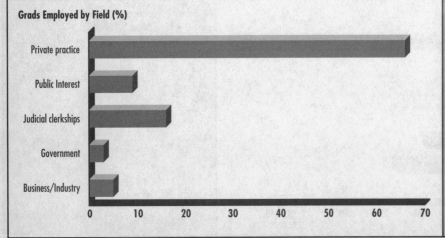

Rate of Placement: 100%
Employers Who Frequently Hire Grads: Private law firms, public interest organizations, government agencies, corporations, and pubic accounting firms
Prominent Alumni: Paul Tagliabue, commissioner, National Football League; Rudolph Giuliani, mayor, City of New York; Hon. Judith Kaye, chief judge, New York State Court of Appeals

NORTH CAROLINA CENTRAL UNIVERSITY
School of Law

Admissions Contact: Admissions Coordinator, Jacqueline Faucett
1512 South Alston Avenue, Durham, NC 27707
Admissions Phone: 919-560-5243 • Admissions Fax: 919-560-6339
Web Address: www.nccu.edu/law

INSTITUTIONAL INFORMATION

Public/Private: Public
Environment: Urban
Academic Calendar: Semester
Schedule: Full time or part time
Student/Faculty Ratio: 25:1
Total Faculty: 22
% Female: 56
% Minority: 59

PROGRAMS

Academic Specialties: Civil and Criminal Litigation, Family Law, Civil Rights
Combined Degrees Offered: JD/MBA (4 years), JD/MLS (4 years)
Clinical Programs: Civil Litigation Clinic, Civil Rights Clinic, Criminal Litigation Clinic, Family Law Clinic, Pro Bono Legal Clinic
Grading System: A to F
Legal Writing/Methods Course Requirements: Writing classes taken every semester

STUDENT INFORMATION

Enrollment of Law School: 371
% Male/Female: 61/39
% Full Time: 68
% Full Time That Are International: 0
% Minority: 37

EXPENSES/FINANCIAL AID

Annual Tuition (Residents/Nonresidents): $2,071/$10,998
Room and Board (On/Off Campus): $4,200/$6,850
Books and Supplies: $1,250
Average Loan: $8,500
% Receiving Some Sort of Aid: 73
Average Debt: $25,500

ADMISSIONS INFORMATION

Application Fee: $30
Regular Application Deadline: Rolling
Regular Notification: Rolling
LSDAS Accepted? No
Average GPA: 3.0
Range of GPA: 2.8–3.3
Average LSAT: 149
Range of LSAT: 146–152
Transfer Students Accepted? Yes
Other Schools to Which Students Applied: University of North Carolina, Campbell University, Wake Forest University, Howard University, Duke University, University of South Carolina, Texas Southern University, Emory University
Other Admissions Factors Considered: The school reviews the complete application.
Number of Applications Received: 1,058
Number of Applicants Accepted: 222
Number of Applicants Enrolled: 135

INTERNATIONAL STUDENTS

TOEFL Required of International Students? Yes

EMPLOYMENT INFORMATION

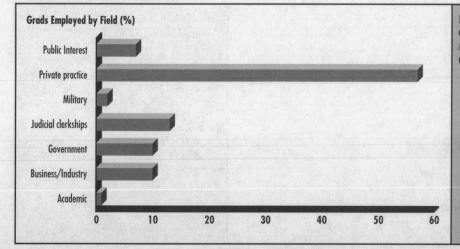

Prominent Alumni: Michael Easley, North Carolina attorney general; Willie Gary, attorney (Florida); Judge Clifton Johnson (retired), North Carolina Court of Appeal

NORTHEASTERN UNIVERSITY
School of Law

Admissions Contact: Assistant Dean and Director of Admissions, Paul D. Bauer
400 Huntington Avenue, Boston, MA 02115
Admissions Phone: 617-373-2395 • Admissions Fax: 617-373-8865
Admissions E-mail: lawadmissions@nunet.neu.edu • Web Address: www.slaw.neu.edu

INSTITUTIONAL INFORMATION

Public/Private: Private
Environment: Urban
Academic Calendar: Quarter
Schedule: Full time only
Student/Faculty Ratio: 21:1
Total Faculty: 29
% Part Time: 46
% Female: 52
% Minority: 28

PROGRAMS

Academic Specialties: Northeastern University School of Law offers the only Cooperative Legal Education Program in the country. Specializations include Environmental Law, Intellectual Property, Employment Law, etc. The school offers 6 clinical programs for students interested in hands-on experience during their academic quarters: Certiorari/Criminal Appeals, Criminal Advocacy, Domestic Violence, Poverty Law and Practice, Prisoners' Rights, and Tobacco Control. The faculty combine energetic and innovative teaching, participation in scholarly debate on pressing contemporary issues of law and social policy, and active involvement in the local, national, and international communities.
Combined Degrees Offered: JD/MBA (45 months), JD/MBA/MS Accountancy (42 months)
Clinical Program Required? No
Clinical Programs: The law school offers 6 upper-level offerings in clinical legal education: Certiorari/Criminal Appeals, Criminal Advocacy, Domestic Violence, Poverty Law and Practice, Prisoner's Rights, and Tobacco Control Clinic.

Grading System: Students receive narrative evaluations in each academic course in lieu of letter or number grades. Students also receive narrative evaluations for each of their 4 required co-op placements. All evaluations become part of the student's permanent transcript.
Legal Writing/Methods Course Requirements: Legal Practice is a six-month 2 quarter required first-year writing and research course.

STUDENT INFORMATION

Enrollment of Law School: 614
% Male/Female: 34/66
% Full Time: 100
% Full Time That Are International: 2
% Minority: 27
Average Age of Entering Class: 25

RESEARCH FACILITIES

Computers/Workstations Available: 50

EXPENSES/FINANCIAL AID

Annual Tuition: $24,585
Room and Board (On/Off Campus): $9,855/$11,700
Books and Supplies: $1,000
Financial Aid Application Deadline: 3/1
% Receiving Some Sort of Aid: 83
Average Debt: $63,000

ADMISSIONS INFORMATION

Application Fee: $65
Regular Application Deadline: 3/1
Regular Notification: 4/15
LSDAS Accepted? Yes
Average GPA: 3.2
Range of GPA: 2.9–3.4
Average LSAT: 157
Range of LSAT: 153–160
Transfer Students Accepted? Yes
Other Schools to Which Students Applied: Boston College, Boston University, Suffolk University, Fordham University, New England School of Law, American University, Georgetown University, New York University
Other Admissions Factors Considered: The admissions committee is particularly interested in candidates who, in addition to possessing solid academic credentials, have a significant amount of work and/or community service experience. The diversity of applicants background is also important.
Number of Applications Received: 1,922
Number of Applicants Accepted: 691
Number of Applicants Enrolled: 195

INTERNATIONAL STUDENTS

TOEFL Required of International Students? Yes

EMPLOYMENT INFORMATION

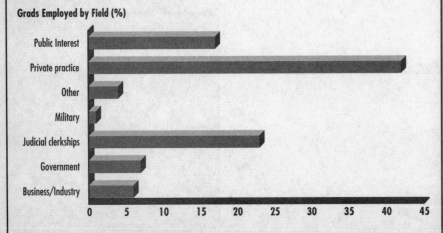

Grads Employed by Field (%)

Rate of Placement: 94%
Average Starting Salary: $46,488
Employers Who Frequently Hire Grads: Mintz, Levin, Cohen, Ferris, Glovsky & Popeo, PC; Massachusetts Superior Court; New Hampshire Public Defenders Office; Testa, Hurwitz & Thibeault, PC; Committee for Public Counsel Services
Prominent Alumni: Hon. Janet Bond Arterton, U.S. District Court justice for the District of Connecticut; Andrew Ketterer, attorney general for the State of Maine; Dana Fabe, Supreme Court of Alaska

NORTHERN ILLINOIS UNIVERSITY
College of Law

Admissions Contact: Director of Admissions and Financial Aid, Judith L. Malen
Swen Parson Hall, Room 276, DeKalb, IL 60115-2890
Admissions Phone: 815-753-8595 • Admissions Fax: 815-753-4501
Admissions E-mail: lawadm@niu.edu • Web Address: www.niu.edu/col

INSTITUTIONAL INFORMATION

Public/Private: Public
Environment: Suburban
Academic Calendar: Semester
Schedule: Full time only
Student/Faculty Ratio: 12:1
Total Faculty: 34%
% Part Time: 35
Female: 29
% Minority: 18

PROGRAMS

Academic Specialties: Public Interest and Corporate Law, Mediation and Alternative Dispute Resolution Lawyering Skills, Trial Advocacy
Combined Degrees Offered: JD/MBA (4 years) is the formal program, though other joint degrees have and can be done by any student so requesting, including JD/MPA, JD/EdD.
Clinical Program Required? No
Clinical Programs: Criminal and Civil Externship Programs, Judicial Externship
Grading System: Letter grades with a 4.0 to 0.0 numerical grading scale
Legal Writing/Methods Course Requirements: Full year, 4 credits

STUDENT INFORMATION

Enrollment of Law School: 281
% Male/Female: 59/41
% Full Time: 90
% Full Time That Are International: 0
% Minority: 24
Average Age of Entering Class: 27

RESEARCH FACILITIES

Computers/Workstations Available: 600
School-Supported Research Centers: Westlaw/Dow Jones and Nexis/Lexis; through interlibrary loan, students have access to library resources nationwide and abroad. Internet access also available.

EXPENSES/FINANCIAL AID

Annual Tuition (Residents/Nonresidents): $5,877/$11,774
Room and Board (On/Off Campus): $4,744/$5,644
Books and Supplies: $1,000
Financial Aid Application Deadline: 3/1
Average Grant: $2,944
Average Loan: $12,500
% of Aid That Is Merit-Based: 7
% Receiving Some Sort of Aid: 71
Average Total Aid Package: $15,300

ADMISSIONS INFORMATION

Application Fee: $40
Regular Application Deadline: Rolling
Regular Notification: Rolling
LSDAS Accepted? Yes
Average GPA: 3.1
Range of GPA: 2.7–3.5
Average LSAT: 153
Range of LSAT: 150–156
Transfer Students Accepted? Yes
Other Schools to Which Students Applied: John Marshall Law School, Southern Illinois University, Loyola University Chicago, Illinois Institute of Technology, University of Illinois, University of Iowa, University of Wisconsin, Marquette University
Other Admissions Factors Considered: Personal statement, letters of recommendation, professional experience, good citizenship, integrity
Number of Applications Received: 834
Number of Applicants Accepted: 46
Number of Applicants Enrolled: 99

INTERNATIONAL STUDENTS

TOEFL Required of International Students? Yes
Minimum TOEFL: 600

EMPLOYMENT INFORMATION

Rate of Placement: 93%
Employers Who Frequently Hire Grads: State's attorneys, public defenders, Illinois attorney general, private medium-size firms
Prominent Alumni: Michael Glawe, board of directors, United Airlines; Brian McGough, VP, Chicago Capital Markets; Kathleen Zellner, Criminal Attorney

NORTHERN KENTUCKY UNIVERSITY
Salmon P. Chase College of Law

Admissions Contact: Admissions Specialist, Gina Bray
Nunn Hall, Room 539, Highland Heights, KY 41099
Admissions Phone: 606-572-6476 • Admissions Fax: 606-572-6081
Admissions E-mail: brayg@nku.edu • Web Address: www.nku.edu

INSTITUTIONAL INFORMATION

Public/Private: Public
Environment: Urban
Academic Calendar: Semester
Schedule: Full time or part time
Student/Faculty Ratio: 26:1
Total Faculty: 93
% Part Time: 59
% Female: 26
% Minority: 1

PROGRAMS

Advanced Degrees Offered: None
Combined Degrees Offered: JD/MBA (3 years full time, 4 years part time)
Clinical Program Required? No
Grading System: Letter system on a 4.3 scale with designations for Incomplete, Satisfactory, Unsatisfactory, Pass, Credit, No Credit, Withdrew, and Audit
Legal Writing/Methods Course Requirements: 2 semesters

STUDENT INFORMATION

Enrollment of Law School: 358
% Male/Female: 57/43
% Full Time: 52
% Full Time That Are International: 0
% Minority: 3%
Average Age of Entering Class: 28

RESEARCH FACILITIES

Computers/Workstations Available: 41
Computers Labs: 1
Campuswide Network? Yes
School-Supported Research Centers: Department of Local Government in Frankfort; Kentucky League of Cities; Kentucky Association of Counties; North Kentucky Area Development District; Hamilton County Solicitors

EXPENSES/FINANCIAL AID

Annual Tuition (Residents/Nonresidents): $5,976/$15,888
Room and Board (On/Off Campus): $5,174/$5,400
Books and Supplies: $500
Financial Aid Application Deadline: 4/1
Average Grant: $5,630
Average Loan: $15,840
Average Total Aid Package: $17,544
Average Debt: $65,244

ADMISSIONS INFORMATION

Application Fee: $30
Regular Application Deadline: 3/1
Regular Notification: Rolling
LSDAS Accepted? Yes
Average GPA: 3.2
Range of GPA: 2.7–3.7
Average LSAT: 153
Range of LSAT: 150–157
Transfer Students Accepted? Yes
Other Schools to Which Students Applied: University of Kentucky, University of Louisville, University of Cincinnati, University of Dayton, Ohio State University, University of Akron, Capital University, University of Toledo
Other Admissions Factors Considered: Undergraduate institution, undergraduate major, work experience, writing ability
Number of Applications Received: 620
Number of Applicants Accepted: 275
Number of Applicants Enrolled: 111

EMPLOYMENT INFORMATION

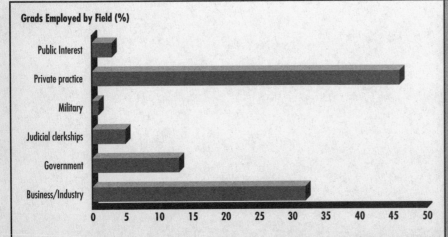

Grads Employed by Field (%)

Public Interest
Private practice
Military
Judicial clerkships
Government
Business/Industry

0 5 10 15 20 25 30 35 40 45 50

Rate of Placement: 93%
Average Starting Salary: $42,875
Employers Who Frequently Hire Grads: Commonwealth of Kentucky, Hamilton County Prosecutor, Lexis/Nexis and Cinergy Corp.
Prominent Alumni: Dr. Jacobus C. Rasser, vice president and general counsel, Patent P&G Worldwide; Steve Chabot, U.S congressman from Ohio; Robert P. Ruwe, federal judge, tax court, Washington, D.C.; Hon. Jack Sherman, magistrate judge, United States District Court
State for Bar Exam: KY
Number Taking Bar Exam: 67
Pass Rate for First-Time Bar: 83%

NORTHWESTERN UNIVERSITY
School of Law

Admissions Contact: Assistant Dean of Admissions and Financial Aid, Donald L. Rebstock
357 East Chicago Avenue, Chicago, IL 60611
Admissions Phone: 312-503-8465 • Admissions Fax: 312-503-0178
Admissions E-mail: nulawadm@nwu.edu • Web Address: www.law.nwu.edu

INSTITUTIONAL INFORMATION

Public/Private: Private
Environment: Urban
Academic Calendar: Semester
Schedule: Full time only
Student/Faculty Ratio: 11:1
Total Faculty: 210
% Part Time: 68
% Female: 25
% Minority: 5

PROGRAMS

Academic Specialties: Civil Rights, Constitutional Law, Contracts, Corporate Law, Criminal Law, Dispute Resolution, Employment/Labor Law, Environmental Law, Feminist Legal Theory, Health Law, International Private Law, International Human Rights, Intellectual Property, Jury Selection/Psychology, Law and Economics, Legal History, Public Interest, Torts, Trial Advocacy
Advanced Degrees Offered: JD (3 years), LLM (1 year), SJD (2 years)
Combined Degrees Offered: JD/MBA (3 years), JD/PhD (5 years), JD/MA (4 years), JD/MSJ (4 years), LLM/Certificate in Management (1 year)
Clinical Program Required? No
Grading System: Letter grades A to F including plus and minus
Legal Writing/Methods Course Requirements: 2 semesters of legal writing required during the first year

STUDENT INFORMATION

Enrollment of Law School: 650
% Male/Female: 50/50
% Full Time: 100
% Full Time That Are International: 2
% Minority: 30
Average Age of Entering Class: 25

RESEARCH FACILITIES

Computers/Workstations Available: 25
Computer Labs: 3
Campuswide Network? Yes
School-Supported Research Centers: Center for Urban Affairs and Policy Research, Anneaberg Washington Program in Communications Policy Studies, Senior Research Program, Center for Health Policy Research, Bartlett Center for Trial Strategy

EXPENSES/FINANCIAL AID

Annual Tuition: $26,850
Room and Board: $10,214
Books and Supplies: $6,038
Financial Aid Application Deadline: 3/15
Average Grant: $11,000
Average Loan: $24,000
% of Aid That Is Merit-Based: 30
% Receiving Some Sort of Aid: 75
Average Total Aid Package: $35,000
Average Debt: $67,000

ADMISSIONS INFORMATION

Application Fee: $80
Regular Application Deadline: 2/15
Regular Notification: Rolling
LSDAS Accepted? Yes
Average GPA: 3.5
Range of GPA: 3.3–3.7
Average LSAT: 167
Range of LSAT: 164–168
Transfer Students Accepted? Yes
Other Schools to Which Students Applied: Harvard University, University of Chicago, Georgetown University, University of Michigan, Loyola University Chicago, Columbia University, Yale University, New York University
Other Admissions Factors Considered: Stated interest in and knowledge of us
Number of Applications Received: 4,103
Number of Applicants Accepted: 744
Number of Applicants Enrolled: 205

EMPLOYMENT INFORMATION

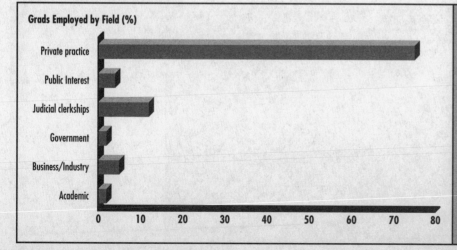

Grads Employed by Field (%)

Rate of Placement: 99%
Average Starting Salary: $90,000
Employers Who Frequently Hire Grads: Sidley and Austin; Kirkland and Ellis; Latham and Watkins; Jones, Day, Reavis and Pogue; Katten, Muchin and Zavis; Morrison and Foerster; Winston and Strawn; Baker and McKenzie; Mayer, Brown and Platt; Schiff, Iturdin and Waite; Holleb and Coff
Prominent Alumni: John Paul Stevens, Associate Supreme Court justice; Arthur Goldberg, Associate Supreme Court justice Newton Minnow, former chairman of the FCC

NORTHWESTERN UNIVERSITY

Founded in 1859, Northwestern University School of Law is a nationally oriented private institution dedicated to advancing the understanding of law and to producing graduates prepared to excel in a rapidly changing world. Legal education at Northwestern uniquely blends a rigorous intellectual environment within a collegial and supportive community. With one of the lowest student/faculty ratios in the country, Northwestern provides students with unusually close contact with full-time professors who are noted scholars

Northwestern's lakefront location in the heart of downtown Chicago provides a truly spectacular setting in which to study law. The School of Law's proximity to courts, commerce, and public interest groups allows students to experience the law in operation.

CURRICULUM

Northwestern offers a curriculum designed to develop fundamental legal skills and an understanding of the contexts in which the law operates. Northwestern's broad and flexible curriculum gives students the opportunity to plan a general course of study or to concentrate in particular areas of legal interest. Northwestern offers concentrations in Business Associations (Corporate Law), Civil Litigation and Dispute Resolution, Health Law, and International Law. A concentration in Law and Social Policy is currently being considered by the faculty.

The School of Law's size enables students to have one-on-one relationships with professors. Over half of the required first-year courses are taught in sections of 50 students or less. Thereafter, students make take courses or seminars in new areas of the law or in student-selected subjects. The Senior Research Program enables third-year students to do individual research under the supervision of a professor, using library, field, and interdisciplinary research methods.

Northwestern's nationally recognized clinical program enables students not only to obtain practical experience but also to understand and challenge the fairness of legal institutions. In the Bluhm Legal Clinic, attorneys and students handle both civil and criminal cases and are intensively involved in juvenile court work. The Small Business Opportunity Clinic brings together students from the Law School and the Kellogg Graduate School of Management to provide assistance to entrepreneurs, start-up companies, and not-for-profit organizations. The recently established Center for International Human Rights allows students to work alongside faculty, staff, volunteer lawyers, and visiting fellows to carry out the activities of the center, which include working on field missions, providing technical assistance to international governments and nongovernmental organizations, drafting *amicus curiae* briefs, and litigating before international courts and other bodies.

SPECIAL PROGRAMS

Northwestern offers a combined program in law and business with The University's J. L. Kellogg Graduate School of Management in which students earn both a JD and a MBA degree in three years. Since the program utilizes a summer session, it is also faster than the four years typically found at other universities. Through the JD/MBA program, students receive a thorough grounding in management and the law. They complete a core curriculum with elective course work in areas such as Enterpreneurship, Finance, International Business Law, Real Estate, and Tax Law. Students may also enroll in a joint JD/PhD program with the law school and one of Northwestern's graduate schools.

The Graduate and International Program awards a masters of law (LLM) degree to outstanding graduates of foreign law schools who pursue a one-year program of advanced study to expand their knowledge of American law and legal processes as well as international law. The Graduate Program in Law and Business, a joint program of the law school and the J. L. Kellogg Graduate School of Management, offers students educated outside the United States an opportunity to study both business law and management techniques. Graduates of this 12-month program are awarded an LLM degree from the law school and a certificate in management from Kellogg.

School of Law

ADMISSION

The admissions process at Northwestern is highly selective. Northwestern seeks a student body diverse in experience, background, and perspective. Northwestern looks at the total applicant—no one element is determinative. Each application is reviewed regardless of the LSAT score or the GPA.

In addition to academic prowess and achievement, Northwestern seeks students with strong interpersonal skills, ambition, and life experience, and substantial maturity. Northwestern maintains an active interviewing program, both on campus and through its alumni throughout the nation and world. Applicants are encouraged to provide information about their personal background and special characteristics they deem pertinent.

Entering Class Profile (2000–2001)	
TOTAL APPLICANTS	4,214
APPLICANTS INTERVIEWED	2,100
ENROLLING STUDENTS	205
LSAT PERFORMANCE	
Median Score	167
Middle 50%	163–168
UNDERGRADUATE RECORD	
Median GPA	3.6
Middle 50%	3.3–3.7
GEOGRAPHIC DISTRIBUTION	
Midwest	33%
Northeast	25%
West	19%
South	19%
FEMALE	50%
MINORITY	33%
WORK EXPERIENCE	
0 Years	23%
1–2 Years	36%
>2 Years	41%

STUDENT ACTIVITIES

Northwestern law students take an intense and energetic interest in their community and their education. Several scholarly journals are available for research, writing, and editing, including the *Northwestern University Law Review*, *Journal of Criminal Law and Criminology*, and *Northwestern Journal of International Law & Business*.

Over 30 student-run organizations enrich the community, ranging from advocacy groups to those focused on careers to social organizations. A weekly student newspaper and an active student-focused website also inform and enliven the community.

CAREER SERVICES

The full-time staff of the Center for Career Strategy and Advancement works actively to assist students in obtaining summer and permanent employment and in developing strategies to benefit them over their long-term careers. The Center schedules student interviews with employers and offers training workshops, individual counseling, and other services to help students pursue their professional goals. In the fall of 2000, over 300 employers came to Northwestern, 30 percent from the Northeast, 24 percent from the West, 30 percent from the Midwest, and 16 percent from the South. Six months after graduation, 99 percent of the class of 1999 was employed, 76 percent in private practice, 19 percent in public service or government, and 5 percent in business.

Admissions Contact: Assistant Dean of Admissions and Financial Aid, Donald L. Rebstock,
357 East Chicago Avenue, Chicago, IL 60611
Admissions Phone: 312-503-8465 • Admissions Fax: 312-503-0178
Admissions E-mail: nulawadm@nwu.edu • Web Address: www.law.nwu.edu

NOVA SOUTHEASTERN UNIVERSITY
Shepard Broad Law Center

Admissions Contact: Director of Admissions, Nancy Kelly Sanguigni
3305 College Avenue, Fort Lauderdale, FL 33314
Admissions Phone: 954-452-6115 • Admissions Fax: 954-452-6109
Admissions E-mail: admission@nsu.law.nova.edu • Web Address: www.nsulaw.nova.edu

INSTITUTIONAL INFORMATION

Public/Private: Private
Environment: Urban
Academic Calendar: Semester
Schedule: Full time or part time
Student/Faculty Ratio: 16:1
Total Faculty: 93
% Part Time: 48
% Female: 32
% Minority: 13

PROGRAMS

Clinical Program Required? No

STUDENT INFORMATION

Enrollment of Law School: 953
% Male/Female: 54/46
% Full Time: 82
% Full Time That Are International: 3
% Minority: 28
Average Age of Entering Class: 27

RESEARCH FACILITIES

School-Supported Research Centers: Environmental and Land Use Law Center, Inter American Center for Human Rights

EXPENSES/FINANCIAL AID

Annual Tuition: $19,770
Room and Board (On/Off Campus): $12,668/$13,435
Books and Supplies: $1,200
Average Grant: $6,166
Average Loan: $20,882
% of Aid That Is Merit-Based: 6
% Receiving Some Sort of Aid: 90
Average Total Aid Package: $25,739
Average Debt: $78,889
Fees Per Credit: $820

ADMISSIONS INFORMATION

Regular Application Deadline: 2/15
Regular Notification: March–April
LSDAS Accepted? Yes
Average GPA: 2.9
Range of GPA: 2.5–3.1
Average LSAT: 147
Range of LSAT: 143–151
Transfer Students Accepted? Yes
Other Schools to Which Students Applied: University of Miami, St. Thomas University, Florida State University, University of Florida, Stetson University, Georgia State University, New York Law School, Emory University
Other Admissions Factors Considered: Age; trend of grades; hardships overcome; distinctive cultural point of view or life; socioeconomic, educational or personal experiences; other factors indicating motivation and discipline

EMPLOYMENT INFORMATION

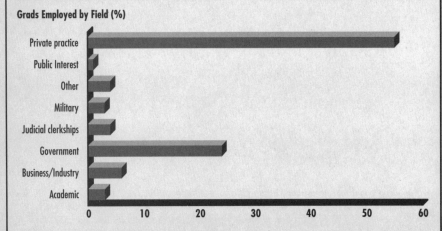

Rate of Placement: 86%
Average Starting Salary: $39,354
Employers Who Frequently Hire Grads: Private law firms, local and state agencies, State Attorney's Office, Public Defender's Office
Prominent Alumni: Hon. Rex Ford, U.S. Immigration judge; Hon. John Rodstrom, chair, Broward County Commission; Hon. Ilene Lieberman, Broward County commissioner

OHIO NORTHERN UNIVERSITY
Claude W. Pettit College of Law

Admissions Contact: Assistant Director of Law Admissions, Grant Keener
Ohio Northern University College of Law, Ada, OH 45810-1599
Admissions Phone: 419-772-2211 • Admissions Fax: 419-772-1487
Admissions E-mail: g-keener@onu.edu • Web Address: www.law.onu.edu

INSTITUTIONAL INFORMATION

Public/Private: Private
Affiliation: Methodist
Environment: Suburban
Academic Calendar: Semester
Schedule: Full time only
Student/Faculty Ratio: 14:1
Total Faculty: 19
% Part Time: 30
% Female: 32
% Minority: 0

PROGRAMS

Clinical Program Required? Yes
Legal Writing/Methods Course Requirements:
All first year students are required to take a year-long course in Legal Research and Writing. Throughout the course, students are required to complete a number of research and drafting assignments, including client memos, motions, discovery materials, an appellate brief, and an oral argument based on the appellate brief.

STUDENT INFORMATION

Enrollment of Law School: 283
% Male/Female: 60/40
% Full Time: 100
% Full Time That Are International: 1
% Minority: 15
Average Age of Entering Class: 26

RESEARCH FACILITIES

Computers/Workstations Available: 450
Computer Labs: 20
Campuswide Network? Yes
School-Supported Research Centers: Lexis-Nexis and Westlaw

EXPENSES/FINANCIAL AID

Annual Tuition: $18,980
Room and Board: $5,650
Books and Supplies: $900
Average Grant: $8,500
Average Loan: $22,270
% of Aid That Is Merit-Based: 20
% Receiving Some Sort of Aid: 95
Average Total Aid Package: $26,810
Average Debt: $65,000

ADMISSIONS INFORMATION

Application Fee: $40
Regular Application Deadline: Rolling
Regular Notification: Rolling
LSDAS Accepted? Yes
Average GPA: 3.0
Range of GPA: 2.6–3.3
Average LSAT: 150
Range of LSAT: 147–155
Transfer Students Accepted? Yes
Other Schools to Which Students Applied:
Capital University, Ohio State University, University of Dayton, University of Toledo, Northern Kentucky University, University of Akron, University of Pittsburgh, University of Cincinnati
Other Admissions Factors Considered: Quality of undergraduate/graduate school(s), type of degree(s) earned, diversity of background and heritage, transcript, degree interpretation for international students
Number of Applications Received: 1,106
Number of Applicants Accepted: 584
Number of Applicants Enrolled: 108

EMPLOYMENT INFORMATION

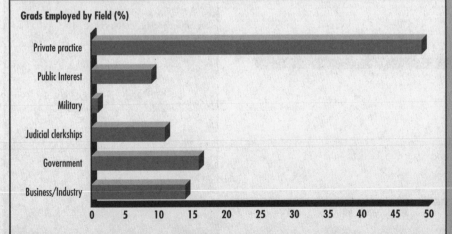

Grads Employed by Field (%)

Rate of Placement: 78%
Average Starting Salary: $35,000
Prominent Alumni: Anthony J. Celebrezze, Sr., retired judge of 6th Circuit U.S. Court of Appeals; R. Micheal Dewine, U.S. Senator

OHIO STATE UNIVERSITY
College of Law

Admissions Contact: Assistant Dean, Kathy Northern
55 West 12th Avenue, Columbus, OH 43210
Admissions Phone: 614-292-8810 • Admissions Fax: 614-292-1492
Admissions E-mail: lawadmin@osu.edu • Web Address: www.osu.edu/units/law

INSTITUTIONAL INFORMATION

Public/Private: Public
Environment: Urban
Academic Calendar: Semester
Schedule: Full time only
Student/Faculty Ratio: 14:1
Total Faculty: 41
% Female: 32
% Minority: 15

PROGRAMS

Clinical Program Required? No

STUDENT INFORMATION

Enrollment of Law School: 640
% Male/Female: 52/48
% Full Time: 99
% Minority: 18
Average Age of Entering Class: 24

RESEARCH FACILITIES

Computers/Workstations Available: 75

EXPENSES/FINANCIAL AID

Annual Tuition (Residents/Nonresidents):
$8,424/$18,288
Room and Board: $8,184
Books and Supplies: $1,588
Financial Aid Application Deadline: 3/1
Average Grant: $2,135
% of Aid That Is Merit-Based: 2
% Receiving Some Sort of Aid: 70
Average Debt: $40,000

ADMISSIONS INFORMATION

Application Fee: $30
Regular Application Deadline: 3/15
Regular Notification: Rolling
LSDAS Accepted? Yes
Average GPA: 3.6
Range of GPA: 3.3–3.8
Average LSAT: 157
Range of LSAT: 153–160
Transfer Students Accepted? Yes
Other Schools to Which Students Applied: Case Western Reserve University, University of Cincinnati, University of Michigan, Georgetown University, George Washington University, University of Wisconsin, University of Dayton, Harvard University
Other Admissions Factors Considered: Resume, personal statement
Number of Applications Received: 1,482
Number of Applicants Accepted: 583
Number of Applicants Enrolled: 215

INTERNATIONAL STUDENTS

TOEFL Required of International Students? Yes
Minimum TOEFL: 600

EMPLOYMENT INFORMATION

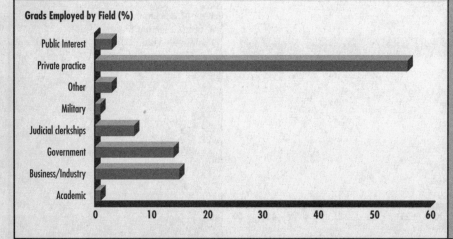

Grads Employed by Field (%)

Rate of Placement: 96%
Average Starting Salary: $50,419
Prominent Alumni: Howard Metzenbaum, U.S. senator; George Voinovich, U.S. senator; Thomas Moyer, chief justice, Ohio Supreme Court; Robert Duncan, former federal district court judge; Erin Moriarty, *CBS News* correspondent

OKLAHOMA CITY UNIVERSITY

School of Law

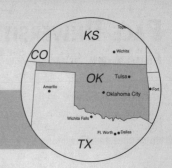

Admissions Contact: Assistant Dean for Admissions, Gary Mercer
PO Box 61310, Oklahoma City, OK 73146-1310
Admissions Phone: 405-521-5354 • Admissions Fax: 405-521-5802
Admissions E-mail: ladmissions@frodo.okcu.edu • Web Address: www.okcu.edu/law

INSTITUTIONAL INFORMATION

Public/Private: Private
Affiliation: United Methodist
Environment: Metropolis
Academic Calendar: Semester
Schedule: Full time or part time
Student/Faculty Ratio: 17:1
Total Faculty: 45
% Part Time: 25
% Female: 26
% Minority: 13

PROGRAMS

Clinical Program Required? No

STUDENT INFORMATION

Enrollment of Law School: 534
% Male/Female: 62/38
% Full Time: 71
% Full Time That Are International: 1
% Minority: 18
Average Age of Entering Class: 27

RESEARCH FACILITIES

School-Supported Research Centers: All state and county libraries, and libraries at other universities in the area

EXPENSES/FINANCIAL AID

Annual Tuition: $15,120
Room and Board (On/Off Campus):
$6,509/$8,791
Books and Supplies: $750
Average Grant: $4,297
Average Loan: $19,357
% of Aid That Is Merit-Based: 5
% Receiving Some Sort of Aid: 88
Average Total Aid Package: $20,167
Average Debt: $42,042
Fees Per Credit: $504

ADMISSIONS INFORMATION

Application Fee: $35
Regular Application Deadline: Rolling
Regular Notification: Rolling
LSDAS Accepted? Yes
Average GPA: 2.9
Range of GPA: 2.5–4.0
Average LSAT: 147
Range of LSAT: 143–165
Transfer Students Accepted? Yes
Other Schools to Which Students Applied: University of Oklahoma, University of Tulsa, South Texas College of Law, Texas Tech University, St. Mary's University, University of Texas, University of Houston, Southern Methodist University
Other Admissions Factors Considered: We try to identify the level of motivation, tenacity, and integrity of each applicant through personal statements and letters of recommendation.
Number of Applications Received: 893
Number of Applicants Accepted: 616
Number of Applicants Enrolled: 191

INTERNATIONAL STUDENTS

TOEFL Required of International Students? Yes
Minimum TOEFL: 560

EMPLOYMENT INFORMATION

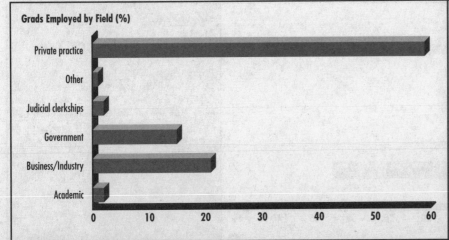

Rate of Placement: 78%
Average Starting Salary: $35,930
Employers Who Frequently Hire Grads: Small to medium-size law firms, government agencies
Prominent Alumni: Mickey Edwards, lecturer in public policy, Kennedy School of Government, Harvard University; former U.S. congressman and House Republican leader; Hon. Yvonnne Kauger, chief justice, Oklahoma Supreme Court; Emmanuel Edem, prominent trial attorney; Robert Ravitz, public defender, Oklahoma County; Tom Quinn, vice president and tax counsel, New England Life Insurance Company; Dr. Rita Raman, professor of pediatrics, fellow, United States Food and Drug Administration

PACE UNIVERSITY
Pace Law School

Admissions Contact: Assistant Dean and Director of Admissions, Cathy Alexander
78 North Broadway, White Plains, NY 10603
Admissions Phone: 914-422-4210 • Admissions Fax: 914-422-4010
Admissions E-mail: admissions@law.pace.edu • Web Address: www.law.pace.edu

INSTITUTIONAL INFORMATION

Public/Private: Private
Environment: Urban/suburban
Academic Calendar: Semester
Schedule: Full time or part time
Student/Faculty Ratio: 16:1
Total Faculty: 75
% Part Time: 52
% Female: 37
% Minority: 5

PROGRAMS

Advanced Degrees Offered: SJD Environmental Law (1 year), LLM Environmental Law (1–2 years), LLM Comparative Legal Studies (1 year)
Clinical Program Required? No
Legal Writing/Methods Course Requirements: Criminal Law Analysis and Writing I and II. This course is an integrated, 2-semester, 6-credit offering that explores the substantive aspects of criminal law through legal analysis and writing. Students learn about the criminalization decision, goals of punishment, elements of criminal conduct, and defenses to criminal charges by reading statutes and using and distinguishing cases. Students also learn about legal research and the legislative process, and complete numerous writing exercises in the area of criminal law. This course cumulates in writing an appellate brief and arguing before a moot court.

STUDENT INFORMATION

Enrollment of Law School: 752
% Male/Female: 66/34
% Full Time: 60
% Minority: 25
Average Age of Entering Class: 27

RESEARCH FACILITIES

Computers/Workstations Available: 80
School-Supported Research Centers: All computer facilities and libraries of Pace University—on campuses in New York City, downtown White Plains, and Pleasantville—are accessible to Pace law students. In addition, the Law Library is a member of a number library consortia that allow our students and faculty to use all the libraries of all the academic institutions in Westchester County and most of the law libraries in the New York area.

EXPENSES/FINANCIAL AID

Annual Tuition: $24,000
Room and Board (On/Off Campus): $9,600/$10,200
Books and Supplies: $1,000
Financial Aid Application Deadline: 2/1
Average Grant: $7,916
Average Loan: $21,060
% of Aid That Is Merit-Based: 61
% Receiving Some Sort of Aid: 81
Average Total Aid Package: $21,500
Average Debt: $66,330
Fees Per Credit: $730

ADMISSIONS INFORMATION

Application Fee: $55
Regular Application Deadline: 2/15
Regular Notification: Rolling
LSDAS Accepted? Yes
Average GPA: 3.1
Range of GPA: 2.9–3.4
Average LSAT: 152
Range of LSAT: 148–155
Transfer Students Accepted? Yes
Other Schools to Which Students Applied: Fordham University, Seton Hall University, New York Law School, St. John's University, Brooklyn Law School, Hofstra University, Touro College
Other Admissions Factors Considered: Undergraduate course work, community service
Number of Applications Received: 1,694
Number of Applicants Accepted: 885
Number of Applicants Enrolled: 261

INTERNATIONAL STUDENTS

TOEFL Required of International Students? Yes
Minimum TOEFL: 600

EMPLOYMENT INFORMATION

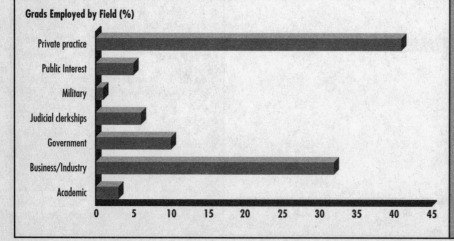

Grads Employed by Field (%)

Rate of Placement: 86%
Average Starting Salary: $60,356
Employers Who Frequently Hire Grads: Law firms and District Attorney's Offices
Prominent Alumni: Hon. Terry J. Ruderman, judge, New York State Claims Court; John P. Cahill, commissioner, New York State Department of Environmental Conservation; Michael Finnegan, managing director of JP Morgan Securities; Hon. Bruce Cozzens, justice of Supreme Court of the State of New York

PENNSYLVANIA STATE UNIVERSITY

The Dickinson School of Law

Admissions Contact: Director of Law Admissions, Barbara W. Guillaume
150 South College Street, Carlisle, PA 17013
Admissions Phone: 717-240-5207 • Admissions Fax: 717-241-3503
Admissions E-mail: dsladmit@psu.edu • Web Address: www.dsl.edu

INSTITUTIONAL INFORMATION

Public/Private: Public
Environment: Suburban
Schedule: Full time only
Student/Faculty Ratio: 15:1
Total Faculty: 92
% Part Time: 62
% Female: 23
% Minority: 2

PROGRAMS

Advanced Degrees Offered: JD (3 years), LLM Comparative Law (1 year)
Clinical Program Required? No
Clinical Programs: Family Law; Disability Law; Art, Sports, and Entertainment Law; externships in judges' chambers, District Attorney's and Public Defender's Offices, government agencies, legal services offices
Grading System: Course grades reported and recorded on numerical basis: Distinguished (90 and above), Excellent (89–85), Good (84–75), Qualified (74–70), Poor (69–65), Failing (below 65)
Legal Writing/Methods Course Requirements: First two semesters involve small-group instruction on legal research and prescriptive and persuasive writing. Third semester centers on appellate advocacy, written and oral.

STUDENT INFORMATION

Enrollment of Law School: 528
% Male/Female: 58/42
% Full Time: 99
% Full Time That Are International: 1
% Minority: 7
Average Age of Entering Class: 25

RESEARCH FACILITIES

Computers/Workstations Available: 80
School-Supported Research Centers: Agricultural Law Center

EXPENSES/FINANCIAL AID

Annual Tuition: $15,850
Room and Board (On/Off Campus): $6,200/ $7,700
Books and Supplies: $800
Financial Aid Application Deadline: 2/15
Average Grant: $5,986
Average Loan: $19,480
% of Aid That Is Merit-Based: 10
% Receiving Some Sort of Aid: 85
Average Total Aid Package: $20,430
Average Debt: $55,894
Fees Per Credit: $730

ADMISSIONS INFORMATION

Application Fee: $50
Regular Application Deadline: 3/1
Regular Notification: Rolling
LSDAS Accepted? Yes
Average GPA: 3.2
Range of GPA: 2.9–3.5
Average LSAT: 153
Range of LSAT: 150–155
Transfer Students Accepted? Yes
Other Schools to Which Students Applied: University of Pittsburgh, Villanova University, Temple University, Widener University, American University
Other Admissions Factors Considered: Evidence of maturity, leadership, and initiative
Number of Applications Received: 1,320
Number of Applicants Accepted: 691
Number of Applicants Enrolled: 188

EMPLOYMENT INFORMATION

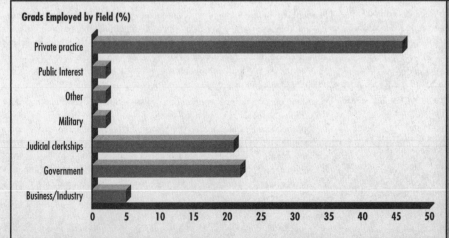

Grads Employed by Field (%)

Rate of Placement: 94%
Average Starting Salary: $39,049
Employers Who Frequently Hire Grads: Dickinson graduates are hired by a variety of employers each year including leading law firms, smaller firms, federal and state judges, and other entities.
Prominent Alumni: Tom Ridge, governor of Pennsylvania; Rick Santorum, U.S. senator; Helen S. Balick, recently retired U.S. bankruptcy judge, Delaware; H. Jesse Arnelle, co-founder of nation's largest minority-owned law firm

PEPPERDINE UNIVERSITY

THE UNIVERSITY AT A GLANCE

Pepperdine University is an independent, medium-size university with a reputation for academic and athletic excellence. In addition to the School of Law, the University includes the highly selective undergraduate Seaver College, the Graziadio School of Business and Management, the Graduate School of Education and Psychology, and the School of Public Policy.

The School of Law is fully approved by the American Bar Association and holds membership in the Association of American Law Schools. Forty percent of its students come from states other than California, with students representing nearly 260 colleges and universities throughout the United States and Canada.

Approximately 650 law students, 60 MPP students, 200 MBA students, and 2,800 undergraduate students share an 830-acre campus on the slopes of the Santa Monica Mountains overlooking the Pacific Ocean in Malibu, California. An additional 3,000 students attend the University's School of Business and Management and the Graduate School of Education and Psychology, located elsewhere in the Los Angeles area.

LOCATION AND ENVIRONMENT

Pepperdine's location in Malibu, California—just 30 miles from downtown Los Angeles—makes it a conducive environment for the intense study of law. Considered one of the most desirable residential communities in the world, Malibu offers an almost rural setting, yet is an integral part of greater Los Angeles, providing access to one of the largest legal communities in the world. A focal point for the emerging Pacific Rim, Los Angeles serves as a center for international trade and finance. Thriving trade in business, entertainment, communications, multimedia, international relations, and public service provides law students with hands-on experience outside the classroom and creates a large potential job market.

THE FACILITIES

The Odell McConnell Law Center, situated on one of the highest points on campus, overlooks the undergraduate school and athletic facilities.

The tri-level building contains a large auditorium classroom, law library, classrooms, seminar rooms, conference areas, atrium, administrative center, appellate courtroom, trial courtroom, cafeteria, bookstore, and offices for student services and activities.

The Jerene Appleby Harnish Law Library strives to meet the research needs of students, faculty, and staff, using both traditional resources and the latest in electronic technology. In addition to its collection of more than 285,000 scholarly and legal volumes, the library boasts three innovative computer labs offering curricular and practice-oriented software and services. The labs feature full Internet access, high-end computer operating systems and software, roaming network profiles, student notebook connectivity, and high-speed printers.

Across the street from the law center stands the George Page Residential Complex. The 72-unit complex houses graduate students in two- and four-bedroom apartments. Many of the apartments offer a spectacular view of the Pacific Ocean, while others face the Santa Monica Mountains.

Law students have year-round use of campus athletic facilities giving them the chance to enjoy tennis, aerobics, an Olympic-size swimming pool, racquetball, basketball, weight training, soccer, track, and equestrian activities. The school also hosts NCAA intercollegiate sporting events.

THE ACADEMIC PROGRAM

The Pepperdine law curriculum has more required courses than the vast majority of law schools. Although 14 curricular tracks allow students to emphasize fields ranging from Entertainment to Criminal Law, the first objective is to ensure that every student has a broad understanding of the law. The classroom environment encourages a lively interchange of ideas between students and professors.

In addition to the JD, the School of Law offers a certificate and a master's degree in Dispute Resolution through the Straus Institute for Dispute Resolution, a pioneer in the alternative dispute resolution movement. A combined Juris Doctor and Master of Dispute Resolution degree (JD/MDR) is also available.

In conjunction with Pepperdine's Graziadio School of Business and Management, the JD/MBA joint degree program allows students to compress a five-year course of study into just four years.

Two joint degree programs are available with the School of Public Policy. The JD/MPP (Master of Public Policy) joint degree permits the student to complete in four years what would ordinarily take five years. The MDR/MPP requires a completion of 26 Dispute Resolution units and 56 units from the Public Policy curriculum.

THE FACULTY

The faculty has an uncommon depth of concern for each individual student. Here, professors walk in partnership with students. They know them by name. Having participated in their selective admission to this rigorous program, the faculty work hard to see students exceed the requirements for practice in every state and join the legal profession as colleagues.

The credentials of the law faculty reflect training in the nation's finest schools and a record of professional service that extends throughout the country. Although the faculty have distinguished themselves through scholarly research and writing as well as leadership positions in prestigious legal organizations, the faculty's primary mission is to teach, to help students see the structure of legal thought, and to be available as professional examples of a multifaceted profession. In addition to the regular faculty, students are exposed to nationally recognized judges, authors, and scholars who serve each year as distinguished visiting professors, practitioners, and jurists-in-residence.

STUDENT CO-CURRICULAR ACTIVITIES

Student Bar Association: Each member of the student body is a member of the Student Bar Association (SBA). The SBA serves the student body by sponsoring social and educational functions during the year and by representing the students in matters involving the school administration.

Student Journals: The *Pepperdine Law Review* is a legal journal edited and published by students selected on the basis of scholarship and/or the ability to do creative research and writing. Students write comments and notes on legal developments and significant cases, as well as edit the lead articles and book reviews written by teachers, lawyers, judges, legislators, and other scholars.

The *Pepperdine Dispute Resolution Law Journal* is published biannually and provides practitioners and academics with an insightful perspective on the rapidly developing dispute resolution field.

Student Advocacy: Pepperdine has a national reputation for excellence in training law students to be advocates. Upper-division students compete for positions on the Moot Court Board and teams that Pepperdine fields for interschool appellate and trial competitions. Considered an outstanding honor, membership on the Moot Court Board and interschool teams allows students to develop excellent advocacy skills.

National Organizations and Student Associations: Several national legal fraternities—such as Phi Alpha Delta and Phi Delta Phi—and other student organizations have local chapters on campus. Students are encouraged to apply for membership in the Law Student Division of the American Bar Association and are eligible in their last year of school to become student members of local bar associations. This enables students to make valuable contacts with practicing members of the profession and benefit from the associations' activities.

School of Law

OFF-CAMPUS OPPORTUNITIES

Clinical Placements: Four clinical law programs provide students with the opportunity to further refine their professional lawyering skills under the supervision of faculty, lawyers, and judges. The majority of clinical law opportunities are with the district attorneys, public defenders, and state and federal judges of Los Angeles and Ventura counties. In addition, there are a number of smaller programs offering experience in corporate and securities law, tax law, juvenile law, family law, labor law, consumer protection, environmental law, and trade regulation. Students have worked with state and federal legislators and on legislative committee staffs. There are also placements within the film, television, and music industries.

Public Interest Opportunities: Pepperdine has recently partnered with the Los Angeles Union Rescue Mission to develop the Pepperdine-Union Rescue Mission Legal Aid Clinic. Located in downtown Los Angeles, the mission provides emergency food and shelter, health services, recovery programs, education, job training, and counseling within a Christian context.

Another outreach program for law students is the Pepperdine-Lanterman Special Education Law Clinic, which assists families with children who have special needs in receiving proper accommodations in public schools. The clinic allows students to gain valuable experience advocating for children with disabilities and ensuring they receive appropriate education and related services as required by law.

The Center for Community Development and Service assists troubled youth in the California Youth Authority camps, as well as adults and teenagers in a variety of inner-city programs. The goal of the Center is not to be a legal clinic that helps one "beat the rap," but to provide training in life skills, such those needed to finish a GED, write a résumé, and dress for a job interview.

London Program: Students and visiting students have the opportunity to study law in historic London at Pepperdine's Univeristy-owned facility in the museum district of South Kensington. An enriching international experience for law students, the London Program takes advantage of its location and a distinguished international faculty.

While in London, students may participate in moot court competitions with English law students at one of the famous Inns of Court and extern in clinical placements with barristers, solicitors, American law firms, and international organiza)ôons.

TUITION AND ROOM FEES

Tuition: $12,410 per semester

Campus housing is charged on a semester basis:

Double occupancy: $3,200

Single occupancy: $4,510

FINANCIAL AID

The School of Law conducts and active financial aid program that provides more than 85 percent of the student body with some type of financial assistance. Financial aid awards are generally a combination of grants, loans, and work-study employment. A substantial number of scholarships and grants are awarded each year, which are made available through endowed funds, gifts from friends and alumni, and allocations of University general funds.

Merit scholarship awards are based on the student's academic record and are awarded to both entering and returning students.

All applicants for admission to the law school are eligible for the prestigious Faculty Scholars Award, which is based on merit without regard to financial need. Five members of each class will be designated as Faculty Scholars. An award of $30,000 is granted to each scholar for the first year of law school, and the scholarship is renewed each year conditioned upon satisfactory academic performance.

Entering students are likely to receive a Dean's Scholarship if they have achieved an undergraduate GPA of at least 3.5 and an LSAT score in approximately the 90th percentile. The amounts of this award will range from approximately one-fourth tuition to full tuition. All Dean's awards are made on a yearly basis, but are renewable contingent upon the student being in the top quarter of the class at the end of the academic year.

ADMISSIONS PROCESS AND REQUIREMENTS

Pepperdine seeks to attract students who will bring variety, diversity, and excellence to the study of law. Admission is based on the applicant's academic record, LSAT score, written personal statement, and other information that reflects outstanding academic and professional promise.

Admission is selective. Because of the limited first-year enrollment, only those applicants who show strong potential of successfully completing the study of law are accepted. The Faculty Admissions Committee evaluates completed applications on the basis of the applicant's undergraduate grade point average, LSAT score, employment experience, extracurricular activities, community involvement, commitment to high standards of morality and ethics, reasons for wanting to study law, competence in writing and speaking, emotional stability, initiative, motivation, and other relevant information.

The admission process is guided by the view that a student body that reflects broad and rich diversity provides a superior educational environment. For this reason, admissions decisions may be based on consideration of other unique factors that include racial and ethnic origin, unique work experience, a history of overcoming disadvantage, or unusual life experiences.

APPLICATION INSTRUCTIONS

Applicants for admission the first-year class should have received a bachelor's degree from an approved college or university prior to registration. Applicants must include:

- Completed, signed, and dated application
- Personal statement
- Résumé
- Mission statement
- $50 application fee in the form of check or money order payable to Pepperdine University School of Law
- Registrations with LSDAS (request official transcripts and letters of recommendation be sent directly to LSDAS)
- Self-addressed, stamped acknowledgement postcards

Admissions Contact: Director of Admissions, Ms. Shannon Phillips
24255 Pacific Coast Highway, Malibu, CA 90263
Admissions Phone: 310-456-4631 • Admissions Fax: 310-317-1668
Admissions E-mail: soladmis@pepperdine.edu • Web Address: law.pepperdine.edu

Pepperdine University

School of Law

Admissions Contact: Director of Admissions, Ms. Shannon Phillips
24255 Pacific Coast Highway, Malibu, CA 90263
Admissions Phone: 310-456-4631 • Admissions Fax: 310-317-1668
Admissions E-mail: soladmis@pepperdine.edu • Web Address: law.pepperdine.edu

INSTITUTIONAL INFORMATION

Public/Private: Private
Affiliation: Church Of Christ
Environment: Urban
Academic Calendar: Semester
Schedule: Full time only
Student/Faculty Ratio: 20:1
Total Faculty: 77
% Female: 27
% Minority: 9

PROGRAMS

Clinical Program Required? No
Clinical Programs: Public Interest Dispute Resolution, Commercial and International Dispute Resolution, Domestic Relations Dispute Resolution, Dispute Resolution in Education
Grading System: Letter and numerical system on a 100 to 55 point scale; students must maintain a 72 average to remain in good standing
Legal Writing/Methods Course Requirements: Identification, description, and use of source materials for the solution of legal problems; introduction to the law library and its use. Each student will be required to produce one or more papers dealing with approved legal subjects and to engage in oral argument thereon.

STUDENT INFORMATION

Enrollment of Law School: 652
% Male/Female: 55/45
% Full Time: 100
% Full Time That Are International: 1
% Minority: 16
Average Age of Entering Class: 23

EXPENSES/FINANCIAL AID

Annual Tuition: $23,810
Room and Board: $10,004
Books and Supplies: $700
Average Grant: $8,975
Average Loan: $24,560
% of Aid That Is Merit-Based: 60
% Receiving Some Sort of Aid: 84
Average Total Aid Package: $32,000
Average Debt: $74,515
Tuition Per Credit: $845
Fees Per Credit: $730

ADMISSIONS INFORMATION

Application Fee: $50
Regular Application Deadline: 3/1
Regular Notification: Rolling
LSDAS Accepted? Yes
Average GPA: 3.3
Range of GPA: 3.0–3.5
Average LSAT: 157
Range of LSAT: 154–160
Transfer Students Accepted? Yes
Other Schools to Which Students Applied: UCLA School of Law, Loyola Marymount University, University of Southern California, University of San Diego, Southwestern University, Santa Clara University, University of California—Hastings, Whittier College
Other Admissions Factors Considered: Community service, work experience
Number of Applications Received: 1,176

INTERNATIONAL STUDENTS

TOEFL Required of International Students? Yes

EMPLOYMENT INFORMATION

Rate of Placement: 92%
Average Starting Salary: $64,234
Employers Who Frequently Hire Grads: Gibson, Dunn & Crutcher; Latham & Watkins; Jones, Day, Reavis, & Pogue; McKenna & Cuneo; Los Angeles and Ventura County District Attorney's Offices and various other law firms and governmental agencies
Prominent Alumni: James K. Hahn, city attorney of Los Angeles; Terry Giles, trial lawyer, youngest person to be admitted to Horatio Alger Society; Mark Hiepler, trial lawyer, tried and received jury verdicts in significant cases against Health Maintenance Organizations

QUEEN'S UNIVERSITY
Faculty of Law

Admissions Contact: Registrar of Law, Merrilees Muir
Macdonald Hall, Faculty of Law, Queens University, Kingston, ON K7L 3N6 Canada
Admissions Phone: 613-533-2220 • Admissions Fax: 613-533-6611
Admissions E-mail: LLB@qsilver.queensu.ca • Web Address: http://qsilver.queensu.ca/law/

INSTITUTIONAL INFORMATION

Public/Private: Public
Total Faculty: 77
% Part Time: 59
% Female: 36

PROGRAMS

Advanced Degrees Offered: LLM
Combined Degrees Offered: MIR/LLB (4 years), Co-op
Clinical Program Required? No
Clinical Programs: Clinical Correctional Law, Clinical Litigation, Clinical Family, Advanced Mediation
Grading System: Letter grades, not on a curve

STUDENT INFORMATION

Enrollment of Law School: 478
% Male/Female: 43/57
% Full Time: 98

EXPENSES/FINANCIAL AID

Annual Tuition: $3,657
Books and Supplies: $690

ADMISSIONS INFORMATION

Regular Application Deadline: 11/1
Regular Notification: Rolling
Average GPA: 3.0
Average LSAT: 158
Transfer Students Accepted? No
Number of Applications Received: 1,781
Number of Applicants Accepted: 623
Number of Applicants Enrolled: 162

QUINNIPIAC UNIVERSITY
School of Law

Admissions Contact: Dean of Law School Admissions, John J. Noonan
275 Mount Carmel Avenue, Hamden, CT 06518-1948
Admissions Phone: 203-287-3400 • Admissions Fax: 203-287-3339
Admissions E-mail: ladm@quinnipiac.edu • Web Address: http://law.quinnipiac.edu/academics/law.asp

INSTITUTIONAL INFORMATION

Public/Private: Private
Environment: Suburban
Academic Calendar: Semester
Schedule: Full time or part time
Student/Faculty Ratio: 18:1
Total Faculty: 63
% Part Time: 40
% Female: 27
% Minority: 5

PROGRAMS

Academic Specialties: Rich curriculum, outstanding teaching faculty, exceptional facilities, specialized practice courses, skills training, hands-on experience
Advanced Degrees Offered: JD (3 years full time, 4 years part time)
Combined Degrees Offered: JD/MBA (4 years), JD/MHA (4 years)
Clinical Program Required? No
Clinical Programs: Civic Clinic, Appellate Clinic, Health Clinic, Tax Clinic, Criminal Justice Clinic
Grading System: Letter grades with a quality point equivalent based on a 4.0 system
Legal Writing/Methods Course Requirements: Year-long course trains students in the fundamentals of legal writing, analysis, and research

STUDENT INFORMATION

Enrollment of Law School: 793
% Male/Female: 54/46
% Full Time: 63
% Full Time That Are International: 0
% Minority: 14
Average Age of Entering Class: 27

RESEARCH FACILITIES

Computers/Workstations Available: 105

EXPENSES/FINANCIAL AID

Annual Tuition: $21,200
Room and Board (On/Off Campus): $7,250
Books and Supplies: $1,000
Average Grant: $7,500
Average Loan: $18,805
% of Aid That Is Merit-Based: 20
% Receiving Some Sort of Aid: 85
Average Total Aid Package: $25,000
Average Debt: $65,000
Fees Per Credit: $850

ADMISSIONS INFORMATION

Application Fee: $40
Regular Application Deadline: Rolling
Regular Notification: Rolling
LSDAS Accepted? Yes
Average GPA: 2.9
Range of GPA: 2.5–3.2
Average LSAT: 147
Range of LSAT: 144–152
Transfer Students Accepted? Yes
Other Schools to Which Students Applied: University of Connecticut, Western New England College, New England School of Law, Pace University, New York Law School, Touro College, Seton Hall University, Suffolk University
Other Admissions Factors Considered: Personal statement, recommendations, interview (optional)
Number of Applications Received: 2,004
Number of Applicants Accepted: 1,045
Number of Applicants Enrolled: 258

EMPLOYMENT INFORMATION

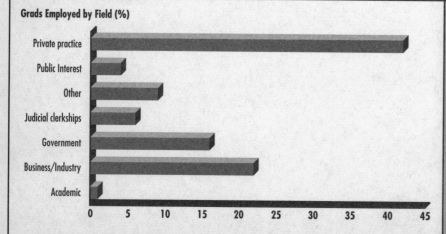

Rate of Placement: 90%
Average Starting Salary: $35,000
Employers Who Frequently Hire Grads: Law firms, corporations, Public Defender's Offices, Prosecutor's Offices, and various government and public interest organizations
State for Bar Exam: CT
Pass Rate for First-Time Bar: 86%

REGENT UNIVERSITY
School of Law

Admissions Contact: Director of Admissions, Bonnie G. Creef
1000 Regent University Drive, R.H. 239, Virginia Beach, VA 23464
Admissions Phone: 757-226-4584 • Admissions Fax: 757-226-4139
Admissions E-mail: lawschool@regent.edu • Web Address: www.regent.edu/acad/schlaw/admit/home.html

INSTITUTIONAL INFORMATION

Public/Private: Private
Affiliation: Nondenominational
Student/Faculty Ratio: 20:1
Total Faculty: 27
% Part Time: 0
% Female: 19
% Minority: 30

PROGRAMS

Academic Specialties: The opportunity to work alongside attorneys for the American Center for Law and Justice; one of the nation's foremost public interest law firms in developing legal strategies to defend life, liberty, and family; the opportunity for selected third-year students to meet regularly with federal and state judges, leading attorneys, and law faculty in the James Kent American Inn of Court; a spacious facility equipped with the latest technology featuring computer-oriented classroom instruction and the use of electronic casebooks; a national reputation for equipping students with the fundamental skills necessary to the effective practice of law, as evidenced by student accomplishments and championships in several national competitions
Advanced Degrees Offered: LLM International Tax (2 years)
Combined Degrees Offered: JD/MBA, JD/MPA, JD/MPP (all are 4 years)
Clinical Program Required? No
Clinical Programs: Students may experience live-client contact through externships at the Tidewater Legal Society and the American Center for Law and

Justice. In addition, third-year students may qualify to represent clients in court through externships at the Tidewater.
Grading System: A+ (4.00), A (4.00) Superior, A– (3.67), B+ (3.33), B (3.00) Good, B– (2.67), C+ (2.33), C (2.00) Satisfactory, C– (1.67), D+ (1.33), D (1.00) Poor, D– (0.67), F (0.00) Failing. A student who fails a required course must repeat the course in order to graduate.
Legal Writing/Methods Course Requirements: The required legal research and writing program consists of 2 sequential, 2-hour courses in the first year of law school.

STUDENT INFORMATION

Enrollment of Law School: 491
% Male/Female: 54/46
% Full Time: 84
% Full Time That Are International: 2
% Minority: 17
Average Age of Entering Class: 28

RESEARCH FACILITIES

Computers/Workstations Available: 78
School-Supported Research Centers: The Law Library is a member of the Tidewater Consortium. This membership allows students to obtain circulation privileges at most other Tidewater area libraries. Additionally, 24 other library catalogs can be accessed from the Regent University Law Library online catalog.

EXPENSES/FINANCIAL AID

Annual Tuition: $16,480
Room and Board (Off Campus): $10,500

Books and Supplies: $1,000
Financial Aid Application Deadline: 3/1
Average Grant: $3,200
Average Loan: $20,893
% of Aid That Is Merit-Based: 40
% Receiving Some Sort of Aid: 95
Average Total Aid Package: $27,347
Average Debt: $61,271
Tuition Per Credit: $515
Fees Per Credit: $0

ADMISSIONS INFORMATION

Application Fee: $40
Regular Application Deadline: 6/1
Regular Notification: Rolling
LSDAS Accepted? Yes
Average GPA: 3.1
Range of GPA: 2.7–3.5
Average LSAT: 148
Range of LSAT: 144–153
Transfer Students Accepted? Yes
Other Schools to Which Students Applied: University of Richmond, George Mason University, College of William and Mary, St. Thomas University, Thomas Cooley Law School, Quinnipiac University, Nova Southeastern University, Widener University
Number of Applications Received: 566
Number of Applicants Accepted: 367
Number of Applicants Enrolled: 219

INTERNATIONAL STUDENTS

TOEFL Required of International Students? Yes
Minimum TOEFL: 550

EMPLOYMENT INFORMATION

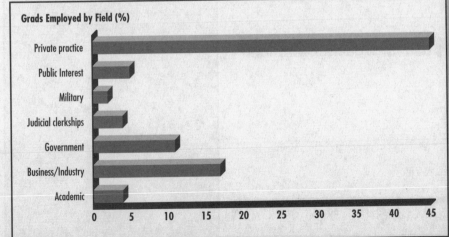

Grads Employed by Field (%)

Rate of Placement: 85%
Average Starting Salary: $36,073
Employers Who Frequently Hire Grads: Winters, King and Associates; Davis and Brynteson; American Center for Law and Justice; Virginia Attorney General
Prominent Alumni: Brad DeSandro, partner, law firm in Utah; Brian Dinning, member, law firm in Virginia; Robert McDonnell, partner, law firm in Virginia and Virginia state delegate; Sherrise Powers, assistant commandant, Virginia Military Institute; Judge Juan Gonzalez, Del Rio, TX; Mark Goins, House of Representatives, TN

ROGER WILLIAMS UNIVERSITY
Ralph R. Papitto School of Law

Admissions Contact: Director of Admissions, Nanci Tessier
Ten Metacom Avenue, Bristol, RI 02809-5171
Admissions Phone: 800-633-2727 • Admissions Fax: 401-254-4516
Admissions E-mail: admissions@rwulaw.rwu.edu • Web Address: http://law.rwu.edu

INSTITUTIONAL INFORMATION
Public/Private: Private
Environment: Suburban
Schedule: Full time or part time
Student/Faculty Ratio: 13:1
Total Faculty: 57
% Part Time: 56
% Female: 29
% Minority: 2

PROGRAMS
Academic Specialties: 4-part Legal Methods sequence, research resources, computer labs, and library staff to offer assistance when conducting legal methods research
Advanced Degrees Offered: JD (3 years full time, 4 years part time)
Combined Degrees Offered: JD/MCP (4 years), JD/MMA (3.5 years)
Clinical Program Required? No
Clinical Programs: Family Law, Criminal Defense
Legal Writing/Methods Course Requirements: 4 separate courses over first two years of law school: Analysis, Research and Writing; Mock Court; Interviewing and Client Counseling; Trial Advocacy

STUDENT INFORMATION
Enrollment of Law School: 394
% Male/Female: 50/50
% Full Time: 58
% Full Time That Are International: 0
% Minority: 11
Average Age of Entering Class: 28

RESEARCH FACILITIES
Computers/Workstations Available: 76
School-Supported Research Centers: Access to law libraries of other schools that participate in New England Law Library Consortium; access to libraries that participate in consortium of RI academic research libraries.

EXPENSES/FINANCIAL AID
Annual Tuition: $20,100
Room and Board: $12,900
Books and Supplies: $1,000
Financial Aid Application Deadline: 5/15
Average Grant: $3,000
% of Aid That Is Merit-Based: 10
% Receiving Some Sort of Aid: 90
Average Total Aid Package: $20,000
Average Debt: $82,000
Fees Per Credit: $635

ADMISSIONS INFORMATION
Application Fee: $60
Regular Application Deadline: 5/15
Regular Notification: Rolling
LSDAS Accepted? Yes
Average GPA: 3.0
Range of GPA: 2.6–3.3
Average LSAT: 148
Range of LSAT: 143–153
Transfer Students Accepted? Yes
Other Admissions Factors Considered: Graduate work
Number of Applications Received: 661
Number of Applicants Accepted: 396
Number of Applicants Enrolled: 143

INTERNATIONAL STUDENTS
TOEFL Required of International Students? Yes
Minimum TOEFL: 600

EMPLOYMENT INFORMATION

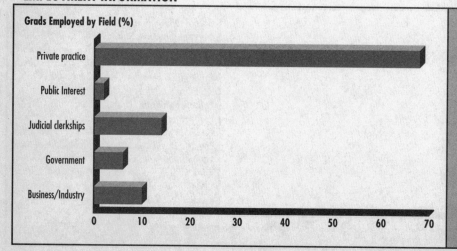

Grads Employed by Field (%)

Rate of Placement: 94%
Average Starting Salary: $43,000

RUTGERS UNIVERSITY — CAMDEN
Rutgers School of Law at Camden

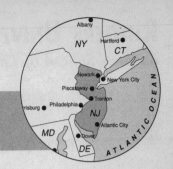

Admissions Contact: Associate Dean of Enrollment and Projects, Camille S. Andrews
406 Penn Street, Third Floor, Camden, NJ 08102-1203
Admissions Phone: 856-225-6102 • Admissions Fax: 856-225-6537
Admissions E-mail: admissions@camlaw.rutgers.edu • Web Address: www-camden.rutgers.edu

INSTITUTIONAL INFORMATION

Public/Private: Public
Environment: Urban
Academic Calendar: Semester
Schedule: Full time or part time
Student/Faculty Ratio: 14:1
Total Faculty: 108
% Part Time: 60
% Female: 31
% Minority: 3

PROGRAMS

Academic Specialties: Sex Discrimination Law, Commercial Law, State Constitutional Law, Criminal Law, Civil Procedure, Admiralty, Legal History, Jurisprudence, International and Comparative Law, Family Law and Domestic Violence, Health Law, and Lawyering Skills and Advocacy.
Advanced Degrees Offered: JD (3 years full time, 4 years part time)
Combined Degrees Offered: JD/MBA (4 years), JD/MPA (4 years), JD/MSW (4 years), JD/MS Public Policy (3.5 years), JD/MCRP (4 years), JD/MD with University of Medicine and Dentistry of New Jersey, JD/MPA Public Administration in Health Care Management and Policy (4 years)
Clinical Program Required? No
Clinical Programs: In-House live-client civil practice clinic and small business clinic. The law school's Domestic Violence Project is a pro bono/public interest program designed to assist victims of domestic violence.
Grading System: A+, A, B+, B, C+, C, D+, D, F

Legal Writing/Methods Course Requirements: Required year-long graded course covering research, analysis, writing, and oral advocacy; every student takes an average of 1 course every semester that includes an intensive writing experience.

STUDENT INFORMATION

Enrollment of Law School: 749
% Male/Female: 50/50
% Full Time: 81
% Full Time That Are International: 1
% Minority: 16
Average Age of Entering Class: 26

RESEARCH FACILITIES

Computers/Workstations Available: 46
School-Supported Research Centers: Pro Bono Program working with domestic violence, bankruptcy, and mediation; Civil Practice Clinic or Externship Program during third year; Camden County Family Court; Camden Regional Legal Services; Community Health Law Project; Philadelphia VIP; AIDS Law Project of Philadelphia; Homeless Advocacy Project; Rutgers-Camden VITA Chapter (tax assistance for low-income residents); LEAP charter schools and other mentoring in public schools; The Rutgers Mediation Project; Camden Municipal Court

EXPENSES/FINANCIAL AID

Room and Board (On Campus): $4,368
Books and Supplies: $1,000
Financial Aid Application Deadline: 4/1
Average Grant: $4,000

Average Loan: $15,000
% of Aid That Is Merit-Based: 10
% Receiving Some Sort of Aid: 83
Average Total Aid Package: $17,000
Average Debt: $48,500

ADMISSIONS INFORMATION

Regular Application Deadline: 3/1
Regular Notification: 4/15
LSDAS Accepted? Yes
Average GPA: 3.2
Range of GPA: 2.8–3.5
Average LSAT: 157
Range of LSAT: 154–159
Transfer Students Accepted? Yes
Other Schools to Which Students Applied: Temple University, Seton Hall University, Villanova University, Rutgers University—Newark, George Washington University, University of Pennsylvania, Pennsylvania State University, Fordham University
Other Admissions Factors Considered: Quality of undergraduate and graduate institutions, undergraduate major, graduate schools and GPA, general background
Number of Applications Received: 1,744
Number of Applicants Accepted: 624
Number of Applicants Enrolled: 206

INTERNATIONAL STUDENTS

TOEFL Required of International Students? Yes
Minimum TOEFL: 600

EMPLOYMENT INFORMATION

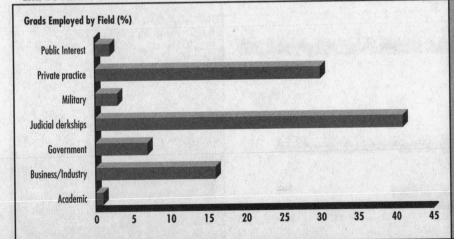

Grads Employed by Field (%)

Public Interest
Private practice
Military
Judicial clerkships
Government
Business/Industry
Academic

0 5 10 15 20 25 30 35 40 45

Rate of Placement: 96%
Average Starting Salary: $64,100
Employers Who Frequently Hire Grads: All major Philadelphia, New Jersey, and Delaware law firms, and numerous prestigious firms from New York City, Washington D.C., California, and other major metropolitan areas. Rutgers also ranks third in the country in placing its law graduates in highly desirable judicial clerkships.
Prominent Alumni: William J. Hughes, ambassador to Panama and former member of the U.S. House of Representatives; Hon. James Florio, former governor of New Jersey and former U.S. congressman; Pennsylvania Supreme Court Justice Nigro

RUTGERS UNIVERSITY — NEWARK
Rutgers School of Law at Newark

Admissions Contact: Director of Admissions, Anita Walton
123 Washington Street, Newark, NJ 07102
Admissions Phone: 973-353-5554 • Admissions Fax: 973-353-3459
Admissions E-mail: geddis@andromeda.rutgers.edu • Web Address: www.rutgers.edu

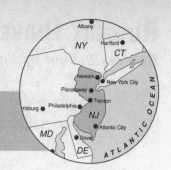

INSTITUTIONAL INFORMATION

Public/Private: Public
Environment: Urban
Academic Calendar: Semester
Schedule: Full time or part time
Student/Faculty Ratio: 16:1
Total Faculty: 68
% Part Time: 44
% Female: 34
% Minority: 19

PROGRAMS

Academic Specialties: Strengths include a diverse faculty with specialties over a broad range of topics. Public Interest Law is a point of intersection for many faculty members and is a driving commitment of the school.
Combined Degrees Offered: JD/MBA (4 years), JD/MBA (6 years), JD/PhD Jurisprudence (5 years), JD/MA Criminal Justice (4 years), JD/MCRP (4 years)
Clinical Program Required? No
Clinical Programs: Constitutional Litigation Clinic, Environmental Law Clinic, Federal Tax Clinic, Urban Legal Clinic, Women's Rights Clinic, Animal Rights Clinic, Women and AIDS, and Special Education Clinic
Grading System: Semester system; 4.0 cumulative system; mandatory curve in first year
Legal Writing/Methods Course Requirements: 1 year, 3 credits, first year

STUDENT INFORMATION

Enrollment of Law School: 685
% Male/Female: 51/49
% Full Time: 74
% Full Time That Are International: 2
% Minority: 42
Average Age of Entering Class: 27

EXPENSES/FINANCIAL AID

Annual Tuition (Residents/Nonresidents): $10,106/$14,828
Room and Board (On/Off Campus): $7,000/$8,490
Books and Supplies: $3,618
Average Grant: $2,045
Average Loan: $17,992
% of Aid That Is Merit-Based: 39
% Receiving Some Sort of Aid: 80
Average Debt: $33,455

ADMISSIONS INFORMATION

Regular Application Deadline: 3/15
Regular Notification: Rolling
LSDAS Accepted? Yes
Average GPA: 3.2
Range of GPA: 2.9–3.4
Average LSAT: 157
Range of LSAT: 151–160
Transfer Students Accepted? Yes
Other Schools to Which Students Applied: Seton Hall University, New York University, Fordham University, George Washington University, Temple, Columbia University, Rutgers University—Camden, Boston College
Other Admissions Factors Considered: Graduate degree, work experience, socio-economic factors, community activities, personal essay, letters of recommendation
Number of Applications Received: 2,001
Number of Applicants Accepted: 910
Number of Applicants Enrolled: 289

INTERNATIONAL STUDENTS

Minimum TOEFL: 610

EMPLOYMENT INFORMATION

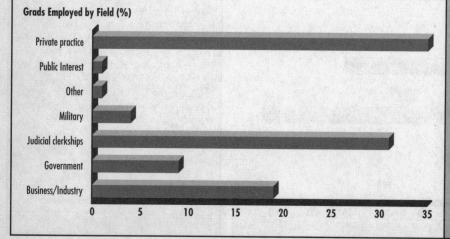

Rate of Placement: 98%
Average Starting Salary: $60,737
Employers Who Frequently Hire Grads: Federal judges, New Jersey State Court judges, large New Jersey and New York law firms, medium New Jersey firms, New York and New Jersey corporations, legal services
Prominent Alumni: Robert Torricelli, U.S. senator; Ida Castro, chair, Equal Employment Opportunity Commission; Louis Freeh, FBI director
State for Bar Exam: NJ
Number Taking Bar Exam: 175
Pass Rate for First-Time Bar: 80%

St. John's University

School of Law

Admissions Contact: Assistant Dean, Gloria Y. Rivera
8000 Utopia Parkway, Jamaica, NY 11439
Admissions Phone: 718-990-6611 • Admissions Fax: 718-990-2526
Admissions E-mail: rsvp@sjulaw.stjohns.edu • Web Address: www.stjohns.edu/law

INSTITUTIONAL INFORMATION

Public/Private: Private
Affiliation: Catholic
Environment: Urban
Academic Calendar: Semester
Schedule: Full time or part time
Total Faculty: 108
% Part Time: 57

PROGRAMS

Academic Specialties: Securities Law, Government Service, Labor Law, Real Estate, Bankruptcy, Criminal Law, Taxation, Environmental Law, Domestic and International Commercial Law, Legal Philosophy
Advanced Degrees Offered: JD (3 years day, 2.5 years day, 4 years evening), LLM Bankruptcy (1 year full time, 2–3 years part time)
Combined Degrees Offered: JD/MBA, JD/MA(MS), BA(BS)/JD
Clinical Program Required? No
Clinical Programs: Elder Law Clinic, Civil, Criminal, Judicial, and Domestic Violence Clinics
Grading System: Letter grades
Legal Writing/Methods Course Requirements: Small class settings throughout the first year

STUDENT INFORMATION

Enrollment of Law School: 1,016
% Male/Female: 55/45
% Full Time: 73
% Full Time That Are International: 2
% Minority: 20

RESEARCH FACILITIES

School-Supported Research Centers: Staten Island Campus of St. John's University

EXPENSES/FINANCIAL AID

Annual Tuition: $22,000
Room and Board: $8,500
Average Grant: $6,904
Average Loan: $16,911
% of Aid That Is Merit-Based: 17
% Receiving Some Sort of Aid: 89
Average Total Aid Package: $18,496
Average Debt: $53,619
Tuition Per Credit: $800

ADMISSIONS INFORMATION

Application Fee: $50
Regular Application Deadline: Rolling
Regular Notification: Rolling
LSDAS Accepted? Yes
Average GPA: 3.1
Range of GPA: 2.8–3.5
Average LSAT: 154
Range of LSAT: 150–157
Transfer Students Accepted? Yes
Other Schools to Which Students Applied: Brooklyn Law School, Fordham University, Hofstra University, New York Law School, New York University, Pace University, Yeshiva University, Columbia University
Other Admissions Factors Considered: Undergraduate major, undergraduate educational institution, graduate work
Number of Applications Received: 2,384
Number of Applicants Accepted: 1,168

EMPLOYMENT INFORMATION

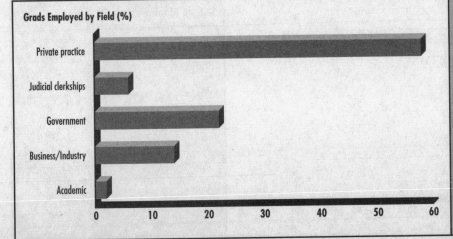

Rate of Placement: 94%
Average Starting Salary: $57,912
Employers Who Frequently Hire Grads: Private law firms
Prominent Alumni: Mario Cuomo, former governor of New York; George Deukmejian, former governor of California; Charles B. Rangel, U.S. congressman

ST. LOUIS UNIVERSITY
School of Law

Admissions Contact: Assistant Director of Admissions, Michael Kolnik
3700 Lindell Boulevard, St. Louis, MO 63108
Admissions Phone: 314-977-2800 • Admissions Fax: 314-977-3966
Admissions E-mail: admissions@law.slu.edu • Web Address: law.slu.edu

INSTITUTIONAL INFORMATION

Public/Private: Private
Affiliation: Catholic
Environment: Urban
Academic Calendar: Semester
Schedule: Full time or part time
Student/Faculty Ratio: 20:1
Total Faculty: 67
% Part Time: 41
% Female: 31
% Minority: 6

PROGRAMS

Academic Specialties: Certificate programs in Employment Law, Health Law, and International and Comparative Law
Advanced Degrees Offered: LLM Health Law (1 year full time, 2 years part time), LLM for foreign lawyers (1 year full time)
Combined Degrees Offered: JD/MBA (3.5–4 years), JD/MHA (4 years), JD/MAPA, JD/MAUA (3–3.5 years), JD/MPH (4 years)
Clinical Program Required? No
Clinical Programs: Trial Advocacy I and II, Moot Court I and II, Client Counseling I and II, Judicial Process, Civil Clinic, Criminal Clinic
Grading System: Letter and numerical system on a 4.0 scale

STUDENT INFORMATION

Enrollment of Law School: 777
% Male/Female: 52/48
% Full Time: 71
% Full Time That Are International: 1
% Minority: 13
Average Age of Entering Class: 27

RESEARCH FACILITIES

Computers/Workstations Available: 425
Computer Labs: 47

EXPENSES/FINANCIAL AID

Annual Tuition: $20,540
Room and Board (On/Off Campus): $9,964/$10,864
Books and Supplies: $900
Financial Aid Application Deadline: 5/1
Average Grant: $6,578
Average Loan: $21,920
% of Aid That Is Merit-Based: 20
% Receiving Some Sort of Aid: 92
Average Total Aid Package: $21,919
Average Debt: $67,323
Tuition Per Credit: $970

ADMISSIONS INFORMATION

Application Fee: $55
Regular Application Deadline: Rolling
Regular Notification: Rolling
LSDAS Accepted? Yes
Average GPA: 3.3
Range of GPA: 3.0–3.6
Average LSAT: 154
Range of LSAT: 150–157
Transfer Students Accepted? Yes
Other Schools to Which Students Applied: Washington University, University of Missouri—Kansas City, University of Missouri—Columbia, University of Illinois, Southern Illinois University, Creighton University, Loyola University Chicago, Northwestern University
Other Admissions Factors Considered: Graduate degrees earned, undergraduate institution
Number of Applications Received: 1,046
Number of Applicants Accepted: 597
Number of Applicants Enrolled: 250

INTERNATIONAL STUDENTS

Minimum TOEFL: 577

EMPLOYMENT INFORMATION

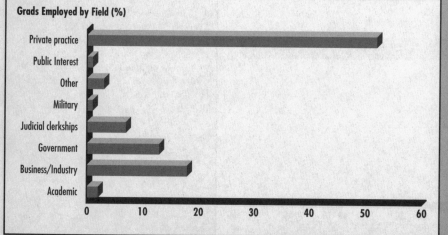

Grads Employed by Field (%)

Rate of Placement: 93%
Average Starting Salary: $43,188

ST. MARY'S UNIVERSITY
School of Law

Admissions Contact: Associate Dean for Enrollment Management, Director of Admissions, Yvonne Cherena-Pacheco
One Camino Santa Maria, San Antonio, TX 78228-8601
Admissions Phone: 210-436-3523 • Admissions Fax: 210-431-4202
Admissions E-mail: admissions@law.stmarytx.edu • Web Address: www.stmarylaw.stmarytx.edu

INSTITUTIONAL INFORMATION

Public/Private: Private
Affiliation: Roman Catholic
Environment: Urban
Academic Calendar: Semester
Schedule: Full time only
Student/Faculty Ratio: 20:1
Total Faculty: 65
% Part Time: 41
% Female: 26
% Minority: 17

PROGRAMS

Academic Specialties: Certificate programs in Employment Law, Health Law, and International and Comparative Law
Advanced Degrees Offered: LLM International and Comparative Law for U.S.-educated graduates, LLM American Legal Studies for foreign-educated graduates.
Clinical Program Required? No
Clinical Programs: Civil Justice Clinic, Community Development Clinic, Criminal Justice Clinic, Immigration Clinic, Human Rights Clinic
Grading System: Letter grades on a 4.0 scale, 10-tier system
Legal Writing/Methods Course Requirements: First-year course taken over 2 semesters

STUDENT INFORMATION

Enrollment of Law School: 749
% Male/Female: 53/47
% Full Time: 100
% Minority: 46
Average Age of Entering Class: 28

RESEARCH FACILITIES

Computer Labs: 3

EXPENSES/FINANCIAL AID

Annual Tuition: $16,950
Room and Board (On/Off Campus): $2,548/$4,500
Books and Supplies: $1,100
Financial Aid Application Deadline: 4/1
Average Grant: $800
Average Loan: $18,500
% of Aid That Is Merit-Based: 3
% Receiving Some Sort of Aid: 85
Average Total Aid Package: $20,000
Average Debt: $70,000
Fees Per Credit: $915

ADMISSIONS INFORMATION

Application Fee: $45
Regular Application Deadline: 3/1
Regular Notification: 5/1
LSDAS Accepted? Yes
Average GPA: 3.0
Range of GPA: 2.6–3.2
Average LSAT: 149
Range of LSAT: 145–152
Transfer Students Accepted? Yes
Other Schools to Which Students Applied: University of Texas, University of Houston, Texas Tech University, Southern Methodist University, Texas A&M University, Baylor University, University of Denver, Columbia University
Number of Applications Received: 1,046
Number of Applicants Accepted: 603
Number of Applicants Enrolled: 263

EMPLOYMENT INFORMATION

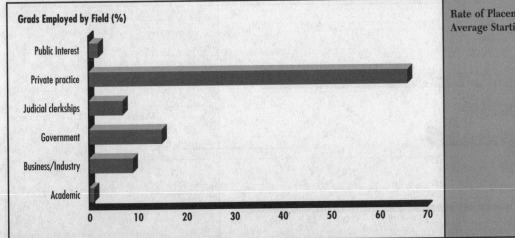

Rate of Placement: 90%
Average Starting Salary: $44,000

St. Thomas University
School of Law

Admissions Contact: Assistant Dean for Enrollment Services, Lydia Amy
16400 Northwest 32nd Avenue, Miami, FL 33054
Admissions Phone: 305-623-2310 • Admissions Fax: 305-623-2357
Admissions E-mail: admitme@stu.edu • Web Address: www.stu.edu

INSTITUTIONAL INFORMATION

Public/Private: Private
Affiliation: Roman Catholic
Student/Faculty Ratio: 16:1
Total Faculty: 31
% Part Time: 39
% Female: 39
% Minority: 23

PROGRAMS

Academic Specialties: Broad General Curriculum, faculty publishes prolifically and in well-regarded law reviews
Clinical Program Required? No
Clinical Programs: Immigration Clinic (8 credits), Appellate Litigation Clinic (8 credits), Family Court Clinic (8 credits), Field Placement Clinic (8 credits)
Grading System: A, B+, B, C+, C, C–, D, F
Legal Writing/Methods Course Requirements: 3-credit Legal Analysis, Writing, and Research required first semester; 2-credit Advanced Legal Research and Writing required forth semester; Senior Writing Requirement

STUDENT INFORMATION

Enrollment of Law School: 487
% Male/Female: 55/45
% Full Time: 100
% Full Time That Are International: 1
% Minority: 47
Average Age of Entering Class: 27

RESEARCH FACILITIES

Computers/Workstations Available: 30

EXPENSES/FINANCIAL AID

Annual Tuition: $21,741
Room and Board (On/Off Campus): $7,600/$8,750
Books and Supplies: $900
Financial Aid Application Deadline: 5/1
Average Grant: $7,012
Average Loan: $23,967
% of Aid That Is Merit-Based: 11
% Receiving Some Sort of Aid: 93
Average Total Aid Package: $24,948
Average Debt: $82,600
Fees Per Credit: $865

ADMISSIONS INFORMATION

Application Fee: $40
Regular Application Deadline: Rolling
Regular Notification: Rolling
LSDAS Accepted? Yes
Average GPA: 2.7
Range of GPA: 2.4–3.0
Average LSAT: 146
Range of LSAT: 143–148
Transfer Students Accepted? Yes
Other Schools to Which Students Applied: Nova Southeastern University, University of Miami, University of Florida, Florida State University, Stetson University, California Western University, Georgia State University, Quinnipiac University
Number of Applications Received: 1,524
Number of Applicants Accepted: 965
Number of Applicants Enrolled: 210

INTERNATIONAL STUDENTS

Minimum TOEFL: 550

EMPLOYMENT INFORMATION

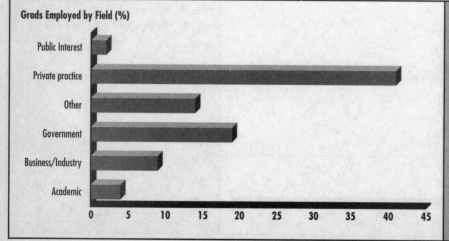

Grads Employed by Field (%)

Rate of Placement: 85%
Average Starting Salary: $45,000
Employers Who Frequently Hire Grads: St. Thomas University School of Law places it's graduates with prominent Florida law firms, corporations, and in federal and state judicial clerkships.
Prominent Alumni: Judge Samuel J. Slom, Dadae County state judge; Richard A. Morgan, Esq., partner, Ruden McColsky; Martin Kofsky, Esq., general counsel, John Aiden Insurance

SAMFORD UNIVERSITY
Cumberland School of Law

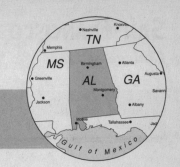

Admissions Contact: Assistant Dean for Admissions and Alumni, Mitzi S. Davis
800 Lakeshore Drive, Birmingham, AL 35229
Admissions Phone: 205-726-2702 • Admissions Fax: 205-726-2057
Admissions E-mail: law.admission@samford.edu • Web Address: http://cumberland.samford.edu

INSTITUTIONAL INFORMATION

Public/Private: Private
Affiliation: Southern Baptist
Environment: Urban
Academic Calendar: 4-1-4
Schedule: Full time only
Student/Faculty Ratio: 18:1
Total Faculty: 71
% Part Time: 55
% Female: 25
% Minority: 13

PROGRAMS

Advanced Degrees Offered: Master of Comparative Law; LLM/SJD in Law, Religion, and Culture
Combined Degrees Offered: JD/MAcc, JD/MBA, JD/MDiv, JD/MPA, JD/MPH, JD/MS Environmental Management (all 3.5 to 4 years)
Clinical Program Required? No
Clinical Programs: State court judges, federal court judges, corporate, U.S. Attorney's Office and IRS Legal Internship, District Attorney's Office (Adult Prosecution, Juvenile Prosecution), Public Defender's Office, Legal Services, Legal Aid Society (Criminal Defense, Juvenile Defense, Family Court)
Grading System: System of letter grades with assigned quality points
Legal Writing/Methods Course Requirements: 1 full year, graded

STUDENT INFORMATION

Enrollment of Law School: 586
% Male/Female: 58/42
% Full Time: 100
% Full Time That Are International: 0
% Minority: 8
Average Age of Entering Class: 24

EXPENSES/FINANCIAL AID

Annual Tuition: $19,550
Room and Board (On Campus): $9,330
Books and Supplies: $1,110
Financial Aid Application Deadline: 3/1
Average Grant: $2,761
Average Loan: $24,384
% of Aid That Is Merit-Based: 4
% Receiving Some Sort of Aid: 86
Average Total Aid Package: $19,199
Average Debt: $63,498

ADMISSIONS INFORMATION

Application Fee: $40
Regular Application Deadline: Rolling
Regular Notification: Rolling
LSDAS Accepted? Yes
Average GPA: 3.0
Range of GPA: 2.7–3.3
Average LSAT: 152
Range of LSAT: 150–154
Transfer Students Accepted? Yes
Other Schools to Which Students Applied: Mercer University, Florida State University, University of Mississippi, University of Alabama, University of Tennessee, Stetson University, Georgia State University, University of Georgia
Other Admissions Factors Considered: Undergraduate major, grade trend, graduate studies, cultural or ethnic diversity, clarity and content of personal statement
Number of Applications Received: 838

INTERNATIONAL STUDENTS

TOEFL Required of International Students? Yes
Minimum TOEFL: 550

EMPLOYMENT INFORMATION

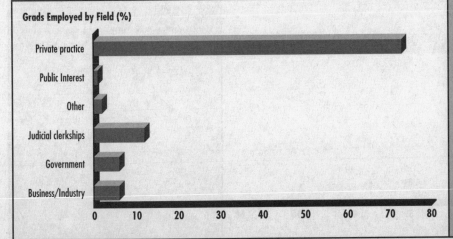

Grads Employed by Field (%)

Rate of Placement: 92%
Average Starting Salary: $40,861
Employers Who Frequently Hire Grads: Bradley, Arant, Rose & White; Burr & Forman; Balch & Birgham; Lange, Simpson, Robinson & Somerville; Carbaniss, Johnston, Gardner, Dumas & O'Neal; Sirote & Permutt; Attorney General's Office; Hand & Arendall, Lyons, Pipes, & Cook; Leitner, Williams, Dooley & Neopolitan; Watkins & Ludlam
Prominent Alumni: Cordell Hull, founder of United Nations; Howell E. Jackson, U.S. Supreme Court; Horace H. Lurton, U.S. Supreme Court

SAN FRANCISCO LAW SCHOOL
College of Law

Admissions Contact: Director of Admissions, Randa Shatara
20 Haight Street, San Francisco, CA 94102
Admissions Phone: 415-626-5550 • Admissions Fax: 415-626-5584
Admissions E-mail: admin@sfls.edu • Web Address: www.sfls.edu

INSTITUTIONAL INFORMATION

Public/Private: Private
Academic Calendar: Semester
Schedule: Part time only
Student/Faculty Ratio: 5:1
Total Faculty: 32
% Part Time: 100
% Female: 31
% Minority: 9

PROGRAMS

Academic Specialties: All faculty is adjunct and are practicing judges and attorneys who teach in their field.
Clinical Program Required? No
Grading System: Numerical system up to 100

STUDENT INFORMATION

Enrollment of Law School: 150
% Full Time: 0
% Minority: 36
Average Age of Entering Class: 34

RESEARCH FACILITIES

Computers/Workstations Available: 4

EXPENSES/FINANCIAL AID

Annual Tuition: $5,775
Books and Supplies: $250
Tuition Per Credit: $275

ADMISSIONS INFORMATION

Regular Application Deadline: 6/15
LSDAS Accepted? No
Transfer Students Accepted? Yes
Other Schools to Which Students Applied: Golden Gate University, University of San Francisco, University of California—Berkeley, University of California—Davis, Gonzaga University, Northwestern University, Santa Clara University, St. Mary's University

INTERNATIONAL STUDENTS

TOEFL Required of International Students? Yes

EMPLOYMENT INFORMATION

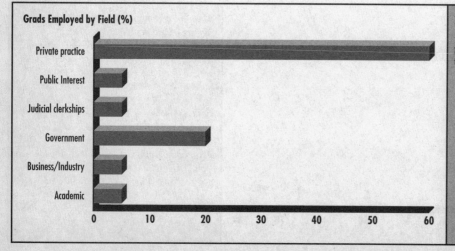

Grads Employed by Field (%)

Prominent Alumni: The late Senator Milton Marks; Edmund G. Brown, the late California governor; Joseph Salgado, former under secretary of U.S. Department of Energy

SAN JOAQUIN COLLEGE OF LAW

Admissions Contact: Admissions Officer, Joyce Morodomi
901 5th Street, Clovis, CA 93612
Admissions Phone: 559-323-2100 • Admissions Fax: 559-323-5566
Admissions E-mail: jcanalin@sjcl.org • Web Address: www.sjcl.org

INSTITUTIONAL INFORMATION

Public/Private: Private
Environment: Urban
Academic Calendar: Semester
Schedule: Full time or part time
Student/Faculty Ratio: 16:1
Total Faculty: 36
% Part Time: 83
% Female: 45
% Minority: 14

PROGRAMS

Academic Specialties: Practice-orientated curriculum with many skills classes. Law review devoted to issues surrounding agriculture.
Advanced Degrees Offered: JD (3–5 years), MS Taxation (2 years)
Clinical Program Required? Yes
Clinical Programs: Alternative Dispute Resolution, Small Claims
Grading System: A (100–85), B (84–75), C (74–65), D (64–55), F (54–0)
Legal Writing/Methods Course Requirements: Legal analysis/research writing

STUDENT INFORMATION

Enrollment of Law School: 185
% Male/Female: 54/46
% Full Time: 13
% Minority: 26
Average Age of Entering Class: 33

EXPENSES/FINANCIAL AID

Annual Tuition: $8,910
Books and Supplies: $550
Average Grant: $1,600
Average Loan: $14,500
% of Aid That Is Merit-Based: 12
% Receiving Some Sort of Aid: 75
Average Total Aid Package: $18,500
Average Debt: $55,000
Tuition Per Credit: $9,504
Fees Per Credit: $405

ADMISSIONS INFORMATION

Application Fee: $40
Regular Application Deadline: 6/30
Regular Notification: Rolling
LSDAS Accepted? No
Average GPA: 2.9
Range of GPA: 1.8–3.9
Average LSAT: 148
Range of LSAT: 139–174
Transfer Students Accepted? Yes
Number of Applications Received: 135
Number of Applicants Accepted: 108
Number of Applicants Enrolled: 91

EMPLOYMENT INFORMATION

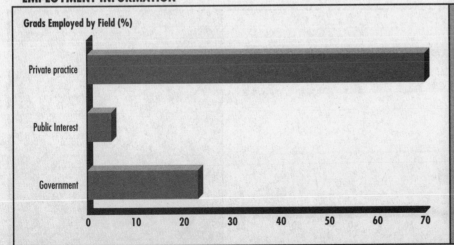

Employers Who Frequently Hire Grads: Local District Attorney and District Defender's Offices; various small firms
Prominent Alumni: Ed Hunt, Fresno Co. district attorney; Phil Cline, Tulare Co. district attorney; Gary Austin, Fresno Co. judge

SANTA BARBARA COLLEGE OF LAW

Admissions Contact: Associate Director, Jeanette Leach
Law Admissions, 500 El Camino Road, Santa Clara, CA 95053
Admissions Phone: 408-554-5048 • Admissions Fax: 408-554-7897
Admissions E-mail: admissions@scu.edu • Web Address: www.santabarbaralaw.edu

INSTITUTIONAL INFORMATION

Public/Private: Private
Academic Calendar: Semester
Schedule: Part time only
Student/Faculty Ratio: 22:1
% Female: 40
% Minority: 11

PROGRAMS

Clinical Program Required? Yes

STUDENT INFORMATION

Enrollment of Law School: 917
% Male/Female: 51/49

EXPENSES/FINANCIAL AID

Annual Tuition: $22,000
Room and Board: $9,787
Books and Supplies: $903
Average Grant: $8,071
Average Debt: $60,379
Tuition Per Credit: $225

ADMISSIONS INFORMATION

Application Fee: $40
Regular Application Deadline: Rolling
Regular Notification: Rolling
Average GPA: 3.2
Range of GPA: 3.0–3.5
Average LSAT: 156
Range of LSAT: 153–158
Transfer Students Accepted? No
Other Schools to Which Students Applied: University of California, Golden Gate University, University of the Pacific, Stetson University
Number of Applications Received: 2,528
Number of Applicants Accepted: 1,265
Number of Applicants Enrolled: 291

EMPLOYMENT INFORMATION

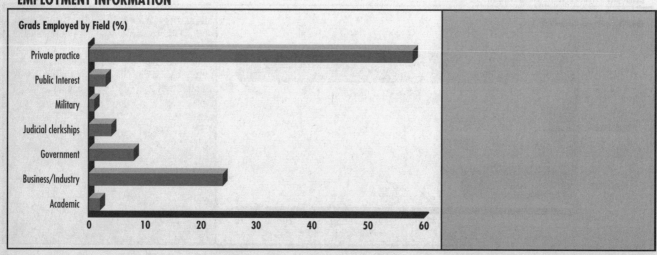

Grads Employed by Field (%)

SANTA CLARA UNIVERSITY
School of Law

Admissions Contact: Associate Director Student Services/Admissions, Jeanette J. Leach
Law Admissions, 500 El Camino Real, Santa Clara, CA 95053
Admissions Phone: 408-554-5048 • Admissions Fax: 408-554-7897
Admissions E-mail: lawadmissions@scu.edu • Web Address: www.scu.edu/law

INSTITUTIONAL INFORMATION

Public/Private: Private
Affiliation: Jesuit
Environment: Urban
Academic Calendar: Semester
Schedule: Full time or part time
Student/Faculty Ratio: 22:1
Total Faculty: 59
% Part Time: 28
% Female: 40
% Minority: 11

PROGRAMS

Academic Specialties: 1) Law and Technology: rich curriculum, law journal, specialty certificate; 2) International and Comparative Law: extensive summer programs in 13 nations, specialty certificate; 3) Public Interest Law: certification, centers, financial support
Advanced Degrees Offered: LLM for foreign lawyers
Combined Degrees Offered: JD/MBA (3.5–4 years)
Clinical Program Required? Yes
Clinical Programs: Law Clinic, East San Jose Community Law Center
Grading System: A to F: A (4.33), B (3.33), C (2.33) etc. A student must achieve and maintain a 2.33 GPA to graduate.

STUDENT INFORMATION

Enrollment of Law School: 917
% Male/Female: 51/49
% Full Time: 69
% Minority: 30
Average Age of Entering Class: 27

EXPENSES/FINANCIAL AID

Annual Tuition: $22,000
Room and Board: $9,787
Books and Supplies: $903
Average Grant: $8,071
Average Loan: $21,877
% of Aid That Is Merit-Based: 7
% Receiving Some Sort of Aid: 85
Average Total Aid Package: $24,089
Average Debt: $60,379
Fees Per Credit: $760

ADMISSIONS INFORMATION

Application Fee: $40
Regular Application Deadline: Rolling
Regular Notification: Rolling
LSDAS Accepted? Yes
Average GPA: 3.2
Range of GPA: 3.0–3.4
Average LSAT: 156
Range of LSAT: 153–160
Transfer Students Accepted? Yes
Other Schools to Which Students Applied: University of California—Hastings, University of San Francisco, University of California—Berkeley, University of California—Davis, University of the Pacific, UCLA School of Law, Stanford University, Golden Gate University
Other Admissions Factors Considered: Academic record, including course of study and quality of institution; graduate work; employment history; maturity; community activities; extracurricular achievments; honors and awards; personal statement

EMPLOYMENT INFORMATION

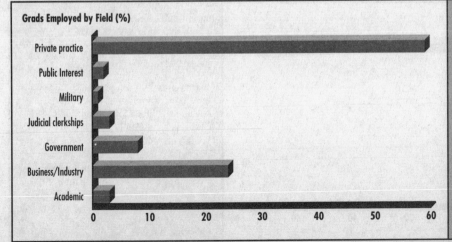

Grads Employed by Field (%)

Private practice
Public Interest
Military
Judicial clerkships
Government
Business/Industry
Academic

0 10 20 30 40 50 60

Rate of Placement: 96%
Average Starting Salary: $58,000
Employers Who Frequently Hire Grads: Cooley, Godward, McCutchen Doyle; Crosby Heafey; Morrison Foerster; Skyerven Morrill; Brobeck, Phleger and Harrison
Prominent Alumni: Leon Panetta, former chief of staff to President Clinton; Edward Panelli, California Supreme Court justice, retired; Zoe Lofgren, U.S. House of Representatives

SEATTLE UNIVERSITY
School of Law

Admissions Contact: Director of Admission, Carol Cochran
900 Broadway, Seattle, WA 98122
Admissions Phone: 206-398-4200 • Admissions Fax: 206-398-4058
Admissions E-mail: lawadmis@seattleu.edu • Web Address: www.law.seattleu.edu

INSTITUTIONAL INFORMATION

Public/Private: Private
Affiliation: Jesuit
Environment: Urban
Academic Calendar: Semester
Schedule: Full time or part time
Student/Faculty Ratio: 21:1
Total Faculty: 80
% Part Time: 44
% Female: 41
% Minority: 16

PROGRAMS

Academic Specialties: Focus areas in Business, Tax, Civil Advocacy, Commercial Law, Criminal Practice, Environmental Law, Estate Planning, Intellectual Property, Labor and Employment Law, Poverty Law, Real Estate
Advanced Degrees Offered: Law School offers JD degrees (3 years). Seattle University offers the following graduate degrees: MBA; MSN; EdD; MPA; MAS in Psychology, Applied Economics Education, and Pastoral Studies; and MS in Software Engineering, Finance, and International Business
Combined Degrees Offered: JD/MBA, JD/MA Applied Economics, JD/MIB, or JD/MS Finance; program can be completed in 4 years
Clinical Program Required? Yes
Clinical Programs: Law Practice Clinic, Bankruptcy Clinic, Immigration, Health, Law and Psychology, Housing Law, Ethics, Environmental Law, Intellectual Property, Administrative Law, and Trust and Estates

Grading System: A+ (4.33), A (4.00), A– (3.67), with grades B to F following the same pattern. Upper-level classes are governed by a presumptive grade curve, and first-year courses have a mandatory grade curve. Pass/fail grades are awarded for limited number of classes.
Legal Writing/Methods Course Requirements: 3 semesters

STUDENT INFORMATION

Enrollment of Law School: 895
% Male/Female: 43/57
% Full Time: 79
% Minority: 21
Average Age of Entering Class: 28

RESEARCH FACILITIES

Computers/Workstations Available: 20

EXPENSES/FINANCIAL AID

Annual Tuition: $20,190
Room and Board (Off Campus): $8,748
Books and Supplies: $625
Average Grant: $5,319
Average Loan: $20,729
% of Aid That Is Merit-Based: 36
% Receiving Some Sort of Aid: 92
Average Total Aid Package: $21,418
Average Debt: $60,000
Fees Per Credit: $637

ADMISSIONS INFORMATION

Application Fee: $50
Regular Application Deadline: 4/1
Regular Notification: Rolling
LSDAS Accepted? Yes
Average GPA: 3.2
Range of GPA: 3.2–3.3
Average LSAT: 156
Range of LSAT: 152–156
Transfer Students Accepted? Yes
Other Schools to Which Students Applied: University of Washington, Gonzaga University, Lewis and Clark College, University of Oregon, University of the Pacific, Willamette University, University of California, University of San Diego
Other Admissions Factors Considered: In all cases, personal accomplishments weigh heavily in the admission decision. Such factors may include, but are not limited to, exceptional professional achievement or community service, outstanding performance in a rigorous program of study, or unique talent.
Number of Applications Received: 1,212
Number of Applicants Accepted: 724
Number of Applicants Enrolled: 324

INTERNATIONAL STUDENTS

Minimum TOEFL: 600

EMPLOYMENT INFORMATION

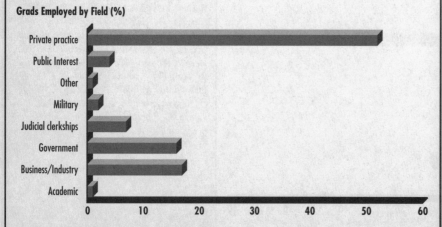

Grads Employed by Field (%)

Rate of Placement: 86%
Average Starting Salary: $44,079
Employers Who Frequently Hire Grads: Perkins Coie; Lane Powell Spears Lubersky; King County Prosecutor's Office; Washington Attorney General's Office; Williams, Kastner and Gibbs; Cozen and O'Connor; Public Defender's Office; Graham and James; Ridell Williams; Foster Pepper Shefelman
Prominent Alumni: Justice Charles Johnson, Washington Supreme Court; Annette Sandberg chief of Washington State Patrol, first woman in country to be chief of state patrol; William Wagner, partner, Gibson, Dunn and Crutcher; Philip Clements, partner, Coopers and Lybrand in New York City

SETON HALL UNIVERSITY
School of Law

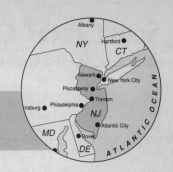

Admissions Contact: Acting Director of Admissions, Kenneth G. Stevenson
One Newark Center, Newark, NJ 07102-5210
Admissions Phone: 973-642-8747 • Admissions Fax: 973-642-8876
Admissions E-mail: admitme@shu.edu • Web Address: www.shu.edu/law

INSTITUTIONAL INFORMATION

Public/Private: Private
Environment: Urban
Academic Calendar: Semester
Schedule: Full time or part time
Student/Faculty Ratio: 24:1
Total Faculty: 47
% Female: 39
% Minority: 15

PROGRAMS

Advanced Degrees Offered: JD (3 years full time, 4 years part time)
Combined Degrees Offered: JD/MBA (4 years full time)
Grading System: Letter and numerical grading system ranging from A+ (4.5) to F (0.0)

STUDENT INFORMATION

Enrollment of Law School: 1,194
% Male/Female: 57/43
% Full Time: 73
% Minority: 15
Average Age of Entering Class: 26

EXPENSES/FINANCIAL AID

Annual Tuition: $20,940
Room and Board: $10,800
Books and Supplies: $850
Average Loan: $18,500
% of Aid That Is Merit-Based: 34
% Receiving Some Sort of Aid: 95
Average Total Aid Package: $20,500
Fees Per Credit: $698

ADMISSIONS INFORMATION

Application Fee: $50
Regular Application Deadline: 4/1
Regular Notification: 1/1
Average GPA: 3.2
Range of GPA: 2.8–3.4
Average LSAT: 154
Range of LSAT: 151–157
Transfer Students Accepted? Yes
Other Schools to Which Students Applied: New York Law School, New York University, Rutgers University—Newark, Fordham University, Brooklyn Law School, St. John's University, Temple University
Other Admissions Factors Considered: Life experiences
Number of Applications Received: 2,116
Number of Applicants Accepted: 973
Number of Applicants Enrolled: 379

EMPLOYMENT INFORMATION

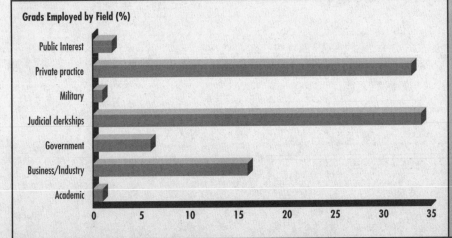

Grads Employed by Field (%)

Average Starting Salary: $48,977
Employers Who Frequently Hire Grads: Graduates are frequently hired by the nation's most prestigious firms, all national and state government agencies, public interest organizations, and state federal judges nationwide.
Prominent Alumni: Lawrence Codey, president and CEO, PSE&G; Katherine Sweeney Hayden, judge, District Court of New Jersey; William McGuire, immediate past president, New Jersey State Bar Association; Donald DiFrancesco, president, New Jersey State Senate

SOUTH TEXAS COLLEGE OF LAW
of Texas A&M University

Admissions Contact: Director of Admissions, Alicia K. Cramer
1303 San Jacinto, Houston, TX 77002-7000
Admissions Phone: 713-646-1810 • Admissions Fax: 713-659-3807
Admissions E-mail: acramer@stcl.edu • Web Address: www.stcl.edu

INSTITUTIONAL INFORMATION
Public/Private: Private
Environment: Urban
Academic Calendar: Semester
Schedule: Full time or part time
Student/Faculty Ratio: 20:1
Total Faculty: 91
% Part Time: 40
% Female: 22

PROGRAMS
Academic Specialties: Emerging programs in International and Environmental Law, and in Dispute Resolution, as well as a nationally recognized program in Advocacy and leading legal research and writing programs. Hands-on live-client clinics provide both a community service and valuable practical experience to students.
Combined Degrees Offered: None
Clinical Program Required? No
Clinical Programs: General Civil Clinic, Criminal Process Clinic, Judicial Process Clinic, Public and Governmental Interest Clinic, Mediation Clinic
Grading System: Alphabetical system of grading; select courses graded Honors Pass, Pass, or Fail
Legal Writing/Methods Course Requirements: 2 courses, 1 semester each, for a total of 4 credits

STUDENT INFORMATION
Enrollment of Law School: 1,220
% Male/Female: 70/30
% Full Time: 70
% Minority: 16
Average Age of Entering Class: 27

EXPENSES/FINANCIAL AID
Annual Tuition: $16,260
Room and Board (Off Campus): $7,272
Books and Supplies: $5,600
Financial Aid Application Deadline: 5/1
Average Grant: $2,120
Average Loan: $16,125
% of Aid That Is Merit-Based: 2
% Receiving Some Sort of Aid: 91
Average Total Aid Package: $19,097
Average Debt: $61,591
Fees Per Credit: $495

ADMISSIONS INFORMATION
Application Fee: $50
Regular Application Deadline: 2/25
Regular Notification: 5/25
LSDAS Accepted? No
Average GPA: 3.0
Range of GPA: 2.6–3.3
Average LSAT: 153
Range of LSAT: 146–153
Transfer Students Accepted? Yes
Other Admissions Factors Considered: Information provided in the essay regarding personal background, accomplishments, and/or achievements; letters of recommendation speaking strongly on the applicant's behalf; improved LSAT scores; upward grade trend over a significant number of hours
Number of Applications Received: 1,539
Number of Applicants Accepted: 1,035
Number of Applicants Enrolled: 385

INTERNATIONAL STUDENTS
TOEFL Required of International Students? Yes

EMPLOYMENT INFORMATION
Rate of Placement: 82%
Prominent Alumni: Sam Nuchia, justice, 1st Court of Appeals for the state of Texas; Robert Eckels, judge, Harris County, Texas; Janis Jack, Judge, Corpus Christi, Texas

SOUTHERN CALIFORNIA INSTITUTE OF LAW

College of Law

Admissions Contact: Dean, Dr. Stanislaus Pulle
877 S. Victoria, Ventura, CA 93003
Admissions Phone: 805-644-2327 • Admissions Fax: 805-644-2367
Web Address: www.lawdegree.com

INSTITUTIONAL INFORMATION
Public/Private: Private
Affiliation: Conservative
Academic Calendar: Semester
Student/Faculty Ratio: 5:1
% Part Time: 75
% Female: 50
% Minority: 10

PROGRAMS
Academic Specialties: Strong emphasis on legal writing. Professors teach in subjects in which they have a specialized practice.

STUDENT INFORMATION
Enrollment of Law School: 50
% Male/Female: 60/40
% Full Time: 0
% Minority: 15
Average Age of Entering Class: 32

RESEARCH FACILITIES
School-Supported Research Centers: Local courthouse library

EXPENSES/FINANCIAL AID
Annual Tuition: $6,480
Books and Supplies: $500
% of Aid That Is Merit-Based: 100
Tuition Per Credit: $200
Fees Per Credit: $200

ADMISSIONS INFORMATION
LSDAS Accepted? No
Transfer Students Accepted? No
Other Schools to Which Students Applied: Ventura College of Law, San Francisco Law School, Santa Barbara College of Law, Western State University
Other Admissions Factors Considered: Working professionals

INTERNATIONAL STUDENTS
TOEFL Required of International Students? Yes

EMPLOYMENT INFORMATION
Average Starting Salary: $30,000
Employers Who Frequently Hire Grads: Local law firms, government and state agencies
Prominent Alumni: Dr. Michael Clare, vice president, HCIA; Sally La Macchia, associate general counsel, National Association of Government Employees; Dr. Jim Forrest, senior scientist, P.E. Muger Base

SOUTHERN ILLINOIS UNIVERSITY
School of Law

Admissions Contact: Assistant Dean, Michael Ruiz
SIUC School of Law, Carbondale, IL 62901-6804
Admissions Phone: 618-453-8858 • Admissions Fax: 618-453-8769
Admissions E-mail: lawadmit@siu.edu • Web Address: www.siu.edu/~lawsch

INSTITUTIONAL INFORMATION
Public/Private: Public
Environment: Suburban
Academic Calendar: Semester
Schedule: Full time only
Student/Faculty Ratio: 10:1
Total Faculty: 37
% Part Time: 27
% Female: 33
% Minority: 0

PROGRAMS
Academic Specialties: Environmental Law, Health Law, Alternative Dispute Resolution
Advanced Degrees Offered: JD (3 years)
Combined Degrees Offered: JD/MD (6 years), JD/MBA (4 years), JD/MPA (4 years), JD/MAcc (4 years), JD/MSW (varies), JD/PhD (varies)
Clinical Program Required? No
Clinical Programs: Elderly Clinic, Alternative Dispute Resolution Clinic, Externship Clinic, Domestic Violence Clinic
Grading System: 4.0 scale with a fixed median
Legal Writing/Methods Course Requirements: Required lawyering skills program including: Legal Research, Writing, Argumentation, and Negotiation

STUDENT INFORMATION
Enrollment of Law School: 381
% Male/Female: 63/37
% Full Time: 100
% Full Time That Are International: 1
% Minority: 8
Average Age of Entering Class: 26

RESEARCH FACILITIES
Computers/Workstations Available: 20

EXPENSES/FINANCIAL AID
Annual Tuition (Residents/Nonresidents): $4,800/$9,600
Room and Board: $7,565
Books and Supplies: $810
Average Grant: $2,143
Average Loan: $12,500
% of Aid That Is Merit-Based: 99
% Receiving Some Sort of Aid: 99
Average Total Aid Package: $14,000
Average Debt: $43,000
Tuition Per Credit (Residents/Nonresidents): $160/$480

ADMISSIONS INFORMATION
Application Fee: $25
Regular Application Deadline: Rolling
Regular Notification: Rolling
LSDAS Accepted? No
Average GPA: 3.1
Range of GPA: 2.8–3.5
Average LSAT: 153
Range of LSAT: 149–158
Transfer Students Accepted? Yes
Other Schools to Which Students Applied: University of Illinois, Northern Illinois University, John Marshall Law School, St. Louis University, Illinois Institute of Technology, Drake University, Washington University, DePaul University
Other Admissions Factors Considered: Leadership ability, character, maturity, motivation, ability to contribute to diversity, obstacles overcome
Number of Applications Received: 670
Number of Applicants Accepted: 388
Number of Applicants Enrolled: 144

INTERNATIONAL STUDENTS
TOEFL Required of International Students? Yes
Minimum TOEFL: 580

EMPLOYMENT INFORMATION

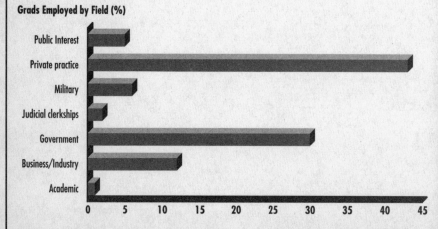

Grads Employed by Field (%)

Rate of Placement: 94%
Average Starting Salary: $35,309
Employers Who Frequently Hire Grads: Peper Martin, Sandberg Phoenix, Hinshaw & Culbertson
Prominent Alumni: G. Patrick Murphy, judge, U.S. District Court; David Herndon, judge, U.S. District Court; Sue Myerscough, justice, Illinois Appellate Court

SOUTHERN METHODIST UNIVERSITY

School of Law

Admissions Contact: Assistant Dean and Director of Admissions, Lynn Switzer Bozalis
PO Box 750110, Dallas, TX 75275-0110
Admissions Phone: 214-768-2550 • Admissions Fax: 214-768-2549
Admissions E-mail: lawadmit@mail.smu.edu • Web Address: www.law.smu.edu/

INSTITUTIONAL INFORMATION

Public/Private: Private
Affiliation: Methodist
Environment: Urban
Academic Calendar: Semester
Schedule: Full time or part time
Student/Faculty Ratio: 20:1
Total Faculty: 38
% Part Time: 2
% Female: 29
% Minority: 16

PROGRAMS

Academic Specialties: Business, Tax, Securities, International, Litigation, Environmental, Health Care, Internet, Dispute Resolution
Advanced Degrees Offered: LLM Taxation (1 year), LLM (1 year)
Combined Degrees Offered: JD/MBA (4.5 years), JD/MA (4 years)
Clinical Program Required? No
Clinical Programs: Civil, Criminal, Tax
Grading System: Letter and numerical system on a 4.0 scale with no C–, D+, or D–

STUDENT INFORMATION

Enrollment of Law School: 741
% Male/Female: 56/44
% Full Time: 98
% Full Time That Are International: 1
% Minority: 11
Average Age of Entering Class: 25

RESEARCH FACILITIES

Computers/Workstations Available: 80

EXPENSES/FINANCIAL AID

Annual Tuition: $21,684
Books and Supplies: $1,290
Financial Aid Application Deadline: 6/1
Average Grant: $8,000
% of Aid That Is Merit-Based: 90
% Receiving Some Sort of Aid: 85
Average Total Aid Package: $30,000
Average Debt: $60,000

ADMISSIONS INFORMATION

Application Fee: $50
Regular Application Deadline: 2/15
Regular Notification: 4/30
Average GPA: 3.3
Range of GPA: 3.1–3.6
Average LSAT: 157
Range of LSAT: 154–160
Transfer Students Accepted? Yes
Other Schools to Which Students Applied: University of Texas, University of Houston, Baylor University, Texas Tech University, St. Mary's University, Tulane University, South Texas College of Law, Emory University
Other Admissions Factors Considered: Diverse background, student's institutional connections
Number of Applications Received: 1,545
Number of Applicants Accepted: 696
Number of Applicants Enrolled: 253

EMPLOYMENT INFORMATION

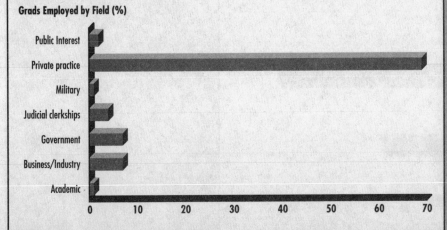

Grads Employed by Field (%)

- Public Interest
- Private practice
- Military
- Judicial clerkships
- Government
- Business/Industry
- Academic

(0, 10, 20, 30, 40, 50, 60, 70)

Rate of Placement: 85%
Average Starting Salary: $60,000
Prominent Alumni: Four justices on the Texas Supreme Court, two justices on the supreme court of Japan

SOUTHERN UNIVERSITY
Law Center

Admissions Contact: Gloria Simon
PO Box 9294, Baton Rouge, LA 70813
Admissions Phone: 225-771-5340 • Admissions Fax: 225-771-7424
Web Address: www.sus.edu

INSTITUTIONAL INFORMATION

Public/Private: Public
Environment: Urban
Academic Calendar: Semester
Schedule: Full time only
Student/Faculty Ratio: 12:1
Total Faculty: 44
% Female: 30
% Minority: 64

PROGRAMS

Academic Specialties: Law and Technology (Artificial Intelligence)
Clinical Program Required? No
Clinical Programs: 4 Clinics: Criminal, Juvenile, Elder Law, Administrative/Civil. Clinical Education Program is restricted to third-year law students in good standing.
Grading System: 4.0 grade point scale; A (90–100), B+ (85–89), B (84–80), C+ (79–75), C (74–70), D+ (69–65), D (64–60), F (59–0)
Legal Writing/Methods Course Requirements: First year: Legal Writing, 2 hours/semester; second year: Advanced Legal Writing 1 hour/semester

STUDENT INFORMATION

Enrollment of Law School: 311
% Male/Female: 50/50
% Full Time: 100
% Minority: 66
Average Age of Entering Class: 27

RESEARCH FACILITIES

School-Supported Research Centers: Through a cooperative aggreement with Paul M. Herbert Law Center at Louisiana State University, students at both institutions have unlimited and free access to each institution's facilities and materials.

EXPENSES/FINANCIAL AID

Annual Tuition (Residents/Nonresidents): $3,128/$7,728

ADMISSIONS INFORMATION

Regular Application Deadline: 3/1
Regular Notification: January–May
Average GPA: 3.6
Average LSAT: 145
Other Schools to Which Students Applied: Loyola University Chicago, Howard University, Tulane University, Texas Southern University, Georgia State University, Florida State University, George Mason University, Georgetown University

EMPLOYMENT INFORMATION

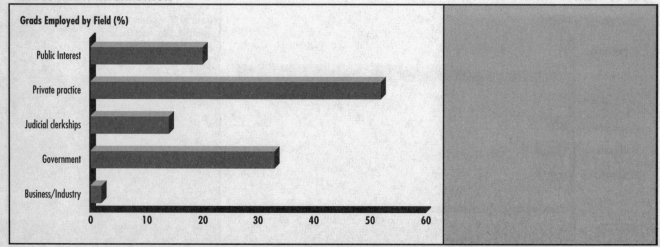

SOUTHWESTERN UNIVERSITY
School of Law

Admissions Contact: Director of Admissions, Anne Wilson
675 South Westmoreland Avenue, Los Angeles, CA 90005
Admissions Phone: 213-738-6717 • Admissions Fax: 213-383-1688
Admissions E-mail: admissions@swlaw.edu • Web Address: www.swlaw.edu

INSTITUTIONAL INFORMATION

Public/Private: Private
Environment: Urban
Academic Calendar: Semester
Schedule: Full time or part time
Student/Faculty Ratio: 17:1
Total Faculty: 87
% Part Time: 43
% Female: 36
% Minority: 20

PROGRAMS

Academic Specialties: Nationally recognized experts in Antitrust, Criminal, Environmental, Family, Housing and Urban Development, Intellectual Property and Entertainment, International, and Taxation Law
Combined Degrees Offered: None
Clinical Program Required? No
Clinical Programs: Externships in over 100 legal settings in judicial, public interest, federal/state/local government, or entertainment entities; clinical/simulation courses on a variety of topics from Alternative Dispute Resolution to White Collar Crime
Grading System: A+/A (4.0) to F (0.0); some courses are P/F
Legal Writing/Methods Course Requirements: Legal Research and Writing, taken in the first year, culminates in Moot Court Intramural Competition

STUDENT INFORMATION

Enrollment of Law School: 867
% Male/Female: 50/50
% Full Time: 70
% Full Time That Are International: 5
% Minority: 33
Average Age of Entering Class: 27

RESEARCH FACILITIES

Computers/Workstations Available: 99
School-Supported Research Centers: Summer Abroad program affiliations: Canada: International Center for Criminal Law Reform and Criminal Justice Policy; Argentina: Universidad de Buenos Aires, Universidad de Salvador; Mexico: Universidad de Guanajuato

EXPENSES/FINANCIAL AID

Annual Tuition: $21,990
Room and Board (Off Campus): $11,000
Books and Supplies: $540
Financial Aid Application Deadline: 6/1
Average Grant: $7,051
Average Loan: $22,066
% of Aid That Is Merit-Based: 30
% Receiving Some Sort of Aid: 87
Average Total Aid Package: $24,525
Average Debt: $82,449
Tuition Per Credit: $634
Fees Per Credit: $733

ADMISSIONS INFORMATION

Application Fee: $50
Regular Application Deadline: 6/30
Regular Notification: Rolling
LSDAS Accepted? Yes
Range of GPA: 2.8–3.4
Range of LSAT: 148–153
Transfer Students Accepted? Yes
Other Schools to Which Students Applied: Loyola Marymount University, UCLA School of Law, University of Southern California, Whittier College, Pepperdine University, University of San Diego, University of California—Hastings, University of the Pacific
Number of Applications Received: 1,975
Number of Applicants Accepted: 1,067
Number of Applicants Enrolled: 353

EMPLOYMENT INFORMATION

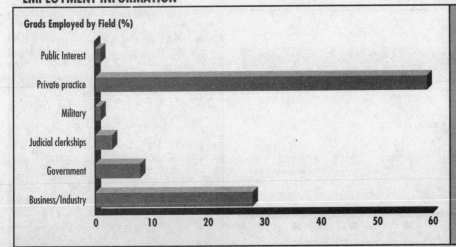

Grads Employed by Field (%)

Rate of Placement: 84%
Average Starting Salary: $50,800
Prominent Alumni: U.S. Senator Gordon Smith, Oregon '79; U.S. Congressman Julian Dixon, California '69; U.S. Congressman Jim Gibbons, Nevada '79; U.S. District Court Judge Ronald S.W. Lew, central district of California '71; California Supreme Court Justice Stanley Mosk '35; California State Treasurer Matthew Fong '85; Hon. Vaino Spencer, presiding justice, California Court of Appeal, 2nd Appellate District, Division 1 '52; late Los Angeles Mayor Tom Bradley '56; California Assemblywoman Denise Moreno Ducheny '79

STANFORD UNIVERSITY
School of Law

Admissions Contact: Associate Dean for Admissions and Financial Aid, Faye K. Deal
559 Nathan Abbott Way, Stanford, CA 94305-8610
Admissions Phone: 650-723-4985 • Admissions Fax: 650-723-0838
Admissions E-mail: law.admissions@forsythe.stanford.edu • Web Address: www.law.stanford.edu/

INSTITUTIONAL INFORMATION

Public/Private: Private
Affiliation: Nondenominational
Environment: Suburban
Academic Calendar: Quarter
Schedule: Full time only
Student/Faculty Ratio: 14:1
Total Faculty: 52
% Female: 21
% Minority: 15

PROGRAMS

Academic Specialties: See http://lawschool.stanford.edu/faculty/index/shtml
Advanced Degrees Offered: MLS (1 year), JSM (1 year), JSD (2 years)
Combined Degrees Offered: JD/MBA (4 years), JD/MA (4 years)
Clinical Program Required? No
Clinical Programs: East Palo Alto Law Project
Grading System: Letter system
Legal Writing/Methods Course Requirements: 1 year

STUDENT INFORMATION

Enrollment of Law School: 545
% Male/Female: 55/45
% Full Time: 100
% Full Time That Are International: 3
% Minority: 32
Average Age of Entering Class: 25

RESEARCH FACILITIES

Computers/Workstations Available: 75

EXPENSES/FINANCIAL AID

Annual Tuition: $26,158
Room and Board (On/Off Campus): $10,332/$14,682
Books and Supplies: $1,254
Financial Aid Application Deadline: 3/15
Average Grant: $9,975
Average Loan: $25,308
% Receiving Some Sort of Aid: 80
Average Total Aid Package: $32,299
Average Debt: $70,000

ADMISSIONS INFORMATION

Application Fee: $65
Regular Application Deadline: Rolling
Regular Notification: 4/30
LSDAS Accepted? No
Average GPA: 3.7
Range of GPA: 3.6–3.9
Average LSAT: 167
Range of LSAT: 165–170
Transfer Students Accepted? Yes
Other Schools to Which Students Applied: Harvard University, Yale University, University of California—Berkeley, UCLA School of Law, Georgetown University, New York University, Columbia University, University of Michigan
Number of Applications Received: 3,824
Number of Applicants Enrolled: 178

EMPLOYMENT INFORMATION

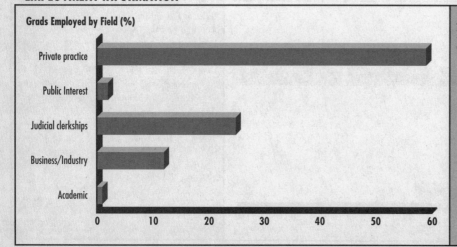

Grads Employed by Field (%)

Average Starting Salary: $76,466
Prominent Alumni: Justice Sandra Day O'Connor, U.S. Supreme Court; Justice William Rehnquist, U.S. Supreme Court

STETSON UNIVERSITY
College of Law

Admissions Contact: Director of Admissions, Pamela B. Coleman
1401 61st Street South, St. Petersburg, FL 33707
Admissions Phone: 813-562-7802 • Admissions Fax: 813-343-0136
Admissions E-mail: lawadmit@law.stetson.edu • Web Address: www.law.stetson.edu

INSTITUTIONAL INFORMATION

Public/Private: Private
Environment: Suburban
Academic Calendar: Semester
Schedule: Full time only
Student/Faculty Ratio: 17:1
Total Faculty: 93
% Part Time: 55
% Female: 27
% Minority: 9

PROGRAMS

Academic Specialties: The Trial Advocacy Program is renowned.
Advanced Degrees Offered: JD (3 years), LLM (1 year)
Combined Degrees Offered: JD/MBA (3.5 years)
Clinical Program Required? No
Clinical Programs: Criminal Defense, Criminal Prosecution, Civil Poverty, Civil Elder Law, Employment Discrimination, Civil Government, Alternative Dispute Resolution
Grading System: 4-point scale
Legal Writing/Methods Course Requirements: 1-year Research and Writing

STUDENT INFORMATION

Enrollment of Law School: 670
% Male/Female: 43/57
% Full Time: 98
% Full Time That Are International: 4
% Minority: 21
Average Age of Entering Class: 25

RESEARCH FACILITIES

Computers/Workstations Available: 100

EXPENSES/FINANCIAL AID

Annual Tuition: $21,165
Room and Board (On/Off Campus): $6,960/$9,225
Books and Supplies: $1,000
Average Grant: $9,500
Average Loan: $24,000
% of Aid That Is Merit-Based: 30
% Receiving Some Sort of Aid: 90
Average Total Aid Package: $35,000
Average Debt: $77,600

ADMISSIONS INFORMATION

Application Fee: $50
Regular Application Deadline: Rolling
Regular Notification: Rolling
LSDAS Accepted? No
Average GPA: 3.3
Range of GPA: 3.0–3.5
Average LSAT: 152
Range of LSAT: 148–155
Transfer Students Accepted? Yes
Other Schools to Which Students Applied: University of Florida, Florida State University, University of Miami, Nova Southeastern University, St. Thomas University, Mercer University, Emory University, Wake Forest University
Other Admissions Factors Considered: Faculty committee reviews personal statements, grade trends, letters of recommendation, campus activities, work experience, diversity factors
Number of Applications Received: 1,943
Number of Applicants Accepted: 748
Number of Applicants Enrolled: 657

INTERNATIONAL STUDENTS

TOEFL Required of International Students? Yes
Minimum TOEFL: 600

EMPLOYMENT INFORMATION

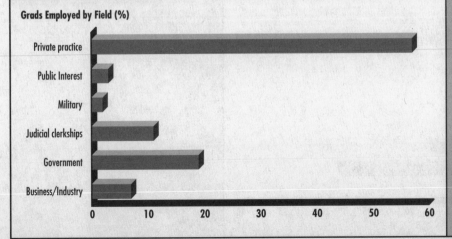

Grads Employed by Field (%)

Rate of Placement: 92%
Average Starting Salary: $43,000
Employers Who Frequently Hire Grads: Small to medium-size firms in the greater Tampa Bay area, State Attorney's Offices, Public Defenders Office

SUFFOLK UNIVERSITY
School of Law

Admissions Contact: Dean of Admissions, Gail N. Ellis
120 Tremont Street, Boston, MA 02108
Admissions Phone: 617-523-8144 • Admissions Fax: 617-523-1367
Admissions E-mail: lawadm@admin.suffolk.edu • Web Address: www.law.suffolk.edu

INSTITUTIONAL INFORMATION

Public/Private: Private
Environment: Urban
Academic Calendar: Semester
Schedule: Full time or part time
Student/Faculty Ratio: 20:1
Total Faculty: 160
% Part Time: 60
% Female: 17
% Minority: 5

PROGRAMS

Academic Specialties: Concentrations in High Technology/Intellectual Property, Health Care Biomedical Law, Financial Services, International Law, Civil Litigation, Tax Law; new study abroad program at University of Lund in Lund, Sweden.
Advanced Degrees Offered: JD (3 years full time, 4 years part time)
Combined Degrees Offered: JD/MBA, JD/MPA, JD/MSIE, JD/MSF; (all 3 years full time, 5 years part time)
Clinical Program Required? No
Clinical Programs: Voluntary Defenders Prosecutor Program, Battered Women's Program, Center for Juvenile Justice, Macaronis Institute for Trial and Appellate Advocacy
Grading System: Letter and numerical system ranging from A+ (4.3) to F (0.0)
Legal Writing/Methods Course Requirements: 2 semesters

STUDENT INFORMATION

Enrollment of Law School: 1,700
% Male/Female: 64/36
% Full Time: 60
% Full Time That Are International: 6
% Minority: 12
Average Age of Entering Class: 25

RESEARCH FACILITIES

Computers/Workstations Available: 102

EXPENSES/FINANCIAL AID

Annual Tuition: $23,270
Room and Board (Off Campus): $13,670
Books and Supplies: $900
Financial Aid Application Deadline: 3/2
Average Grant: $4,000
Average Loan: $18,500
% of Aid That Is Merit-Based: 5
% Receiving Some Sort of Aid: 95
Average Total Aid Package: $4,500
Average Debt: $59,600
Tuition Per Credit: $730

ADMISSIONS INFORMATION

Application Fee: $50
Regular Application Deadline: 3/1
Regular Notification: Rolling
LSDAS Accepted? Yes
Average GPA: 3.2
Range of GPA: 2.9–3.4
Average LSAT: 154
Range of LSAT: 150–157
Transfer Students Accepted? Yes
Other Schools to Which Students Applied: Albany Law School, Boston University, New England School of Law, Northeastern University, University of Connecticut, Temple Law, American University, George Washington University
Other Admissions Factors Considered: Community service
Number of Applications Received: 2,200
Number of Applicants Enrolled: 575

INTERNATIONAL STUDENTS

TOEFL Required of International Students? Yes
Minimum TOEFL: 600

EMPLOYMENT INFORMATION

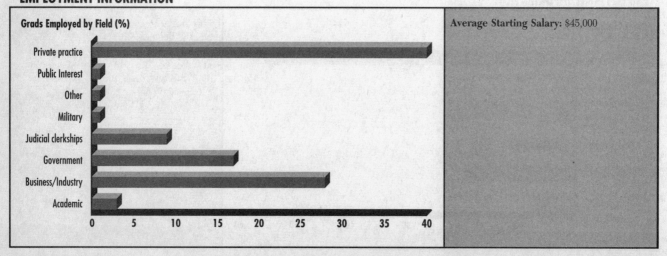

Grads Employed by Field (%)

Field	Value
Private practice	40
Public Interest	1
Other	1
Military	1
Judicial clerkships	9
Government	17
Business/Industry	28
Academic	3

Average Starting Salary: $45,000

SYRACUSE UNIVERSITY
College of Law

Admissions Contact: Director of Admissions, Patricia K. Golla
Office of Admissions, Suite 340, Syracuse, NY 13244-1030
Admissions Phone: 315-443-1962 • Admissions Fax: 315-443-9568
Admissions E-mail: admissions@law.syr.edu • Web Address: www.law.syr.edu

INSTITUTIONAL INFORMATION

Public/Private: Private
Environment: Urban
Academic Calendar: Semester
Schedule: Full time or part time
Student/Faculty Ratio: 17:1
Total Faculty: 85
% Part Time: 52
% Female: 29
% Minority: 6

PROGRAMS

Academic Specialties: Syracuse has developed numerous programs designed to integrate theory and practice. These applied learning opportunities provide hands-on experience in a variety of fields. A number of joint degree programs are also offered with other units on campus. Specializations include Trial Practice; Law, Technology, and Management; Law and Economics; and Clinical Training.
Combined Degrees Offered: JD/MS Accounting, Library Science, Environmental Science, Communications, Speech Communications, News/Magazine, Media, Language Arts, Nutrition; JD/MBA; JD/MA Economics, History, International, Engineering, Geography; JD/PhD Political Science, JD/MSW, JD/MPA
Clinical Program Required? No

Clinical Programs: Housing and Finance, Criminal Law, Public Interest Law, Civil Law, Children's Rights; 3 externship courses: Judicial, Advocacy, and Public Interest Advocacy
Grading System: A, B+, B, C+, C, D, F or pass/fail. Grading is anonymous except in courses like seminars and Trial Practice.
Legal Writing/Methods Course Requirements: First-year, 2-semester course Law Firm

STUDENT INFORMATION

Enrollment of Law School: 751
% Male/Female: 54/46
% Full Time: 98
% Full Time That Are International: 4
% Minority: 24
Average Age of Entering Class: 25

EXPENSES/FINANCIAL AID

Annual Tuition: $23,140
Room and Board: $9,214
Books and Supplies: $1,100
Average Grant: $7,876
% Receiving Some Sort of Aid: 57
Average Debt: $65,000
Fees Per Credit: $1,012

ADMISSIONS INFORMATION

Application Fee: $50
Regular Application Deadline: Rolling
Regular Notification: Rolling
LSDAS Accepted? Yes
Average GPA: 3.2
Range of GPA: 2.9–3.4
Average LSAT: 151
Range of LSAT: 148–154
Transfer Students Accepted? Yes
Other Schools to Which Students Applied: Boston College, American University, George Washington University, Albany Law School of Union University, State University of New York, Boston University, New York Law School, Catholic University School of Law
Other Admissions Factors Considered: Trend of undergraduate performance and course selection; graduate course work and degree, writing ability, overcoming personal hardship including such burdens as poverty or disability, age, race/ethnicity, gender, community activities
Number of Applications Received: 1,714

INTERNATIONAL STUDENTS

TOEFL Required of International Students? Yes
Minimum TOEFL: 600

EMPLOYMENT INFORMATION

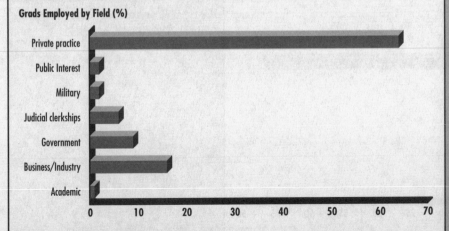

Grads Employed by Field (%)

Rate of Placement: 92%
Average Starting Salary: $48,006
Prominent Alumni: Joseph R. Biden, Jr., U.S. senator; Theodore A. McKee, judge, Federal Court of Appeals, third Circuit; Alfonse M. D'Amato, U.S. senator

TEMPLE UNIVERSITY

James E. Beasley School of Law

Admissions Contact: Director of Admissions, Jodeen M. Hobbs
1719 North Broad Street, Philadelphia, PA 19122
Admissions Phone: 215-204-5949 • Admissions Fax: 215-204-1185
Admissions E-mail: lawadmis@blue.temple.edu • Web Address: www.temple.edu/lawschool

INSTITUTIONAL INFORMATION

Public/Private: Public
Environment: Urban
Academic Calendar: Semester
Schedule: Full time or part time
Student/Faculty Ratio: 19:1
Total Faculty: 57
% Female: 37
% Minority: 25

PROGRAMS

Academic Specialties: Trial Advocacy, Business and Tax Law, International Law, Public Interest Law, Criminal Law, Transactional Law Technology Law/Intellectual Property

Advanced Degrees Offered: JD (3 years full time, 4 years part time), LLM Trial Advocacy (1 year), LLM Taxation (1 year), LLM Transnational Law (1 year), graduate teaching fellowships (1 year), LLM for graduates of foreign law schools (1 year)

Combined Degrees Offered: JD/MBA (approximately 4 years), JD/LLM degree programs in Taxation and Transnational Law (3.5 years), JD with individually designed joint degrees

Clinical Program Required? No

Clinical Programs: Temple has extensive clinical offerings in 25 areas ranging from Civil Litigation to Business and Criminal Law. All students are guaranteed at least 1 clinical offering.

Grading System: 4.0 scale

Legal Writing/Methods Course Requirements: 1-year intensive program that includes drafting briefs, memos, and conducting an oral argument

STUDENT INFORMATION

Enrollment of Law School: 1,104
% Male/Female: 49/51
% Full Time: 69
% Full Time That Are International: 2
% Minority: 25
Average Age of Entering Class: 26

RESEARCH FACILITIES

School-Supported Research Centers: Temple's brand new recreational and exercise facilities, including a student field house

EXPENSES/FINANCIAL AID

Annual Tuition (Residents/Nonresidents): $9,226/$15,990
Room and Board: $6,246
Books and Supplies: $1,200
Financial Aid Application Deadline: 3/1
Average Grant: $2,702
Average Loan: $17,118
% of Aid That Is Merit-Based: 69
% Receiving Some Sort of Aid: 79
Average Total Aid Package: $17,582
Average Debt: $50,785
Fees Per Credit (Residents/Nonresidents): $344/$637

ADMISSIONS INFORMATION

Application Fee: $50
Regular Application Deadline: 3/1
Regular Notification: Rolling
LSDAS Accepted? Yes
Average GPA: 3.2
Range of GPA: 2.9–3.5
Average LSAT: 155
Range of LSAT: 152–159
Transfer Students Accepted? Yes
Other Schools to Which Students Applied: University of Pennsylvania, Villanova University, Rutgers University—Camden, American University, Dickinson School of Law

Other Admissions Factors Considered: Graduate course work; demonstrated leadership ability in college, community, or career activities; economic disadvantage; academic honors; committment to service (Peace Corps, VISTA, military); serious disabilities

Number of Applications Received: 2,732
Number of Applicants Accepted: 1,108
Number of Applicants Enrolled: 343

INTERNATIONAL STUDENTS

TOEFL Required of International Students? Yes
Minimum TOEFL: 600

EMPLOYMENT INFORMATION

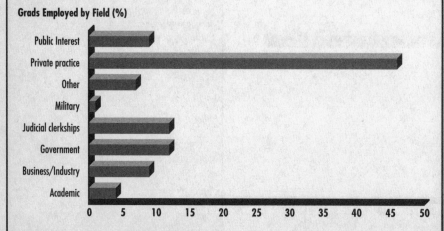

Grads Employed by Field (%)

Rate of Placement: 92%
Average Starting Salary: $52,517

TEXAS SOUTHERN UNIVERSITY
Thurgood Marshall School of Law

Admissions Contact: Dean of Admissions, Edward René
3100 Cleburne Street, Houston, TX 77004
Admissions Phone: 713-313-7114 • Admissions Fax: 713-313-1049
Admissions E-mail: erene@tsulaw.edu • Web Address: www.tsulaw.edu

INSTITUTIONAL INFORMATION
Public/Private: Public
Environment: Urban
Academic Calendar: Semester
Schedule: Full time only
Student/Faculty Ratio: 17:1
Total Faculty: 35
% Female: 20
% Minority: 83

STUDENT INFORMATION
Enrollment of Law School: 541
% Male/Female: 57/43
% Full Time: 100
% Minority: 77

EXPENSES/FINANCIAL AID
Annual Tuition (Residents/Nonresidents):
$4,466/$7,562
Room and Board (Off Campus): $6,000
Books and Supplies: $700
Fees Per Credit (Residents/Nonresidents):
$344/$637

ADMISSIONS INFORMATION
Application Fee: $40
Regular Application Deadline: 4/1
Regular Notification: Rolling
Average GPA: 3.0
Transfer Students Accepted? Yes
Other Schools to Which Students Applied: University of Houston, Texas A&M University, Texas Tech University, University of Texas, St. Mary's University, Southern Methodist University, Southern University, Baylor University
Number of Applications Received: 1,460
Number of Applicants Accepted: 540
Number of Applicants Enrolled: 265

EMPLOYMENT INFORMATION

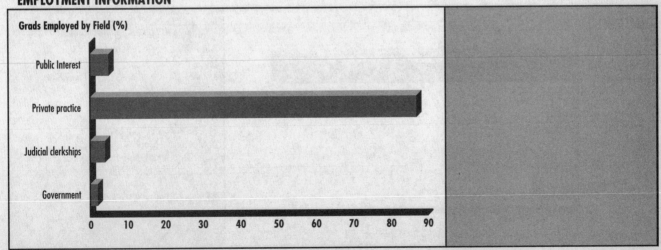

TEXAS TECH UNIVERSITY
School of Law

Admissions Contact: Admissions Assistant, Donna Williams
1802 Hartford Avenue, Lubbock, TX 79409
Admissions Phone: 806-742-3985 • Admissions Fax: 806-742-1629
Admissions E-mail: xydaw@ttacs.ttu.edu • Web Address: www.law.ttu.edu

INSTITUTIONAL INFORMATION

Public/Private: Public
Environment: Urban
Academic Calendar: Semester
Schedule: Full time only
Student/Faculty Ratio: 24:1
Total Faculty: 30
% Female: 30
% Minority: 20

PROGRAMS

Academic Specialties: The faculty offers courses in all the areas of specialization listed below, and a program in Litigation Skills.
Combined Degrees Offered: JD/MBA (3 years), JD/MPA (3.5 years), JD/MS Agriculture and Applied Science (3–3.5 years), JD/MS Accounting (Taxation) (3–3.5 years)
Clinical Program Required? No
Legal Writing/Methods Course Requirements: 2-semester course, 4 total credits, meets in classes of approximately 22

STUDENT INFORMATION

Enrollment of Law School: 555
% Male/Female: 56/44
% Full Time: 100
% Full Time That Are International: 2
% Minority: 10
Average Age of Entering Class: 25

RESEARCH FACILITIES

Computers/Workstations Available: 250
School-Supported Research Centers: In conjunction with Southwestern and the University of New Mexico Law Schools, Texas Tech offers a summer program in Guanajuato, Mexico, with an emphasis on NAFTA. The Universidad de Guanajuato Law School hosts.

EXPENSES/FINANCIAL AID

Annual Tuition (Residents/Nonresidents): $4,800/$9,870
Room and Board: $5,748
Books and Supplies: $849
Average Grant: $3,000
Average Loan: $7,043
% of Aid That Is Merit-Based: 46
% Receiving Some Sort of Aid: 79
Average Debt: $49,000
Fees Per Credit (Residents/Nonresidents): $160/$329

ADMISSIONS INFORMATION

Application Fee: $50
Regular Application Deadline: 2/1
Regular Notification: Rolling
LSDAS Accepted? Yes
Average GPA: 3.3
Range of GPA: 3.1–3.5
Average LSAT: 154
Range of LSAT: 151–158
Transfer Students Accepted? Yes
Other Schools to Which Students Applied: University of Texas, University of Houston, Baylor University, Southern Methodist University, St. Mary's University, Texas A&M University, University of Oklahoma, University of Arizona
Other Admissions Factors Considered: Socioeconomic background of the applicant including the percentage by which the applicant's family is above or below any recognized measure of poverty, the applicant's household income, and the applicant's parent's level of education
Number of Applications Received: 1,079
Number of Applicants Accepted: 536
Number of Applicants Enrolled: 199

INTERNATIONAL STUDENTS

TOEFL Required of International Students? Yes
Minimum TOEFL: 550

EMPLOYMENT INFORMATION

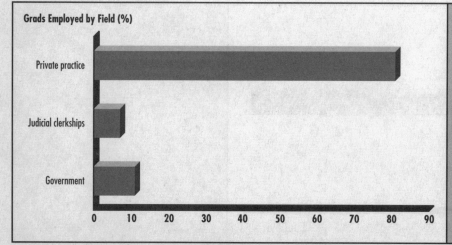

Rate of Placement: 93%
Average Starting Salary: $52,000
Employers Who Frequently Hire Grads: Jones, Day Reavis and Pogue; Thompson and Knight; Haynes and Boone; Thompson and Coe; Cousins and Irons; Strasburger and Price; Cooper and Aldous; Kemp, Smith, Duncan and Hammond; Mehaffy and Weber; Orgain, Bell and Tucker; State and Federal Judiciary
Prominent Alumni: General Walter R. Huffman, Judge Advocate General of the U.S. Army; Justice Mary Ellen Hicks, first African American to sit on the Court of Appeals in Texas; Bill Mateja, president, Texas Young Lawyers Association

TEXAS WESLEYAN UNIVERSITY
School of Law

Admissions Contact: Assistant Director of Admissions, Lynda Culver
1515 Commerce Street, Fort Worth, TX 76102
Admissions Phone: 817-212-4040 • Admissions Fax: 817-212-4002
Admissions E-mail: law_admissions@law.txwes.edu • Web Address: www.txwesleyan.edu/law

INSTITUTIONAL INFORMATION

Public/Private: Private
Affiliation: Methodist
Environment: Urban
Academic Calendar: Semester
Schedule: Full time day, part time night
Student/Faculty Ratio: 17:1
Total Faculty: 29
% Part Time: 22
% Female: 29
% Minority: 12

PROGRAMS

Academic Specialties: Innovative program of skills courses called Practicum Courses—a course of study designed especially for the preparation of practitioners that involves the supervised practical application of previously studied theory
Advanced Degrees Offered: JD degree only (3 years full time, 4 years part time)
Clinical Program Required? No
Clinical Programs: Law Clinic specializing in Social Security Disability Issues, Mediation Clinic, Family Mediation Clinics
Grading System: Numerical system
Legal Writing/Methods Course Requirements: 2-semester course that includes briefing and meets court component

STUDENT INFORMATION

% Male/Female: 100/0
Average Age of Entering Class: 34

EXPENSES/FINANCIAL AID

Annual Tuition: $17,100
Books and Supplies: $1,500
Financial Aid Application Deadline: 4/15
Average Grant: $2,500
Average Loan: $17,681
% of Aid That Is Merit-Based: 18
% Receiving Some Sort of Aid: 82
Average Total Aid Package: $20,000
Average Debt: $56,500
Fees Per Credit: $520

ADMISSIONS INFORMATION

Application Fee: $50
Regular Application Deadline: 3/31
Regular Notification: Rolling
Average GPA: 2.9
Range of GPA: 2.7–3.4
Average LSAT: 150
Range of LSAT: 146–154
Transfer Students Accepted? Yes
Other Schools to Which Students Applied: Southern Methodist University, Texas Tech University, University of Texas—Austin, University of Houston, St. Mary's University, South Texas College of Law
Number of Applications Received: 1,177
Number of Applicants Accepted: 486

INTERNATIONAL STUDENTS

TOEFL Required of International Students? Yes

EMPLOYMENT INFORMATION

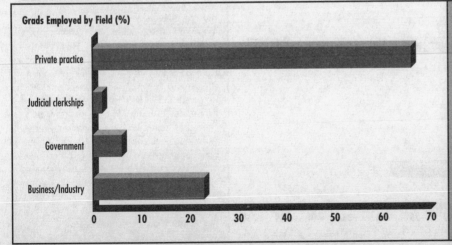

Rate of Placement: 84%
Average Starting Salary: $48
Employers Who Frequently Hire Grads: Small to medium-size private practice firms, District Attorney's Offices, government agencies, various corporations and businesses

THOMAS JEFFERSON SCHOOL OF LAW

Admissions Contact: Assistant Dean, Jennifer Keller
2121 San Diego Avenue, San Diego, CA 92110
Admissions Phone: 619-297-9700 • Admissions Fax: 619-294-4713
Admissions E-mail: adm@tjsl.edu • Web Address: www.tjsl.edu

INSTITUTIONAL INFORMATION

Public/Private: Private
Environment: Urban
Academic Calendar: Semester
Student/Faculty Ratio: 18:1
Total Faculty: 42
% Part Time: 45
% Female: 31
% Minority: 5

PROGRAMS

Academic Specialties: Faculty members specialize in a wide variety of areas, with some emphasis on International Law. The curriculum emphasizes professional skills.
Advanced Degrees Offered: JD (3 years full time, 4 years part time)
Clinical Program Required? No
Clinical Programs: Placements at federal, state, and local levels
Grading System: 4.0 system
Legal Writing/Methods Course Requirements: 2 semesters

STUDENT INFORMATION

Enrollment of Law School: 586
% Male/Female: 61/39
% Full Time: 65
% Full Time That Are International: 35
% Minority: 22
Average Age of Entering Class: 28

RESEARCH FACILITIES

Computers/Workstations Available: 45

EXPENSES/FINANCIAL AID

Annual Tuition: $21,150
Room and Board (Off Campus): $7,074
Books and Supplies: $525
Financial Aid Application Deadline: 6/30
Average Grant: $5,480
Average Loan: $19,158
% of Aid That Is Merit-Based: 100
% Receiving Some Sort of Aid: 95
Average Total Aid Package: $20,576
Average Debt: $64,023
Fees Per Credit: $625

ADMISSIONS INFORMATION

Application Fee: $35
Regular Application Deadline: Rolling
Regular Notification: Rolling
LSDAS Accepted? Yes
Average GPA: 2.8
Range of GPA: 2.4–3.1
Average LSAT: 149
Range of LSAT: 146–154
Transfer Students Accepted? Yes
Other Schools to Which Students Applied: California Western University, University of San Diego, Whittier College, Southwestern University, Golden Gate University, University of San Francisco
Number of Applications Received: 1,590
Number of Applicants Accepted: 1,096
Number of Applicants Enrolled: 192

EMPLOYMENT INFORMATION

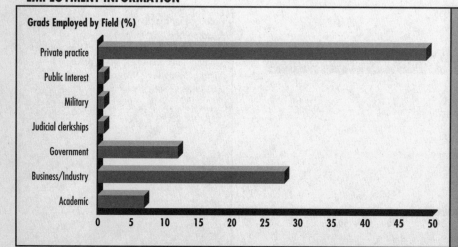

Grads Employed by Field (%)

Rate of Placement: 91%
Average Starting Salary: $47,394
Employers Who Frequently Hire Grads: District Attorney's, Attorney General's, and Public Defender's Offices; various and numerous alumni small firms, and other medium-sized local firms in San Diego and Orange County
Prominent Alumni: Marc D. Adelman, 1998 president, State Bar of California; Duncan Hunter, U.S. congressman; Hon. Lillian Y. Lim of the Municipal Court of the San Diego Judicial District, the first Filipino woman to become a judge in the United States

THOMAS M. COOLEY LAW SCHOOL

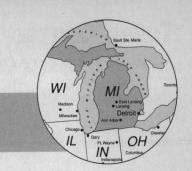

Admissions Contact: Assistant Dean of Admissions, Stephanie Gregg
300 South Capitol Avenue, PO Box 13038, Lansing, MI 48901
Admissions Phone: 517-371-5140 • Admissions Fax: 517-334-5718
Admissions E-mail: admissions@cooley.edu • Web Address: www.cooley.edu

INSTITUTIONAL INFORMATION

Public/Private: Private
Environment: Urban
Academic Calendar: Trimester
Schedule: Full time or part time
Student/Faculty Ratio: 21:1
Total Faculty: 146
% Female: 31
% Minority: 7

PROGRAMS

Academic Specialties: Cooley offers students more scheduling options than most law schools and is dedicated to its mission of providing practical legal education to students from all walks of life.
Advanced Degrees Offered: JD (usually 3 years)
Clinical Program Required? Yes
Clinical Programs: Cooley Law School has an extensive third-year externship program that places senior students in real work situations.
Grading System: Firm but fair. In most courses, grades are based on written final exams, administered and graded under a system that assures student anonymity. Professors adhere to established grade definitions. The Thomas M. Cooley Law School does not practice grade inflation.
Legal Writing/Methods Course Requirements: Intro to Law and Research and Writing are 2 required courses

STUDENT INFORMATION

Enrollment of Law School: 1,694
% Male/Female: 57/43
% Full Time: 24
% Full Time That Are International: 4
% Minority: 29
Average Age of Entering Class: 25

RESEARCH FACILITIES

School-Supported Research Centers: Law students have access to nearby state law library.

EXPENSES/FINANCIAL AID

Annual Tuition: $18,150
Room and Board (Off Campus): $10,328
Books and Supplies: $775
Average Grant: $2,200
Average Loan: $20,000
% Receiving Some Sort of Aid: 92
Average Total Aid Package: $22,000
Average Debt: $63,000
Fees Per Credit: $550

ADMISSIONS INFORMATION

Regular Application Deadline: Rolling
Regular Notification: Rolling
Average GPA: 2.9
Range of GPA: 2.6–3.2
Average LSAT: 144
Range of LSAT: 140–147
Transfer Students Accepted? Yes
Other Schools to Which Students Applied: Wayne State University, John Marshall Law School, Pepperdine University, Whittier College, University of Michigan, Nova Southeastern University, Ohio State University, University of Southern California
Other Admissions Factors Considered: None, other than character and fitness
Number of Applications Received: 2,110
Number of Applicants Accepted: 1,410

EMPLOYMENT INFORMATION

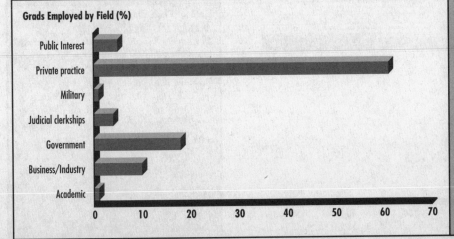

Grads Employed by Field (%)

Average Starting Salary: $36,450
Prominent Alumni: Michigan Governor John Engler; U.S. Senator Spencer Abraham; Michigan Appeals Court Judge Jane Markey

TOURO COLLEGE
Jacob D. Fuchsberg Law Center

Admissions Contact: Director of Recruitment, Bill Imbriale
300 Nassau Road, Huntington, NY 11743
Admissions Phone: 631-421-2244 • Admissions Fax: 631-421-9708
Admissions E-mail: williami@tourolaw.edu • Web Address: www.tourolaw.edu

INSTITUTIONAL INFORMATION

Public/Private: Private
Environment: Urban
Academic Calendar: Semester
Schedule: Full time or part time
Student/Faculty Ratio: 13:1

PROGRAMS

Academic Specialties: Business Law, Criminal Law, Intellectual Property Law, International Law, Public Interest Law, Health Law
Advanced Degrees Offered: JD (3 years full time, 4 years part time), LLM for foreign-trained attorneys (1 year full time), MPS (1 year full time)
Combined Degrees Offered: JD/MBA, JD/MPA, JD/MS, JD/MSW (all require 1 additional year)
Clinical Program Required? No
Clinical Programs: Civil Rights Litigation Clinic, Elder Law Clinic, International Human Rights Litigation Clinic, Family Law Clinic, Judicial Clerkship Clinic, Legal Institutions Clinic—Criminal, Legal Institutions Clinic—Civil

STUDENT INFORMATION

Enrollment of Law School: 684
% Male/Female: 50/50
% Full Time: 60
% Minority: 25
Average Age of Entering Class: 29

EXPENSES/FINANCIAL AID

Annual Tuition: $20,720
Room and Board (On/Off Campus): $5,100/$6,000
Books and Supplies: $750
Average Grant: $4,000
Average Loan: $20,000
% of Aid That Is Merit-Based: 41
% Receiving Some Sort of Aid: 65
Average Total Aid Package: $20,000
Average Debt: $74,000
Fees Per Credit: $775

ADMISSIONS INFORMATION

Application Fee: $50
Regular Application Deadline: Rolling
Regular Notification: Rolling
LSDAS Accepted? Yes
Average GPA: 2.8
Range of GPA: 2.6–3.3
Average LSAT: 147
Range of LSAT: 145–151
Transfer Students Accepted? Yes
Other Schools to Which Students Applied: Hofstra University, St. John's University, New York Law School, Brooklyn Law School, Pace University, Fordham University, Yeshiva University, City University of New York
Other Admissions Factors Considered: Personal statement, work experience, graduate degree
Number of Applications Received: 1,912
Number of Applicants Accepted: 857
Number of Applicants Enrolled: 219

INTERNATIONAL STUDENTS

TOEFL Required of International Students? Yes
Minimum TOEFL: 570

EMPLOYMENT INFORMATION

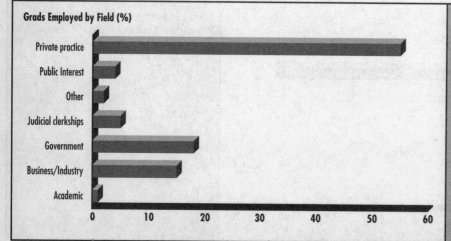

Grads Employed by Field (%)

Rate of Placement: 73%
Average Starting Salary: $45,000
Employers Who Frequently Hire Grads: District Attorney's Offices; public interest employers; small and medium-size law firms
Prominent Alumni: Nina Pozgar, counsel for the U.S. Department of Justice, reporting to U.S. Attorney Janet Reno; Kenneth LaValle, New York state senator; Seymour Liebman, chief financial officer, Canon USA

TULANE UNIVERSITY
School of Law

Admissions Contact: Admission Coordinator, Carl Hudson
Weinmann Hall, 6329 Freret Street, New Orleans, LA 70118-6231
Admissions Phone: 504-865-5930 • Admissions Fax: 504-865-6710
Admissions E-mail: admissions@law.tulane.edu • Web Address: www.law.tulane.edu

INSTITUTIONAL INFORMATION

Public/Private: Private
Environment: Urban
Academic Calendar: Semester
Schedule: Full time only
Student/Faculty Ratio: 20:1
Total Faculty: 50
% Female: 24
% Minority: 12

PROGRAMS

Academic Specialties: International and Comparative Law, Maritime Law, Environmental Law, Intellectual Property
Advanced Degrees Offered: JD (1 to 3 years), LLM (1 year full time), LLM Admiralty (1 year full time, 2 years part time), LLM Energy and Environment (1 year full time, 2 years part time), LLM International and Comparative Law (1 year full time)
Combined Degrees Offered: JD/BA or JD/BS (6 years), JD/MBA (4–4.5 years), JD/MHA (4–4.5 years), JD/MPH (4–4.5 years), LLM/MPH (2 years), JD/MSW (4–4.5 years), JD/MA International Affairs, Latin American Studies (3–3.5 years)
Clinical Program Required? No
Grading System: Letter and numerical system on a 4.0 scale
Legal Writing/Methods Course Requirements: 1 year, taught in 8 sections

STUDENT INFORMATION

Enrollment of Law School: 952
% Male/Female: 50/50
% Full Time: 100
% Full Time That Are International: 1
% Minority: 23
Average Age of Entering Class: 24

RESEARCH FACILITIES

Computers/Workstations Available: 150
Computer Labs: 3
Campuswide Network? Yes

EXPENSES/FINANCIAL AID

Annual Tuition: $23,500
Room and Board (Off Campus): $7,250
Books and Supplies: $1,270
Average Grant: $9,788
Average Loan: $26,837
% Receiving Some Sort of Aid: 86
Average Total Aid Package: $35,128
Average Debt: $65,220

ADMISSIONS INFORMATION

Application Fee: $50
Regular Application Deadline: 8/10
Regular Notification: Rolling
LSDAS Accepted? Yes
Average GPA: 3.3
Range of GPA: 3.0–3.5
Average LSAT: 159
Range of LSAT: 155–161
Transfer Students Accepted? Yes
Other Schools to Which Students Applied: Emory University, American University, Boston University, Vanderbilt University, George Washington University, Georgetown University, Boston College, Loyola University New Orleans
Other Admissions Factors Considered: Membership in a minority group or other group in which the institution is interested, life experience, qualities or characteristics that may be underrepresented and/or that indicate special motivation, leadership skills, industriousness, seriousness of purpose
Number of Applications Received: 2,993
Number of Applicants Accepted: 1,204

EMPLOYMENT INFORMATION

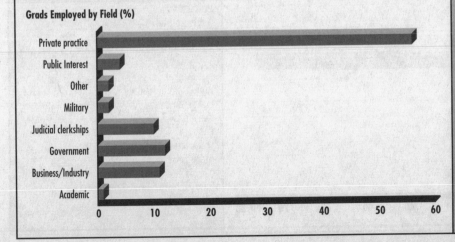

Grads Employed by Field (%)

Average Starting Salary: $56,588
Employers Who Frequently Hire Grads: Fulbright and Jaworski; Skadden Arps; Arnold and Porter; White and Case; Mayer, Brown and Platt; Cleary Gottlieb; Winthrop Stimson; McGlinchey; Adams and Reese; Exxon Co.; U.S. Army; U.S. Department of Justice
Prominent Alumni: Judge J. Wisdom, U.S. 5th Circuit Court of Appeals; Joseph Parkinson, founder, Micron Corp.; Hon. William Suter, clerk of the U.S. Supreme Court
State for Bar Exam: NY
Number Taking Bar Exam: 57
Pass Rate for First-Time Bar: 85%

UCLA School of Law

Admissions Contact: Dean of Admissions, Andrea Sossin-Bergman
71 Dodd Hall, Box 951445, UCLA Law Admissions, Los Angeles, CA 90095-1445
Admissions Phone: 310-825-2080 • Admissions Fax: 310-825-4041
Admissions E-mail: admissions@law.ucla.edu • Web Address: www.law.ucla.edu

INSTITUTIONAL INFORMATION

Public/Private: Public
Environment: Urban
Academic Calendar: Semester
Schedule: Full time only
Student/Faculty Ratio: 15:1
Total Faculty: 108
% Part Time: 25
% Female: 28
% Minority: 10

PROGRAMS

Academic Specialties: The faculty's dedication to teaching and regular, collegial interaction with students; the clinical program, which has long led in its depth, intensity, and innovation; a prominent group of scholars and teachers of Public Law (Constitutional and Criminal Law), intellectual and artistic property (including Entertainment Law), Legal and Moral Philosophy, Communications, Cyber Law, Business Law, Public Interest Law and Policy, a concentration in International Law and Environmental Law; extern program with full-time placements that include the State Department's Office of General Counsel, the White House Counsel, government law offices, public interest law firms, nonprofit agencies, and the chambers of numerous federal judges
Advanced Degrees Offered: 1-year advanced LLM degree program for approximately 10 outstanding foreign scholars
Combined Degrees Offered: JD/MBA, JD/MA Urban Planning, JD/MSW (pending approval), JD/

MA Public Policy (pending), JD/American Indian Studies program (all are 4 years). Students may also create a tailored program within UCLA or with another school.
Clinical Program Required? Yes
Clinical Programs: The required first-year Lawyering Skills course has a clinical component. Beyond that, innovative programs are taught in the state-of-the-art clinical wing, which was designed especially for clinical teaching and student practice.
Grading System: A+ (4.3) to F (0.0) with mandatory curve in all first-year classes and in advanced courses of 40 or more students. There is a recommended distribution of plusses and minuses within each letter grade.
Legal Writing/Methods Course Requirements: Students introduced to fundamentals of legal research, reasoning, client counseling, and fact investigation using clinical methods

STUDENT INFORMATION

Enrollment of Law School: 957
% Male/Female: 49/51
% Full Time: 100
% Minority: 31
Average Age of Entering Class: 24

RESEARCH FACILITIES

School-Supported Research Centers: Partnership with the pro bono Public Counsel, Environmental Law Clinic, program in public interest law and policy, wide variety of volunteer opportunities, such as a recent project in which students represented adoptive parents in dependency court

EXPENSES/FINANCIAL AID

Room and Board (On/Off Campus): $2,475/ $9,009
Books and Supplies: $1,221
Average Grant: $5,401
Average Loan: $17,228
% of Aid That Is Merit-Based: 7
% Receiving Some Sort of Aid: 85
Average Total Aid Package: $20,605
Average Debt: $48,850

ADMISSIONS INFORMATION

Regular Application Deadline: 2/1
Regular Notification: 2/1
LSDAS Accepted? No
Average GPA: 3.6
Range of GPA: 3.5–3.7
Average LSAT: 164
Range of LSAT: 161–166
Transfer Students Accepted? Yes
Other Schools to Which Students Applied: University of Southern California, University of California—Berkeley, University of California—Hastings, Stanford University, Loyola University
Other Admissions Factors Considered: Undergraduate program, graduate study, awards or publications, unusual or exceptional career or personal achievements, diversity characteristics, challenges overcome, or other significant experience
Number of Applications Received: 4,744
Number of Applicants Accepted: 910
Number of Applicants Enrolled: 289

EMPLOYMENT INFORMATION

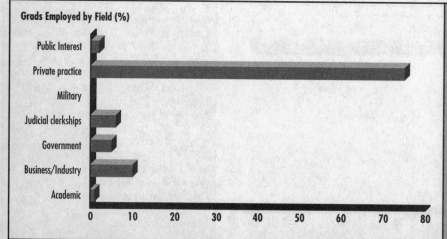

Grads Employed by Field (%)

Rate of Placement: 96%
Average Starting Salary: $63,485
Employers Who Frequently Hire Grads: Latham & Watkins; O'Melveny & Myers; Irell & Manella; Gibson, Dunn & Crutcher; Morrison & Foerster; Skadden, Arps, et al
Prominent Alumni: U.S. Representatives Henry Watman and Howard Berman; U.S. 9th Circuit Court of Appeals Judge and Former Law Dean Dorothy Nelson; Antonia Hernandez, president, MALDEF
State for Bar Exam: CA
Number Taking Bar Exam: 279
Pass Rate for First-Time Bar: 83%

UNIVERSITY AT BUFFALO, STATE UNIVERSITY OF NY

School of Law

Admissions Contact: Associate Dean for Admissions and Financial Aid, Jack D. Cox
309 O'Brian Hall, Buffalo, NY 14260-1100
Admissions Phone: 716-645-2907 • Admissions Fax: 716-645-6676
Admissions E-mail: law-admissions@buffalo.edu • Web Address: www.buffalo.edu/law

INSTITUTIONAL INFORMATION

Public/Private: Public
Environment: Suburban
Academic Calendar: Semester
Schedule: Full time only
Student/Faculty Ratio: 16:1
Total Faculty: 158
% Part Time: 64
% Female: 31
% Minority: 8

PROGRAMS

Academic Specialties: Law and Society, Law and Gender, Litigation, Family Violence, Corporate Finances, International Human Rights, Family Law, Affordable Housing, Labor Law, Health Law and Management, Family Violence, Community Economic Development, Environmental Law, State and Local Government Law, Criminal Law, Business Transactions.
Advanced Degrees Offered: LLM Criminal Law (1 year)
Combined Degrees Offered: JD/MSW (4 years), JD/MBA (4 years), JD/PhD (5 to 6 years)
Clinical Program Required? No
Clinical Programs: Affordable Housing, Community Economic Development, Family and Domestic Violence, Education Law, Environment and Development, Health-Related Legal Concerns of the Elderly, Federal Criminal Practice, Securities Law
Grading System: Letter system: H (Honors), Q+, Q (Qualified), Q–, D, F
Legal Writing/Methods Course Requirements: 6 credits, 2 semester-course taught during first year

STUDENT INFORMATION

Enrollment of Law School: 657
% Male/Female: 52/48
% Full Time: 100
% Full Time That Are International: 1
% Minority: 18
Average Age of Entering Class: 26

RESEARCH FACILITIES

Computers/Workstations Available: 40
School-Supported Research Centers: Access to the research libraries collection through the online library catalog

EXPENSES/FINANCIAL AID

Annual Tuition (Residents/Nonresidents): $9,150/$14,700
Room and Board (On/Off Campus): $6,959/$7,200
Books and Supplies: $1,323
Financial Aid Application Deadline: 3/1
Average Grant: $3,100
Average Loan: $13,500
% of Aid That Is Merit-Based: 41
% Receiving Some Sort of Aid: 85
Average Total Aid Package: $18,500
Average Debt: $35,642

ADMISSIONS INFORMATION

Application Fee: $50
Regular Application Deadline: 3/15
Regular Notification: Rolling
LSDAS Accepted? Yes
Average GPA: 3.2
Range of GPA: 2.9–3.5
Average LSAT: 154
Range of LSAT: 150–157
Transfer Students Accepted? Yes
Other Schools to Which Students Applied: Albany Law School of Union University, Syracuse University, Brooklyn Law School, American University, Cornell University, University of Maryland, Boston College, New York University
Other Admissions Factors Considered: Admissions decisions are influenced by achievements or activities that suggest a high probability of scholastic excellence or distinctive intellectual contribution while in law school.
Number of Applications Received: 885

INTERNATIONAL STUDENTS

TOEFL Required of International Students? Yes
Minimum TOEFL: 630

EMPLOYMENT INFORMATION

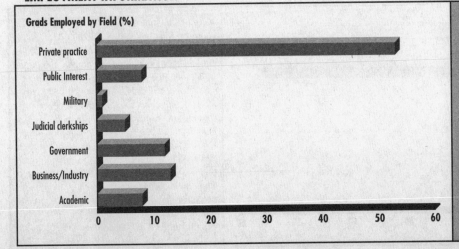

Grads Employed by Field (%)

- Private practice
- Public Interest
- Military
- Judicial clerkships
- Government
- Business/Industry
- Academic

0 10 20 30 40 50 60

Rate of Placement: 96%
Average Starting Salary: $41,894
Employers Who Frequently Hire Grads: LeBoeuf Lamb; Hodgson Russ; New York State Appellate Division 4th Department; Dewey Ballantine; Nixon Hargrave; Phillips Lytle
Prominent Alumni: Herald Price Fahringer, prominent defense attorney and leading constitutional lawyer; Hon. Paul Friedman, U.S. District Court judge for Washington, D.C.; Kenneth B. Forrest, senior partner, Wachtell, Lipton, Rosen and Katz

UNIVERSITY OF AKRON
School of Law

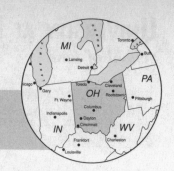

Admissions Contact: Director of Admissions and Financial Assistance, Lauri S. File
The University of Akron School of Law, Akron, OH 44325-2901
Admissions Phone: 800-425-7668 • Admissions Fax: 330-258-2343
Admissions E-mail: lawadmissions@uakron.edu • Web Address: www.uakron.edu/law

INSTITUTIONAL INFORMATION
Public/Private: Public
Environment: Urban
Academic Calendar: Semester
Schedule: Full time or part time
Student/Faculty Ratio: 19:1
Total Faculty: 66
% Part Time: 55
% Female: 44
% Minority: 11

PROGRAMS
Academic Specialties: International Public Law and Business Law, Capital Punishment, Consent Decrees, Constitutional Law, Law and Medicine, Alternative Dispute Resolution. Small sections are offered in all required classes, and the Trial Advocacy, Enriched Intellectual Property, and Intellectual Property Law programs are nationally known.
Combined Degrees Offered: JD/MBA, JD/MT, JD/MPA (all usually take 1 additional semester)
Clinical Program Required? No
Clinical Programs: Legal Clinic, Appellate Review, Inmate Assistance Program
Grading System: A (4.00) to C (2.00). Students must not have less than 2.00 cumulative GPA in order to continue law studies.
Legal Writing/Methods Course Requirements: 3 semesters of Legal writing—3 memos first semester, appellate brief and argument second semester, contract drafting third semester); Legal Method is a 1-credit-hour, week-long intensive course before the first semester of law school.

STUDENT INFORMATION
Enrollment of Law School: 560
% Male/Female: 53/47
% Full Time: 60
% Full Time That Are International: 1
% Minority: 15
Average Age of Entering Class: 29

RESEARCH FACILITIES
Computers/Workstations Available: 71
School-Supported Research Centers: Access to the Center for Research Libraries Collection through the online library catalog; Ohiolink offers access to libraries of most Ohio colleges and universities for direct loan; ASCPL Patent Trademark Office Depository.

EXPENSES/FINANCIAL AID
Annual Tuition (Residents/Nonresidents): $7,428/$13,166
Room and Board: $9,845
Books and Supplies: $820
Financial Aid Application Deadline: 5/1
Average Grant: $4,000
Average Loan: $10,182
% of Aid That Is Merit-Based: 99
% Receiving Some Sort of Aid: 92
Average Total Aid Package: $11,013
Average Debt: $30,000
Tuition Per Credit (Residents): $8
Fees Per Credit (Residents): $232

ADMISSIONS INFORMATION
Application Fee: $35
Regular Application Deadline: Rolling
Regular Notification: Rolling
LSDAS Accepted? Yes
Average GPA: 3.1
Range of GPA: 2.8–3.5
Average LSAT: 151
Range of LSAT: 148–154
Transfer Students Accepted? Yes
Other Schools to Which Students Applied: Case Western Reserve University, Cleveland State University, Ohio State University, University of Dayton, Thomas M. Cooley Law School, Ohio Northern University, University of Toledo, Capital University
Other Admissions Factors Considered: Whether or not the applicant had to overcome special challenges such as economic hardship, educational deprivation, physical disability, discrimination, assimilation to a different culture/society
Number of Applications Received: 1,149
Number of Applicants Accepted: 492
Number of Applicants Enrolled: 202

INTERNATIONAL STUDENTS
TOEFL Required of International Students? Yes
Minimum TOEFL: 600

EMPLOYMENT INFORMATION

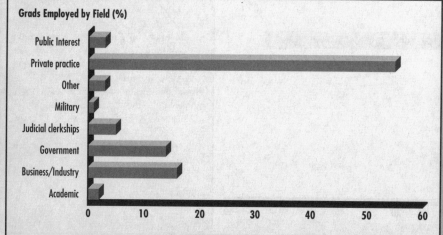

Grads Employed by Field (%)

Rate of Placement: 97%
Average Starting Salary: $45,000
Employers Who Frequently Hire Grads: Buckingham, Doolittle and Burroughs; Brouse and McDowell; Roetzel and Andress; County Prosecutor Offices; Stark and Summit; 9th District Court of Appeals; Ernst and Young; Arthur Anderson
Prominent Alumni: Alice Moore Batchelder, circuit judge, U.S. Court of Appeals for the 6th Circuit; Alex Shumate, Esq. managing partner, Squire, Sanders and Dempsey; Shirley Buccieri, senior vice president and general counsel of Transamerica Corporation
State for Bar Exam: NY
Number Taking Bar Exam: 24
Pass Rate for First-Time Bar: 83%

UNIVERSITY OF ALABAMA

School of Law

Admissions Contact: Admissions Coordinator, Betty McGinley
Box 870382, Tuscaloosa, AL 35487-0382
Admissions Phone: 205-348-5440 • Admissions Fax: 205-348-3917
Admissions E-mail: admissions@law.ua.edu • Web Address: www.law.ua.edu

INSTITUTIONAL INFORMATION

Public/Private: Public
Environment: Urban
Academic Calendar: Semester
Schedule: Full time only
Student/Faculty Ratio: 17:1
Total Faculty: 36
% Part Time: 54
% Female: 23
% Minority: 9

PROGRAMS

Academic Specialties: Business and Tax Law, Criminal Law, Commercial Law, Bankruptcy Law
Advanced Degrees Offered: Master of Comparative Law (1 year), LLM Taxation (2 years part time)
Combined Degrees Offered: MBA/JD (4 years)
Clinical Program Required? No
Clinical Programs: 4 in-house clinics are offered for the 6-credit-hour summer externship program.
Grading System: Letter and numerical system on a 4.0 scale
Legal Writing/Methods Course Requirements: 2 semesters

STUDENT INFORMATION

Enrollment of Law School: 536
% Male/Female: 62/38
% Full Time: 100
% Full Time That Are International: 1
% Minority: 11
Average Age of Entering Class: 24

EXPENSES/FINANCIAL AID

Annual Tuition (Residents/Nonresidents): $4,490/$9,484
Books and Supplies: $600
Average Grant: $3,343
Average Loan: $12,296
% of Aid That Is Merit-Based: 8
% Receiving Some Sort of Aid: 69
Average Total Aid Package: $13,446
Average Debt: $32,481

ADMISSIONS INFORMATION

Application Fee: $25
Regular Application Deadline: 4/1
Regular Notification: Rolling
LSDAS Accepted? Yes
Average GPA: 3.3
Range of GPA: 3.0–3.7
Average LSAT: 158
Range of LSAT: 155–161
Transfer Students Accepted? Yes
Other Schools to Which Students Applied: Samford University, Florida State University, University of Mississippi, University of Arkansas—Little Rock, Baylor University, Pennsylvania State University, University of Tennessee, University of Texas
Other Admissions Factors Considered: Difficulty of undergraduate course work, graduate study, writing ability, trends in academic performance, leadership qualities, career achievement
Number of Applications Received: 621
Number of Applicants Accepted: 311
Number of Applicants Enrolled: 184

INTERNATIONAL STUDENTS

TOEFL Required of International Students? Yes

EMPLOYMENT INFORMATION

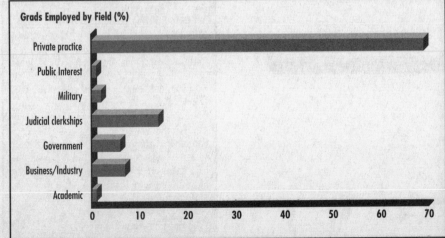

Grads Employed by Field (%)

Rate of Placement: 99%
Average Starting Salary: $44,264
Employers Who Frequently Hire Grads: Private practices, government agencies, public interest agencies
Prominent Alumni: Justice Hugo Black of the U.S. Supreme Court; Howell Heflin, retired member of the U.S. Senate and former chief justice of the Alabama Supreme Court; Judge Frank M. Johnson, Jr., senior judge, U.S. Court of Appeals, 11th Circuit.
State for Bar Exam: AL
Number Taking Bar Exam: 169
Pass Rate for First-Time Bar: 93%

UNIVERSITY OF ARIZONA
James E. Rogers College of Law

Admissions Contact: Assistant Dean for Admissions, Terry Sue Holpert
College of Law, Room 114, PO Box 210176, Tucson, AZ 85721-0176
Admissions Phone: 520-621-3477 • Admissions Fax: 520-621-9140
Admissions E-mail: admissions@nt.law.arizona.edu • Web Address: www.law.arizona.edu

INSTITUTIONAL INFORMATION

Public/Private: Public
Affiliation: Not Applicable
Environment: Urban
Academic Calendar: Semester
Schedule: Full time only
Student/Faculty Ratio: 15:1
Total Faculty: 80
% Part Time: 50
% Female: 33
% Minority: 20

PROGRAMS

Academic Specialties: Outstanding teaching faculty with extraordinary strength in all first-year classes. In addition, there is particular strength in Tax, Estates, and Trust; Corporate and Securities; Indian Law; Water Law; Constitutional Law; Employment Law; Remedies and Trial Advocacy; Family Law; International Trade; International Trade Rights; and Environmental Law.
Advanced Degrees Offered: LLM International Trade Law (24 units, 1 year), JD (85 units, 3 years)
Combined Degrees Offered: JD/PhD in Philosophy, Psychology, or Economics (6 years.), JD/MBA (4 years), JD/MPA (4 years), JD/MA American Indian Studies (4 years), JD/MA Economics (4 years), JD/MA Women's Studies (4 years)
Clinical Program Required? No
Clinical Programs: Criminal Prosecution and Defense, Immigration Law, Domestic Violence, Child Advocacy, Indian/Tribal Law Clinics
Grading System: There is a curve for all courses of 21 or more students: 25% A, 55% B, 20% C, D, and

E. For classes of 20 or less, the mean GPA for courses shall not exceed 3.5.
Legal Writing/Methods Course Requirements: 1-semester Legal Research and Writing class required in the first semester of first year and Research and Writing seminar in second or third year.

STUDENT INFORMATION

Enrollment of Law School: 460
% Male/Female: 50/50
% Full Time: 100
% Full Time That Are International: 1
% Minority: 25
Average Age of Entering Class: 26

RESEARCH FACILITIES

Computers/Workstations Available: 50
School-Supported Research Centers: The University of Arizona is a top-ranked research university with a plethora of library and cultural opportunities and venues for interdisiplinary study and extracurricular involvement.

EXPENSES/FINANCIAL AID

Annual Tuition (Residents/Nonresidents): $5,125/$12,500
Room and Board (On/Off Campus): $6,000/$7,500
Books and Supplies: $750
Financial Aid Application Deadline: 3/1
Average Grant: $4,000
Average Loan: $13,500
% of Aid That Is Merit-Based: 35
% Receiving Some Sort of Aid: 81
Average Total Aid Package: $15,000
Average Debt: $42,000

ADMISSIONS INFORMATION

Application Fee: $45
Regular Application Deadline: 2/15
Regular Notification: Rolling
LSDAS Accepted? Yes
Average GPA: 3.5
Range of GPA: 2.6–4.0
Average LSAT: 161
Range of LSAT: 145–173
Transfer Students Accepted? Yes
Other Schools to Which Students Applied: Arizona State University, UCLA School of Law, University of San Diego, University of Texas, University of Colorado, University of California—Berkeley, University of California—Davis, University of California—Hastings
Other Admissions Factors Considered: The College seeks to enroll a class that is intellectually dynamic and culturally diverse. Each file is therefore reviewed with care and in the context of the student's strengths, background, academic experience, test scores, work experience, community and public service.
Number of Applications Received: 1,667
Number of Applicants Accepted: 420
Number of Applicants Enrolled: 150

INTERNATIONAL STUDENTS

TOEFL Required of International Students? Yes

EMPLOYMENT INFORMATION

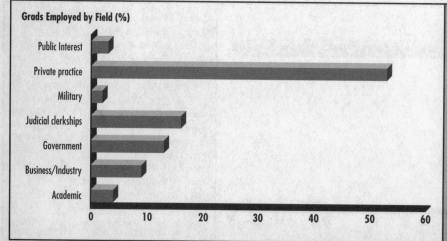

Grads Employed by Field (%)

- Public Interest
- Private practice
- Military
- Judicial clerkships
- Government
- Business/Industry
- Academic

0 10 20 30 40 50 60

Rate of Placement: 94%
Average Starting Salary: $49,031
Employers Who Frequently Hire Grads: Snell and Wilmer; Quarles and Brady; Bryan Cave; Gibson, Dunn and Crutcher; O'Conner Cavanagh; Streich Lang; Squire Sanders; Arizona Supreme Court and court of Appeals; U.S. District and Circuit Courts; Department of Justice; District Attorney's, Public Defender's, City Attorney's Offices
Prominent Alumni: Morris K. Udall, former congressman; Stewart Udall, former congressman and secretary of interior; former Senator Dennis Deconcini
State for Bar Exam: CA/FL/NV/NY/AK/AZ
Number Taking Bar Exam: 137
Pass Rate for First-Time Bar: 93

UNIVERSITY OF ARKANSAS — FAYETTEVILLE

School of Law

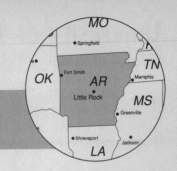

Admissions Contact: Associate Dean for Students, James Miller
Leflar Law Center, Fayetteville, AR 72701-1201
Admissions Phone: 501-575-3102 • Admissions Fax: 501-575-3320
Admissions E-mail: jkmiller@comp.uark.edu • Web Address: www.law.uark.edu

INSTITUTIONAL INFORMATION

Public/Private: Public
Environment: Suburban
Academic Calendar: Semester
Schedule: Full time only
Student/Faculty Ratio: 14:1
Total Faculty: 45
% Part Time: 24
% Female: 24
% Minority: 10

PROGRAMS

Advanced Degrees Offered: LLM Agricultural Law (1 academic year)
Combined Degrees Offered: JD/MBA (3–4 years), JD/MPA (1–2 years), LLM/MPA (3–4 years)
Clinical Program Required? No
Clinical Programs: 4 clinical programs: Civil Clinic, Criminal Clinic, Federal Practice Clinic, Advanced Criminal Clinic
Grading System: A to F
Legal Writing/Methods Course Requirements: 3 semesters of Legal Writing required, for a total of 7 credit hours

STUDENT INFORMATION

Enrollment of Law School: 372
% Male/Female: 56/44
% Full Time: 100
% Full Time That Are International: 2
% Minority: 10
Average Age of Entering Class: 26

RESEARCH FACILITIES

Computers/Workstations Available: 32

EXPENSES/FINANCIAL AID

Annual Tuition (Residents/Nonresidents): $4,752/$10,200
Room and Board: $10,800
Books and Supplies: $1,000
Average Grant: $3,025
Average Loan: $13,901
% of Aid That Is Merit-Based: 5
% Receiving Some Sort of Aid: 78
Average Debt: $33,000

ADMISSIONS INFORMATION

Regular Application Deadline: Rolling
Regular Notification: Rolling
LSDAS Accepted? Yes
Average GPA: 3.3
Range of GPA: 3.0–3.6
Average LSAT: 152
Range of LSAT: 148–156
Transfer Students Accepted? Yes
Other Schools to Which Students Applied: University of Arkansas—Little Rock, Southern Methodist University, Vanderbilt University, University of Texas, Tulane University, University of Tulsa, University of Memphis, University of Oklahoma
Other Admissions Factors Considered: In a small percentage of cases, additional criteria such as ethnicity, vocational or professional experience, graduate work, and progressive improvement in college work are considered by the Admissions Committee.
Number of Applicants Enrolled: 161

INTERNATIONAL STUDENTS

TOEFL Required of International Students? Yes
Minimum TOEFL: 550

EMPLOYMENT INFORMATION

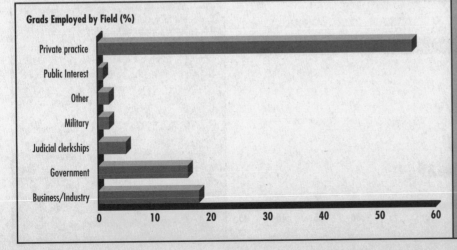

Grads Employed by Field (%)

Rate of Placement: 95%
Average Starting Salary: $37,772
Employers Who Frequently Hire Grads: No concentration—the majority of our grads go into small firms
Prominent Alumni: United States Senator David Pryor; Judge Morris Arnold, U.S. Court of Appeals, 8th Circuit; Ronald T. LeMay, president, Sprint Corporation; Philip S. Anderson, president-elect, American Bar Association; Rodney E. Slater, U.S. Secretary of Education
State for Bar Exam: AR
Number Taking Bar Exam: 125
Pass Rate for First-Time Bar: 82%

UNIVERSITY OF ARKANSAS — LITTLE ROCK
School of Law

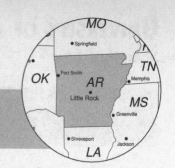

Admissions Contact: Director of Admissions, Jean Probasco
1201 McAlmont, Little Rock, AR 72202-5142
Admissions Phone: 501-324-9903 • Admissions Fax: 501-324-9433
Admissions E-mail: lawadm@ualr.edu • Web Address: www.ualr.edu/~lawschool

INSTITUTIONAL INFORMATION

Public/Private: Public
Environment: Urban
Academic Calendar: Semester
Schedule: Full time or part time
Student/Faculty Ratio: 17:1
Total Faculty: 48
% Part Time: 38
% Female: 38
% Minority: 8

PROGRAMS

Academic Specialties: Faculty publish articles and books in a number of areas. The curriculum offers a strong foundation in traditional areas as well as requiring all students to take trial advocacy.
Combined Degrees Offered: JD/MBA, JD/MPA
Clinical Program Required? No
Clinical Programs: 2 clinics: Litigation and Mediation. Areas of practice include Family Law, Administrative Law, Mental Health Law, and Child Dependency and Neglect.
Grading System: Letter grades converted to a 4.0 scale, substantially all courses graded anonymously.
Legal Writing/Methods Course Requirements: First-year and upper-level requirement

STUDENT INFORMATION

Enrollment of Law School: 406
% Male/Female: 54/46
% Full Time: 64
% Minority: 9
Average Age of Entering Class: 27

RESEARCH FACILITIES

Computers/Workstations Available: 56
School-Supported Research Centers: Special discounts on Internet service through local Internet provider

EXPENSES/FINANCIAL AID

Annual Tuition (Residents/Nonresidents): $4,800/$10,800
Room and Board (Off Campus): $9,000
Books and Supplies: $800
Average Grant: $3,690
Average Loan: $12,004
% of Aid That Is Merit-Based: 5
% Receiving Some Sort of Aid: 62
Average Total Aid Package: $12,500
Average Debt: $21,000

ADMISSIONS INFORMATION

Application Fee: $40
Regular Application Deadline: Rolling
Regular Notification: Rolling
LSDAS Accepted? Yes
Average GPA: 3.2
Range of GPA: 3.0–3.7
Average LSAT: 153
Range of LSAT: 150–156
Transfer Students Accepted? Yes
Other Schools to Which Students Applied: University of Arkansas—Fayetteville, University of Memphis, Vanderbilt University, University of Mississippi, Southern Methodist University, University of Tulsa, Mercer University, Thomas M. Cooley Law School
Other Admissions Factors Considered: Background and experience relevant to success in law school and to diversity of the student body and the profession
Number of Applications Received: 461
Number of Applicants Accepted: 234
Number of Applicants Enrolled: 109

EMPLOYMENT INFORMATION

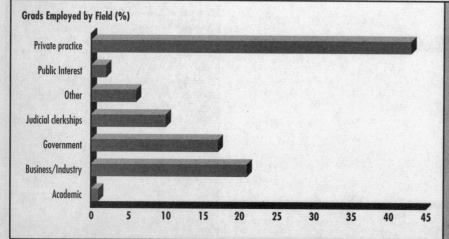

Grads Employed by Field (%)

Field	
Private practice	44
Public Interest	2
Other	6
Judicial clerkships	8
Government	18
Business/Industry	21
Academic	1

Rate of Placement: 95%
Average Starting Salary: $37,290
Employers Who Frequently Hire Grads: Wright, Lindsey and Jennings; Friday, Eldredge and Clark; Prosecuting Attorney; Mitchell, Williams, Selig, Gates and Woodyard; State Supreme Court; State Supreme Court of Appeals
Prominent Alumni: Justice Annabelle Clinton Imber, Arkansas Supreme Court; Judge Mary Davies Scott, U.S. Bankruptcy Court; Michael Wheeler, professor of law, South Texas College of Law
State for Bar Exam: AR
Number Taking Bar Exam: 109
Pass Rate for First-Time Bar: 75%

UNIVERSITY OF BALTIMORE
School of Law

Admissions Contact: Associate Director of Admissions, Claire Valentine
1420 North Charles Street, Baltimore, MD 21201
Admissions Phone: 410-837-4459 • Admissions Fax: 410-837-4450
Admissions E-mail: lwadmiss@ubmail.ubalt.edu • Web Address: www.ubalt.edu/www/law/index.html

INSTITUTIONAL INFORMATION

Public/Private: Public
Environment: Urban
Schedule: Full time or part time
Student/Faculty Ratio: 19:1
Total Faculty: 104
% Part Time: 58
% Female: 32
% Minority: 11

PROGRAMS

Academic Specialties: The law school offers 12 concentrations as well as an LLM in taxation. Specialties include Family, Criminal, Intellectual Property, Evidence, Antitrust, Taxation, Environmental, and International Law.
Advanced Degrees Offered: LLM Taxation
Combined Degrees Offered: JD/MBA, JD/MS Criminal Justice, JD/MPA, JD/PhD Policy Science in conjunction with the University of Maryland at Baltimore, JD/LLM Taxation, JD/MS Negotiation and Conflict Management (most combined degrees add 1 year of study)
Clinical Program Required? No
Clinical Programs: Clinics are offered in the following areas: Family, Criminal, Civil, Community Development, Disability, Appellate
Grading System: A 4.0 quality scale from A to F
Legal Writing/Methods Course Requirements: 1-year program encompassing legal writing and research

STUDENT INFORMATION

Enrollment of Law School: 904
% Male/Female: 48/52
% Full Time: 67
% Full Time That Are International: 1
% Minority: 27
Average Age of Entering Class: 27

EXPENSES/FINANCIAL AID

Annual Tuition (Residents/Nonresidents): $9,027/$16,108
Room and Board (Off Campus): $10,638
Books and Supplies: $850
Average Grant: $4,000
Average Loan: $12,500
% Receiving Some Sort of Aid: 68
Average Debt: $38,300
Fees Per Credit (Residents/Nonresidents): $426/$666

ADMISSIONS INFORMATION

Application Fee: $35
Regular Application Deadline: Rolling
Regular Notification: Rolling
LSDAS Accepted? No
Average GPA: 2.9
Range of GPA: 2.7–3.3
Average LSAT: 149
Range of LSAT: 146–152
Transfer Students Accepted? Yes
Other Schools to Which Students Applied: University of Maryland, American University, George Washington University, Catholic University of America, Georgetown University, Widener University, Seton Hall University, Temple University
Other Admissions Factors Considered: Level of difficulty of the undergraduate major, graduate degrees, work experience, ability to overcome adversity, individual achievement, motivation, character
Number of Applications Received: 1,443
Number of Applicants Accepted: 885
Number of Applicants Enrolled: 305

INTERNATIONAL STUDENTS

TOEFL Required of International Students? Yes

EMPLOYMENT INFORMATION

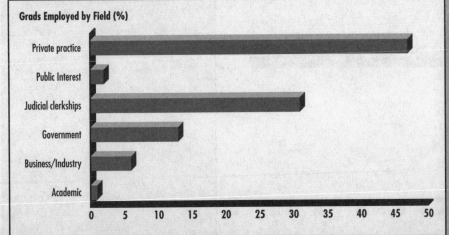

Grads Employed by Field (%)

Rate of Placement: 92%
Average Starting Salary: $39,391
Employers Who Frequently Hire Grads: Law firms, judges, government agencies, corporations
Prominent Alumni: Peter G. Angelos, principal owner, Baltimore Orioles, and one of the nation's leading plantiff attorneys in asbestos and tobacco litigation
State for Bar Exam: MD
Number Taking Bar Exam: 223
Pass Rate for First-Time Bar: 82%

UNIVERSITY OF BRITISH COLUMBIA

Faculty of Law

Admissions Contact: Admissions Office, Elaine Borthwick
1822 East Mall, Vancouver BC V6T 1Z1 Canada
Admissions Phone: 604-822-6303 • Admissions Fax: 604-822-8108
Admissions E-mail: borthwick@law.ubc.ca • Web Address: www.law.ubc.ca

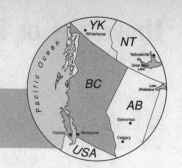

INSTITUTIONAL INFORMATION

Public/Private: Public
Student/Faculty Ratio: 5:1
Total Faculty: 118
% Part Time: 67
% Female: 45

PROGRAMS

Advanced Degrees Offered: LLB (3 years full time), LLM (12 months), PhD (1–2 years)
Combined Degrees Offered: LLB/MBA (4 years)
Clinical Program Required? No
Clinical Programs: Criminal Clinic, First Nations Clinic, Law Students Legal Advice Program
Grading System: Percentage

STUDENT INFORMATION

Enrollment of Law School: 708
% Male/Female: 54/46
% Full Time: 90
% Full Time That Are International: 1
Average Age of Entering Class: 26

RESEARCH FACILITIES

Computers/Workstations Available: 48

EXPENSES/FINANCIAL AID

Annual Tuition (Residents/Nonresidents): $3,199/$14,000
Books and Supplies: $1,300
Financial Aid Application Deadline: 5/15
Average Debt: $25,000

ADMISSIONS INFORMATION

Application Fee: $72
Regular Application Deadline: 2/1
Regular Notification: Rolling
Average GPA: 3.6
Range of GPA: 3.2–4.4
Average LSAT: 163
Range of LSAT: 152–175
Transfer Students Accepted? Yes
Other Schools to Which Students Applied: University of Victoria
Number of Applications Received: 1,351
Number of Applicants Accepted: 462
Number of Applicants Enrolled: 208

EMPLOYMENT INFORMATION

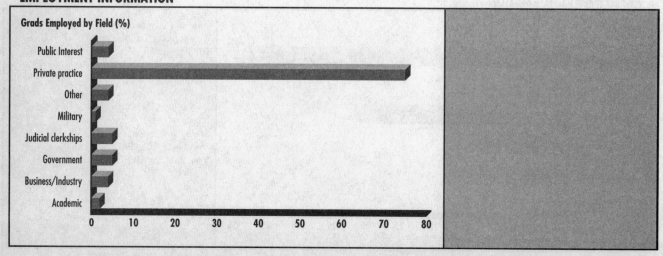

UNIVERSITY OF CALGARY
Faculty of Law

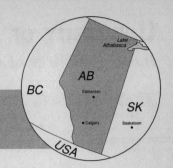

Admissions Contact: Admissions/Student Services Officer, Karen Argento
2500 University Drive NW, Calgary, AB T2N 1NY Canada
Admissions Phone: 403-220-8154 • Admissions Fax: 403-282-8325
Admissions E-mail: law@ucalgary.ca • Web Address: www.ucalgary.ca/faculties/law/

INSTITUTIONAL INFORMATION

Public/Private: Public
Student/Faculty Ratio: 15:1
Total Faculty: 17
% Female: 47

PROGRAMS

Advanced Degrees Offered: LLB (3 years)
Advanced Degrees Offered: LLB (3 years), LLM (15–18 months)
Combined Degrees Offered: LLB/MBA (4 years), LLB/MED
Clinical Program Required? No
Clinical Programs: Criminal Seminar, Family Seminar, Natural Resources Seminar, Business Seminar
Grading System: 11-band grading system, 4-point scale

STUDENT INFORMATION

Enrollment of Law School: 216
% Male/Female: 46/54
% Full Time: 94
Average Age of Entering Class: 28

EXPENSES/FINANCIAL AID

Annual Tuition: $4,488
Room and Board (On/Off Campus): $4,400/ $7,000
Books and Supplies: $1,450

ADMISSIONS INFORMATION

Regular Application Deadline: 2/1
Regular Notification: Rolling
Average GPA: 3.4
Range of GPA: 2.2–3.9
Transfer Students Accepted? No
Other Schools to Which Students Applied: University of Alberta

EMPLOYMENT INFORMATION

Rate of Placement: 90%

UNIVERSITY OF CALIFORNIA
Hastings College of Law

Admissions Contact: Director of Admissions, Akira Ohiroma
200 McAllister Street, San Francisco, CA 94102
Admissions Phone: 415-565-4623 • Admissions Fax: 415-565-4863
Admissions E-mail: admission@uchastings.edu • Web Address: www.uchastings.edu

INSTITUTIONAL INFORMATION
Public/Private: Public
Environment: Urban
Academic Calendar: Semester
Schedule: Full time only
Student/Faculty Ratio: 20:1
Total Faculty: 126
% Part Time: 62
% Female: 36
% Minority: 18

PROGRAMS
Academic Specialties: Civil Litigation, International Law, Public Interest Law, Taxation
Advanced Degrees Offered: JD (3 years)
Combined Degrees Offered: JD/MBA, other master's degrees (4 to 5 years)
Clinical Program Required? No
Clinical Programs: As early as the fourth semester, enrollment is permitted in one of the "clinics." Each clinic contains a class component and placement in a designated Bay Area law office. Current clinics are: Civil Justice Clinic, Criminal Practice Clinic, Environmental Law Clinic.
Grading System: Traditional 4.0 scale, except C– is 1.5 and there are no D+ or D– grades

STUDENT INFORMATION
Enrollment of Law School: 1,122
% Male/Female: 51/49
% Full Time: 100
% Full Time That Are International: 1
% Minority: 30
Average Age of Entering Class: 27

RESEARCH FACILITIES
School-Supported Research Centers: The Land Conservation Institute

EXPENSES/FINANCIAL AID
Annual Tuition (Residents/Nonresidents): $11,200/$20,344
Room and Board (Off Campus): $16,290
Books and Supplies: $840
Average Grant: $4,469
Average Loan: $18,331
% of Aid That Is Merit-Based: 1
% Receiving Some Sort of Aid: 97
Average Total Aid Package: $22,468
Average Debt: $48,343

ADMISSIONS INFORMATION
Application Fee: $40
Regular Application Deadline: 2/16
Regular Notification: 5/1
LSDAS Accepted? Yes
Average GPA: 3.4
Range of GPA: 3.1–3.6
Average LSAT: 162
Range of LSAT: 158–163
Transfer Students Accepted? Yes
Other Schools to Which Students Applied: University of California—Berkeley, UCLA School of Law, University of California—Davis, University of San Francisco, University of Southern California
Other Admissions Factors Considered: Writing ability, obstacles overcome
Number of Applications Received: 3,992
Number of Applicants Accepted: 1,329
Number of Applicants Enrolled: 416

INTERNATIONAL STUDENTS
TOEFL Required of International Students? Yes
Minimum TOEFL: 550

EMPLOYMENT INFORMATION

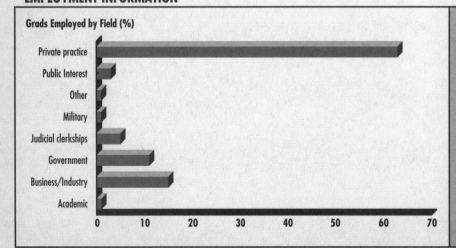

Grads Employed by Field (%)

Rate of Placement: 95%
Average Starting Salary: $65,139
Employers Who Frequently Hire Grads: Major San Francisco and Los Angeles large and medium-size law firms
Prominent Alumni: Willie L. Brown Jr., mayor of San Fransisco and former speaker of the California State Assembly; Robert Matsui, U.S. congressman from California; Marvin R. Baxter; justice, California Supreme Court
State for Bar Exam: CA
Number Taking Bar Exam: 337
Pass Rate for First-Time Bar: 92%

UNIVERSITY OF CALIFORNIA — BERKELEY

Boalt Hall School of Law

Admissions Contact: Director of Admissions, Edward G. Tom
5 Boalt Hall, Berkeley, CA 94720-7200
Admissions Phone: 510-642-2274 • Admissions Fax: 510-643-6222
Admissions E-mail: admissions@law.berkeley.edu • Web Address: www.law.berkeley.edu

INSTITUTIONAL INFORMATION

Public/Private: Public
Environment: Urban
Academic Calendar: Semester
Schedule: Full time only
Student/Faculty Ratio: 16:1
Total Faculty: 166
% Part Time: 61
% Female: 31
% Minority: 9

PROGRAMS

Advanced Degrees Offered: LLM (1 year), JSD, PhD in JSP (6 years)
Combined Degrees Offered: Approximately 12 combined degree programs are offered, including JD/MBA, JD/MPP, JD/MSW (all are 4 years), and JD/PhD Economics and History (7 years)
Clinical Program Required? No
Clinical Programs: Faculty-supervised clinicals, Community Clinics, Professional Lawyering Skills, Field Placement Program.
Grading System: High Honors, Honors, Pass, No credit. In each class the top 40–45 percent of students earn Honors, and the top 10–15 percent earn High Honors. In the first year, percentages are fixed at 40 percent Honors and 10 percent High Honors.

STUDENT INFORMATION

Enrollment of Law School: 866
% Male/Female: 45/55
% Full Time: 100
% Minority: 24
Average Age of Entering Class: 24

RESEARCH FACILITIES

School-Supported Research Centers: Many cooperative and interlibrary loan agreements exist with other universities throughout the United States.

EXPENSES/FINANCIAL AID

Annual Tuition: $10,322/$21,000
Room and Board: $10,586
Books and Supplies: $1,126
Financial Aid Application Deadline: 2/1
Average Grant: $6,000
Average Loan: $16,148
% of Aid That Is Merit-Based: 2
% Receiving Some Sort of Aid: 78
Average Total Aid Package: $21,234
Average Debt: $46,448

ADMISSIONS INFORMATION

Application Fee: $40
Regular Application Deadline: 2/1
Regular Notification: Rolling
LSDAS Accepted? Yes
Average GPA: 3.7
Range of GPA: 3.7–3.9
Average LSAT: 167
Range of LSAT: 161–169
Transfer Students Accepted? Yes
Other Schools to Which Students Applied: UCLA School of Law, Stanford University, Harvard University, Yale University, University of California—Hastings, Columbia University, University of Michigan, University of California—Davis
Other Admissions Factors Considered: Refer to the Boalt Hall Catalog or visit its website at www.law.berkeley.edu.
Number of Applications Received: 5,241
Number of Applicants Accepted: 639
Number of Applicants Enrolled: 269

EMPLOYMENT INFORMATION

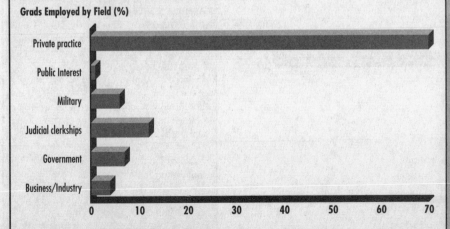

Grads Employed by Field (%)

- Private practice
- Public Interest
- Military
- Judicial clerkships
- Government
- Business/Industry

Rate of Placement: 96%
Average Starting Salary: $67,643
Employers Who Frequently Hire Grads: Over 300 empolyers recruit on campus each fall
Prominent Alumni: Leigh Steinberg, Sports and Entertainment; Larry Sonsini, partner, Wilson, Sonsini, Goodrich and Rosati; Jami Floyd, Court TV, Former White House fellow
State for Bar Exam: CA
Number Taking Bar Exam: 220
Pass Rate for First-Time Bar: 89%

UNIVERSITY OF CALIFORNIA — DAVIS
School of Law

Admissions Contact: Director of Admission, Sharon L. Pinkney
School of Law, 400 Mrak Hall Drive, Davis, CA 95616-5201
Admissions Phone: 530-752-6477 • Admissions Fax: 530-752-4704
Admissions E-mail: lawadmissions@ucdavis.edu • Web Address: www.kinghall.ucdavis.edu

INSTITUTIONAL INFORMATION

Public/Private: Public
Environment: Suburban
Academic Calendar: Quarter
Schedule: Full time only
Student/Faculty Ratio: 15:1
Total Faculty: 76
% Part Time: 50
% Female: 45
% Minority: 19

PROGRAMS

Academic Specialties: International, Immigration, Public Interest, Skills Training, Environmental, Civil Rights, International Criminal, Human Rights, Clinical Programs
Advanced Degrees Offered: LLM (1 year)
Combined Degrees Offered: JD/MBA (4 years), JD/MA, JD/MS (4 years)
Clinical Program Required? No
Clinical Programs: 2 types of clinical programs are offered: in-house clinical programs working with staff attorneys in the law school, and outside externships.
Grading System: A to F including plus and minus grades, with some courses graded S/U (Satisfactory/Unsatisfactory). Some skills courses are graded P/F.
Legal Writing/Methods Course Requirements: Legal Writing—lecture for 2 hours, instruction in the form and substance of writing. A variety of law-related documents will be discussed and drafted.

STUDENT INFORMATION

Enrollment of Law School: 511
% Male/Female: 48/52
% Full Time: 100
% Full Time That Are International: 1
% Minority: 23
Average Age of Entering Class: 26

RESEARCH FACILITIES

Computers/Workstations Available: 40

EXPENSES/FINANCIAL AID

Room and Board (On/Off Campus): $7,239/$7,572
Books and Supplies: $915
Financial Aid Application Deadline: 3/2
Average Grant: $4,863
Average Loan: $14,503
% of Aid That Is Merit-Based: 1
% Receiving Some Sort of Aid: 87
Average Total Aid Package: $17,915
Average Debt: $41,490

ADMISSIONS INFORMATION

Regular Application Deadline: 2/1
Regular Notification: Rolling
LSDAS Accepted? Yes
Average GPA: 3.4
Range of GPA: 3.2–3.6
Average LSAT: 159
Range of LSAT: 156–162
Transfer Students Accepted? Yes
Other Schools to Which Students Applied: University of California—Hastings, University of California—Berkeley, UCLA School of Law, Santa Clara University, University of Southern California
Other Admissions Factors Considered: Rigor of undergraduate course of study, undergraduate school attended, advanced degrees or coursework, diversity of background and experiences, significant work experience
Number of Applications Received: 2,290
Number of Applicants Accepted: 796
Number of Applicants Enrolled: 161

INTERNATIONAL STUDENTS

TOEFL Required of International Students? Yes
Minimum TOEFL: 600

EMPLOYMENT INFORMATION

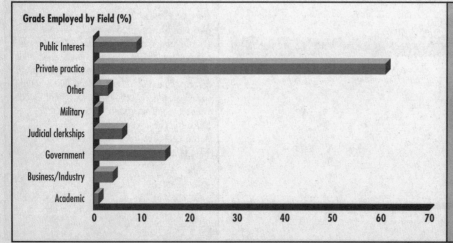

Grads Employed by Field (%)

Average Starting Salary: $54,370
Employers Who Frequently Hire Grads: State of California, private law firms, District Attorney's and Public Defender's Offices, public interest entities
Prominent Alumni: George W. Miller, representative for California, U.S. Congress; Dean Pregerson, U.S. district judge, Central District of California; Phil Satre, CEO, Harrah's Entertainment, Inc.
State for Bar Exam: CA
Number Taking Bar Exam: 149
Pass Rate for First-Time Bar: 93%

UNIVERSITY OF CHICAGO
Law School

Admissions Contact: Dean of the JD and Graduate Programs, Anna Praschma and Genita Robinson
1111 East 60th Street, Chicago, IL 60637
Admissions Phone: 773-702-9484 • Admissions Fax: 773-834-0942
Admissions E-mail: admissions@law.uchicago.edu • Web Address: www.law.uchicago.edu

INSTITUTIONAL INFORMATION
Public/Private: Private
Environment: Urban
Academic Calendar: Quarter
Schedule: Full time only
Student/Faculty Ratio: 19:1
Total Faculty: 30
% Female: 17
% Minority: 13

PROGRAMS
Academic Specialties: Interdisciplinary Studies
Advanced Degrees Offered: LLM (1 year), JSD (length depends on dissertation)
Combined Degrees Offered: JD/MBA (4 years), JD/PhD (length depends on dissertation)
Clinical Program Required? No
Clinical Programs: Anti-Poverty, Employment Discrimination, Criminal Justice, Child Support, Mental Health, Homelessness Assistance, Entrepreneurship
Grading System: A (80 and above), B (79–74), C (73–68), D (67–60), F (59–55)
Legal Writing/Methods Course Requirements: Year-long program during first year—students are divided into 6 sections of 30 and taught by full-time fellows.

STUDENT INFORMATION
Enrollment of Law School: 565
% Male/Female: 58/42
% Full Time: 100
% Full Time That Are International: 1
% Minority: 20
Average Age of Entering Class: 24

EXPENSES/FINANCIAL AID
Annual Tuition: $27,276
Room and Board: $10,100
Books and Supplies: $1,300
Average Grant: $8,000
% Receiving Some Sort of Aid: 82

ADMISSIONS INFORMATION
Application Fee: $60
Regular Application Deadline: 2/1
Regular Notification: 3/30
LSDAS Accepted? Yes
Average GPA: 3.7
Range of GPA: 3.5–3.8
Average LSAT: 170
Range of LSAT: 165–172
Transfer Students Accepted? Yes
Other Schools to Which Students Applied: Harvard University, Yale University, University of Michigan, Stanford University, Columbia University, New York University, Duke University, Georgetown University
Other Admissions Factors Considered: Quality of undergraduate school, quality of academic record, interview

INTERNATIONAL STUDENTS
TOEFL Required of International Students? Yes
Minimum TOEFL: 600

EMPLOYMENT INFORMATION

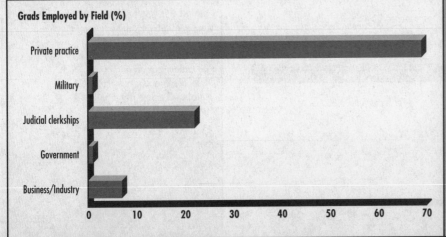

Grads Employed by Field (%)

Private practice
Military
Judicial clerkships
Government
Business/Industry

0 10 20 30 40 50 60 70

Rate of Placement: 99%
Average Starting Salary: $125,000
Employers Who Frequently Hire Grads: Cravath, Swain and Moore; Mayer, Brown and Platt; Gibson, Dunn and Crutcher; Sidley and Austin; Kirkland and Ellis; Skadden, Arps, Slate, Meagher and Flom
State for Bar Exam: IL
Number Taking Bar Exam: 77
Pass Rate for First-Time Bar: 97%

UNIVERSITY OF CINCINNATI
College of Law

Admissions Contact: Assistant Dean and Director of Admission and Financial Aid, Al Watson
PO Box 210040, Cincinnati, OH 45221-0040
Admissions Phone: 513-556-6805 • Admissions Fax: 513-556-2391
Admissions E-mail: admissions@law.uc.edu • Web Address: www.law.uc.edu

INSTITUTIONAL INFORMATION

Public/Private: Public
Environment: Urban
Academic Calendar: Quarter
Schedule: Full time only
Student/Faculty Ratio: 15:1
Total Faculty: 25
% Female: 36
% Minority: 16

PROGRAMS

Academic Specialties: For a small law school enrollment-wise, there is a well-balanced curriculum taught by a good teaching faculty.
Advanced Degrees Offered: JD (3 years), JD/MBA (4 years), JD/MA Women's Studies (3.5-4 years), JD/MCP (4 years)
Combined Degrees Offered: JD/MBA (4 years), JD/MCP (4 years), JD/MA Women's Studies (3.5-4 years)
Clinical Program Required? No
Clinical Programs: A very wide range of internships and judicial externships is offered.
Grading System: Numerical system on a 4.0 scale. First-year courses are graded on a curve; after the first year there is no mandatory curve.

STUDENT INFORMATION

Enrollment of Law School: 371
% Male/Female: 48/52
% Full Time: 99
% Full Time That Are International: 1
% Minority: 19
Average Age of Entering Class: 26

EXPENSES/FINANCIAL AID

Annual Tuition (Residents/Nonresidents): $8,530/$16,362
Room and Board: $6,429
Books and Supplies: $4,478
Average Grant: $4,000
% Receiving Some Sort of Aid: 75
Average Debt: $43,000

ADMISSIONS INFORMATION

Application Fee: $35
Regular Application Deadline: 4/1
Regular Notification: Rolling
LSDAS Accepted? No
Average GPA: 3.4
Range of GPA: 3.0-3.7
Average LSAT: 159
Range of LSAT: 154-161
Transfer Students Accepted? Yes
Other Schools to Which Students Applied: Ohio State University, University of Dayton, Northern Kentucky University, Case Western Reserve University, Indiana University—Bloomington, University of Notre Dame, Vanderbilt University
Other Admissions Factors Considered: Quality of applicant's previous education, trend of academic performance, community service, graduate work
Number of Applications Received: 953
Number of Applicants Accepted: 416

INTERNATIONAL STUDENTS

TOEFL Required of International Students? Yes

EMPLOYMENT INFORMATION

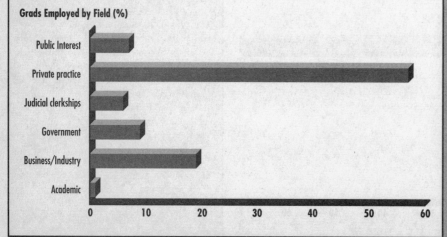

Grads Employed by Field (%)

Rate of Placement: 95%
Average Starting Salary: $46,545
Employers Who Frequently Hire Grads: All major law firms in Cincinnati specifically and Ohio generally
State for Bar Exam: OH
Number Taking Bar Exam: 103
Pass Rate for First-Time Bar: 93%

UNIVERSITY OF COLORADO
School of Law

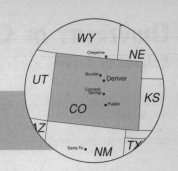

Admissions Contact: Director of Admissions, Carol Nelson-Douglas
Campus Box 403, Fleming Law Building, Boulder, CO 80309-0403
Admissions Phone: 303-492-7203 • Admissions Fax: 303-492-1200
Admissions E-mail: lawadmin@stripe.colorado.edu • Web Address: www.colorado.edu/law

INSTITUTIONAL INFORMATION

Public/Private: Public
Environment: Urban
Academic Calendar: Semester
Schedule: Full time only
Student/Faculty Ratio: 14:1
Total Faculty: 72
% Part Time: 28
% Female: 25
% Minority: 11

PROGRAMS

Academic Specialties: The faculty have particular strengths in Natural Resources and Environmental Law, Constitutional Law, Legal Theory, Corporate Law, Tax Law, and American Indian Law. The curriculum reflects these strengths.
Advanced Degrees Offered: JD (3 years)
Combined Degrees Offered: JD/MBA (4 years), JD/MPA (4 years), Tax Certificate, (3 years), Environmental Policy Certificate, (3 years)
Clinical Program Required? No
Clinical Programs: Legal Aid Civil Practice I and II, Legal Aid Criminal Practice I and II, American Indian Law Clinic, Natural Resources Litigation Clinic, Appellate Advocacy Clinic
Grading System: Letter and numerical system on a 4.0 and 99–59 scale. Designations offered for Incomplete, No Credit, Audit Pass, Transfer Credit, Withdrew.

Legal Writing/Methods Course Requirements: A first-year legal writing course is required for all students. It is taught by full-time professional writing instructors and receives 4 hours of credit. In addition, there is a "small-section program" (35 or fewer class members) in the first year, which requires a writing assignment. Upper-division students are required to take 1 or more seminars that include a substantial legal research and writing requirement. Each upper-division course of 35 or fewer students includes a writing component, either compulsory or optional.

STUDENT INFORMATION

Enrollment of Law School: 491
% Male/Female: 49/51
% Full Time: 100
% Minority: 17
Average Age of Entering Class: 26

RESEARCH FACILITIES

Computers/Workstations Available: 55

EXPENSES/FINANCIAL AID

Room and Board (On/Off Campus): $5,488/ $8,325
Books and Supplies: $675

Average Grant: $2,219
Average Loan: $15,595
% of Aid That Is Merit-Based: 5
% Receiving Some Sort of Aid: 86
Average Total Aid Package: $19,162
Average Debt: $42,110

ADMISSIONS INFORMATION

Application Fee: $45
Regular Application Deadline: 2/15
Regular Notification: Rolling
LSDAS Accepted? Yes
Average GPA: 3.5
Range of GPA: 3.3–3.7
Average LSAT: 160
Range of LSAT: 158–164
Transfer Students Accepted? Yes
Other Schools to Which Students Applied: University of Denver, University of California—Hastings, University of Arizona, George Washington University, University of Washington, UCLA School of Law, University of Michigan, University of Oregon
Other Admissions Factors Considered: Work experience
Number of Applications Received: 1,947
Number of Applicants Accepted: 594
Number of Applicants Enrolled: 168

EMPLOYMENT INFORMATION

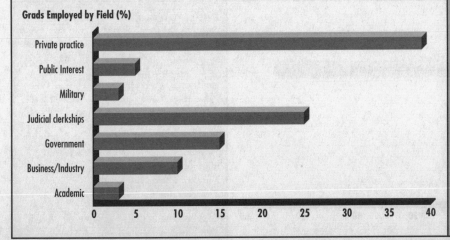

Grads Employed by Field (%)

Rate of Placement: 87%
Average Starting Salary: $38,607
Employers Who Frequently Hire Grads: Arnold and Porter; Cooley Godward, Castro, Huddleson and Tatum; Davis, Graham and Stubbs, LLP; Dorsey and Whitney; Gibson, Dunn and Crutcher, LLP; Holland and Hart; Lyon and Lyon, LLP; Morrison and Foerster, LLP; U.S. Department of Justice; U.S. Department of Transportation
Prominent Alumni: Wiley B. Rutledge, associate justice U.S. Supreme Court; Luis D. Rovira, chief justice (retired), Colorado Supreme Court; Roy Romer, Governor of Colorado
State for Bar Exam: CO
Number Taking Bar Exam: 122
Pass Rate for First-Time Bar: 97%

UNIVERSITY OF CONNECTICUT
School of Law

Admissions Contact: Assistant Dean, Ellen Rutt
55 Elizabeth Street, Hartford, CT 06015
Admissions Phone: 860-570-5100 • Admissions Fax: 860-570-5153
Admissions E-mail: admit@law.ucon.edu • Web Address: www.law.uconn.edu

INSTITUTIONAL INFORMATION

Public/Private: Public
Environment: Urban
Schedule: Full time or part time
Student/Faculty Ratio: 11:1
Total Faculty: 126
% Part Time: 59
% Female: 29
% Minority: 11

PROGRAMS

Academic Specialties: Full range of specializations among faculty and in the curriculum.
Advanced Degrees Offered: LLM (1 year), JD (3 to 4 years), UM Insurance (1 year)
Combined Degrees Offered: JD/MA Public Policy Studies, JD/MBA, JD/MLS, JD/MPA, JD/MSW, JD/MPH
Clinical Program Required? No
Clinical Programs: Clinic and externship programs in Administrative Law, Civil Rights, Disability Law, Criminal Law, Tax Law, Street Law, Judicial Clerkship, Women's Rights, Children's Rights, Labor Relations, Mediation, Poverty Law, Health Law, and Legslative Process
Grading System: Letter system with pass/fail designation available
Legal Writing/Methods Course Requirements: One year-long lawyering process course: writing and lawyering skills. Moot Court component is a separate required course during the first year.

STUDENT INFORMATION

Enrollment of Law School: 585
% Male/Female: 54/46
% Full Time: 69
% Full Time That Are International: 1
% Minority: 18
Average Age of Entering Class: 25

EXPENSES/FINANCIAL AID

Annual Tuition (Residents/Nonresidents): $10,948/$23,092
Room and Board (Off Campus): $8,152
Books and Supplies: $964
Financial Aid Application Deadline: 4/1
Average Grant: $6,639
Average Loan: $18,761
% of Aid That Is Merit-Based: 6
% Receiving Some Sort of Aid: 74
Average Total Aid Package: $19,871
Average Debt: $36,316

ADMISSIONS INFORMATION

Application Fee: $30
Regular Application Deadline: 4/1
Regular Notification: Rolling
LSDAS Accepted? Yes
Average GPA: 3.3
Range of GPA: 3.1–3.6
Average LSAT: 159
Range of LSAT: 157–161
Transfer Students Accepted? Yes
Other Schools to Which Students Applied: Boston College, Boston University, Yale University, Western New England College, Harvard University, New York University, Suffolk University, Fordham University
Other Admissions Factors Considered: Quality and maturity of written essays, strength of undergraduate/graduate curriculum
Number of Applications Received: 1,939
Number of Applicants Accepted: 625
Number of Applicants Enrolled: 184

EMPLOYMENT INFORMATION

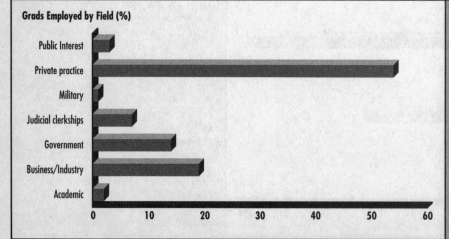

Grads Employed by Field (%)

- Public Interest
- Private practice
- Military
- Judicial clerkships
- Government
- Business/Industry
- Academic

Rate of Placement: 96%
Average Starting Salary: $55,500
Prominent Alumni: Thomas J. Meskill, former governor of Connecticut and chief judge of 2nd Circuit Court of Appeals; Alfred V. Covello and Christopher F. Droney, U.S. District Court judges; Robert I. Berdon, Joette Katz and Richard Palmer, justices of the Connecticut Spreme Court; Thomas Ritter, Speaker of the House, Connecticut State Legislature; W. Randall Pinkson, Washington Bureau, CBS News
State for Bar Exam: CT
Number Taking Bar Exam: 166
Pass Rate for First-Time Bar: 86%

UNIVERSITY OF DAYTON
School of Law

Admissions Contact: Director of Admission and Financial Aid, Janet L. Hein
300 College Park, Dayton, OH 45469-2760
Admissions Phone: 937-229-3555 • Admissions Fax: 937-229-4194
Admissions E-mail: lawinfo@udayton.edu • Web Address: www.law.udayton.edu

INSTITUTIONAL INFORMATION

Public/Private: Private
Affiliation: Catholic
Environment: Suburban
Academic Calendar: Semester
Schedule: Full time only
Student/Faculty Ratio: 18:1
Total Faculty: 28
% Part Time: 15
% Female: 37
% Minority: 8

PROGRAMS

Advanced Degrees Offered: JD (3 years)
Combined Degrees Offered: JD/MBA (4 years)
Clinical Program Required? No
Clinical Programs: Civil and Criminal
Grading System: Numerical system on a 4.0 scale
Legal Writing/Methods Course Requirements: There are 3 required semesters of legal research, writing, and analysis under the title Legal Profession I, II, and III (total of 8 letter-graded credits). The courses are client-simulation driven and introduce students to research in several media, objective writing, and persuasive writing and oral argument at the trial and appellate level.

STUDENT INFORMATION

Enrollment of Law School: 453
% Male/Female: 57/43
% Full Time: 100
% Full Time That Are International: 2
% Minority: 17
Average Age of Entering Class: 26

RESEARCH FACILITIES

Computers/Workstations Available: 70

EXPENSES/FINANCIAL AID

Annual Tuition: $19,860
Room and Board: $6,500
Books and Supplies: $900
Financial Aid Application Deadline: 3/1
Average Grant: $9,500
% of Aid That Is Merit-Based: 30
Average Total Aid Package: $27,000
Average Debt: $51,011
Tuition Per Credit: $794

ADMISSIONS INFORMATION

Application Fee: $40
Regular Application Deadline: 5/1
Regular Notification: Rolling
LSDAS Accepted? Yes
Average GPA: 3.1
Range of GPA: 2.8–3.4
Average LSAT: 152
Range of LSAT: 147–154
Transfer Students Accepted? Yes
Other Schools to Which Students Applied: University of Cincinnati, Ohio State University, Case Western Reserve University, Capital University, Ohio Northern University, Pennsylvania State University, Northern Kentucky University, University of Toledo
Other Admissions Factors Considered: Diversity of experiences, leadership, motivation, ability to overcome hardships, breadth and depth of skills and interests
Number of Applications Received: 1,190
Number of Applicants Accepted: 762
Number of Applicants Enrolled: 167

INTERNATIONAL STUDENTS

Minimum TOEFL: 625

EMPLOYMENT INFORMATION

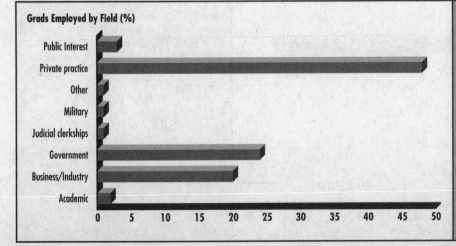

Rate of Placement: 88%
Average Starting Salary: $40,243
Employers Who Frequently Hire Grads: Procter and Gamble; Porter, Wright, Morris, & Arthur; Thompson, Hine, & Ploury; Dinsmore & Shohl; Hine and Flory; Chernesky; Heyman and Kress; Faruki, Gilliam and Ireland; Sebaly; Shillito A. Dyer; Lexis-Nexis
Prominent Alumni: Stephen Powell, 12th District Court of Appeals of Ohio; Nancy Michaud, vice president and general counsel, Huffy Corp.; Mishael Anderson, vice president, Fidelity Investments
State for Bar Exam: OH
Number Taking Bar Exam: 64
Pass Rate for First-Time Bar: 75%

UNIVERSITY OF DENVER
College of Law

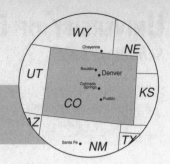

Admissions Contact: Director, Forrest Stanford
7039 East 18th Avenue, Denver, CO 80220
Admissions Phone: 303-871-6135 • Admissions Fax: 303-871-6100
Admissions E-mail: admissions@law.du.edu • Web Address: www.law.du.edu

INSTITUTIONAL INFORMATION
Public/Private: Private
Environment: Urban
Academic Calendar: Semester
Schedule: Full time only
Student/Faculty Ratio: 17:1
Total Faculty: 61
% Female: 30
% Minority: 16

PROGRAMS
Combined Degrees Offered: Business, Geography, History, International Management, International Studies, Legal Administration, Mass Communications, Professional Psychology, Psychology, Social Work, Sociology
Clinical Program Required? Yes
Clinical Programs: Natural Resources, Public Interest, Transportation, Litigation
Legal Writing/Methods Course Requirements: 2 semesters

STUDENT INFORMATION
Enrollment of Law School: 1,049
% Male/Female: 48/52
% Full Time: 74
% Full Time That Are International: 2
% Minority: 9
Average Age of Entering Class: 28

RESEARCH FACILITIES
Computers/Workstations Available: 100

EXPENSES/FINANCIAL AID
Annual Tuition: $22,000
Room and Board (On Campus): $10,000
Books and Supplies: $700
Average Grant: $10,000
Average Loan: $18,300
% of Aid That Is Merit-Based: 33
% Receiving Some Sort of Aid: 80
Average Debt: $45,000
Tuition Per Credit: $572

ADMISSIONS INFORMATION
Application Fee: $45
Regular Application Deadline: 5/30
Regular Notification: Rolling
LSDAS Accepted? Yes
Average GPA: 3.1
Range of GPA: 2.4–3.4
Average LSAT: 153
Range of LSAT: 149–156
Transfer Students Accepted? Yes
Other Schools to Which Students Applied: University of Colorado, Tulane University, Lewis and Clark College, University of Wyoming, American University, University of San Diego, University of Arizona, Gonzaga University
Other Admissions Factors Considered: Resume is required
Number of Applications Received: 1,739
Number of Applicants Enrolled: 316

INTERNATIONAL STUDENTS
TOEFL Required of International Students? Yes
Minimum TOEFL: 580

EMPLOYMENT INFORMATION

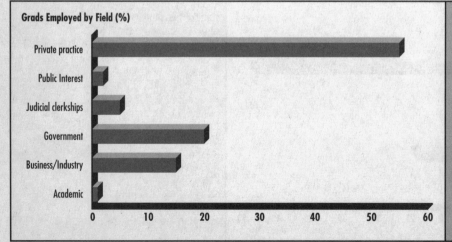

Grads Employed by Field (%)

Rate of Placement: 87%
Average Starting Salary: $42,175
Employers Who Frequently Hire Grads: Small, medium, and large law firms; government agencies such as District Attorney's and Attorney General's Offices; corporations
Prominent Alumni: Daniel Mase, former Denver city attorney; Caroline Turner, general counsel/ VP, Adolph Coors Co.; Donald Sturm, owner, Bank of Colorado and many other businesses; Jim Nicholson, former chairman, Republican National Committee
State for Bar Exam: CO
Number Taking Bar Exam: 204
Pass Rate for First-Time Bar: 77%

UNIVERSITY OF DETROIT MERCY

School of Law

Admissions Contact: Admissions Counselor, Bernard Dobranski
651 East Jefferson Avenue, Detroit, MI 48226
Admissions Phone: 313-596-9848 • Admissions Fax: 313-596-0280
Admissions E-mail: udmlawao@udmercy.edu • Web Address: www.law.udmercy.edu

INSTITUTIONAL INFORMATION

Public/Private: Private
Affiliation: Society of Jesus
Schedule: Full time or part time
Total Faculty: 24
% Part Time: 50
% Female: 20
% Minority: 9

PROGRAMS

Academic Specialties: London Law Program available fall and winter semesters
Advanced Degrees Offered: JD (3 years full time), JD/MBA (4 years)
Combined Degrees Offered: JD/MBA (3.5–4 years full time), JD/LLB (2 years), JD for Canadian lawyers (1 year full time)
Clinical Program Required? No
Clinical Programs: 4-credit in-house Urban Law Clinic, numerous externships
Grading System: 4.5 system
Legal Writing/Methods Course Requirements: Full year, 5 credits, integrated with contracts course

STUDENT INFORMATION

Enrollment of Law School: 429
% Male/Female: 50/50
% Full Time: 57
% Full Time That Are International: 1
% Minority: 11
Average Age of Entering Class: 29

EXPENSES/FINANCIAL AID

Annual Tuition : $18,000
Books and Supplies: $900
Average Grant: $8,000
% of Aid That Is Merit-Based: 5
Average Debt: $55,541
Fees Per Credit: $600

ADMISSIONS INFORMATION

Regular Application Deadline: 4/15
Regular Notification: Rolling
Average GPA: 3.2
Average LSAT: 150
Transfer Students Accepted? Yes
Other Schools to Which Students Applied: Wayne State University, University of Michigan, Detroit College of Law at Michigan State University, Thomas M. Cooley Law School, University of Notre Dame, Loyola University Chicago, DePaul University, University of Toledo
Other Admissions Factors Considered: Strong writing skills, undergraduate course work

EMPLOYMENT INFORMATION

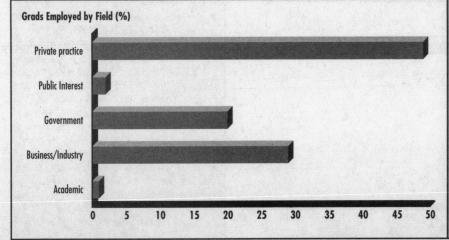

Grads Employed by Field (%)

Rate of Placement: 86%
Average Starting Salary: $439,000
Employers Who Frequently Hire Grads: County prosecutors; Dickinson Wright, PLLC; Dykema Gossett, PLLC; Michigan Court of Appeals; Butzel Long; Bodman Longley; Howard and Howard; Michigan Supreme Court
Prominent Alumni: Hon. Michael F. Cacanagh, Michigan Supreme Court; Hon. James H. Brickley, Michigan Supreme Court; Hon. Maura D. Corrigan, Michigan Supreme Court
State for Bar Exam: MI
Number Taking Bar Exam: 142
Pass Rate for First-Time Bar: 57%

UNIVERSITY OF FLORIDA
Levin College of Law

Admissions Contact: Assistant Dean for Admissions, J. Michael Patrick
Box 117622, Gainesville, FL 32611
Admissions Phone: 904-392-2087 • Admissions Fax: 904-392-8727
Admissions E-mail: patrick@law.ufl.edu • Web Address: www.law.ufl.edu

INSTITUTIONAL INFORMATION

Public/Private: Public
Environment: Urban
Academic Calendar: Semester
Schedule: Full time only
Student/Faculty Ratio: 15:1
Total Faculty: 74
% Female: 35
% Minority: 9

PROGRAMS

Academic Specialties: Centers or degree programs in Taxation, International and Comparative Law, Environmental and Land Use Law, Intellectual Property, Dispute Resolution and Race, and Race Relations
Advanced Degrees Offered: LLM Taxation (1 year), LLM Comparative Law (1 year), SJD in Taxation
Combined Degrees Offered: JD/MA Urban and Regional Planning, JD/MBA, JD/MA Political Science–Public Administration, JD/MA Sociology, JD/PhD History, JD/MA Accounting, JD/MA Mass Communication, JD/PhD Psychology, JD/PhD Mass Communication, JD/MA Forest Conservation, JD/PhD Education Leadership, JD/MA Sports Management, JD/MD, JD/MA Biotechnology, JD/MA Environmental Engineering, JD/MA Latin American Studies
Clinical Program Required? No
Clinical Programs: Civil, Criminal, Mediation, Juvenile, Pro Se Clinic, Conservation Clinic

Grading System: Letter and numerical system on a 4.0 scale. Minimum 2.0 GPA required for good academic standing and graduation.
Legal Writing/Methods Course Requirements: Legal Research and Writing is taken in the first semester of the first year, Appelate Advocacy is taken in the second semester of the first year, and Legal Drafting is taken in the second year.

STUDENT INFORMATION

Enrollment of Law School: 1,140
% Male/Female: 52/48
% Full Time: 100
% Full Time That Are International: 6
% Minority: 26
Average Age of Entering Class: 25

RESEARCH FACILITIES

Computers/Workstations Available: 71

EXPENSES/FINANCIAL AID

Annual Tuition (Residents/Nonresidents): $4,970/$16,510
Room and Board (On/Off Campus): $6,130/$6,540
Books and Supplies: $3,690
Financial Aid Application Deadline: 3/15
Average Grant: $8,300
Average Loan: $10,500
% of Aid That Is Merit-Based: 87
% Receiving Some Sort of Aid: 80
Average Total Aid Package: $12,000
Average Debt: $49,000

Tuition Per Credit (Residents/Nonresidents): $166/$550
Fees Per Credit (Residents/Nonresidents): $166/$550

ADMISSIONS INFORMATION

Application Fee: $20
Regular Application Deadline: 2/1
Regular Notification: 4/1
LSDAS Accepted? Yes
Average GPA: 3.5
Range of GPA: 3.3–3.8
Average LSAT: 154
Range of LSAT: 152–161
Transfer Students Accepted? Yes
Other Schools to Which Students Applied: Florida State University, University of Miami, Stetson University, Emory University, Georgetown University, American University, George Washington University, Tulane University
Other Admissions Factors Considered: Undergraduate or other academic performance; undergraduate institution; post-bachelor's-degree course work; leadership or other relevant activities; maturing experiences; and racial, ethnic, and economic background
Number of Applications Received: 1,659
Number of Applicants Accepted: 502
Number of Applicants Enrolled: 200

INTERNATIONAL STUDENTS

TOEFL Required of International Students? Yes
Minimum TOEFL: 550

EMPLOYMENT INFORMATION

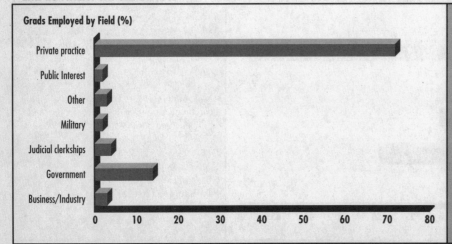

Grads Employed by Field (%)

Rate of Placement: 81%
Average Starting Salary: $45,000
Employers Who Frequently Hire Grads: Foley and Lardner; King and Spalding; Holland and Knight; Troutman Sanders; Steel, Hector and Davis; Gunster Yoakley; Powell Goldstein; Lowndes Drosdick; Kilpatrick Stockton
Prominent Alumni: Rosemary Barkett, former Florida Supreme Court justice, currently judge, U.S. Court of Appeals for 11th Circuit; Carol Browner, head of the Department of Environmental Protection; John Dasburg, president of Northwest Airlines
State for Bar Exam: FL
Number Taking Bar Exam: 196
Pass Rate for First-Time Bar: 91%

UNIVERSITY OF GEORGIA
School of Law

Admissions Contact: Director of Law Admissions, Giles Kennedy
University of Georgia School of Law, Athens, GA 30602-6012
Admissions Phone: 706-542-7060 • Admissions Fax: 706-542-5556
Admissions E-mail: ugajd@arches.uga.edu • Web Address: www.lawsch.uga.edu

INSTITUTIONAL INFORMATION

Public/Private: Public
Environment: Urban
Academic Calendar: Quarter
Schedule: Full time only
Student/Faculty Ratio: 17:1
Total Faculty: 84
% Part Time: 43
% Female: 17
% Minority: 2

PROGRAMS

Advanced Degrees Offered: LLM (1 year)
Combined Degrees Offered: JD/MBA (4 years),
JD/Master of Historic Preservation (4 years)
Clinical Program Required? No
Clinical Programs: Legal Aid Clinic, Prosecutorial
Clinic, Civil Clinic, Public Interest Practicum, civil
externships, Family Violence Clinic
Legal Writing/Methods Course Requirements:
2 semesters, 2 hours per semester

STUDENT INFORMATION

Enrollment of Law School: 640
% Male/Female: 53/47
% Full Time: 100
% Full Time That Are International: 1
% Minority: 12
Average Age of Entering Class: 25

RESEARCH FACILITIES

Computers/Workstations Available: 50

EXPENSES/FINANCIAL AID

Annual Tuition (Residents/Nonresidents):
$4,736/$17,084
Room and Board (On/Off Campus): $6,726/
$8,714
Books and Supplies: $1,000
Financial Aid Application Deadline: 3/1

ADMISSIONS INFORMATION

Application Fee: $30
Regular Application Deadline: 3/1
Regular Notification: Rolling
Average GPA: 3.6
Range of GPA: 3.3–3.8
Average LSAT: 161
Range of LSAT: 157–164
Transfer Students Accepted? Yes
Number of Applications Received: 1,680

EMPLOYMENT INFORMATION

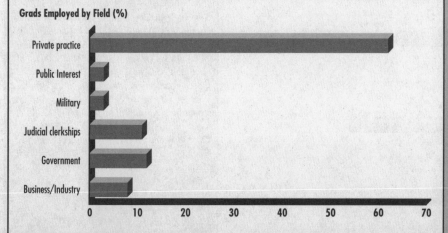

Rate of Placement: 98%
Average Starting Salary: $47,957
State for Bar Exam: GA
Number Taking Bar Exam: 190
Pass Rate for First-Time Bar: 93%

UNIVERSITY OF HAWAII—MANOA
William S. Richardson School of Law

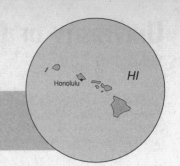

Admissions Contact: Assistant Dean, Joanne K. Punu
Admissions Office, 2515 Dole Street, Honolulu, HI 96822
Admissions Phone: 808-956-7966 • Admissions Fax: 808-956-3813
Admissions E-mail: lawadm@hawaii.edu • Web Address: www.hawaii.edu/law

INSTITUTIONAL INFORMATION
Public/Private: Public
Environment: Urban
Academic Calendar: Semester
Schedule: Full time only
Student/Faculty Ratio: 13:1
Total Faculty: 18
% Female: 44
% Minority: 22

PROGRAMS
Academic Specialties: Pacific-Asian Legal Studies with emphasis on China, Japan, Pacific Rim; Environmental Law Studies with emphasis on ocean and water resources
Advanced Degrees Offered: JD (3 years)
Combined Degrees Offered: JD/Environmental Law (3 years.), JD/Pacific-Asian Legal Studies (3 years), JD/Grad. Ocean Policy (varies), JD/MA (varies), JD/MBA (varies), JD/MS (varies), JD/MSW (varies)
Clinical Program Required? Yes
Clinical Programs: Elder Law, Family, Prosecution, Mediation, Native Hawaiian Rights, Estate Planning
Grading System: Grades are given on a "C+/B–" curve, and this grading standard is in effect for all classes except writing. The median GPA is 2.60. Grading allowances within curve are: A (0%–15%), B (25%–45%), C (40%–65%), D (0%–20%), and F (0%–10%).
Legal Writing/Methods Course Requirements: First semester, 3 credits

STUDENT INFORMATION
Enrollment of Law School: 240
% Male/Female: 48/52
% Full Time: 100
% Full Time That Are International: 1
% Minority: 69
Average Age of Entering Class: 27

EXPENSES/FINANCIAL AID
Annual Tuition (Residents/Nonresidents): $8,016/$14,112
Room and Board (On/Off Campus): $6,400/$8,900
Books and Supplies: $2,800
Average Grant: $6,720
Average Loan: $10,789
% of Aid That Is Merit-Based: 22
% Receiving Some Sort of Aid: 67
Average Total Aid Package: $12,680
Average Debt: $29,500

ADMISSIONS INFORMATION
Application Fee: $30
Regular Application Deadline: 3/1
Regular Notification: 4/1
LSDAS Accepted? Yes
Average GPA: 3.3
Range of GPA: 3.1–3.6
Average LSAT: 157
Range of LSAT: 154–160
Transfer Students Accepted? Yes
Other Schools to Which Students Applied: University of California—Hastings, Stanford University, Santa Clara University, UCLA School of Law, Harvard University, University of California—Berkeley, George Washington University, University of Washington
Other Admissions Factors Considered: Personal factors such as writing ability, work experience, volunteer or community involvement, letters of recommendation, honors, and awards as well as a history of overcoming adversity are all considered in the admissions process.
Number of Applications Received: 468

INTERNATIONAL STUDENTS
TOEFL Required of International Students? Yes
Minimum TOEFL: 600

EMPLOYMENT INFORMATION

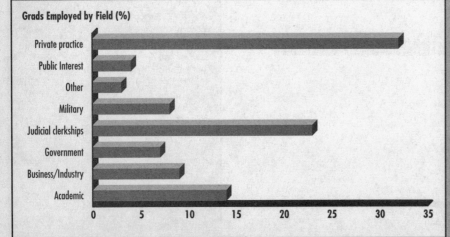

Grads Employed by Field (%)

- Private practice
- Public Interest
- Other
- Military
- Judicial clerkships
- Government
- Business/Industry
- Academic

Rate of Placement: 96%
Average Starting Salary: $42,500
Employers Who Frequently Hire Grads: Office of the Prosecuting Attorney; Public Defender's Office; Ashford & Wriston; Carlsmith, Ball, Whichman, Case & Ichiki; Goodsil, Anderson, Quinn & Stifel; Cades, Schutte, Fleming & Wright
Prominent Alumni: John Waihee, former governor of Hawaii; Mari Matsuda, professor, Georgetown University Law Center; Lawrence Enomoto, senior international affairs officer, National Environmental Satellite Data and Information Services
State for Bar Exam: HI
Number Taking Bar Exam: 61
Pass Rate for First-Time Bar: 84%

UNIVERSITY OF HOUSTON
Law Center

Admissions Contact: Assistant Dean for Admissions, Sondra Richardson
University of Houston Law Center Office of Admissions, Houston, TX 77204-6371
Admissions Phone: 713-743-2280 • Admissions Fax: 713-743-2194
Admissions E-mail: admissions@www.law.uh.edu • Web Address: www.law.uh.edu

INSTITUTIONAL INFORMATION

Public/Private: Public
Environment: Urban
Academic Calendar: Semester
Schedule: Full time or part time
Student/Faculty Ratio: 19:1
Total Faculty: 165
% Part Time: 59
% Female: 20
% Minority: 13

PROGRAMS

Academic Specialties: Health Law, Intellectual Property, International Law, Corporate and Taxation Law
Advanced Degrees Offered: LLM Health, Intellectual Property, Tax, Energy and Natural Resources, International Law (24 credit hours); Foreign (for International Students)
Combined Degrees Offered: JD/MBA (4 years), JD/MPH (3.5 years), JD/MA History (4 years), JD/PhD (Medical Humanities)
Clinical Program Required? No
Clinical Programs: Family and Poverty Law Clinic, Criminal Defense, Criminal Prosecution, Health, Judicial, Environmental, Mediations
Grading System: A (4.00), A– (3.67), B+ (3.33), B (3.00), B– (2.67), C+ (2.33), C (2.00), C– (1.67), D+ (1.33), D (1.00), D– (0.67), F (0.00)
Legal Writing/Methods Course Requirements: First-year legal research and writing includes small group instruction.

STUDENT INFORMATION

Enrollment of Law School: 989
% Male/Female: 51/49
% Full Time: 77
% Full Time That Are International: 1
% Minority: 21
Average Age of Entering Class: 25

EXPENSES/FINANCIAL AID

Annual Tuition (Residents/Nonresidents): $4,960/$10,540
Room and Board (On/Off Campus): $4,624/$6,180
Books and Supplies: $824
Financial Aid Application Deadline: 4/1
Average Grant: $2,908
Average Loan: $14,560
% of Aid That Is Merit-Based: 23
% Receiving Some Sort of Aid: 79
Average Total Aid Package: $14,279
Average Debt: $36,880
Tuition Per Credit (Residents/Nonresidents): $160/$340
Fees Per Credit: $237

ADMISSIONS INFORMATION

Application Fee: $50
Regular Application Deadline: 2/15
Regular Notification: 5/15
LSDAS Accepted? Yes
Average GPA: 3.3
Range of GPA: 3.0–3.5
Average LSAT: 158
Range of LSAT: 155–162
Transfer Students Accepted? Yes
Other Schools to Which Students Applied: University of Texas, Texas A&M University, Southern Methodist University, Texas Tech University, Baylor University, Tulane University, St. Mary's University, South Texas University
Number of Applications Received: 2,440
Number of Applicants Accepted: 880
Number of Applicants Enrolled: 289

INTERNATIONAL STUDENTS

TOEFL Required of International Students? Yes
Minimum TOEFL: 600

EMPLOYMENT INFORMATION

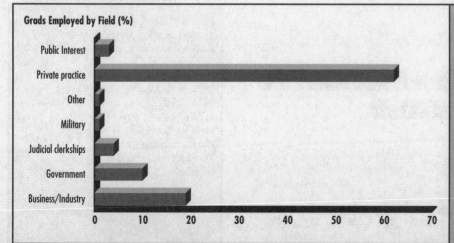

Grads Employed by Field (%)

Rate of Placement: 96%
Average Starting Salary: $60,116
Employers Who Frequently Hire Grads: Baker and Botts; Locke, Liddel and Sapp; Fulbright and Jaworski; Arthur Andersen; Jenkins Gilcrest; Bracewell and Patterson; Harris Co. District Attorney; Weil, Gotshal and Manges
Prominent Alumni: John O'Quinn, Richard Racehorse Haynes, Clarence Bradford
State for Bar Exam: TX
Number Taking Bar Exam: 255
Pass Rate for First-Time Bar: 91%

UNIVERSITY OF IDAHO

College of Law

Admissions Contact: Admissions Coordinator, Amy E. DeWitt
PO Box 442321, Moscow, ID 83844-2321
Admissions Phone: 208-885-6423 • Admissions Fax: 208-885-5709
Admissions E-mail: lawadmit@uidaho.edu • Web Address: www.uidaho.edu/law

INSTITUTIONAL INFORMATION

Public/Private: Public
Environment: Suburban
Academic Calendar: Semester
Schedule: Full time only
Student/Faculty Ratio: 14:1
Total Faculty: 21
% Female: 20
% Minority: 0

PROGRAMS

Academic Specialties: Business Law, Environmental and Natural Resource Law, Professional and Litigation Skills
Combined Degrees Offered: JD/MA in Environmental Science (4 years)
Clinical Program Required? No
Clinical Programs: Appellate Clinic, Tribal Clinic, General Legal Aid Clinic, Extern Program
Grading System: A (4.00), A– (3.67), B+ (3.33), B (3.00), B– (2.67), etc.
Legal Writing/Methods Course Requirements: 1 year for all first-year students

STUDENT INFORMATION

Enrollment of Law School: 300
% Male/Female: 70/30
% Full Time: 100
% Minority: 6
Average Age of Entering Class: 28

RESEARCH FACILITIES

School-Supported Research Centers: Students may enroll in graduate-level courses at Washington State University. Six graduate-level credits may be accepted towards the JD.

EXPENSES/FINANCIAL AID

Annual Tuition (Residents/Nonresidents): $4,416/$10,416
Room and Board (On Campus): $6,444
Books and Supplies: $700
Financial Aid Application Deadline: 2/15
Average Grant: $1,200
% of Aid That Is Merit-Based: 20
Average Debt: $38,770

ADMISSIONS INFORMATION

Application Fee: $40
Regular Application Deadline: 2/1
Regular Notification: 4/1
LSDAS Accepted? No
Average GPA: 3.3
Range of GPA: 3.1–3.6
Average LSAT: 154
Range of LSAT: 149–156
Transfer Students Accepted? Yes
Other Schools to Which Students Applied: Gonzaga University, Brigham Young University, University of Oregon, University of Utah, Willamette University, Seattle University, University of Washington, Lewis and Clark College
Number of Applications Received: 479
Number of Applicants Accepted: 307
Number of Applicants Enrolled: 100

INTERNATIONAL STUDENTS

TOEFL Required of International Students? Yes
Minimum TOEFL: 560

EMPLOYMENT INFORMATION

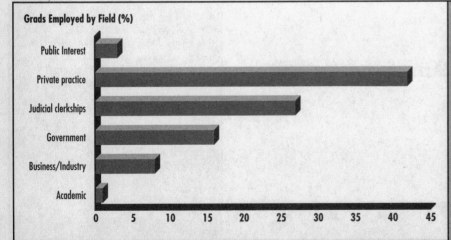

Rate of Placement: 97%
Average Starting Salary: $35,390
Employers Who Frequently Hire Grads: Employers with offices in Idaho, Washington, Oregon, Utah
Prominent Alumni: Frank Shrontz, former CEO, Boling Co., Linda Copple Trout, chief justice, Idaho Supreme Court
State for Bar Exam: ID
Number Taking Bar Exam: 43
Pass Rate for First-Time Bar: 65%

UNIVERSITY OF ILLINOIS
College of Law

Admissions Contact: Director of Admissions, Ana K. Perry
504 East Pennsylvania Avenue, Champaign, IL 61820
Admissions Phone: 217-244-6415 • Admissions Fax: 217-244-1478
Admissions E-mail: admissions@law.uiuc.edu • Web Address: www.law.uiuc.edu

INSTITUTIONAL INFORMATION

Public/Private: Public
Environment: Urban
Academic Calendar: Semester
Schedule: Full time only
Student/Faculty Ratio: 14:1
Total Faculty: 68
% Part Time: 20
% Female: 39
% Minority: 19

PROGRAMS

Advanced Degrees Offered: LLM (1 year)
Combined Degrees Offered: JD/MBA (4 years),
JD/MA (4 years), JD/PhD (varies), JD/DVM (6
years), JD/MD (6 years), JD/MALIR (3.5 years),
JD/MUP (4 years)
Clinical Program Required? No
Clinical Programs: Public Interest Law including
live-client Civil Clinic
Grading System: Letter and numerical system on a
4.0 scale

STUDENT INFORMATION

Enrollment of Law School: 596
% Male/Female: 60/40
% Full Time: 100
% Minority: 30
Average Age of Entering Class: 24

EXPENSES/FINANCIAL AID

Annual Tuition (Residents/Nonresidents):
$8,024/$18,884
Room and Board: $6,950
Books and Supplies: $930
Average Grant: $5,242
Average Loan: $10,500
% of Aid That Is Merit-Based: 13
% Receiving Some Sort of Aid: 95
Average Total Aid Package: $18,500
Average Debt: $36,700

ADMISSIONS INFORMATION

Regular Application Deadline: 3/15
LSDAS Accepted? Yes
Average GPA: 3.4
Range of GPA: 3.2–3.8
Average LSAT: 160
Range of LSAT: 157–164
Transfer Students Accepted? Yes
Other Schools to Which Students Applied:
Northwestern University, University of Michigan,
Loyola University Chicago, DePaul University, University of Wisconsin, University of Chicago, Illinois
Institute of Technology, Washington University
Other Admissions Factors Considered: Graduate work in other fields, demontrated leadership
ability
Number of Applications Received: 1,837
Number of Applicants Accepted: 580

INTERNATIONAL STUDENTS

TOEFL Required of International Students? Yes
Minimum TOEFL: 600

EMPLOYMENT INFORMATION

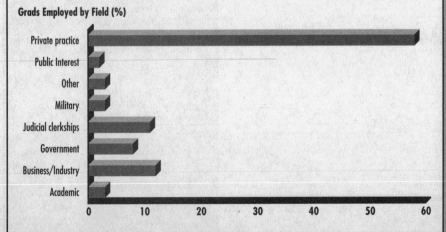

Average Starting Salary: $58,327
Employers Who Frequently Hire Grads:
Sidley & Austin; Jenner & Block; Mayer, Brown &
Platt; Kirkland & Ellis; McDermott, Will &
Emory; Katten, Muchin & Zairs
State for Bar Exam: IL
Number Taking Bar Exam: 143
Pass Rate for First-Time Bar: 95%

UNIVERSITY OF IOWA
College of Law

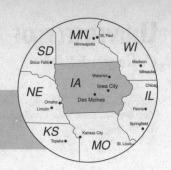

Admissions Contact: Director of Admissions, Camille deJorna
284 Boyd Law Building, Melrose at Byington Streets, Iowa City, IA 52242
Admissions Phone: 319-335-9095 • Admissions Fax: 319-335-9019
Admissions E-mail: law-admissions@uiowa.edu • Web Address: www.uiowa.edu/~lawcoll

INSTITUTIONAL INFORMATION

Public/Private: Public
Environment: Suburban
Academic Calendar: Semester
Schedule: Full time only
Student/Faculty Ratio: 13:1
Total Faculty: 50
% Part Time: 2
% Female: 26
% Minority: 14

PROGRAMS

Advanced Degrees Offered: LLM International and Comparative Law (24 hours of academic credit and a thesis)
Combined Degrees Offered: JD/MBA (4 years), JD/MA (4 years)
Clinical Program Required? No
Grading System: Letter and numerical system with a 90–55 range

STUDENT INFORMATION

Enrollment of Law School: 654
% Male/Female: 61/39
% Full Time: 100
% Full Time That Are International: 2
% Minority: 19
Average Age of Entering Class: 25

EXPENSES/FINANCIAL AID

Annual Tuition (Residents/Nonresidents): $6,822/$17,384
Room and Board (Off Campus): $5,220
Books and Supplies: $1,350
Average Grant: $5,254
Average Debt: $40,947

ADMISSIONS INFORMATION

Application Fee: $30
Regular Application Deadline: 3/1
Regular Notification: Rolling
LSDAS Accepted? Yes
Average GPA: 3.4
Range of GPA: 3.2–3.7
Average LSAT: 158
Range of LSAT: 155–161
Transfer Students Accepted? Yes
Other Schools to Which Students Applied: University of Minnesota, University of Wisconsin, Drake University, Northwestern University, University of Illinois, University of Michigan, Indiana University—Bloomington, Georgetown University
Other Admissions Factors Considered: Letters of recommendation reflecting academic or professional ability, extracurricular activities, or any other information that addresses the applicant's potential for law study
Number of Applications Received: 1,119
Number of Applicants Accepted: 538
Number of Applicants Enrolled: 227

INTERNATIONAL STUDENTS

TOEFL Required of International Students? Yes
Minimum TOEFL: 580

EMPLOYMENT INFORMATION

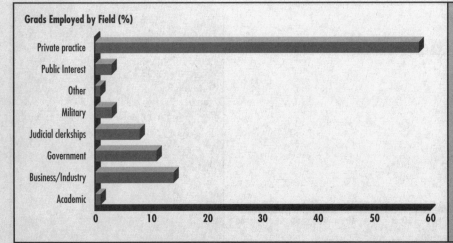

Employers Who Frequently Hire Grads: National law firms, government agencies, state and federal judges
Prominent Alumni: Judge Donald P. Lay, U.S. Court of Appeals; Justice Arthur A. McGiverin, Iowa Supreme Court; Richard C. Levitt, banking and finance
State for Bar Exam: IA
Number Taking Bar Exam: 76
Pass Rate for First-Time Bar: 83%

UNIVERSITY OF KANSAS

School of Law

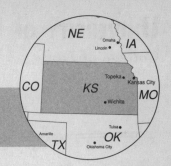

Admissions Contact: Director of Admissions, Diane Lindeman
15th and Burdick Drive, Lawrence, KS 66045
Admissions Phone: 785-864-4378 • Admissions Fax: 785-864-5054
Admissions E-mail: lindeman@law.wpo.ukans.edu • Web Address: www.law.ukans.edu

INSTITUTIONAL INFORMATION

Public/Private: Public
Environment: Suburban
Academic Calendar: Semester
Schedule: Full time only
Student/Faculty Ratio: 20:1
Total Faculty: 31
% Part Time: 8
% Female: 23
% Minority: 13

PROGRAMS

Academic Specialties: Tax and Business Law, Criminal Law, Family Law, Environmental/Natural Resource Law, Constitutional Law
Advanced Degrees Offered: JD
Combined Degrees Offered: JD/MBA, JD/MA Economics, JD/MPA, JD/MA Philosophy, JD/MSW, JD/MUP, JD/MHSA (all are 4 years)
Clinical Program Required? No
Clinical Programs: Legal Aid, Judicial Clerkship, Criminal Justice, Defender Project, Elder Law, Public Policy, Legislative, Media Law
Grading System: Letter grading system ranging from A to F, assigned on the basis of examination scores or on the basis of performance in seminars or courses with writing requirements. Some courses are graded on a Credit/No Credit, A/Credit/No Credit, or A/Credit/F basis.
Legal Writing/Methods Course Requirements: 1 semester, legal/writing exercises implemented

STUDENT INFORMATION

Enrollment of Law School: 543
% Male/Female: 59/41
% Full Time: 100
% Full Time That Are International: 1
% Minority: 11
Average Age of Entering Class: 24

EXPENSES/FINANCIAL AID

Annual Tuition (Residents/Nonresidents): $6,937/$14,433
Room and Board (On/Off Campus): $6,500/$7,000
Books and Supplies: $650
Financial Aid Application Deadline: 3/1
Average Grant: $8,500
Average Loan: $8,500
% of Aid That Is Merit-Based: 85
% Receiving Some Sort of Aid: 80
Average Total Aid Package: $14,500
Average Debt: $35,000

ADMISSIONS INFORMATION

Application Fee: $40
Regular Application Deadline: 3/15
Regular Notification: Rolling
Average GPA: 3.3
Range of GPA: 2.5–4.0
Average LSAT: 155
Range of LSAT: 143–171
Transfer Students Accepted? Yes
Other Schools to Which Students Applied: University of Missouri—Kansas City, University of Texas, University of Iowa, Washburn University
Other Admissions Factors Considered: Admissions decisions also influenced by demonstrated ability to overcome cultural, financial, or other disadvantages. Kansas residents receive preference.
Number of Applications Received: 682
Number of Applicants Accepted: 410
Number of Applicants Enrolled: 186

INTERNATIONAL STUDENTS

TOEFL Required of International Students? Yes
Minimum TOEFL: 550

EMPLOYMENT INFORMATION

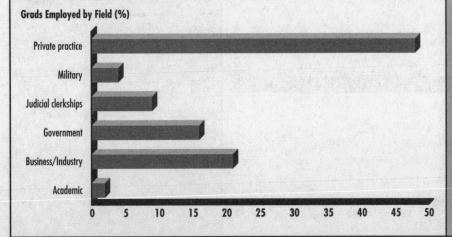

Rate of Placement: 96%
State for Bar Exam: KS
Number Taking Bar Exam: 89
Pass Rate for First-Time Bar: 88%

UNIVERSITY OF KENTUCKY
College of Law

Admissions Contact: Associate Dean, Drusilla V. Bakert
209 Law Building, Lexington, KY 40506-0048
Admissions Phone: 859-257-1678 • Admissions Fax: 859-323-1061
Admissions E-mail: dbakert@pop.uky.edu • Web Address: www.uky.edu/law

INSTITUTIONAL INFORMATION

Public/Private: Public
Environment: Urban
Academic Calendar: Semester
Schedule: Full time only
Student/Faculty Ratio: 16:1
Total Faculty: 27
% Part Time: 13
% Female: 30
% Minority: 7

PROGRAMS

Academic Specialties: Advocacy, Constructive Law, Family Law, Fair Housing Law, Bankruptcy Law
Advanced Degrees Offered: None
Combined Degrees Offered: JD/MPA (4 years), JD/MBA (4 years)
Clinical Program Required? No
Clinical Programs: Elder Law Clinic; Judicial Clerkship; Prison, Prosecutorial, and Environmental Mediation externships
Grading System: A+ to E (0.0 to 4.3) scale
Legal Writing/Methods Course Requirements: Small-group sessions in the first year

STUDENT INFORMATION

Enrollment of Law School: 402
% Male/Female: 55/45
% Full Time: 100
% Full Time That Are International: 1
% Minority: 6
Average Age of Entering Class: 23

RESEARCH FACILITIES

Computers/Workstations Available: 50
School-Supported Research Centers: Law Library is a member of the National Law Library Consortium. Students also have access to the State Loan Library and State Library System.

EXPENSES/FINANCIAL AID

Annual Tuition (Residents/Nonresidents): $5,876/$15,450
Room and Board: $7,200
Books and Supplies: $550
Financial Aid Application Deadline: 4/1
Average Grant: $5,000
Average Loan: $14,000
% Receiving Some Sort of Aid: 75
Average Debt: $40,000

ADMISSIONS INFORMATION

Regular Application Deadline: 3/1
Regular Notification: Rolling
LSDAS Accepted? Yes
Average GPA: 3.5
Range of GPA: 3.2–3.7
Average LSAT: 158
Range of LSAT: 155–161
Transfer Students Accepted? Yes
Other Schools to Which Students Applied: University of Louisville, Northern Kentucky University, Vanderbilt University, Wake Forest University, University of Virginia, University of Cincinnati, Emory University, University of Tennessee
Other Admissions Factors Considered: Geographic, racial, ethnic diversity; diversity of experience
Number of Applications Received: 843
Number of Applicants Accepted: 320
Number of Applicants Enrolled: 124

EMPLOYMENT INFORMATION

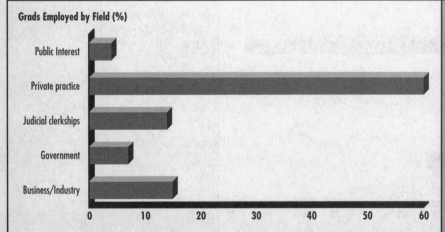

Grads Employed by Field (%)

Rate of Placement: 98%
Average Starting Salary: $41,000
Employers Who Frequently Hire Grads: Five largest Kentucky firms; major firms in Cincinnati, Nashville, West Virginia, and Atlanta
Prominent Alumni: Mitch McConnell, U.S. senator; Edward T. Breathitt, former governor; James E. Rogers Jr., president and CEO, Cinergy Corporation
State for Bar Exam: KY
Number Taking Bar Exam: 90
Pass Rate for First-Time Bar: 92%

University of La Verne

College of Law

Admissions Contact: Director of Admissions, John Osborne
1950 3rd Street, La Verne, CA 91715
Admissions Phone: 909-596-1848 • Admissions Fax: 909-392-2707
Admissions E-mail: osborne@ulv.edu • Web Address: www.ulv.edu

INSTITUTIONAL INFORMATION

Public/Private: Private
Academic Calendar: Semester
Schedule: Full time or part time
Student/Faculty Ratio: 25:1

PROGRAMS

Advanced Degrees Offered: JD (3 years full time, 4 years part time)
Clinical Program Required? No
Grading System: A to F
Legal Writing/Methods Course Requirements:
Legal Analysis, 2-unit class

STUDENT INFORMATION

Enrollment of Law School: 160
% Male/Female: 50/50
% Full Time: 50

EXPENSES/FINANCIAL AID

Books and Supplies: $1,500
Tuition Per Credit: $575

ADMISSIONS INFORMATION

Regular Application Deadline: 8/1
Transfer Students Accepted? Yes

EMPLOYMENT INFORMATION

Employers Who Frequently Hire Grads:
County government and law firms

UNIVERSITY OF LOUISVILLE
Louis D. Brandeis School of Law

Admissions Contact: Assistant Dean for Admissions, Jerie Torbeck
Law Admissions Office, Louisville, KY 40292
Admissions Phone: 502-852-6364 • Admissions Fax: 502-852-0862
Admissions E-mail: gjjack01@ulkyvm.louisville.edu • Web Address: www.louisville.edu/brandeislaw/

INSTITUTIONAL INFORMATION

Public/Private: Public
Environment: Urban
Academic Calendar: Semester
Schedule: Full time or part time
Student/Faculty Ratio: 12:1
Total Faculty: 32
% Part Time: 13
% Female: 39
% Minority: 16

PROGRAMS

Advanced Degrees Offered: JD (3 years full time, 4 years part time)
Combined Degrees Offered: JD/MBA, JD/MDiv (4–5 years)
Clinical Program Required? Yes
Clinical Programs: Public Service Program and 6 externship programs
Grading System: Numerical system on a 4.0 scale
Legal Writing/Methods Course Requirements: Basic Legal Skill, 1 year, 3 credits; Research and Writing first semester, 1 credit

STUDENT INFORMATION

Enrollment of Law School: 383
% Male/Female: 57/43
% Full Time: 73
% Full Time That Are International: 1
% Minority: 14
Average Age of Entering Class: 24

RESEARCH FACILITIES

Computers/Workstations Available: 51

EXPENSES/FINANCIAL AID

Annual Tuition (Residents/Nonresidents): $5,977/$16,050
Room and Board (On/Off Campus): $4,986/$5,988
Books and Supplies: $752
Financial Aid Application Deadline: 7/1
Average Grant: $3,000
Average Loan: $13,660
% of Aid That Is Merit-Based: 13
% Receiving Some Sort of Aid: 79
Average Total Aid Package: $16,980
Average Debt: $22,750
Tuition Per Credit (Residents/Nonresidents): $249/$669
Fees Per Credit (Residents/Nonresidents): $15/$15

ADMISSIONS INFORMATION

Regular Application Deadline: Rolling
Regular Notification: Rolling
LSDAS Accepted? Yes
Average GPA: 3.4
Range of GPA: 2.9–3.7
Average LSAT: 157
Range of LSAT: 151–159
Transfer Students Accepted? Yes
Other Schools to Which Students Applied: University of Kentucky, Northern Kentucky University, University of Cincinnati, University of Dayton, Vanderbilt University, University of Memphis, Indiana University—Bloomington
Other Admissions Factors Considered: Academic improvement, adversity overcome, community service
Number of Applications Received: 830
Number of Applicants Accepted: 290
Number of Applicants Enrolled: 125

EMPLOYMENT INFORMATION

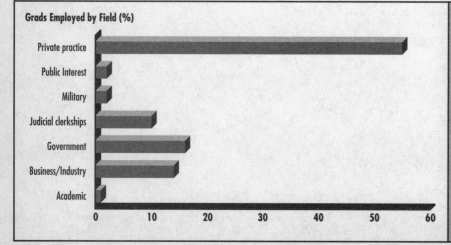

Grads Employed by Field (%)

Rate of Placement: 94%
Average Starting Salary: $36,000
Employers Who Frequently Hire Grads: Brown, Todd and Heyburn; Dinsmore and Shohl; Greenebaum, Doll and McDonald; Wyatt, Tarrant and Combs
Prominent Alumni: Ernest E. Allen, CEO of the National Center for Missing and Exploited Children; Christopher J. Dodd, U.S. senator from Connecticut; L. Stanley Chauvin, former president, American Bar Association
State for Bar Exam: KY
Number Taking Bar Exam: 112
Pass Rate for First-Time Bar: 90%

UNIVERSITY OF MARYLAND
School of Law

Admissions Contact: Associate Dean, James F. Forsyth
515 West Lombard Street, Baltimore, MD 21201
Admissions Phone: 410-706-3492 • Admissions Fax: 410-706-4045
Admissions E-mail: admissions@law.umaryland.edu • Web Address: www.law.umaryland.edu

INSTITUTIONAL INFORMATION
Public/Private: Public
Environment: Urban
Academic Calendar: Semester
Schedule: Full time or part time
Student/Faculty Ratio: 14:1
Total Faculty: 121
% Part Time: 56
% Female: 30
% Minority: 24

PROGRAMS
Academic Specialties: Integration of theory and faculty-supervised, live-client representation for student attorneys
Advanced Degrees Offered: JD (3 years full time day, 4 years evening)
Combined Degrees Offered: JD/PhD Policy Sciences (7 years), JD/MBA (4 years), JD/MA Public Management (4 years), JD/MA Criminal Justice (3.5–4 years), JD/MSW (3.5–4 years), JD/MA Liberal Education (4 years)
Clinical Program Required? Yes
Clinical Programs: Intellectual Property/Tech Transfer, Law and Health Care, AID Environmental, Economic and Community Development, Disability and Homelessness, Criminal (Defense), Criminal (Prosecution), Family and Children, and others varying on an annual basis
Grading System: Letter A through F and numerical equivalent on 4.0 scale
Legal Writing/Methods Course Requirements: Fall research and writing; spring moot court

STUDENT INFORMATION
Enrollment of Law School: 883
% Male/Female: 45/55
% Full Time: 70
% Full Time That Are International: 1
% Minority: 26
Average Age of Entering Class: 26

RESEARCH FACILITIES
Computers/Workstations Available: 250
School-Supported Research Centers: Research resources available through proximity to federal government in Washington, D.C., and state resources in Annapolis, MD.

EXPENSES/FINANCIAL AID
Annual Tuition (Residents/Nonresidents): $9,982/$18,254
Room and Board (On/Off Campus): $7,254/$8,820
Books and Supplies: $1,200
Financial Aid Application Deadline: 5/1
Average Grant: $3,647
Average Loan: $17,402
% Receiving Some Sort of Aid: 83
Average Total Aid Package: $19,048
Average Debt: $55,101

ADMISSIONS INFORMATION
Application Fee: $50
Regular Application Deadline: Rolling
Regular Notification: Rolling
LSDAS Accepted? Yes
Average GPA: 3.3
Range of GPA: 2.8–3.6
Average LSAT: 156
Range of LSAT: 151–160
Transfer Students Accepted? Yes
Other Schools to Which Students Applied: University of Baltimore, George Washington University, American University, Georgetown University, Catholic University of America, Boston College, Boston University, Temple University
Other Admissions Factors Considered: Race and ethnicity; gender; geographic origin; language and cultural background; social, disability, and economic barriers overcome; interpersonal skills; extracurricular activities; work or service experience, leadership record, and potential for service to the community as an attorney
Number of Applications Received: 2,579
Number of Applicants Accepted: 666
Number of Applicants Enrolled: 301

INTERNATIONAL STUDENTS
Minimum TOEFL: 600

EMPLOYMENT INFORMATION

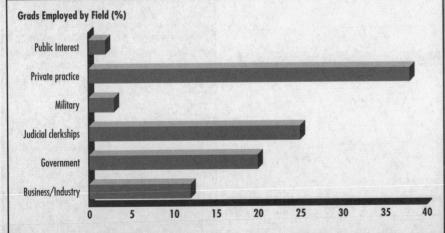

Grads Employed by Field (%)

Rate of Placement: 94%
Average Starting Salary: $45,856
Employers Who Frequently Hire Grads: Department of Justice; Dickstein, Shapiro and Morin, LLP; Hogan and Hartson; Miles and Stockbridge; Ober, Kaler, Grimes and Shriver; Piper and Marbury, LLP; Public Defender's Office; State of Maryland Attorney General's Office; Venable, Baetjer & Howard, LLP; Whiteford, Taylor and Preston, LLP
Prominent Alumni: Christine A. Edwards, executive vice president, chief legal officer, and secretary of Morgan Stanley Dean Witter and Co.; Alvin Krongard, counselor to the director, Central Intelligence Agency; Benjamin Cardin, United States congressman

UNIVERSITY OF MEMPHIS
Cecil C. Humphreys School of Law

Admissions Contact: Director of Law Admissions and Recruitment, Sidney S. Evans
Law Admissions, 207 Humphreys Law Building, Memphis, TN 38152
Admissions Phone: 901-678-5403 • Admissions Fax: 901-678-5210
Admissions E-mail: uofmlaw@memphis.edu • Web Address: www.law.memphis.edu

INSTITUTIONAL INFORMATION

Public/Private: Public
Environment: Urban
Academic Calendar: Semester
Schedule: Full time or part time
Student/Faculty Ratio: 18:1
Total Faculty: 55
% Part Time: 56
% Female: 33
% Minority: 13

PROGRAMS

Academic Specialties: Curriculum is designed to prepare students for general practice in civil and criminal matters. A special strength of the curriculum is the required courses, which expose students to all major facets of the practice of law.
Advanced Degrees Offered: JD (6 semesters)
Combined Degrees Offered: JD/MBA (4 years, 8 semesters)
Clinical Program Required? No
Clinical Programs: Civil Litigation, Child Advocacy, Elder Law
Grading System: A+ to F, and in some courses E (Excellent), S (Satisfactory) and U (Unsatisfactory). A grade of D or better is passing, less than D is failing, below C is unsatisfactory.
Legal Writing/Methods Course Requirements: 3 credit hours in first year and upperclass research requirement

STUDENT INFORMATION

Enrollment of Law School: 443
% Male/Female: 58/42
% Full Time: 95
% Minority: 13
Average Age of Entering Class: 26

RESEARCH FACILITIES

Computers/Workstations Available: 1,100
Computer Labs: 50
School-Supported Research Centers: Interlibrary loan programs with other law schools

EXPENSES/FINANCIAL AID

Annual Tuition (Residents/Nonresidents): $4,834/$12,990
Room and Board : $6,570
Books and Supplies: $1,300
Financial Aid Application Deadline: 4/1
Average Grant: $1,992
Average Loan: $13,406
% of Aid That Is Merit-Based: 15
% Receiving Some Sort of Aid: 75
Average Total Aid Package: $13,423
Average Debt: $51,336
Tuition Per Credit (Residents/Nonresidents): $220/$574
Fees Per Credit (Residents/Nonresidents): $206/$501

ADMISSIONS INFORMATION

Application Fee: $25
Regular Application Deadline: 2/15
Regular Notification: 4/15
LSDAS Accepted? Yes
Average GPA: 3.2
Range of GPA: 2.8–3.6
Average LSAT: 154
Range of LSAT: 151–157
Transfer Students Accepted? Yes
Other Schools to Which Students Applied: University of Tennessee, Vanderbilt University, University of Mississippi, University of Georgia, Mississippi College, Samford University, Mercer University, Georgia State University
Number of Applications Received: 897
Number of Applicants Enrolled: 139

INTERNATIONAL STUDENTS

TOEFL Required of International Students? Yes
Minimum TOEFL: 550

EMPLOYMENT INFORMATION

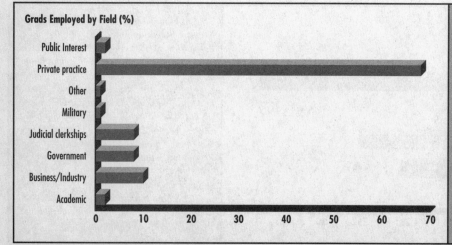

Grads Employed by Field (%)

Rate of Placement: 95%
Average Starting Salary: $42,500
Employers Who Frequently Hire Grads: Major area law firms, Tennessee Attorney General's Office, Public Defender's Office, Tennessee Supreme Court and Court of Appeals, major area corporate legal depts., city and county government
Prominent Alumni: John S. Wilder, lieutenant governor of Tennessee; Hon. Bernice B. Donald, U.S. district judge for the western district of Tennessee; Hon. David S. Kennedy and Hon. G. Harvey Boswell, judges, U.S. Bankrupcy Court, western district of Tennessee

UNIVERSITY OF MIAMI
School of Law

Admissions Contact: Director of Student Recruiting, Therese Lambert
PO Box 248087, Coral Gables, FL 33124-8087
Admissions Phone: 305-284-6746 • Admissions Fax: 305-284-2795
Admissions E-mail: admissions@law.miami.edu • Web Address: www.law.miami.edu

INSTITUTIONAL INFORMATION

Public/Private: Private
Environment: Suburban
Academic Calendar: Semester
Schedule: Full time or part time
Student/Faculty Ratio: 16:1
Total Faculty: 50
% Female: 23
% Minority: 10

PROGRAMS

Academic Specialties: Traditional classroom courses, specialized legal skills courses, seminars designed to provide intensive research and writing opportunities, workshops that enable students to apply theoretical skills to practical problems, and courses that deal with timely issues. Miami is known for being exceptionally strong in International Law (currently offering 3 courses taught in Spanish), Taxation, and Litigation Skills, and is also very strong in many other areas including Labor Law, Entertainment and Sports Law, Computer Law, Estate Planning (the only school in the country with an LLM program in this area), Human Rights, Public Interest, and many courses that deal with cutting-edge issues.
Advanced Degrees Offered: LLM in Comparative Law (for graduates of foreign law schools), Estate Planning, Inter-American Law, International Law, Ocean and Coastal Law, Real Property Development, Taxation (all 1 year full time)
Combined Degrees Offered: JD/MBA, JD/MPH, JD/MS Marine Affairs (all approximately 3.5 years)

Clinical Program Required? No
Grading System: Letter system, with Pass/Fail offered in some courses
Legal Writing/Methods Course Requirements: In addition to the required first year (small sections each semester), an advanced legal and writing course and several sections of advanced legal research are offered

STUDENT INFORMATION

Enrollment of Law School: 1,164
% Male/Female: 54/46
% Full Time: 85
% Full Time That Are International: 7
% Minority: 31
Average Age of Entering Class: 26

RESEARCH FACILITIES

Computers/Workstations Available: 147

EXPENSES/FINANCIAL AID

Annual Tuition: $23,760
Room and Board: $9,360
Books and Supplies: $1,000
Financial Aid Application Deadline: 3/1
Average Grant: $13,760
Average Loan: $37,064
% of Aid That Is Merit-Based: 29
% Receiving Some Sort of Aid: 90
Average Total Aid Package: $33,500
Average Debt: $71,707
Tuition Per Credit: $1,037

ADMISSIONS INFORMATION

Application Fee: $50
Regular Application Deadline: 7/31
Regular Notification: Rolling
LSDAS Accepted? Yes
Average GPA: 3.2
Range of GPA: 2.9–3.4
Average LSAT: 154
Range of LSAT: 150–157
Transfer Students Accepted? Yes
Other Schools to Which Students Applied: University of Florida, Florida State University, Nova Southeastern University, Tulane University, Emory University, American University, George Washington University, St. Thomas University
Other Admissions Factors Considered: Undergraduate institution and major, LSAT writing sample, pattern and trend of grades, work and internship experience, graduate work, and diversity. The above criteria is not ranked—each file is considered individually.
Number of Applications Received: 2,430
Number of Applicants Accepted: 1,389
Number of Applicants Enrolled: 435

INTERNATIONAL STUDENTS

TOEFL Required of International Students? Yes
Minimum TOEFL: 600

EMPLOYMENT INFORMATION

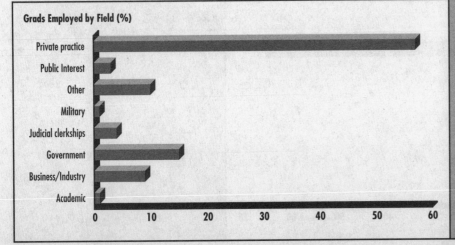

Grads Employed by Field (%)

Rate of Placement: 89%
Average Starting Salary: $53,827
Employers Who Frequently Hire Grads: Steel, Hector and Davis; Holland and Knight; Greenberg Traurig; Dade County State Attorney's Office; Dade County Public Defender's Office
Prominent Alumni: Roy Black, one of the nation's most prominent criminal defense Attorneys; Patricia Ireland, president, National Organization of Women; Alex Penelas, mayor of Miami-Dade County, one of the nation's most prominent Hispanic politicians

UNIVERSITY OF MICHIGAN
Law School

Admissions Contact: Acting Director, Erica Munzel
Reading Room, Ann Arbor, MI 48109-1215
Admissions Phone: 734-764-0537 • Admissions Fax: 734-647-3218
Admissions E-mail: law.jd.admissions@umich.edu • Web Address: www.law.umich.edu

INSTITUTIONAL INFORMATION
Public/Private: Public
Environment: Urban
Academic Calendar: Semester
Schedule: Full time only
Student/Faculty Ratio: 14:1
Total Faculty: 125
% Part Time: 41
% Female: 30
% Minority: 7

PROGRAMS
Academic Specialties: Strong interdisciplinary legal scholarship and teaching and diverse clinical offerings, including several litigation clinics, an appellate clinic, and a transactional clinic
Advanced Degrees Offered: LLM, MCL, SJD
Combined Degrees Offered: JD/MBA (4 years), JD/PhD Economics (5 years), JD/AM Middle Eastern and North African Studies (3.5–4 years), JD/Master of Public Policy (4 years), JD/MS Natural Resources (4 years), JD/MHSA (9 terms), JD/AM Russian and East European Studies (3.5 years), JD/AM Political Science (3.5 years), JD/MSW (8 terms), JD/MSI (8 terms)
Clinical Program Required? No
Clinical Programs: General Clinic (6 faculty), Child Advocacy Law Clinic, Legal Assistance or Urban Communities Program, Environmental Law Clinic, Criminal Appellate Seminar. In addition, there are student-run advocacy programs in which students volunteer to represent clients.
Legal Writing/Methods Course Requirements: Required first-year course, taken sequentially

STUDENT INFORMATION
Enrollment of Law School: 1,067
% Male/Female: 57/43
% Full Time: 100
% Full Time That Are International: 1
% Minority: 23
Average Age of Entering Class: 24

RESEARCH FACILITIES
Computers/Workstations Available: 161

EXPENSES/FINANCIAL AID
Annual Tuition (Residents/Nonresidents): $18,930/$24,900
Room and Board: $7,995
Books and Supplies: $800
Average Grant: $10,412
Average Loan: $18,500
% of Aid That Is Merit-Based: 34
% Receiving Some Sort of Aid: 86
Average Total Aid Package: $21,915
Average Debt: $65,000

ADMISSIONS INFORMATION
Application Fee: $70
Regular Application Deadline: 2/15
Regular Notification: Rolling
LSDAS Accepted? Yes
Average GPA: 3.6
Range of GPA: 3.4–3.8
Average LSAT: 165
Range of LSAT: 163–167
Transfer Students Accepted? Yes
Other Schools to Which Students Applied: Harvard University, Yale University, University of Chicago, Stanford University, Columbia University, Duke University
Number of Applications Received: 3,335
Number of Applicants Enrolled: 343

EMPLOYMENT INFORMATION

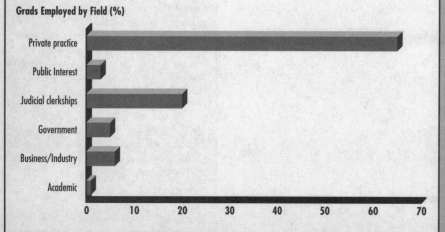

Grads Employed by Field (%)

Rate of Placement: 99%
Average Starting Salary: $72,800

UNIVERSITY OF MINNESOTA
Law School

Admissions Contact: Director of Admissions, Collins B. Byrd, Jr.
229 19th Avenue South, Minneapolis, MN 55455
Admissions Phone: 612-625-5005 • Admissions Fax: 612-625-2011
Admissions E-mail: umnlsadm@tc.umn.edu • Web Address: www.law.umn.edu

INSTITUTIONAL INFORMATION

Public/Private: Public
Environment: Urban
Academic Calendar: Semester
Schedule: Full time only
Student/Faculty Ratio: 16:1
Total Faculty: 44
% Part Time: 100
% Female: 30
% Minority: 11

PROGRAMS

Academic Specialties: Public Law, Public and Private International Law, Constitutional Law, Criminal Law, Corporate and Business Law, Regulatory Law, Legislation, Human Rights Law, Legal Philosophy, Law Clinic
Advanced Degrees Offered: LLM for foreign lawyers (1 year)
Combined Degrees Offered: JD/MBA, JD/MPA, joint degrees available with most graduate programs (all are 4 years)
Clinical Program Required? No
Clinical Programs: 16 separate clinics, including Bankruptcy, Child Advocacy, Civil Litigation, Criminal Appeals, Disability, Domestic Abuse, Federal Prosecution, Federal Taxation, Housing, Immigration, Indian Child Welfare, Law and Violence Against Women, Legal Assistance
Grading System: Numerical system on a 4 to 16 scale
Legal Writing/Methods Course Requirements: 3 years of writing requirements

STUDENT INFORMATION

Enrollment of Law School: 744
% Male/Female: 53/47
% Full Time: 100
% Full Time That Are International: 2
% Minority: 17
Average Age of Entering Class: 24

RESEARCH FACILITIES

School-Supported Research Centers: 6 international exchanges programs in France, Germany, Ireland, the Netherlands, Spain, and Sweden

EXPENSES/FINANCIAL AID

Annual Tuition (Residents/Nonresidents): $9,000/$15,300
Average Grant: $6,300
Average Loan: $17,500
% Receiving Some Sort of Aid: 91
Average Debt: $38,000

ADMISSIONS INFORMATION

Application Fee: $40
Regular Application Deadline: 3/1
Regular Notification: Rolling
LSDAS Accepted? Yes
Average GPA: 3.6
Range of GPA: 3.3–3.8
Average LSAT: 162
Range of LSAT: 158–164
Transfer Students Accepted? Yes
Other Schools to Which Students Applied: University of Wisconsin, University of Michigan, William Mitchell College of Law, Hamline University, Yale University, Harvard University, Georgetown University, University of Iowa
Number of Applications Received: 1,467

INTERNATIONAL STUDENTS

TOEFL Required of International Students? Yes

EMPLOYMENT INFORMATION

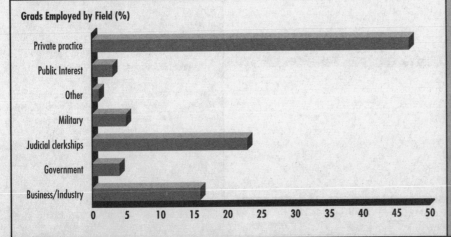

Grads Employed by Field (%)

Rate of Placement: 99%
Average Starting Salary: $60,000
Prominent Alumni: Walter Mondale, former vice president and ambassador to Japan; James Blanchard, former governor of Michigan and ambassador to Canada; Constance Barry Newman, director of the U.S. Office of Personnel Management; Robert Stein, executive director of the American Bar Association; A. W. Clausen, former president of the World Bank, and CEO of Bank America; Michael Sullivan, president of International Dairy Queen; Michael Wright, President of SUPERVALU Inc.; over 250 federal and state court judges nationwide

UNIVERSITY OF MISSISSIPPI SCHOOL OF LAW
Lamar Law Center

Admissions Contact: Coordinator of Admissions, Barbara Vinson
School of Law, Room 310, University, MS 38677
Admissions Phone: 662-915-6910 • Admissions Fax: 662-915-1289
Admissions E-mail: lawmiss@olemiss.edu • Web Address: www.olemiss.edu/depts/law_school/law-hom.html

INSTITUTIONAL INFORMATION

Public/Private: Public
Environment: Suburban
Academic Calendar: Semester
Schedule: Full time only
Student/Faculty Ratio: 22:1
Total Faculty: 27
% Part Time: 25
% Female: 22
% Minority: 15

PROGRAMS

Academic Specialties: The School provides a solid legal education in all areas, with particular strength in Tax and Business and International and Environmental Law.
Combined Degrees Offered: JD/MBA (4 years)
Clinical Program Required? No
Clinical Programs: Public service internships (3–6 hours). Students work as legal assistants with prosecutors, defenders, judges, or attorneys in public service agencies with established internship programs.
Grading System: A (4.0), B+ (3.5), B (3.0), C+ (2.5), C (2.0), D+ (1.5), D (1.0), F (0.0), Z (Pass), X (Audit), W (Withdraw)
Legal Writing/Methods Course Requirements: 1 year of Legal Research and Writing, advanced skills writing requirement

STUDENT INFORMATION

Enrollment of Law School: 479
% Male/Female: 63/37
% Full Time: 99
% Minority: 15
Average Age of Entering Class: 24

RESEARCH FACILITIES

Computers/Workstations Available: 32
School-Supported Research Centers: The Mississippi Law Research Institute, or MLRI, is located in the Law Center, and is the state's advisory law revision, research and reform agency. It operates much like an unbiased, nonpolitical law firm for the legislature and every state agency. The Mississippi Judicial College (MJC) is also headquartered at the Lamar Law Center and is the first full-time state judicial education effort in the nation. Whether holding mock trials in public schools and in communities to promote understanding of the judicial system, or offering stress management seminars and topics such as law and literature to judges, MJC meets the needs and provides resources for the state's judicial system, which will benefit all Mississippians. The American Academy of Judicial Education is also located at the University of Mississippi, and provides continuing education for judges throughout the United States.

EXPENSES/FINANCIAL AID

Annual Tuition (Residents/Nonresidents): $4,810/$9,822
Room and Board: $9,828
Books and Supplies: $1,200
Average Grant: $1,700
Average Loan: $15,334
% Receiving Some Sort of Aid: 81
Average Total Aid Package: $15,417
Average Debt: $38,134
Fees Per Credit (Residents/Nonresidents): $179/$375

ADMISSIONS INFORMATION

Application Fee: $25
Regular Application Deadline: 3/1
Regular Notification: 4/15
LSDAS Accepted? Yes
Average GPA: 3.2
Range of GPA: 3.0–3.5
Average LSAT: 152
Range of LSAT: 149–156
Transfer Students Accepted? Yes
Other Schools to Which Students Applied: Mississippi College, Vanderbilt University, University of Georgia, Tulane University, University of Memphis, University of Tennessee, Georgia State University, Samford University
Number of Applications Received: 1,122
Number of Applicants Accepted: 469
Number of Applicants Enrolled: 194

INTERNATIONAL STUDENTS

TOEFL Required of International Students? Yes
Minimum TOEFL: 625

EMPLOYMENT INFORMATION

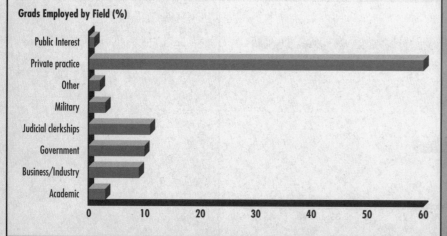

Rate of Placement: 96%
Average Starting Salary: $42,000
Employers Who Frequently Hire Grads: Top regional employers from across the South
Prominent Alumni: John Grisham, author; Trent Lott, U.S. congressman; Robert C. Khayat, chancellor of the University of Mississippi

UNIVERSITY OF MISSOURI — COLUMBIA
School of Law

Admissions Contact: Associate Dean, Kenneth Dean
103 Hulston Hall, Columbia, MO 65211
Admissions Phone: 573-882-6042 • Admissions Fax: 573-882-9625
Admissions E-mail: umclawadmissions@missouri.edu • Web Address: www.law.missouri.edu

INSTITUTIONAL INFORMATION
Public/Private: Public
Environment: Suburban
Academic Calendar: Semester
Schedule: Full time or part time
Student/Faculty Ratio: 18:1
Total Faculty: 51
% Part Time: 29
% Female: 31
% Minority: 10

PROGRAMS
Academic Specialties: Dispute Resolution
Advanced Degrees Offered: LLM Dispute Resolution
Combined Degrees Offered: JD/MBA (4 years), JD/MPA (4 years), JD/MA Economics (4 years), JD/MA Human Development and Family Studies (4 years), JD/MA Educational Leadership and Policy Analysis (4 years)
Clinical Program Required? No
Grading System: Numerical system ranging 55 to 100; minimum 70 GPA required for graduation
Legal Writing/Methods Course Requirements: 2 hours fall, 2 hours winter of first year

STUDENT INFORMATION
Enrollment of Law School: 555
% Male/Female: 59/41
% Full Time: 99
% Full Time That Are International: 1
% Minority: 10
Average Age of Entering Class: 24

RESEARCH FACILITIES
Campuswide Network? No

EXPENSES/FINANCIAL AID
Room and Board: $6,830
Books and Supplies: $1,200
Average Grant: $3,000
Average Loan: $13,300
% of Aid That Is Merit-Based: 10
% Receiving Some Sort of Aid: 80
Average Debt: $39,434
Fees Per Credit (Residents/Nonresidents): $315/$629

ADMISSIONS INFORMATION
Regular Application Deadline: Rolling
Regular Notification: Rolling
LSDAS Accepted? Yes
Average GPA: 3.3
Range of GPA: 3.0–3.6
Average LSAT: 155
Range of LSAT: 152–158
Transfer Students Accepted? Yes
Other Schools to Which Students Applied: University of Missouri—Kansas City, Washington University, St. Louis University, University of Illinois, University of Iowa, Vanderbilt University, University of Arkansas—Little Rock, University of Kansas
Other Admissions Factors Considered: Applicant's suitability for career
Number of Applications Received: 792
Number of Applicants Accepted: 445
Number of Applicants Enrolled: 177

INTERNATIONAL STUDENTS
TOEFL Required of International Students? Yes
Minimum TOEFL: 600

EMPLOYMENT INFORMATION

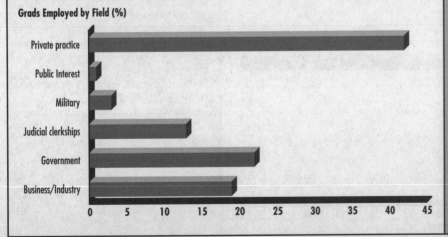

Grads Employed by Field (%)

Rate of Placement: 85%
Average Starting Salary: $40,583
Employers Who Frequently Hire Grads: Shook, Hardy and Bacon; Attorney General of Missouri; Missouri Court of Appeals; WD&ED; Brown and James; KCMO and STL; Thompson Coburn, STL
Prominent Alumni: Mel Carnahan, Governor of Missouri

UNIVERSITY OF MISSOURI—KANSAS CITY

School of Law

Admissions Contact: Director of Admissions, Jean Klosterman
5100 Rockhill Road, Kansas City, MO 64110-2499
Admissions Phone: 816-235-1644 • Admissions Fax: 816-235-5276
Admissions E-mail: klostermanm@umkc.edu • Web Address: www.law.umkc.edu

INSTITUTIONAL INFORMATION

Public/Private: Public
Environment: Urban
Academic Calendar: Semester
Schedule: Full time or part time
Student/Faculty Ratio: 18:1
Total Faculty: 33
% Part Time: 33
% Female: 33
% Minority: 6

PROGRAMS

Advanced Degrees Offered: LLM (1–3 years)
Combined Degrees Offered: JD/MBA (3–4 years), JD/LLM (3.5–4 years)
Clinical Program Required? No
Grading System: A, B, C, D, F

STUDENT INFORMATION

Enrollment of Law School: 485
% Male/Female: 51/49
% Full Time: 94
% Full Time That Are International: 1
% Minority: 12

EXPENSES/FINANCIAL AID

Annual Tuition (Residents/Nonresidents): $8,540/$17,077
Room and Board (On/Off Campus): $9,690/$11,770
Books and Supplies: $1,520
Financial Aid Application Deadline: 3/1
Average Grant: $4,310
Average Loan: $16,755
% Receiving Some Sort of Aid: 85
Average Total Aid Package: $17,288

ADMISSIONS INFORMATION

Application Fee: $25
Regular Application Deadline: Rolling
Regular Notification: Rolling
Average GPA: 3.2
Range of GPA: 2.1–4.0
Average LSAT: 154
Range of LSAT: 150–156
Transfer Students Accepted? Yes
Other Schools to Which Students Applied: University of Kansas, University of Missouri, Columbia University, Washburn University, St. Louis University
Other Admissions Factors Considered: Extracurricular activities, work experience, advanced degrees, efforts to overcome societally imposed disadvantages
Number of Applications Received: 712

INTERNATIONAL STUDENTS

TOEFL Required of International Students? Yes

EMPLOYMENT INFORMATION

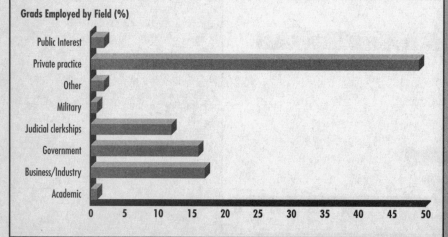

Rate of Placement: 93%
Average Starting Salary: $39,118
Employers Who Frequently Hire Grads: Jackson County, Missouri, Shook, Hardy and Bacon, small law firms
Prominent Alumni: Donald Fehr, Executive Director and General Counsel, Major League Baseball Players Association; H. Howard Stephenson, Chairman and CEO, Bank of Hawaii

UNIVERSITY OF MONTANA

School of Law

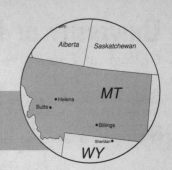

Admissions Contact: Director of Admissions, Heidi Fanslow
University of Montana School of Law, Missoula, MT 59812
Admissions Phone: 406-243-2698 • Admissions Fax: 406-243-2576
Admissions E-mail: lawadmis@selway.umt.edu • Web Address: www.umt.edu/law/

INSTITUTIONAL INFORMATION

Public/Private: Public
Environment: Urban
Academic Calendar: Semester
Schedule: Full time only
Student/Faculty Ratio: 15:1
Total Faculty: 22
% Part Time: 18
% Female: 32
% Minority: 5

PROGRAMS

Academic Specialties: Competency-based curriculum, Environmental and Indian Law
Advanced Degrees Offered: JD (3 years)
Combined Degrees Offered: JD/MPA (4 years), JD/MS Environmental Studies (4 years)
Clinical Program Required? Yes
Clinical Programs: Criminal Defense, Indian Law, Prosecution, Legal Aid, Disability, Judicial
Grading System: Students are not graded on mandatory curve.

STUDENT INFORMATION

Enrollment of Law School: 235
% Male/Female: 58/42
% Full Time: 100
% Minority: 7
Average Age of Entering Class: 28

RESEARCH FACILITIES

Computers/Workstations Available: 45

EXPENSES/FINANCIAL AID

Annual Tuition (Residents/Nonresidents): $6,882/$12,484
Room and Board: $7,510
Books and Supplies: $910
Average Grant: $1,457
Average Loan: $14,349
% of Aid That Is Merit-Based: 3
% Receiving Some Sort of Aid: 87
Average Total Aid Package: $14,619
Average Debt: $35,507

ADMISSIONS INFORMATION

Application Fee: $60
Regular Application Deadline: 3/1
Regular Notification: Rolling
LSDAS Accepted? Yes
Average GPA: 3.2
Range of GPA: 3.0–3.4
Average LSAT: 153
Range of LSAT: 149–157
Transfer Students Accepted? Yes
Other Schools to Which Students Applied: Lewis and Clark College, University of Oregon, Gonzaga University, University of Idaho, Willamette University, University of Colorado, University of Wyoming, University of Denver
Other Admissions Factors Considered: Ability to overcome economic or other disadvantage
Number of Applications Received: 362
Number of Applicants Accepted: 225
Number of Applicants Enrolled: 73

INTERNATIONAL STUDENTS

TOEFL Required of International Students? Yes
Minimum TOEFL: 600

EMPLOYMENT INFORMATION

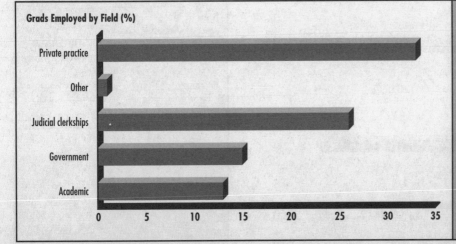

Grads Employed by Field (%)

Rate of Placement: 93%
Average Starting Salary: $34,149
Employers Who Frequently Hire Grads: Church, Harris, Johnson and Williams; Moulton, Bellingham, Longo & Mather; Crowley, Haughy, Hanson, Toole & Dietrich
Prominent Alumni: Governor Marc Racicot; Hon. James R. Browning, 9th Circuit Court of Appeals; Hon. William J. Jameson (deceased) former American Bar Association president, former president of American Judicature Society, recipent of the American Bar Association Medal

UNIVERSITY OF NEBRASKA — LINCOLN
College of Law

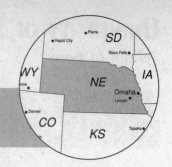

Admissions Contact: Assistant Dean, Glenda J. Pierce
PO Box 830902, Lincoln, NE 68583-0902
Admissions Phone: 402-472-2161 • Admissions Fax: 402-472-5185
Admissions E-mail: lawadm@unl.edu • Web Address: www.unl.edu/lawcoll

INSTITUTIONAL INFORMATION

Public/Private: Public
Environment: Urban
Academic Calendar: Semester
Schedule: Full time only
Student/Faculty Ratio: 14:1
Total Faculty: 52
% Part Time: 46
% Female: 21
% Minority: 7

PROGRAMS

Academic Specialties: Faculty with national/international reputations in Tort Law, Intellectual Property Law, and Labor and Employment Law; clinical programs supervised by in-house faculty
Advanced Degrees Offered: JD (3 years), MLS (1 year)
Combined Degrees Offered: JD/PhD Psychology (6 years); JD/MA Economics, JD/MBA, JD/MPA, JD/Political Science, JD/Community of Regional Planning (all are 4 years), JD/PhD Education Administration (5 years), JD/MA International Affairs (4 years)
Clinical Program Required? No
Clinical Programs: Civil Clinic, Criminal Prosecution Clinic
Grading System: 9 (A+), 8 (A), 7 (B+), 6 (B), 5 (C+), 4 (C), 3 (D+), 2 (D), 0 (F)
Legal Writing/Methods Course Requirements: 6 credit hours, 2 semesters during the first year

STUDENT INFORMATION

Enrollment of Law School: 378
% Male/Female: 59/41
% Full Time: 100
% Full Time That Are International: 1
% Minority: 8
Average Age of Entering Class: 26

RESEARCH FACILITIES

Computers/Workstations Available: 55
School-Supported Research Centers: Lincoln is the state capital; students have access to government offices and courts.

EXPENSES/FINANCIAL AID

Annual Tuition (Residents/Nonresidents): $4,086/$10,485
Room and Board (On/Off Campus): $8,280/$9,496
Books and Supplies: $990
Financial Aid Application Deadline: 3/1
Average Grant: $3,405
Average Loan: $11,933
% of Aid That Is Merit-Based: 48
% Receiving Some Sort of Aid: 59
Average Debt: $35,000

ADMISSIONS INFORMATION

Application Fee: $25
Regular Application Deadline: 3/1
Regular Notification: Rolling
LSDAS Accepted? Yes
Average GPA: 3.5
Range of GPA: 3.2–3.8
Average LSAT: 153
Range of LSAT: 150–158
Transfer Students Accepted? Yes
Other Schools to Which Students Applied: Creighton University, University of Iowa, University of Kansas, Drake University, Washburn University, University of South Dakota, University of Colorado, Arizona State University
Other Admissions Factors Considered: Major, courses taken and their level of difficulty, upward or downward trend in undergraduate GPA, graduate study
Number of Applications Received: 530
Number of Applicants Accepted: 320
Number of Applicants Enrolled: 133

INTERNATIONAL STUDENTS

TOEFL Required of International Students? Yes
Minimum TOEFL: 600

EMPLOYMENT INFORMATION

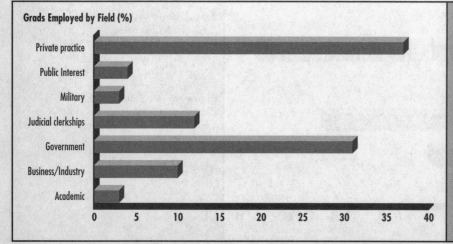

Grads Employed by Field (%)

Rate of Placement: 96%
Average Starting Salary: $37,770
Employers Who Frequently Hire Grads: Law firms with 2–10 attorneys; District Attorneys, Attorney Generals' Offices
Prominent Alumni: Theodore Sorenson, author/attorney, former presidential advisor; Clayton Yeutter, former U.S. secretary of agriculture, chair of Republican National Committee; John Hendry, chief justice of the Nebraska Supreme Court

UNIVERSITY OF NEW MEXICO
School of Law

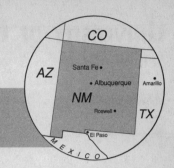

Admissions Contact: Administrative Assisitant, Susan Mitchell
1117 Stanford NE, Albuquerque, NM 87131-1431
Admissions Phone: 505-277-0958 • Admissions Fax: 505-277-9958
Admissions E-mail: admissions@law.unm.edu • Web Address: www.unm.edu/~unmlaw/lawsch.html

INSTITUTIONAL INFORMATION

Public/Private: Public
Environment: Urban
Academic Calendar: Semester
Schedule: Full time only
Student/Faculty Ratio: 12:1
Total Faculty: 34
% Female: 44
% Minority: 27

PROGRAMS

Advanced Degrees Offered: JD (3 years)
Combined Degrees Offered: JD/MA, JD/MS, JD/PhD, JD/MAPA, JD/MA Latin American Studies (4 years)
Clinical Program Required? Yes
Clinical Programs: Southwest Indian Clinic, DA Clinic, Law Practice Clinic, Community Lawyering Clinic
Grading System: 4.0 scale; students must maintain a GPA of at least 2.0
Legal Writing/Methods Course Requirements: Legal Research/Writing course required during first year

STUDENT INFORMATION

Enrollment of Law School: 354
% Male/Female: 42/58
% Full Time: 100
% Minority: 38
Average Age of Entering Class: 26

RESEARCH FACILITIES

Computers/Workstations Available: 55

EXPENSES/FINANCIAL AID

Annual Tuition (Residents/Nonresidents): $4,382/$14,672
Room and Board (On/Off Campus): $4,936/$6,430
Books and Supplies: $824
Financial Aid Application Deadline: 3/1
Average Grant: $4,000

ADMISSIONS INFORMATION

Application Fee: $40
Regular Application Deadline: 2/15
Regular Notification: Rolling
LSDAS Accepted? Yes
Average GPA: 3.2
Range of GPA: 2.9–3.5
Average LSAT: 153
Range of LSAT: 150–160
Transfer Students Accepted? Yes
Other Admissions Factors Considered: Decided preference given to New Mexico residents
Number of Applications Received: 737
Number of Applicants Accepted: 256
Number of Applicants Enrolled: 120

INTERNATIONAL STUDENTS

TOEFL Required of International Students? Yes

EMPLOYMENT INFORMATION

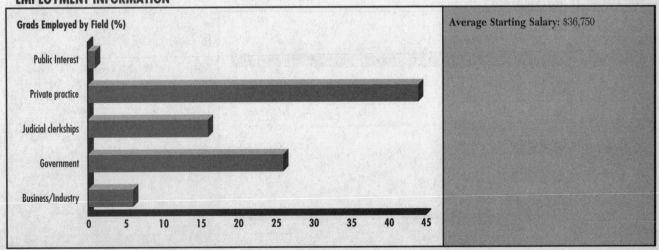

Grads Employed by Field (%)

Average Starting Salary: $36,750

UNIVERSITY OF NORTH CAROLINA — CHAPEL HILL

School of Law

Admissions Contact: Assistant Dean for Admissions, J. Elizabeth Furr
Campus Box 3380, Chapel Hill, NC 27599-3380
Admissions Phone: 919-962-5109 • Admissions Fax: 919-962-1170
Admissions E-mail: law_admission@unc.edu • Web Address: www.law.unc.edu

INSTITUTIONAL INFORMATION

Public/Private: Public
Environment: Suburban
Academic Calendar: Semester
Schedule: Full time only
Student/Faculty Ratio: 15:1
Total Faculty: 84
% Part Time: 47
% Female: 38
% Minority: 6

PROGRAMS

Combined Degrees Offered: JD/MBA (4 years), JD/MPA (4 years), JD/MPPS (4 years), JD/MPH (4 years), JD/MRP (4 years), JD/MSW (4 years)
Clinical Program Required? No
Clinical Programs: Live-client Clinics in Criminal and Civil Law, simulation programs in Trial advocacy, Dispute Resolution
Grading System: Numerical system ranging from 4.3 to 0.0

STUDENT INFORMATION

Enrollment of Law School: 690
% Male/Female: 50/50
% Full Time: 100
% Full Time That Are International: 1
% Minority: 20

EXPENSES/FINANCIAL AID

Annual Tuition (Residents/Nonresidents): $3,169/$15,269
Room and Board (On Campus): $7,695
Books and Supplies: $700
Average Grant: $2,800
Average Debt: $33,982

ADMISSIONS INFORMATION

Application Fee: $60
Regular Application Deadline: Rolling
Regular Notification: Rolling
LSDAS Accepted? Yes
Average GPA: 3.5
Range of GPA: 3.3–3.8
Average LSAT: 159
Range of LSAT: 153–164
Transfer Students Accepted? Yes
Other Schools to Which Students Applied: Duke University, Wake Forest University, University of Virginia, Georgetown University, Emory University, Vanderbilt University, George Washington University, College of William and Mary

INTERNATIONAL STUDENTS

TOEFL Required of International Students? Yes
Minimum TOEFL: 600

EMPLOYMENT INFORMATION

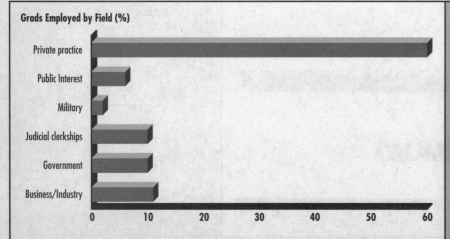

Grads Employed by Field (%)

Rate of Placement: 98%
Average Starting Salary: $51,417
Prominent Alumni: Julius Chambers, former legal counsel to NAACP and present chancellor of North Carolina Central University; Boyden Gray, former legal counsel to President Bush; James Hunt, current North Carolina governor; Stephen Cowper, former governor of Alaska; Judge David Sentelle, U.S. Circuit Court of Appeals for D.C.; Judge James Dickson Phillips, Jr., U.S. Circuit Judge, 4th Circuit; John Edward, North Carolina U.S. senator

UNIVERSITY OF NORTH DAKOTA
School of Law

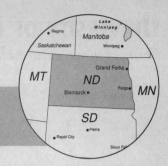

Admissions Contact: Admissions and Records Associate, Linda D. Kohoutek
PO Box 9003, Grand Forks, ND 58202
Admissions Phone: 701-777-2104 • Admissions Fax: 701-777-2217
Admissions E-mail: mark.brickson@thor.law.und.nodak.edu • Web Address: www.law.und.nodak.edu

INSTITUTIONAL INFORMATION

Public/Private: Public
Environment: Suburban
Academic Calendar: Semester
Schedule: Full time only
Student/Faculty Ratio: 10:1
Total Faculty: 19
% Female: 42
% Minority: 1

PROGRAMS

Advanced Degrees Offered: JD (3 years)
Clinical Program Required? No
Grading System: A to F system
Legal Writing/Methods Course Requirements:
Fall and spring of first year

STUDENT INFORMATION

Enrollment of Law School: 188
% Male/Female: 57/43
% Full Time: 100
% Full Time That Are International: 6
% Minority: 4

EXPENSES/FINANCIAL AID

Annual Tuition (Residents/Nonresidents):
$2,900/$7,744
Room and Board: $7,200
Books and Supplies: $800
Financial Aid Application Deadline: 4/15
Average Grant: $500
Average Loan: $11,000
% of Aid That Is Merit-Based: 1
% Receiving Some Sort of Aid: 90
Average Total Aid Package: $11,500
Average Debt: $37,800

ADMISSIONS INFORMATION

Application Fee: $35
Regular Application Deadline: 4/1
Regular Notification: Rolling
Average GPA: 3.2
Range of GPA: 3.0–3.5
Average LSAT: 151
Range of LSAT: 147–154
Transfer Students Accepted? Yes
Other Schools to Which Students Applied: University of Minnesota, William Mitchell College of Law, Hamline University, University of South Dakota, Arizona State University, University of Arizona, University of Idaho, University of Iowa
Number of Applications Received: 217
Number of Applicants Accepted: 129
Number of Applicants Enrolled: 64

EMPLOYMENT INFORMATION

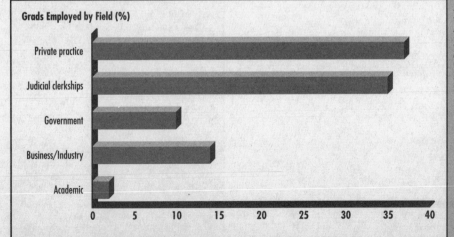

Grads Employed by Field (%)

Rate of Placement: 100%
Average Starting Salary: $33,400
Employers Who Frequently Hire Grads: Judicial systems of North Dakota and Minneapolis; Private firms in North Dakota and Minneapolis
Prominent Alumni: Maj. General Bryan Hawley, TJAG, U.S. Air Force; Congressman Earl Pomeroy, U.S. House of Representatives; Hon. H.F. Gierk III, MS Court of Military Justice

UNIVERSITY OF NOTRE DAME

Notre Dame Law School

Admissions Contact: Acting Director of Admissions, Rev. James E. McDonald
PO Box 959, Notre Dame, IN 46556-0959
Admissions Phone: 219-631-6626 • Admissions Fax: 219-631-3980
Admissions E-mail: law.bulletin.1@nd.edu • Web Address: www.law.nd.edu

INSTITUTIONAL INFORMATION

Public/Private: Private
Affiliation: Catholic
Environment: Rural
Academic Calendar: Semester
Schedule: Full time only
Student/Faculty Ratio: 16:1
Total Faculty: 85
% Part Time: 55
% Female: 20
% Minority: 13

PROGRAMS

Academic Specialties: Trial Advocacy, International Human Rights Law, Comparative Law, Law and Religion, Professionalism and Ethics
Advanced Degrees Offered: LLM International Human Rights (1 year), JSD International Human Rights (3–5 years, including 1 year of residency), LLM International Comparative Law (London campus only) (1 academic year)
Combined Degrees Offered: JD/MBA (4 years), JD/ME (3–4 years), JD/MA English (3–4 years), JD/MA Peace Studies (3–4 years)
Clinical Program Required? No
Clinical Programs: Students are not required to participate in any clinical programs, but the Law School offers a Legal Aid Clinic Program, Immigration Clinic Program, Public Defender's Office Externship, and Prosecutor's Office Externship.
Grading System: No mandated grading curve, students are not ranked. Grades issued on the following scale: A (4.000), A– (3.667), B+ (3.333), B (3.000), B– (2.667), C+ (2.333), C (2.000), C– (1.667), D

(1.000), F (0.000). Faculty regard C as indicating satisfactory work, and therefore, a C is a respectable grade. The median grade point average is 3.0 for the first year, 3.1 for the second year, and 3.3 for the third year.
Legal Writing/Methods Course Requirements: 2-credit legal writing course in the first semester followed by a 2-credit Legal Research and Writing program (Moot Court) in the second semester

STUDENT INFORMATION

Enrollment of Law School: 550
% Male/Female: 61/39
% Full Time: 100
% Minority: 20
Average Age of Entering Class: 23

RESEARCH FACILITIES

Computers/Workstations Available: 70
Computers/Work Stations: 7
Campuswide Network? Yes
School-Supported Research Centers: National Institute for Trial Advocacy, trial advocacy training; Trillium Group, alternative dispute resolution training

EXPENSES/FINANCIAL AID

Annual Tuition: $23,780
Room and Board (On/Off Campus): $3,200/$4,800
Books and Supplies: $1,200
Financial Aid Application Deadline: 3/1
Average Grant: $9,500
Average Loan: $10,000
Average Debt: $62,778

ADMISSIONS INFORMATION

Application Fee: $55
Regular Application Deadline: 3/1
Regular Notification: Rolling
LSDAS Accepted? Yes
Average GPA: 3.4
Range of GPA: 3.2–3.6
Average LSAT: 163
Range of LSAT: 160–165
Transfer Students Accepted? Yes
Other Schools to Which Students Applied: Northwestern University, Georgetown University, University of Michigan, Boston College, Harvard University, Duke University, George Washington University, University of Chicago
Other Admissions Factors Considered: The admissions committee gives strong weight to an applicant's demonstrated leadership, record of participation in extracurricular activities and/or work experience, commitment to community service, and strength of the personal statement. Numerical data such as LSAT and GPA represent only two of the many criteria considered in evaluating each application.

INTERNATIONAL STUDENTS

TOEFL Required of International Students? Yes

EMPLOYMENT INFORMATION

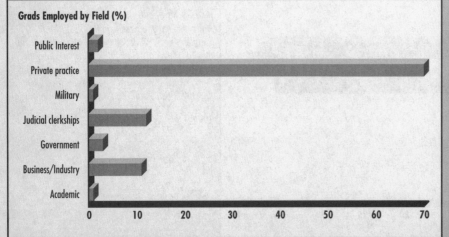

Grads Employed by Field (%)

Rate of Placement: 98%
Average Starting Salary: $65,738
Employers Who Frequently Hire Grads: Major law firms in locations throughout the country and abroad, judges at all levels, government agencies, corporations, and public interest organizations
State for Bar Exam: IL
Pass Rate for First-Time Bar: 89%

UNIVERSITY OF OKLAHOMA

College of Law

Admissions Contact: Admissions and Recruitment Advisor, Kathie Madden
300 Timberdell Road, Norman, OK 73019
Admissions Phone: 405-325-4726 • Admissions Fax: 405-325-0502
Admissions E-mail: kmadden@ou.edu • Web Address: www.law.ou.edu

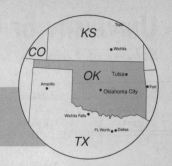

INSTITUTIONAL INFORMATION

Public/Private: Public
Environment: Urban
Academic Calendar: Semester
Schedule: Full time only
Student/Faculty Ratio: 23:1
Total Faculty: 51
% Part Time: 30
% Female: 22
% Minority: 8

PROGRAMS

Advanced Degrees Offered: None
Clinical Program Required? No

STUDENT INFORMATION

Enrollment of Law School: 572
% Male/Female: 58/42
% Full Time: 100
% Full Time That Are International: 0
% Minority: 16
Average Age of Entering Class: 24

RESEARCH FACILITIES

Computers/Workstations Available: 35

EXPENSES/FINANCIAL AID

Annual Tuition (Residents/Nonresidents):
$4,472/$13,000
Room and Board (On/Off Campus): $9,673/
$11,265
Books and Supplies: $808
Financial Aid Application Deadline: 3/1
Average Grant: $1,000
Average Loan: $13,000
% of Aid That Is Merit-Based: 25
% Receiving Some Sort of Aid: 80
Average Total Aid Package: $13,000

ADMISSIONS INFORMATION

Application Fee: $50
Regular Application Deadline: 3/15
Regular Notification: Rolling
LSDAS Accepted? Yes
Average GPA: 3.4
Range of GPA: 3.1–3.6
Average LSAT: 153
Range of LSAT: 149–157
Transfer Students Accepted? Yes
Other Schools to Which Students Applied:
Oklahoma City University, University of Tulsa, University of Texas, Southern Methodist University, Baylor University, University of Arkansas—Little Rock, University of Houston, University of Denver
Other Admissions Factors Considered: Undergraduate institution attended, curriculum taken, upward trend in GPA
Number of Applications Received: 605
Number of Applicants Accepted: 317
Number of Applicants Enrolled: 179

EMPLOYMENT INFORMATION

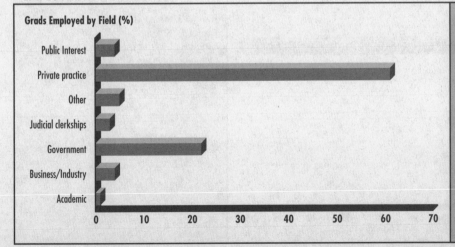

Grads Employed by Field (%)

Public Interest
Private practice
Other
Judicial clerkships
Government
Business/Industry
Academic

0   10   20   30   40   50   60   70

Rate of Placement: 89%
Average Starting Salary: $40,000
Employers Who Frequently Hire Grads: Hartzog, Conger and Cason; McAfee and Taft; Crowe and Dunlevy; McKinney and Stringer
Prominent Alumni: Andrew M. Coats, dean of the College of Law and past president of the American College of Trial Lawyers; David L. Boren, former governor of Oklahoma, former U.S. senator from Oklahoma, and now president of the University of Oklahoma; William Paul, president elect, American Bar Association

UNIVERSITY OF OREGON

School of Law

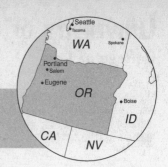

Admissions Contact: Admissions Director, Katherine Jernberg
1221 University of Oregon, Eugene, OR 97403
Admissions Phone: 541-346-3846 • Admissions Fax: 541-346-1564
Admissions E-mail: kjernber@law.uoregon.edu • Web Address: www.law.uoregon.edu

INSTITUTIONAL INFORMATION
Public/Private: Public
Environment: Urban
Academic Calendar: Quarter
Schedule: Full time only
Student/Faculty Ratio: 18:1
Total Faculty: 42
% Female: 38
% Minority: 13

PROGRAMS
Clinical Program Required? No

STUDENT INFORMATION
Enrollment of Law School: 530
% Male/Female: 49/51
% Full Time: 100
% Full Time That Are International: 1
% Minority: 15
Average Age of Entering Class: 27

EXPENSES/FINANCIAL AID
Annual Tuition (Residents/Nonresidents):
$10,238/$13,986
Books and Supplies: $800
Average Grant: $1,344
Average Loan: $18,500
% Receiving Some Sort of Aid: 90
Average Total Aid Package: $18,500
Average Debt: $43,000

ADMISSIONS INFORMATION
Application Fee: $50
Regular Application Deadline: 4/1
Regular Notification: Rolling
Average GPA: 3.4
Average LSAT: 157
Transfer Students Accepted? Yes
Other Schools to Which Students Applied:
Lewis and Clark College, University of Washington, University of Arizona, University of California—Hastings, University of California—Davis, University of California—Berkeley, University of Colorado, Seattle University
Number of Applications Received: 1,071

EMPLOYMENT INFORMATION

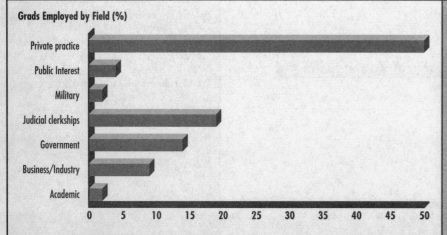

Grads Employed by Field (%)

Rate of Placement: 87%
Average Starting Salary: $43,224
Prominent Alumni: Helen J. Frye, U.S. District judge, Oregon; Alfred T. Goodwin, former chief justice, U.S. Court of Appeals, 9th Circuit; Ron Wyden, U.S. senator

UNIVERSITY OF PENNSYLVANIA
Law School

Admissions Contact: Assistant Dean to Admissions, Janice Austin
3400 Chestnut Street, Philadelphia, PA 19104
Admissions Phone: 215-898-7400 • Admissions Fax: 215-573-2025
Admissions E-mail: admissions@law.upenn.edu • Web Address: www.law.upenn.edu

INSTITUTIONAL INFORMATION

Public/Private: Private
Environment: Urban
Academic Calendar: Semester
Schedule: Full time only
Student/Faculty Ratio: 15:1
Total Faculty: 100
% Part Time: 46
% Female: 30
% Minority: 9

PROGRAMS

Academic Specialties: Administrative Law, Commercial Law, Constitutional Law, Criminal Law, Jurisprudence, Law and Economics
Advanced Degrees Offered: JD (3 years), LLM (1 year), SJD (at least 1 year), LLCM (1 year)
Combined Degrees Offered: JD/MBA (4 years), JD/MA or PhD in Economics (4 years or more), JD/MA or PhD in Public Policy and Management (4 years or more), JD/MA or PhD in Philosophy (6 years), JD/MA in Islamic Studies (3 years or more), JD/MCP (4 years), JD/MSW (4 years), JD/MD, others as approved.
Clinical Program Required? No
Clinical Programs: Civil Practice Clinic, Advanced Civil Practice Clinic, Small Business Clinic, Mediation Clinic, Criminal Defense Clinic, Legislative Clinic
Grading System: A+, A, B+, B, C, F, with mandatory distribution in first-year courses

STUDENT INFORMATION

Enrollment of Law School: 766
% Male/Female: 57/43
% Full Time: 100
% Full Time That Are International: 2
% Minority: 25
Average Age of Entering Class: 24

RESEARCH FACILITIES

Computers/Workstations Available: 200

EXPENSES/FINANCIAL AID

Annual Tuition: $26,650
Room and Board: $9,020
Books and Supplies: $850
Average Grant: $9,780
Average Loan: $25,663
% of Aid That Is Merit-Based: 5
% Receiving Some Sort of Aid: 74
Average Total Aid Package: $9,477
Average Debt: $54,000

ADMISSIONS INFORMATION

Application Fee: $65
Regular Application Deadline: 3/1
Regular Notification: Rolling
LSDAS Accepted? Yes
Average GPA: 3.6
Range of GPA: 3.4–3.8
Average LSAT: 166
Range of LSAT: 163–167
Transfer Students Accepted? Yes
Other Schools to Which Students Applied: Harvard University, Georgetown University, New York University, Columbia University, Yale University, Duke University, Cornell University, Stanford University
Other Admissions Factors Considered: Completion of advanced degrees (rigorous program), interest in interprofessional/joint degree programs
Number of Applications Received: 3,390
Number of Applicants Accepted: 918
Number of Applicants Enrolled: 230

INTERNATIONAL STUDENTS

TOEFL Required of International Students? Yes
Minimum TOEFL: 600

EMPLOYMENT INFORMATION

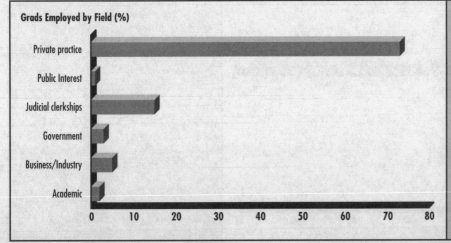

Grads Employed by Field (%)

Rate of Placement: 98%
Average Starting Salary: $74,194
Employers Who Frequently Hire Grads: Variety of major corporate law firms nationwide, prestigious national fellowship organizations and public onterest organizations; federal and state judges
Prominent Alumni: Charles Heimbold, chairman, president, and CEO, Bristol-Myers Squibb Co.; Hon. Dolores Sloviter, judge, United States Court of Appeals for the 3rd Circuit; Gerald M. Levin, chairman and CEO, Time Warner, Inc.; Henry R. Silverman, president and CEO, Cendant Corp.

UNIVERSITY OF PITTSBURGH

School of Law

Admissions Contact: Assistant Dean for Admissions and Financial Aid, Fredi G. Miller
3900 Forbes Avenue, Pittsburgh, PA 15260
Admissions Phone: 412-648-1412 • Admissions Fax: 412-648-2647
Admissions E-mail: admissions@law.pitt.edu • Web Address: www.law.pitt.edu

INSTITUTIONAL INFORMATION

Public/Private: Public
Environment: Urban
Academic Calendar: Semester
Schedule: Full Time only
Student/Faculty Ratio: 20:1
Total Faculty: 99
% Part Time: 59
% Female: 36
% Minority: 9

PROGRAMS

Academic Specialties: Health Law Certificate Program and Center for International Legal Education are special curricular strengths. Academic specialties include Health Law, International Law, Elder Law, Family Law, Environmental Law and Criminal Law.
Advanced Degrees Offered: LLM for foreign-trained attorneys—a 2-semester program that allows foreign-trained lawyers to study common law in a U.S. context
Combined Degrees Offered: JD/MPA (4 years), JD/MPIA (International Affairs) (4 years), JD/MBA (3.5 years), JD/MPH (3.5 years), JD/MA Medical Ethics (3.5 years), JD/MSIA (4 years), JD/MS Public Management (4 years), JD/MAM (4 years)
Clinical Program Required? No
Clinical Programs: Child Welfare Law Clinic, Corporate Counsel Clinic, Lawyering Process Clinic, Health Law Clinic, Elder Law Clinic, Disability Law Clinic

Grading System: Letter grades for most courses ranging from A to F, with some seminars and clinics graded on Honors/Pass/Fail basis
Legal Writing/Methods Course Requirements: 2-semester first-year course taught in small sections

STUDENT INFORMATION

Enrollment of Law School: 685
% Male/Female: 52/48
% Full Time: 100
% Full Time That Are International: 1
% Minority: 10
Average Age of Entering Class: 24

RESEARCH FACILITIES

Computers/Workstations Available: 75
School-Supported Research Centers: Students have access to the Carnegie Mellon University Library and the Carnegie Public Library, both within walking distance of School of Law.

EXPENSES/FINANCIAL AID

Annual Tuition (Residents/Nonresidents): $12,388/$19,362
Room and Board (Off Campus): $9,970
Books and Supplies: $500
Financial Aid Application Deadline: 3/1
Average Grant: $5,700
Average Loan: $18,500
% of Aid That Is Merit-Based: 29
% Receiving Some Sort of Aid: 32
Average Total Aid Package: $24,000
Average Debt: $60,000

ADMISSIONS INFORMATION

Application Fee: $50
Regular Application Deadline: 3/1
Regular Notification: Rolling
LSDAS Accepted? Yes
Average GPA: 3.2
Range of GPA: 2.9–3.5
Average LSAT: 155
Range of LSAT: 151–157
Transfer Students Accepted? Yes
Other Schools to Which Students Applied: Duquesne University, Pennsylvania State University, Temple University, Villanova University
Other Admissions Factors Considered: Writing ability, community service
Number of Applications Received: 1,220
Number of Applicants Accepted: 765
Number of Applicants Enrolled: 263

INTERNATIONAL STUDENTS

TOEFL Required of International Students? Yes
Minimum TOEFL: 600

EMPLOYMENT INFORMATION

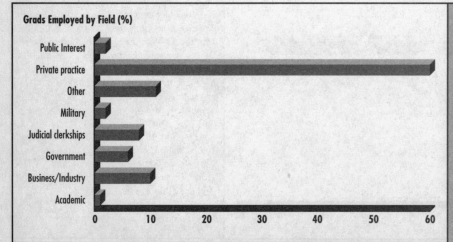

Grads Employed by Field (%)

Public Interest
Private practice
Other
Military
Judicial clerkships
Government
Business/Industry
Academic

0   10   20   30   40   50   60

Rate of Placement: 94%
Average Starting Salary: $50,198
University of Pittsburgh
Employers Who Frequently Hire Grads: Buchanan Ingersoll; Kirkpatrick & Lockhart; Reed, Smith, Shaw & McClay; Morgan, Lewis & Bockius; Jones, Day, Reavis & Pogue; Pepper Hamilton
Prominent Alumni: Derrick Bell Jr., Weld Professor of Law, New York University, and first black professor to earn tenure at Harvard Law School; Hon. Richard Thornburgh, civil rights activist and author; Hon. John P. Flaherty, chief justice of Pennsylvania Supreme Court
State for Bar Exam: PA
Number Taking Bar Exam: 177
Pass Rate for First-Time Bar: 73%

UNIVERSITY OF RICHMOND
School of Law

Admissions Contact: Director of Admissions, Michelle L. Rahman
University of Richmond, Richmond, VA 23173
Admissions Phone: 804-289-8189 • Admissions Fax: 804-287-6516
Admissions E-mail: admissions@uofrlaw.richmond.edu • Web Address: law.richmond.edu

INSTITUTIONAL INFORMATION

Public/Private: Private
Environment: Suburban
Academic Calendar: Semester
Schedule: Full time
Student/Faculty Ratio: 16:1
Total Faculty: 101
% Part Time: 63
% Female: 33
% Minority: 12

PROGRAMS

Academic Specialties: First Law School in the country to require all students to have a laptop computer; numerous International and Comparative Law courses; several courses focusing on lawyering skills (advanced trial practice, interviewing, counseling, negotiations, business transactions)
Advanced Degrees Offered: JD (3 years)
Combined Degrees Offered: JD/MBA, JD/MURP, JD/MHA, JD/MSW (all are 4 years)
Clinical Program Required? No
Clinical Programs: Clinical Externship Program (Civil, Criminal Judicial, Business), Youth Advocacy Clinic, Mental Disability Clinic
Grading System: 4.0 scale
Legal Writing/Methods Course Requirements: 4 semesters, Lawyering Skills

STUDENT INFORMATION

Enrollment of Law School: 474
% Male/Female: 53/47
% Full Time: 100
% Full Time That Are International: 1
% Minority: 18
Average Age of Entering Class: 25

RESEARCH FACILITIES

Computers/Workstations Available: 500
Computers/Work Stations: 24
Campuswide Network? Yes
School-Supported Research Centers: Center for Computer-Assisted Legal Instruction, Westlaw, Lexis Loislaw electronic indices to legal periodical literature, electronic access to career services package

EXPENSES/FINANCIAL AID

Annual Tuition: $19,940
Room and Board (On/Off Campus): $4,325/$7,020
Books and Supplies: $900
Financial Aid Application Deadline: 2/25
Average Grant: $4,675
Average Loan: $22,050
% of Aid That Is Merit-Based: 32
% Receiving Some Sort of Aid: 96
Average Total Aid Package: $23,970
Average Debt: $58,020
Tuition Per Credit: $995

ADMISSIONS INFORMATION

Application Fee: $35
Regular Application Deadline: 1/15
Regular Notification: 4/15
LSDAS Accepted? Yes
Average GPA: 3.2
Range of GPA: 2.9–3.5
Average LSAT: 157
Range of LSAT: 154–160
Transfer Students Accepted? Yes
Other Schools to Which Students Applied: College of William and Mary, University of Virginia, George Mason University, Washington and Lee University, American University, Wake Forest University, George Washington University
Number of Applications Received: 1,246
Number of Applicants Accepted: 914
Number of Applicants Enrolled: 156

INTERNATIONAL STUDENTS

Minimum TOEFL: 650

EMPLOYMENT INFORMATION

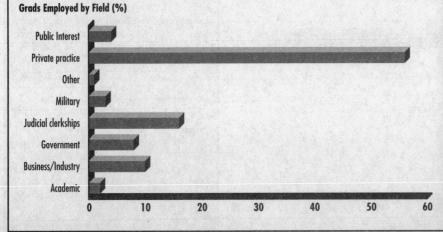

Grads Employed by Field (%)

Rate of Placement: 99%
Average Starting Salary: $48,460
Employers Who Frequently Hire Grads: Hunton and Williams; Williams, Mullen, Christian and Dobbins; McGuire, Woods, Battle and Booth; Kaufman and Canoles; Mays and Valentine; Woods, Rogers and Hazlegrove
Prominent Alumni: Hon. Robert R. Merhige, Jr.; U.S. District Court judge, Eastern District of Virginia; Hon. Frederick P. Stamp, Jr.; judge, U.S. District Court, Northern District of West Virginia; Hon. Harvey E. Schlesinger, U.S. district judge, U.S. District Court, Middle District of Florida

UNIVERSITY OF SAN DIEGO
School of Law

Admissions Contact: Director of Admissions and Financial Aid, Carl Eging
5998 Alcala Park, San Diego, CA 92110-2492
Admissions Phone: 619-260-4528 • Admissions Fax: 619-260-2218
Admissions E-mail: jdinfo@acusd.edu • Web Address: www.acusd.edu/~usdlaw

INSTITUTIONAL INFORMATION

Public/Private: Private
Affiliation: Roman Catholic
Environment: Urban
Academic Calendar: 4-1-4
Schedule: Full time or part time
Student/Faculty Ratio: 20:1
Total Faculty: 116
% Part Time: 48
% Female: 31
% Minority: 11

PROGRAMS

Academic Specialties: USD's large faculty contains experts in virtually every field of law, and authors of leading case books, treatises, and scholarly monographs published by the best university presses.
Advanced Degrees Offered: JD (3 years day, 4 years evening); LLM General, Taxation, Business, Corporate, International, Comparative Law for Foreign Lawyers (approximately 1 year)
Combined Degrees Offered: JD/MBA, JD/MA International Relations (4–4.5 years), JD/IMBA
Clinical Program Required? No
Clinical Programs: Children's Advocacy, Civil, Criminal, Environmental, Immigration, Mental Health, Public Interest, Judicial Internship, Land Development Clinic

Grading System: Letter and numerical system on a 93–65 point scale. Some courses may be graded Pass/Fail or Honors/Pass/Low Pass/Fail.
Legal Writing/Methods Course Requirements: Lawyering Skills I and II: 1 semester each, with small section, and student/faculty ratios.

STUDENT INFORMATION

Enrollment of Law School: 980
% Male/Female: 58/42
% Full Time: 73
% Full Time That Are International: 1
% Minority: 24
Average Age of Entering Class: 24

RESEARCH FACILITIES

Computers/Workstations Available: 60

EXPENSES/FINANCIAL AID

Annual Tuition: $23,510
Room and Board: $12,862
Books and Supplies: $750
Financial Aid Application Deadline: 3/1
Average Grant: $12,878
% Receiving Some Sort of Aid: 76
Average Total Aid Package: $35,472
Average Debt: $64,000
Fees Per Credit: $770

ADMISSIONS INFORMATION

Application Fee: $40
Regular Application Deadline: Rolling
Regular Notification: Rolling
LSDAS Accepted? Yes
Average GPA: 3.3
Average LSAT: 160
Transfer Students Accepted? Yes
Other Schools to Which Students Applied: UCLA School of Law, Loyola Marymount University, Tulane University, Pepperdine University, University of California—Davis, University of Southern California, University of California—Hastings, Santa Clara University.
Other Admissions Factors Considered: The full application file is reviewed by the Admissions Committee.
Number of Applications Received: 2,935

INTERNATIONAL STUDENTS

TOEFL Required of International Students? Yes
Minimum TOEFL: 600

EMPLOYMENT INFORMATION

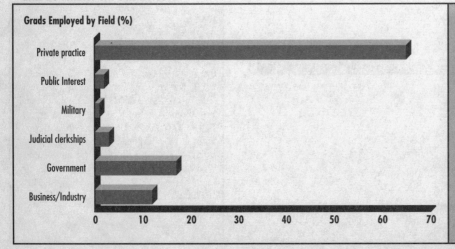

Grads Employed by Field (%)

Rate of Placement: 89%
Employers Who Frequently Hire Grads: Gibson, Dunn & Crutcher; Brobeck, Phleger & Harrison; Cooley, Godward, Castro, Huddleson & Tatum; Fulbright & Jaworski; Gray, Cary, Ware & Freidenrich; Littler, Mendelson, Castiff, Tichy & Mathiason; Pillsbury, Madison & Sutro; Department of Justice; Luce, Forward, Hamilton & Scripps
Prominent Alumni: Congressman David Camp; Steve Altman, vice president, general counsel, and general manager of technology transfer and strategic alliance division, Qualcomm Inc.; Hon. Judy Keep, presiding judge, U.S. District Court, Southern District of California

UNIVERSITY OF SAN FRANCISCO
School of Law

Admissions Contact: Law Admissions Contact, Josie Martin
2130 Fulton Street, KND #203, San Francisco, CA 94117-1080
Admissions Phone: 415-422-6586 • Admissions Fax: 415-422-6433
Admissions E-mail: lawadmissions@usfca.edu • Web Address: www.usfca.edu

INSTITUTIONAL INFORMATION

Public/Private: Private
Affiliation: Catholic
Environment: Urban
Academic Calendar: Semester
Schedule: Full time or part time
Student/Faculty Ratio: 20:1
Total Faculty: 39
% Part Time: 38
% Female: 30
% Minority: 20

PROGRAMS

Academic Specialties: The law school's full-time faculty is comprised of accomplished and dedicated scholar-teachers who are committed to providing a quality legal education and to developing each student's fullest potential. They are augmented by a number of adjunct professors drawn from the finest legal and judicial talent in the San Francisco Bay Area. Together, they bring broad expertise that supports a curriculum strong in virtually every area of law. The educational program is especially rich, offering Trial Advocacy and Dispute Resolution courses taught by faculty nationally recognized as experts in these fields. Similarly, the school has a significant concentration of courses in the Intellectual Property area taught by leading attorneys from firms and corporations in Silicon Valley, as well as by full-time faculty, one of whom is recognized as a preeminent international authority in these subjects. There is also a large number of offerings in International Law, again taught by full-time faculty experts in the field as well as by practitioners and

scholars from the Bay Area and from abroad. In addition, the school offers many courses in Maritime Law and publishes 1 of only 2 journals devoted to the subject.
Advanced Degrees Offered: LLM International Transactions and Comparative Law (1 year)
Combined Degrees Offered: JD/MBA (4 years)
Clinical Program Required? No
Clinical Programs: Criminal Law Clinic, Civil Law Clinic, and Investigation Law Clinic; judicial externships
Grading System: Letter and numerical system on a 4.0 scale. Credit/No Credit available for some courses

STUDENT INFORMATION

Enrollment of Law School: 645
% Male/Female: 54/46
% Full Time: 80
% Minority: 22
Average Age of Entering Class: 25

RESEARCH FACILITIES

Computers/Workstations Available: 60
School-Supported Research Centers: Other ABA law schools in the San Francisco Bay Area

EXPENSES/FINANCIAL AID

Annual Tuition: $22,938
Room and Board (On/Off Campus): $7,838/$9,900
Books and Supplies: $750
Average Grant: $9,721

Average Loan: $18,500
% of Aid That Is Merit-Based: 90
% Receiving Some Sort of Aid: 94
Average Total Aid Package: $21,500
Average Debt: $63,131
Tuition Per Credit: $675
Fees Per Credit: $770

ADMISSIONS INFORMATION

Application Fee: $40
Regular Application Deadline: 4/1
Regular Notification: Rolling
LSDAS Accepted? Yes
Average GPA: 3.1
Range of GPA: 3.0–3.4
Average LSAT: 156
Range of LSAT: 153–159
Transfer Students Accepted? Yes
Other Schools to Which Students Applied: University of California—Hastings, Santa Clara University, University of California—Berkeley, University of California—Davis, Golden Gate University, UCLA School of Law, University of San Diego, University of the Pacific
Number of Applications Received: 2,325

INTERNATIONAL STUDENTS

TOEFL Required of International Students? Yes
Minimum TOEFL: 600

EMPLOYMENT INFORMATION

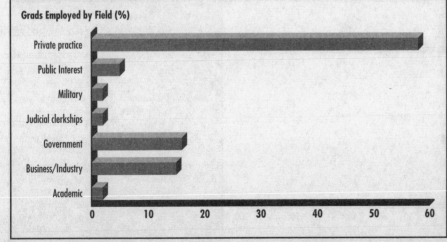

Grads Employed by Field (%)

- Private practice
- Public Interest
- Military
- Judicial clerkships
- Government
- Business/Industry
- Academic

Rate of Placement: 77%
Employers Who Frequently Hire Grads: Brobeck, Phleger & Harrison; Sedgewick, Detert, Moran & Arnold; Landels, Ripley & Diamond; Keesel, Young & Logan; Hanson, Bridgett, Marcus, Vlahos & Rudy; McCutchen, Doyle, Brown & Enersen; Miller, Starr & Regalia; Orrick, Herrington & Sutcliffe
Prominent Alumni: Ming Chin, associate justice, Supreme Court of California; Saundra Brown Armstrong, judge, U.S. District Court; Nettie Hogue, executive director TURN (Toward Utility Rate Normalization); Michael Yamaguchi, U.S. attorney, Northern California
State for Bar Exam: CA
Number Taking Bar Exam: 163
Pass Rate for First-Time Bar: 71%

UNIVERSITY OF SOUTH CAROLINA
School of Law

Admissions Contact: Assistant Dean for Admissions, John S. Benfield
Corner of Greene and Main Street, Columbia, SC 29208
Admissions Phone: 803-777-6605 • Admissions Fax: 803-777-7751
Admissions E-mail: usclaw@law.law.sc.edu • Web Address: www.law.sc.edu

INSTITUTIONAL INFORMATION

Public/Private: Public
Environment: Urban
Academic Calendar: Semester
Schedule: Full time only
Student/Faculty Ratio: 21:1
Total Faculty: 43
% Female: 4
% Minority: 2

PROGRAMS

Academic Specialties: Criminal Law, Constitutional Law, Clinical Legal Education, Environmental Law. Clinical Legal Education programs afford students the opportunity to gain practical experience while enrolled in the School of Law.
Advanced Degrees Offered: JD (3 years)
Combined Degrees Offered: JD/MIB (4 years), JD/MBA (4 years), JD/MPA (4 years), JD/Master's in Criminal Justice (4 years), JD/Master's in Economics (4 years), JD/MAcc (4 years), JD/MSW (4 years), JD/Master's in Environmental Sciences (4 years)
Clinical Program Required? No
Grading System: Letter and numerical system on a 4.0 scale, A to F
Legal Writing/Methods Course Requirements: 2 semesters first year

STUDENT INFORMATION

Enrollment of Law School: 708
% Male/Female: 56/44
% Full Time: 100
% Minority: 10
Average Age of Entering Class: 25

RESEARCH FACILITIES

Computers/Workstations Available: 80
Computers/Work Stations: 3
Campuswide Network? Yes
School-Supported Research Centers: None

EXPENSES/FINANCIAL AID

Annual Tuition (Residents/Nonresidents): $7,548/$15,616
Room and Board: $10,000
Books and Supplies: $500
Financial Aid Application Deadline: 4/15
Average Grant: $1,000
Average Loan: $18,000
% of Aid That Is Merit-Based: 15
% Receiving Some Sort of Aid: 69
Average Total Aid Package: $18,525
Average Debt: $40,000
Tuition Per Credit (Residents/Nonresidents): $319/$654

ADMISSIONS INFORMATION

Regular Application Deadline: 2/15
Regular Notification: Rolling
LSDAS Accepted? Yes
Average GPA: 3.2
Average LSAT: 156
Range of LSAT: 152–159
Transfer Students Accepted? Yes
Other Schools to Which Students Applied: University of Georgia, Mercer University, Wake Forest University, University of Virginia, Campbell University, University of North Carolina, Duke University, Washington and Lee University
Other Admissions Factors Considered: Undergraduate institution, undergraduate major, graduate work, diversity, whether the individual is a joint degree candidate, maturity
Number of Applications Received: 1,159
Number of Applicants Accepted: 619
Number of Applicants Enrolled: 321

INTERNATIONAL STUDENTS

TOEFL Required of International Students? Yes

EMPLOYMENT INFORMATION

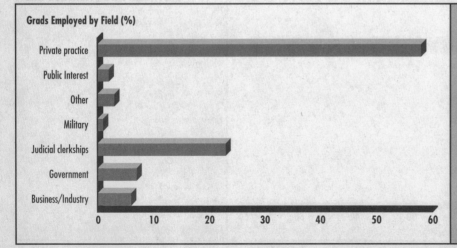

Rate of Placement: 90%
Average Starting Salary: $44,961
Employers Who Frequently Hire Grads: Nelson, Mullins, Riley and Scarborough; Ness, Motley, Loadholt, Richardson and Poole; Kennedy, Covington, Labdell and Hickman
Prominent Alumni: Richard W. Riley, secretary U.S. Department of Education; Ernest F. Hollings, U.S. Senate; Ronald L. Motley, Ness, Motley, Loadholt, Richardson and Poole
State for Bar Exam: SC
Number Taking Bar Exam: 200
Pass Rate for First-Time Bar: 80%

UNIVERSITY OF SOUTH DAKOTA
School of Law

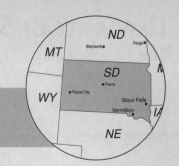

Admissions Contact: Registrar, Jean Henriques
414 East Clark, Vermilion, SD 57069-2390
Admissions Phone: 605-677-5443 • Admissions Fax: 605-677-5417
Admissions E-mail: lawreq@usd.edu • Web Address: www.usd.edu/law

INSTITUTIONAL INFORMATION

Public/Private: Public
Environment: Suburban
Academic Calendar: Semester
Schedule: Full time only
Student/Faculty Ratio: 14:1
Total Faculty: 17
% Part Time: 1
% Female: 17
% Minority: 5

PROGRAMS

Academic Specialties: Indian Law—Professor Pommersheim and Associate Professor John Lavelle; Environmental Law—Professor John Davidson; opportunity to write for Great Plains Natural Resources Journal
Advanced Degrees Offered: None
Combined Degrees Offered: JD/MBA, JD/MPA (Professional Accountancy), JD/Master's in Education Administration, JD/Master's in English, JD/Master's in History, JD/Master's in Political Science, JD/Master's in Public Administration, JD/Master's in Psychology
Clinical Program Required? No
Clinical Programs: USD Law Clinic
Grading System: A (99–90), B (89–80), C (79–70), D (69–60), F (59–50)
Legal Writing/Methods Course Requirements: First-year course—Legal Research and Writing, semester 1; Appellate Advocacy, semester 2

STUDENT INFORMATION

Enrollment of Law School: 184
% Male/Female: 53/47
% Full Time: 100
% Minority: 3
Average Age of Entering Class: 27

RESEARCH FACILITIES

Computers/Workstations Available: 40

EXPENSES/FINANCIAL AID

Annual Tuition (Residents/Nonresidents): $3,210/$9,304
Room and Board (On/Off Campus): $3,700/$5,500
Books and Supplies: $800
Financial Aid Application Deadline: 4/15
Average Grant: $2,690
Average Loan: $13,984
% of Aid That Is Merit-Based: 80
Average Debt: $34,982
Fees Per Credit (Residents/Nonresidents): $99/$287

ADMISSIONS INFORMATION

Application Fee: $15
Regular Application Deadline: Rolling
Regular Notification: Rolling
LSDAS Accepted? Yes
Average GPA: 3.2
Range of GPA: 2.7–3.7
Average LSAT: 152
Range of LSAT: 146–155
Transfer Students Accepted? Yes
Other Schools to Which Students Applied: University of Minnesota, University of Nebraska, Creighton University, University of Iowa, University of Wyoming, Hamline University, William Mitchell College of Law, University of North Dakota
Number of Applications Received: 221
Number of Applicants Accepted: 116
Number of Applicants Enrolled: 45

INTERNATIONAL STUDENTS

TOEFL Required of International Students? Yes
Minimum TOEFL: 600

EMPLOYMENT INFORMATION

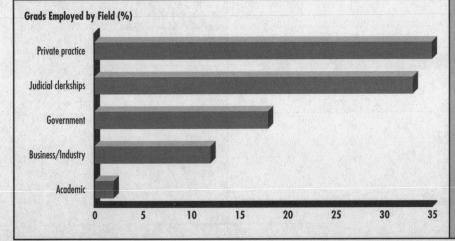

Grads Employed by Field (%)

Average Starting Salary: $28,500
Employers Who Frequently Hire Grads: U.S. 8th Circuit Court of Appeals; U.S. District Court; South Dakota Supreme Court; South Dakota Circuit Court; Minnehaha Public Defender's Office
Prominent Alumni: Hon. Tim Johnson, U.S. senator; Roger L. Wollman, U.S. 8th Circuit Court of Appeals; Bill Janklow, governor of South Dakota

UNIVERSITY OF SOUTHERN CALIFORNIA
The Law School

Admissions Contact: Assistant Dean, William Hoye
University Park, Los Angeles, CA 90089-0071
Admissions Phone: 213-740-7331 • Admissions Fax: 213-740-4570
Admissions E-mail: admissions@law.usc.edu • Web Address: www.usc.edu/law/

INSTITUTIONAL INFORMATION

Public/Private: Private
Environment: Urban
Academic Calendar: Semester
Schedule: Full time only
Student/Faculty Ratio: 13:1
Total Faculty: 110
% Part Time: 40
% Female: 21
% Minority: 14

PROGRAMS

Academic Specialties: USC Law School has achieved national recognition both for its innovative, interdisciplinary-oriented faculty and for its leadership in clinical education. Numerous courses are offered by well-known faculty experts in the areas of Corporations and Business-Government Relationships, Bioethics, International Law, Civil Rights and Liberties, Taxation, and Clinicals.
Advanced Degrees Offered: JD (3 years)
Combined Degrees Offered: JD/MBA (3.5–4 years), JD/MPA (3 years), JD/PhD Economics (5 years), JD/MA Economics (3 years), JD/MA International Relations (3 years), JD/MA Communications Management (3 years), JD/MA Philosophy (3 years), JD/MA Religion (3 years), JD/MSW (4 years), JD/Master of Real Estate Development (3.5 years), JD/Master of Business Taxation (3.5–4 years), JD/MS Gerontology (4 years), JD/MPP (3 years), JD/PhD with California Institute of Technology (5 years)
Clinical Program Required? No

Clinical Programs: Post-Conviction Justice Project, Children's Legal Issues, Small Business Advice, Externship/Internship Program, Trial Advocacy, Pretrial Advocacy, Negotiations
Grading System: A numerical grading system is employed with grades from 90–65
Legal Writing/Methods Course Requirements: First-year, year-long course develops analytic and communication skills. Students draft legal office memos and court documents, and participate in moot court.

STUDENT INFORMATION

Enrollment of Law School: 621
% Male/Female: 54/46
% Full Time: 100
% Full Time That Are International: 1
% Minority: 40
Average Age of Entering Class: 25

RESEARCH FACILITIES

Computers/Workstations Available: 98
School-Supported Research Centers: Caltech; International Gay/Lesbian Archives

EXPENSES/FINANCIAL AID

Annual Tuition: $27,814
Room and Board: $7,758
Books and Supplies: $1,284
Average Grant: $10,000
% Receiving Some Sort of Aid: 87
Average Total Aid Package: $37,000
Fees Per Credit: $952

ADMISSIONS INFORMATION

Application Fee: $60
Regular Application Deadline: 2/1
Regular Notification: March—April
LSDAS Accepted? Yes
Average GPA: 3.5
Range of GPA: 3.2–3.6
Average LSAT: 164
Range of LSAT: 159–166
Transfer Students Accepted? Yes
Other Schools to Which Students Applied: UCLA School of Law, Loyola Marymount University, University of California—Hastings, University of California—Berkeley, Georgetown University, University of California—Davis, Stanford University, New York University
Other Admissions Factors Considered: The primary goal of the admissions process is to enroll students who demonstrate outstanding academic and professional promise and whose background and experience will enhance the diversity of the student body or the profession.

EMPLOYMENT INFORMATION

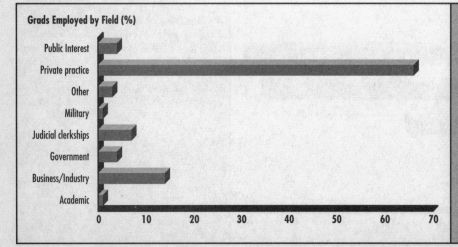

Grads Employed by Field (%)

Employers Who Frequently Hire Grads: Private firms, corporations, federal judges, government and public interest nonprofits
Prominent Alumni: Joyce Luther Kennard, associate justice, California Supreme Court; Larry Flax, CEO and co-founder, California Pizza Kitchen; Conrad Mallett, chief justice, Michigan Supreme Court

UNIVERSITY OF SOUTHERN MAINE

University of Maine School of Law

Admissions Contact: Assistant Dean, Barbara Gauditz
246 Deering Avenue, Portland, ME 04102
Admissions Phone: 207-780-4341 • Admissions Fax: 207-780-4239
Admissions E-mail: law@usm.maine.edu • Web Address: www.law.usm.maine.edu

INSTITUTIONAL INFORMATION

Public/Private: Public
Environment: Urban
Schedule: Full time only
Student/Faculty Ratio: 17:1
Total Faculty: 17
% Female: 35

PROGRAMS

Advanced Degrees Offered: JD
Combined Degrees Offered: JD/MA
Clinical Program Required? No
Clinical Programs: General Practice Clinic, Criminal Law Practicum, Family Law Clinic
Grading System: Letter system
Legal Writing/Methods Course Requirements: 3 credits first semester, 2 credits second semester

STUDENT INFORMATION

Enrollment of Law School: 262
% Male/Female: 57/43
% Full Time: 97
% Full Time That Are International: 2
% Minority: 5
Average Age of Entering Class: 30

RESEARCH FACILITIES

School-Supported Research Centers: CalTech; International Gay/Lesbian Archives

EXPENSES/FINANCIAL AID

Annual Tuition (Residents/Nonresidents):
$9,900/$17,790
Room and Board: $7,496
Books and Supplies: $1,050
Average Grant: $2,961
Average Loan: $16,442
% of Aid That Is Merit-Based: 20
% Receiving Some Sort of Aid: 80
Average Debt: $38,000
Tuition Per Credit (Residents/Nonresidents):
$276/$548
Fees Per Credit: $952

ADMISSIONS INFORMATION

Application Fee: $25
Regular Application Deadline: 2/15
Regular Notification: Rolling
LSDAS Accepted? Yes
Average GPA: 3.1
Range of GPA: 2.8–3.4
Average LSAT: 155
Range of LSAT: 149–157
Transfer Students Accepted? Yes
Other Schools to Which Students Applied: Vermont Law School, Suffolk University, Boston College, Northeastern University, Franklin Pierce Law Center, Boston University, Western New England College, American University
Other Admissions Factors Considered: Overall academic record, difficulty of courses taken, undergraduate institution, professional background
Number of Applicants Enrolled: 77

INTERNATIONAL STUDENTS

TOEFL Required of International Students? Yes

EMPLOYMENT INFORMATION

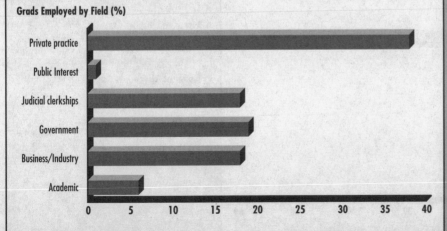

Rate of Placement: 77%
State for Bar Exam: ME
Number Taking Bar Exam: 52
Pass Rate for First-Time Bar: 71%

UNIVERSITY OF TENNESSEE
College of Law

Admissions Contact: Director of Admissions and Career Services, Karen R. Britton
1505 West Cumberland Avenue, Knoxville, TN 37996-1810
Admissions Phone: 865-974-4131 • Admissions Fax: 865-974-1572
Admissions E-mail: lawadmit@libra.law.utk.edu • Web Address: www.law.utk.edu

INSTITUTIONAL INFORMATION
Public/Private: Public
Environment: Urban
Academic Calendar: Semester
Schedule: Full time only
Student/Faculty Ratio: 16:1
Total Faculty: 57
% Part Time: 47
% Female: 32
% Minority: 5

PROGRAMS
Academic Specialties: Concentrations in Business Transactions, Advocacy and Dispute Resolution
Advanced Degrees Offered: JD (3 years, 6 semesters)
Combined Degrees Offered: JD/MBA (4 years), JD/MPA (4 years)
Clinical Program Required? No
Clinical Programs: Civil, Criminal, Mediation
Grading System: Letter system, with Pass/Fail available for some courses

STUDENT INFORMATION
Enrollment of Law School: 484
% Male/Female: 55/45
% Full Time: 100
% Full Time That Are International: 1
% Minority: 13
Average Age of Entering Class: 25

EXPENSES/FINANCIAL AID
Annual Tuition (Residents/Nonresidents): $4,626/$12,932
Room and Board: $5,666
Books and Supplies: $1,172
Financial Aid Application Deadline: 3/1
Average Grant: $4,873
Average Loan: $13,282
% of Aid That Is Merit-Based: 18
% Receiving Some Sort of Aid: 79
Average Total Aid Package: $13,940
Average Debt: $36,163

ADMISSIONS INFORMATION
Application Fee: $15
Regular Application Deadline: 2/15
Regular Notification: 3/15
LSDAS Accepted? Yes
Average GPA: 3.5
Range of GPA: 3.3–3.7
Average LSAT: 155
Range of LSAT: 152–160
Transfer Students Accepted? Yes
Other Schools to Which Students Applied: Vanderbilt University, University of Memphis, University of Georgia, Emory University, University of North Carolina, University of South Carolina, Alabama University, University of Mississippi
Other Admissions Factors Considered: Academic factors; employment; activities and service; economic, social or cultural background; evidence of maturity, responsibility and motivation; circumstances that may have affected an applicant's undergraduate GPA or LSAT scores
Number of Applications Received: 1,049
Number of Applicants Accepted: 387
Number of Applicants Enrolled: 168

INTERNATIONAL STUDENTS
TOEFL Required of International Students? Yes
Minimum TOEFL: 550

EMPLOYMENT INFORMATION

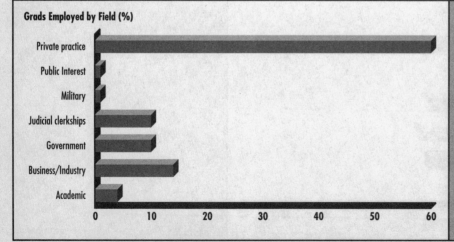

Grads Employed by Field (%)

Rate of Placement: 93%
Average Starting Salary: $42,683
Employers Who Frequently Hire Grads: Law firms and judges across the Southeast and the United States
Prominent Alumni: Howard H. Baker, former United States Senate majority leader and White House chief of staff; Lyle Reid, former Tennessee Supreme Court justice; Joel Katz, partner of Greenberg Traurig in Atlanta; Arthur Stolnitz, executive vice president of Warner Brothers TV; Penny White, former Tennessee Supreme Court justice

UNIVERSITY OF TEXAS — AUSTIN

The University of Texas School of Law

Admissions Contact: Assistant Dean for Admissions, Shelli Soto
727 East Dean Keeton Street Austin, TX 78705
Admissions Phone: 512-232-1200 • Admissions Fax: 512-471-6988
Admissions E-mail: admissions@mail.law.utexas.edu • Web Address: www.utexas.edu/law

INSTITUTIONAL INFORMATION

Public/Private: Public
Environment: Urban
Academic Calendar: Semester
Student/Faculty Ratio: 18:1
Total Faculty: 198
% Part Time: 63
% Female: 25
% Minority: 9

PROGRAMS

Academic Specialties: Very prestigious, multitalented/published faculty world-renowned for legal expertise; very broad and diverse curriculum
Advanced Degrees Offered: LLM (1 year)
Combined Degrees Offered: JD/MBA; JD/MPAFF; JD/MA Latin American Studies; JD/MS Community and Regional Planning; JD/MA Russian, East European, and European Studies; JD/MA Middle Eastern Studies; 3 programs leading to the JD and PhD in Government, History, or Philosophy
Clinical Program Required? No
Clinical Programs: Mediation Clinic, Housing Law Clinic, Domestic Violence Clinic, Capital Punishment Clinic, Children's Rights, Criminal Defense, Elder Law, Juvenile Justice Clinic, Mental Health Clinic, Immigration Clinic
Grading System: A+ (4.3), A (4.0), A– (3.7), B+ (3.3), B (3.0), B– (2.7), C+ (2.3), C (2.0), D (1.7), F (1.3)
Legal Writing/Methods Course Requirements: 1 semester

STUDENT INFORMATION

Enrollment of Law School: 1,387
% Male/Female: 53/47
% Full Time: 100
% Full Time That Are International: 1
% Minority: 17
Average Age of Entering Class: 25

RESEARCH FACILITIES

Computers/Workstations Available: 160

EXPENSES/FINANCIAL AID

Annual Tuition (Residents/Nonresidents): $6,000/$15,060
Room and Board (On/Off Campus): $6,216/$6,982
Books and Supplies: $882
Average Grant: $2,150
Average Loan: $14,500
% of Aid That Is Merit-Based: 25
% Receiving Some Sort of Aid: 93
Average Total Aid Package: $21,396
Average Debt: $45,000
Fees Per Credit (Residents): $475

ADMISSIONS INFORMATION

Application Fee: $65
Regular Application Deadline: 2/1
LSDAS Accepted? No
Average GPA: 3.6
Range of GPA: 3.4–3.8
Average LSAT: 161
Range of LSAT: 158–164
Transfer Students Accepted? Yes
Other Schools to Which Students Applied: University of Houston, Southern Methodist University, Harvard University, Georgetown University, Baylor University, Yale University, University of Virginia, Texas Tech University
Other Admissions Factors Considered: Admissions aims to identify students with the greatest probability of success in law school, giving due weight to proven predictors; and to identify students who exhibit demonstrated commitment to public service, leadership, and other qualities.
Number of Applications Received: 3,284
Number of Applicants Accepted: 1,088
Number of Applicants Enrolled: 483

INTERNATIONAL STUDENTS

TOEFL Required of International Students? Yes
Minimum TOEFL: 550

EMPLOYMENT INFORMATION

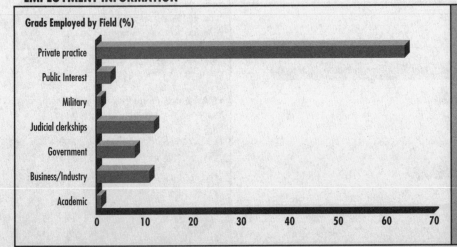

Rate of Placement: 97%
Average Starting Salary: $61,626
Employers Who Frequently Hire Grads: Akin, Gump, Strauss, Hauer and Feld; Baker and Botts; Fulbright and Jaworski; Haynes and Boone; Jones, Day, Reavis and Pogue; Vinson and Elkins, Locke Liddle; Texas Attorney General's Office; Bracewell and Patterson
Prominent Alumni: James Baker, former secretary of state; Tom Clark, former justice of the U.S. Supreme Court; Robert Strauss, former U.S. ambassador to the Soviet Union; Ron Kirk, mayor of Dallas; U.S. Senator Kay Bailey Hutchinson; Secretary of Energy Frederico Pena

UNIVERSITY OF THE DISTRICT OF COLUMBIA

David A. Clarke School of Law

Admissions Contact: Director of Admissions, Vivian Canty
4200 Connecticut Avenue NW, Washington, DC 20008
Admissions Phone: 202-274-7336 • Admissions Fax: 202-274-5583
Admissions E-mail: vcanty@law.udc.edu • Web Address: www.udc.edu

INSTITUTIONAL INFORMATION

Public/Private: Public
Student/Faculty Ratio: 17:1
Total Faculty: 38
% Part Time: 35
% Female: 50
% Minority: 50

PROGRAMS

Academic Specialties: Public Interest and Civil Rights Law emphasis, 14 required credits in clinic serving indigent D.C. residents
Advanced Degrees Offered: JD (3 years)
Clinical Program Required? Yes
Clinical Programs: Legislative, Juvenile/Special Education, Public Entitlements, HIV/AIDS, Housing and Consumer
Grading System: 4-point scale: A (4.0), B (3.0), C (2.0), D (1.0)
Legal Writing/Methods Course Requirements: Small sections, 1 year

STUDENT INFORMATION

Enrollment of Law School: 172
% Male/Female: 47/53
% Full Time: 100
% Minority: 74
Average Age of Entering Class: 30

RESEARCH FACILITIES

School-Supported Research Centers: Library of Congress

EXPENSES/FINANCIAL AID

Annual Tuition (Residents/Nonresidents): $7,000/$14,000
Room and Board (Off Campus): $18,700
Books and Supplies: $2,000
Average Grant: $4,500
Average Loan: $18,500
% of Aid That Is Merit-Based: 12
% Receiving Some Sort of Aid: 96
Average Total Aid Package: $25,000
Average Debt: $55,000
Fees Per Credit (Residents/Nonresidents): $250/$500

ADMISSIONS INFORMATION

Application Fee: $35
Regular Application Deadline: 4/1
Regular Notification: Rolling
LSDAS Accepted? Yes
Average GPA: 2.7
Range of GPA: 2.3–2.8
Average LSAT: 144
Range of LSAT: 141–147
Transfer Students Accepted? Yes
Other Schools to Which Students Applied: Howard University, Thomas M. Cooley Law School, City University of New York, American University
Other Admissions Factors Considered: Goals, family background, community involvment, graduate work if applicable, college attended, college major
Number of Applications Received: 386
Number of Applicants Accepted: 131
Number of Applicants Enrolled: 60

EMPLOYMENT INFORMATION

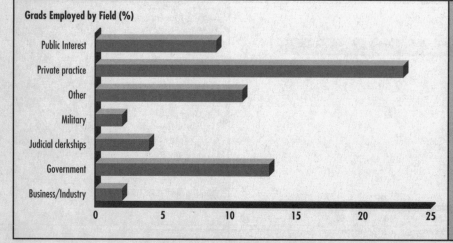

Grads Employed by Field (%)

Rate of Placement: 66%
Average Starting Salary: $33,000
Employers Who Frequently Hire Grads: District of Columbia Council, various U.S. agencies, legal services providers, smaller litigation-oriented law firms
Prominent Alumni: Hon. Rafael Diaz, D.C. Superior Court; Hon. Stephen Milliken, D.C. Superior Court; Jan May, executive director, Legal Counsel for the Elderly, Washington, D.C.

UNIVERSITY OF THE PACIFIC
McGeorge School of Law

Admissions Contact: Dean of Students, Admissions Office
3200 Fifth Avenue, Sacramento, CA 95817
Admissions Phone: 916-739-7105 • Admissions Fax: 916-739-7134
Admissions E-mail: admissionsmcgeorge@uop.edu • Web Address: www.mcgeorge.edu

INSTITUTIONAL INFORMATION
Public/Private: Private
Environment: Urban
Academic Calendar: Semester
Schedule: Full time or part time
Student/Faculty Ratio: 22:1
Total Faculty: 103
% Part Time: 57
% Female: 14
% Minority: 5

PROGRAMS
Academic Specialties: Governmental Affairs program offers certificate concurrently with JD degree; particular faculty strengths in areas of Criminal Law, Trial and Appellate Advocacy, Environmental Law, Taxation, Child and Elder Law, International Business Law, Government Affairs
Advanced Degrees Offered: JD (3–4 years), LLM Transnational Business Practice (1 year)
Combined Degrees Offered: JD/MBA, JD/MPPA, JD/MA or MS upon approval
Clinical Program Required? No
Clinical Programs: 5 on-campus live-client clinics and over 50 internships with local, state, and federal offices and courts.
Grading System: Letter and numerical system, A+ to F; A+ (4.33)
Legal Writing/Methods Course Requirements: First-year, year-long program offered in small sections

STUDENT INFORMATION
Enrollment of Law School: 1,050
% Male/Female: 51/49
% Full Time: 66
% Full Time That Are International: 0
% Minority: 25
Average Age of Entering Class: 25

RESEARCH FACILITIES
Computers/Workstations Available: 70
School-Supported Research Centers: California State University—Sacramento and the Eberhardt School of Business of the University of the Pacific for joint degree programs.

EXPENSES/FINANCIAL AID
Annual Tuition: $22,956
Room and Board: $8,883
Books and Supplies: $610
Average Grant: $4,969
Average Loan: $18,500
% Receiving Some Sort of Aid: 92
Average Total Aid Package: $28,813
Average Debt: $64,409
Fees Per Credit: $739

ADMISSIONS INFORMATION
Application Fee: $40
Regular Application Deadline: 5/15
Regular Notification: Rolling
LSDAS Accepted? Yes
Average GPA: 3.0
Range of GPA: 2.7–3.3
Average LSAT: 151
Range of LSAT: 148–154
Transfer Students Accepted? Yes
Other Schools to Which Students Applied: University of California—Davis, Santa Clara University, University of San Diego, University of San Francisco, University of California—Hastings, Loyola Marymount University, Golden Gate University, Southwestern University
Other Admissions Factors Considered: Career experiences, graduate study, extracurricular leadership activities, recommendation letters, factors that contribute to student body diversity
Number of Applications Received: 1,680
Number of Applicants Accepted: 1,174
Number of Applicants Enrolled: 364

INTERNATIONAL STUDENTS
TOEFL Required of International Students? Yes
Minimum TOEFL: 600

EMPLOYMENT INFORMATION

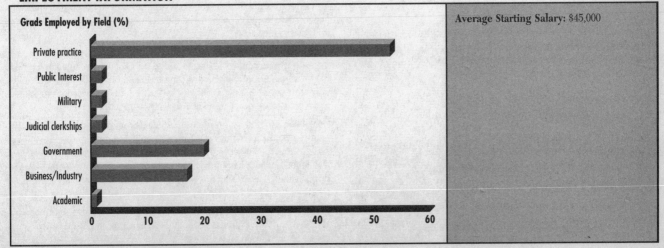

Grads Employed by Field (%)

Average Starting Salary: $45,000

UNIVERSITY OF TOLEDO

SCHOOL OVERVIEW

The College of Law at the University of Toledo is a public law school that provides a quality legal education with a personal touch at an affordable price. The nationally recognized faculty emphasizes classroom teaching and student accessibility as its primary function. The College of Law is committed to providing total student support.

First and foremost, the College of Law offers a quality academic program that produces superior results. It's proud of its small classes and the personal student-to-faculty engagement that takes place in and beyond the classroom. At the College of Law, students are not just a product of the educational process; they are in many ways the process itself. This means that students are challenged to be the best that they can be.

The faculty and administration constantly strive to create the best learning environment. For example, in response to the changing nature of the practice of law, the College of Law has added numerous new courses and changed the scope of many existing ones. The faculty incorporates the latest technology into courses. Computer labs and computer-assisted legal research are freely available. In addition, the College of Law has created joint degree programs with other colleges at the University of Toledo to prepare students for more specialized careers.

Unlike many public law schools, the composition of the law faculty and student body is truly national. Nearly all the faculty and two-thirds of the student body hail from outside the local area. This diversity exposes students to an interesting, stimulating, and creative atmosphere, where insights and ideas flourish. Diversity is reflected in student groups and activities representing a broad spectrum of social, political, ethnic, and religious perspectives.

Our unique placement program takes advantage of this diversity when assisting students or alumni. Students have opportunities to participate in clinical and externship programs, and to seek part-time employment. These opportunities to gain practical experience, coupled with a superb legal education and supportive alumni network, result in excellent employment opportunities throughout the country.

The College of Law works hard to provide an affordable legal education without sacrificing quality. Every effort is made to ensure that students graduate without large financial obligations that may take years to repay. The College of Law awards scholarships totaling in excess of $1,000,000 each year to first-year students. The goal of the financial aid program is to ensure that graduates become the lawyers they want to be, and not the lawyers that they have to be to repay financial obligations.

ACADEMIC PROGRAMS

The College of Law requires the successful completion of 89 semester hours for graduation. Students are evaluated on a grading scale of A–F and must maintain a minimum 2.0 grade point average to remain in good standing. Because of a favorable student/faculty ratio and the wide-ranging interests of the faculty, the College of Law is able to offer a great variety of courses. Like most national law schools, the curriculum in the first year of the full-time and the first two years of the part-time program consists of required courses. Upper-level students may select from a broad range of courses including Commercial Law, Corporate Law, Cyberlaw, Family Law, Environmental Law, Intellectual Property Law, International Law, Tax Law, Tort Law, or Labor Law.

The College of Law is extremely proud of its new and innovative writing program. In addition to taking legal writing and research courses during the first year, students have an opportunity for at least five other substantive writing experiences as upper-level students. This gives the student the opportunity to research and write in those areas of law that most interest the student. In addition, students prepare a portfolio of research and writing samples that will assist them in the employment process.

A pioneer in clinical legal education, the College of Law provides an atmosphere for learning basic lawyering techniques and allows students the opportunity to further sharpen their skills. Advanced students appear in court under the close supervision of clinical faculty in both criminal and civil cases. Some students may elect to spend the summer working with law firms and barristers in London, England. In addition to litigation skills, students may also learn mediation or transactional skills in the clinical program.

For students with an interest, opportunities exist to participate in the work of the Great Lakes Institute. The Great Lakes Institute supports research, maintains publications, publishes a scholarly journal, and sponsors conferences on the legal, economic, and social issues of importance to the Great Lakes Region of the United States and Canada. In order to recognize increasing specialization in the practice of law, the College of Law has introduced certificate programs in three of the fastest growing areas of law: Environmental Law, International Law, and Intellectual Property Law.

Finally, the College of Law has joint degree programs with the College of Engineering and the College of Business leading to a Master of Science in Engineering or Master of Business Administration, respectively. These programs allow a student to earn an additional degree in as little as one additional year and to gain additional qualifications to achieve related career goals or for personal growth.

ACADEMIC LIFE

An extensive and ever-growing curriculum covers the traditional subjects of legal education as well as the cutting-edge environmental law, international law, and cyberlaw subjects, and incorporates the development of professional legal skills and values.

Unlike many law schools, all of the upper-level standard program and the vast majority of other courses are taught by full-time faculty. Occasionally, to add to the breath of the curriculum, distinguished members of the legal community, judges, or government officials with specialized expertise are invited to teach highly specialized or technical courses in their area of competence.

In addition to traditional course work, students have the opportunity to participate in several activities that also earn academic credit: the *University of Toledo Law Review*; the *Toledo Journal of the Great Lakes' Law, Science, and Policy*; and Moot Court. Highly motivated students may create their own courses through the Independent Study Program or work with faculty as research assistants.

Faculty teaching first-year courses employ teaching assistants. Teaching assistants are upper-level students who are available for additional tutorial work, review sessions, or to provide other academic support services.

College of Law

CAMPUS LIFE AND FACILITIES

The College of Law is located in a suburban residential neighborhood. The University of Toledo has the distinct advantage of being located in a thriving midwestern city on the shores of Lake Erie. Toledo was recently named one of 10 All-American City Award winners, and the city's proximity to the Great Lakes is an excellent source of entertainment. The College of Law is only a few miles from downtown Toledo, the waterfront, courthouses, headquarters of several Fortune 500 companies, and some of the most prestigious law firms in the United States. Toledo's other attractions include a splendid zoo, world class art museum, nationally known symphony, and of course the Toledo Mud Hens baseball franchise.

The University of Toledo is ranked as one of the safest among comparable universities, has been noted for its landscaping and recognized by *Wired* magazine for its use of technology. There is an active social and intellectual life on campus. Recent events have included performances by Boyz II Men, Kenny G, Elton John, Lord of the Dance, Pearl Jam, and Yanni. Nationally known speakers have included President Bill Clinton, Vice President Al Gore, and author Maya Angelou. Recreational facilities include a $17.3 million Student Recreation Center acclaimed as one of the best in the country by *USA Today*.

The College of Law also has an active intellectual life outside class. Recent speakers have included Judge Abner J. Mikva, Constance Baker Motley, Nadine Strossen, Max Boot, John Stossel, Richard Epstein, James Q. Wilson, and many others who provide the College of Law and the general public with a timely discussion of legal and policy issues.

FACULTY INFORMATION

The faculty's primary emphasis is to provide a quality legal education for each of its students through a meaningful classroom experience. Teaching at the College of Law begins with the construction of a solid foundation in basic legal rules and principles, and then progresses to an examination of difficult concepts and theories. Students are taught to think and write clearly, to reason abstractly, and to be effective advocates. The faculty, therefore, blends an emphasis on "practical" learning with a concentration on the "theoretical" analysis that is needed for a successful career and is essential to intellectual growth. The faculty also boasts an impressive number of nationally recognized publications.

STUDENT ADVANTAGES

The College of Law provides a private law school education at a public law school price as well as small classes, numerous course offerings, activities outside of class, and effective career placement services.

A variety of student activities and student organizations form the foundation of a student's nonclassroom intellectual and social environment. Students are actively involved in the governance of the law school and serve on many committees. Law student organizations include the Student Bar Association, American Civil Liberties Union, Arab-American Law Student Organization, Black Law Student Association, Business Law Society, Christian Legal Society, Delta Theta Phi, Environmental Law Students Association, Federalist Society, Health Law Association, Hispanic Law Students Association, Intellectual Property Law Association, International Law Society, Jewish Law Students Association, Kappa Beta Phi, Lavender Law Student Association, Phi Alpha Delta, Phi Delta Phi, Progressive Policy Institute, and the Women's Law Students Association.

PLACEMENT INITIATIVES

The Career Placement Office assists students in finding jobs while in law school and after graduation. The College of Law has placed graduates throughout the United States and in foreign countries. Graduates can be found in major law firms, government offices, the judiciary, and in public interest positions in practically every state in the Union. Graduates also can be found in Asia, Europe, and Africa. Many students find local part-time employment on the job bulletin board. The Career Placement Office coordinates mass mailings to employers, arranges interviews, helps students to attend job fairs, and provides access to computerized job search tools.

ADMISSION INFORMATION

The Admissions Committee considers each application carefully and on its own merits. Applicants must have received or have completed all the requirements for a bachelor's degree from an accredited college or university before the first day of law classes. The median LSAT score is generally in the 153–155 range, and the median GPA is approximately 3.2 on a 4.0 scale. The full-time entering class ranges from 115–125 students and the part-time class from 30–35 students. The College of Law does not require any particular major or pre-law curriculum.

The College of Law encourages applications from students with backgrounds or with life experiences that may not be typically represented in law school. Students are encouraged to visit the campus and law school, talk to the students and faculty, and time permitting, to attend a class. The College of Law has a rolling admissions policy and encourages students to apply early. The College of Law waives the online application fee (www.utlaw.edu/admissions/index.htm).

Admissions Contact: Assistant Dean for Admissions, Carol Frendt
2801 West Bancroft, Toledo, OH 43606
Admissions Phone: 419-530-4131 • Admissions Fax: 419-530-4345
Admissions E-mail: lawinfo@pop3.utoledo.edu • Web Address: www.utlaw.edu

SCHOOL SAYS . . . • 287

UNIVERSITY OF TOLEDO
College of Law

Admissions Contact: Assistant Dean for Admissions, Carol Frendt
2801 West Bancroft, Toledo, OH 43606
Admissions Phone: 419-530-4131 • Admissions Fax: 419-530-4345
Admissions E-mail: lawinfo@pop3.utoledo.edu • Web Address: www.utlaw.edu

INSTITUTIONAL INFORMATION

Public/Private: Public
Environment: Urban
Academic Calendar: Semester
Schedule: Full time or part time
Student/Faculty Ratio: 17:1
Total Faculty: 43
% Part Time: 33
% Female: 31
% Minority: 7

PROGRAMS

Academic Specialties: The College curriculum reflects the interest in the Great Lakes region, with numerous courses and seminars in Environmental and International Law as well as a course on Law and the Great Lakes. The *University of Toledo Law Review* annually devotes an issue to legal problems of the Great Lakes. A Criminal Law Practice Program is offered (prosecutor intern).
Advanced Degrees Offered: JD (3–4 years)
Combined Degrees Offered: JD/MBA
Clinical Program Required? No
Clinical Programs: The Legal Clinic focuses on development of legal skills such as interviewing, counseling, negotiation, drafting, trial and appellate work, and the application of those skills to the problems of individuals
Grading System: A (4.0) to F (0.0), DR (0.0), W (0.0)

Legal Writing/Methods Course Requirements: 2 semesters—An intensive study of research tools and techniques and their utilization in the preparation of memoranda of law; researching and writing a brief and presenting an oral argument to an appellate court of faculty and students; Instruction through class meetings and individual conference

STUDENT INFORMATION

Enrollment of Law School: 521
% Male/Female: 54/46
% Full Time: 72
% Full Time That Are International: 1
% Minority: 8
Average Age of Entering Class: 27

RESEARCH FACILITIES

School-Supported Research Centers: Toledo Lucas County Public Library; Medical College of Ohio; Toledo Museum of Art

EXPENSES/FINANCIAL AID

Room and Board (Off Campus): $5,344
Books and Supplies: $1,025
Average Grant: $7,852
Average Loan: $15,427
% of Aid That Is Merit-Based: 12
% Receiving Some Sort of Aid: 83
Average Total Aid Package: $18,854
Average Debt: $43,072
Fees Per Credit (Residents/Nonresidents): $264/$548

ADMISSIONS INFORMATION

Regular Application Deadline: Rolling
Regular Notification: Rolling
LSDAS Accepted? No
Average GPA: 3.1
Range of GPA: 2.8–3.5
Average LSAT: 152
Range of LSAT: 146–157
Transfer Students Accepted? Yes
Other Schools to Which Students Applied: Ohio State University, University of Akron, University of Cincinnati, University of Dayton, Cleveland State University, Capital University, Ohio Northern University, Case Western Reserve University
Number of Applications Received: 733
Number of Applicants Accepted: 427
Number of Applicants Enrolled: 190

EMPLOYMENT INFORMATION

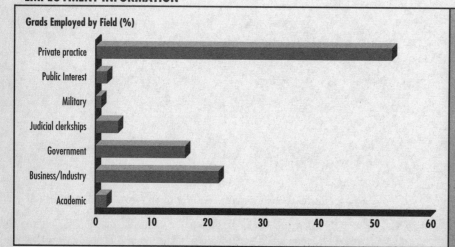

Grads Employed by Field (%)

Rate of Placement: 90%
Average Starting Salary: $41,887
Employers Who Frequently Hire Grads: Spengler Nathanson; Shumaker, Loop and Kendrik; Eastman and Smith; DeNune and Killam; Gallon and Takacs; Wagoner and Steinberg; Kalniz, Iorio and Feldstein; Connelly, Soutar and Jackson; Marshall and Melhorn; Cooper, Walinski and Cramer; Fuller and Henry; Robison, Curphey and O'Connell; Newcomer Shaffer and Spangler; Watkins, Bates and Carey; Williams, Jilek, Lafferty and Gallagher; Brown, Schlageter, Craig and Shindler

UNIVERSITY OF TORONTO
Faculty of Law

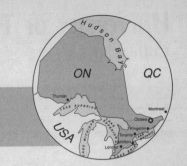

Admissions Contact: Admissions Officer, Judy Finlay
78 Queen's Park, Toronto, ON M5N 1L7 Canada
Admissions Phone: 416-978-3716 • Admissions Fax: 416-978-7899
Admissions E-mail: law.admissions@utoronto.ca • Web Address: www.law.utoronto.ca

INSTITUTIONAL INFORMATION

Public/Private: Public
Student/Faculty Ratio: 9:1
Total Faculty: 54
% Female: 30

PROGRAMS

Academic Specialties: After the first year, the choice of courses is entirely optional, within certain academic requirements. The breadth of courses, both theoretical and practical, offered means that students specialize only to the extent to which they wish. There is no one "focus" among the courses offered to upper-year students. An extensive selection of courses is offered in the following areas: Administrative Law and Regulation Business Law, including Corporations, Commercial Law, and Taxation; Constitutional Law; Crime and Criminology; Family Law; Intellectual Property and Technology Law; International and Comparative Law; Labor Law and Social Justice Law; Law and Economics; Legal Research and Writing; Legal Theory; Litigation and Dispute Settlement; Women's Studies. Three aspects of the upper-year curriculum promote the intellectual initiatives of the law school: every upper-year student must engage in a substantial legal research and writing project under the supervision of a faculty member; upper-year students must take a perspective course, which is one concerned with the nature, sources, and purposes of legal regulation in general rather than with the study of legal doctrine in a particular area; and upper-year students also benefit from the Distinguished Visiting Professors program, in which some of the

world's outstanding legal scholars and law teachers visit the school for several weeks and engage in lively and stimulating debate with students and faculty in classes and workshops.
Advanced Degrees Offered: LLM (1 year), SJD (1 year plus thesis), MSL (1 year)
Combined Degrees Offered: LLB/MBA (4 years), LLB/MSW (4 years), LLB/MA Criminology (3 years), LLB/MA Economics (3 years), LLB/MA Political Science, Collaborative Program in International Relations (3 years), LLB/MA Russian and East European Studies (4 years), Collaborative Program in Environmental Studies (3 years), LLB/PhD Economics (4 years plus dissertation), LLB/PhD Philosophy (4 years plus dissertation)
Clinical Program Required? Yes
Clinical Programs: The U of T does not require students to participate in a clinic program, but several clinical opportunities are offered, and a vast majority of students take part in at least 1 clinic program: Centre for Spanish-Speaking People.
Grading System: Letter grades and overall standing for the year of A, B, or C
Legal Writing/Methods Course Requirements: The cornerstone of the first-year curriculum is the "small group," which permits students to study one of the first-year subjects with a member of the faculty and 15 classmates. The "small group" introduces students to the techniques of legal research and writing in a personal and direct setting with a member of the teaching faculty.

STUDENT INFORMATION

Enrollment of Law School: 526
% Male/Female: 50/50
% Full Time: 98
% Minority: 23
Average Age of Entering Class: 25

RESEARCH FACILITIES

Computers/Workstations Available: 30
Computers/Work Stations: 1
Campuswide Network? Yes

EXPENSES/FINANCIAL AID

Annual Tuition (Residents/Nonresidents): $10,000/$16,500
Room and Board (On Campus): $8,500
Books and Supplies: $1,000
Financial Aid Application Deadline: 9/30
Average Grant: $3,000
Average Loan: $5,500
% of Aid That Is Merit-Based: 2
% Receiving Some Sort of Aid: 28

ADMISSIONS INFORMATION

Application Fee: $50
Regular Application Deadline: 11/1
Regular Notification: 1/4
Average GPA: 3.8
Range of GPA: 3.3–4.0
Average LSAT: 165
Range of LSAT: 163–169
Transfer Students Accepted? Yes
Number of Applications Received: 1,619
Number of Applicants Accepted: 273
Number of Applicants Enrolled: 180

EMPLOYMENT INFORMATION

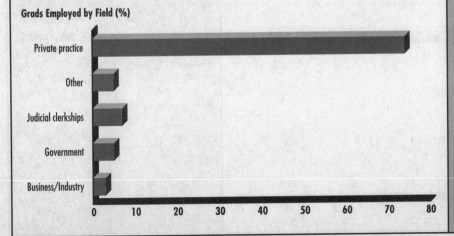

Grads Employed by Field (%)

Rate of Placement: 95%
Average Starting Salary: $48,000
Employers Who Frequently Hire Grads: All major Toronto law firms; many large New York and Boston law firms; large and midsize Vancouver, Halifax, and Calgary law firms
Prominent Alumni: Hon. Madam Justice Rosalie Abella, Court of Appeal for Ontario; Hon. Mr. Justice Ian Binnie, Supreme Court of Canada; Mr. Robert Pritchard, president, University of Toronto; Mr. Bob Rae, former premier, Province of Ontario

UNIVERSITY OF TULSA
College of Law

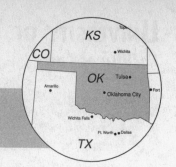

Admissions Contact: Director of Admissions, George A. Justice, Jr.
3120 East Fourth Place, Tulsa, OK 74104-2499
Admissions Phone: 918-631-2406 • Admissions Fax: 918-631-3630
Admissions E-mail: george-justice@utulsa.edu • Web Address: www.utulsa.edu/law

INSTITUTIONAL INFORMATION

Public/Private: Private
Affiliation: Presbyterian Church
Environment: Urban
Academic Calendar: Semester
Schedule: Full time or part time
Student/Faculty Ratio: 15:1
Total Faculty: 93
% Part Time: 58
% Female: 36
% Minority: 15

PROGRAMS

Academic Specialties: Certificate programs in Alternative Methods of Dispute Resolution; Comparative and International Law; Health Law; Native American Public Policy and Regulation; and Resources, Energy, and Environmental Law. The Legal Clinic gives students an opportunity to handle actual cases and develop professional skills under the close supervision of faculty supervisors.
Combined Degrees Offered: History, Industrial/Organizational Psychology, Geosciences, Biological Sciences, Anthropology, Accounting, Taxation, Business Administration, Clinical Psychology, English
Clinical Program Required? No
Clinical Programs: Elder Law Clinic, Health Law Clinic
Grading System: A– (4.0), B+ (3.5), B (3.0), C+ (2.5), C (2.0), D+ (1.5), D (1.0), F (0.0)

STUDENT INFORMATION

Enrollment of Law School: 561
% Male/Female: 56/44
% Full Time: 79
% Full Time That Are International: 1
% Minority: 18
Average Age of Entering Class: 27

RESEARCH FACILITIES

Computers/Workstations Available: 50

EXPENSES/FINANCIAL AID

Annual Tuition: $17,750
Room and Board (On/Off Campus): $5,020/$7,210
Books and Supplies: $1,500
Financial Aid Application Deadline: 4/1
Average Grant: $6,300
Average Loan: $24,468
% of Aid That Is Merit-Based: 8
% Receiving Some Sort of Aid: 89
Average Total Aid Package: $22,538
Average Debt: $69,021

ADMISSIONS INFORMATION

Application Fee: $30
Regular Application Deadline: Rolling
Regular Notification: Rolling
LSDAS Accepted? Yes
Average GPA: 3.0
Range of GPA: 2.0–4.0
Average LSAT: 150
Range of LSAT: 140–169
Transfer Students Accepted? Yes
Other Schools to Which Students Applied: Oklahoma City University, University of Oklahoma, Texas Tech University, University of Houston, University of Texas, Southern Methodist University, St. Mary's University, University of Missouri—Kansas City
Number of Applications Received: 787
Number of Applicants Accepted: 518
Number of Applicants Enrolled: 181

INTERNATIONAL STUDENTS

TOEFL Required of International Students? Yes

EMPLOYMENT INFORMATION

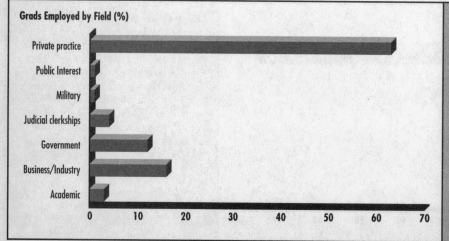

Grads Employed by Field (%)

Rate of Placement: 87%
Average Starting Salary: $39,521
Employers Who Frequently Hire Grads: Williams, local law firms
Prominent Alumni: Justice Robert E. Lavender, state of Oklahoma Supreme Court; David Waller, deputy director general of the International Atomic Energy Agency

UNIVERSITY OF UTAH
College of Law

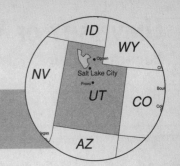

Admissions Contact: Coordinator, Laura Gormley
332 South 1400 East Front, Salt Lake City, UT 84112-0730
Admissions Phone: 801-581-7479 • Admissions Fax: 801-581-6897
Admissions E-mail: admissions@law.utah.edu • Web Address: www.law.utah.edu

INSTITUTIONAL INFORMATION

Public/Private: Public
Environment: Urban
Academic Calendar: Semester
Schedule: Full time only
Student/Faculty Ratio: 15:1
Total Faculty: 65
% Part Time: 36
% Female: 27
% Minority: 17

PROGRAMS

Academic Specialties: Environmental, Resource, and Energy Law
Advanced Degrees Offered: LLM Environmental Law (1 year)
Combined Degrees Offered: JD/MPA (4 years), JD/MBA (4 years), others by petition
Clinical Program Required? No
Clinical Programs: Environmental, Health, Civil, Criminal, Judicial
Grading System: 4.0 scale
Legal Writing/Methods Course Requirements: 2 semesters, 4 credits, 1 year

STUDENT INFORMATION

Enrollment of Law School: 369
% Male/Female: 57/43
% Full Time: 100
% Full Time That Are International: 1
% Minority: 14
Average Age of Entering Class: 27

RESEARCH FACILITIES

Computers/Workstations Available: 60

EXPENSES/FINANCIAL AID

Annual Tuition (Residents/Nonresidents): $5,176/$11,908
Room and Board: $6,102
Books and Supplies: $1,150
Financial Aid Application Deadline: 3/15
Average Grant: $3,790
Average Loan: $12,000
% of Aid That Is Merit-Based: 30
% Receiving Some Sort of Aid: 79
Average Total Aid Package: $16,000
Average Debt: $42,000

ADMISSIONS INFORMATION

Regular Application Deadline: 2/1
Regular Notification: Rolling
LSDAS Accepted? Yes
Average GPA: 3.5
Range of GPA: 3.3–3.7
Average LSAT: 158
Range of LSAT: 155–162
Transfer Students Accepted? Yes
Other Schools to Which Students Applied: Brigham Young University, Lewis and Clark College, Arizona State University, University of Washington, Stanford University, University of Arizona, University of Idaho, University of Oregon
Other Admissions Factors Considered: Personal statement, letter of recommendation
Number of Applications Received: 805
Number of Applicants Accepted: 304
Number of Applicants Enrolled: 125

INTERNATIONAL STUDENTS

TOEFL Required of International Students? Yes
Minimum TOEFL: 600

EMPLOYMENT INFORMATION

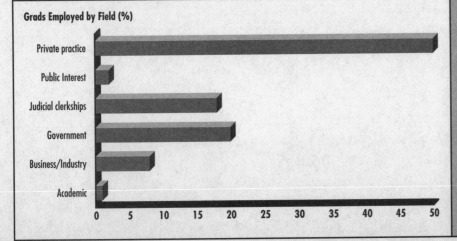

Grads Employed by Field (%)

Rate of Placement: 95%
Average Starting Salary: $39,400
Employers Who Frequently Hire Grads: Utah Attorney General's Office; Van Cott, Bagley Cornwall and McCarthy; Ray, Quinney and Nebeker; Jones, Waldo, Holbrook and Mconough
Prominent Alumni: James Rawlings, former ambassador to Zimbabwe; Honorable Stephen Anderson, U.S. Court of Appeals, 10th Circuit; Hon. Michael Zinmerman, chief justice, Utah Supreme Court

UNIVERSITY OF VICTORIA
Faculty of Law

Admissions Contact: Admissions Assistant, Neela Cumming
PO Box 2400, Victoria, BC V8W 3H7 Canada
Admissions Phone: 250-721-8151 • Admissions Fax: 250-721-6390
Admissions E-mail: lawadmss@uvic.ca • Web Address: www.law.uvic.ca

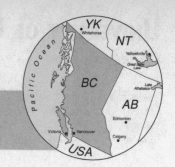

INSTITUTIONAL INFORMATION

Public/Private: Public
Student/Faculty Ratio: 7:1
Total Faculty: 59
% Part Time: 56
% Female: 24
% Minority: 5

PROGRAMS

Advanced Degrees Offered: No graduate program offered at this point in time.
Combined Degrees Offered: LLB/MPA (4 years), LLB/MBA (4 years), LLB/MIA (3.5 years), LLB/BCL (4.5 years)
Clinical Program Required? No
Clinical Programs: Full time term (4 months) in Community Legal and Environmental Law course = 1 course credit; Business Law Clinic = 1 course credit
Grading System: 9-point system: 9 (A+), 8 (A), 7 (A–), 6 (B+), 5 (B), 4 (B–), 3 (C+), 2 (C) 1 (D), 0 (F)
Legal Writing/Methods Course Requirements: Full year (8 months) during first year

STUDENT INFORMATION

Enrollment of Law School: 390
% Male/Female: 50/50
% Full Time: 97
% Minority: 20
Average Age of Entering Class: 29

RESEARCH FACILITIES

Computers/Workstations Available: 25
Campuswide Network? Yes

EXPENSES/FINANCIAL AID

Annual Tuition (Residents/Nonresidents): $2,900/$8,700
Room and Board (On/Off Campus): $6,000/$8,000
Books and Supplies: $1,000
Financial Aid Application Deadline: 10/15
Average Grant: $2,500
% of Aid That Is Merit-Based: 77
Average Debt: $30,000

ADMISSIONS INFORMATION

Application Fee: $50
Regular Application Deadline: 2/1
Regular Notification: 5/31
Average GPA: 3.8
Range of GPA: 3.2–4.3
Average LSAT: 165
Range of LSAT: 153–175
Transfer Students Accepted? Yes
Number of Applications Received: 964
Number of Applicants Accepted: 230
Number of Applicants Enrolled: 104

INTERNATIONAL STUDENTS

TOEFL Required of International Students? Yes
Minimum TOEFL: 600

EMPLOYMENT INFORMATION

Rate of Placement: 90%
Employers Who Frequently Hire Grads: Attorney General and Justice Departments as well as law firms across Canada
Prominent Alumni: Andrew Petter, Provincial Cabinet minister; Moe Sihota, Provincial Cabinet minister; Jean Harvey, Provincial Court judge

UNIVERSITY OF VIRGINIA
School of Law

Admissions Contact: Associate Dean for Admissions and Career Services, Albert R. Turnbull
580 Massie Road, Charlottesville, VA 22903-1789
Admissions Phone: 804-924-7351 • Admissions Fax: 804-982-2128
Admissions E-mail: lawadmit@virginia.edu • Web Address: www.law.virginia.edu

INSTITUTIONAL INFORMATION
Public/Private: Public
Environment: Urban
Academic Calendar: Semester
Schedule: Full time only
Student/Faculty Ratio: 15:1
Total Faculty: 127
% Part Time: 49
% Female: 18
% Minority: 6

PROGRAMS
Academic Specialties: Comprehensive
Advanced Degrees Offered: LLM (1 year), LLM Judicial Process, SJD
Combined Degrees Offered: JD/MBA (4 years); several JD/MA, JD/MS, JD/PhD programs
Clinical Program Required? No
Grading System: Letter and numerical system. Faculty policy requires adherence to a mean grade of B+ in most classes.
Legal Writing/Methods Course Requirements: 2 semesters; small sections; research, writing, and oral argument

STUDENT INFORMATION
Enrollment of Law School: 1,090
% Male/Female: 57/43
% Full Time: 100
% Minority: 15
Average Age of Entering Class: 24

RESEARCH FACILITIES
Computers/Workstations Available: 102
Computers/Work Stations: 1
Campuswide Network? Yes
School-Supported Research Centers: First Amendment Center

EXPENSES/FINANCIAL AID
Annual Tuition (Residents/Nonresidents): $14,201/$20,600
Room and Board (Off Campus): $10,465
Books and Supplies: $800
Financial Aid Application Deadline: 2/15
Average Grant: $6,900
Average Loan: $20,307
% Receiving Some Sort of Aid: 75
Average Total Aid Package: $23,623

ADMISSIONS INFORMATION
Application Fee: $65
Regular Application Deadline: 1/15
Regular Notification: 4/15
LSDAS Accepted? Yes
Average GPA: 3.7
Range of GPA: 2.7–4.1
Average LSAT: 165
Range of LSAT: 150–178
Transfer Students Accepted? Yes
Other Schools to Which Students Applied: Harvard University, Georgetown University, Yale University, Duke University, Stanford University, William and Mary, Columbia University, University of Pennsylvania
Other Admissions Factors Considered: Maturing effect of some years away from formal education, rising trend in academic performance, financial pressure requiring employment as undergraduate, significant personal achievement
Number of Applications Received: 3,368
Number of Applicants Accepted: 975
Number of Applicants Enrolled: 353

INTERNATIONAL STUDENTS
TOEFL Required of International Students? Yes

EMPLOYMENT INFORMATION

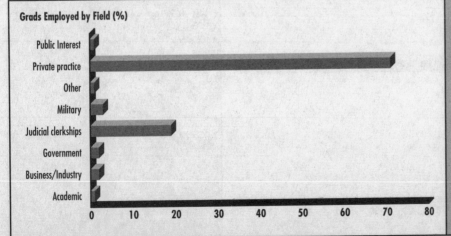

Grads Employed by Field (%)

Rate of Placement: 99%
Average Starting Salary: $85,000
Employers Who Frequently Hire Grads: Graduates are in all top 100 firms in the country
State for Bar Exam: VA
Number Taking Bar Exam: 95
Pass Rate for First-Time Bar: 96%

UNIVERSITY OF WASHINGTON
School of Law

Admissions Contact: Admissions Supervisor, Kathy Swinehart
1100 Northeast Campus Parkway, Seattle, WA 98105-6617
Admissions Phone: 206-543-4078 • Admissions Fax: 206-543-5671
Admissions E-mail: admissions@law.washington.edu • Web Address: www.law.washington.edu

INSTITUTIONAL INFORMATION

Public/Private: Public
Environment: Urban
Academic Calendar: Quarter
Schedule: Full time only
Student/Faculty Ratio: 13:1
Total Faculty: 47
% Female: 31
% Minority: 8

PROGRAMS

Advanced Degrees Offered: LLM in Asian Law, Law and Marine Affairs, Law of Sustainable International Development, Taxation
Combined Degrees Offered: Can be set up with 90 graduate programs at UW.
Clinical Program Required? No
Clinical Programs: Refer to Admissions Bulletin
Grading System: A to F

STUDENT INFORMATION

Enrollment of Law School: 500
% Male/Female: 50/50
% Full Time: 100
% Minority: 22%
Average Age of Entering Class: 25

EXPENSES/FINANCIAL AID

Annual Tuition (Residents/Nonresidents): $6,210/$15,320
Room and Board: $8,001
Books and Supplies: $900
Financial Aid Application Deadline: 2/28
Average Grant: $4,413
Average Loan: $12,696
% of Aid That Is Merit-Based: 6
% Receiving Some Sort of Aid: 88
Average Debt: $33,000

ADMISSIONS INFORMATION

Application Fee: $50
Regular Application Deadline: 1/15
Regular Notification: 4/1
Average GPA: 3.6
Range of GPA: 3.4–3.8
Average LSAT: 162
Range of LSAT: 159–165
Transfer Students Accepted? Yes
Other Schools to Which Students Applied: University of California—Berkeley, Georgetown University, Harvard University, Stanford University, University of Michigan, UCLA School of Law, Seattle University, University of California—Hastings
Number of Applications Received: 1,642
Number of Applicants Accepted: 437
Number of Applicants Enrolled: 165

EMPLOYMENT INFORMATION

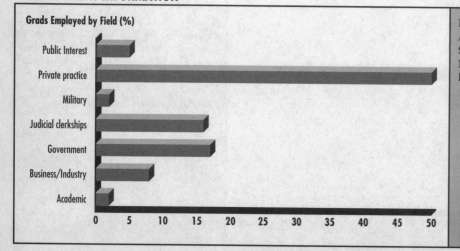

Rate of Placement: 94%
Average Starting Salary: $46,000
State for Bar Exam: WA
Number Taking Bar Exam: 140
Pass Rate for First-Time Bar: 91%

UNIVERSITY OF WEST LOS ANGELES

School of Law

Admissions Contact: Director of Admissions, Lynda Freeman
1155 West Arbor Vitae, Inglewood, CA 90301
Admissions Phone: 310-342-5254 • Admissions Fax: 310-342-5295
Admissions E-mail: uwlalawreview@juno.com • Web Address: www.uwla.edu

INSTITUTIONAL INFORMATION

Public/Private: Private
Academic Calendar: Semester
Schedule: Full time or part time
Student/Faculty Ratio: 50:1
Total Faculty: 40
% Part Time: 80
% Female: 15
% Minority: 15

PROGRAMS

Advanced Degrees Offered: JD (3 years full time, 4 years part time)
Clinical Program Required? No
Clinical Programs: Credit for judicial externships and lawyer-supervised internships
Grading System: Letter grade (4-point scale)
Legal Writing/Methods Course Requirements: 15 weeeks of first semester

STUDENT INFORMATION

Enrollment of Law School: 378
% Male/Female: 61/39
% Part Time: 80
% Full Time: 20
% Minority: 53
Average Age of Entering Class: 35

RESEARCH FACILITIES

Computers/Workstations Available: 23

EXPENSES/FINANCIAL AID

Annual Tuition: $9,620
Books and Supplies: $900
Financial Aid Application Deadline: 3/1
Average Grant: $18,500
Average Loan: $18,500
% Receiving Some Sort of Aid: 90
Average Total Aid Package: $18,500
Average Debt: $70,000
Fees Per Credit: $370

ADMISSIONS INFORMATION

Application Fee: $45
LSDAS Accepted? No
Transfer Students Accepted? Yes
Other Admissions Factors Considered: If an applicant has completed less than 60 academic semester units, three General CLEP exams are required.
Number of Applications Received: 163
Number of Applicants Accepted: 93
Number of Applicants Enrolled: 55

INTERNATIONAL STUDENTS

TOEFL Required of International Students? Yes
Minimum TOEFL: 550

UNIVERSITY OF WEST LOS ANGELES

PROGRAMS OF STUDY

The School of Law offers the J.D. (Juris Doctor) degree upon completion of 84 semester units. The program satisfies the guidelines promulgated by the Committee of Bar Examiners. Students are required to complete all California Bar Exam subjects in addition to school required courses. Copies of course sequences are available from the Admissions Office.

Students are encouraged to participate in the Clinical Studies or Judicial Externship programs to gain practical experience. Advanced students assist clients in the on-campus Legal Aid Clinic, under the supervision of an experienced practitioner faculty member.

An extensive academic support program is available to help students improve their testing and analytical skills. Students with a cumulative GPA below a stated minimum are required to participate. Exceptional students are recognized by being placed on the Dean's List, participating on the Law Review Board, or graduating with honors.

Classes are offered for both full-time and part-time students. The admission requirements are the same for both programs. Full-time students generally carry 12 units per semester and attend daytime classes. Advanced full-time students are permitted to take electives that are offered in the evening. This program takes three years to complete, including summer sessions. Students in the full-time program should devote all of their time to their studies. Part-time students take a minimum of 8 units each semester and one course each summer. The program is designed to accommodate students who must work or have limited time to devote to their studies. Part-time students may attend in the day or evening. This program takes four years to complete, including summers. Students who must work while in school should apply part-time. Although there are no restrictions on outside employment, students who work long hours may need to adjust their work schedules in order to have adequate study time.

RESEARCH FACILITIES

The University of West Los Angeles (UWLA) is proud of its full-service Kelton Law Library. The collection contains federal and state materials in addition to providing access to computerized legal research databases (Lexis and Westlaw). It offers materials on CD-ROM, videotape, and microfiche and includes a Computer Learning Center. Students have access to word-processing computers and printers and tutorials. Study group meeting rooms and periodical reading rooms are available. Students have access to legal software commonly found in law offices. The new Computer Lab, located in the classroom building, provides many of the same functions as the library Computer Center. It has Internet access, and future plans include providing e-mail to faculty, staff members, and students. The Computer Lab is an instructional lab, is used as a classroom, and has limited hours for student use. UWLA employs a full-time and part-time professional librarian and provides reference assistance to meet the needs of library patrons. The library is open daily, with the exception of legal holidays and a two-week period between semesters.

COST OF STUDY 2000–2001

In the academic year, tuition is $450 per unit. Fees charged include sums for computer use and library use amounting to $140 per term. Books and materials range from approximately $50 to $100 per course

LIVING AND HOUSING COST

UWLA is a commuter institution and does not provide housing. However, there is ample apartment housing in the immediate area surrounding the University.

FINANCIAL AID

The Financial Aid Office assists students in finding resources to finance their education. The governmental programs available to students include Federal Stafford Student Loans and benefits available through government sources to veterans of the U.S. armed forces. To apply for financial assistance, applicants must file a Free Application for Federal Student Aid (FAFSA), which is available from UWLA's Financial Aid Office.

A number of scholarships, some funded by alumni of the School, are available to students. Each year the School offers a program of scholarships to qualified students.

STUDENT GROUP

UWLA serves a student body whose composition reflects the rich cultural and ethnic diversity of the Los Angeles community. Students come to UWLA from all walks of life, and the University is proud of its high enrollment of members of minority groups, women, and nontraditional students. Some are entering law as a second or third career, and others are returning to school and work after raising families.

STUDENT OUTCOMES

The most recent graduate survey shows a high job satisfaction rate (more than 80 percent of those surveyed). Graduates are employed in private firms and by the government, and close to 30 percent are sole practitioners. Close to two dozen are members of the bench, serving as commissioners or judges in municipal or superior court.

LOCATION

UWLA is located on a 4.5-acre campus northeast of the Los Angeles International Airport. Freeways make the campus convenient to all parts of the Los Angeles basin. The campus is situated approximately three miles from the Pacific Ocean to the west and one mile from the San Diego Freeway to the east. It offers convenient on-site free parking.

THE UNIVERSITY AND THE SCHOOL

As a small, private institution specializing in legal education, UWLA offers a distinctive educational experience designed to expose students to the practical application of law. The learning environment is serious and professional. The faculty consists of a small core of full-time professors and a large group of adjunct professors who are experienced practicing attorneys. Because of its size, UWLA is able to give students personal attention—from admissions counseling to graduate placement assistance—in a friendly and supportive atmosphere. Small classes, special counseling, tutoring, and other support programs are an integral part of UWLA's commitment to its students.

APPLYING

Applications are accepted on a rolling basis and may be submitted at any time. Applicants are notified of admission decisions promptly once all transcripts and test scores have been received. All applicants must take the Law School Admissions Test (LSAT) and earn a score at or above the 31st percentile. The School does not average scores; only the highest score is considered. Applicants are also required to come to the campus to write an essay and be interviewed.

School of Law

THE FACULTY

The School prides itself on its faculty, which includes several full-time professors as well as about 40 adjunct professors who are practitioners bringing the real world of current legal practice into the classroom. Since class size is often small, professors need not rely solely on lecture methods to convey information. Professors are committed to sharing with students the academic challenges found in learning the law and the practical necessities found in daily legal work. The faculty reflects the same diverse communities as the student body; they come from different age groups and racial and ethnic backgrounds from legal institutions throughout the country.

Faculty members include:

- Marilyn W. Alper, Adjunct Professor, M.P.A. from USC and J.D. from University of West Los Angeles. Women and the Law.

- Anne E. Arvin, Associate Dean of Academic Affairs, M.A. from Abilene Christian and J.D. from Pepperdine. Litigation Procedure.

- Sara Berman-Barrett, Full-Time Professor, J.D. from UCLA. Criminal Procedure, Criminal Law.

- Ira E. Bilson, Adjunct Professor, LL.B. from NYU. Constitutional Law, Income Tax, Trusts and Estates.

- Roy Eugene Boggs Jr., Full-Time Professor, J.D. from Berkeley. Contracts, Employment Law.

- Steve Bracci, Full-Time Professor, J.D. from Whittier. Contracts, Torts.

- Clifford S. Dicker, Adjunct Professor, LL.B. from Southwestern University. Community Property, Family Law.

- Lynn B. Feldman, Adjunct Professor, J.D. University of West Los Angeles. Legal Research, Introduction to Legal Studies.

- Paul A. Jacobs, Adjunct Professor, J.D. from Loyola. Local Government Law, Ethical Lawyering.

- Andrew H. Kopkin, Full-Time Professor, M.A. from Oxford and LL.M. from Cambridge. Constitutional Law, International Business, Transactions, Public International Law.

- Eugene Kramer, Adjunct Professor and Director of Federal Judicial Externship Program, J.D. from DePaul. Federal Trial Advocacy.

- Bruce G. Landau, Dean of the School of Law, J.D. from Whittier. Real Estate Transactions, Real Property.

- Lionel P. Levin, Adjunct Professor, J.D. from Villanova. Constitutional Law.

- Marilyn H. Mackel, Adjunct Professor, M.A. from CUNY John Jay College of Criminal Justice and J.D. from Georgetown. Juvenile Law.

- Mark Oring, Full-Time Professor, M.A. from Indiana and J.D. from Hastings Law. Remedies, Torts.

- Perry M. Polski, Dean Emeritus and Adjunct Professor, M.A. from Minnesota and J.D. from University of West Los Angeles. Criminal Law.

- Tayo A. Popoola, Adjunct Professor, M.B.A. from Georgia State and J.D. from Connecticut. Criminal Law.

- John T. Schooler, Adjunct Professor, J.D. from University of West Los Angeles. Trusts and Estates.

- Bruce E. Schwartz, Adjunct Professor, J.D. from San Diego. Evidence.

- Kenneth P. Sherman, Adjunct Professor and Director of Legal Aid Clinic, J.D. from Southwestern Law.

- Lawrence S. Silverman, Adjunct Professor and Director of Clinical Studies; J.D., Southwestern Law.

- David Starleaf, Adjunct Professor and Associate Director of Legal Aid Clinic, J.D. from Loyola.

- Peter C. Swarth, Adjunct Professor, J.D. from Loyola. Trial Skills.

- Vince Tassinari, Adjunct Professor, J.D. from Golden Gate and LL.M. from John Marshall Law. Intellectual Property, Federal Legislative Process.

- Nicholas B. Waite, Full-Time Professor, J.D. from Michigan. Civil Procedure, Products Liability, Torts.

Admissions Contact: Director of Admissions, Lynda Freeman
1155 West Arbor Vitae, Inglewood, CA 90301
Admissions Phone: 310-342-5254 • Admissions Fax: 310-342-5295
Web Address: www.uwia.edu

UNIVERSITY OF WINDSOR

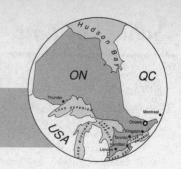

Admissions Contact: Michelle Pilutti
401 Sunset Ave, Windsor, ON N8S 2R3 Canada
Admissions Phone: 519-253-3000 • Admissions Fax: 519-973-7064
Admissions E-mail: pilutt1@uwindsor.ca • Web Address: www.lawadmit.com

INSTITUTIONAL INFORMATION

Public/Private: Public
Total Faculty: 23
% Female: 30
% Minority: 10

PROGRAMS

Advanced Degrees Offered: LLB program only, no graduate degrees
Combined Degrees Offered: MBA/LLB (3–4 years)
Clinical Program Required? Yes
Clinical Programs: Legal Assistance of Windsor/ Legal Aid Clinics, Community Legal Aid

STUDENT INFORMATION

Enrollment of Law School: 423
% Male/Female: 43/57
% Full Time: 98
Average Age of Entering Class: 26

EXPENSES/FINANCIAL AID

Annual Tuition (Residents/Nonresidents): $6,000/$895
Room and Board (On Campus): $5,287
Books and Supplies: $1,000
Average Grant: $750
Average Loan: $8,626
% of Aid That Is Merit-Based: 100
% Receiving Some Sort of Aid: 49
Average Total Aid Package: $8,626

ADMISSIONS INFORMATION

Application Fee: $50
Regular Notification: Rolling
Transfer Students Accepted? Yes
Number of Applications Received: 1,462
Number of Applicants Accepted: 381
Number of Applicants Enrolled: 155

EMPLOYMENT INFORMATION

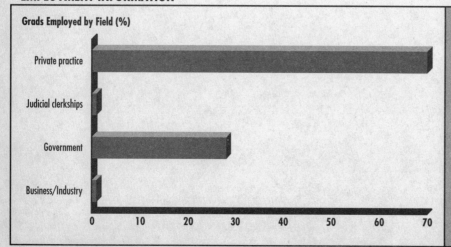

Rate of Placement: 98%
Employers Who Frequently Hire Grads: Law firms
Prominent Alumni: Hon. Charles Harnick, attorney general, Province of Ontario; Donna C. McGillis, judge, Federal Court of Canada; Pater Farmor, president and CEO of Dennison Mines

UNIVERSITY OF WISCONSIN
Law School

Admissions Contact: Chair of Admissions and Financial Aid Committee, Professor William H. Clune
975 Bascom Mall, Madison, WI 53716
Admissions Phone: 608-262-5914 • Admissions Fax: 608-262-5914
Admissions E-mail: admissions@law.wisc.edu • Web Address: www.law.wisc.edu

INSTITUTIONAL INFORMATION

Public/Private: Public
Environment: Urban
Academic Calendar: Semester
Schedule: Full time or part time
Student/Faculty Ratio: 20:1
Total Faculty: 49
% Female: 20
% Minority: 15

PROGRAMS

Advanced Degrees Offered: LLM (2 years), SJD (1 year)
Combined Degrees Offered: Law and Environmental Studies (4 years), JD/MBA (4 years), Law and Industrial Relations (4 years), Law and Ibero-American Studies (4 years), Law and Sociology (4 years)
Grading System: Letter and numerical system ranging 65–95

STUDENT INFORMATION

Enrollment of Law School: 841
% Male/Female: 54/46
% Part Time: 10
% Full Time That Are International: 2
% Minority: 23
Average Age of Entering Class: 25

EXPENSES/FINANCIAL AID

Annual Tuition (Residents/Nonresidents): $5,910/$15,442
Room and Board: $5,360
Books and Supplies: $1,670
Average Grant: $1,000
Average Loan: $12,797
% of Aid That Is Merit-Based: 10
% Receiving Some Sort of Aid: 42
Average Debt: $31,708

ADMISSIONS INFORMATION

Regular Application Deadline: February 1
Regular Notification: Rolling
Average GPA: 3.4
Average LSAT: 158
Transfer Students Accepted? Yes
Other Schools to Which Students Applied: Marquette University, University of Minnesota, Washington University, Georgetown University, University of Michigan, University of California—Berkeley, George Washington University, Loyola University Chicago
Other Admissions Factors Considered: Residency, trend of college grades, graduate study, time interval between college graduation and application to law school, undergraduate institution, college grading and course selection patterns

EMPLOYMENT INFORMATION

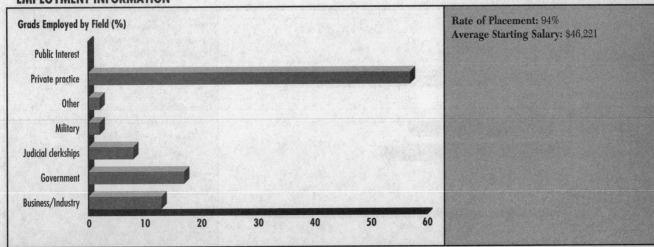

Grads Employed by Field (%)

Rate of Placement: 94%
Average Starting Salary: $46,221

UNIVERSITY OF WYOMING
College of Law

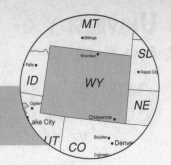

Admissions Contact: Associate Dean, Brad Saxton
PO Box 3035, Laramie, WY 82071-3035
Admissions Phone: 307-766-6416 • Admissions Fax: 307-766-6417
Admissions E-mail: lawadmis@uwyo.edu • Web Address: www.uwyo.edu/law/law.htm

INSTITUTIONAL INFORMATION

Public/Private: Public
Environment: Suburban
Academic Calendar: Semester
Schedule: Full time only
Student/Faculty Ratio: 15:1
Total Faculty: 16
% Female: 38

PROGRAMS

Combined Degrees Offered: JD/MPA (3.5 years), JD/MBA (3.5–4 years)
Clinical Program Required? No
Clinical Programs: Defender Aid, Legal Services, Prosecution Assistance
Grading System: Grades are assigned on a plus/minus letter system (A–F), and grades of Incomplete (X) and Withdrawn (W) are disregarded. The grade of Satisfactory (S) or Unsatisfactory (U) may be granted if the student so requests at the time of registration. Courses taken for S/U credit do not count toward hours required for graduation unless the course is offered for the S/U grade only.

STUDENT INFORMATION

Enrollment of Law School: 229
% Male/Female: 58/42
% Full Time: 100
% Minority: 5
Average Age of Entering Class: 27

EXPENSES/FINANCIAL AID

Annual Tuition (Residents/Nonresidents): $4,172/$9,252
Room and Board (On Campus): $4,568
Books and Supplies: $800
Financial Aid Application Deadline: 3/1
Average Grant: $1,675
Average Loan: $9,000
% of Aid That Is Merit-Based: 46
% Receiving Some Sort of Aid: 75
Average Debt: $30,000

ADMISSIONS INFORMATION

Application Fee: $35
Regular Application Deadline: 3/15
Regular Notification: 4/15
Average GPA: 3.2
Range of GPA: 3.0–3.5
Average LSAT: 152
Range of LSAT: 148–156
Transfer Students Accepted? Yes
Other Schools to Which Students Applied: University of Denver, University of Colorado, University of Utah, Creighton University, University of Montana, University of Arizona, Gonzaga University, University of Idaho
Other Admissions Factors Considered: Grade progression
Number of Applications Received: 379
Number of Applicants Accepted: 249
Number of Applicants Enrolled: 84

INTERNATIONAL STUDENTS

TOEFL Required of International Students? Yes

EMPLOYMENT INFORMATION

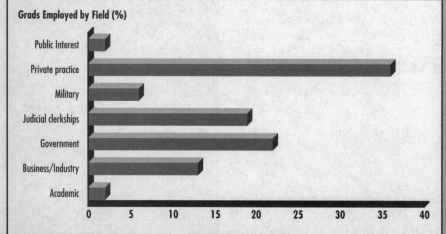

Grads Employed by Field (%)

Rate of Placement: 97%
Average Starting Salary: $34,575
Prominent Alumni: Alan Simpson, retired U.S. senator; Michael Sullivan, former governor of Wyoming, ambassador to Ireland; Gerry Spence, trial lawyer
State for Bar Exam: WY
Number Taking Bar Exam: 33
Pass Rate for First-Time Bar: 64%

VALPARAISO UNIVERSITY
School of Law

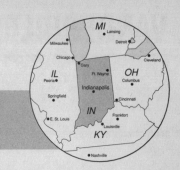

Admissions Contact: Assistant Dean of Admissions and Student Services, Heike Spahn
Wesemann Hall, Valparaiso, IN 46383
Admissions Phone: 219-465-7829 • Admissions Fax: 219-465-7808
Admissions E-mail: valpolaw@valpo.edu • Web Address: www.valpo.edu/law/

INSTITUTIONAL INFORMATION

Public/Private: Private
Affiliation: Lutheran
Environment: Suburban
Academic Calendar: Semester
Schedule: Full time or part time
Student/Faculty Ratio: 17:1
Total Faculty: 72
% Part Time: 51
% Female: 38
% Minority: 4

PROGRAMS

Academic Specialties: Opportunity to select a minor or concentration area including course work, practical experience, and a scholarly paper
Advanced Degrees Offered: JD (3 years full time, 5 years part time), LLM (1 year full time, 2 years part time)
Combined Degrees Offered: JD/MA Psychology (4 years)
Clinical Program Required? No
Grading System: Numerical and letter system ranging from A (4.0) to F (0.0)
Legal Writing/Methods Course Requirements: Legal writing required each of the 3 years

STUDENT INFORMATION

Enrollment of Law School: 420
% Male/Female: 54/46
% Full Time: 87
% Full Time That Are International: 1
% Minority: 13
Average Age of Entering Class: 26

RESEARCH FACILITIES

Computers/Workstations Available: 285
Computers/Work Stations: 14
Campuswide Network? Yes

EXPENSES/FINANCIAL AID

Annual Tuition: $18,940
Room and Board: $6,600
Books and Supplies: $750
Average Grant: $11,502
Average Loan: $20,200
% Receiving Some Sort of Aid: 90
Average Total Aid Package: $23,210
Average Debt: $56,916
Tuition Per Credit: $740

ADMISSIONS INFORMATION

Application Fee: $30
Regular Application Deadline: 4/15
Regular Notification: Rolling
LSDAS Accepted? Yes
Average GPA: 3.2
Range of GPA: 2.9–3.5
Average LSAT: 152
Range of LSAT: 148–157
Transfer Students Accepted? Yes
Other Schools to Which Students Applied: Indiana University—Bloomington, Loyola University Chicago, John Marshall Law School, Marquette University, University of Notre Dame, University of Dayton, DePaul University, Indiana University—Indianapolis
Other Admissions Factors Considered: Undergraduate institution, undergraduate major, graduate work, life/work experience
Number of Applications Received: 692
Number of Applicants Accepted: 491
Number of Applicants Enrolled: 167

INTERNATIONAL STUDENTS

TOEFL Required of International Students? Yes
Minimum TOEFL: 550

EMPLOYMENT INFORMATION

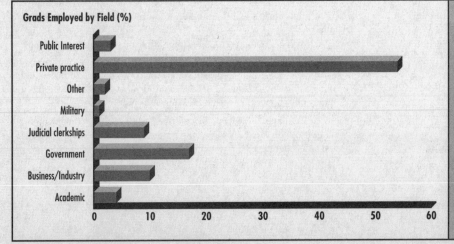

Grads Employed by Field (%)

Rate of Placement: 96%
Average Starting Salary: $44,588
Employers Who Frequently Hire Grads: Sidley and Austin; Barnes and Thornburg; Baker and Daniels; May, Oberfell and Lorber; Hoeppner, Wagner and Evans; Ruman, Clements, Tobin and Holub; Kightlinger and Gray; Hinshaw and Culbertson; Querrey and Harrow
Prominent Alumni: Deborah Schavey Ruff, partner, Mayer, Brown and Platt, intellectual property attorney; Stephen E. Buyer, U.S House of Representatives; Justice Robert Rucker, Indiana Supreme Court
State for Bar Exam: IN

VANDERBILT UNIVERSITY

INTRODUCTION

Vanderbilt University Law School offers the Juris Doctor degree to a small group of academically talented students. These students learn in an environment combining the rigors of serious intellectual study with collegial relationships. The faculty is committed to excellence in both teaching and scholarship. As prolific writers who publish regularly in leading law reviews and journals, Vanderbilt professors bring a breadth of interdisciplinary training and research interests to the classroom. The student/faculty ratio of 15:1, and the faculty's open-door policy encourages regular interaction between students and their professors.

More than 225 colleges and universities are represented in the 559-member student body. A typical class will have students from 40 states and several foreign countries.

Founded in 1874, the Law School is part of the beautiful Vanderbilt University campus, designated a National Arboretum. The campus is two miles from Nashville's business center. A recent $22.5 million expansion to the Law School building provides state-of-the-art facilities and focuses on providing student-centered spaces. Vanderbilt is a major research university with approximately 10,000 students in its undergraduate, graduate, and professional schools. A state capital of 1.5 million, Nashville is home to the executive and legislative branches of Tennessee state government and many federal agencies. Trial and appellate courts at both the state and federal levels are accessible to students.

Nashville is listed regularly among the best cities in which to live and work. It has the vitality and attractions of a major city—professional sports, theater, ballet, symphony—and the grace of a smaller town with friendly and welcoming citizens.

ENROLLMENT/STUDENT BODY

- 2,428 applicants
- 613 admitted
- 182 enrolled in—first-year class 2000
- Median GPA: 3.62
- Median LSAT: 162
- 559 total full time
- 29 percent minority—first-year class 2000
- 23 percent minority—entire student body
- 52 percent women—first-year class 2000
- 110 undergraduate institutions represented

FACULTY

- 76 total
- 47 percent full time
- 53 percent part time or adjunct
- 33 percent women
- 8 percent minorities

LIBRARY AND PHYSICAL FACILITIES

- 582,072 volumes and equivalents
- Library hours: Monday–Sunday, 7:00 A.M.–Midnight
- Lexis-Nexis
- Westlaw
- Infotrac
- CD-based systems
- 10 full-time librarians
- Library seats 431

The Alyne Queener Massey law library is one of the primary research centers in the Southeast. The collection primarily supports the curriculum and research interests of the faculty, and its strengths include corporate law, intellectual property law, bioethics, international trade, and general international and foreign law. All other University libraries, containing more than 2.3 million volumes, are available to law students.

CURRICULUM

- 88 credits required to graduate
- 148 courses available
- Degrees available: JD/MDiv, MBA/JD, JD/MTS, LLM for International Students pending acquiescence by the ABA and University approval

The first-year required courses include the foundation courses of legal study in addition to an innovative course on legal process and the institutions of lawmaking. The year-long legal writing course, teaching the fundamentals of writing, analysis, and research, is taught in small groups of 23 students. With the exception of Professional Responsibility and an independent research writing class or seminar, all upper-level courses are electives.

The curriculum is broad, offering students the opportunity to gain exposure to the fundamental knowledge necessary to become a competent professional, while focusing on areas of special interest.

SPECIAL PROGRAMS

Clinical programs offer students the chance to represent clients in civil, family, criminal, and juvenile cases while earning academic credit. Through cooperative arrangements with the Legal Aid Society of Middle Tennessee, the District Attorney's Office, the Public Defender, and juvenile court, students perform a number of legal services under the supervision of clinical professors.

The Joe C. Davis Foundation Program in Law and Economics features regular workshops involving leading scholars from around the nation.

Vanderbilt University is home to the First Amendment Center, a nationally recognized institute where journalists and legal scholars do research and write on issues involving freedoms granted in the first amendment to the Constitution. The Vanderbilt Institute for Policy Studies offers faculty and students from departments throughout the University a place to work cooperatively on issues ranging from health care policy to international trade.

STUDENT ACTIVITIES

Students continue their learning outside the classroom through opportunities to serve on the editorial boards of the *Vanderbilt Law Review*, *The Journal of Entertainment Law and Practice*, and *The Journal of Transnational Law*; participation on moot court teams and the Moot Court Board; and through the activities of more than 28 student organizations. Educational programs add to the intellectual life of the School and social events bring students together regularly.

The Moot Court Board administers a program of brief-writing and oral advocacy to enhance students' courtroom lawyering skills. Moot court teams compete in national and international tournaments each year and the board hosts the nationally acclaimed First Amendment Moot Court competition, which draws teams from 32 other law schools each year.

The Hyatt Speakers Fund has been established to enhance the intellectual experience of students by supporting symposia and educational programs of student organizations.

Law School

EXPENSES AND FINANCIAL AID

- Full-time tuition and fees: $25,550

- Estimated additional expenses: $14,500 (housing, food, books, travel, etc.)

- Need-based and merit-based scholarships available

- Participation in several federal and private loan programs; FAFSA and the Vanderbilt University Law School Financial Aid Statement required by February 28; the CSS/Financial Aid PROFILE also required for all entering students; those age 28 and younger must provide parental information.

A substantial amount of scholarship aid is available for law students. Financial aid packages are awarded before the admission response deadlines. Scholarship awards are made for three years, conditioned on good-standing. Approximately 85 percent of entering students receive financial aid. Vanderbilt participates in federal, university, and private loan programs to assist students in funding their legal education. A good credit history is essential for borrowing from private loan programs.

Vanderbilt offers a loan forgiveness program to graduates who take public-interest positions.

HOUSING

While the University offers limited on-campus housing, most law students elect to live in apartments and off-campus houses. The Admission Office assists incoming students during the summer months with roommate lists and housing information.

CAREER SERVICES

Vanderbilt graduates enjoy an outstanding reputation in the legal profession. In addition to the on-campus recruiting program, several hundred employers write annually to solicit résumés from Vanderbilt students.

In the fall of 1999, over 600 employers visited Vanderbilt to recruit students participating in the on-campus recruiting program. They came from more than 36 states, and Vanderbilt graduates accepted positions throughout the country. The Career Services Office maintains a staff of professional counselors to assist students individually with their career goals. The placement rate six months following graduation is 98 percent. The same percentage of second-year students worked in legal jobs during the summer. An on-campus interviewing program is held for first-year students in the spring, and more than 92 percent of first-year students had a legal job last summer, 60 percent of which were paid positions.

ADMISSION

- Bachelor's degree from an accredited college or university required

- Application deadline: March 1

- LLM application deadline: March 1

- Early decision deadline: November 1

- LSAT, LSDAS required

- Application fee: $50

The Admission Committee thoroughly evaluates each application, considering the candidate's academic record, LSAT score, letters of recommendation, personal statements, extracurricular/civic activities, GPA, and work experience. The Committee takes into account any elements in the applicant's background that will add depth to the student body or that indicate leadership promise.

The full-file review process yields a group of students that has developed the ability to speak and write clearly; to think precisely; and to analyze complex issues. A broad cultural background is also important since lawyers must serve a multifaceted society. The entering class is limited to approximately 185 students. Because the students work in a cooperative and mutually respectful environment, Vanderbilt attracts students with diverse interests, but who are academically serious about studying the legal processes of the law.

Admissions Contact: Assistant Dean, Sonya G. Smith, EdD, JD
131 21st Avenue South, Suite 207, Nashville, TN 37203
Admissions Phone: 615-322-6452 • Admissions Fax: 615-322-1531
Admissions E-mail: admissions@law.vanderbilt.edu • Web Address: www.vanderbilt.edu/law/

VANDERBILT UNIVERSITY
Law School

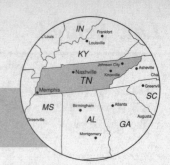

Admissions Contact: Assistant Dean, Sonya G. Smith, EdD, JD
131 21st Avenue South, Suite 207, Nashville, TN 37203
Admissions Phone: 615-322-6452 • Admissions Fax: 615-322-1531
Admissions E-mail: admissions@law.vanderbilt.edu • Web Address: www.vanderbilt.edu/law/

INSTITUTIONAL INFORMATION
Public/Private: Private
Environment: Urban
Academic Calendar: Semester
Schedule: Full time only
Student/Faculty Ratio: 17:1
Total Faculty: 76
% Part Time: 53
% Female: 33
% Minority: 8

PROGRAMS
Academic Specialties: Public and Constitutional Law, Corporate Law, Intellectual Property, Entertainment Law and Practice, Cyberspace and Technology Law
Combined Degrees Offered: JD/MBA (4 years), JD/MA (5 years), JD/PhD (7 years), JD/MDiv (5 years), JD/MTS (4 years)
Clinical Program Required? No
Grading System: A+ to F
Legal Writing/Methods Course Requirements: 2 semesters in the first year

STUDENT INFORMATION
Enrollment of Law School: 559
% Male/Female: 52/48
% Full Time: 100
% Full Time That Are International: 2
% Minority: 21
Average Age of Entering Class: 24

RESEARCH FACILITIES
Campuswide Network? Yes
School-Supported Research Centers: Vanderbilt Institute for Public Policy Studies, First Ammendment Center

EXPENSES/FINANCIAL AID
Annual Tuition: $24,350
Room and Board: $14,500
Books and Supplies: $1,100
Financial Aid Application Deadline: 2/1
Average Loan: $22,000
% of Aid That Is Merit-Based: 20
% Receiving Some Sort of Aid: 80
Average Total Aid Package: $25,500
Average Debt: $62,000

ADMISSIONS INFORMATION
Application Fee: $50
Regular Application Deadline: 3/1
Regular Notification: 4/15
LSDAS Accepted? Yes
Average GPA: 3.6
Range of GPA: 3.4–3.8
Average LSAT: 162
Range of LSAT: 160–165
Transfer Students Accepted? Yes
Other Schools to Which Students Applied: University of Virginia, Emory University, Duke University, Georgetown University, Harvard University, Yale University, Northwestern University, University of Michigan
Other Admissions Factors Considered: Letters of recommendation, personal statements, rigor of academic courses, extracurricular activities, work experience
Number of Applications Received: 2,387
Number of Applicants Accepted: 760
Number of Applicants Enrolled: 182

INTERNATIONAL STUDENTS
TOEFL Required of International Students? Yes
Minimum TOEFL: 640

EMPLOYMENT INFORMATION

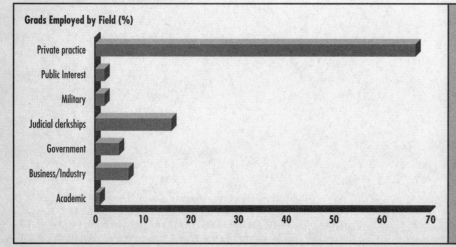

Grads Employed by Field (%)

Rate of Placement: 91%
Average Starting Salary: $36,440

VENTURA COLLEGE OF LAW

Admissions Contact: Assistant Dean, Barbara Doyle
4475 Market Street, Ventura, CA 93003
Admissions Phone: 805-658-0511 • Admissions Fax: 805-658-0529
Admissions E-mail: bdoyle@venturalaw.edu • Web Address: www.venturalaw.edu

INSTITUTIONAL INFORMATION

Public/Private: Private
Student/Faculty Ratio: 6:1
Total Faculty: 19
% Part Time: 100
% Female: 10
% Minority: 10

PROGRAMS

Academic Specialties: All faculty are practicing attorneys or judges.
Advanced Degrees Offered: JD (4 year part-time evening program)
Combined Degrees Offered: None
Clinical Program Required? Yes
Clinical Programs: Family Law and Bankruptcy legal clinics
Grading System: Letter system A to F on a 4.0 scale
Legal Writing/Methods Course Requirements: Consists of 5 separate courses over the 4-year curriculum

STUDENT INFORMATION

Enrollment of Law School: 100
% Part Time: 100
Average Age of Entering Class: 33

RESEARCH FACILITIES

Computers/Workstations Available: 5

EXPENSES/FINANCIAL AID

Books and Supplies: $400
Average Grant: $750
Fees Per Credit: $225

ADMISSIONS INFORMATION

Application Fee: $45
Regular Application Deadline: 8/1
Regular Notification: Rolling
LSDAS Accepted? No
Average GPA: 3.0
Range of GPA: 2.1–3.9
Transfer Students Accepted? Yes
Other Schools to Which Students Applied: Southwestern University, University of California—Berkeley, Pepperdine University, Tulane University, Whittier College, San Francisco Law School
Other Admissions Factors Considered: Work and life experience
Number of Applications Received: 29
Number of Applicants Accepted: 24
Number of Applicants Enrolled: 19

EMPLOYMENT INFORMATION

Employers Who Frequently Hire Grads: County of Ventura District Attorney and Public Defender Offices
Prominent Alumni: Colleen Toy White, judge of the Superior Court, County of Ventura; David Long, judge of the Superior Court, County of Ventura

VERMONT LAW SCHOOL

Admissions Contact: Assistant Dean for Admissions, Michelle D. Mason
PO Box 96, Chelsea Street, South Royalton, VT 05068
Admissions Phone: 800-227-1395 • Admissions Fax: 802-763-7071
Admissions E-mail: admiss@vermontlaw.edu • Web Address: www.vermontlaw.edu

INSTITUTIONAL INFORMATION

Public/Private: Private
Environment: Suburban
Academic Calendar: Semester
Schedule: Full time only
Student/Faculty Ratio: 14:1
Total Faculty: 68
% Part Time: 45
% Female: 40
% Minority: 5

PROGRAMS

Academic Specialties: Clinical/experiential programs, Environmental Law specialty, Public Interest Law specialties, General Practice Program Certificate, Canadian Studies Program, First Nations Environmental Law Program
Advanced Degrees Offered: JD (3 years), MSEL (1 year), LLM Environmental Law (1 year)
Combined Degrees Offered: JD/MSEL (3 years total: 6 regular semesters and 2 summer semesters)
Clinical Program Required? No
Clinical Programs: South Royalton Legal Clinic, Semester in Practice, Environmental Semester in Washington, Legislation Clinic, Environmental Law Clinic, etc.
Grading System: A to F
Legal Writing/Methods Course Requirements: 4 courses over 3 years

STUDENT INFORMATION

Enrollment of Law School: 486
% Male/Female: 52/48
% Full Time: 100
% Full Time That Are International: 2
% Minority: 8
Average Age of Entering Class: 27

RESEARCH FACILITIES

Computers/Workstations Available: 35

EXPENSES/FINANCIAL AID

Annual Tuition: $20,958
Room and Board (Off Campus): $7,975
Books and Supplies: $780
Average Grant: $5,500
Average Loan: $18,500
% of Aid That Is Merit-Based: 50
% Receiving Some Sort of Aid: 90
Average Total Aid Package: $27,500
Average Debt: $72,000

ADMISSIONS INFORMATION

Application Fee: $50
Regular Application Deadline: 2/1
Regular Notification: 3/15
LSDAS Accepted? Yes
Average GPA: 3.2
Range of GPA: 2.8–3.3
Average LSAT: 151
Range of LSAT: 148–156
Transfer Students Accepted? Yes
Other Schools to Which Students Applied: Lewis and Clark College, Pace University, Boston University, University of Oregon, Suffolk University, University of Colorado, George Washington University, Boston College
Number of Applications Received: 781
Number of Applicants Enrolled: 180

INTERNATIONAL STUDENTS

TOEFL Required of International Students? Yes
Minimum TOEFL: 575

EMPLOYMENT INFORMATION

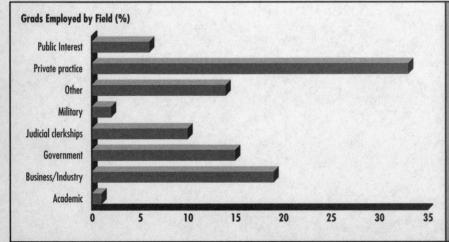

Rate of Placement: 89%
Average Starting Salary: $37,900
Employers Who Frequently Hire Grads: Department of Justice; Environmental Protection Agency; various nonprofit legal aid organizations and advocacy groups; various state and federal appellate and trial court systems
Prominent Alumni: Glenn J. Berger, partner, Skadden, Arps, Slate, Meagher and Flom; Shirley Ann Jefferson, associate at Wilhelmina, Jackson, Rolark and general counsel for United Black Fund, Inc.; Steven Stitzel, partner, Stitzel and Page

VILLANOVA UNIVERSITY
School of Law

Admissions Contact: Director of Admissions, David Pallozzi
299 North Spring Mill Road, Villanova, PA 19085
Admissions Phone: 610-519-7010 • Admissions Fax: 610-519-6291
Admissions E-mail: shaiko@law.vill.edu • Web Address: vls.law.vill.edu

INSTITUTIONAL INFORMATION

Public/Private: Private
Affiliation: Roman Catholic
Environment: Suburban
Academic Calendar: Semester
Schedule: Full time only
Student/Faculty Ratio: 16:1
Total Faculty: 84
% Part Time: 46
% Female: 32
% Minority: 8

PROGRAMS

Advanced Degrees Offered: JD (3 years), LLM Tax (24 credits)
Combined Degrees Offered: JD/MBA (3–4.5 years), JD/PhD Psychology (7–8 years)
Clinical Program Required? No
Clinical Programs: Tax Clinic, Informational Law Clinic, Juvenile Justice Clinic, Villanova Community Legal Services, externships, Law and Entrepreneurship, Immigration Law Clinic
Grading System: 4.00 scale

STUDENT INFORMATION

Enrollment of Law School: 710
% Male/Female: 53/47
% Full Time: 100
% Full Time That Are International: 2
% Minority: 15
Average Age of Entering Class: 24

EXPENSES/FINANCIAL AID

Annual Tuition: $20,000
Room and Board (Off Campus): $10,990
Books and Supplies: $1,000
Average Grant: $6,414
Average Loan: $26,003
% Receiving Some Sort of Aid: 74
Average Total Aid Package: $26,893
Average Debt: $73,076

ADMISSIONS INFORMATION

Application Fee: $75
Regular Application Deadline: 3/1
Regular Notification: Rolling
Average GPA: 3.3
Range of GPA: 3.0–3.5
Average LSAT: 157
Range of LSAT: 153–158
Transfer Students Accepted? Yes
Other Schools to Which Students Applied: Temple University, George Washington University, University of Pennsylvania, Boston University, Boston College

EMPLOYMENT INFORMATION

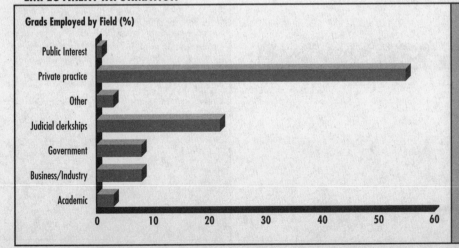

Rate of Placement: 86%
Average Starting Salary: $55,000
Employers Who Frequently Hire Grads: State judges and government law firms in Philadelphia, New York, New Jersey, Washington, D.C., and Delaware
Prominent Alumni: Ed Rendell, Mayor of Philadelphia; Mattew McHugh, former U.S. congressman, now general counsel to the World Bank; Sandra Schultz Newman, first elected woman to Supreme Court of Pennsylvania; Mattew Ryan, Speaker of the Pennsylvania House of Representatives; John J. LaFalce, U.S. congressman; William Green, Former U.S. congressman and former mayor of Philadelphia

WAKE FOREST UNIVERSITY
School of Law

Admissions Contact: Director of Admissions and Financial Aid, Melaine E. Nutt
PO Box 7206, Reynolda Station, Winston-Salem, NC 27109
Admissions Phone: 910-759-5437 • Admissions Fax: 910-759-4632
Admissions E-mail: admissions@law.wfu.edu • Web Address: www.law.wfu.edu

INSTITUTIONAL INFORMATION
Public/Private: Private
Environment: Urban
Academic Calendar: Semester
Schedule: Full time only
Student/Faculty Ratio: 14:1
Total Faculty: 28
% Part Time: 18
% Female: 32
% Minority: 4

PROGRAMS
Advanced Degrees Offered: LLM in American Law for foreign lawyers only
Combined Degrees Offered: JD/MBA
Clinical Program Required? Yes
Clinical Programs: Although not required, over 50 percent of students participate in either the Traditional Clinic or Elder Care Clinic, and approximately 80 students participate in a Domestic Advocacy project.
Grading System: A (100–91), B (90–81), C (80–71), D (70–66), and F (65–59)

STUDENT INFORMATION
Enrollment of Law School: 465
% Male/Female: 61/39
% Full Time: 98
% Full Time That Are International: 1
% Minority: 10
Average Age of Entering Class: 24

RESEARCH FACILITIES
Computers/Workstations Available: 150

EXPENSES/FINANCIAL AID
Annual Tuition: $20,450
Room and Board (Off Campus): $11,000
Books and Supplies: $700
Financial Aid Application Deadline: 5/1
Average Grant: $13,734
Average Loan: $18,500
% of Aid That Is Merit-Based: 40
% Receiving Some Sort of Aid: 80
Average Total Aid Package: $32,240
Average Debt: $66,600

ADMISSIONS INFORMATION
Application Fee: $60
Regular Application Deadline: 3/15
Regular Notification: Rolling
Range of GPA: 2.9–4.0
Average LSAT: 160
Range of LSAT: 156–162
Transfer Students Accepted? Yes
Other Schools to Which Students Applied: University of North Carolina, College of William and Mary, George Washington University, Vanderbilt University, Emory University, Duke University, University of Richmond, Washington and Lee University

INTERNATIONAL STUDENTS
TOEFL Required of International Students? Yes
Minimum TOEFL: 600

EMPLOYMENT INFORMATION

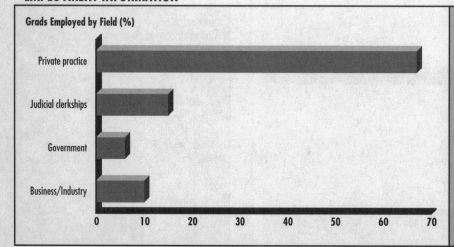

Grads Employed by Field (%)

Rate of Placement: 99%
Average Starting Salary: $51,952
Prominent Alumni: Judge Sam Wilson, federal district judge, Western District of Virginia; Justice Major Harding, justice, Supreme Court of the State of Florida; Hon. Dennis Wicker, Lieutenant Governor, State of North Carolina

WASHBURN UNIVERSITY
School of Law

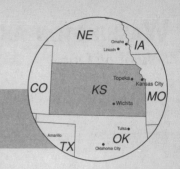

Admissions Contact: Director of Admissions, Janet K. Kerr
1700 College, Topeka, KS 66621
Admissions Phone: 785-231-1185 • Admissions Fax: 785-232-8087
Admissions E-mail: admissions@washburnlaw.edu • Web Address: washburnlaw.edu

INSTITUTIONAL INFORMATION

Public/Private: Public
Environment: Urban
Academic Calendar: Semester
Schedule: Full time only
Student/Faculty Ratio: 14:1
Total Faculty: 29
% Female: 31
% Minority: 21

PROGRAMS

Advanced Degrees Offered: JD (90 credit hours, 3 years)
Combined Degrees Offered: MBA may be completed in conjunction with the JD; 9 hours of the 30 hours required for the MBA are met by completing the JD, leaving only 21 hours of MBA course work to complete. This may be completed within the 3-year JD program or can extend an additional semester or two. MCJ may be completed with JD. Up to 18 hours of 36 hours required for the MCJ may be met by JD courses, leaving only 12 hours of course work and 6 hours of thesis or practicum to complete.
Clinical Program Required? No
Clinical Programs: Washburn has one of the oldest clinical programs in the country, offering a General Practice Clinic that also includes a strong mediation program. It is staffed by 5 full-time faculty and is housed in a model law office building adjacent to the law school.

Grading System: A (4.0), B+ (3.5), C+ (2.5), C (2.0), D+ (1.5), D (1.0), F (0.0). Must have 2.0 GPA or above to graduate. Some courses may be designated as Outstanding, Credit, or No Credit rather than graded.

STUDENT INFORMATION

Enrollment of Law School: 411
% Male/Female: 58/42
% Full Time: 100
% Full Time That Are International: 2
% Minority: 15
Average Age of Entering Class: 27

RESEARCH FACILITIES

Computers/Workstations Available: 110

EXPENSES/FINANCIAL AID

Annual Tuition (Residents/Nonresidents): $8,220/$12,750
Room and Board (On/Off Campus): $3,500/$7,000
Books and Supplies: $800
Financial Aid Application Deadline: 4/1
Average Grant: $3,454
Average Loan: $17,500
% of Aid That Is Merit-Based: 95
% Receiving Some Sort of Aid: 90
Average Total Aid Package: $17,950
Average Debt: $37,000
Fees Per Credit (Residents/Nonresidents): $251/$378

ADMISSIONS INFORMATION

Application Fee: $30
Regular Application Deadline: 3/15
Regular Notification: 6/1
Average GPA: 3.1
Range of GPA: 2.8–3.5
Average LSAT: 151
Range of LSAT: 146–154
Transfer Students Accepted? Yes
Other Schools to Which Students Applied: University of Kansas, University of Missouri—Kansas City, Creighton University, University of Tulsa, Oklahoma State University, Drake University, University of Nebraska, University of Missouri—Columbia
Number of Applications Received: 543
Number of Applicants Accepted: 353
Number of Applicants Enrolled: 141

EMPLOYMENT INFORMATION

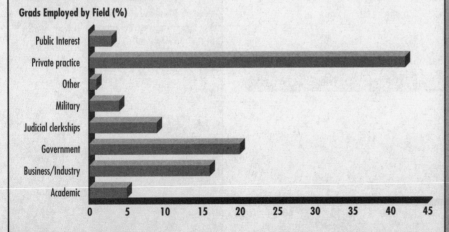

Grads Employed by Field (%)

Rate of Placement: 91%
Average Starting Salary: $36,440
Employers Who Frequently Hire Grads: Koch Industries, many large law firms in the Kansas City and Wichita areas, various state and federal courts
Prominent Alumni: Bob Dole, former majority leader of the U.S. Senate, 1996 Republican presidential nominee; Delano Lewis, former CEO and president of the National Public Radio and current nominee for U.S. ambassador to South Africa; Ronald K. Richey, CEO and president of Torchmark Corporation; Bill Kurtis, broadcast journalist

WASHINGTON AND LEE UNIVERSITY

School of Law

Admissions Contact: Associate Dean for Student Affairs, Susan Palmer
Sydney Lewis Hall, Lexington, VA 24450
Admissions Phone: 540-463-8504 • Admissions Fax: 540-463-8586
Admissions E-mail: lawadm@wlu.edu • Web Address: www.law.wlu.edu

INSTITUTIONAL INFORMATION

Public/Private: Private
Environment: Suburban
Academic Calendar: Semester
Schedule: Full time only
Student/Faculty Ratio: 11:1
Total Faculty: 52
% Part Time: 21
% Female: 15
% Minority: 12

PROGRAMS

Advanced Degrees Offered: None
Combined Degrees Offered: None
Clinical Program Required? No
Clinical Programs: The Prison Practicum, a legal services clinic at a federal women's prison; the Black Lung Administrative/Labor Law clinic; the Virginia Capital Case Clearinghouse, a death-penalty clinic; Public Defender Service; U.S. Attorney's Prosecutorial Clinic; Legal Aid Society; and judicial clerkships in a trial, juvenile and domestic relations, or federal bankruptcy court
Grading System: A, A–, B, B–, C+, C, C–, D+, D, D–, F, I (Incomplete)

STUDENT INFORMATION

Enrollment of Law School: 360
% Male/Female: 58/42
% Full Time: 100
% Full Time That Are International: 1
% Minority: 9
Average Age of Entering Class: 25

RESEARCH FACILITIES

Computers/Workstations Available: 79

EXPENSES/FINANCIAL AID

Annual Tuition: $18,790
Room and Board (On Campus): $6,100
Books and Supplies: $600
Financial Aid Application Deadline: 2/15
Average Grant: $7,000
Average Loan: $18,300
% Receiving Some Sort of Aid: 90
Average Debt: $58,000

ADMISSIONS INFORMATION

Application Fee: $40
Regular Application Deadline: 2/1
Regular Notification: 4/1
Average GPA: 3.4
Range of GPA: 3.2–3.8
Average LSAT: 164
Range of LSAT: 161–166
Transfer Students Accepted? Yes
Other Schools to Which Students Applied: University of Virginia, College of William and Mary, Vanderbilt University, George Washington University, Boston College, Cornell University, Duke University, Georgetown University
Number of Applications Received: 1,282
Number of Applicants Accepted: 488
Number of Applicants Enrolled: 130

EMPLOYMENT INFORMATION

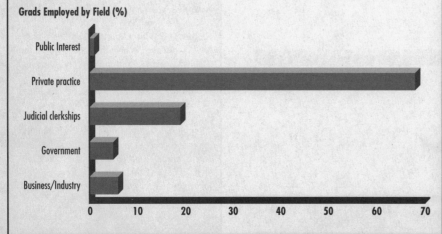

Rate of Placement: 97%
Average Starting Salary: $52,514
State for Bar Exam: VA
Number Taking Bar Exam: 35
Pass Rate for First-Time Bar: 89%

WASHINGTON UNIVERSITY
School of Law

Admissions Contact: Assistant Dean for Admissions and Financial Aid, Janet Laybold Bolin
One Brookings Drive, Campus Box 1120, St. Louis, MO 63130
Admissions Phone: 314-935-4525 • Admissions Fax: 314-935-6493
Admissions E-mail: admiss@wulaw.wustl.edu • Web Address: ls.wustl.edu

INSTITUTIONAL INFORMATION

Public/Private: Private
Environment: Urban
Academic Calendar: Semester
Schedule: Full time only
Student/Faculty Ratio: 16:1
Total Faculty: 124
% Part Time: 62
% Female: 38
% Minority: 3

PROGRAMS

Advanced Degrees Offered: JD (3 years), JSD, LLM, MJS
Combined Degrees Offered: JD/MA in East Asian Studies, Political Science, European Studies, and Islamic Studies; JD/PhD; JD/MBA; JD/MHA; JD/MSW; JD/MS in Engineering and Policy, Economics
Clinical Program Required? No
Grading System: 65–100 with a mandatory median of 82–84

STUDENT INFORMATION

Enrollment of Law School: 607
% Male/Female: 53/47
% Full Time: 100
% Full Time That Are International: 1
% Minority: 21
Average Age of Entering Class: 24

RESEARCH FACILITIES

Computers/Workstations Available: 40

EXPENSES/FINANCIAL AID

Annual Tuition: $25,690
Room and Board (Off Campus): $8,500
Books and Supplies: $1,700
Financial Aid Application Deadline: 3/1
Average Grant: $9,547
Average Loan: $25,000
% of Aid That Is Merit-Based: 100
% Receiving Some Sort of Aid: 75
Average Total Aid Package: $40,000
Average Debt: $60,000

ADMISSIONS INFORMATION

Application Fee: $50
Regular Application Deadline: 3/1
Regular Notification: 4/15
Average GPA: 3.4
Range of GPA: 3.0–3.6
Average LSAT: 161
Range of LSAT: 156–163
Transfer Students Accepted? Yes
Other Schools to Which Students Applied: St. Louis University, Vanderbilt University, Emory University, Northwestern University, Georgetown University, Tulane University, Boston University, University of Iowa
Number of Applications Received: 1,961
Number of Applicants Accepted: 813
Number of Applicants Enrolled: 212

INTERNATIONAL STUDENTS

TOEFL Required of International Students? Yes
Minimum TOEFL: 600

EMPLOYMENT INFORMATION

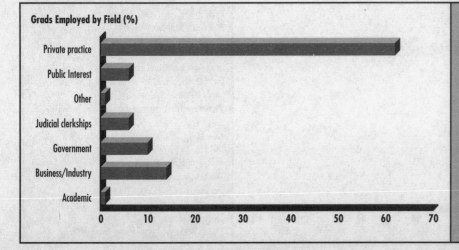

Grads Employed by Field (%)

Rate of Placement: 98%
Average Starting Salary: $50,303
State for Bar Exam: MO
Number Taking Bar Exam: 105
Pass Rate for First-Time Bar: 85%

WAYNE STATE UNIVERSITY
Law School

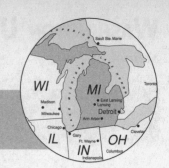

Admissions Contact: Assistant Dean for Recruitment and Admissions, Linda Fowler Sims
468 West Ferry Mall, Detroit, MI 48202
Admissions Phone: 313-577-3937 • Admissions Fax: 313-577-6000
Admissions E-mail: lawinquire@wayne.edu • Web Address: www.law.wayne.edu/

INSTITUTIONAL INFORMATION

Public/Private: Public
Environment: Urban
Academic Calendar: Semester
Schedule: Full time or part time
Total Faculty: 39
% Part Time: 41
% Female: 33
% Minority: 10

PROGRAMS

Advanced Degrees Offered: JD (3 years full time), LLM (1 year full time)
Combined Degrees Offered: JD/MBA (4 years), JD/MA History and Political Science (4 years)
Clinical Program Required? No
Clinical Programs: Free Legal and Clinic, Commercial Law Clinic, Bankruptcy Reorganization Clinic, Criminal Appellate Practice
Grading System: A to E for courses and seminars, High Pass to Fail for Legal Writing

STUDENT INFORMATION

Enrollment of Law School: 746
% Male/Female: 53/47
% Full Time: 70
% Minority: 15
Average Age of Entering Class: 26

EXPENSES/FINANCIAL AID

Annual Tuition (Residents/Nonresidents): $7,038/$14,778
Room and Board: $8,645
Average Grant: $2,000
Average Loan: $8,500
% of Aid That Is Merit-Based: 15
% Receiving Some Sort of Aid: 80
Average Total Aid Package: $20,000
Average Debt: $27,000
Fees Per Credit (Residents/Nonresidents): $230/$488

ADMISSIONS INFORMATION

Application Fee: $20
Regular Application Deadline: Rolling
Regular Notification: Rolling
Average GPA: 3.2
Range of GPA: 3.0–3.5
Average LSAT: 155
Range of LSAT: 151–159
Transfer Students Accepted? Yes
Other Schools to Which Students Applied: University of Detroit, University of Michigan, Michigan State University, Ohio State University, Thomas M. Cooley Law School, Case Western Reserve University, Loyola University Chicago, DePaul University

INTERNATIONAL STUDENTS

TOEFL Required of International Students? Yes
Minimum TOEFL: 600

EMPLOYMENT INFORMATION

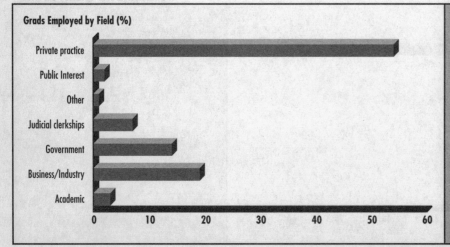

Grads Employed by Field (%)

Rate of Placement: 93%
Average Starting Salary: $42,095
Employers Who Frequently Hire Grads: Leading law firms throughout Michigan; major multinational corporations based in Michigan; federal, state, and local courts and governmental agencies and legal service providers
Prominent Alumni: Hon. Damon J. Keith, Sr., judge U.S. Court of Appeals, 6th Circuit; William Davidson, president, Guardian Industries, Inc. and a principal in the Detroit Pistons and Palace of Auburn Hills; Tyrone Fahner, former Illinois attorney general, now with Mayer, Brown and Platt
State for Bar Exam: MI
Number Taking Bar Exam: 199
Pass Rate for First-Time Bar: 95%

WEST VIRGINIA UNIVERSITY
College of Law

Admissions Contact: Assistant Dean of Admissions and Student Affairs, Janet L. Armistead
PO Box 6130, Morgantown, WV 26506
Admissions Phone: 304-293-5304 • Admissions Fax: 304-293-6891
Admissions E-mail: devince@wvnvm.wvnet.edu • Web Address: www.wvu.edu/~law

INSTITUTIONAL INFORMATION

Public/Private: Public
Environment: Suburban
Academic Calendar: Semester
Schedule: Full time or part time
Student/Faculty Ratio: 16:1
Total Faculty: 51
% Part Time: 4
% Female: 31
% Minority: 4

PROGRAMS

Advanced Degrees Offered: JD (3 years)
Combined Degrees Offered: JD/MPA (4 years),
JD/MBA (4 years)
Clinical Program Required? No
Clinical Programs: Students learn the skills of interviewing, counseling, drafting, litigation planning, negotiation, and trial advocacy. In addition, they confront issues of ethics and the professional role, and handle cases of violence and social security disability.
Grading System: 4.3 scale

STUDENT INFORMATION

Enrollment of Law School: 439
% Male/Female: 58/42
% Full Time: 96
% Minority: 6
Average Age of Entering Class: 26
Number of Applications Received: 610

EXPENSES/FINANCIAL AID

Annual Tuition (Residents/Nonresidents):
$5,296/$12,568
Room and Board (Off Campus): $9,130
Books and Supplies: $853
Average Grant: $4,111
Average Loan: $13,945
% of Aid That Is Merit-Based: 1
% Receiving Some Sort of Aid: 88
Average Total Aid Package: $13,196
Average Debt: $36,373
Fees Per Credit (Residents/Nonresidents):
$258/$662

ADMISSIONS INFORMATION

Application Fee: $45
Regular Application Deadline: Rolling
Regular Notification: Rolling
Average GPA: 3.3
Range of GPA: 3.0–3.7
Average LSAT: 154
Range of LSAT: 150–157
Transfer Students Accepted? Yes
Other Schools to Which Students Applied:
Duquesne University, University of Pittsburgh, Washington and Lee University, University of Dayton, Pennsylvania State University, Georgetown University, University of Virginia, University of Akron
Number of Applications Received: 610

INTERNATIONAL STUDENTS

TOEFL Required of International Students? Yes
Minimum TOEFL: 600

EMPLOYMENT INFORMATION

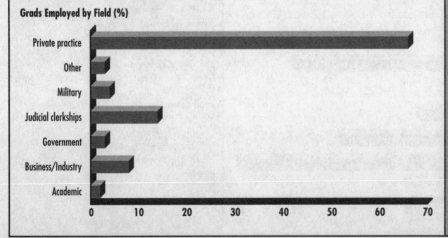

Rate of Placement: 92%
Average Starting Salary: $38,741
Employers Who Frequently Hire Grads: Law firms, government
Prominent Alumni: Major General Kenneth G. Gray; John T. Chambers, president and CEO, Cisco Systems

WESTERN NEW ENGLAND COLLEGE

School of Law

Admissions Contact: Assistant Dean and Director of Admissions, Eric James Eden
1215 Wilbraham Road, Springfield, MA 01119
Admissions Phone: 413-782-1406 • Admissions Fax: 413-796-2067
Admissions E-mail: lawadmis@wnec.edu • Web Address: www.law.wnec.edu

INSTITUTIONAL INFORMATION

Public/Private: Private
Environment: Suburban
Academic Calendar: Semester
Schedule: Full time or part time
Student/Faculty Ratio: 9:1
Total Faculty: 63
% Part Time: 54
% Female: 30
% Minority: 3

PROGRAMS

Combined Degrees Offered: JD/MRP with the University of Massachusetts (4 years), JD/MSW with Springfield College
Clinical Program Required? No
Clinical Programs: Criminal, Legal Services, Discrimination Consumer Protection, Disabilities
Grading System: Numerical system ranging from 99–55, with a minimum of 70 required for graduation. Pass/Fail available for some courses.

STUDENT INFORMATION

Enrollment of Law School: 570
% Male/Female: 50/50
% Full Time: 56
% Minority: 12
Average Age of Entering Class: 27

RESEARCH FACILITIES

Computers/Workstations Available: 40

EXPENSES/FINANCIAL AID

Annual Tuition: $20,589
Room and Board: $9,180
Books and Supplies: $1,100
Average Grant: $4,486
Average Loan: $17,791
% of Aid That Is Merit-Based: 7
% Receiving Some Sort of Aid: 85
Average Total Aid Package: $20,401
Average Debt: $59,983

ADMISSIONS INFORMATION

Application Fee: $45
Regular Application Deadline: Rolling
Regular Notification: Rolling
Average GPA: 3.1
Range of GPA: 2.7–3.4
Average LSAT: 148
Range of LSAT: 142–153
Transfer Students Accepted? Yes
Other Schools to Which Students Applied: New England School of Law, University of Connecticut, Suffolk University, Quinnipiac University, Boston College, Syracuse University, Northeastern University, Boston University
Number of Applications Received: 961
Number of Applicants Accepted: 135
Number of Applicants Enrolled: 55

INTERNATIONAL STUDENTS

TOEFL Required of International Students? Yes

EMPLOYMENT INFORMATION

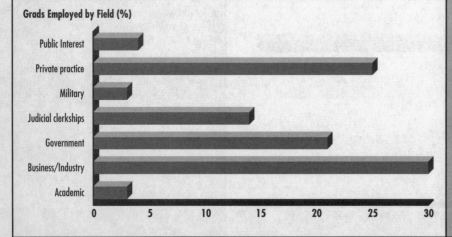

Grads Employed by Field (%)

Rate of Placement: 88%
Average Starting Salary: $39,732
Employers Who Frequently Hire Grads: Law firms (e.g. Skadden, Arps, Slate, Meagher and Flom; Robinson and Cole; Shipman and Goodwin); accounting firms; insurance companies; government agencies
Prominent Alumni: Phillip Harris, partner, Skadden, Arps, Slate, Meagher and Flom; John Greaney, chief, computers and finance section, U.S. Department of Justice, Antitrust Division; Nancy Linck, solicitor, U.S. Patent and Trademark Office

WESTERN STATE UNIVERSITY
College of Law

Admissions Contact: Dean of Admissions, Joel Goodman
1111 North State College Boulevard, Fullerton, CA 92831
Admissions Phone: 714-738-1000 • Admissions Fax: 714-441-1748
Admissions E-mail: adm@wsulaw.edu • Web Address: www.wsulaw.edu

INSTITUTIONAL INFORMATION

Public/Private: Private
Student/Faculty Ratio: 21:1
Total Faculty: 20
% Part Time: 60
% Female: 46
% Minority: 30

PROGRAMS

Academic Specialties: Entrepreneurial Law Center, Professional Skills, Academic Support Program, Academic Success and Enrichment Program
Advanced Degrees Offered: JD (3 years full time, 4 years part time)
Clinical Program Required? Yes
Clinical Programs: 6 units of advanced professional skills—externships and simulation courses—no in-house programs
Grading System: Based on a 4.0 scale
Legal Writing/Methods Course Requirements: Required professional skills courses with upper-division professor

STUDENT INFORMATION

Enrollment of Law School: 600
% Male/Female: 55/45
% Full Time: 50
% Full Time That Are International: 1
% Minority: 35
Average Age of Entering Class: 30

RESEARCH FACILITIES

Computers/Workstations Available: 60
Computers/Work Stations: 1
Campuswide Network? Yes
School-Supported Research Centers: Affiliation with Cal State University—Fullerton

EXPENSES/FINANCIAL AID

Annual Tuition: $20,800
Room and Board (Off Campus): $16,114
Books and Supplies: $810
Financial Aid Application Deadline: 4/14
Average Grant: $14,898
Average Loan: $22,523
% of Aid That Is Merit-Based: 13
% Receiving Some Sort of Aid: 88
Average Total Aid Package: $56,843
Average Debt: $53,069

ADMISSIONS INFORMATION

Application Fee: $50
Regular Application Deadline: Rolling
Regular Notification: Rolling
LSDAS Accepted? Yes
Average GPA: 3.0
Range of GPA: 2.7–3.3
Average LSAT: 148
Range of LSAT: 145–153
Transfer Students Accepted? Yes
Other Schools to Which Students Applied: Chapman University, Whittier University, Southwestern University, Thomas Jefferson School of Law
Other Admissions Factors Considered: Diversity Outreach Program
Number of Applications Received: 1,000
Number of Applicants Accepted: 500
Number of Applicants Enrolled: 200

EMPLOYMENT INFORMATION

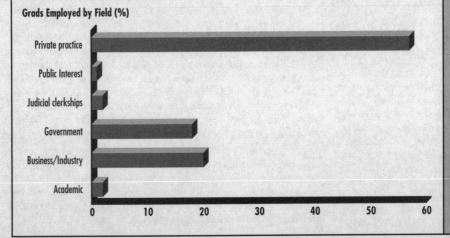

Rate of Placement: 37%
Average Starting Salary: $51,800
Employers Who Frequently Hire Grads: Medium-size law firms; District Attorneys' Offices; Public Defenders' Offices; Corporations

WESTERN STATE UNIVERSITY

AT A GLANCE

The mission of the Western State University College of Law is to provide the highest quality legal education, based on an innovative program of studies designed to develop the tools of careful legal analysis and to foster a broad understanding of law, law practice, and legal theory.

The College of Law emphasizes the study and practice of lawyering skills required for the ethical, skillful, and professional practice of law, and is particularly committed to meeting the educational needs of those who seek to practice in small- to medium-sized law offices, corporate law departments, and governmental and other public service settings. To further its mission, the College of Law will pursue student and faculty diversity, both to enhance the educational program of the school and to address important needs of the legal profession and of society as a whole.

Western State University College of Law became the nation's newest American Bar Association law school in August 1998, when the ABA House of Delegates voted unanimously to grant the law school provisional approval at its annual meeting. Under the terms of provisional approval, the ABA will review and monitor Western State's academic and administrative operations annually for the next two years. The ABA cannot grant full approval upon initial application. Once Western State earns full approval, the ABA will evaluate the law school every seven years.

The Accrediting Commission for Senior Colleges and Universities Western Association of Schools and Colleges has accredited Western State since 1976.

First accredited by the Committee of Bar Examiners of the State Bar of California in 1972, Western State was one of the premier state-accredited law schools for 26 years.

LOCATION AND ENVIRONMENT

Western State is in Orange County, California, midway between Los Angeles and San Diego. With its 42 miles of coastline and easy access to mountain and desert resorts, the region is nirvana for recreation enthusiasts. Winter weekends find our students skiing Snow Summit, windsurfing off Newport, or sipping *cafe lattes* while they watch the sun set over the Pacific.

The campus is situated in Fullerton within the city's university district, home to five institutions of higher education. Outdoor concerts and art exhibits, plays, musical recitals, orchestral and rock concerts, comedians, and lectures on the adjoining Cal State Fullerton campus provide students a welcome break from study. Western State students may also join the University Recreation Services for access to its pools, weight rooms, and basketball and tennis courts.

THE FACILITIES

The new, tri-level library houses classic law volumes side-by-side with a wealth of state-of-the-art electronic resources. Virtually every seat has computer-network ports. Working with remote online databases, CD-ROM services, and research software, our students hone their lawyering skills in this dynamic atmosphere. The law library also maintains a consortium relationship with Cal State, giving our students access to CSUF's 1.5 million–volume collection.

THE ACADEMIC PROGRAM

Western State's hands-on curriculum emphasizes the effective combination of legal theory and professional skills training, which focuses on the techniques and strategies needed for client representation. The faculty tailors specific courses to assist students in bridging the gap between classroom learning and real-time practice. In upper-division electives, professors weave actual courtroom scenarios into the teaching of substantive law via a sequence of integrated advanced-skills texts. Students also have the opportunity to apply their skills training in several externship programs, working directly with a supervising attorney or judge. These one-on-one partnerships give students a crucial insider's perspective into the law as it is actually practiced. The law school's emphasis on professional skills equips graduates with the training necessary for a lifetime of legal practice in a constantly changing environment.

FACULTY

Vital student-teacher interaction enhances the Socratic and case-study methods of teaching. Our faculty members are talented individuals whose personal passions infuse their work and bring the law to life in their classrooms. They are scholars whose articles and books affect the judiciary, have an impact on a wide array of industries, and explore the nature of law and legal education. They are activists and humanitarians committed to their local communities and the world community. But above all, they are committed to teaching and to seeing students succeed.

Because Western State is a small, private school, our professors take a personal interest in their students. They provide constant feedback and they are readily accessible outside the classroom.

Our faculty is also notable for its diversity. As a result, full-time faculty members bring to the program an impressive range of scholarly expertise and life experiences. Western State currently ranks second in California in percentage of women faculty members and in the top 5 percent of ABA law schools in percentage of minority faculty.

STUDENT GROUPS

Western State University College of Law students can enhance their law school education by participating in one of 20 student groups.

CRIMINAL LAW PRACTICE CENTER

Western State University College of Law has created a cutting-edge program that expands the teaching of criminal law far beyond the traditional law school curriculum. The Criminal Law Practice Center (CLPC) brings together in the law school legal scholars, practicing criminal attorneys, prosecutors, legislators, law enforcement officers, and community leaders who contribute a tremendous amount of experience and diversity of perspectives to the educational experience of students. By weaving contemporary societal issues into the criminal law curriculum and providing a forum to examine those issues, the CLPC exposes students to the many facets of the criminal justice system. This fusion of the practical and theoretical is reinforced with course work ranging from advanced criminal trial practice, criminal evidence, and criminal appellate advocacy to seminars on domestic violence and the death penalty.

Students enrolled in the CLPC have the opportunity to research and write scholarly articles and to participate in public policy and legislative development discussions. At the same time, they develop working relations with prominent criminal defense attorneys, prosecutors, and judges. Students also participate in police "ride-alongs"; visit the county jail, coroner's office and crime lab; and tour state and federal courts as part of their overview of the actual day-to-day workings of the criminal justice system.

ENTREPRENEURIAL LAW CENTER

Western State University College of Law has created a client-centered legal studies program for law students who want to acquire the specialized skills necessary to represent and guide small businesses and entrepreneurs. This law school program is the first of its kind at a California law school. The Entrepreneurial Law Center (ELC), which offers WSU students a curriculum focused on the effective representation, guidance, and leadership of small or start-up businesses, is a response to the continuing explosion of small businesses in California. News reports indicate that small, start-up, or entrepreneurial businesses are an important trend of the future. In 1997, according to the U.S. Small Business Administration, 99.2 percent of California's 837,802 businesses with employees fall in the category of "small business."

The Entrepreneurial Law Center is a natural extension of the College of Law's innovative skills curriculum. Because many business lawyers spend little, if any, time in court, students focus on developing competence in transactional matters such as drafting and negotiating contracts and other types of legal documents and counseling clients. An important goal of the program is learning "preventive law" to help clients avoid litigation.

College of Law

Many Western State students already have a keen understanding of the business world. Their interest in law is often inspired by their professional experience. Coupling those prior experiences with the ELC curriculum will provide these graduates with a combination of legal skills, theory, and practical experiences for entering the field of business law or even reentering the world of business.

EXTERNSHIPS

Externships offer hands-on experience. Students have the opportunity to translate their training into real-world experience by participating in externships with appellate and trial judges in federal and state courts, the Attorney General's Office, district attorneys, public defenders, and lawyers in a variety of private- and public-interest practices. Students in the externship programs spend 15 to 40 hours a week working directly with a supervising attorney or judge. This one-on-one partnership gives the extern a crucial insider's perspective into the law as it is actually practiced. Our students do far more than merely observe. By making decisions that affect real people, Western State's students gain confidence quickly.

TUITION

- Full time: $21,840 per year
- Part time: $7,350 per semester
- Summer Session: $735 per unit

FINANCIAL AID DEPARTMENT

Western State University participates in financial assistance programs to help students finance their law study. The Financial Assistance Office, helps students obtain loans and scholarships from state, federal, institutional, and private funding sources. Our Financial Assistance Handbook supplies detailed information on the types of assistance available. It also includes a calendar of important deadlines.

Because financial assistance guidelines and programs change frequently, students should maintain regular contact with the financial assistance staff. Look for new information on the financial assistance bulletin board or on the website.

It is imperative that students and applicants who anticipate a need for financial assistance arrange an appointment as soon as possible to avoid unnecessary delays and funding limitations. Applicants to Western State should begin their financial assistance paperwork immediately. Western State strongly recommends early application.

The Office of Financial Aid may be reached by dialing 714-738-1000, ext. 2350 or by e-mailing wsu406@wsulaw.edu.

ADMISSIONS PROCESS AND REQUIREMENTS

The Admissions Committee bases its judgment on all of the information available; no one item, such as the LSAT score, grades, or letters of recommendation, is conclusive. Western State grants to each applicant a full and careful review of the information submitted. Western State strives for a diverse student body and seeks to admit individuals who through their personal, intellectual, or professional background and experience will contribute to the diversity of the law school community, the legal profession, and society as a whole. Western State uses an inclusive philosophy in reviewing candidates for admission. The Admissions Committee views the diversity of the student body broadly. For example, it might view the following applicants as potentially contributing to the diversity of the student body: an applicant who has struggled against adversity or other social hardships; an applicant who possesses unusual career goals, employment history, or educational background (including graduate study); or an applicant who demonstrates unusual extracurricular achievement (including school or community service). The Committee will consider any of these areas, or others, that an applicant wishes to have considered on a voluntary basis. Applicants should submit information in writing to the Admissions Office as part of the application package.

While the Committee reviews each application on an individual basis, applicants with strong academic records and high test scores are the most likely to gain admission. The Admission Committee's primary concern is with the applicant's potential as a law student. The Committee will review an applicant's college grades, academic major, selection of courses, and significant academic achievements. The Committee considers the average LSAT score(s). When LSAT score(s) submitted are for exams taken more than five years prior to application, it is usually the policy of the Committee to require a candidate to sit for the test again.

Personal statements are given careful attention as a source of more complete and detailed information about the applicant. The Committee is particularly interested in the applicant's motivation to study law, future career plans, and clarification of any weaknesses in the academic record. The personal statement also serves as a sample of the applicant's writing ability.

Letters of recommendation are used as an evaluation of an applicant's academic potential and to further the information available about the applicant. The faculty members of the Admissions Committee highly value the insight and evaluation provided by those who write the letters of recommendation.

Applications for the first-year class are accepted for the fall and spring semesters. Transfer students who seek admission may apply either semester. Admissions offers are made on a rolling basis as soon as files are complete and ready for review.

If you have any questions about the admissions process, please contact the Admissions Office at 714-738-1000, ext. 2600.

APPLICATION INSTRUCTIONS

To be considered for admission to Western State University College of Law, each applicant must submit:

1. An application with all requested information and applicant's signature
2. An official copy of applicant's LSDAS report
3. Two letters of recommendation via LSDAS or mailed directly to WSU
4. A personal statement

Transfer applicants have the following additional requirements:

1. A statement of reasons for requesting the transfer
2. An official transcript of all work taken at the previous law school(s)
3. A letter of from the dean or the registrar at the current or last attended law school verifying student was in good standing
4. A letter of recommendation from a professor at the current or last attended law school

Additional information may be rquested upon review of the file.

Admissions Contact: Dean of Admissions, Joel Goodman
1111 North State College Boulevard, Fullerton, CA 92831
Admissions Phone: 714-738-1000 • Admissions Fax: 714-441-1748
Admissions E-mail: adm@wsulaw.edu
Web Address: www.wsulaw.edu

WHITTIER COLLEGE
Whittier Law School

Admissions Contact: Director of Admissions, Alexis Boles
3333 Harbor Boulevard, Costa Mesa, CA 92626
Admissions Phone: 714-444-4141 • Admissions Fax: 714-444-0250
Admissions E-mail: info@law.whittier.edu • Web Address: www.law.whittier.edu

INSTITUTIONAL INFORMATION

Public/Private: Private
Environment: Urban
Academic Calendar: 4-1-4
Schedule: Full time or part time
Student/Faculty Ratio: 18:1
Total Faculty: 29
% Part Time: 29
% Female: 11
% Minority: 18

PROGRAMS

Academic Specialties: Health Law Symposium, International Law Symposium, Center for Children's Rights, Intellectual Property
Advanced Degrees Offered: JD (3 years full time, 4 years part time), LLM Foreign Legal Studies (24 credits, 1 year)
Clinical Program Required? No
Clinical Programs: Externship program allows students to receive academic credit for work performed in trial/appellate courts and government agencies.
Grading System: Letter and numerical system on a 100-point scale. Cumulative grade of 77 required for good standing.
Legal Writing/Methods Course Requirements: 5 units of legal writing are required for graduation

STUDENT INFORMATION

Enrollment of Law School: 660
% Male/Female: 48/52
% Full Time: 58
% Full Time That Are International: 2
% Minority: 39
Average Age of Entering Class: 26

RESEARCH FACILITIES

Computers/Workstations Available: 75
School-Supported Research Centers: Whittier College undergraduate resources

EXPENSES/FINANCIAL AID

Annual Tuition: $21,900
Room and Board (Off Campus): $9,325
Books and Supplies: $675
Financial Aid Application Deadline: 4/15
Average Grant: $10,250
Average Loan: $27,600
% of Aid That Is Merit-Based: 96
% Receiving Some Sort of Aid: 90
Average Total Aid Package: $21,000
Average Debt: $71,573
Fees Per Credit: $701

ADMISSIONS INFORMATION

Application Fee: $50
Regular Application Deadline: Rolling
Regular Notification: Rolling
LSDAS Accepted? Yes
Average GPA: 2.9
Range of GPA: 2.5–3.3
Average LSAT: 150
Range of LSAT: 146–152
Transfer Students Accepted? Yes
Other Schools to Which Students Applied: Southwestern University, UCLA School of Law, Loyola Marymount University, University of Southern California, Pepperdine University, California Western, University of San Diego, Golden Gate University
Other Admissions Factors Considered: Maturity, capacity for self-discipline, work record, year-to-year progress in college, courses completed, graduate work, employment, participation in student organizations and/or volunteer work
Number of Applications Received: 1,275
Number of Applicants Accepted: 834

INTERNATIONAL STUDENTS

TOEFL Required of International Students? Yes
Minimum TOEFL: 550

EMPLOYMENT INFORMATION

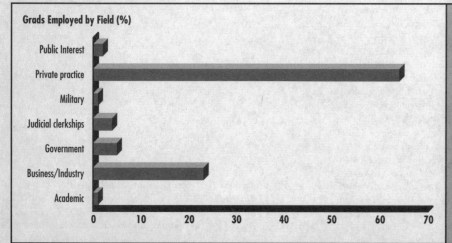

Grads Employed by Field (%)

Rate of Placement: 88%
Average Starting Salary: $51,479
Prominent Alumni: Miriam Vogel, justice, California Court of Appeals; Regina Shanney-Saborsky, partner, Mitchell, Silberberg and Knupp; Diane Tebelius, assistant U.S. attorney
State for Bar Exam: CA
Number Taking Bar Exam: 109
Pass Rate for First-Time Bar: 42%

WIDENER UNIVERSITY
School of Law, Delaware Campus

Admissions Contact: Assistant Dean for Admissions, Barbara Ayars
4601 Concord Pike, Wilmington, DE 19803
Admissions Phone: 888-943-3637 • Admissions Fax: 302-477-2224
Admissions E-mail: law.admissions@law.widener.edu • Web Address: www.law.widener.edu

INSTITUTIONAL INFORMATION
Public/Private: Private
Environment: Urban
Academic Calendar: Semester
Schedule: Full time or part time
Total Faculty: 92
% Part Time: 41
% Female: 33
% Minority: 2

PROGRAMS
Academic Specialties: Health Law (Health Law Institute), Corporate Law and Finance, Environmental Law (Environmental Law Clinic), Intellectual Property, Constitutional Law (H. Albert Young Fellowship), International Law, Trial Advocacy (Intensive Trial Advocacy Program). Curriculum Strengths include Health Law, Corporate Law, International Law, Environmental Law, and Trial Advocacy, as evidenced by the number of courses offered in these areas.
Advanced Degrees Offered: LLM Corporate Law and Finance (24 credits), LLM Health Law (24 credits), MJ (30 credits), SJD Health Law, DL Health Law
Combined Degrees Offered: JD/PsyD (6 years), JD/MBA (4 years), JD/Master of Marine Policy in conjunction with University of Delaware Graduate College of Marine Studies
Clinical Program Required? No
Clinical Programs: Consumer Credit, Civil Law, Domestic Violence, Environmental Law, Criminal Defense

Grading System: 4.00 to 0.00 (A to F)
Legal Writing/Methods Course Requirements: 2 courses taken in the first 2 semesters of law school, 3 credits each

STUDENT INFORMATION
Enrollment of Law School: 1,112
% Male/Female: 52/48
% Full Time: 55
% Full Time That Are International: 2
% Minority: 9
Average Age of Entering Class: 27

RESEARCH FACILITIES
Computers/Workstations Available: 80
School-Supported Research Centers: Computer labs available on the main campus in Chester

EXPENSES/FINANCIAL AID
Annual Tuition: $20,200
Room and Board: $7,500
Books and Supplies: $1,000
Financial Aid Application Deadline: 3/1
Average Grant: $6,442
Average Loan: $19,303
% of Aid That Is Merit-Based: 85
% Receiving Some Sort of Aid: 39
Average Total Aid Package: $20,460
Average Debt: $53,336
Fees Per Credit: $620

ADMISSIONS INFORMATION
Application Fee: $60
Regular Application Deadline: 5/15
Regular Notification: Rolling
LSDAS Accepted? Yes
Average GPA: 3.0
Range of GPA: 2.7–3.2
Average LSAT: 147
Range of LSAT: 145–151
Transfer Students Accepted? Yes
Other Schools to Which Students Applied: Temple University, New York Law School, Rutgers University—Camden, Pennsylvania State University, Seton Hall University, University of Baltimore, New England School of Law, Quinnipiac University
Other Admissions Factors Considered: The admissions committee reviews each applicant's entire file, including all material submitted in support of the application. The committee considers the personal essay, work experience, life experiences, extracurricular activities, and letters of recommendation.
Number of Applications Received: 1,305
Number of Applicants Enrolled: 375

INTERNATIONAL STUDENTS
Minimum TOEFL: 600

EMPLOYMENT INFORMATION

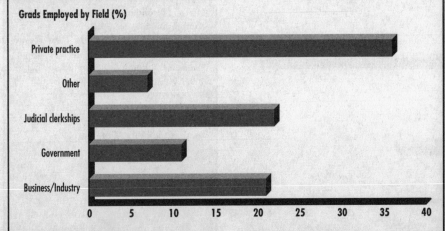

Grads Employed by Field (%)

Private practice
Other
Judicial clerkships
Government
Business/Industry

0 5 10 15 20 25 30 35 40

Rate of Placement: 91%
Average Starting Salary: $42,665
Employers Who Frequently Hire Grads: Law firms, judges, and other government employers
Prominent Alumni: Fred DiBona, president of Independence Blue Cross of the state of Pennsylvania; Andrew Jefferson, CEO, Ameristar Technologies, Hon. Paul R. Panepinto, administrative judge, Philadelphia Family Court
State for Bar Exam: PA
Number Taking Bar Exam: 66
Pass Rate for First-Time Bar: 69%

WIDENER UNIVERSITY
School of Law, Pennsylvania Campus

Admissions Contact: Assistant Dean of Admissions, Barbara Ayars
3800 Vartan Way, Harrisburg, PA 17110-9450
Admissions Phone: 888-943-3637 • Admissions Fax: 717-541-3999
Admissions E-mail: law.admissions@law.widener.edu • Web Address: www.law.widener.edu

INSTITUTIONAL INFORMATION

Public/Private: Private
Student/Faculty Ratio: 17:1
Total Faculty: 37
% Part Time: 43
% Female: 41
% Minority: 3

PROGRAMS

Academic Specialties: Administrative Law, Constitutional Law, Trial Advocacy, Law and Government, Public Interest Law, Legislation/Legislative Drafting
Clinical Program Required? No
Clinical Programs: Environmental Law, Public Interest Law, Civil Law
Grading System: 4.0 to 0.0 (A to F)
Legal Writing/Methods Course Requirements: 2 courses taken in the first 2 semesters, 3 credits each

STUDENT INFORMATION

Enrollment of Law School: 383
% Male/Female: 55/45
% Full Time: 60
% Minority: 17
Average Age of Entering Class: 28

RESEARCH FACILITIES

Computers/Workstations Available: 31

EXPENSES/FINANCIAL AID

Annual Tuition: $20,200
Room and Board (Off Campus): $7,500
Books and Supplies: $1,000
Financial Aid Application Deadline: 3/1
Average Grant: $6,647
Average Loan: $19,601
% of Aid That Is Merit-Based: 82
% Receiving Some Sort of Aid: 40
Average Total Aid Package: $20,959
Average Debt: $55,742

ADMISSIONS INFORMATION

Application Fee: $60
Regular Application Deadline: 5/15
Regular Notification: Rolling
Average GPA: 2.9
Range of GPA: 2.7–3.2
Average LSAT: 147
Range of LSAT: 143–151
Transfer Students Accepted? Yes
Other Schools to Which Students Applied: Temple University, Pennsylvania State University, Rutgers University—Camden, University of Baltimore, Seton Hall University, New England School of Law, New York Law School, Quinnipiac University
Number of Applications Received: 607
Number of Applicants Enrolled: 145

INTERNATIONAL STUDENTS

Minimum TOEFL: 600

EMPLOYMENT INFORMATION

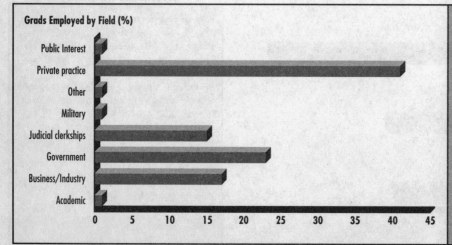

Grads Employed by Field (%)

Rate of Placement: 87%
Average Starting Salary: $37,379
Employers Who Frequently Hire Grads: Law firms, judges, and other government employers
Prominent Alumni: Pennsylvania State Representatives David Mayernick, Mark Cohen, Terry E. VanHorn
State for Bar Exam: PA
Number Taking Bar Exam: 169
Pass Rate for First-Time Bar: 59%

WILLAMETTE UNIVERSITY
College of Law

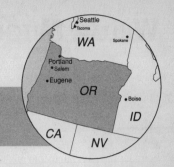

Admissions Contact: Director of Admissions, Lawrence Seno Jr.
900 State Street, Salem, OR 97301
Admissions Phone: 503-370-6282 • Admissions Fax: 503-370-6375
Admissions E-mail: law-admission@willamette.edu • Web Address: www.willamette.edu/wucl

INSTITUTIONAL INFORMATION

Public/Private: Private
Affiliation: Historically related to United Methodist Church
Environment: Urban
Academic Calendar: Semester
Schedule: Full time only
Student/Faculty Ratio: 18:1
Total Faculty: 28
% Part Time: 43
% Female: 32
% Minority: 1

PROGRAMS

Academic Specialties: Law and Government, International Law
Advanced Degrees Offered: None
Clinical Program Required? No
Clinical Programs: Live-client Clinic internship programs
Grading System: Letter grades A to F
Legal Writing/Methods Course Requirements:
2 semesters, 2 hours per semester

STUDENT INFORMATION

Enrollment of Law School: 416
% Male/Female: 55/45
% Full Time: 98
% Full Time That Are International: 1
% Minority: 13
Average Age of Entering Class: 26

RESEARCH FACILITIES

Computer Labs: 2

EXPENSES/FINANCIAL AID

Annual Tuition: $18,300
Room and Board: $9,950
Books and Supplies: $1,250
Average Grant: $8,000
Average Loan: $20,638
% of Aid That Is Merit-Based: 15
% Receiving Some Sort of Aid: 94
Average Total Aid Package: $24,758
Average Debt: $66,428

ADMISSIONS INFORMATION

Application Fee: $50
Regular Application Deadline: 4/1
LSDAS Accepted? No
Average GPA: 3.1
Range of GPA: 2.9–3.5
Average LSAT: 154
Range of LSAT: 150–157
Transfer Students Accepted? Yes
Other Schools to Which Students Applied:
Lewis and Clark College, University of Oregon, University of Washington, Seattle University
Other Admissions Factors Considered: Some additional consideration is given to candidates who have strong ties to Oregon or to the Pacific Northwest and who intend to practice in the state or region.
Number of Applications Received: 715
Number of Applicants Accepted: 467
Number of Applicants Enrolled: 150

INTERNATIONAL STUDENTS

TOEFL Required of International Students? Yes
Minimum TOEFL: 575

EMPLOYMENT INFORMATION

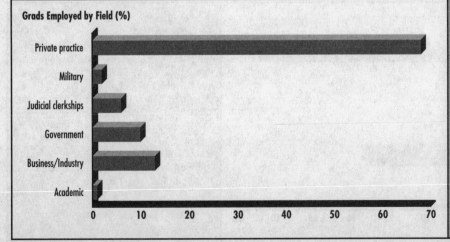

Average Starting Salary: $43,858
Employers Who Frequently Hire Grads: Stoel Rives; Marion, Lane, and Pierce Counties; Schwabe, Williamson & Wyatt; Lane Powell; Dunn Carney
Prominent Alumni: Honorable Wallace P. Carson Jr., chief justice Oregon Supreme Court; Honorable Caroline Glassman, justice, Maine Supreme Court; Bruce Botelho, attorney general of Alaska
State for Bar Exam: WY
Number Taking Bar Exam: 33
Pass Rate for First-Time Bar: 64%

WILLIAM MITCHELL COLLEGE OF LAW

Admissions Contact: Dean of Students, Dr. James H. Brooks
875 Summit Avenue, St. Paul, MN 55105
Admissions Phone: 612-290-6329 • Admissions Fax: 612-290-7535
Admissions E-mail: admissions@wmitchell.edu • Web Address: www.wmitchell.edu

INSTITUTIONAL INFORMATION

Public/Private: Private
Environment: Urban
Academic Calendar: Semester
Schedule: Full time or part time
Total Faculty: 245
% Part Time: 85
% Female: 38

PROGRAMS

Academic Specialties: Specialties in skills, IP, Business/Commercial, Tort, and Tax; strengths in lawyering skills and clinic programs
Advanced Degrees Offered: LLM Taxation (2 years part time)
Clinical Program Required? No
Clinical Programs: Business Law Clinic, Civil Advocacy Clinic, Criminal Appeals Clinic, Immigration Clinic, Legal Assistance to Minnesota Prisoners, Misdemeanor Clinic, Administrative Law Clinic, Attorney General Clinic, Civil and Human Rights Clinic, Court of Appeals
Grading System: Letter and numerical system on a 4.0 scale
Legal Writing/Methods Course Requirements: Research, Writing and Reasoning, small groups of approximately 13 students

STUDENT INFORMATION

Enrollment of Law School: 1,019
% Male/Female: 52/48
% Full Time: 51
% Full Time That Are International: 1
% Minority: 10
Average Age of Entering Class: 25

RESEARCH FACILITIES

Computers/Workstations Available: 81
School-Supported Research Centers: None

EXPENSES/FINANCIAL AID

Annual Tuition: $19,000
Books and Supplies: $725
Average Grant: $3,846
Average Loan: $17,642
% of Aid That Is Merit-Based: 9
% Receiving Some Sort of Aid: 91
Average Total Aid Package: $18,364
Average Debt: $54,661
Fees Per Credit: $750

ADMISSIONS INFORMATION

Application Fee: $45
Regular Application Deadline: 6/30
Regular Notification: Rolling
LSDAS Accepted? Yes
Average GPA: 3.2
Range of GPA: 2.8–3.5
Average LSAT: 152
Range of LSAT: 148–156
Transfer Students Accepted? Yes
Other Schools to Which Students Applied: Hamline University, University of Minnesota, Drake University, University of Wisconsin, University of North Dakota, Marquette University, University of Iowa
Other Admissions Factors Considered: Motivation, interpersonal skills, work experience, extracurricular activities, community service, overcoming disadvantage
Number of Applications Received: 972
Number of Applicants Accepted: 638
Number of Applicants Enrolled: 352

INTERNATIONAL STUDENTS

TOEFL Required of International Students? Yes
Minimum TOEFL: 600

EMPLOYMENT INFORMATION

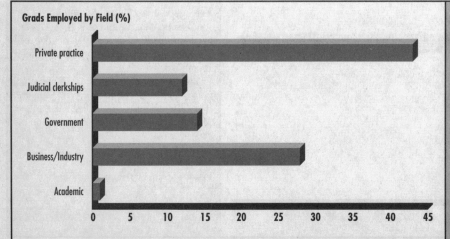

Grads Employed by Field (%)

Rate of Placement: 94%
Average Starting Salary: $42,601
Employers Who Frequently Hire Grads: Briggs and Morgan; Robins, Kaplan, Miller and Ciresi; Gray, Plant, Mooty; The St. Paul Companies; Merchant and Gould
Prominent Alumni: Warren E. Burger, chief justice of U.S.; Justice Rosalie Wahl, Minnesota Supreme Court (retired); Chief Justice Douglas Amdahl, Minnesota Supreme Court (retired)
State for Bar Exam: MN
Number Taking Bar Exam: 183
Pass Rate for First-Time Bar: 85%

YALE UNIVERSITY
Yale Law School

Admissions Contact: Associate Director of Admissions, Lauretta Tremblay
PO Box 208329, New Haven, CT 06520-8329
Admissions Phone: 203-432-4995 • Admissions Fax: 203-432-7093
Admissions E-mail: admissions@mail.law.yale.edu • Web Address: www.law.yale.edu

INSTITUTIONAL INFORMATION

Public/Private: Private
Environment: Urban
Academic Calendar: Semester
Schedule: Full time only
Total Faculty: 117
% Part Time: 55
% Female: 24
% Minority: 12

PROGRAMS

Advanced Degrees Offered: JD (3 years), LLM (1 year), MSL (1 year), JSD (up to 5 years)
Combined Degrees Offered: JD/PhD History, JD/PhD Political Science, JD/MS Forestry, JD/MS Sociology, JD/MS Statistics, JD/MBA (with Yale School of Management), and others
Clinical Program Required? No
Grading System: Honors (work done in the course is significantly superior), Pass (successful performance of the work in the course), Low Pass (work done in the course is below the level of performance), Credit (indicates that the course has been completed satisfactorily without further specification of level of performance), Failure (no credit is given for the course)

STUDENT INFORMATION

Enrollment of Law School: 593
% Male/Female: 57/43
% Full Time: 100
% Full Time That Are International: 2
% Minority: 33
Average Age of Entering Class: 25

EXPENSES/FINANCIAL AID

Annual Tuition: $26,950
Books and Supplies: $780
Average Grant: $9,300
Average Loan: $22,500
% Receiving Some Sort of Aid: 75
Average Debt: $58,000

ADMISSIONS INFORMATION

Application Fee: $65
Regular Application Deadline: 2/15
Regular Notification: Rolling
LSDAS Accepted? Yes
Average GPA: 3.8
Range of GPA: 3.8–4.0
Average LSAT: 171
Range of LSAT: 168–175
Transfer Students Accepted? Yes
Other Admissions Factors Considered: TOEFL is required for foreign applicants to LLM program
Number of Applications Received: 3,215

EMPLOYMENT INFORMATION

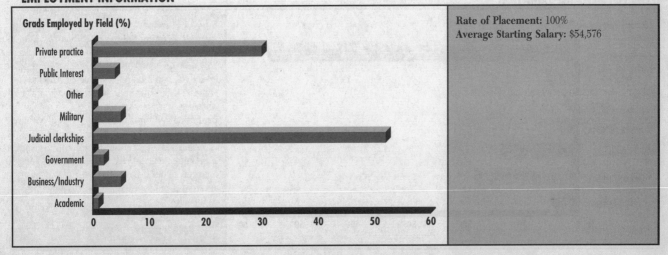

Rate of Placement: 100%
Average Starting Salary: $54,576

YESHIVA UNIVERSITY
Benjamin N. Cardozo School of Law

Admissions Contact: Director of Admissions, Robert L. Schwartz
55 5th Avenue, New York, NY 10003
Admissions Phone: 212-790-0274 • Admissions Fax: 212-790-0482
Admissions E-mail: lawinfo@ymail.yu.edu • Web Address: www.cardozo.yu.edu

INSTITUTIONAL INFORMATION

Public/Private: Private
Affiliation: Jewish
Environment: Urban
Academic Calendar: Semester
Schedule: Full time only
Student/Faculty Ratio: 17:1
Total Faculty: 104
% Part Time: 54
% Female: 31
% Minority: 4

PROGRAMS

Academic Specialties: Faculty specialties are broad and diverse, and the faculty is particularly deep in Intellectual Property, Corporate Law, Criminal Law and Litigation, and Legal Theory.
Advanced Degrees Offered: JD (3 academic years, or 2.5 years, or 2 academic years and 2 summers), LLM Intellectual Property Law and General Studies (1 year)
Combined Degrees Offered: JD/MSW (about 4 years), JD/MA (about 4 years)
Clinical Program Required? No
Clinical Programs: 15 clinical programs offered
Grading System: A+ to D by third (i.e. A+, A, A–) then F. A curve applies in all 1L and large upper-level classes.
Legal Writing/Methods Course Requirements: 1-year, small-group legal writing course; semester-long legal methods course

STUDENT INFORMATION

Enrollment of Law School: 915
% Male/Female: 52/48
% Full Time: 100
% Minority: 21
Average Age of Entering Class: 23

RESEARCH FACILITIES

Computers/Workstations Available: 55
School-Supported Research Centers: Students may take courses and use the facilities at other divisions of Yeshiva University and at the neighboring New School University. Library has cooperative on-site access arrangements with other area academic libraries.

EXPENSES/FINANCIAL AID

Annual Tuition: $23,936
Room and Board (Off Campus): $18,133
Books and Supplies: $960
Financial Aid Application Deadline: 4/15
Average Grant: $5,000
Average Loan: $2,000
% of Aid That Is Merit-Based: 41
% Receiving Some Sort of Aid: 70
Average Total Aid Package: $22,000
Average Debt: $70,000
Fees Per Credit: $985

ADMISSIONS INFORMATION

Application Fee: $60
Regular Application Deadline: 4/1
Regular Notification: Rolling
LSDAS Accepted? Yes
Average GPA: 3.3
Range of GPA: 2.2–4.1
Average LSAT: 157
Range of LSAT: 154–159
Transfer Students Accepted? Yes
Other Schools to Which Students Applied: Brooklyn Law School, Fordham University, New York University, New York Law School, Columbia University, St. John's University, Boston University, George Washington University
Number of Applications Received: 2,506
Number of Applicants Accepted: 1,075
Number of Applicants Enrolled: 347

EMPLOYMENT INFORMATION

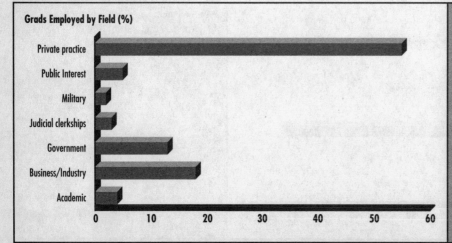

Grads Employed by Field (%)

Rate of Placement: 96%
Average Starting Salary: $60,378
Employers Who Frequently Hire Grads: Law firms in New York metropolitan area; federal, state, and local judges; District Attorneys' Offices; federal, state, and local government agencies
Prominent Alumni: Hon. Sandra Feuerstein, New York State Supreme Court judge, Clifton Elgarten, partner, Crowell and Morning, former U.S. Supreme Court clerk. These graduates are examples of our distinguished alumni who have achieved prominence in all facets of the legal community.
State for Bar Exam: NY
Pass Rate for First-Time Bar: 74%

York University
Osgoode Hall Law School

Admissions Contact: Admissions Coordinator, Ms. Louise Resendes
4700 Keele Street, York, ON M3J IP3 Canada
Admissions Phone: 416-736-6571 • Admissions Fax: 416-736-5736
Admissions E-mail: admit@yorku.ca • Web Address: www.yorku.ca/osgoode

INSTITUTIONAL INFORMATION

Public/Private: Private
Total Faculty: 55

PROGRAMS

Advanced Degrees Offered: LLM, DJUR
Combined Degrees Offered: LLB/MBA (4 years)
Clinical Program Required? No
Clinical Programs: Public, Criminal, Housing, Immigration
Grading System: A+, A, B+, B, etc.

STUDENT INFORMATION

Enrollment of Law School: 825
% Male/Female: 48/52
% Full Time: 100
Average Age of Entering Class: 25

EXPENSES/FINANCIAL AID

Annual Tuition: $3,400
% of Aid That Is Merit-Based: 10
% Receiving Some Sort of Aid: 10

ADMISSIONS INFORMATION

Application Fee: $75
Regular Application Deadline: 11/1
Regular Notification: Rolling
Average GPA: 3.7
Range of GPA: 3.3–4.3
Average LSAT: 75
Transfer Students Accepted? No
Other Schools to Which Students Applied: University of Toronto
Number of Applications Received: 2,413
Number of Applicants Accepted: 217
Number of Applicants Enrolled: 141

EMPLOYMENT INFORMATION

Province for Bar Exam: ON (Ontario)
Number Taking Bar Exam: 300
Pass Rate for First-Time Bar: 98%

INDEXES

ALPHABETICAL LIST OF SCHOOLS

A

Albany Law School	100
American University	101-103
Arizona State University	104

B

Baylor University	105
Boston College	106
Boston University	107
Brigham Young University	108
Brooklyn Law School	109

C

Cal Northern School of Law	110
California Pacific School of Law	111
California Western School of Law	112-114
Campbell University	115
Capital University	116
Case Western Reserve University	117
Catholic University of America	118
City University of New York	119
Cleveland State University	120
College of William & Mary	121
Columbia University	122
Cornell University	123
Creighton University	124

D

Dalhousie University	125
DePaul University	126-128
Drake University	129
Duke University	130
Duquesne University	131

E

Emory University	132
Empire College	133

F

Florida Coastal School of Law	134
Florida State University	135
Fordham University	136
Franklin Pierce Law Center	137

G

George Mason University	138
George Washington University	139
Georgetown University	140
Georgia State University	141
Golden Gate University	142-144
Gonzaga University	145

H

Hamline University	146
Harvard University	147
Hofstra University	148-150
Howard University	151
Humphreys College	152

I

Illinois Institute of Technology	153
Indiana University—Bloomington	154
Indiana University—Indianapolis	155

J

John F. Kennedy University	156
The John Marshall Law School	157-159

L

Lewis and Clark College	160
Lincoln Law School of Sacramento	161
Louisiana State University	162
Loyola Marymount University	163
Loyola University Chicago	164
Loyola University New Orleans	165

M

Marquette University	166
Mercer University	167
Michigan State University	168
Mississippi College	169
Monterey College of Law	170

N

New College of California	171
New England School of Law	172
New York Law School	173
New York University	174
North Carolina Central University	175
Northeastern University	176
Northern Illinois University	177
Northern Kentucky University	178
Northwestern University	179-181
Nova Southeastern University	182

O

Ohio Northern University	183
Ohio State University	184
Oklahoma City University	185

P

Pace University	186
Pennsylvania State University	187
Pepperdine University	188-190

Q

Queen's University	191
Quinnipiac University	192

R

Regent University   193
Roger Williams University   194
Rutgers University—Camden   195
Rutgers University—Newark   196

S

St. John's University   197
St. Louis University   198
St. Mary's University   199
St. Thomas University   200
Samford University   201
San Francisco Law School   202
San Joaquin College of Law   203
Santa Barbara College of Law   204
Santa Clara University   205
Seattle University   206
Seton Hall University   207
South Texas College of Law   208
Southern California
   Institute of Law   209
Southern Illinois University   210
Southern Methodist University   211
Southern University   212
Southwestern University   213
Stanford University   214
Stetson University   215
Suffolk University   216
Syracuse University   217

T

Temple University   218
Texas Southern University   219
Texas Tech University   220
Texas Wesleyan University   221
Thomas Jefferson School of Law   222
Thomas M. Cooley Law School   223
Touro College   224
Tulane University   225

U

UCLA School of Law   226
University at Buffalo, State
   University of New York   227
University of Akron   228
University of Alabama   229
University of Arizona   230
University of Arkansas—
   Fayetteville   231

University of Arkansas—
   Little Rock   232
University of Baltimore   233
University of British Columbia   234
University of Calgary   235
University of California   236
University of California—Berkeley 237
University of California—Davis   238
University of Chicago   239
University of Cincinnati   240
University of Colorado   241
University of Connecticut   242
University of Dayton   243
University of Denver   244
University of Detroit Mercy   245
University of Florida   246
University of Georgia   247
University of Hawaii—Manoa   248
University of Houston   249
University of Idaho   250
University of Illinois   251
University of Iowa   252
University of Kansas   253
University of Kentucky   254
University of La Verne   255
University of Louisville   256
University of Maryland   257
University of Memphis   258
University of Miami   259
University of Michigan   260
University of Minnesota   261
University of Mississippi
   School of Law   262
University of Missouri—Columbia 263
University of Missouri—
   Kansas City   264
University of Montana   265
University of Nebraska—Lincoln   266
University of New Mexico   267
University of North Carolina—
   Chapel Hill   268
University of North Dakota   269
University of Notre Dame   270
University of Oklahoma   271
University of Oregon   272
University of Pennsylvania   273
University of Pittsburgh   274
University of Richmond   275
University of San Diego   276
University of San Francisco   277
University of South Carolina   278
University of South Dakota   279
University of Southern California 280
University of Southern Maine   281
University of Tennessee   282
University of Texas—Austin   283
University of the District
   of Columbia   284
University of the Pacific   285
University of Toledo   286-288
University of Toronto   289
University of Tulsa   290
University of Utah   291
University of Victoria   292
University of Virginia   293
University of Washington   294
University of West Los Angeles 295-297

University of Windsor   298
University of Wisconsin   299
University of Wyoming   300

V

Valparaiso University   301
Vanderbilt University   302-304
Ventura College of Law   305
Vermont Law School   306
Villanova University   307

W

Wake Forest University   308
Washburn University   309
Washington and Lee University   310
Washington University   311
Wayne State University   312
West Virginia University   313
Western New England College   314
Western State University   315-317
Whittier College   318
Widener University (DE)   319
Widener University (PA)   320
Willamette University   321
William Mitchell College of Law 322

Y

Yale University   323
Yeshiva University   324
York University   325

Law Program Name

James E. Beasley School of Law   218
Boalt Hall School of Law   237
Louis D. Brandeis School of Law   256
Shepard Broad Law Center   182
Benjamin N. Cardozo
   School of Law   324
Salmon P. Chase College of Law   178
Chicago-Kent College of Law   153
J. Reuben Clark Law School   108
David A. Clarke School of Law   284
Cleveland-Marshall School of Law   120
Columbus School of Law   118
Cumberland School of Law   201
Detroit College of Law   168
The Dickinson School of Law   187
Jacob D. Fuchsberg Law Center   224
Walter F. George School of Law   167
Hastings College of Law   236
Paul M. Hebert Law Center   162
Cecil C. Humphreys School of Law   258
Lamar Law Center   262
Levin College of Law   246
Thurgood Marshall
   School of Law   219
McGeorge School of Law   285
Northwestern School of Law   160
Osgoode Hall Law School   325
Ralph R. Papitto School of Law   194
Claude W. Pettit College of Law   183
William S. Richardson
   School of Law   248
James E. Rogers College of Law   230
of Texas A&M University   208
of Union University   100
Washington College of Law   101-103
Norman Adrian Wiggins
   School of Law   115

LOCATION

ALABAMA

Samford University   201
University of Alabama   229

ARIZONA

Arizona State University   104
University of Arizona   230

ARKANSAS

University of Arkansas—
   Fayetteville   231
University of Arkansas—
   Little Rock   232

CALIFORNIA

Cal Northern School of Law   110
California Pacific School of Law   111
California Western
   School of Law   112-114
Empire College   133
Golden Gate University   142-144
Humphreys College   152
John F. Kennedy University   156
Lincoln Law School of Sacramento   161
Loyola Marymount University   163
Monterey College of Law   170
New College of California   171
Pepperdine University   188-190
San Francisco Law School   202
San Joaquin College of Law   203
Santa Barbara College of Law   204
Santa Clara University   205
Southern California
   Institute of Law   209
Southwestern University   213
Stanford University   214
Thomas Jefferson School of Law   222
UCLA School of Law   226
University of California   236
University of California—Berkeley 237
University of California—Davis   238
University of La Verne   255
University of San Diego   276
University of San Francisco   277
University of Southern California   280
University of the Pacific   285
University of West Los Angeles 295-297
Ventura College of Law   305
Western State University   315-317
Whittier College   318

COLORADO

University of Colorado   241
University of Denver   244

CONNECTICUT

Quinnipiac University   192
University of Connecticut   242
Yale University   323

DELAWARE

Widener University   319
District of Columbia
American University   101-103
Catholic University of America   118
George Washington University   139
Georgetown University   140
Howard University   151
University of the District of
   Columbia   284

DISTRICT OF COLUMBIA

American University   101-103
Catholic University of America   118
George Washington University   139
Georgetown University   140
Howard University   151
University of the District
   of Columbia   284

FLORIDA

Florida State University   135
Nova Southeastern University   182
St. Thomas University   200
Stetson University   215
University of Florida   246
University of Miami   259

GEORGIA

Emory University   132
Georgia State University   141
Mercer University   167
University of Georgia   247

HAWAII

University of Hawaii—Manoa   248

IDAHO

University of Idaho   250

ILLINOIS

DePaul University   126-128
Illinois Institute of Technology   153
The John Marshall Law School   157-159
Loyola University Chicago   164
Northern Illinois University   177
Northwestern University   179-181
Southern Illinois University   210
University of Chicago   239
University of Illinois   251

INDIANA

Indiana University—Bloomington   154
Indiana University—Indianapolis   155
University of Notre Dame   270
Valparaiso University   301

IOWA

Drake University	129
University of Iowa	252

KANSAS

University of Kansas	253
Washburn University	309

KENTUCKY

Northern Kentucky University	178
University of Kentucky	254
University of Louisville	256

LOUISIANA

Louisiana State University	162
Loyola University New Orleans	165
Southern University	212
Tulane University	225

MAINE

University of Southern Maine	281

MARYLAND

University of Baltimore	233
University of Maryland	257

MASSACHUSETTS

Boston College	106
Boston University	107
Harvard University	147
New England School of Law	172
Northeastern University	176
Suffolk University	216
Western New England College	314

MICHIGAN

Michigan State University	168
Thomas M. Cooley Law School	223
University of Detroit Mercy	245
University of Michigan	260
Wayne State University	312

MINNESOTA

Hamline University	146
University of Minnesota	261
William Mitchell College of Law	322

MISSISSIPPI

Mississippi College	169
University of Mississippi School of Law	262

MISSOURI

St. Louis University	198
University of Missouri—Columbia	263
University of Missouri—Kansas City	264
Washington University	311

MONTANA

University of Montana	265

NEBRASKA

Creighton University	124
University of Nebraska—Lincoln	266

NEW HAMPSHIRE

Franklin Pierce Law Center	137

NEW JERSEY

Rutgers University—Camden	195
Rutgers University—Newark	196
Seton Hall University	207

NEW MEXICO

University of New Mexico	267

NEW YORK

Albany Law School	100
Brooklyn Law School	109
City University of New York	119
Columbia University	122
Cornell University	123
Fordham University	136
Hofstra University	148-150
New York Law School	173
New York University	174
Pace University	186
St. John's University	197
Syracuse University	217
Touro College	224
University at Buffalo, State University of New York	227
Yeshiva University	324

NORTH CAROLINA

Campbell University	115
Duke University	130
North Carolina Central University	175
University of North Carolina—Chapel Hill	268
Wake Forest University	308

NORTH DAKOTA

University of North Dakota	269

OHIO

Capital University   116
Case Western Reserve University   117
Ohio Northern University   183
Ohio State University   184
University of Akron   228
University of Cincinnati   240
University of Dayton   243
University of Toledo   286-288

OKLAHOMA

Oklahoma City University   185
University of Oklahoma   271
University of Tulsa   290

OREGON

Lewis and Clark College   160
University of Oregon   272
Willamette University   321

PENNSYLVANIA

Duquesne University   131
Pennsylvania State University   187
Temple University   218
University of Pennsylvania   273
University of Pittsburgh   274
Villanova University   307

RHODE ISLAND

Roger Williams University   194

SOUTH CAROLINA

University of South Carolina   278

SOUTH DAKOTA

University of South Dakota   279

TENNESSEE

University of Memphis   258
University of Tennessee   282
Vanderbilt University   302-304

TEXAS

Baylor University   105
St. Mary's University   199
South Texas College of Law   208
Southern Methodist University   211
Texas Southern University   219
Texas Tech University   220
Texas Wesleyan University   221
University of Houston   249
University of Texas—Austin   283

UTAH

Brigham Young University   108
University of Utah   291

VERMONT

Vermont Law School   306

VIRGINIA

College of William & Mary   121
George Mason University   138
Regent University   193
University of Richmond   275
University of Virginia   293
Washington and Lee University   310

WASHINGTON

Gonzaga University   145
Seattle University   206
University of Washington   294

WEST VIRGINIA

West Virginia University   313

WISCONSIN

Marquette University   166
University of Wisconsin   299

WYOMING

University of Wyoming   300

CANADA

Dalhousie University   125
Queen's University   191
University of British Columbia   234
University of Calgary   235
University of Toronto   289
University of Victoria   292
University of Windsor   298
Widener University   320
York University   325

COST

(IN-STATE TUITION)

$0 TO $9,999

Arizona State University	104
Brigham Young University	108
Cal Northern School of Law	110
California Pacific School of Law	111
City University of New York	119
Dalhousie University	125
Drake University	129
Empire College	133
Georgia State University	141
Humphreys College	152
John F. Kennedy University	156
Lincoln Law School of Sacramento	161
Louisiana State University	162
Monterey College of Law	170
New College of California	171
North Carolina Central University	175
Northern Illinois University	177
Queen's University	191
San Francisco Law School	202
Southern California Institute of Law	209
Southern Illinois University	210
Southern University	212
Texas Southern University	219
Texas Tech University	220
University of Alabama	229
University of Arizona	230
University of Arkansas—Fayetteville	231
University of Arkansas—Little Rock	232
University of British Columbia	234
University of Calgary	235
University of Houston	249
University of Idaho	250
University of Memphis	258
University of Mississippi School of Law	262
University of Montana	265
University of Nebraska—Lincoln	266
University of New Mexico	267
University of North Carolina—Chapel Hill	268
University of North Dakota	269
University of Oklahoma	271
University of South Dakota	279
University of Tennessee	282
University of Utah	291
University of Victoria	292
University of West Los Angeles	295-297
University of Windsor	298
University of Wyoming	300
Ventura College of Law	305
West Virginia University	313
York University	325

$10,000 TO $19,999

Baylor University	105
Campbell University	115
Capital University	116
Cleveland State University	120
College of William & Mary	121
Creighton University	124
Duquesne University	131
Florida Coastal School of Law	134
Florida State University	135
Franklin Pierce Law Center	137
George Mason University	138
Gonzaga University	145
Hamline University	146
Howard University	151
Indiana University—Bloomington	154
Indiana University—Indianapolis	155
Loyola University New Orleans	165
Marquette University	166
Mercer University	167
Michigan State University	168
Mississippi College	169
New England School of Law	172
Northern Kentucky University	178
Nova Southeastern University	182
Ohio Northern University	183
Ohio State University	184
Oklahoma City University	185
Pennsylvania State University	187
Regent University	193
St. Mary's University	199
Samford University	201
San Joaquin College of Law	203
San Joaquin College of Law	203
South Texas College of Law	208
Temple University	218
Texas Wesleyan University	221
Thomas M. Cooley Law School	223
University at Buffalo, State University of New York	227
University of Akron	228
University of Akron	228
University of Baltimore	233

University of California	236
University of California—Berkeley	237
University of Cincinnati	240
University of Connecticut	242
University of Dayton	243
University of Detroit Mercy	245
University of Florida	246
University of Georgia	247
University of Hawaii—Manoa	248
University of Illinois	251
University of Iowa	252
University of Kansas	253
University of Kentucky	254
University of Louisville	256
University of Maryland	257
University of Minnesota	261
University of Missouri—Kansas City	264
University of Oregon	272
University of Pittsburgh	274
University of Richmond	275
University of South Carolina	278
University of Southern Maine	281
University of Texas—Austin	283
University of the District of Columbia	284
University of Toronto	289
University of Tulsa	290
University of Virginia	293
University of Washington	294
University of Wisconsin	299
Valparaiso University	301
Washburn University	309
Washington and Lee University	310
Wayne State University	312
Willamette University	321
William Mitchell College of Law	322

$20,000+

Albany Law School	100
American University	101-103
Boston College	106
Boston University	107
Brooklyn Law School	109
California Western School of Law	112-114
Case Western Reserve University	117

Catholic University of America 118
Columbia University 122
Cornell University 123
DePaul University 126-128
Duke University 130
Emory University 132
Fordham University 136
George Washington University 139
Georgetown University 140
Golden Gate University 142-144
Harvard University 147
Hofstra University 148-150
Illinois Institute of Technology 153
The John Marshall Law School 157-159
Lewis and Clark College 160
Loyola Marymount University 163
Loyola University Chicago 164
New York Law School 173
New York University 174
Northeastern University 176
Northwestern University 179-181
Pace University 186
Pepperdine University 188-190
Quinnipiac University 192
Roger Williams University 194
St. John's University 197
St. Louis University 198
St. Thomas University 200
Santa Barbara College of Law 204
Seattle University 206
Seton Hall University 207
Southern Methodist University 211
Southwestern University 213
Stanford University 214
Stetson University 215
Suffolk University 216
Syracuse University 217
Thomas Jefferson School of Law 222
Touro College 224
Tulane University 225
University of Chicago 239
University of Denver 244
University of Miami 259
University of Michigan 260
University of Notre Dame 270
University of Pennsylvania 273
University of San Diego 276
University of San Francisco 277
University of Southern California 280
University of the Pacific 285
Vanderbilt University 302-304
Vermont Law School 306
Villanova University 307
Wake Forest University 308
Washington University 311
Western New England College 314
Western State University 315-317
Whittier College 318
Widener University (DE) 319
Widener University (PA) 320
Yale University 323
Yeshiva University 324

ENROLLMENT OF LAW SCHOOL

0 TO 499

Arizona State University	104
Baylor University	105
Brigham Young University	108
Cal Northern School of Law	110
California Pacific School of Law	111
Campbell University	115
City University of New York	119
Creighton University	124
Dalhousie University	125
Drake University	129
Empire College	133
Franklin Pierce Law Center	137
Gonzaga University	145
Hamline University	146
Howard University	151
Humphreys College	152
John F. Kennedy University	156
Lincoln Law School of Sacramento	161
Mercer University	167
Mississippi College	169
Monterey College of Law	170
New College of California	171
North Carolina Central University	175
Northern Illinois University	177
Northern Kentucky University	178
Ohio Northern University	183
Queen's University	191
Regent University	193
Roger Williams University	194
St. Thomas University	200
San Francisco Law School	202
Southern California Institute of Law	209
Southern Illinois University	210
Southern University	212
Texas Wesleyan University	221
University of Arizona	230
University of Arkansas— Fayetteville	231
University of Arkansas— Little Rock	232
University of Calgary	235
University of Cincinnati	240
University of Colorado	241
University of Dayton	243
University of Detroit Mercy	245
University of Hawaii—Manoa	248
University of Idaho	250
University of Kentucky	254
University of La Verne	255
University of Louisville	256
University of Memphis	258
University of Mississippi School of Law	262
University of Missouri— Kansas City	264
University of Montana	265

University of Nebraska—Lincoln	266
University of New Mexico	267
University of North Dakota	269
University of Richmond	275
University of South Dakota	279
University of Southern Maine	281
University of Tennessee	282
University of the District of Columbia	284
University of Utah	291
University of Victoria	292
University of West Los Angeles	295-297
University of Windsor	298
University of Wyoming	300
Valparaiso University	301
Ventura College of Law	305
Vermont Law School	306
Wake Forest University	308
Washburn University	309
Washington and Lee University	310
West Virginia University	313
Widener University (PA)	320
Willamette University	321

500 TO 749

Albany Law School	100
California Western School of Law	112-114
Case Western Reserve University	117
College of William & Mary	121
Cornell University	123
Duke University	130
Duquesne University	131
Emory University	132
Florida Coastal School of Law	134
Florida State University	135
George Mason University	138
Georgia State University	141
Golden Gate University	142-144
Indiana University—Bloomington	154
Lewis and Clark College	160
Louisiana State University	162
Loyola University Chicago	164
Loyola University New Orleans	165
Marquette University	166
Michigan State University	168
Northeastern University	176
Northwestern University	179-181
Ohio State University	184
Oklahoma City University	185
Pennsylvania State University	187
Pepperdine University	188-190
Rutgers University—Camden	195
Rutgers University—Newark	196
St. Mary's University	199
Samford University	201

San Joaquin College of Law	203
San Joaquin College of Law	203
Southern Methodist University	211
Stanford University	214
Stetson University	215
Texas Southern University	219
Texas Tech University	220
Thomas Jefferson School of Law	222
Touro College	224
University at Buffalo, State University of New York	227
University of Akron	228
University of Akron	228
University of Alabama	229
University of British Columbia	234
University of California—Davis	238
University of Chicago	239
University of Connecticut	242
University of Georgia	247
University of Illinois	251
University of Iowa	252
University of Kansas	253
University of Minnesota	261
University of Missouri—Columbia	263
University of North Carolina— Chapel Hill	268
University of Notre Dame	270
University of Oklahoma	271
University of Oregon	272
University of Pittsburgh	274
University of San Francisco	277
University of South Carolina	278
University of Southern California	280
University of Toledo	286-288
University of Toronto	289
University of Tulsa	290
University of Washington	294
Vanderbilt University	302-304
Villanova University	307
Washington University	311
Wayne State University	312
Western New England College	314
Western State University	315-317
Whittier College	318
Yale University	323

750+

American University	101-103
Boston College	106
Boston University	107
Brooklyn Law School	109
Capital University	116
Catholic University of America	118
Cleveland State University	120
Columbia University	122
DePaul University	126-128

Fordham University 136
George Washington University 139
Georgetown University 140
Harvard University 147
Hofstra University 148-150
Illinois Institute of Technology 153
Indiana University—Indianapolis 155
The John Marshall Law School 157-159
Loyola Marymount University 163
New England School of Law 172
New York Law School 173
New York University 174
Nova Southeastern University 182
Pace University 186
Quinnipiac University 192
St. John's University 197
St. Louis University 198
Santa Barbara College of Law 204
Santa Clara University 205
Seattle University 206
Seton Hall University 207
South Texas College of Law 208
Southwestern University 213
Suffolk University 216
Syracuse University 217
Temple University 218
Thomas M. Cooley Law School 223
Tulane University 225
UCLA School of Law 226
University of Baltimore 233
University of California 236
University of California—Berkeley 237
University of Denver 244
University of Florida 246
University of Houston 249
University of Maryland 257
University of Miami 259
University of Michigan 260
University of Pennsylvania 273
University of San Diego 276
University of Texas—Austin 283
University of the Pacific 285
University of Virginia 293
University of Wisconsin 299
Widener University (DE) 319
William Mitchell College of Law 322
Yeshiva University 324
York University 325

AVERAGE LSAT

120 TO 152

Albany Law School	100
California Pacific School of Law	111
California Western School of Law	112-114
Capital University	116
City University of New York	119
Cleveland State University	120
Creighton University	124
Franklin Pierce Law Center	137
Gonzaga University	145
Howard University	151
Humphreys College	152
The John Marshall Law School	157-159
Lincoln Law School of Sacramento	161
Loyola University New Orleans	165
Mississippi College	169
Monterey College of Law	170
North Carolina Central University	175
Nova Southeastern University	182
Ohio Northern University	183
Oklahoma City University	185
Pace University	186
Quinnipiac University	192
Regent University	193
Roger Williams University	194
St. Mary's University	199
St. Thomas University	200
Samford University	201
San Joaquin College of Law	203
Southern University	212
Stetson University	215
Syracuse University	217
Texas Southern University	219
Thomas Jefferson School of Law	222
Thomas M. Cooley Law School	223
Touro College	224
University of Akron	228
University of Baltimore	233
University of Dayton	243
University of Detroit Mercy	245
University of Idaho	250
University of North Dakota	269
University of Oklahoma	271
University of South Dakota	279
University of the District of Columbia	284
University of Toledo	286-288
University of Tulsa	290
Valparaiso University	301
Ventura College of Law	305
Washburn University	309
Western New England College	314

Western State University	315-317
Whittier College	318
Widener University	319
William Mitchell College of Law	322

153 TO 157

American University	101-103
Brooklyn Law School	109
Campbell University	115
Case Western Reserve University	117
Catholic University of America	118
DePaul University	126-128
Drake University	129
Duquesne University	131
Florida State University	135
George Mason University	138
Georgia State University	141
Golden Gate University	142-144
Hamline University	146
Hofstra University	148-150
Illinois Institute of Technology	153
Indiana University—Indianapolis	155
Louisiana State University	162
Marquette University	166
Mercer University	167
Michigan State University	168
New York Law School	173
Northeastern University	176
Northern Illinois University	177
Northern Kentucky University	178
Ohio State University	184
Pennsylvania State University	187
Pepperdine University	188-190
Rutgers University—Camden	195
Rutgers University—Newark	196
St. John's University	197
St. Louis University	198
Santa Clara University	205
Seattle University	206
Seton Hall University	207
South Texas College of Law	208
Southern Illinois University	210
Southern Methodist University	211
Suffolk University	216
Temple University	218
Texas Tech University	220
University at Buffalo, State University of New York	227
University of Alabama	229
University of Arkansas— Fayetteville	231

University of Arkansas— Little Rock	232
University of Denver	244
University of Hawaii—Manoa	248
University of Kansas	253
University of Louisville	256
University of Maryland	257
University of Memphis	258
University of Miami	259
University of Mississippi School of Law	262
University of Missouri—Columbia	263
University of Missouri— Kansas City	264
University of Montana	265
University of Nebraska—Lincoln	266
University of New Mexico	267
University of Pittsburgh	274
University of Richmond	275
University of San Francisco	277
University of South Carolina	278
University of Southern Maine	281
University of Tennessee	282
University of Wyoming	300
Vermont Law School	306
Wayne State University	312
West Virginia University	313
Willamette University	321
Yeshiva University	324

158 TO 180

Arizona State University	104
Baylor University	105
Boston College	106
Boston University	107
Brigham Young University	108
College of William & Mary	121
Columbia University	122
Cornell University	123
Emory University	132
Fordham University	136
George Washington University	139
Georgetown University	140
Harvard University	147
Indiana University—Bloomington	154
Lewis and Clark College	160
Loyola Marymount University	163
Loyola University Chicago	164
New York University	174
Northwestern University	179-181
Stanford University	214

Tulane University 225
UCLA School of Law 226
University of Arizona 230
University of California 236
University of California—Berkeley 237
University of California—Davis 238
University of Chicago 239
University of Cincinnati 240
University of Colorado 241
University of Connecticut 242
University of Florida 246
University of Georgia 247
University of Houston 249
University of Illinois 251
University of Iowa 252
University of Kentucky 254
University of Michigan 260
University of Minnesota 261
University of North Carolina—
  Chapel Hill 268
University of Notre Dame 270
University of Oregon 272
University of Pennsylvania 273
University of San Diego 276
University of Southern California 280
University of Texas—Austin 283
University of Utah 291
University of Virginia 293
University of Washington 294
University of Wisconsin 299
Vanderbilt University 302-304
Villanova University 307
Wake Forest University 308
Washington and Lee University 310
Washington University 311
Yale University 323

AVERAGE UNDERGRAD GPA

0 TO 3.10

Albany Law School	100
California Pacific School of Law	111
California Western	
School of Law	112-114
Campbell University	115
Capital University	116
City University of New York	119
Cleveland State University	120
Creighton University	124
Franklin Pierce Law Center	137
George Mason University	138
Golden Gate University	142-144
Gonzaga University	145
Howard University	151
Humphreys College	152
The John Marshall Law School	157-159
Lincoln Law School of Sacramento	161
Loyola University New Orleans	165
Marquette University	166
Mercer University	167
Michigan State University	168
Mississippi College	169
Monterey College of Law	170
New York Law School	173
North Carolina Central University	175
Northern Illinois University	177
Nova Southeastern University	182
Ohio Northern University	183
Oklahoma City University	185
Pace University	186
Quinnipiac University	192
Regent University	193
Roger Williams University	194
St. Mary's University	199
St. Thomas University	200
Samford University	201
San Joaquin College of Law	203
Seton Hall University	207
South Texas College of Law	208
Texas Southern University	219
Thomas Jefferson School of Law	222
Thomas M. Cooley Law School	223
Touro College	224
University of Baltimore	233
University of Dayton	243
University of Denver	244
University of Memphis	258
University of San Francisco	277
University of the District of	
Columbia	284
University of Toledo	286-288
University of Tulsa	290
Valparaiso University	301
Ventura College of Law	305
Vermont Law School	306

Western New England College	314
Western State University	315-317
Whittier College	318
Widener University (DE)	319
Willamette University	321

3.11 TO 3.30

American University	101-103
Arizona State University	104
Catholic University of America	118
College of William & Mary	121
DePaul University	126-128
Drake University	129
Duquesne University	131
Florida State University	135
Georgia State University	141
Hamline University	146
Hofstra University	148-150
Illinois Institute of Technology	153
Indiana University—Indianapolis	155
Lewis and Clark College	160
Louisiana State University	162
Loyola Marymount University	163
Loyola University Chicago	164
Northeastern University	176
Northern Kentucky University	178
Pennsylvania State University	187
Pepperdine University	188-190
Rutgers University—Camden	195
Rutgers University—Newark	196
St. John's University	197
St. Louis University	198
Santa Clara University	205
Seattle University	206
Southern Illinois University	210
Southern Methodist University	211
Stetson University	215
Suffolk University	216
Syracuse University	217
Temple University	218
Tulane University	225
University at Buffalo, State	
University of New York	227
University of Akron	228
University of Arkansas—	
Fayetteville	231
University of Arkansas—	
Little Rock	232
University of Connecticut	242
University of Detroit Mercy	245
University of Hawaii—Manoa	248
University of Houston	249
University of Idaho	250
University of Louisville	256

University of Miami	259
University of Missouri—Columbia	263
University of Missouri—	
Kansas City	264
University of Montana	265
University of New Mexico	267
University of Oklahoma	271
University of Pittsburgh	274
University of Richmond	275
University of San Diego	276
University of South Carolina	278
University of South Dakota	279
University of Southern Maine	281
University of Wyoming	300
Washburn University	309
Wayne State University	312
West Virginia University	313
William Mitchell College of Law	322
Yeshiva University	324

3.31 TO 4.00

Baylor University	105
Boston College	106
Boston University	107
Brigham Young University	108
Brooklyn Law School	109
Case Western Reserve University	117
Columbia University	122
Cornell University	123
Emory University	132
Empire College	133
Fordham University	136
George Washington University	139
Georgetown University	140
Harvard University	147
Indiana University—Bloomington	154
New York University	174
Northwestern University	179-181
Ohio State University	184
Southern University	212
Stanford University	214
Texas Tech University	220
UCLA School of Law	226
University of Alabama	229
University of Arizona	230
University of California	236
University of California—Berkeley	237
University of California—Davis	238
University of Chicago	239
University of Cincinnati	240
University of Colorado	241
University of Florida	246
University of Georgia	247
University of Illinois	251

University of Iowa   252
University of Kansas   253
University of Kentucky   254
University of Maryland   257
University of Michigan   260
University of Minnesota   261
University of Mississippi
    School of Law   262
University of Nebraska—Lincoln   266
University of North Carolina—
    Chapel Hill   268
University of North Dakota   269
University of Notre Dame   270
University of Oregon   272
University of Pennsylvania   273
University of Southern California   280
University of Tennessee   282
University of Texas—Austin   283
University of Utah   291
University of Virginia   293
University of Washington   294
University of Wisconsin   299
Vanderbilt University   302-304
Villanova University   307
Washington and Lee University   310
Washington University   311
Yale University   323

ENVIRONMENT

RURAL

Campbell University	115
College of William & Mary	121
Ohio Northern University	183
Pennsylvania State University	187
Roger Williams University	194
Stetson University	215
University of Arkansas— Fayetteville	231
University of Idaho	250
University of Mississippi School of Law	262
University of South Dakota	279
University of Wyoming	300
Vermont Law School	306
Washington and Lee University	310

SUBURBAN

Cornell University	123
Franklin Pierce Law Center	137
Hofstra University	148-150
Northern Illinois University	177
Quinnipiac University	192
Southern Illinois University	210
Stanford University	214
University at Buffalo, State University of New York	227
University of California—Davis	238
University of Dayton	243
University of Iowa	252
University of Kansas	253
University of Miami	259
University of Missouri—Columbia	263
University of North Carolina— Chapel Hill	268
University of North Dakota	269
University of Richmond	275
Valparaiso University	301
Villanova University	307
West Virginia University	313
Western New England College	314

URBAN

Albany Law School	100
American University	101-103
Arizona State University	104
Baylor University	105
Boston College	106
Boston University	107
Brigham Young University	108
Brooklyn Law School	109
California Western School of Law	112-114
Capital University	116
Case Western Reserve University	117
Catholic University of America	118
City University of New York	119
Columbia University	122
Creighton University	124
DePaul University	126-128
Drake University	129
Duke University	130
Duquesne University	131
Emory University	132
Florida State University	135
Fordham University	136
George Mason University	138
George Washington University	139
Georgetown University	140
Georgia State University	141
Golden Gate University	142-144
Gonzaga University	145
Hamline University	146
Harvard University	147
Howard University	151
Illinois Institute of Technology	153
Indiana University—Bloomington	154
Indiana University—Indianapolis	155
The John Marshall Law School	157-159
Lewis and Clark College	160
Lincoln Law School of Sacramento	161
Louisiana State University	162
Loyola Marymount University	163
Loyola University Chicago	164
Loyola University New Orleans	165
Marquette University	166
Mercer University	167
Michigan State University	168
Mississippi College	169
New England School of Law	172
New York Law School	173
New York University	174
North Carolina Central University	175
Northeastern University	176
Northern Kentucky University	178
Northwestern University	179-181
Nova Southeastern University	182
Ohio State University	184
Oklahoma City University	185
Pace University	186
Pepperdine University	188-190
Rutgers University—Camden	195
Rutgers University—Newark	196
St. John's University	197
St. Louis University	198
St. Mary's University	199
Samford University	201
San Joaquin College of Law	203
Santa Clara University	205
Seattle University	206
Seton Hall University	207
South Texas College of Law	208
Southern Methodist University	211
Southern University	212
Southwestern University	213
Suffolk University	216
Syracuse University	217
Temple University	218
Texas Southern University	219
Texas Tech University	220
Texas Wesleyan University	221
Thomas Jefferson School of Law	222
Thomas M. Cooley Law School	223
Touro College	224
Tulane University	225
UCLA School of Law	226
University of Akron	228
University of Alabama	229
University of Arizona	230
University of Arkansas— Little Rock	232
University of Baltimore	233
University of California	236
University of California—Berkeley	237
University of Chicago	239
University of Cincinnati	240
University of Colorado	241
University of Connecticut	242
University of Denver	244
University of Florida	246
University of Georgia	247
University of Hawaii—Manoa	248
University of Houston	249
University of Illinois	251
University of Kentucky	254
University of Louisville	256
University of Maryland	257
University of Memphis	258
University of Michigan	260
University of Minnesota	261
University of Missouri— Kansas City	264
University of Montana	265
University of Nebraska—Lincoln	266
University of New Mexico	267
University of Notre Dame	270
University of Oklahoma	271
University of Oregon	272
University of Pennsylvania	273
University of Pittsburgh	274
University of San Diego	276
University of San Francisco	277
University of South Carolina	278
University of Southern California	280
University of Southern Maine	281
University of Tennessee	282
University of Texas—Austin	283
University of the Pacific	285

University of Toledo   286-288
University of Tulsa   290
University of Utah   291
University of Virginia   293
University of Washington   294
University of Wisconsin   299
Vanderbilt University   302-304
Wake Forest University   308
Washburn University   309
Washington University   311
Wayne State University   312
Whittier College   318
Widener University (DE)   319
Willamette University   321
William Mitchell College of Law   322
Yale University   323
Yeshiva University   324

Pass Rate for First-Time Bar

0% TO 82%

American University	101-103
California Western School of Law	112-114
Capital University	116
Case Western Reserve University	117
Catholic University of America	118
City University of New York	119
Cleveland State University	120
Duquesne University	131
Florida State University	135
George Mason University	138
Golden Gate University	142-144
Hofstra University	148-150
Howard University	151
Illinois Institute of Technology	153
The John Marshall Law School	157-159
Lewis and Clark College	160
Loyola University New Orleans	165
Michigan State University	168
University of Arkansas—Fayetteville	231
University of Arkansas—Little Rock	232
University of Baltimore	233
University of Dayton	243
University of Denver	244
University of Detroit Mercy	245
University of Idaho	250
University of Iowa	252
University of South Carolina	278

83% TO 90%

Arizona State University	104
Boston University	107
Brooklyn Law School	109
Creighton University	124
DePaul University	126-128
Drake University	129
Fordham University	136
Franklin Pierce Law Center	137
George Washington University	139
Georgetown University	140
Gonzaga University	145
Indiana University—Indianapolis	155
Loyola Marymount University	163
Northern Kentucky University	178
Pennsylvania State University	187
Quinnipiac University	192
Tulane University	225
UCLA School of Law	226
University of Akron	228
University of California—Berkeley	237
University of Connecticut	242
University of Hawaii—Manoa	248
University of Kansas	253
University of Louisville	256

91% TO 100%

Baylor University	105
Boston College	106
Brigham Young University	108
Campbell University	115
Cornell University	123
Duke University	130
Emory University	132
Georgia State University	141
Hamline University	146
Harvard University	147
Indiana University—Bloomington	154
Loyola University Chicago	164
University of Alabama	229
University of Arizona	230
University of California	236
University of California—Davis	238
University of Chicago	239
University of Cincinnati	240
University of Colorado	241
University of Florida	246
University of Georgia	247
University of Houston	249
University of Illinois	251
University of Kentucky	254
University of Notre Dame	270
University of Virginia	293

Average Starting Salary

$0 TO $42,999

California Pacific School of Law	111
Creighton University	124
Drake University	129
Florida State University	135
Gonzaga University	145
Hamline University	146
Lewis and Clark College	160
Lincoln Law School of Sacramento	161
Louisiana State University	162
Mercer University	167
Mississippi College	169
Northern Kentucky University	178
Nova Southeastern University	182
Ohio Northern University	183
Oklahoma City University	185
Pennsylvania State University	187
Quinnipiac University	192
Regent University	193
Samford University	201
Southern California Institute of Law	209
Southern Illinois University	210
Texas Wesleyan University	221
Thomas M. Cooley Law School	223
University at Buffalo, State University of New York	227
University of Arkansas—Fayetteville	231
University of Arkansas—Little Rock	232
University of Baltimore	233
University of Colorado	241
University of Dayton	243
University of Denver	244
University of Hawaii—Manoa	248
University of Idaho	250
University of Kansas	253
University of Kentucky	254
University of Louisville	256
University of Memphis	258
University of Mississippi School of Law	262
University of Missouri—Columbia	263
University of Missouri—Kansas City	264
University of Montana	265
University of Nebraska—Lincoln	266
University of New Mexico	267
University of North Dakota	269
University of Oklahoma	271
University of South Dakota	279
University of Tennessee	282
University of the District of Columbia	284
University of Toledo	286-288
University of Tulsa	290
University of Utah	291
University of Wyoming	300
Vanderbilt University	302-304
Vermont Law School	306
Washburn University	309
Wayne State University	312
West Virginia University	313
Western New England College	314
Widener University	320
Widener University	319
Willamette University	321
William Mitchell College of Law	322

$43,000 TO $51,999

Albany Law School	100
American University	101-103
Arizona State University	104
Brigham Young University	108
California Western School of Law	112-114
Capital University	116
Catholic University of America	118
Cleveland State University	120
College of William & Mary	121
DePaul University	126-128
Duquesne University	131
Franklin Pierce Law Center	137
Georgia State University	141
Golden Gate University	142-144
Hofstra University	148-150
Illinois Institute of Technology	153
Indiana University—Indianapolis	155
The John Marshall Law School	157-159
Marquette University	166
Michigan State University	168
New England School of Law	172
Northeastern University	176
Ohio State University	184
Roger Williams University	194
St. Louis University	198
St. Mary's University	199
St. Thomas University	200
San Joaquin College of Law	203
Seattle University	206
Seton Hall University	207
Southwestern University	213
Stetson University	215
Suffolk University	216
Syracuse University	217
Thomas Jefferson School of Law	222
Touro College	224
University of Akron	228
University of Alabama	229
University of Arizona	230
University of Cincinnati	240

University of Florida	246
University of Georgia	247
University of Maryland	257
University of North Carolina—Chapel Hill	268
University of Oregon	272
University of Pittsburgh	274
University of Richmond	275
University of South Carolina	278
University of the Pacific	285
University of Toronto	289
University of Washington	294
University of Wisconsin	299
Valparaiso University	301
Wake Forest University	308
Washington University	311
Western State University	315-317
Whittier College	318

$52,000+

Baylor University	105
Boston College	106
Brooklyn Law School	109
Case Western Reserve University	117
Columbia University	122
Cornell University	123
Duke University	130
Emory University	132
Fordham University	136
George Mason University	138
George Washington University	139
Georgetown University	140
Harvard University	147
Howard University	151
Indiana University—Bloomington	154
Loyola Marymount University	163
Loyola University Chicago	164
New York Law School	173
Northwestern University	179-181
Pace University	186
Pepperdine University	188-190
Rutgers University—Camden	195
Rutgers University—Newark	196
St. John's University	197
Santa Clara University	205
Southern Methodist University	211
Stanford University	214
Temple University	218
Texas Tech University	220
Tulane University	225
UCLA School of Law	226
University of California	236
University of California—Berkeley	237
University of California—Davis	238
University of Connecticut	242
University of Detroit Mercy	245

University of Houston   249
University of Illinois   251
University of Miami   259
University of Michigan   260
University of Minnesota   261
University of Notre Dame   270
University of Pennsylvania   273
University of Texas—Austin   283
University of Virginia   293
Villanova University   307
Washington and Lee University   310
Yale University   323
Yeshiva University   324

ABOUT THE AUTHOR

Eric Owens has taught courses and worked in various capacities for The Princeton Review since 1994. He attended Cornell College and Loyola University Chicago School of Law. He currently lives in Chicago and is studying (hard) for his bar exam. And with any luck, he'll have passed the bar by the time you read this.

NOTES

NOTES

NOTES

NOTES

www.review.com

Expert Advice

Talk About It

www.review.com

Pop Surveys

Paying for it

www.review.com

The Princeton Review

Getting in

Word du Jour

www.review.com

Find-O-Rama School & Career Search

www.review.com

Finding it

Best Schools

www.review.com

FIND US...

International

Hong Kong
4/F Sun Hung Kai Centre
30 Harbour Road, Wan Chai,
Hong Kong
Tel: (011)85-2-517-3016

Japan
Fuji Building 40, 15-14
Sakuragaokacho, Shibuya Ku,
Tokyo 150, Japan
Tel: (011)81-3-3463-1343

Korea
Tae Young Bldg, 944-24,
Daechi- Dong, Kangnam-Ku
The Princeton Review- ANC
Seoul, Korea 135-280,
South Korea
Tel: (011)82-2-554-7763

Mexico City
PR Mex S De RL De Cv
Guanajuato 228 Col. Roma
06700 Mexico D.F., Mexico
Tel: 525-564-9468

Montreal
666 Sherbrooke St.
West, Suite 202
Montreal, QC H3A 1E7 Canada
Tel: (514) 499-0870

Pakistan
1 Bawa Park - 90 Upper Mall
Lahore, Pakistan
Tel: (011)92-42-571-2315

Spain
Pza. Castilla, 3 - 5° A, 28046
Madrid, Spain
Tel: (011)341-323-4212

Taiwan
155 Chung Hsiao East Road
Section 4 - 4th Floor,
Taipei R.O.C., Taiwan
Tel: (011)886-2-751-1243

Thailand
Building One, 99 Wireless Road
Bangkok, Thailand 10330
Tel: (662) 256-7080

Toronto
1240 Bay Street, Suite 300
Toronto M5R 2A7 Canada
Tel: (800) 495-7737
Tel: (716) 839-4391

Vancouver
4212 University Way NE,
Suite 204
Seattle, WA 98105
Tel: (206) 548-1100

National (U.S.)
We have over 60 offices around the U.S. and
run courses in over 400 sites. For courses and locations
within the U.S. call 1 (800) 2/Review and you will be
routed to the nearest office.

MORE EXPERT ADVICE FROM THE PRINCETON REVIEW

I f you want to give yourself the best chance for getting into the law school of your choice, we can help you get the highest test scores, make the most informed choices, and make the most of your experience once you get there. We can also help you make the career move that will let you use your skills and education to their best advantage.

CRACKING THE LSAT
2001 EDITION
0-375-75628-0 $20.00

CRACKING THE LSAT WITH SAMPLE TESTS ON CD-ROM
2001 EDITION
0-375-75629-9 $34.95
MAC AND WINDOWS COMPATIBLE

LSAT/GRE ANALYTIC WORKOUT
0-679-77358-4 $16.00

THE COMPLETE BOOK OF LAW SCHOOLS
2001 EDITION
0-375-76155-1 $21.95

PRE-LAW SCHOOL COMPANION
0-679-77372-X $15.00

LAW SCHOOL COMPANION
0-679-76150-0 $15.00

ALTERNATIVE CAREERS FOR LAWYERS
0-679-77870-5 $15.00